Acknowledgments

I HAD THE PLEASURE OF MEETING AND WORKING with many people in the creation of this work. And it would not be complete without the assistance I received from them.

Primary recognition should go to the authors of the first guidebooks to the High Sierra: Walter A. Starr, Jr., Hervey Voge, Andy Smatko, and Steve Roper. Walter A. Starr, Jr., had nearly completed his *Guide to the John Muir Trail and the High Sierra Region* before his untimely death in the Minarets in 1933. During the course of my research I located a copy of his climbing notes and rediscovered some of his routes that have been overlooked in the past. In the early 1950s, Hervey Voge accepted the job of collating the work of twenty-three authors to create the first *Climber's Guide to the High Sierra*. The 1954 and 1965 editions of this work were logically oriented and extremely accurate, and many climbers considered it the only authoritative book describing the approaches and routes in the range. It is regrettable that Hervey Voge died in 1990, prior to the publication of this book. The 1972 edition of Voge's work was titled *Mountaineer's Guide to the High Sierra;* edited by Andy Smatko, it included descriptions of many previously overlooked peaks. The first modern climber's guide, written by Steve Roper in 1976, included technical rock climbing descriptions of routes done in Tuolumne Meadows and the High Sierra during the 1960s and early 1970s. Steve Roper graciously allowed me to review his notes that would have updated his work, and this book is much stronger because of his assistance. In the following introduction I have used, with permission, numerous ideas, as well as some of the phraseology, from two of Steve Roper's books, *The Climber's Guide to the High Sierra* and *Timberline Country: The Sierra High Route,* both published by the Sierra Club.

I am also grateful for the assistance I received from the staffs of several institutions. These include the Pasadena Public Library, the Milliken Library of the California Institute of Technology, the Honnold Library of the Claremont Colleges, Sequoia and Kings Canyon National Parks, and the United States Geological Survey's Ice and Climate Project at the University of Puget Sound in Tacoma, Washington. David Hirst of the Ice and Climate Project sent me the aerial photographs of the glaciers of the High Sierra at record speed, and I am especially grateful for the attention he gave to this work.

Alan Bartlett patiently answered my questions on the remote rock walls of Northern Yosemite, and John Moynier pointed out to me some previously overlooked peaks and pinnacles in the Rock Creek area. But John Fischer, formerly of the Palisade School of Mountaineering, deserves the most credit for filling in my gaps of knowledge in the Palisades. John reviewed the first draft of that chapter, and provided me with information on cross-country and climbing routes that somehow had escaped my attention. He is the outstanding authority on this region of the High Sierra.

But most of the credit should go to those individuals who provided me with a few bits of information that eventually added up to the bulk of this book. Some of these people are close friends whom I have known for years; others I met only briefly when our paths crossed in the High Sierra, and some I have never met. But they all took the time to give me their route descriptions and answer my questions. It breaks my heart to reduce this to an alphabetical list: Bob Ayers, Mike Baca, How Bailey, Scott Bailey, Bob Bandy, Allan Bard, Ron Bartell, Dick Beach, Rick Beatty, Don Borad, Bill Bradley, Graham Breakwell, Tom Brogan, Lloyd Brown, Harry Brumer, Cameron Burns, Jim Butler, Pat Butler, Fred Camphausen, Miguel Carmona, Jim Cervenka, Pat Christie, Gerry Cox, Fred Crostic, Peter Cummings, Glen Dawson, Diana Dee, Jeff Dozier, Tom Duryea, Dave Dykeman, Bob Emerick, the late Arkel Erb, Jim Erb, Tim Forsell, Andy Fried, Howard Gates, Rich Gnagy, Nancy Gordon, Vi Grasso, Arnold Green, Gary Guenther, Todd Handy, David Harden, Bob Hartunian, the late Carl Heller, John Hellman, Rich Henke, Larry Hoak, Fred Hoeptner, Ellen Holden, Delores Holladay, Gerry Holleman, Pat Holleman, Stan Horn, Marty Hornick, George Hubbard, Ron Hudson, Sigrid Hutto, Bill Hunt, Robin

Ingraham, Jr., Jon Inskeep, Rick Jali, Mike Jelf, Horton Johnson, Ron Jones, Walton Kabler, Jerry Keating, Chris Keith, Bruce Knudtson, Bill Krause, Barbara Lilley, Bob Lindgren, Mike Loughman, Larry Machleder, Gordon MacLeod, Barbara Magnuson, Roy Magnuson, Mark Maier, Owen Maloy, Igor Mamedalin, Doug Mantle, Harry Marinakis, Gene Mauk, David Mazel, Rob Roy McDonald, the late John Mendenhall, the late Ruth Mendenhall, Rene MeVay, Frank Meyers, Mary Sue Miller, Kathy Moore, Jim Murphy, Tom Naves, Ti Neff, Edward Nunez, Bart O'Brien, Bill Oliver, Donna O'Shaughnessy, the late Bruce Parker, Dave Petzold, Don Pies, Allan Pietrasanta, Steve Porcella, Phil Rabichow, Tom Randall, Cuno Ranschau, Barbara Reber, John Reed, John Ripley, Jim Roberts, Bob Rockwell, Steve Rogero, Casey Rohn, Maggie Rohn, the late Norm Rohn, Galen Rowell, LeRoy Russ, Bill T. Russell, Theresa Rutherford, Jim Shirley, Don Slager, Ursula Slager, Alois Smrz, Robert Somoano, Chuck Stein, Maria Steinberg, Reiner Stenzel, Tina Stough, Bill Stronge, Scott Sullivan, Steve Thaw, Bill Thomas, Larry Tidball, George Toby, Ed Treacy, Maris Valkass, Dale Van Dalsem, Dave Vandervoet, Greg Vernon, Roy Ward, Ron Webber, John Wedberg, Vieve Weldon, the late Fred Wing, Diana Worman, Pete Yamagata, Nozomu Yamanaka, and Chuck Yeager.

And I am grateful to the publishing staff of The Mountaineers, under the direction of Donna DeShazo, not only for supporting this project, but also for working with me in creating the final copy of this work. Rick May served as this book's editor, and the production details were coordinated by Marge Mueller and Lynne Fischer.

R. J. Secor
Pasadena, California

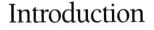

Introduction

THE HIGH SIERRA, WHICH I HAVE DEFINED AS the region between the southern boundary of Sequoia National Park and the northern boundary of Yosemite National Park, is the best place in the world for the practice of mountains.[1] By the practice of mountains, I am referring to hiking, cross-country rambling, peak bagging, rock climbing, ice climbing, and ski touring. The High Sierra is the highest mountain range in the contiguous United States, yet the enviable California climate almost guarantees excellent weather for an extended mountain journey. The High Sierra has an excellent system of trails, and cross-country travel is relatively easy among the alpine meadows, lakes, and talus slopes near timberline. This alpine region has a natural beauty that is unequaled, and the streams and lakes make this area a fishing paradise. It is an unspoiled wilderness, and it is possible to start a hike in the desert of the eastern Sierra and finish the trip among the lush redwood groves on the western slope. Cross-country skiers can find a stable snowpack during most of the winter, and will enjoy outstanding backcountry skiing over perfect corn snow during the spring. The mountains, crags, and domes of the High Sierra inspire the climber, who will find sound rock among these aretes, faces, and chimneys.

All who wander the area will take away treasured memories. Here are some of mine: the distant sound of a roaring stream as I descended a trail into the Middle Fork of the Kings River; the mechanical movements of my axe, hammer, and crampons as I climbed an ice gully in the autumn; skiing velvet snow across a high plateau during the spring; looking out over the range while giving an upper belay at the end of a difficult pitch over rough, yet solid alpine granite; climbing a peak and discovering that the summit register predates the twentieth century; and enjoying hundreds of timberline camps, with the sky filled with more starlight than air.

One of my goals in life is to go around the world three times and visit every mountain range twice. But whenever I have wandered other mountains, I have been homesick for the High Sierra. I am a hopeless romantic, and therefore my opinions cannot be regarded as objective. But how can I be objective while discussing the mountains that I love?

History

The first humans to explore the High Sierra were the Native Americans. The Paiutes from the Owens Valley and the Mono Indians from the Mono Lake region crossed the range to trade with the tribes in the Central Valley: the western Mono, Miwok, and Yokut tribes. The Indians typically crossed the Sierra crest at Mono Pass (north), Mammoth Pass, Mono Pass (south), Taboose Pass, and Kearsarge Pass. These crossings of the range were usually done by men and women in small parties during the summer and fall. Trading was usually conducted outside of the mountains in the home grounds of the host tribe.

It should be stressed that the Indians used many other routes and passes aside from those listed above, which were the main routes used by heavily laden parties. The

---

1. This excellent expression has been borrowed from the title of Andrea Mead Lawrence's and Sara Burnaby's book, *A Practice of Mountains*, Seaview Books, New York, 1980.

objective of most Native American parties was to cross the High Sierra easily and quickly with heavy loads of goods.

Signs of Indians have been found throughout the range, in the most remote canyons and atop the highest peaks. I believe that it can be safely said that Native Americans had visited all major and most minor river drainages, crossed all of the major passes, and may have climbed a few of its peaks.

The first systematic, scientific exploration of the High Sierra itself (as opposed to simply finding a way across the mountains) took place in 1863 and 1864. The California Geological Survey, under the direction of Josiah Dwight Whitney, visited Yosemite Valley, and then moved north, where in 1863 Whitney, Charles Hoffman, and William Brewer made the first ascent of Mt. Hoffman—the first recorded first ascent in the High Sierra.

The year 1864 was the banner year in the early exploration of the High Sierra. The Whitney Survey headed for the South Fork of the Kings River and visited the rival of Yosemite, Kings Canyon. On July 2, Hoffman and Brewer climbed a high peak that could be seen to the east of their camp along Roaring River. This peak was subsequently named Mt. Brewer by other members of the survey, but the two climbers were astounded by the view of higher peaks to the east and southeast. This discovery excited Clarence King in particular, who along with Richard Cotter volunteered to explore this area.

Cotter and King spent five days crossing the Kings–Kern Divide, traversing the headwaters of the Kern River, and climbing Mt. Tyndall. From the summit of Mt. Tyndall, King swept the horizon with his level and discovered the highest peak in the Sierra Nevada, Mt. Whitney, named in honor of the leader of the California Geological Survey. After returning to their camp along the Roaring River, King temporarily left the survey on one of his many attempts to climb Mt. Whitney.

The next major explorers of the High Sierra were the shepherds. There were many large flocks of sheep in California's Central Valley in the 1850s. The land was cheap, and the mild climate combined with ample pasturage led many owners of these flocks to great riches, especially during the Civil War. Farmers proceeded to buy up the land in the

Central Valley in the late 1860s, and the shepherds were forced to move into the meadowlands in the foothills of the Coast Range and the western Sierra Nevada. These were the American shepherds, who had first claim on the most favorable pasturage available. Shepherds who were recruited from Europe—French, Basque, Spanish, Portuguese, Italian—had to search for less desirable forage that was far up in the High Sierra. These shepherds were amazingly industrious, and probably led their sheep to every high mountain meadow in existence. Sheep grazed in one of the most remote areas of the High Sierra, Goddard Creek, prior to 1879.

This was in the days before there was control over public lands, and the damage caused by the sheep was overwhelming. Prior to overgrazing, High Sierra meadows had shoulder-high grass; this is a rare sight to this day. The shepherds brought in far too many sheep, and took these flocks to the highest meadows as soon as the snow had melted. The meadows were wet at this time, and the grass had not yet reached its full height as it would later in the summer. Hooves trampled the wet ground, exposing the grass roots, and the animals finished off the meadow quickly due to the short grass. The flock moved on to the next meadow, and the process was repeated. The hot, dry Sierra summer soon dried out the ground, and the grass roots died, leaving bare, dusty patches, which were taken over by weeds, brush, and eventually trees. The worst cases had such severe water and wind erosion that other plants could not take root, and the meadows became a sand flats within five years. Also, domestic sheep introduced diseases that the native bighorn sheep had no immunity to, and the bighorn herds were soon decimated.

The most famous shepherd was John Muir, and it could be said that this experience led to his becoming America's foremost conservationist of the late nineteenth and early twentieth centuries. In 1869 he guided two thousand sheep to Tuolumne Meadows. Muir was shocked by the damage caused by the sheep, which ate and trampled out wide scars through the high grass and flowers of the meadows. He called the sheep "hoofed locusts," and wrote, "To let sheep trample so divinely fine a place seems barbarous!"

It was only a matter of time before the

shepherds were forced out of business either by exhaustion of their forage or by governmental protection of public lands, which began in the 1890s with the creation of Yosemite National Park, Sequoia National Park, and the Sierra Forest Preserve. Control gradually came over the land, but the damage had been done. Some meadows disappeared forever under cover of forests; others now consist of open spaces marked by sand, dust, and weeds. They haven't recovered to this day.

Shepherds have been almost universally detested in the literature of the American West. Although the shepherds of the High Sierra used the mountains with no concern for the future, it must be remembered that they explored the farthest reaches of the range, establishing trails and cross-country routes along the way, and provided hospitality and route information to the mountaineers from the cities (including John Muir) who started to visit the High Sierra in the latter part of the nineteenth century.

After his brief tenure as a shepherd, John Muir worked for a time at a sawmill in Yosemite Valley (logging was another destroyer of the Sierra Nevada, but the loggers confined their activities to the western slopes, rather than the more remote High Sierra). Other odd jobs followed, and Muir continued to explore the High Sierra. The purpose of his journeys had more to do with biological and geological discoveries than geographical surveys of watersheds and the heights of peaks. It is known that he climbed Cathedral Peak, Mt. Ritter, and Mt. Whitney, and may have made the first ascent of Mt. Humphreys or Mt. Darwin. But instead of creating a "macro-record" of his journeys, he made a "micro-record" of the things he saw in nature, and was the first to recognize the important role that glaciers played in the creation of the High Sierra landscape.

Mountaineers from the city, interested in mountain exploration and conquest for its own sake, began to visit the High Sierra in the 1890s. One of these individuals was Theodore Solomons, who first had the idea of a trail along the Sierra crest (now known as the John Muir Trail) in 1884 at the age of fourteen. In 1892 he set out on his first expedition, accompanied only by a mule, exploring Tuolumne Meadows, the Lyell Fork of the Tuolumne River, and the forks of the San

Joaquin River. He returned to the mountains in 1894 with Leigh Bierce, son of newspaperman Ambrose Bierce, and continued south from the southernmost point of his 1892 journey, ascending Mono Creek and Bear Creek and climbing Seven Gables. Solomons returned to the Bear Creek region again in 1895 in the company of Ernest Bonner. They moved to the South Fork of the San Joaquin River, where they left their pack animals with a shepherd. Shouldering heavy packs, they ascended Evolution Creek, which was named by Solomons as were the great peaks at its head, after the prominent evolutionists. They climbed Mt. Wallace, attempted Mt. Darwin, and then retraced their steps to the South Fork of the San Joaquin River. From its head they climbed Mt. Goddard and then proceeded down the Enchanted Gorge (one of the most remote parts of the High Sierra even today) to the Middle Fork of the Kings River. They descended to Tehipite Valley before crossing the Monarch Divide via Granite Pass and dropping down to Kings Canyon.

While Solomons and Bonner were exploring the Middle Fork of the Kings River, Bolton Brown climbed out of Kings Canyon and crossed the Monarch Divide on the first of his three expeditions to the Kings River area. From Simpson Meadow, Brown climbed Mt. Woodworth and sketched the Palisades. Brown then ascended Cartridge Creek and climbed Mt. Ruskin from Cartridge Pass. From the summit, Brown saw and named Split Mountain to the east and Arrow Peak to the south. The latter peak was an irresistible siren for him, and he climbed its northeast spur, a route that, to the best of my knowledge, has never been repeated.

The following summer, 1896, Brown and his bride, Lucy, explored the Bubbs Creek drainage and the upper Kern River area. The newlyweds crossed the Kings–Kern Divide in pouring rain via a sheep route over Harrison Pass. After a miserable bivouac, they trekked across the upper Kern River basin to climb Mt. Williamson. (This was the first time that any reliable witnesses had visited this region since the journey of Clarence King in 1864.) A few days later, they climbed Mt. Ericsson atop the Kings–Kern Divide. On the same day, Brown continued on alone to the summit of Mt. Stanford, which he named after his university, where he was a professor of fine arts. Later during the same summer, Brown made a solo ascent of Mt. Clarence King from Paradise Valley. This was the most difficult rock climb done in North America in the nineteenth century. The climb was accomplished solo, by means of artificial chockstones (in this case, a knot in the end of a rope) and a final lasso of the summit block. The Browns returned to the Kings River area again in 1899, this time accompanied by their two-year-old daughter, Eleanor. They explored the beautiful Rae Lakes area east of Mt. Clarence King, and Eleanor discovered the delicious taste of trout.

But the greatest explorer of the High Sierra during the late nineteenth and early twentieth centuries was Joseph "Little Joe" LeConte. In all, he made forty-four extended trips to the High Sierra from 1892 to 1930. His scientifically drawn maps, the first to accurately portray the High Sierra, made a significant contribution to further exploration of the range. In 1898, he and Clarence Cory traveled from Yosemite to Kings Canyon. They followed Solomons' route south from Yosemite and climbed Red Slate Mountain and Mt. Goddard, with LeConte setting up his plane table and transit on each summit to measure other Sierra peaks. They were unable to find a route for their animals across the Goddard Divide, but after consulting a nearby shepherd they found a route across the barrier now known as the LeConte Divide, and eventually arrived in Kings Canyon. But LeConte had viewed the distant Palisades during this trip, and he decided to explore them over the next few years.

In 1902, LeConte, his wife, Helen Marion Gompertz LeConte, and Curtis Lindley crossed the Monarch Divide from Kings Canyon and ascended the Middle Fork of the Kings River and Cartridge Creek—Bolton Brown's route of 1895. From the lake at the head of the creek, which LeConte named Marion Lake, they crossed what is now known as Frozen Lake Pass and ascended Split Mountain. Their supplies were almost exhausted, however, and only Lindley and LeConte were able to make a short side trip to the north to Observation Peak to scout out the approaches to the Palisades. LeConte returned the following year, and with James Hutchinson, James Moffitt, and Robert Pike, he again went north from Marion Lake,

skirting the eastern slopes of Observation Peak, descended to Palisade Creek, and made camp along Glacier Creek. They climbed to the Sierra crest the next day, and looked down onto the Palisade Glacier, the largest in the range. Turning towards the greatest prize of all, North Palisade, they found their way blocked by a huge gap—the U Notch. Disappointed, they turned in the opposite direction and climbed Mt. Sill, a peak that LeConte had spotted and named seven years earlier. The next day, July 25, 1903, the men hiked to the base of the southwest face of North Palisade and climbed the prominent chute leading to the U Notch. The upper part of the chute was blocked by cliffs, but upon descending the chute, LeConte spotted a ledge that climbers have sought ever since. This led to easier climbing, and LeConte and his friends soon found themselves atop North Palisade, an enviable first ascent.

George Davis of the United States Geological Survey (USGS) was responsible for overseeing the production of detailed, 2-miles-to-the-inch, 30-minute maps of the High Sierra in the early 1900s. The last of these was published in 1912, and the unknown territory that once characterized the High Sierra had now been charted, and soon exploration gave way to to the sport of mountaineering.

James Hutchinson was the most prominent mountaineer in the High Sierra in the early twentieth century, making first ascents of Matterhorn Peak, Mt. Mills, Mt. Abbot, Mt. Humphreys, and the Black Kaweah, in addition to the first ascent of North Palisade. Perhaps the most obscure but almost omnipresent climber during this period was Charles Michael, the assistant postmaster of Yosemite Valley. A complete record of his climbs has never been located, but he reveled in solo climbs of class 3 and 4 routes, including Michael Minaret, Devil's Crag No. 1, the second ascent of North Palisade, and Michael's Pinnacle in the Kaweahs. Walter A. Starr, Jr. was a young man who loved the High Sierra passionately, climbing forty-two peaks and covering at least 2,000 miles of trails and cross-country routes while researching his *Guide to the John Muir Trail and the High Sierra Region,* published posthumously in 1934. (Starr had died from a fall while attempting a solo ascent of Michael Minaret the year before.)

The mountaineer who lived in both the ages of the pioneers and the rock climbers was the legendary Norman Clyde. He made the first of his first ascents in 1914, and from 1920 to 1946 he came to totally dominate climbing in the High Sierra. It can be safely said that he made at least one thousand ascents of peaks in the range, and of these approximately 120 were either first ascents of unclimbed peaks or new routes on previously climbed mountains. Clyde was a scholar of the classics, and he would spend hours reading Homer in classical Greek at a timberline campsite, with occasional glances toward the surface of a lake to see if the trout were rising. He was famous for his huge packs, which seldom weighed less than ninety pounds. These packs contained numerous cast iron pots, books in foreign languages ("They last longer that way," he once explained), guns, skis, a small anvil to repair hobnailed boots, ski boots, hiking boots, tennis shoes for rock climbing, camp slippers, five cameras, two fishing rods, reels, plus other essential impedimenta that was necessary to live in the mountains for months on end. Clyde was an eccentric, and many people believed that his equipment was strange (perhaps because he carried no stove, fuel, or water purification system) but as his old friend Smoke Blanchard once pointed out, "Norman was not just visiting the mountains or passing through the peaks. He lived there."

It is a matter of great debate among alpine historians of the High Sierra as to when ropes were first *properly* used to safeguard a party making a difficult ascent. Clarence King and Richard Cotter used ropes while crossing the Kings–Kern Divide in 1864, as did George Anderson on Half Dome in 1875, and Bolton Brown during his first ascent of Mt. Clarence King in 1896. It is my belief that the first proper roped climb in the High Sierra occurred on September 7, 1930, when John Mendenhall and Max Van Patten climbed the northeast face of Laurel Mountain. Mendenhall wrote in the 1931 *Sierra Club Bulletin:* "My companion and I were roped, moved one at a time, and employed the belays." The proper use of the rope in rock climbing became common after 1931. In that year, Robert L. M. Underhill visited the High Sierra from the East Coast and taught proper rope management to members of the Sierra Club during its annual High Trip. After this outing, a grand tour of the High Sierra was arranged, and Underhill and other prominent climbers made ascents of the north face of Temple Crag, Thunderbolt Peak, and the east face of Mt. Whitney. Rock Climbing Sections of the Sierra Club were soon organized in the San Francisco and Los Angeles areas, and climbers such as Jules Eichorn, Oliver Kehrlein, Glen Dawson, David Brower, Raffi Bedayn, Richard Leonard, Bestor Robinson, and Hervey Voge, as well as many others, made difficult ascents in the High Sierra in the 1930s, at a standard never dreamed of by LeConte or Hutchinson, in relative safety.

The Sierra Club was founded in 1892, but the first annual outing of the club occurred in 1901 at Tuolumne Meadows. This annual event came to be known as the "High Trip" and it reached its height in the 1930s. The trip was six weeks long, divided into three two-week segments, and participants (as many as two hundred) would travel from one end of the Sierra to the other. Packers would relay food and equipment between camps on layover days, while the members of the party would either take in the mountain scene in the valley ("The Meadoweers") or frantically leave the valley and climb peaks ("The Polemonium Club"). A commissary staff ("The Management") fed everyone, using sheepherder stoves. After dinner the group would gather around a large campfire to hear lectures by renowned men of science, performances by talented musicians, or tales of adventure by mountaineers. It is common for mountain travelers of today to look down on this method of travel that was enjoyed so long ago. The Sierra Club High Trips should not be despised. The pity is that they will never return to those days of glory.

After World War II, rock climbers who had learned their craft on the big walls of Yosemite Valley turned their attention to the more remote walls of the High Sierra backcountry. The main character behind these endeavors was Warren Harding, and his ascents of the southwest face of Mt. Conness and the east face of Keeler Needle were far ahead of their time. There was a resurgence of interest in some of the fine alpine climbs available in the High Sierra in the late 1960s and early 1970s. The leaders of these efforts were Galen Rowell and expatriate Briton Chris Jones, who discovered classic lines on the west face of Mt. Russell, on the south face of Lone Pine Peak, and Charlotte Dome.

In 1974, *Ascent,* the Sierra Club mountaineering journal, stopped publishing the traditional climbing notes on new routes, due to a feeling on the part of its editors that "the Sierra is too close to losing its remaining mystery and its remaining promise." It appears that this action occurred too soon, for although all of the major and most of the minor peaks of the High Sierra had been climbed, there were still countless fine climbs waiting to be discovered. Some of the discoverers included Alan Bartlett, Bart O'Brien, Steve Porcella, Vern Clevenger, Peter Cummings, Alan Roberts, Mike Strassman, Cameron Burns, Craig Peer, Eddie Joe, Dick Leversee, Mike Graber, Herb Laeger, Eve Laeger, David Wilson, and Greg Vernon. Even if exploratory rock climbing continues at its present rate, I believe that the mystery the range has to offer will not be exhausted for another hundred years.

Are there any unclimbed peaks left in the High Sierra? In 1938 Richard Leonard published a list of peaks for which no records then existed, as an appendix to *Mountain Records of the Sierra Nevada.* I have checked, double-checked, and cross-checked this list many times while preparing this book, and I have come to the conclusion that, yes, there are still some unclimbed peaks in the High Sierra. Most of these will involve hours of drudgery for rather dubious rewards, but a scant few are beautifully contoured on the map. Maybe I'll see you on some of these peaks!

Safety

Mountains are extraordinarily dangerous places. But the High Sierra is a rather benevolent place in comparison with the other great ranges of the world. There are no man-eating animals, killer storms are so rare that when they do occur they get newspaper coverage, the rock is relatively solid, and the glaciers are well behaved. The High Sierra is a gentle wilderness. But there are some things that hikers and climbers should be aware of in the gentle wilderness. What follows is simply a checklist of the most common hazards in the High Sierra, and some tips regarding them. It is no substitute

for proper training in outdoor safety.

Stream Crossings. A remarkable number of people have drowned while crossing streams in the High Sierra. The force of water should never be underestimated. Water moving at 5 miles per hour (or 7 feet per second) exerts 103 pounds of pressure on 1.2 square feet of the surface of the human body. Also, your weight advantage is negated by the buoyant effect of the water.

It is perhaps unnecessary to say that the best way to cross a stream is on a bridge or a log. Lacking these, cross the stream in the morning, preferably upstream from a confluence, where the stream is wide and shallow. Some people carry old tennis shoes to protect their feet during a crossing. Next best is to remove socks and only wear boots in the water. Only hardy individuals cross barefoot in swift, cold water—sharp rocks on the streambed could damage feet.

Some believe that the safe way to cross a swift and deep stream is by using ropes—a dangerous practice. If someone attempts a crossing while being belayed and stumbles, the belayer will be unable to pull the victim upstream; if the victim is lucky, the current will push him or her back to the bank where the belayer is located. More likely, the rope will snag on a rock on the streambed, and the victim has only one direction to go: down, underwater. Others may say that the solution is to have two belayers, one on each side of the stream. This is even more dangerous, because if the victim stumbles, the ropes will assume a V shape, and each side will keep the victim from being pulled ashore. Neither belayer will have the strength to pull the victim to safety, and the victim has only one direction to go: down, underwater. Never use ropes to cross a stream.

Lightning. Being struck by lightning is a very real hazard in the High Sierra. It goes without saying that you should flee from summits or ridges when thunder is heard in the distance. Lightning can also occur when there aren't any distant signs of an electrical storm approaching. I climbed a peak once during a cloudy day when there weren't any signs of electrical activity. That is, until I reached the summit, when a spark of electricity shot from the summit register to my hand. I didn't sign the register on that peak!

If a party is caught high on a peak during a thunderstorm, the best tactic is to move off of the ridge as far as possible and to sit or squat on packs, coiled ropes, foam pads, or other insulators. Don't take shelter under talus, in a rock crevice, or in a cave. Electrical currents go through these places; it is better to keep as low as possible on the surface. It is a myth that lightning is attracted to metal, and it is pointless to throw away climbing hardware to prevent a direct strike. Those who survive this experience will witness tremendous flashes of light with thunder louder than the roar of sixteen-inch guns, painful hail storms, and the air buzzing and crackling overhead. A few have been really lucky to survive after witnessing St. Elmo's fire glowing off of rocks, equipment, and themselves.

Hypothermia. The most dangerous part of a solo trip in the High Sierra is that you may have hypothermia and not know it. Death by exposure usually begins when a tired and hungry hiker pushes his or her limits during cold, wet, and windy weather. The victim will have trouble keeping warm, become weak and cranky, and start to shiver uncontrollably. When the shivering stops, death is imminent. Anybody who starts to exhibit these symptoms should get into a tent or other windproof shelter, remove wet clothes, and slide into a sleeping bag. Consumption of hot drinks and high-energy foods usually speeds recovery. If the victim is or has been shivering uncontrollably, it may be necessary to provide external heat by building a fire or having someone strip off his or her clothes and climb into the sleeping bag with the victim.

Rockfall. Natural rockfall is rather rare in the High Sierra. It ordinarily happens in chutes during strong rain showers, or in snow or ice couloirs with the melting and freezing of ice. The most common type of rockfall is that produced by members of a climbing party. This is best avoided by not knocking off any loose rocks. Other tactics include spreading the party out horizontally or keeping everyone close together so that the impact of a falling rock is minimized. Shout out "rock!" when a missile is dislodged, and take cover when you hear this signal.

The typical Sierra peak is composed of "a pile of bricks." This means that the rock is heavily fractured. The rock itself is solid, but the big rocks that make up the peak seem to have been stacked by the Great Architect. Many of these huge blocks are loose even though they appear to be solid. A common accident in the High Sierra is when a climber pulls him- or herself up onto one of these blocks, upsetting its balance, and the rock falls, taking the climber with it. You should expect talus to be loose, no matter what its size, or where it is located.

Altitude Sickness. The thin air at high altitudes does strange things to people. The most common illness is known as Acute Mountain Sickness. Symptoms include headache, no appetite, nausea, and poor or no sleep. (In other words, symptoms similar to a hangover.) This illness can usually be prevented by gaining altitude slowly. Those susceptible should take a day to gain each 1,000 feet of altitude (this refers to the sleeping altitude). Those with the illness should take the day off, rest, relax, and drink a lot of fluids. (That is, do what you would do if you had a hangover.) If symptoms persist, do not continue ascending; ignoring these warning signs may mean serious consequences.

A more dangerous form of altitude illness is High Altitude Pulmonary Edema. This can cause death quickly. Symptoms include shortness of breath, weakness, a high pulse, vomiting, and a cough with frothy, then bloody sputum. The most telltale clue is a gurgling or bubbling sound from the chest, which can be heard by most people without the aid of a stethoscope. If anyone exhibits these symptoms, get him or her down to a lower elevation *immediately*, regardless of inconvenience, the time of day or night, or the weather. Rescuers should be notified immediately, and a helicopter with oxygen should be dispatched.

Fortunately this illness is rather rare, but it has been observed in the High Sierra. I once met a man displaying all of the symptoms at 10,850 feet. He had taken four days to reach that altitude from the trailhead at 7,300 feet.

Weather. Winter typically comes to the High Sierra in mid-November, after the snowfall of a major autumn storm fails to melt. During some years this storm occurs as early as mid-October; other years, it happens as late as mid-January.

Generally speaking, air temperatures during the winter in the High Sierra are relatively mild (at least when compared to those of the other great mountain ranges in the contigu-

The Sierra Wave above Onion Valley (photo by Norm Rohn)

ous United States). The average minimum overnight temperature is approximately 15 degrees F.; daytime highs are near freezing in the shade; the air is much warmer in the sunlight.

Although the winter temperatures in the High Sierra are relatively mild, nature usually makes up for this by the amount of snowfall. The May 1915 *Monthly Weather Review* reads: "California, usually thought of as a land of fruit, sunshine, and flowers, also has within its borders the region of greatest snowfall in the United States." Other regions have since been found to receive greater snowfall, but the point remains valid: The High Sierra can receive a phenomenal amount of snow. In the winter of 1969, the town of Mammoth Lakes was buried under snow. I remember opening the door of a ski lodge, taking two steps down the front steps, and then *climbing up* twenty-five steps to see the roof barely visible above the snow.

Winter weather is typically influenced by the low-pressure system in the Gulf of Alaska, the Pacific High, and a high-pressure system of varying strength that usually exists over the middle of the North American continent. During fall and winter, the Pacific High gradually moves south (in August, the northern edge of the Pacific High is at 40 degrees north latitude, the approximate latitude of Cape Mendocino; in November, its northern edge is at 32 degrees north latitude, a latitude that is south of San Diego). Gulf of Alaska or Aleutian storms (low-pressure areas) move southeast, are blocked by the Pacific High, and may move east over the Sierra Nevada, depending on the strength and location of the high pressure system over North America. This is the situation in a nutshell.

But there are some variables. An Alaskan storm may move directly southeast, and bring cold temperatures (perhaps 10 to 20 degrees F.) and some snow to the northern part of the High Sierra. Skiers hope that these storms move south at first, and are stalled over the Pacific Ocean for a while before moving onshore. These storms are warmed by the ocean, pick up more moisture, and bring relatively warm temperatures (perhaps 20 to 30 degrees F.) and dump a lot of snow in the High Sierra. But there may be a strong high-pressure area over the Great Basin, and this would divert some storms to the Pacific Northwest. This strong high-pressure system over the Great Basin can also force air outward from its center. This may take the form of a strong, cold wind blowing out of the east, which is readily felt atop the Sierra crest. (In Southern California, this is known as a Santa Ana wind, which usually feels much warmer because of the low elevation along the coast.)

So, good weather signs in winter may include a wind out of the east, crisp, cold air, and unlimited visibility. An old joke is that the wind changes direction so that it can go back and bring more snow. Does a wind out of the west mean that a storm is on its way? Maybe. Mountains create their own wind patterns, so wind direction by itself may not mean much; but if there are gusty winds coming from many directions, it may be a sign of approaching storm activity. It is colder at night, so cold air should flow (i.e., wind should blow) downhill at night. A west-facing valley with the wind blowing uphill (out of the west) at night may be a storm sign. It may be hazy, perhaps due to a storm pushing air pollution forward into the High Sierra from the Central Valley. High, cirrus clouds (especially those with mares' tails) may mean that the weather will change in a few days. Rings around the sun and/or moon may mean that a storm is due within 24 hours (if the storm arrives in less than 24 hours, then it may be short-lived; if the storm arrives later, then it may last awhile). Low, dark clouds usually mean that a storm is imminent.

But most of the winter is quite pleasant and the sun seems to shine every day all day long. It is interesting to note that professional skiers at Mammoth Mountain are routinely used as subjects in experiments investigating the cause and prevention of skin cancer.

Spring typically lasts from April until June. A winter-type storm (out of the Gulf of Alaska or the Aleutians) is still possible at this time of year. The northern edge of the Pacific High is at 37 degrees north latitude in May, the approximate latitude of Santa Cruz on the California coast and Taboose Pass in the High Sierra. One type of spring storm starts east of Japan and crosses the Pacific Ocean, gaining strength along the way before making a landfall on the West Coast. If there is a weak high-pressure system over the Great Basin, this storm would cross over into the High Sierra, dropping a lot of snow, sometimes even more than the total winter snowfall. Experienced ski mountaineers have learned to study weather maps of the entire northern Pacific Ocean prior to a trans-Sierra ski tour. In some years there have been as many as five storms lined up along the 37th parallel across the Pacific. It is foolhardy to enter the High Sierra under these conditions.

Please don't think that I am not recommending spring as a time to visit the High Sierra. When the weather is good, it is an excellent time for properly equipped and experienced skiers and mountaineers. The corn snow can be perfect for skiing in April and May, and climbers will find beautiful snow slopes up the peaks rather than miles of talus. In the morning, the snow will be frozen, making upward travel relatively easy. In the early afternoon, the bottom drops out of the snow, just in time for glissades or downhill skiing. The snow-covered mountains give the High Sierra an alpine flavor, and I know some individuals who consider spring to be the only time to visit the High Sierra.

Throughout the winter and spring, you may see snow surveyors making their rounds in the High Sierra. These are men and women who are paid to ski cross-country in the wilderness. They visit snow courses in the backcountry, and measure the depth and density of the snow to enable the state Department of Water Resources to accurately predict the amount of runoff that farmers and local water departments can expect during the spring and summer, when the snowpack melts. The High Sierra could be considered a vast reservoir which delivers water for the economic benefit and well-being of the citizens of California. If it weren't for the Sierra Nevada, California would just be another desert.

The Department of Water Resources makes runoff forecasts in April and May, and this information is published in the local media. This is useful information for the hiker, as it gives him or her an idea of how much snow and how much high water can be expected during a visit to the mountains. These forecasts are expressed in a percentage of normal, based on a fifty-year average. For example, I once hiked for a week in the High

Sierra in the middle of June when the snowpack was 43 percent of normal. An ice axe wasn't needed to cross a pass, and I never got my feet wet, even when crossing a major river. A few years later I repeated the same hike at the same time of year but the snowpack was 205 percent of normal. I had great difficulty crossing the same pass due to a huge cornice, and the river was in flood stage. Generally speaking, you can expect passes that cross the Sierra crest to be more or less snow free by July 1 in normal (i.e., 100 percent) snow years. During that 205 percent of normal snow year, some passes did not become passable to ordinary mortals until the middle of August.

Summer in the High Sierra lasts from the end of June through the middle of September. (By the way, mosquitos are usually present only in the early part of the summer.) It is usually quite pleasant, with daily shade temperatures ranging from 50 to 70 degrees F., with night temperatures from 30 to 45 degrees F. The temperature in the sun is much higher due to the high altitude, low humidity, and lack of dust. Protection against glare and sunburn is usually needed. Afternoon showers may be experienced, and the refrain that "it never rains at night in the Sierra" seems to have some validity.

The northern edge of the Pacific High is at 40 degrees north latitude in August, the approximate latitude of Cape Mendocino and Lassen Peak. This effectively blocks any storm from moving in from the Gulf of Alaska or Japan to California. The big weather concern during the summer is the tropical storms that may bring moist, unstable air into California or the Great Basin from the west coast of Mexico. This storm is not a local phenomenon but rather can cover the entire range with rain (or snow and hail at higher elevations). Signs of such a storm include clouds moving out of the southwest and toward the northeast, relatively high humidity, and the presence of thick clouds that cover almost the entire sky at night. Rain at night is an almost sure sign that a major tropical storm has arrived. Tropical Storm Norman made a landfall in September 1978 near Los Angeles, and this storm brought much grief to those in the High Sierra at that time.

A more typical weather phenomenon is the afternoon thunderstorm cycle. After several days of perfectly clear weather, some scattered clouds may appear in the afternoon but disappear by sundown. During the next few days the clouds appear earlier and earlier and grow in size, but still disappear before the end of the day. After about five days of this, cumulus "fair-weather" clouds appear in the late morning. By midafternoon these clouds join into thunderheads, which shoot upward far into the sky. The sun disappears behind these clouds and the temperature drops. You can hear thunder in the distance, and then the clouds drop their loads of rain, hail, and snow amidst flashes of lightning, terrific crashes of thunder, and winds that seem to come from all directions. The precipitation gradually lightens (indicating that the life of the thunderstorm is about to end), and soon the sun reappears. Tents and rain gear are soon drying, and everyone wonders what all of the fuss was about. Afternoon thunderstorms may continue for a few more days before the cycle is completed.

Autumn in the High Sierra typically lasts from the middle of September to the first major winter storm, which usually happens in mid-November. In many ways fall is the best season to be in the High Sierra. Mosquitos are completely absent, the nights are crisp and cold, and it seems as if the traveler has the mountains all to him- or herself. Storms during this season can deposit several inches of snow, but the usual Indian summer weather soon returns and what snow is left quickly disappears. Everyone traveling in the High Sierra should carry warm clothing and a stormproof tent, and make certain that their camps are positioned so that a convenient escape route leads them to safety, rather than into higher elevations, should the first major winter storm occur.

A meteorological landmark of the High Sierra is the Sierra Wave. This beautiful, long, lenticular cloud may run along the Sierra crest for over 200 miles. It is formed when high, strong winds out of the west hit the western slope of the High Sierra. This forces the moving air upward, where it cools, condenses, and forms a cloud. The wind descends on the east side of the range, where it warms, expands, and becomes clear air. The appearance of a Sierra Wave means only one thing for certain: there are high winds aloft. There may be rain or snow in the wave,

or it may be simply overcast. The Sierra Wave can appear in any season, and it can also appear in the absence of other storm signs; this usually indicates that it is only a local phenomenon. (In this case, you can find better weather by simply moving away from the Sierra crest.) But when it appears along with other storm signs, it is another piece of data to consider when you are deciding whether to stay put, to move camp to ensure that a high pass does not separate the party from safety, or go home and watch television.

Avalanches. The High Sierra has a well-deserved reputation of having a low avalanche danger. This just means that the danger is low, not that it is nonexistent. What follows are my observations of avalanche conditions in the High Sierra. New snow in the High Sierra is damp and is commonly known as "Sierra Cement" by skiers. But the effects of the day and night gradually thaw and freeze the snowpack until it turns into a beautiful layer of corn snow, which is God's gift to ski mountaineers. This action also coincidentally creates a stable snowpack, and I believe that this is why there are so few avalanche accidents among backcountry skiers in the High Sierra. In my experience, when the skiing is bad, so are the avalanche conditions; when the skiing is good, the avalanche conditions are usually minimal.

Avalanches occur most frequently following a snowfall of 4 inches or more. In this situation, it is best to avoid steep (30 degrees or so) terrain for at least a day. During winters of normal snowfall, avalanches tend to occur on north-facing slopes, especially in couloirs or chutes. The sun warms the snow on south-facing slopes, and it soon thaws and freezes into a stable slope.

But in winters of heavy snowfall, avalanches occur in unexpected places. South-facing slopes may have a deep snowpack, with many unstable layers covering a rough talus base. This entire slope may avalanche in a slab, taking not only the snowpack but underlying rocks and trees with it, creating a spectacular path of destruction in its wake.

Most ski mountaineering takes place in April and May, when the conditions are optimal. One warning sign of instability during this time is overnight temperatures above freezing. During April and May, daytime

Close call! Avalanches in Armstrong Canyon (photo by R. J. Secor)

temperatures will usually be quite warm and pleasant, with evening temperatures below freezing. Overnight temperatures above freezing create a dangerous situation, and heavy rainfall combined with overnight temperatures above freezing increases the danger.

The most important rule to remember about avalanches is that there are no rules. This does not mean that it is impossible to learn why, when, or where avalanches are likely to occur. Instruction in this art is available, and I encourage anyone who is heading out into the High Sierra in the winter or spring to try to learn all they can about the "White Death." The art of avalanche prediction is 60 percent hard facts, 30 percent practice and judgment, and 10 percent luck.

Rescue. Requests for assistance should be directed to the rangers in the national parks, or to the county sheriff outside of the parks.

In the final analysis, safety is in the character of the individual rather than in the use of equipment or knowledge of specialized techniques. The judgment of a party can make all of the difference between a pleasurable journey and a preventable tragedy.

Conservation

Astronomers at the Lick Observatory atop Mt. Hamilton in the Coast Range at one time were able to point their telescope towards the Sierra Nevada and photograph the peaks and passes. This was an interesting diversion for them at sunset, before they began their nightly explorations of the heavens. It is rare today for the astronomers to see the High Sierra from Mt. Hamilton due to the pervasive air pollution in the Central Valley.

California is the most populated state in the country. The effects of having too many people in one place—traffic congestion and air and water pollution—are apparent. It might appear that most of these city problems would be absent in the wilderness of the High Sierra, but California's large population is having its effect in the mountains as well. All of us, i.e., *you* and *I*, must make the extra effort to leave the mountains unspoiled for the enjoyment of future generations. We must leave no traces of our passing through the mountains, and have as little effect on the terrain as possible.

Go Light. This means to travel as lightly as possible, in terms of the weight on your back or on the pack animal, and to go light on the terrain. This is a matter of learning to be at home in the wilderness with a few pieces of equipment, rather than carrying and living in an elaborate camp. It is possible to get along with less than you think—in travel, as in life, often "less is more." You will be more comfortable and less tired, and will make the effort to take care of the mountains.

This also applies to those who travel with horses, mules, or burros. Too much equipment translates into more animals that must be rounded up in the morning, fed, groomed, loaded, guided during the day's travel, unloaded, picketed or hobbled, and so on. Too many animals can translate into even more animals to carry their feed!

Low-Profile Camping. Keep your group small, and try to camp at least 100 feet away from a trail, preferably in an area that is screened from the trail by the terrain or vegetation. Colorful equipment may have caught your eye in the store, but it can be visually offensive in the wilderness, and wildlife will see you long before you ever have a chance to see it. Keep the "improvements" to your camp to a minimum. Trenches around tents and hip holes lead to erosion. And pack out all refuse. Unless each and every one of us starts to show some class, camping in the High Sierra wilderness will be no different from camping at a roadside campground.

Also, you should select "hard" campsites. Meadows, lakeshores, and streamsides cannot take the wear and tear of camping. These soils are moist and soft, and will rapidly disappear from the effects of too many campers, just as meadows disappeared in the nineteenth century from too many sheep. Campsites should be placed at least 100 feet away from any water source, but even this is not enough distance in popular areas.

Fires. Large campfires are passé. At timberline, down wood is being burnt up faster than it is produced. The beautiful snags left standing after lightning strikes are part of the unique scenery of the High Sierra, but even these are being torn apart in the search for more wood. In some places these trees have disappeared completely. Many hikers don't know that they were ever there. Wood at timberline is a finite resource, and it must be used sparingly in the few locales where fires are allowed.

Instead of a wood fire, cook on a white gas, butane, or kerosene stove. Cooking is much easier and usually faster, and the weight penalty is negligible. If a fire *must* be built,

keep it small. The best fireplace is the one used throughout rural areas of developing countries: three rocks approximately the size of grapefruits, arranged in a triangle with 6-inch sides. The fire is kept small and easy to control for cooking, with a minimal waste of wood. When camp is broken, let the coals burn down and out, pulverize the ashes to a fine powder, cover the hearth with clean sand, and return the stones to their places of origin. Scatter the surplus wood. The fireplace should be completely gone when you leave.

But consider using a stove. Some stoves have as much personality as a campfire, and the best way to get to know the night is to crawl into your sleeping bag for complete warmth and watch the heavens circle overhead.

Water. Protect water quality in the High Sierra by burying human waste at least 4 inches deep and at least 100 feet from water sources. Please be willing to walk a little farther and dig and cover a little more carefully. Do all washing at least 100 feet from water. Purify all drinking water (no matter how pure it may look) by means of boiling, filters, or an iodine-based chemical purifier.

Ducks and Blazes. These markers appear regularly along High Sierra routes. Ducks are also known as cairns; a duck is a small cairn, erected by well-meaning hikers to show the correct route to those who follow. The problem with ducks is that they seldom actually show the easiest route. They also have a tendency to direct all cross-country hikers onto the same path. This leads to the creation of a use trail, which usually scars the land above timberline. There are a lot of use trails in the High Sierra (in fact, some are described in this book) but we must do everything we can to prevent more use trails from being created. I believe that anyone who leaves the trail and sets out cross-country should be capable of finding the correct route on his or her own without the assistance of ducks. Don't build ducks, and destroy all ducks encountered.

In a similar manner, a party hiking cross-country should spread out when crossing a meadow. It is tempting to "stay on the trail" and follow the leader's footsteps. But this leads to the creation of a rut across the meadow, which would soon become a permanent scar. It is much better and often easier to go around a meadow. If this is impossible, the party should spread out and each individual should make his or her own path, one that at least stands a chance of healing. And don't cut switchbacks while hiking on established trails.

Blazes are scars that have been made on trees to mark the route of a trail or cross-country route. Blazes reached an art form in the late nineteenth century in Yosemite, when the new national park was being patrolled by the cavalry. The common blazes seen in Yosemite are the "T" (for trail) blazes in northern Yosemite, and the pointed "Obelisk" blazes in the southern part of the park. Today's hikers should admire these blazes, but not create any new ones.

Bears. Grizzly bears are extinct in California, except on the state flag. Black bears (which may actually be black, brown, or blue) are present throughout the High Sierra. In most cases, they are basically timid creatures that are very clever at obtaining hikers' food, and have the potential of causing great bodily harm. Don't ever store food in a tent. Some backcountry campsites have metal food-storage lockers, or overhead cables to aid in hanging food out of a bear's reach. Lacking these, you must hang food from trees using the counterbalance method. Find a tree with a live, slightly down-sloping branch that extends 10 feet from the trunk, and is at least 20 feet above the ground. The end of the branch must be at least an inch thick so that it will support the weight of the food, but not a bear cub. Weight a cord with a rock or stick to give it enough momentum and toss one end over the branch and back down to the ground. Divide the food into two separate stuff sacks, weighing no more than ten pounds each. Tie the rope to one sack, and hoist it to the branch. Tie the other sack as high on the cord as possible, and also tie a loop of cord to this sack to aid in retrieval. Use a long stick to push the second sack upward until it is level with the first sack. The sacks of food should be at least 12 feet above the ground. The food is retrieved by using a long stick to hook the loop of cord on the second sack. Pull the stick and sack down slowly to avoid tangles, untie the second sack, and lower the first sack down to the ground.

This procedure becomes quite easy with practice. A few other pointers: Make camp early, and hang food before it is too dark and you are too tired to do a proper job. Find a tree with a branch that runs parallel to a nearby granite slab. This provides an extra reach, but make sure that the slab is not positioned to give a bear an extra reach as well. Bears are attracted to anything with an odor, so soap, toothpaste, sunscreen, toothbrushes, cosmetics, and garbage should also go in the stuff sacks. Packs should be left on the ground with all pockets, zippers, and flaps open so that the bear doesn't tear it open to find nothing to eat. It is a deadly practice to attempt to scare a grizzly bear away, but the black bears of the High Sierra are generally very shy. If a bear approaches your camp, everyone should yell, scream, bang pots, and throw rocks at the bear, taking care to miss your friends. Of course, beware of a mother bear with cubs—always maintain a safe distance. Never attempt to retrieve food or gear from a bear; wait until the bear has left the area. There has never been a report of an unprovoked attack by a black bear in the High Sierra (but all too many reports of tourists being injured while intentionally feeding a bear). An aware, realistic attitude by everyone toward bears in the High Sierra will help keep these creatures wild.

Historical Artifacts. National Park Service policy defines any object made by humans that is more than fifty years old as a historical artifact; these artifacts are the property of the National Park Service. Typical items are arrowheads, mortar holes, sheepherder stoves, cavalry relics, animal traps, and even the garbage dumps established by the Sierra Club High Trips! It is illegal to remove these artifacts from national parks. Any artifacts found should be left where they are, and their location reported to the National Park Service.

Climbing Ethics. Avoid placing bolts and fixed pitons wherever possible. The rock on the high peaks is heavily fractured and eminently well suited for the use of runners and chocks. Chalk marks on the rock make the art of climbing a "paint by the numbers" exercise. Its use diminishes the pleasure of those who follow, and it interferes with the discovery of a route's secrets. Graffiti, of course, has no place in the mountains. Make brief comments in the summit registers, not on the mountains.

Wilderness Permits. The United States Forest Service (USFS) and the National Park Service (NPS) maintain control over the lands under their jurisdictions by issuing permits. Wilderness Permits or Backcountry Use Permits have two purposes: They enable the authorities to educate wilderness users on minimum impact camping techniques, and they also limit the number of hikers that enter the wilderness during the most popular season, or quota period, which lasts from the end of June to mid-September in most locations. During this period, permits can be obtained by making reservations far in advance, but in some places a small number of first-come, first-served permits are saved to be issued each day. The trick to gain entry to the wilderness during the quota period is to be flexible enough to change trailheads and trails (and perhaps dates) from your first choices. Hikers who visit the High Sierra outside of the quota period should have no problem obtaining a wilderness permit.

It must be stressed that all parties need to have a wilderness permit in their possession while they are in a wilderness area or a national park backcountry, regardless of the time of year. Those without permits will be cited by the rangers who regularly patrol the backcountry and wilderness; this involves a fine or an order to appear in court, and a verbal order from the issuing officer to leave the wilderness or backcountry immediately.

Addresses of the ranger stations that issue permits are given in each chapter. Contact them for the most up-to-date information regarding quotas and advance reservations. A request for a wilderness permit must include the date and place of entry and exit from the wilderness, method of travel (on foot, ski, or horseback), the number of people in the group, and the number of pack animals that will be taken.

How to Use This Book

The region described has been divided into thirteen chapters, generally based upon the drainage patterns of each area. Each chapter has a brief overview of the area being discussed, a list of that area's land managers, a list of pertinent maps, and descriptions of roads, trails, established cross-country routes, and routes on the peaks.

Sketch maps, drawings, and photographs are also provided to enable the reader to better understand the terrain being discussed.

These show features, routes, and place names that may not be on the USGS maps, but should not be used as substitutes for these maps.

Special mention should be made of what I call "Wrinkles." It is a rare mountain traveler who is interested only in one single destination during a journey in the mountains. The Wrinkles sections show the reader alternative routes or how various places can be linked together in ways that may not be apparent during home study.

You may notice that no mention of campsites has been made in this guide. This is because the great increase in the numbers of mountain travelers over the last generation has resulted in tremendous human impact on the High Sierra's popular campsites. Besides, in this age of high-tech camping equipment and lightweight stoves, you can camp almost anywhere in relative comfort.

Maps. This book has been written under the assumption that the reader will be using it along with a detailed topographic map that shows the region being discussed. After all, the purpose of this book is to provide the wilderness user with information not provided by a map, and to correct map information that is in error.

The USGS has produced extremely detailed 1:24,000 scale (1 inch = 2,000 feet; the *7.5-minute series*) maps of the entire Sierra Nevada. These maps will eventually replace the older 1:62,500 scale (1 inch = approximately 1 mile; the *15-minute series*) maps that have been available in the past. The problem with these newer, large-scale maps is that they are actually *too* detailed. Previously, you could enjoy an extended trip in the mountains and carry only four maps; when the 15-minute maps are no longer available, it may be necessary to carry sixteen maps to cover the same area. Several maps may be needed to identify a distant landmark, and it is inconvenient to orient oneself on a map in combination with other maps.

Another problem has to do with feet and meters. The older maps showed elevations exclusively in feet. Some of the new maps show elevations in meters, but an adjacent map may show the elevations in feet! These maps would be more useful if every map showed elevations in either meters or feet.

Fortunately, the map situation has been somewhat resolved by the Forest Service's publication of 1:63,360 (1 inch = exactly 1 mile) maps of the Golden Trout Wilderness, the John Muir Wilderness and the Sequoia and Kings Canyon National Parks Backcountry, the Ansel Adams Wilderness, and the Hoover Wilderness. These maps are true bargains; they show sufficient, up-to-date detail. And each covers such a large area that it seems as if they were made for home study during winter evenings. They are available from Forest Service ranger stations and National Park Service visitor centers.

Also of use are the USGS special series maps of Sequoia and Kings Canyon National Parks and of Yosemite National Park. The scale of these maps is 1:125,000 (1 inch = 2 miles) and they are not quite as detailed as those maps mentioned above. But they enable you to get the "big picture" on a reasonably sized piece of paper.

The Forest Service also publishes recreation maps of the national forests, showing roads, trails, campgrounds, and other man-made and natural landmarks, but no topographic detail. These, combined with local road maps issued by automobile clubs, may be useful for finding remote trailheads.

Place Names. Many of the place names used in this book may not appear on the USGS maps of the High Sierra. Some of these names have been in use for years by hikers, climbers, fishermen, rangers, and packers, and have not yet been officially recognized by the Board of Geographic Names. Forty-five of the names used in this book are my own creations. These are usually named after a nearby feature, or after someone who has made a significant contribution to the exploration of the Sierra Nevada. I have taken the liberty of naming a few places after my friends. Place names that are my own creation include: Alpine Pass, Bard Pass, Bilko Pass, Blackcap Pass, Clinch Pass, Confusion Pass, Conness Pass, Courte-Echelle, Cox Col, Dancing Bear Pass, Davis Lake Pass, Deadhorse Pass, Dykeman Pass, Fleming Pass, Franklin Col, Goddard Creek Pass, Grasshopper Pass, Gunsight Pass, Haeckel Col, Lane Pass, Lilley Pass, Lobe Pass, Mantle Pass, McDonald Pass, McGee Lakes Pass, Merriam Pass, Midway Pass, Mt. Mendenhall, Packsaddle Pass, Pete's Col, Post Corral Pass, Pterodactyl Pass, The Right Pass, Rohn Pass, Royce Pass, Russell Pass, Seven Gables Pass, Solomons Pass, Ski Mountaineers Pass, Steel-head Pass, Treasure Col, Two Passes, Ursula Pass, Valor Pass, and Wallace Col.

At first glance it may appear that I have gone crazy in naming the features of the High Sierra. But this list is not excessive when you consider that some 1,860 places are described in this book; also, I only named twelve of the places after my friends.

Some may say that naming physical features implies that humans have mastery over the land. My reply to this is that, from a guidebook author's point of view, a place without a name isn't a place.

Route Descriptions. I once tried to follow a route description that someone gave me for a remote High Sierra peak. The description said to look for an upside-down "W" and I finally gave up and climbed past an "M." What I am trying to say here is that no matter how good the route description, the hiker's or climber's route-finding ability is the essential ingredient for a safe and successful trip.

The information in this book has come from my personal experiences, input from friends, articles and notes that have appeared in semipopular magazines, mountaineering journals, and the newsletters of many small but serious outdoor clubs—and in four cases, rumor, gossip, hearsay, and speculation. The record of exploration of the High Sierra is incomplete, and I am certain that many places worthy of inclusion in this book have been inadvertently omitted.

Roads are usually described in this book from the point of view of driving up into the mountains. Mileage logs are provided, telling the reader when to turn left or right to a tenth of a mile from a prominent starting point along the road.

Trails are usually described the same way. The mileage is given to the nearest quarter-mile. The mileage in this book may differ from the signs at trailheads or along the trail. These signs are frequently inaccurate, and I have instead given my best estimate of the distance covered by a trail. If a trail seemed to me to be X number of miles, then that is the distance that I recorded, regardless of what a sign said.

Cross-country routes are described in the direction that they are normally traveled.

The headings for each cross-country and peak route may be confusing; examples with explanations are given below.

Disappointment Peak

(4242 m; 13,917 ft)

This place is named on the map, and its elevations from the new 7.5-minute map and old 15-minute map, respectively, are listed.

Please note that when two elevations are given, they are the *new and old elevations,* and not the English/metric equivalents.

"Whitney–Russell Pass"

(3980 m+; 13,040 ft+; 0.4 miles NE of Mt. Whitney; UTM 898493)

The quotation marks indicate that this place is not named on the map. The old and new elevations are listed; the plus sign indicates that its exact elevation is not on the map. In this case the summit elevation is not exactly 4000 meters or 13,120 feet (which would be the next contour line on the map), but is higher than 3980 meters or 13,040 feet (which is the last contour line found). The location is then given respective to a place named on the map.

Universal Transverse Mercator (UTM) grid coordinates are sometimes listed to help locate ambiguous places. The grid is defined on the new maps by the fine black lines that are drawn on the map itself. On older maps, the grid is identified by the fine blue tick marks that are spaced 1 kilometer apart in the margins of the map. As far as this book is concerned, only the two larger (in size of typeface, not numeration) numbers are used. These numbers indicate the easterly and northerly coordinates to the nearest kilometer. A location is identified by a six-digit number. The first three digits indicate the easterly coordinate to the nearest 100 meters and the last three digits are the northerly coordinate. In this case, Whitney–Russell Pass is located 800 meters east of the line marked "89" and 300 meters north of the line marked "49" on the Mt. Whitney 7.5- and 15-minute maps.

Perhaps the most speculative information is the first-ascent party listed for routes on the peaks. The earliest recorded ascent is given credit as the first, when this information can be determined. The party listed may not actually have been the first to climb that peak or route, but were the first to *publish* their ascent of the peak or route.

Almost everybody now knows that the Vikings were the first Europeans to visit North America. But Columbus gets all of the credit because he was the first to publish his discovery.

First-ascent information is included at the start of the route description for a route on a peak because it contains facts that may be of use to the savvy mountaineer. A first ascent done in June or July would probably have a description of snow or ice cover, which may be absent in August or September. A first ascent of a route done in the 1930s probably has shorter pitches than one done in later decades. Listing the names of the first-ascent party also helps to identify the correct route; this is especially true on crowded faces, such as the west face of Mt. Russell. The main purpose of including first-ascent information is to make the book more useful, not to glorify these individuals.

Routes on peaks are usually named by their direction from the summit (e.g., southwest slope or north face). In some cases routes have earned new names through popular usage (e.g., the Swiss Arete on Mt. Sill) or they have been renamed by a guidebook author who worships heroes (e.g., the LeConte Route on North Palisade). Route directions (e.g., turn left) are stated from the point of view of facing the summit. If these may be ambiguous, a compass direction is also given: traverse right (south). I usually specify if a traverse is slight (i.e., slightly more vertical than horizontal), diagonal (equal amounts of vertical and horizontal), or horizontal (level).

Many route descriptions are not overly detailed, and a statement that reads, "Follow the south ridge to the summit," should not be taken too literally. The best route will likely involve a number of variations on both sides of the ridge, rather than stubbornly staying directly on the crest of the ridge in difficult places.

Rating System

The Yosemite Decimal System has been used to rate the difficulty of the terrain being described. This system is complex and illogical, and can be confusing to beginners and experts alike. On a more positive note, it seems to have been accepted nationwide by rock climbers and mountaineers, so there may be some basis of understanding among the readers of this book. It also applies to all terrain, from horizontal ground to beyond-the-vertical rock.

Class 1 is walking. Mt. Whitney via the trail and the south slope of Mt. Kaweah fall into this category.

Class 2 is defined here as difficult cross-country travel. In the High Sierra this is usually talus hopping, which requires the occasional use of hands for balance. Hikers who are not used to class 2 terrain will soon become tired, especially if carrying a heavy pack. Talus can be unstable, and the danger of class 2 terrain is that you may stumble among these blocks—and it is also possible for a boulder to dislodge and roll over a hiker. Split Mountain (via the north ridge) is an example of class 2.

Class 3 is where the climbing begins. Hands and feet are used not just for balance, but to hang onto the rock. Steep or large talus can be rated as class 3. Class 3 is more common on steep faces or along ridges and aretes. Novices may feel uncomfortable, but the holds are large and easy to locate. A rope should be available to give a belay to anyone who requests it. Class 3 can be compared to climbing a steep, narrow staircase on the side of a tall building. No guard rail is present, and the climbing is easy but scary. The east face of Middle Palisade and Mt. Mills via the east couloir are examples of class 3.

Class 4 is on steep rock, with smaller holds, and a lot of exposure. ("Exposure" is a euphemism for the amount of air beneath your feet.) Ropes and belays should come into continuous use, because a fall will probably be fatal. Class 4 can be loosely compared to climbing a ladder on the side of a tall building. The handholds and footholds are there, but if you let go, then that is the end. Mt. Humphreys via the southwest slope and northwest face is class 4.

Class 5 is steep and difficult rock climbing, involving the use of protection placed between the leader and the belayer. Holds are small to tiny, and the best holds must be sought by the climber. Types of protection include: *runners* (loops of nylon webbing placed around flakes, blocks, and natural chockstones); *chocks* (placed in cracks); *pitons* (hammered into cracks); and *bolts* (drilled into solid rock).

Class 5 spans a wide range of difficulty, and so has been divided into several categories. A rating of 5.0 is the easiest class 5 climbing, and 5.14 is the most difficult rating currently known (the scale does not have an upper limit). Mathematically oriented minds would assume that 5.14 is easier than 5.2, but this is not the case. The upper ranges of class 5 have been further divided into four subcategories: a, b, c, and d.

Aid climbing, where the climber quite literally hangs from the equipment that has been placed on the rock, was once known as class 6, but this is now rated from A1 to A5. An A1 placement is very simple and will hold a small truck; an A5 placement may be a nest of pitons or stacked nuts that barely supports the climber's weight.

Some technical climbs have been classified into grades, identified as Roman numerals from I to VI. The grade indicates the overall difficulty of the route, i.e., the length, commitment, exposure, continuity, and other factors that give the climber an indication of the seriousness of the route. Generally speaking, a grade I climb takes a couple of hours, grade II a half day, and grade III most of a day. Grade IV would take a full day with some serious pitches, and grades V and VI are big walls, with a lot of difficult free (i.e., class 5) and aid climbing. Grades have fallen out of style recently, but they have been continued here because of their usefulness.

Snow and ice climbs are comparatively rare in the High Sierra during the height of the summer. Ice axes probably won't be needed after the first of July during a normal snow year, and crampons are seldom really essential. Unless, of course, the climber wants to climb snow or ice. Snow and ice climbs have not been rated in this book. Instead, they are described in terms of angle and length. In the late spring and early summer, these climbs will consist of frozen nevé; in the autumn the ice will be brick hard, and will get harder until a substantial snowfall in the middle of the winter starts a new cycle. Rating this plastic medium is quite impossible.

The class number of a climb in this book may mean nothing. It is entirely possible that someone will follow a class 2 route and discover it to be class 3 in reality. Or a class 3 climb may turn out to include a lot of class 4 pitches. Class 4 may include moves up to 5.6 in the real world. And class 4 may turn out to be class 3, class 3 may turn out to be class 2, and so on. (For further information, please see Appendix B.)

This is because there has never been a

general agreement on what each class really means. For over fifty years, climbers in the High Sierra have had different ideas of what each classification means. Readers should put their own judgments ahead of this book. If a route turns out to be more difficult than what this book says, the user should recognize that it may have been incorrectly classified in the first place (or that the user may be off route). And a relatively low rating for a climb should never keep a climber from backing off from a climb in the interest of safety.

Peaks and Registers

Previous guidebooks to the High Sierra have covered some peaks that are not in this book, and vice versa. These other authors were either extremely diligent, and included every closed contour circle no matter how insignificant the peak, or they applied specific criteria to a peak (altitude, routes on it, etc.) before including it.

I have included a peak in this book when I thought it was worthy of mention. This may sound rather arbitrary, but in the final analysis, it is the same criteria that other guidebook authors have used.

Almost all of the peaks in the High Sierra (and a few of the passes) have summit registers. These may be either a few scraps of paper inserted into a pair of nesting tin cans, or the elaborate cast-aluminum boxes with bound blank books that were placed by the Sierra Club many years ago. I never cease to be amazed by these registers. A register may have been placed fifty years ago and be no more than one-third full. It is not uncommon to have three generations sign the same book. I have seen the simple entries made by Bolton Brown, Norman Clyde, Walter A. Starr, Jr., Nobel laureates, and Pulitzer Prize winners in the registers on a few peaks and the grandiose entries made by some who draw pictures, write poems, insult the entries of other climbers, curse guidebook authors, and so on.

Peak baggers usually place a code after their names in a register. For example, a number inside a mountain indicates that this is the nth Sierra peak that he or she has climbed. An entry that reads "2X" or "3X" means that this is his or her second or third ascent of that peak. "SPS" means that the climber is a member of the Sierra Peaks

Section of the Angeles Chapter of the Sierra Club. "PCS" refers to the Peak Climbing Section, Loma Prieta Chapter, Sierra Club. "RCS" is the Rock Climbing Section of many chapters of the Sierra Club. "NAS" is the Northern Alpine Section, Mother Lode Chapter, Sierra Club. "Yeti" is the mascot of the Vagmarken Mountaineering Club. "SAC" refers to the Stanford Alpine Club. "CMC" can refer to the Colorado Mountain Club, the Chicago Mountaineering Club, or the California Mountaineering Club. "AMC" is the Appalachian Mountain Club, and "AAC" is the American Alpine Club. Contrary to popular belief, "SCMA" does not mean Sierra Club My A**, but rather identifies the Southern California Mountaineers Association. "MGS" stands for the Mountaineering Guide Service, and "PSOM" is the Palisade School of Mountaineering; these entries are frequently seen in the Palisades.

It has been a long-standing policy of the Sierra Club to remove summit registers when full and place them in the Sierra Club archives kept in the Bancroft Library at the University of California, Berkeley. My personal view is to keep summit registers on the summits forever. This policy won't work on Mt. Whitney, Mt. Dana, and other popular peaks, but it has worked quite well on some of the "lesser peaks," such as Mt. Stanford or the Devil's Crags.

A Note About Safety

Safety is an important concern in all outdoor activities. No guidebook can alert you to every hazard or anticipate the limitations of every reader. Therefore, the descriptions of roads, trails, routes, and natural features in this book are not representations that a particular place or excursion will be safe for your party. When you follow any of the routes described in this book, you assume responsibility for your own safety. Under normal conditions, such excursions require the usual attention to traffic, road and trail conditions, weather, terrain, the capabilities of your party, and other factors. Keeping informed on current conditions and exercising common sense are the keys to a safe, enjoyable outing.

The Mountaineers

The Whitney Region

For the purposes of this book, the Whitney region includes the Sierra crest from Shepherd Pass to Cottonwood Pass; it is bounded on the west by the Kern River. This area contains some of the highest peaks in California, as well as deep, glaciated canyons, cirques, hanging valleys, sharp ridges, and high passes, which are all the more dramatic in contrast to the views of the desert to the east.

History

As soon as Clarence King discovered Mt. Whitney from the summit of Mt. Tyndall in 1864, the race was on to be the first to climb it. After he and Richard Cotter had returned to the California Geological Survey's camp along Roaring River, King begged the field leader, William Brewer, for permission to make another attempt. Realizing that this would be a first-rate opportunity to fill in more blanks on the map, Brewer gave his permission to King, plus $100 and an escort of two soldiers. King and the soldiers left Visalia and followed the Hockett Trail up the South Fork of the Kaweah River. They crossed the Great Western Divide, descended to the Kern River, and followed a canyon north of what King called "Sheep Rock" (Mt. Langley). This route put him too far to the east (the most difficult side of Mt. Whitney), and he was forced to retreat.

King returned to the eastern Sierra in 1871 and immediately set out for a prominent peak, assuming that it was Mt. Whitney. He and Paul Pinson reached the summit during a storm that obscured the view of surrounding peaks, but they felt confident that the summit of Mt. Whitney had finally been reached. King soon returned to civilization and spread the word that the highest mountain in the United States had been conquered.

As it turned out, King wasn't on the summit of Mt. Whitney after all. In reality, he and Pinson had climbed Mt. Langley, and this error was discovered in late July of 1873. King, on the east coast at the time, immediately headed west and on September 19, 1873, he finally stood on the summit. Unfortunately, two parties had preceded him, both consisting of individuals from the Owens Valley. Mt. Whitney was first climbed on August 18, 1873, by "The Fishermen," John Lucas, Charles D. Begole, and Albert H. Johnson. The second ascent was on August 20, 1873, by William Crapo and Abe Leyda. There was a modest proposal to rename the mountain "Fishermen's Peak," but the name first proposed by William Brewer nine years before remained.

The highest mountain in the United States became the site for many scientific experiments. The first was in 1881, when Samuel P. Langley used the summit for solar heat observations. For the next twenty years the summit was a military reservation, under the control of the U.S. Army Signal Corps, the weather service of the age. A stock trail was constructed to the summit in 1904, and in 1909 a shelter was constructed on the summit by the Smithsonian Institution for the use of its astronomers.

The other peaks in the region were eventually climbed, but Mt. Russell, only 1 mile north of Mt. Whitney, became one of the last 14,000-foot peaks to be climbed in California, in 1926.

One of the first roped rock climbs to be done in the High Sierra was the east face of Mt. Whitney, in 1931. The other faces of the Whitney massif soon saw roped ascents, and the age of rock climbing had begun.

Maps

United States Geological Survey: 7.5-

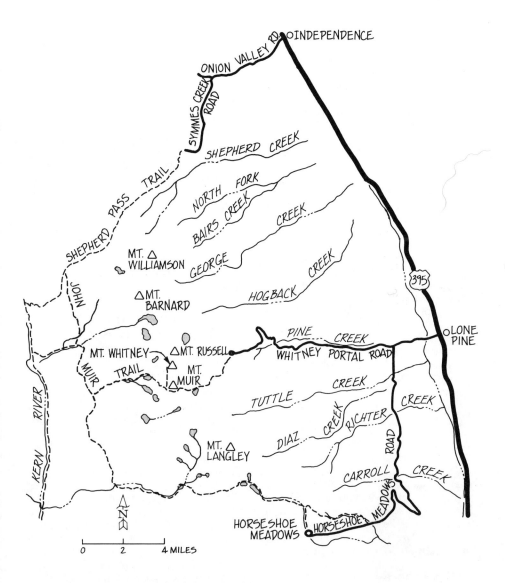

minute series: Cirque Peak, Johnson Peak, Chagoopa Falls, Mt. Langley, Mount Whitney, Mt. Kaweah, Manzanar, Mt. Williamson, Mt. Brewer; 15-minute series: Olancha, Kern Peak, Lone Pine, Mount Whitney; national park maps: Sequoia and Kings Canyon National Parks and Vicinity (1:125,000).

United States Forest Service: Golden Trout Wilderness and South Sierra Wilderness (1:63,360); John Muir Wilderness and the Sequoia–Kings Canyon National Parks Backcountry (1:63,360).

Wilderness Permits

For east-side entry to the Golden Trout Wilderness and John Muir Wilderness: Inyo National Forest, Mt. Whitney Ranger District, Lone Pine, CA 93545.

Roads

Horseshoe Meadows Road

The Horseshoe Meadows Road leads to the Cottonwood Lakes and New Army Pass trailheads. The road starts 3.2 miles. Head west from Lone Pine along the Whitney

Portal Road for 3.2 miles. The Horseshoe Meadows Road goes south, passes Granite View Drive after 2.0 miles, and comes to a gate (locked in winter) 4.7 miles later. The road then starts to climb via a few huge switchbacks and comes to the trailhead for the Cottonwood Lakes/New Army Pass Trail after another 13.0 miles. It continues another 0.3 mile to Horseshoe Meadows, with its campgrounds, and the trailhead for Cottonwood Pass.

Granite View Drive

Granite View Drive serves as the approach to the Tuttle Creek Trailhead. Drive west up the Whitney Portal Road 3.2 miles from Lone Pine to the Horseshoe Meadows Road. Drive south on the Horseshoe Meadows Road, past the Tuttle Creek Campground, to Granite View Drive, 2.0 miles south of the Horseshoe Meadows–Whitney Portal junction. Turn right (west) on the dirt road, and after 2.3 miles the road forks. Go right, and continue another 2.0 miles to a sandy parking area on a flat that overlooks Tuttle Creek. High-clearance, four-wheel-drive vehicles can continue another 0.5 mile, but the road is steep and loose.

Whitney Portal Road

The Whitney Portal Road leads from Lone Pine to the Meysan Lakes and Mt. Whitney trailheads. Drive west up the road from Lone Pine, passing the Horseshoe Meadows Road after 3.2 miles, and continue up the steep grade to Whitney Portal. At 11.3 miles from Lone Pine the road passes the Meysan Lakes Trailhead, and the Mt. Whitney Trailhead at 12.1 miles. The road ends in a loop 0.2 mile beyond the Mt. Whitney Trailhead.

George Creek Road

The only thing harder than hiking up rugged George Creek is driving the last 0.5 mile to the trailhead. This road begins 5.3 miles south of Independence on Highway 395, or 10.3 miles north of Lone Pine on the same highway. Head west on the dirt road, pass a gate (leave it as you found it, i.e., either open or closed), and follow the road as it gradually turns south. Drive past the Manzanar Cemetery to a fork 2.6 miles from the highway. Turn right, and continue driving toward the mountains for 5.0 miles to another fork. Turn left (most people park

somewhere along the next 0.5 mile) and drive to the trailhead after another 1.3 miles. The last 0.5 mile of the road is the worst; only high-clearance, four-wheel-drive vehicles are suitable.

Symmes Creek Road

The Symmes Creek Road leads to the Shepherd Pass Trailhead. Drive west from Independence on the Onion Valley Road for 4.5 miles to Foothill Road. Turn left (south) onto the dirt road, and turn right at a fork after 1.3 miles. Continue another 1.6 miles to a corral. This is the stock trailhead; hikers should continue driving to the next fork, 0.4 mile farther. Turn right (west) and drive another 0.5 mile to another fork. Go right, and continue another 0.9 mile to the Shepherd Pass Trailhead for hikers.

Trails

Cottonwood Pass Trail and the Pacific Crest Trail (19½ miles)

This trail leads from the end of the Horseshoe Meadows Road to the summit of Cottonwood Pass in 3½ miles. The Cottonwood Pass Trail continues downhill to the southwest, through Big Whitney Meadow, where it eventually meets the Siberian Pass Trail. One branch of the Pacific Crest Trail heads south and east from Cottonwood Pass to Trail Pass, and, ultimately, to Mexico.

From Cottonwood Pass, the Pacific Crest Trail traverses the southern slopes of Cirque Peak before climbing and then descending to a junction with the Siberian Pass Trail after 5 miles. Siberian Pass is 1 mile to the south, and you can meet the New Army Pass Trail by hiking ¾ mile north. Continuing westward, the Pacific Crest Trail gradually descends for 4 miles to meet the end of the New Army Pass Trail. The Pacific Crest Trail continues down Rock Creek another ½ mile, where it crosses to the north side of the creek. The trail then climbs to the saddle northeast of Mt. Guyot, goes through Guyot Flat, and descends to lower Crabtree Meadow after 6 miles.

From lower Crabtree Meadow, a short-cut trail gradually climbs to the northeast on the north side of Whitney Creek for 1 mile, where it meets the John Muir Trail near Crabtree Ranger Station.

The Pacific Crest Trail heads north for ¹/₂ mile from lower Crabtree Meadow to a junction with the John Muir Trail.

Cottonwood Lakes Trail and New Army Pass Trail *(16 miles)*

This is the shortest and most direct trail leading from Horseshoe Meadows to New Army Pass. From the trailhead along the Horseshoe Meadows Road, the trail makes a level traverse to Cottonwood Creek and on to Golden Trout Camp for 2 miles. It continues up the creek another 2 miles to Cottonwood Lakes basin, where many use trails have appeared, leading fishermen to their favorite spots. Wood campfires are prohibited within 300 feet of water in Cottonwood Lakes basin, and special fishing regulations have also been established.

The trail to New Army Pass leads to the west, passes Long Lake and High Lake, and after a short, steep climb, it pops out onto the plateau marking the western side of New Army Pass; the summit of the pass is approximately 3 miles beyond Cottonwood Lakes basin. The trail descends the western slope for 2¹/₂ miles to the Siberian Pass Trail. The trail goes north for ¹/₂ mile, crossing one of the tributaries of Rock Creek. One trail goes northeast from here, leading to the "Soldier Lakes" southwest of The Major General. The New Army Pass Trail continues down Rock Creek another 6 miles to a junction with the Pacific Crest Trail.

Mention should be made of two other, older trails leading to Cottonwood Lakes. One trail leaves the Horseshoe Meadows Road near the old pack station and ascends Little Cottonwood Creek before descending to Golden Trout Camp after 4 miles. The other trail, which leaves the Horseshoe Meadows Road below the new trailhead and climbs up Cottonwood Creek to Golden Trout Camp, is ¹/₄ mile longer than the current New Army Pass Trail, and it involves an extra 500 feet of gain.

At one time there was a trail over Army Pass (0.4 mi NE of New Army Pass) but it has been abandoned. The northeastern aspect of the Army Pass Trail left it packed with snow all summer long after heavy winters, and rockfall was a continuous hazard. Even though the New Army Pass Trail involves an extra 700 feet of gain, it is a much better route.

Meysan Lakes Trail *(3 miles)*

The trailhead for the Meysan Lakes Trail is located 11.3 miles from Lone Pine along the Whitney Portal Road. Walk past the lower Whitney Portal Campground, through the summer-home area, following the signs directing hikers to the correct trail, which starts its climb up the north side of Meysan Creek. The actual trail ends just before Meysan Lake, but there are many use trails around the lake, and cross-country travel is easy in the upper part of this basin.

This trail is heavily used, and wood fires are prohibited in the entire Meysan Creek drainage.

The Mt. Whitney Trail *(9 miles)*

This is one of the most heavily used trails in the High Sierra. Wood fires and pack and saddle stock are prohibited along the trail. Camping is prohibited at Mirror Lake and along Trailside Meadow.

The trail starts at the lower end of the road loop at the end of the Whitney Portal Road. It gradually climbs the north slope of the canyon and crosses the North Fork of Lone Pine Creek 1 mile from the trailhead. The trail then climbs for 2 miles, crosses to the south side of Lone Pine Creek, until meeting the junction with the Lone Pine Lake Trail. The Mt. Whitney Trail continues another mile to Bighorn Park (also known as "Ibex Park," "Whitney Outpost," and "Outpost Camp"). The trail crosses to the north side of the creek, and after ¹/₂ mile it reaches Mirror Lake, where camping is prohibited. The trail continues another mile to "Trailside Meadow" (no camping) and after another mile it reaches Trail Camp, which is the last water. Many hikers take their minds off of the tedium of the next 2 miles to Trail Crest by counting the number of switchbacks encountered. The Mt. Whitney Trail meets the John Muir Trail ¹/₂ mile beyond Trail Crest.

It is another 2 miles along the John Muir Trail to the summit of Mt. Whitney.

The John Muir Trail *(18¹/₂ miles)*

The John Muir Trail goes south from its junction with the Shepherd Pass Trail along Tyndall Creek and makes a gradual ascent to the Bighorn Plateau, with wonderful views in all directions. After 6 miles it meets the High Sierra Trail along Wallace Creek. The John Muir Trail makes a steep ascent to the south, crosses Sandy Meadow, and meets the Pacific Crest Trail before turning east and descending to Whitney Creek and the Crabtree Ranger Station after 4¹/₂ miles. The trail continues up the south side of the creek for ¹/₂ mile before crossing the creek, and ¹/₂ mile beyond this it reaches Timberline Lake, where camping is prohibited. Guitar Lake is 1 mile farther, where the trail climbs to the southeast for another 3 miles to meet the Mt. Whitney Trail. The John Muir Trail turns north, with many impressive views through the "windows" between the pinnacles south of Mt. Whitney. It eventually arrives at the summit of Mt. Whitney, 2 miles from the Mt. Whitney Trail junction. There is a hut on the summit, but it should not be used as a shelter during a thunderstorm because it does not offer protection from lightning.

The High Sierra Trail (4 miles)

The High Sierra Trail actually begins near Giant Forest at Crescent Meadow, but this chapter's description starts 1 mile north of Junction Meadow along the Kern River.

From the Kern River, the High Sierra Trail adopts a moderate grade and ascends the Wallace Creek drainage to meet the John Muir Trail just north of where it crosses Wallace Creek.

The Shepherd Pass Trail (12 miles)

The Shepherd Pass Trail has a reputation of being long, steep, and difficult. This reputation is well deserved. In the middle part of the trail, which is east of the Sierra crest, there is 500 feet of loss (or gain, depending on direction). On a more positive note, this trail offers the most direct access to the upper Kern River Basin. There are two trailheads for the Shepherd Pass Trail, one for hikers and the other for stock (see the description of the Symmes Creek Road). Those hiking the stock trail will hike an extra 1¹/₄ miles.

From the hikers' trailhead, the trail crosses Symmes Creek four times before beginning its long, steep climb across a ridge and then descending to the Shepherd Creek drainage. At 6 miles from the hikers' trailhead, the trail crosses Shepherd Creek near Anvil Camp. Wood campfires are prohibited in the vicinity of Anvil Camp. The trail crosses the creek again after another ³/₄ mile at The Pothole; an abandoned trail leads over Junction Pass from here. The Shepherd Pass Trail contin-

ues through moraines, and sometimes snowfields, to Shepherd Pass. The trail then descends the Tyndall Creek drainage 4 miles to join with the John Muir Trail just south of where the John Muir Trail crosses Tyndall Creek.

The Shepherd Pass Trail passes through the California Bighorn Sheep Zoological Area, east of the Sierra crest. Dogs are prohibited in this area.

Cross-Country Routes

"Diaz Pass"

(4040 m+; 13,280 ft+; 0.4 mi SE of Mt. Langley)

Class 2. This is an old shepherds' route which ascends Diaz Creek from the floor of Owens Valley to cross the Sierra crest just south of Mt. Langley. The New Army Pass Trail is much easier!

Tuttle Creek and "Tuttle Pass"

(3900 m+; 12,880 ft+)

This route serves as the approach to the north side of Mt. Langley, the eastern approach to Mt. Corcoran, the southeastern approach to Mt. LeConte, and the southern approaches to Peak 3985m (Peak 12,960+) and Lone Pine Peak.

From the end of Granite View Drive go up the canyon on a trail to the abandoned stone house that once served the needs of fundamentalist Christians or utopian nudists, depending on which story you believe. Climb about 100 feet directly above the house, and follow an old pipeline that leads to the southwest. Just before reaching the south fork of Tuttle Creek, a faint use trail can be found. This use trail avoids most of the brush and remains on the north side of the stream until 9,600 feet, where it crosses the creek and disappears. Climb onto a rib on the south side of the canyon, and stay on top of it while hiking up the Tuttle Creek drainage.

Tuttle Pass is a class 2, talus-infested pass crossing the Sierra crest between Mt. Corcoran and Mt. Langley. It leads between Tuttle Creek and Rock Creek. It involves almost 7,000 feet of gain in a rugged, mostly trailless canyon on its east side. It is for adventurous hikers only.

Arc Pass (3920 m+; 12,880 ft+)

Class 2–3. This is a convenient route be-

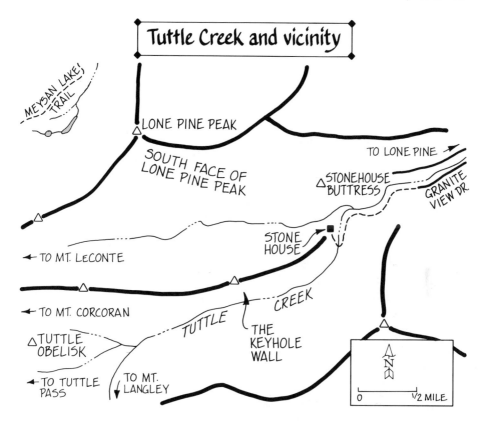

Tuttle Creek and vicinity

tween the Mt. Whitney Trail and the upper reaches of Rock Creek. Follow the eastern shore of Consultation Lake and make a gradual ascending traverse to the low point of the pass, east of Mt. McAdie. A direct ascent from Consultation Lake to the pass involves much loose rock over steep terrain; it is better to approach the pass from the east. The south side of the pass is easy, as long as you circle Sky Blue Lake on its eastern side.

Crabtree Pass *(3820 m+; 12,560 ft+)*

Class 2. This pass has also been called "Miter Pass." Crabtree Pass is the low point of the ridge between Mt. McAdie and Mt. Newcomb. It provides access between Crabtree Lakes and upper Rock Creek. A good use trail leads from upper Crabtree Meadow to the Crabtree Lakes. From the highest lake in the basin, ascend a short, steep section of talus to the pass. Descend to Lake 3697m (Lake 12,125), and pass Sky Blue Lake on its east side. Descend Rock Creek on its west bank. A use trail is eventu-

ally encountered, which leads down to the New Army Pass Trail.

Whitney Pass *(4040 m+; 13,280 ft+)*

Class 1–2. At one time the Mt. Whitney Trail crossed Whitney Pass, but this portion of the trail has been abandoned for a long time. This pass is included here only for the record. Discovery Pass is the preferred route.

"Discovery Pass"

(4160 m+; 13,400 ft+; 0.1 mi ESE of Discovery Pinnacle)

Class 2. Strictly speaking, this is not a pass. It crosses the southeast ridge of Discovery Pinnacle. It is the easiest, most direct route between the Mt. Whitney Trail and the Crabtree Creek drainage, and has also been used to climb Mt. Hitchcock. From the highest switchback of the Mt. Whitney Trail, simply leave the trail and cross the Sierra crest southeast of Discovery Pinnacle. The southeast slopes of the "pass" are sandy, and it is easy to descend to Crabtree Lakes.

"Pinnacle Pass"

(3720 m+; 12,160 ft+; UTM 863482)

Class 3. This pass gives access to the North Fork of Lone Pine Creek from the Mt. Whitney Trail. From Mirror Lake, hike up a wide canyon to the northwest, near the base of the cliffs to the north. After ³/₄ mile, ledges lead up and right (east) to the pass, located immediately to the east of Pinnacle Pass Needle, which is visible from Mirror Lake. The first part of the descent is class 3 on ledges and leads eastward. The lower portion descends diagonally to the west.

From Iceberg Lake to Mirror Lake, climb talus at the first place where the boulders rise prominently against the north face of Pinnacle Ridge. From the top of the talus, climb up the ledges that lead to the pass.

North Fork of Lone Pine Creek

Class 2. This is the approach for the routes on Mt. Whitney's east face. This cross-country route starts approximately 1 mile up the Mt. Whitney Trail, where the trail crosses the North Fork of Lone Pine Creek. Leave the trail and hike up the north side of the stream for approximately ¹/₄ mile. Cross to the south bank of the stream, continue up the canyon another ¹/₄ mile, and cross to the north bank of the stream near a Matterhorn-shaped rock. Climb up the steep slope above this rock for about 100 feet to the Ebersbacher Ledges. Head east on the ledges until it is possible to turn west on another ledge and continue hiking upstream. The route remains on the north side of the creek to the outlet of Lower Boy Scout Lake. Cross to the south side of the creek and climb up a talus slope to the southwest. The stream forks near Clyde Meadow; cross to the north side of the creek and hike to the outlet of Upper Boy Scout Lake. Cross the outlet and climb the steep, tiring talus slope that is due south from the outlet of the lake. Turn right (west) at the top of this slope, and hike for about ¹/₂ mile to the cliff just below Iceberg Lake. This cliff is often wet and/or icy, and it is best to continue west a little farther and climb a cruddy chute to Iceberg Lake.

Wood campfires are prohibited in the entire North Fork of Lone Pine Creek drainage.

"Whitney–Russell Pass"

(3980 m+; 13,040 ft+; 0.4 mi NE of Mt. Whitney; UTM 898493)

This pass is *not* the low point between Mt. Whitney and Mt. Russell, but rather the notch immediately northwest of Iceberg Lake. (The low point between Mt. Russell and Mt. Whitney can be crossed, but it is class 3 on its east side and requires some creative route finding. Whitney–Russell Pass is the preferred route.)

Class 2 slopes lead from Iceberg Lake to the pass. The western slopes of the pass are gentle, with the exception of some talus. From Arctic Lake, it is easy cross-country hiking to reach the John Muir Trail at Guitar Lake.

When crossing the pass from west to east, remember to head for the southern, higher notch, and not the lower, northern notch.

"Russell–Carillon Pass"

(4040 m+; 13,280 ft+)

Class 2–3. This route provides a direct route between the North Fork of Lone Pine Creek and the Wallace Creek drainage by way of Tulainyo Lake. From Clyde Meadow, ascend sandy slopes to the northwest to the saddle between Mt. Russell and Mt. Carillon. The north side of the pass is steep, and care must be taken while descending to Tulainyo Lake. It is best to approach Wallace Lake from the south, rather than the southeast.

"Cleaver Col"

(3960 m+; 12,560 ft+; 0.25 mi NE of Mt. Carillon)

Class 3. This is a steep, difficult, cross-country route connecting the lower portion of the North Fork of Lone Pine Creek with Tulainyo Lake. Leave the North Fork where a stream descends from the northwest at approximately 10,000 feet and follow it uphill. In the upper part of this drainage, move to the left (west) and climb up to the pass. It is best to circle around Tulainyo Lake on its south side.

Wallace Creek

At one time a trail led from the John Muir Trail to Wallace Lake, but it has not been maintained for many years. This is now considered a cross-country route, although portions of the trail are still visible.

Leave the John Muir Trail just north of Wallace Creek, where the High Sierra Trail comes in from the west. Hike up to the north side of Wallace Creek to approximately

10,800 feet and cross Wallace Creek to its south side. (This is at UTM 792514—a landmark for this crossing is a small meadow just downstream from where the creek draining Wales Lake enters Wallace Creek.) After crossing Wallace Creek, cross the tributary leading from Wales Lake, and continue hiking up the south side of Wallace Creek to the outlet of Wallace Lake.

The easiest approach to Wales Lake is to first head south from the inlet of Wallace Lake and then head southwest to the eastern shore of Wales Lake.

Vacation Pass *(3860 m+; 12,640 ft+)*

Class 2–3. This pass crosses the Sierra crest and leads between George Creek and Wallace Creek. The easiest crossing is ¹/₂ mile north of the low point.

George Creek

George Creek is a difficult cross-country route. It is used as the eastern approach to climb Mt. Williamson, Trojan Peak, and Mt. Barnard. This area is open only from April 15 to May 15 and from December 15 to January 1 due to Bighorn Sheep Zoological Area restrictions. Any enthusiastic Sierra mountaineer should climb up George Creek at least once. It is one of the classic bushwhacks of the High Sierra.

From the end of the George Creek Road, hike up the north bank of the stream for about ¹/₄ mile to where a cliff bars further progress. Cross to the south side of George Creek on a small logjam. Continue up the south side of the stream for another ¹/₄ mile, where you cross to the north side of the stream on a big log, just below some small waterfalls. Hike up the north side of the creek for about ¹/₂ mile to where a stream enters George Creek from the right (northwest), with a sharp little ridge between two streams. Hike over the ridge (30 feet of gain) and follow the main course of George Creek about 200 yards, and cross to the south side on a log. The route continues up the south bank of the creek to approximately 8,800 feet, where a stream enters George Creek from the left (southwest). (This is the departure point for Vacation Pass.) Cross to the north side of George Creek and hike up to approximately 9,800 feet, where the creek forks. Those headed for Trojan Peak and Mt. Barnard head left (southwest) from here; if

Mt. Williamson is the objective, go right (northwest). The upper reaches of George Creek are free of brush, and it is easy to pick out a route.

"Tyndall Col" *(3980 m+; 12,960 ft+)*

Class 2. This pass crosses the Sierra crest between Mt. Tyndall and Mt. Versteeg, and it leads from the upper reaches of Wright Creek to the lakes of Williamson Bowl. Williamson Bowl is closed from December 15 to July 15 due to Bighorn Sheep Zoological Area restrictions.

Peaks

Cirque Peak *(12,900 ft; 12,900 ft)*

This peak has a fine view from the summit. It is class 1 from either the New Army Pass Trail or the Pacific Crest Trail. It is also class 1 from Cirque Lake; climb to the saddle south of the peak, then up the ridge to the summit.

Mt. Langley *(4274 m; 14,042 ft)*

This is the southernmost 14,000-foot peak in the High Sierra. Clarence King and Paul Pinson climbed it in 1871, believing that they were making the first ascent of Mt. Whitney. They found a cairn with an arrow on the summit.

South Slopes. First winter ascent January 4, 1929, by Orland Bartholomew. Class 1 from the New Army Pass Trail.

West Face. Class 2. Climb a wide chute from the Rock Creek drainage. This chute ends approximately ¹/₄ mile north of The Major General. From the top of this chute, climb an easy ridge to the northeast which leads to the summit plateau.

North Face. Class 3. First ascent August 1937 by Howard S. Gates and Nelson P. Nies. Climb a chimney with a chockstone at its head. Leave the chimney in its upper reaches via a ledge, and traverse east to a ridge. Follow the ridge to the summit.

Northeast Chute. Class 2–3. From Tuttle Creek, approach this chute east of Point 3620m (11,940 ft) and climb it to the crest of the east ridge of Mt. Langley.

East Slope. Class 2. Follow Diaz Creek to its head and ascend the eastern slopes to the summit of Mt. Langley.

Southeast Face of Southeast Peak. III, class 5. First ascent April 1977 by Fred Beckey and

Will Crjenko. This route has been reported as having eight leads of moderate to serious rock climbing. It ends atop Peak 3878m (12,722 ft), which has been called "Mt. Wooly Back."

The Major General
(3780 m+; 12,400 ft+)
Class 3. First ascent August 1937 by Chester Versteeg and Elizabeth Versteeg. This point is southwest of Mt. Langley, and the approach to the summit block is class 2 from all directions. It is hardly worth the effort.

Mt. Guyot *(3749 m; 12,300 ft)*
Class 1. First ascent 1881 by William Wallace. The preferred route of ascent is from the Pacific Crest Trail, which crosses the saddle northeast of the peak. As would be expected, the high point of the summit is at the far southwestern end of the ridge.

Joe Devel Peak *(4062 m; 13,325 ft)*
Southwest Slopes. Class 1. First ascent September 1875 by members of the Wheeler Survey. This is a sand climb.
Northeast Ridge from Mt. Pickering. Class 2. This traverse starts on the east side of the ridge from Mt. Pickering and ends on the west slope of Joe Devel Peak.

Mt. Pickering *(4107 m; 13,485 ft)*
First ascent July 1936 by Chester Versteeg, Tyler Van Degrift, and Oliver Kehrlein.
North Ridge from Mt. Newcomb. Class 3. Keep to the west side of the ridge.
West Slope. Class 2 from the upper reaches of Perrin Creek.
Southwest Ridge from Joe Devel Peak. Class 2. Begin this traverse on the west slope of Joe Devel Peak and finish on the east side of the ridge.
South Slopes. Class 2. These consist of talus and sand. An excellent descent route heads southeast from the summit of Mt. Pickering to a sandy chute that leads to Erin Lake.
Southeast Slopes. Class 2 from Primrose Lake.
East Slope. Class 2. From Sky Blue Lake hike to the highest small lake to the west, and climb to the saddle east of Mt. Pickering. Climb up the slope to the summit.

The Miter *(3880 m+; 12,770 ft)*
Southeast Face. Class 3–4. First ascent July 18, 1938, by Sam Fink. From Iridescent Lake or Sky Blue Lake, scramble to the notch immediately south of the The Miter's twin summits. Climb over flakes to a large platform, and traverse right (northeast) across small cracks on the exposed slabs to a shallow chute that heads left (northwest) to the top of an arete. Follow the arete to the buttress of the south summit. Work up ledges and chimneys on the southeast face of the buttress to the south summit. The traverse to the higher north summit is easy class 3, with the low point of the notch between the two summits being reached by crawling to the right (east) of a large boulder.
The northwest chute of the north summit has been reported as being class 3.

Mt. Corcoran
(4180 m+; 13,760 ft+; UTM 882442)
There has been considerable discussion as to which of the four summits of this peak is the actual high point. The true summit is immediately south of the prominent notch between Mt. Corcoran and Mt. LeConte. Mt. Corcoran has also been called "Comb Ridge."
North Notch from the West. Class 2–3. First ascent 1933 by Howard S. Gates. From Iridescent Lake, climb the chute leading to the notch north of Mt. Corcoran. This chute divides twice near the top; take the right branch both times. The north notch is reached after passing under a huge chockstone. Traverse south 150 feet on ledges west of the crest and then climb a chute that leads to the summit area. There is much loose rock on this route.
North Notch from the East. Class 2–3. First ascent 1958 by Carl Heller. From 11,000 feet on the south fork of Tuttle Creek, climb slabs leading to a canyon to the northwest. Stay high and well to the north to avoid talus, and move into the northernmost of two basins at the head of the canyon. Climb the broad chute leading to the notch between Mt. LeConte and Mt. Corcoran. Just below the crest, turn to the south (left) and climb a short pitch with a small chockstone to the top of the crest. Traverse south 150 feet on ledges on the west side of the crest, and climb a chute leading to the summit.
Traverse from Mt. LeConte. Class 3. A traverse from Mt. LeConte to Mt. Corcoran has been done, but it requires skilled route finding. Descend the Northwest Chute of Mt.

LeConte, and stop at the top of the Waterfall Pitch. Traverse south 50 feet on a ledge into the next chute. Descend about 150 feet in this chute, and traverse south on ledges, descending slightly and crossing two ribs to the chute leading to the notch between Mt. LeConte and Mt. Corcoran.

A common mistake made on this traverse is to stay too high after leaving the top of the Waterfall Pitch. This could lead a peak bagger into big air!

Northeast Face. IV, 5.10, A2. This route starts in a crack system to the right of the buttress.

Sharktooth, Southeast Face. II, 5.7. First ascent May 2, 1972, by Hooman Aprin and Fred Beckey. The Sharktooth is the sharp peak (Peak 4160m+) south of the high point of Mt. Corcoran. This climb has been de-scribed as having a number of class 4 and class 5 leads. The climbs begins at the base of Mt. Corcoran and climbs a giant dihedral on The Sharktooth itself.

There is also a 5.5 route on the right side of the upper southeast face of The Sharktooth.

South Ridge. Class 4. This is a traverse of the four main summits of Mt. Corcoran. The southernmost summit (Peak 4151m) was first climbed July 20, 1938, from Tuttle Pass by Sam Fink. The complete traverse of the four summits was done by Galen Rowell in August 1970. The two southern summits are class 2 from Tuttle Pass. The Sharktooth is class 4 on its west side. From the saddle south of The Sharktooth, descend about 300 feet on the west side of the crest, and traverse north across class 4 rock to the chute leading to the summit area.

Mt. Corcoran and Mt. LeConte from northeast (photo by F. E. Matthes, #1409, USGS Photographic Library, Denver, CO)

Mt. LeConte and Mt. Corcoran from west

Mt. LeConte

(4220 m+; 13,960 ft+; UTM 880446)

There is a large plateau between Mt. LeConte and Mt. Mallory. This plateau can be reached from upper Meysan Lake by climbing a loose, narrow chute that leads to a point on the plateau between these two peaks, or by traversing southwest from Mt. Mallory. A large cairn has been built on top of the plateau at the base of the north face of Mt. LeConte. This landmark serves as the starting point for three of the routes described here.

Northwest Chute. Class 3. First ascent June 1935 by Norman Clyde. This route has been referred to as the "Northwest Ridge," which is not exactly correct. From the plateau between Mt. LeConte and Mt. Mallory, follow the ridge to the base of the cliffs of Mt. LeConte. Drop 200 feet in elevation and climb the chute on the northwest side of Mt. LeConte. A 15-foot class 3 pitch is encountered just below the summit. In early season it may be covered with running water and/or verglas, and it is commonly referred to as the Waterfall Pitch. The summit is a short scramble above.

North Face. I, 5.3. First ascent August 29, 1971, by Carl Heller and Bill Stronge. This route follows cracks directly above the large cairn at the base of the north face of Mt. LeConte.

Northeast Face. Class 3. First ascent September 7, 1952, by Steve Wilkie, Barbara Lilley, Wes Cowan, George Wallerstein, and June Kilbourne. From the cairn at the base of the north face, traverse east along an easy but exposed ledge for 400 feet to an area of vertical cracks and small ledges; this is the first break in the otherwise smooth face. Approximately 200 feet of exposed class 3 leads to the summit.

East Arete. Class 3. First ascent June 12, 1937, by Gary Leech, Smoke Blanchard, and Hubert North. The east arete is reached by continuing farther along the ledge of the Northeast Face route. Access to the arete is via a chimney. Leave the chimney near the summit, and finish the climb via the arete. This route is less exposed than the Northeast Face.

Southwest Ridge. II, 5.6. First ascent August 1970 by Galen Rowell. From the notch north of Mt. Corcoran, follow the ridge to the summit of Mt. LeConte.

Traverse from Mt. Corcoran. Class 3. First ascent July 15, 1973, by a party led by Ed Treacy. From the notch north of Mt. Corcoran, descend the chute on the west side of the crest for approximately 250 feet. Traverse across the west side of Mt. LeConte, ascending slightly and crossing two ridges, to a large couloir. Ascend the couloir about 150 feet to a ledge leading left (north). This ledge ends after 50 feet at a point above the Waterfall Pitch of the Northwest Chute route, and it is a short scramble from there to the summit.

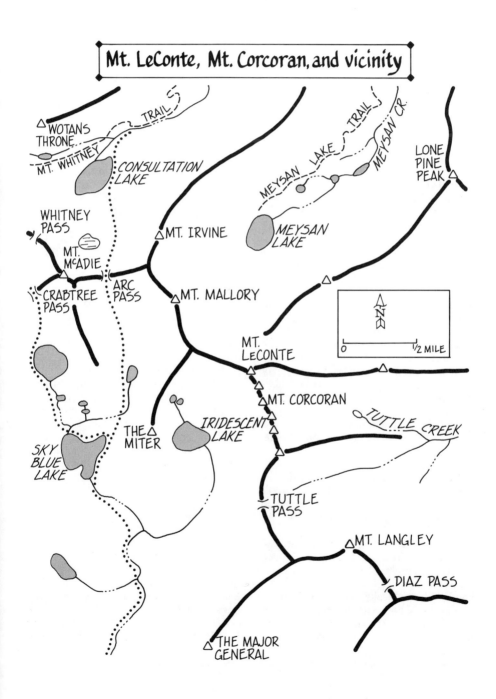

Mt. LeConte, Mt. Corcoran, and vicinity

West Couloir. Class 3. First ascent July 17, 1936, by Oliver Kehrlein, Tyler Van Degrift, and Chester Versteeg. A large couloir descends the west side of Mt. LeConte to a point just north of Iridescent Lake. Ascend the couloir to the ledge that leads left (north) to a point above the level of the Waterfall Pitch of the Northwest Chute route.

Peak 3925m

(12,880 ft+; 1.5 mi SSW of Lone Pine Peak)

Southwest Slopes. Class 2. First ascent September 24, 1967, by Ed Lane and Alice Lewis.

West Ridge. Class 4. First ascent August 1970 by Galen Rowell. There is a lot of loose rock on this ridge.

"The Tuttle Obelisk"

This is the striking white tower near the head of the south fork of Tuttle Creek.

Rowell-Jones Route. III, 5.9. First ascent April 1970 by Chris Jones and Galen Rowell. This route begins in a dihedral directly beneath the summit on the obelisk's south side. The first pitch is a 5.9 crack, followed by four more pitches of 5.5 to 5.7. The final pitch dead-ends against the summit block; a hand traverse to the right leads to a ledge that provides access to the top.

School's Out. III, 5.9. First ascent June 1979 by Brent Norum and Alan Bartlett. This route starts a few hundred feet to the right of the Rowell-Jones Route. Climb a right-slanting ramp 200 feet to the base of a large corner. Two pitches up the corner lead to a huge ledge. Climb to the right up a curving crack to the final pitch of the Rowell-Jones Route.

"The Keyhole Wall"

This nice cliff has also been called "The Keystone," after the formation in the middle of the face with two facing dihedrals that lead up to an overhang at its apex. It is south of Point 3233m (10,067 ft).

Saumnambulist. II, 5.8+. First ascent 1980 by Dick Saum, Herb Laeger, and Eve Laeger. This route climbs the left side of The Keyhole Wall. The first pitch consists of a fine 5.7 hand crack that breaks a small roof. The crux is not the roof but some face moves near the end of the climb. The climb ends on a ledge that leads left to a large inside corner, where rappels lead to the ground.

Master Key. II, 5.8. First ascent July 1984 by Greg Vernon, Herb Laeger, and Jim Murray. This three-pitch route climbs cracks that are about 200 feet left of The Locksmith Route. The route begins with 5.8 moves up a fist crack, followed by 5.7 climbing up cracks to a large water groove. Continue climbing the groove; the crux is passing some vegetation on the second pitch. The climb ends with an easy class 5 third pitch in the groove that leads to some brushy ledges. Traverse right along the ledges and rappel The Locksmith Route.

Bushmaster. II, 5.9. First ascent July 1984 by Greg Vernon, Herb Laeger, and Jim Murray. This route is immediately right of the Master Key route. Begin by climbing the 5.8 fist crack of Master Key. From the top of this crack, go up and right, with thin face and crack climbing past a bush (5.9), and belay from an off-width chimney. Continue up the chimney for another pitch. The third pitch goes up the chimney before moving right and up the face, with excellent jugs, to a series of brushy ledges. Walk right along the ledges and rappel The Locksmith Route.

The Locksmith Route. III, 5.9. First ascent May 18, 1975, by Fred Beckey and Jack Roberts. This route has finger jams, cracks, and face-climbing problems. It climbs the left side of The Keystone. The first two pitches are in a white, right-facing open book. The second pitch ends on a ledge with a tree, which is beyond the left side of the open book. The third pitch goes up and right and over some buckets to an off-width chimney, which ends on a brushy ledge with trees. Move to the right a short distance, beyond a dead tree, and rappel the route with two 165-foot rappels. The first rappel ends near the very bottom of the off-width chimney, at the upper left-hand corner of The Keystone. One more rappel leads straight down to the ground.

The Keystone. III, 5.8. First ascent March 1970 by Galen Rowell and Chris Jones. Climb the left-facing dihedral on the right side of The Keystone to its top. The route ends via an off-width chimney on the brushy ledges that mark the top of The Locksmith Route. Move left along the brushy ledges and rappel The Locksmith Route.

Clean Willy's Escape. III, 5.9. First ascent June 1976 by Alan Roberts and Alan Bartlett. This classic route follows the prominent crack-and-chimney system that makes up the right side of The Keystone. Climb the right-facing dihedral (5.8), then a crack that leads out onto the face. Ascend this crack (5.8), followed by some difficult face moves (5.9) beneath an overhang. This leads to a chimney (5.8) which ends on a large brushy ledge with broken rock above. Go left along this ledge and rappel The Locksmith Route.

Pass Key. II, 5.7. First ascent January 15, 1976, by Fred Beckey and Jack Roberts. Climb a short open book, which is 100 yards east of The Locksmith Route, and ascend a continuous crack-and-chimney system to the top of the cliff.

Yellow Face. II, 5.8. First ascent July 16, 1983, by Rich Smith, Eve Laeger, and Herb Laeger. This route is on the far right side of the Keyhole Wall. A yellow face can be seen to the right of a right-facing inside corner. A crack-and-chimney system leads up to this face (5.4). Four pitches on the yellow face itself (5.6, 5.8, 5.7, and 5.4, respectively) lead to the top. Climb down a few feet on the left to a tree. Rappel with two ropes from the tree to a large gully. Another long rappel leads to the ground after some down-climbing.

Hangin' Out. III, 5.10. First ascent 1980 by Eve Laeger and Herb Laeger. This route climbs the crack near the edge of the east face of The Keyhole Wall (the wall itself faces south). This route is four pitches long, and the first pitch is the crux.

Peak 3985m

(12,960 ft+ and 13,016 ft; 1.2 mi SW of Lone Pine Peak)

East Ridge. Class 2–3 from Lone Pine Peak.

Kearney Route. V, 5.9, A2. First ascent May 1976 by Shari Nelson, Jay Foster, and Alan Kearney. This route ascends a large chimney system just to the right of center on the south face. The climb finishes through a crack system slightly left of the chimney at its end. One bolt was placed during the two and a half days of its first ascent.

South Face. V, 5.8, A2. First ascent May 1970 by Chris Jones, Joe Faint, and Galen Rowell. This route begins by climbing a ramp that leads to the left from the center of the south face. From the ramp, there are two short aid sections on this otherwise free climb. At one point it is necessary to traverse to avoid an area of rotten rock. You come to a pillar just below the final summit wall. Rappel to the right to a ledge. The climb finishes by climbing the right side of the face. The first ascent took one and a half days.

Red Baron Tower. III, 5.7, A2. First ascent May 19, 1972, by Fred Beckey and Barry Hagen. This route is to the left of the South Face route, and ends atop a flat platform. Two aid pitches lead to interesting free climbing along a buttress to the platform.

West Ridge. Class 4. First ascent 1988 by Marty Hornick. There is a lot of loose rock on this ridge.

Lone Pine Peak *(3945 m; 12,944 ft)*

This is an impressive peak when viewed from Lone Pine. The north ridge is a striking sight to the mountaineer, and rock climbers are intrigued by the mile-wide, 3,000-foot-high big wall on the peak's south face.

From Meysan Lake. Class 2. First ascent July 1947 by Murray Bruch and Fred Johnson. Climb a chute filled with sand, scree, and talus on the northwest slope of the peak. Walk northeast across the summit plateau to the summit.

North Ridge. III, 5.4. First ascent September 1952 by Art Lembeck and Ray Van Aken. This is an interesting, lengthy, and not too difficult route. Few parties climb this route in one day.

Hike up the Meysan Lakes Trail to just below Little Meysan Lake. Cross Meysan Creek, and climb up and left along a series of ledges and boulders until the crest of the north ridge is reached. Follow the crest upward, pass through a small notch on the crest, and drop 100 feet to a gully at the base of the first tower. Climb the gully for 75 feet and move right to the top of the ridge. Follow the crest of the ridge to an overhanging headwall, which is passed (5.2) via a small gully on the left. This is soon followed by another headwall, which is climbed via an open book (5.4) on the left. Climb cracks and small ledges to the top of the first tower. Cross over to the south side of the tower and follow a countouring ledge system to some sandy ledges that overlook a deep chute at the base of the second tower. This is followed by another class 4 ledge system to an area of polished rock. Climb a gully (5.2) that rises to the right. From the top of the gully, go left and up (5.4). A 300-foot class 3 traverse follows, and leads to a steep chute at the base of the summit headwall. Climb the headwall to a notch on the ridge crest. From this notch, a ledge system contours across the north side of the headwall past the bottom of a large chute (loose rock!) to a small buttress. Climb the buttress (class 3), which forms the right side of the loose chute, and after about 400 feet move left into the chute. Follow the chute up over rock and sandy class 3 ledges and boulders to the summit. *Variation:* First ascent July 12, 1986, by Dick Beach and Bob Good. Instead of approaching the north ridge via the Meysan Lakes Trail, leave the Whitney Portal Road at an elevation of 6,200 feet (where it begins the steep climb to Whitney Portal). Follow the ridge up from the base in the Owens Valley, staying to the east side of the ridge near the top. At a large, ball-shaped boulder, cross to the west side of the ridge at a notch to a system of ledges. Class 3 steps lead down to a ledge with a lone pine tree. Another 1,000 feet of scrambling lead to the small notch near the base of the first tower, where the real climbing begins. This variation involves over 7,000 feet of gain. Incredibly, it was climbed in one day on the first ascent. *Variation:* Class 4. First ascent June 23, 1973, by Bill Stronge, Al Green, Bill Sweatt, and Scott Charlton. Climb toward the north ridge from the Meysan Lakes Trail approach. Before reaching the ridge, however, turn right and go around a brushy slope to an arete leading to the notch in the ridge at the summit headwall.

Bastille Buttress. V, 5.8, A3. First ascent April 1969 by Fred Beckey, Joe Brown, and Chuck Haas. This 2,000-foot buttress is in the Inyo Creek drainage, and it ends at an elevation of 10,500 feet on the north ridge of Lone Pine Peak. This is a deceiving, complex, and difficult route with an arduous approach. The best approach begins along the Meysan Lakes Trail. Leave the trail at the 8,400-foot level, cross Meysan Creek, and contour around the lower north ridge of Lone Pine Peak to Inyo Creek. The buttress is apparent from the Inyo Creek drainage.

Begin by scrambling up a gully on the right side of the buttress, then go up and left to a ledge that is 50 feet above the toe of the buttress. The first roped pitch goes up a crack past a small tree to a larger belay tree, and is followed by a short, easy pitch to a big ledge. Climb the face, which is to the left of a left-facing open book, to belay from a flake beneath a roof. Pass the roof on the right, where easy face climbing leads to a belay

beneath a large black knob. Climb up and right to a crack, which leads up and left, then face climb up and right to a crack that leads to a small ledge. Another poorly protected pitch then ascends a crack up and right to a belay from the face beneath another large black knob. A bat-hook-and-bolt ladder section follows, and then a lonely 175-foot crack (A1) on the prow of the buttress ends at the bottom of a deep, strenuous chimney. From the top of the chimney, the crux consists of two flared, overhanging pitches of aid and free climbing, which go up and left before moving right to an exposed outside corner. Continue up this edge to some overhanging flakes, which are bypassed on the left with a tension traverse and friction. Climb straight up before traversing left to a bolt on a sharp outside corner, and climb straight up again to the bottom of a chimney. From the top of this chimney, face climb up and left (passing several bolts and a shallow trough) to a belay tree. This is followed by a class 4 tunnel that ends atop a large ledge. Go to the left side of the ledge. An aid move off of a bolt leads to some free climbing. Move up and left, passing several more bolts, to another large ledge. Class 3 leads to the last roped pitch: a crack that leads to the crest of the north ridge of Lone Pine Peak.

The gully to the north of the buttress may be followed for descent, or the north ridge of Lone Pine Peak may be descended back to the Meysan Lakes Trail. Further reading: *Summit,* April 1972, pp. 2–5; *Summit,* November–December 1983, pp. 12–13.

Northeast Ridge. III, 5.5. First ascent July 10–11, 1982, by Phil Warrender and Gary Valle. This is the first major ridge to the left of the north ridge of Lone Pine Peak. The ridge is 3 miles long and over 1 mile high, with many short to long technical pitches. Follow the crest of the ridge from the Owens Valley, with deviations on each side to bypass many towers. Leave the crest beneath the final headwall, and traverse right several hundred yards to a gully that leads to the summit plateau.

East Face. Class 4, with rappels. First ascent July 1952 by Warren Harding. Climb the second chute south of the north ridge on the east face of Lone Pine Peak. Class 4 pitches lead to a point about 400 feet below the summit. Rappel 200 feet to the next chute south, and ascend this chute to the summit.

Three Arrows. III, 5.9, A2. First ascent April 1976 by Randy Grandstaff, Hooman Aprin, and Fred Beckey. This route climbs to a sharp rock crest on the east side of Lone Pine Peak. The summit of this formation, as seen from Lone Pine, looks like arrows. The route begins by climbing a southeast-facing trough/dihedral, then a deep, difficult chimney. There are two short aid sections, and three bolts were placed on the first ascent.

East Slopes. Class 2. First ascent 1925 by Norman Clyde. Go northwest from the Tuttle Creek trailhead to some cliffs that guard the summit plateau. The cliffs can be overcome by way of some class 2 gullies. (This is the usual descent route for routes on the south side of Lone Pine Peak.)

Stonehouse Buttress, Jeanne Neale Route. IV, 5.8, A2. First ascent March 4, 1972, by Dan Hurd and David Boyd. This buttress is the large formation across Tuttle Creek from the stone house. The name of this route commemorates an unfortunate fall by a young woman on another nearby route during an early attempt. Warning: The rock on Stonehouse Buttress is loose! Begin climbing the southeast face of the buttress just left of an obvious, large, triangular flake. Climb a jam crack, which leads to a small flake, and traverse down and right from a bolt, then climb a crack left of an overhang and dogleg right. This first pitch ends at the bottom of a flared, overhanging chimney visible from below. Climb the chimney, using some aid at its top, and belay in slings from a bolt left of the overhang. Mixed climbing goes left and up to a small ledge with a bush. A bolt protects a move to another ledge. Climb to the right to the only comfortable belay on the climb. Traverse right and climb a dihedral with two mixed pitches, and turn the overhang on its left. Climb the left of two cracks to a dead tree. One more pitch leads to the unroping spot, and a few hundred feet of scrambling leads to the summit of Stonehouse Buttress. The first-ascent party used many big pitons on this climb: four 2-inch, three 2½-inch, two 3-inch, and one 4-inch bong.

Stonehouse Buttress, Chimney Route. IV, 5.8. First ascent January 1970 by Joe Faint and Galen Rowell. This route starts several hundred feet to the left of the Jeanne Neale Route, in a prominent, narrow chimney that curves to the right. After passing some chockstones in the upper part of the chim-

ney, move left onto a steep, crackless face and climb chickenheads to the summit of the buttress.

Stonehouse Buttress, Milky Way Chimney. IV, 5.10+. First ascent April 29, 1973, by Jack Roberts, Hooman Aprin, and Fred Beckey. First free ascent May 10, 1980, by Herb Laeger, Eve Laeger, and Mike Jaffe. This is the main left chimney on Stonehouse Buttress. Follow the Chimney Route for two and a half pitches, to the bottom of the narrow chimney. Climb a crack that leads up and left into the main left chimney. Leave the chimney on the left side, and ascend the corner of the buttress.

Stonehouse Buttress, Dynamo-Hum. IV, 5.10+. First ascent November 1978 by Dick Swindon and Jack Roberts. This is the first right-facing dihedral to the right of the Club Alpin Francais Route on the proper south face of Lone Pine Creek. Climb the dihedral for three 5.10 pitches and turn the roof atop the dihedral to the left. Follow the upper crack system for four pitches. Above these cracks, follow a line of small, right-facing cracks to the top.

Club Alpin Francais Route. IV, 5.9, A1. First ascent July 13, 1973, by Henri Agresti and Tom Birtley. The east side of the south face of Lone Pine Peak features a brush-covered ledge area. This route scrambles up to the left of these ledges to a huge ledge visible from below. From the huge ledge, follow the ridge above the left corner of the ledge and descend from a small notch to the next chute to the left. Climb the chute for 300 feet, and then ascend the ridge to the right of the chute for the remaining fourteen pitches to the summit plateau. The first overhang is turned by its left chimney (5.7), the second and third overhangs are bypassed to the left (A1 both times), and the fourth overhang is avoided by traversing right (5.6) and then up a chimney (5.9).

Winter Route. IV, 5.7. First ascent March 1970 by Chris Jones and Galen Rowell. Climb the prominent chute that diagonally ascends from right to left across the south face of Lone Pine Peak. After 1,000 vertical feet, climb a narrow gully with slabs. From the top of a rib at a notch, rappel 60 feet to the left to a ledge. Six pitches of 5.3 to 5.7 then lead up to the long summit plateau.

Direct South Face. V, 5.7, A1. First ascent May 1970 by Eric Bjornstad and Fred Beckey.

This climb begins about 1 mile upstream from the stone house of Tuttle Creek. Climb a large, 1,000-foot-long gully, which leads up and right to end behind a prominent tower. (This gully is behind a small ridge on the west side of the tower.) From the top of this gully, climb a large right-facing dihedral for five pitches (class 4 to 5.7). The route now overlooks a prominent gully, and it stays to the right of this gully for four more pitches until the route goes left across the top of the gully. Climb a left-facing dihedral, and from its top go left to the edge of a broad chute. Class 3 and 4 climbing leads up and left for 500 feet to a smaller gully with a hole at its top. Pass through the eye of the needle to some sandy ledges. Walk right along the ledges for approximately 200 feet to the base of a steep chimney, which leads up to a gully. Start climbing again to the left of this chimney by going up slightly left to a crack, and then belay from some boulders. Continue up the crack, and tension-traverse right (the only aid on the route) to a gully. Climb the gully for two more pitches and move right along a sharp ridge that overlooks a big drop-off. The last pitch starts with a traverse across the face to the right before going up to a crack.

This is probably the easiest grade V in the United States. (The "direct" in the route name is a misnomer, and the rating has been maintained here to keep many weekend warriors from having broken hearts.) Most of this climb is moderate class 5 (5.4 to 5.5) with three leads of 5.7 and a simple tension traverse. But this climb is a great test piece for the recreational climber who wants to apply his or her crag skills on a wilderness big wall. There are many bivouac ledges, and in early season, snow may be available for water. Further reading: *Summit*, April 1972, pp. 2-5; *Summit*, November–December 1983, pp. 12–13.

South Gully. Class 4. Descended May 1970 by Galen Rowell, Joe Faint, and Chris Jones. There is a break in the cliffs at the western end of the south face of Lone Pine Peak. This has been used as a descent route from the south face, but it is better to descend the east slopes of Lone Pine Peak.

Mt. Mallory   (4220 m; 13,850 ft)

East Slopes. Class 2. Climb an obvious chute that is south of the east ridge of Mt. Mallory. This chute leads to the plateau southeast of the peak. *Variation:* Class 2. The plateau can be reached from Tuttle Creek by climbing to the saddle between Mt. LeConte and Peak 3925m (12,880+). This is more difficult than the approach from Meysan Lake.

West Slope. Class 2. From the basin south of Arc Pass, climb a chute that leads to the plateau southeast of the peak. A landmark for this chute is a prominent peak on the western edge of the plateau. The chute ends to the north of this prominent peak.

From Arc Pass. Class 2. First ascent July 18, 1936, by Oliver Kehrlein, Chester Versteeg, and Tyler Van Degrift. Climb a broad chute from Arc Pass to the ridge between Mt. Mallory and Mt. Irvine. Follow the ridge southeast to the summit of Mt. Mallory, passing over its lower north summit.

Traverse from Mt. Irvine. Class 2. First ascent June 1925 by Norman Clyde. From Mt. Irvine, traverse around the upper reaches of the east ridge of Mt. Mallory, and hike up the plateau to the summit. *Variation:* Class 3. The ridge between Mt. Irvine and Mt. Mallory can also be followed.

Mt. Irvine   (4200 m+; 13,770 ft)

From Arc Pass. Class 1. First ascent June 1925 by Norman Clyde. Climb the broad chute leading to the ridge between Mt. Irvine and Mt. Mallory. Cross the ridge and descend slightly on its east side. Climb to the summit via the easy southeast slope.

West Face. Class 2–3. First ascent 1957 by Charles House. Ascend the fourth chute south of Consultation Lake. Be forewarned: As a descent route, this chute is impossible to find from the summit of Mt. Irvine.

North Slopes. Class 1. This is a simple climb from the Mt. Whitney Trail.

East Buttress. III, 5.7. First ascent September 5, 1971, by Bill Stronge and Arold Greene. This seventeen-pitch route starts in a flaky chimney just to the left of the toe of the buttress. Bypass the towers on the buttress until confronted by a wall. Down-climb a few feet to a ledge on the right, and climb the crack (5.7) at the end of the ledge. The final tower is climbed on the right side. Scrambling then leads to the summit.

East Couloir. Class 4. First ascent 1969 by John Mendenhall and Bill Dixon. This couloir is to the south of the East Buttress.

Mt. Irvine, East Face (photo by R. J. Secor)

East Slopes. Class 2. Climb the chute north of the east ridge of Mt. Mallory from Meysan Lake.

Mt. McAdie *(4206 m; 13,680 ft+)*

The north peak is the high point.

Northeast Face. III, class 5. First ascent July 1978 by Mike Daugherty, Jeff Lee, and Woody Stark. From Consultation Lake, traverse from the east (class 4) into a recess below a bowl on the northeast face. Climb class 3 and 4 rock to the bowl. Exit the bowl to the left and climb directly up for two and a half pitches. After gaining the east buttress, climb to the summit on the north side of the east buttress.

From Arc Pass. Class 3. First ascent 1922 by Norman Clyde. Ascend the obvious chute leading to the middle peak from Arc Pass. Just before reaching the summit of the middle peak, traverse right (north) through or around a tunnel formed by a leaning slab. Climb up and then down in one of the two class 3 chimneys to a ledge that overlooks the breathtaking notch between the north and middle peaks. Descend the class 3 northwest face of the middle peak for approximately 100 feet, to a point just below the notch. Climb up to the notch, over a rock outcrop, and climb out of the notch (class 3) by traversing upward around the southwest shoulder of the north peak for 50 feet to a horizontal ledge. Traverse across the ledge for 150 feet to the west side of the north peak. Scramble directly up to the summit from here.

West Face. Class 4. First ascent July 1954 by Jim Koontz, Hervey Voge, Norv LeVene, Claire Millikan, Mike Loughman, Ro Lenel, and Bent Graust. This route has much loose rock. It climbs the rock rib north of the chute that leads to the notch between the middle and north peaks, and ends atop the north peak.

Middle Peak. Class 2. First ascent June 1928 by Norman Clyde. This is a simple scramble from Arc Pass.

South Peak. Class 2. First ascent June 12, 1936, by Oliver Kehrlein, Chester Versteeg, and Tyler Van Degrift. Climb a chute on the southeast side of the peak to the summit.

The middle and south peaks of Mt. McAdie are connected by a class 3 ridge.

Mt. Newcomb   *(4091 m; 13,410 ft)*

Southwest Slopes. Class 2. First ascent August 1936 by Max Eckenburg and Bob Rumohr. This is a simple ascent from the upper reaches of Perrin Creek.

Southwest Ridge. Class 2. This is the ridge between Mt. Newcomb and Mt. Chamberlin. The saddle between the two peaks can be reached from the upper Crabtree Lake via class 2 ledges.

Northeast Ridge. Class 3. Either follow the ridge from Crabtree Pass, or ascend directly to the ridge from the uppermost lake in the Crabtree Creek drainage.

South Ridge from Mt. Pickering. Class 3. Stay on the west side of the ridge when descending from Mt. Pickering.

Mt. Chamberlin   *(4014 m; 13,169 ft)*

East Ridge from Mt. Newcomb. Class 3. The saddle between Mt. Chamberlin and Mt. Newcomb can be reached via class 2 ledges from the upper Crabtree Lake.

West Pillar of the Northeast Face. V, 5.10. First ascent July 1979 by Galen Rowell and Mike Farrell. This route climbs the single, vertical system of cracks that leads directly to the top of the pillar. The first-ascent party took 8 hours to climb the thirteen pitches.

South and West Slopes. Class 1–2. The difficulty depends on whether you encounter sand or talus.

Mt. Hitchcock   *(4019 m; 13,184 ft)*

From Discovery Pass. Class 2. This traverse is unique in that it starts at a higher elevation than the peak itself. It has been called a "boulder whack," but some climbers believe that this is preferable to hiking up the sandy slopes south and west of the peak.

Southwest Slopes. Class 1. Ascend these seemingly interminable slopes from the upper Crabtree Lake.

West Slopes. Class 1. First ascent 1881 by Frederick Wales. From the vicinity of

Crabtree Meadow, ascend the west shoulder of the peak and cross the plateau to the summit. These sandy slopes are usually descended by those who reach the summit via Discovery Pass.

Northeast Face. Class 4. First ascent 1970 by Vern Clevenger. Climb one of the chutes on this face.

Discovery Pinnacle   *(4192 m; 13,680 ft)*

Class 2. First ascent September 19, 1873, by Clarence King and Frank Knowles. This is a simple ascent from Trail Crest or via the south slopes from Crabtree Creek.

Thor Peak   *(3751 m; 12,300 ft)*

The southeast face of this peak is a spectacular sight from the Mt. Whitney Trail near Bighorn Park.

West Arete. Class 2. Descended September 7, 1936, by Robert K. Brinton, Glen Dawson, and William Rice. This ridge can be reached from either Pinnacle Pass or direct from Mirror Lake.

Southwest Slope. Class 2. First ascent by Norman Clyde. From Mirror Lake, climb ledges north to the sloping, sandy plateau southwest of the summit. Cross a notch south of the summit, traverse to the northeast side, and climb up to the summit.

Mirror Point, West Side. Class 1. Mirror Point is the small, detached pinnacle at the far left side of Thor Peak's southeast face.

Mirror Point, Southeast Face. Class 5. First ascent September 6, 1936, by William Rice and Robert K. Brinton. Climb the talus slope northeast of Mirror Lake to an apron. Climb around the apron to its left, and ascend a series of cracks above. The crux is an overhanging 20-foot crack. The route then gradually works to the left (south).

The Shnahz. I, 5.5. First ascent July 9, 1978, by Scott Anderson and Bob Margulis. This route ascends the southwest buttress of Thor Peak. Begin by climbing a ramp to the right of the buttress. This ramp then angles left and leads to a flake near a black watermark. Climb the crack (5.5) and go up and right to the top of the towers on the crest of the buttress. Climb the left and right sides of the buttress for three more pitches of class 3–4 to the summit.

South Crack. III, 5.9. First ascent July 1962 by Tom Condon and Ron Dickenson. Follow the Mt. Whitney Trail above Bighorn Park to the top of the switchbacks. Climb a combination of brush and talus up and to the right. Ascend the crack that separates Mirror Point from Thor Peak. After two pitches, traverse right across a system of ledges. There is a series of cracks above, to the right of the left-hand skyline. Climb the second crack from the left (5.9) to the top of the cliff.

Satan's Delight. Class 5. First ascent September 4, 1937, by Howard Koster, Arthur B. Johnson, and James N. Smith. From the ledge system of the South Crack route, continue traversing on the ledges to a crack that leads to the Pink Perch, a high, red-colored ledge. Descend a crack eastward for approximately 100 feet. A delicate move leads to a vertical crack a few feet out on the face. Climb two pitches up the crack to a shelf behind a gendarme. Go right and make another delicate move for 15 feet where the difficulties ease; this pitch ends after 70 feet.

Climb some fine, high-angle blocks, then traverse left high above the Pink Perch. Climb a series of ledges to a recess under the blocks that mark the top of the cliff. This climb ends about 100 feet east of the southeast point of Thor Peak.

The Pink Perch. Class 4. Descended September 3, 1940, by Carl Jensen, Howard Koster, Wayland Gilbert, and Elsie Strand. This climb ends atop the Pink Perch. It has also been considered as a variation to the beginning of Satan's Delight. Follow the South Crack and Satan's Delight routes to the top of the slope of talus and brush. A wide ledge runs across the southeast face of Thor Peak. Follow this ledge for about two-thirds of its length, then climb the steep, narrow gully leading diagonally left across the face to the Pink Perch.

Truncated Buttress. II, 5.7, A1. First ascent May 7, 1972, by William Putnam, Tom

Thor Peak, South Face (photo by R. J. Secor)

Cosgrove, and Fred Beckey. This route begins a few hundred feet northeast of the Pink Perch route. It starts at the highest pine tree and climbs a series of jam cracks (with one aid pitch) to the left of a prominent, broken, steep ridge.

Principal Dihedral. III, 5.8, A2. First ascent May 1973 by Fred Beckey, Leland Davis, and Mike McGoey. This route is approximately 200 feet northeast of the Truncated Buttress route, in a prominent, long, shallow dihedral. Climb the dihedral for several pitches to where a blank slab is overcome by means of bat hooks. Later, the crux involves jamming a headwall on its left side.

Rainbow Bridge. III, 5.10. First ascent May 1979 by Allan Pietrasanta and Alan Bartlett. This route begins just to the right of the Principal Dihedral route in a long, right-facing dihedral. Two pitches lead to a point just below the top of the dihedral. Go left on a hand traverse to a ledge. A brushy crack leads to another ledge, then go left and up past two bolts to a crack. Three easier pitches lead to the east shoulder of Thor Peak.

Loki. IV, 5.10, A2. First ascent October 1980 by Alan Roberts, Kim Walker, and Alan Bartlett. It is about time that someone used this name for a route on Thor Peak! This route ascends the first major crack system to the right of the Rainbow Bridge route. Five pitches of free climbing lead to a huge ledge. Climb a prominent left-leaning crack. Three more pitches of easier climbing lead to the end of the climb.

The Stemwinder. II, 5.4. First ascent September 7, 1936, by William Rice, Robert K. Brinton, and Glen Dawson. Climb to the highest trees that are to the right of the Loki route on the southeast face. Traverse left on a ledge to the base of a vertical chimney. Ascend the chimney, and follow a ledge back to the right. Climb cracks and ledges to a large, pale red pinnacle standing out from the main face. From the notch between the pinnacle and the face, traverse right to a gully, which slopes up to the left. A broad ledge to the left leads to the top of the climb. This is a fine six-pitch route.

Northeast Slopes. Class 2. Leave the Mt. Whitney Trail just below the junction with the Lone Pine Lake Trail. Climb brush and talus to the summit of Thor Peak.

Warm Leatherette. II, 5.10d. First ascent 1984 by Scott Ayers and Bill Leventhal. This

route climbs the north buttress of Thor Peak from a point above Clyde Meadow on the North Fork of Lone Pine Creek.

Wotan's Throne *(3880 m+; 12,720 ft+)*

South Face. Class 3. From Trail Camp along the Mt. Whitney Trail ascend easy ledges to some broken blocks in the middle of the south face.

Northwest Arete. Class 2. First ascent 1933 by Norman Clyde.

East Chimney. Class 2. First ascent July 10, 1937, by Chester Versteeg. There are three chimneys on the upper part of the southeast face of the peak. Climb the far right-hand chimney to the summit.

Pinnacle Ridge *(3980 m+; 13,040 ft+)*

Traverse. Class 4. First ascent July 10, 1935, by John Mendenhall and Nelson Nies.

So Many Aiguilles, So Little Time. III, 5.10+. First ascent early 1980s by Scott Ayers and Mike Strassman. This route climbs cracks in the center of the south face for six pitches.

"Pinnacle Pass Needle"
(3760 m+; 12,320 ft+)

Northwest Corner. Class 4. First ascent September 7, 1936, by Robert K. Brinton, Glen Dawson, and William Rice. Climb a crack on the side of the needle facing Mt. Whitney and traverse an arete leading to the summit.

"S'brutal Tower"
(4240 m+; UTM 845475)

This is the second tower south of Mt. Muir. It is class 1 from the John Muir Trail.

East Prow. III, 5.9. First ascent early 1980s by Scott Ayers and Mike Strassman. The first three pitches of this climb stay to the left of the prow. The remaining five pitches remain on top of the prow.

"Aiguille Junior"
(4240 m+; UTM 845477)

This is the next tower north of S'brutal Tower. It is an easy boulder hop from the John Muir Trail.

Breathless. III, 5.10a. First ascent early 1980s by Scott Ayers and Mike Strassman. This route climbs the right-hand east buttress for eight pitches. Finish the climb by traversing to the left edge of the tower high on the buttress.

"Aiguille du Paquoir"

(4260 m+; UTM 845478)

This is the next tower north from Aiguille Junior. It is a simple climb from the John Muir Trail.

East Face. IV, 5.9. First ascent early 1980s by Scott Ayers and Mike Strassman. Ascend corners for eleven pitches to the summit.

Mt. Muir *(4271 m; 14,015 ft)*

From the John Muir Trail. Class 3. The summit is about 200 feet above the trail. Leave the trail at an elevation of 13,780 feet; Mt. Hitchcock bears 225 degrees magnetic, Mt. Hale bears 309 degrees magnetic, and the "neck" of Guitar Lake bears 274 degrees magnetic. Climb a shallow chute of loose talus and head toward the ridge on the right, where talus blends with the rocks of the summit pinnacle. Move left and climb a chimney to its head. Traverse left across a sloping ledge, and climb a crack to the small summit.

East Buttress. Class 4. First ascent July 11, 1935, by Nelson P. Nies and John Mendenhall. This is a splendid route. The buttress is obvious from Trail Camp on the Mt. Whitney Trail. From the toe of the buttress, climb to the right of the crest. Approximately halfway up the buttress, move left into a well-fractured chute that leads back to the right, between two gendarmes. Climb large blocks to a notch just beneath the summit. Stay slightly to the left, and climb a steep trough to the summit.

Southeast Face. Class 4. First ascent September 1, 1935, by Arthur Johnson and William Rice. Climb the crest of the east buttress to where the difficulties increase. Traverse left, down a ledge and into a chimney on the southeast face of the buttress. Climb the chimney to the crest of the buttress; a 60-foot squeeze chimney is encountered at the top of the chimney. From the crest of the buttress, climb up and right under a gendarme to the well-fractured chute of the East Buttress route.

"Aiguille Extra"

(4280 m+; 14,000 ft+; UTM 846479)

Class 1 from the John Muir Trail.

East Buttress. V, 5.10, A2. First ascent July 2–3, 1978, by Werner Landry and Kenny Cook. Gain the toe of the buttress by approaching it from the right. Climb the crest of the buttress (5.6) to a good crack to the right of the base of a chimney. Ascend the crack (5.9) to a ledge. Climb a thin crack and use aid to traverse into an off-width crack (A2, 5.9). Go up left through a slot (5.7) beneath some ledges. Some class 3 climbing leads to a large ledge, and then 5.7 climbing tends to the right and ends on another ledge. Class 3 to the left leads to a large ledge at the base of a headwall. Leave the ledge via a hand jam (5.10) next to a large block. A layback is followed by a traverse to the right for 30 feet. The traverse ends with a vertical hand jam, which leads to a good belay ledge atop some large blocks. A corner to the right has some aid moves up an overhang. Easy class 5 climbing leads to the summit.

East Face. V, 5.8, A3. First ascent June 1971 by Bill Sumner and Mike Heath. This route follows the prominent dihedral on the east face. It begins by using aid to leave a small platform that is 40 feet above the talus. Follow cracks to the base of the dihedral. Climb the dihedral to a hanging belay beneath an overhang. Pass this on the right and follow the dihedral for three pitches to a step just below the summit. Broken rock and chimneys lead to the summit.

"Third Needle"

(4300 m+; 14,080 ft+; UTM 847481)

This peak is easily identified from the east because Pinnacle Ridge abuts its east buttress. It is a simple climb from the John Muir Trail.

East Buttress. Class 5, A1. First ascent September 5, 1948, by John Mendenhall, Ruby Wacker, and John Altseimer. Climb the south side of the buttress, starting from where Pinnacle Ridge ends against Third Needle. After 400 feet of class 4, traverse left and climb a chimney using aid. Then move right into a rotten, bottomless chimney. Climb over the buttress to its north side via a crack. A thank-God ledge leads to the notch north of the summit.

East Face, Right Side. Class 5. First ascent September 3, 1939, by John Mendenhall and Ruth Mendenhall. From the saddle at the western end of Pinnacle Ridge, climb class 3 up and to the left into an easy gully. Climb the gully about halfway up, to where it is blocked by an overhang. Bypass this on the right side via a short class 5 traverse. Many class 4 pitches then lead to the notch north of the summit.

Hall of the Yeti King. III, 5.7. First ascent September 12, 1982, by Greg Vernon and George Pfalsy. Climb class 3 up and to the left from the saddle at the western end of Pinnacle Ridge. Instead of climbing the easy gully of the East Face, Right Side route, climb the chute to the right of the gully. Climb this chute for four pitches to the base of a chimney. Climb the chimney for two pitches, and leave it via a ledge. This is followed by an easy pitch that leads back into the chimney. Climb the right wall of the chimney for two more pitches. This route ends a few hundred feet south of the high point of Third Needle.

East Face, Left Side. III, 5.3. First ascent August 1966 by Mike Heath. Follow the East Face, Right Side route to the overhang. Bypass the overhang on the left side and climb a thin buttress, which leads to a narrow, chockstone-filled chimney. Go up and left to a broad ledge that crosses the upper part of the east face. Continue left to a prominent, curving chimney. This leads to the small notch just south of the summit.

"Day Needle"

(4320 m+; 14,080 ft+; UTM 846483)

This is the second needle south of Mt. Whitney. There are no problems encountered while climbing this peak from the John Muir Trail.

East Buttress, Right Side. IV, 5.8. First ascent July 1977 by Ed Conner and John Vawter. Climb the couloir between Day Needle and Keeler Needle (loose rock!) for about 300 feet to a point about 30 feet below and left of a prominent roof. Traverse up and left to the crest of the buttress. Follow the buttress to the summit.

East Buttress, Left Side. IV, 5.7, A2. First ascent September 14–15, 1963, by Fred Beckey and Rick Reese. This route begins at the bottom of the couloir between Day Needle and Third Needle. Climb the couloir a short distance and move to the right over easy rock to where the chimney narrows to the left of the buttress. Climb the chimney for two pitches and emerge onto the crest of the buttress. Ascend the prow of the buttress for several pitches. The crux is a long dihedral, poorly protected, which goes mostly free, with some aid. Later, use aid up a vertical open book that leads out of a chimney. Then make an exposed traverse right (protected by a bolt), which leads into another chimney.

Climb the chimney for one pitch; this ends atop a big belay platform in an exposed and awesome position. Traverse the rim of the drop-off to the north for two leads. Finish the route by climbing through a hole.

Keeler Needle *(4340 m+; 14,240 ft+)*

This is the first needle south of Mt. Whitney. It is an easy climb from the John Muir Trail.

East Face, Right Side. V, 5.9, A2. First ascent 1973 by John Weiland and Jeff Lowe. This route starts on the right side of the east face and climbs six pitches all free except for the last 30 feet, which lead to a large, red dihedral. From the top of the dihedral, work left on ledges to the center of the face below a headwall. The headwall requires steep aid climbing up several different cracks. The aid climbing ends at a ledge, where another pitch up a steep crack leads up the right side of the prow below The Ledge of the Harding Route. Follow the Harding Route to the summit.

Harding Route. V, 5.10b. First ascent July 1960 by Warren Harding, Glen Denny, Rob McKnight, and Desert Frank (a hitchhiker who went a lot farther than he ever expected to). First winter ascent March 1972 by Warren Harding, Galen Rowell, and Tim Auger. First free ascent August 21, 1976, by Galen Rowell, Chris Vandiver, and Gordon Wiltsie. This climb begins on the left side of the east face and climbs a prominent crack system. Begin from the base of the couloir between Day Needle and Keeler Needle. Face climbing on a slab with cracks leads up and slightly to the right. The second pitch is hard, with a tough move over a strenuous overhang (5.10). Continue climbing cracks and dihedrals up to the right, where an off-width crack (5.9) leads up to a series of broken ledges. Two class 4 pitches lead to the top of the broken ledges. More face climbing follows (with a 5.8 move in a crack), up to the base of a red dihedral. Climb the dihedral (5.9) to a ledge. This is followed by a trough, with a 5.8 move to the right and up to a sloping ledge. The crux is a 5.10b off-width crack that leads to a belay from a chockstone in the chimney. The chimney becomes easier and then jogs left to another belay from a chockstone. Climb an obvious flake and crack that goes up and to the right (5.7, with some loose rock) to some big ledges. Improbable (yes, it *will* go) 5.7 climbing continues up and to the right, over a face and flakes to The Ledge on the very prow of the east buttress. Another pitch leads to a 5.7 traverse that leads left under a roof, followed by an easy crack. Climb blocks on the arete (or on either side of it) to the summit. Further reading: *Summit*, May 1972, pp. 18–25; Galen Rowell, *High and Wild*, Lexicos, San Francisco, 1983, pp. 29–35; *American Alpine Journal*, 1972, pp. 276–81; *Rock & Ice*, No. 41, pp. 46–49.

Mt. Whitney *(4417 m; 14,494 ft)*

West Slope. Class 2. First ascent August 18, 1873, by The Fishermen: Charles D. Begole, Albert Johnson, and John Lucas. First winter ascent January 10, 1929, by Orland Bartholomew during his three-month solo ski traverse of the High Sierra. Climb any of the talus chutes to the summit.

Northwest Rib. 5.7. First ascent July 27, 1988, by Galen Rowell. Climb the arete that

Whitney Massif from the east (photo by Austin Post, #72R2-195, USGS Ice and Climate Project, Tacoma, WA)

rises above the outlet of Arctic Lake.

North Slope. Class 2–3. Climb the left side of the north slope, just under the northeast ridge. Ascend some shallow chutes leading to a 50-foot-high wall of broken blocks. Pass through these blocks and climb directly to the summit.

Northeast Ridge. III, 5.10 with a rappel. First ascent July 26, 1982, by Galen Rowell, Claude Fiddler, and Vern Clevenger. This route begins just south of Whitney–Russell Pass. Follow the ridge to the top of the Mountaineer's Route. At one point it is necessary to make a short rappel over an overhang and into a notch.

Cardiovascular Seizure. III, 5.10. First ascent September 1973 by Vern Clevenger and Keith Bell. There is a pillar leaning against the farthest northern portion of the east face, just south of Whitney–Russell Pass. This route begins a short distance north of a chimney on this pillar. Seven difficult pitches lead to the top of the northeast ridge. Either continue up the ridge and descend the Mountaineer's Route or descend a very loose chute south of the climb's finish.

The Rotten Chimney. III, 5.8. First ascent 1973 by Vern Clevenger, Mark Moore, and Julie X. This climbs the chimney on the pillar of Cardiovascular Seizure. Five pitches of difficult crud climbing lead to the top of the northeast ridge.

Mountaineer's Route. Class 3. First ascent October 21, 1873, by John Muir. This is the deep couloir that separates the northeast ridge from the east buttress of Mt. Whitney. There is some loose talus in the couloir, and early in the season it usually has hard, frozen snow or ice, even in the late afternoon. This can complicate matters for those using this as a descent route after climbing one of the routes on the main east face of Mt. Whitney. It may be better to descend the north slope and return to Iceberg Lake via Whitney–Russell Pass, rather than descending steep snow or ice in rock-climbing shoes.

From Iceberg Lake ascend the north side of the couloir to the notch north of the summit of Mt. Whitney. From the notch,

Mt. Whitney from the east (photo by R. J. Secor)

descend slightly toward the west, and then climb a wide chute via ledges and ribs to the summit plateau.

Those using this as a descent route should note that you leave the summit plateau approximately 75 yards northwest of the outhouse.

East Buttress. III, 5.6. First ascent September 5, 1937, by Bob Brinton, Glen Dawson, Richard Jones, Howard Koster, and Muir Dawson. (The first-ascent party called this route the "Sunshine-Peewee Route.") Scramble to the notch between the First Tower and the Second Tower on the East Face route. Rope up here, and climb the east face of the Second Tower until you are about 15 feet below its top. Go right along the north side of the tower to a small ledge and crack

Mt. Whitney, East Buttress (photo by Pete Yamagata)

which lead to the notch behind the Second Tower. The pitch above the notch on the crest of the buttress requires finesse. Follow the buttress upward to the Peewee, a gigantic detached block which, upon closer inspection, could be compared to the Sword of Damocles. Pass the Peewee on its right side. Scramble over blocks (either directly upward or to the right) to the summit. Two weeks after the first ascent, the second-ascent party took 3½ hours to reach the summit from Iceberg Lake; this time is rarely equaled today. *Bard Variation: 5.7.* First ascent by Allan Bard. Continue up and left from the Peewee to a short, right-facing corner. Climb the corner (5.7) to ledges on the crest of the buttress. Climb up and left away from a left-facing corner above the ledges. This leads to the blocks and ledges immediately beneath the summit. Further reading: Allan Bard, *East Buttress of Mt. Whitney,* Shooting Star Guides, Bishop, California, 1991 (a route card).

Peewee's Big Adventure. III, 5.8. First ascent 1986 by Joel Richnak and Mike Carville. This route could be considered the direct east buttress. Start climbing about 100 feet to the right of the notch between the First Tower and Second Tower. Go up and to the right on flakes, then climb left to a block. After a short distance in a gully, ascend an exposed face. Several more pitches, gradually moving to the left, lead to the Peewee. Climb through the crack that splits the roof of the Peewee, and then go over blocks and ledges to the summit.

East Face. III, 5.4. First ascent August 16, 1931, by Robert Underhill, Glen Dawson, Jules Eichorn, and Norman Clyde. From the notch behind the First Tower, traverse across the south face of the Second Tower. This is the Tower Traverse (5.3; first ascent August 17, 1934, by Jules Eichorn and Marjory Bridge). This involves ascending an upward-sloping ledge to a shelf that traverses horizontally to a tight chimney. Move left from the top of this chimney and climb the Washboard, a series of class 3 ledges covered with scree. The Washboard ends at a large alcove with a wall on its southern side. Climb the wall on its left side. Traverse across the southern side of this wall along some ledges to an inside corner. Move up and left, then go around a block to the Fresh Air Traverse. This is a long step-across, with wild exposure, but relatively easy (5.4). Move 20 feet to the left and climb a smooth face to a broken chimney, which gradually goes back to the right. These two pitches end at the Grand Staircase, a series of steep shelves. Ascend the shelves to the wall at the top of the Grand Staircase. Exit this staircase via a tight chimney on the left. Scramble up blocks to the summit. The first-ascent party took an incredible 3¼ hours to finish the climb from the First Tower. Most parties seem to take 6 hours or more to do the route these days. *Variation:* This was the route of the first-ascent party: Instead of taking the Tower Traverse, climb the East Buttress route to the notch behind the Second Tower. Descend a loose chute that leads left (south) to the top of the chimney at the end of the Tower Traverse and the start of the Washboard. *Variation: Shaky-Leg Crack. 5.7.* First ascent June 9, 1936, by Morgan Harris, James N. Smith, and Neil Ruge. There is a large block with a ledge at its top directly above the start of the Fresh Air Traverse. Climb the north inside corner of this block to the large block's ledge, then a flaring crack to a comfortable ledge. Move left and up to the Grand Staircase. This variation is not as exposed as the Fresh Air Traverse, but it is much more strenuous. *Variation: Direct Crack. 5.8.* First ascent July 4, 1953, by John Mendenhall. This is a short, strenuous crack about 40 feet south of the inside corner encountered before the Fresh Air Traverse. (It is right [north] from the Shaky-Leg Crack.) *Escape Route:* If a party backs off of the East Face route, it can probably escape by reversing the Tower Traverse. Another option is to climb the cruddy chute (class 3) that leads up and right from the end of the Tower Traverse, near the bottom of the Washboard. This leads up to the notch behind the Second Tower of the East Buttress route. It is possible to reach the Mountaineer's Route from here via a long rappel (i.e., two 150-foot ropes). Some parties have done this with two short rappels from the small ledge and crack on the north side of the Second Tower of the East Buttress route. Further reading: Allen Steck and Steve Roper, *Fifty Classic Climbs of North America,* Sierra Club Books, San Francisco, 1979, pp. 276–81; *Summit,* May–June 1982, pp. 26–29; Allan Bard, *East Face of Mt. Whitney,* Shooting Star Guides, Bishop, California, 1991 (a route card).

Mt. Whitney, East Face (photo by R. J. Secor)

The Great Book. IV, 5.9. First ascent August 1974 by Gary Colliver and Chris Vandiver. This route starts to the left of the base of the First Tower, on its southern side. Seven pitches of 5.8 and 5.9 and 300 feet of class 3 lead to the top of the Washboard. Climb the large open book that rises above the Washboard. Use the crack on the right, and two pitches of 5.8 and two pitches of 5.9 end 400 feet below the summit. Scramble over blocks and ledges to the summit.

The Hairline. V, 5.10, A3. First ascent August 1987 by Bernie Binder and Alex Schmauss. This route is between the Great Book and the Direct East Face. Climb a 5.10 face with cracks that don't quite reach the ground. (The first part of this is protected with bolts.) Climb the cracks until you are just beneath the Fresh Air Traverse, and continue climbing left of the Great Book. The first-ascent party reported that about 30 percent of the route was aid. Twenty-five pitons should be carried, along with bat hooks, sky hooks, and cams to 5 inches.

Direct East Face. V, 5.9, A3. First ascent July 6, 1959, by Denis Rutovitz and Andrzel Ehrenfeucht. First winter ascent February 1985 by Galen Rowell, Ron Kauk, and Michael Graber. This route follows the enormous crack on the true east face of Mt. Whitney. The climb starts 40 feet to the right of some black watermarks on the apron at the bottom of the crack. Climb broken outside corners up and right for 60 feet to some class 4 ledges.

These ledges lead left to a slanting crack (5.8), followed by a belay. Climb the chimney above it (5.3) to a large terrace. Go up and right from the terrace to a broken gully, which gradually turns into a narrow crack behind a large flake (5.5), and then move left to a belay behind another flake. Climb up and to the right over cracks and edges; this 5.7 pitch is sustained and poorly protected and ends at a small belay ledge. Climb a jam crack before moving left onto the face and continuing to another small ledge (5.3). This is followed by a 5.7 jam crack and a belay at the base of a chimney. This chimney features a chockstone, and gradually narrows into an off-width crack (5.8; large chocks required) to a belay stance (the perfect bivouac cave is 20 feet below and to the left of this stance). Continue climbing the short, wet crack (5.8) to a large, black, damp cave. Aid climbing leads up and right from the cave; an awkward aid move around the nose of an overhang leads to easy rock. A short 5.7 pitch up a large crack is followed by another short pitch (5.5) up blocks and faces on the left to a large ledge. Go right from this ledge up more blocks and faces (5.5) to the final chimney. This chimney can be avoided by climbing up and left and traversing to the right (5.3). Class 3 then leads to the Fresh Air Traverse of the regular East Face route. *Variation:* The first-ascent party climbed 300 feet up and to the left from the bottom of the face to an open book that leads to the large terrace.

Southeast Face. III, Class 5. First ascent October 11, 1941, by John Mendenhall and Ruth Mendenhall. This route begins on the buttress that leans against the southeast face. Class 4 climbing on the buttress leads to a point where you can traverse to the right into a chimney (loose rock!) above an overhang. A thousand feet of class 4 then lead to the top.

Whitney–Keeler Couloir. This is dangerously loose. Three climbers were killed here many years ago.

The John Muir Trail. Class 1. This requires nothing more than stamina.

Further reading: Paul Hellweg and Scott McDonald, *Mount Whitney Guide for Hikers and Climbers,* Canyon Publishing Co., Canoga Park, California, 1990; Walt Wheelock and Tom Condon, *Climbing Mt. Whitney,* La Siesta Press, Glendale, California, 1970.

Mt. Young *(4016 m; 13,177 ft)*

South Slopes. Class 1. First ascent September 7, 1881, by Frederick Wales, William Wallace, and James Wright. A mixture of sand and easy talus leads to the summit.

Traverse from Mt. Hale. Class 1. If climbing Mt. Young and Mt. Hale, it is easier to ascend Mt. Hale first, and then traverse to Mt. Young.

Mt. Hale *(4113 m; 13,440 ft+)*

The author is a proud graduate of George Ellery Hale (for whom the peak was named) Elementary School, Class of '68.

South Slopes. Class 1. First ascent July 24, 1934, by J. H. Czock and Mildred Czock. These slopes are sandy.

Northeast Face. V, 5.9, A3. First ascent July 1973 by Dennis Hennek and Galen Rowell. Begin climbing in the center of the tallest of the two east faces of Mt. Hale. Climb a right-leaning crack system for five pitches of continuously difficult climbing. Direct aid is needed to overcome an overhanging off-width crack. The upper half of the climb has several short but difficult sections.

Hale Pinnacles. First ascent June 1973 by Galen Rowell. There are two 100-foot pinnacles on the ridge between Mt. Hale and Mt. Russell. They are due north of Arctic Lake. The southern pinnacle is 5.6 and the northern one is 5.8.

Peak 3940m+

(12,880 ft+; 0.4 mi S of Mt. Hale)

Arctic Dreams. IV, 5.10b. First ascent July 27, 1988, by Pat O'Donnell and Galen Rowell. This vertical face is next to Arctic Lake. Keep just left of center while climbing the face.

Peak 4245m

(13,920 ft+; 0.5 mi W of Mt. Russell)

The northeast slope is class 2 until the class 3 summit rocks are reached. The east ridge from Mt. Russell is continuous class 3.

Mt. Russell *(4294 m; 14,086 ft)*

This is the finest peak in the Mt. Whitney region. It is high and beautiful, and none of its routes are easy. The peak has two summits; the west peak is the high point.

East Ridge. Class 3. First ascent June 24, 1926, by Norman Clyde. Ascend the north side of the ridge from Russell–Carillon Pass to the east summit of Mt. Russell. It is easy to traverse to the west summit.

Southeast Face, Right Arete. III, 5.10, A1. First ascent July 1984 by Vern Clevenger, Claude Fiddler, and Bob Harrington. Follow

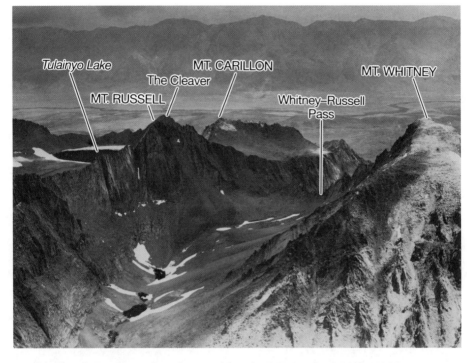

Mt. Russell and Mt. Whitney from the west (photo by F. E. Matthes, #1399, USGS Photographic Library, Denver, CO)

the right-hand arete on the southeast face to the east ridge of Mt. Russell. One rappel is needed to reach a notch high on the route.

Southeast Face, Left Arete. III, 5.8. Follow the left-hand arete to the east ridge. This route ends on the east ridge just before reaching the east summit of Mt. Russell.

South Ridge to East Peak. II, 5.7. First ascent September 15, 1974, by Greg Thomsen, Ed Ehrenfeldt, and Fred Beckey. This ridge follows the Sierra crest from the low point between Mt. Whitney and Mt. Russell to the top of the Mt. Russell's east peak. The route involves climbing over and around the serrated ridge crest. It is simple to leave the ridge at any point by traversing or rappelling off of it to the left.

South Face, Right Side. Class 3. First ascent 1928 by A. E. Gunther. Ascend easy talus slopes immediately left (west) of the south ridge to the headwall beneath the top of the ridge between the east and west summits. Climb the second chimney to the right of the headwall to the top of the ridge. *Variation:* Class 3. First ascent August 7, 1931, by Howard Sloan, Frank Noel, and William

Murray. Climb the headwall by following a ledge that rises diagonally to the left. *Variation:* Class 4. First ascent July 29, 1932, by James Wright. Climb the first chimney to the right of the headwall, and pass over a loose overhang near its top. Traverse right on a ledge, and climb to the ridge between the two summits.

South Face, Left Side. 5.0. First ascent July 1932 by Jules Eichorn, Glen Dawson, Walter Brem, and Hans Leschke. Follow the talus slopes as in the description of South Face, Right Side, but take the left branch. Near the end of the left branch, climb the right wall to a short ridge, which ends just before the west summit.

Fish Hook Arete. III, 5.9. First ascent June 1974 by Gary Colliver and John Cleare. This is the prominent, curved arete that drops immediately below the west summit of Mt. Russell. Follow the arete to the summit. Further reading: John Cleare, *Mountains*, Crown Publishers, New York, 1975, pp. 116–27.

Pilgrimage. III, 5.9. First ascent September 1979 by Allan Pietrasanta and Alan Bartlett.

Mt. Russell, South Face (photo by R. J. Secor)

This and the next two routes are on the south face of the west summit of Mt. Russell. Low on this face is a left-facing broken dihedral. Climb a crack on the left side of this and go past a small roof. Continue up the face for several pitches to easier climbing and the summit.

Direct South Face. III, 5.10. First ascent July 1986 by Rich Romano and Fred Yakulic. This route starts by climbing a hand crack below a large right-facing dihedral. Later, a left-facing dihedral is entered, which is the crux of the climb.

The Mithral Dihedral. III, 5.9. First ascent July 1976 by Alan Bartlett and Alan Roberts. Climb the large left-facing dihedral just to the right of the Southwest Buttress route. This route involves five pitches of sustained, difficult jamming.

Southwest Buttress. III, 5.8. First ascent September 1, 1974, by Gary Colliver, TM Herbert, and Don Lauria. There are two prominent cracks at the base of this buttress.

Climb the left crack (loose rock!). Three more pitches of 5.7 to 5.8 on better quality rock lead to the crest of the buttress, and easier climbing then leads to the summit.

Bloody Corner. III, 5.10. First ascent September 1979 by Alan Bartlett and Allan Pietrasanta. There is a prominent dihedral to the left of the Southwest Buttress route. Climb progressively more difficult rock for a few hundred feet to the dihedral. Two pitches in the dihedral lead to easier climbing and the crest of the buttress.

West Face. IV, 5.10 or 5.9, A2. First ascent June 1971 by Galen Rowell and Chris Jones. First free ascent 1974 by Mark Moore and Julie X. First winter ascent March 1983 by Galen Rowell and Jack Tackle. Climb the crack system on the center of the west face. A landmark for this crack system is a square belay ledge 150 feet above the start of the route. There have been many variations done on this route, notably by Fred Yakulic, Alan Kouzmanoff, and Rich Romano. All of

Mt. Russell, West Face (photo by R. J. Secor)

these variations stay within 100 feet of the main crack system.

Beowulf's Revenge. IV, 5.8. First ascent October 1978 by Marie Grayson, Mark Fielding, and Fred Beckey. This route climbs the left side of the west face. Begin by climbing among some ledges in a loose chimney about 100 feet to the left of an obvious right-leaning arch. The first three pitches go up and left, with continuously improving climbing. The remaining portion of the climb is exposed, and has high-quality rock and roomy belay ledges. The last pitch traverses left on smooth rock and ends with a 5.7 layback.

West Chimney. III, 5.10. First ascent September 5, 1988, by Steve Porcella and Cameron Burns. This steep chimney is on the left side of the west face, but right of the west couloir. The first pitch ends beneath an enormous roof. Climb the face on the left wall (5.8), and climb over the roof (5.9) to a steep hand crack above. This crack is 5.8,

and it leads to a rubble-covered ledge. Continue climbing the main chimney for two more pitches. This is followed by a sustained pitch that climbs a face (loose rock and little protection!) to bypass a rotten roof. The next pitch continues up the chimney over some loose blocks. The seventh pitch is the crux of the climb. It goes up a shallow dihedral and features 5.10 face moves with no protection. One more pitch leads to the summit.

West Couloir. Class 4. Descended July 1932 by Jules Eichorn, Glen Dawson, Walter Brem, and Hans Leschke. This is the deep couloir between the west face and the west arete. Climb the couloir to the west arete, which leads to the west summit.

West Arete. Class 3. Descended July 1932 by Norman Clyde. Follow the ridge leading from Peak 4245m (13,920+).

Northwest Face. Class 3–4. First ascent 1935 by J. H. Czock, Mildred Czock, and Mary Luck. From the small lake near the base of the north ridge, ascend the northwest face near its east side. Go over easy rock to the first ledge that leads out onto the middle of the northwest face. Follow the ledge to the middle of the face and climb directly to the summit ridge midway between the east and west summits.

North Arete. Class 3. Descended June 24, 1926, by Norman Clyde. Climb onto the ridge from Tulainyo Lake. Difficulties can be avoided by keeping to the right of the arete along the ends of the ledges on the northwest face. This route ends atop the east summit.

Northeast Face. III, class 5. First ascent June 10, 1971, by Reed Cundiff and Fred Beckey. Climb steep snow and rock slabs to the right of the main face. This climb ends on the east summit.

Mt. Carillon   *(4120 m+; 13,552 ft)*

From Russell–Carillon Pass. Class 2. First ascent 1925 by Norman Clyde. Either ascend directly from the pass, or from the slopes to the south of the peak.

Northeast Ridge. Class 3. Follow the ridge from Cleaver Col.

East Face. III, 5.8. First ascent July 1968 by Fred Beckey and Chuck Haas. This climb is between a deep crack on the right side of the face and a broad gully on the left. Climb up and left over slabs to an open book that slants up and right. Climb the book to a slab that leads to a narrow crack. A squeeze chimney in a corner and a jam crack lead to a traverse to the left to a cave with orange rock. One more pitch leads to the southeast ridge of Mt. Carillon.

The Impala, South Face. II, 5.7. First ascent June 1968 by Chuck Ray and Brad Fowler. This formation is the sloping pyramid at the base of the long southeast ridge of Mt. Carillon. It is due north of Clyde Meadow on the North Fork of Lone Pine Creek. Climb the obvious chimney in the middle of the south face for two pitches. Cross a left-ascending diagonal chimney system, and climb straight up to a false summit. Easy scrambling leads to the summit of the Impala.

The Impala, Diagonal Route. II, 5.7. First ascent November 1968 by Fred Beckey and Charlie Raymond. Follow the diagonal chimney system that starts at the lower left side of the south face and goes up to the right. Once on the southeast face, go up to the false summit.

The Winged Horse. III, 5.8, A3. First ascent November 17, 1970, by Jack Miller and Fred Beckey. This formation is east of the Impala. The climb begins at the base of the south face, near a pine tree. After a pitch of tricky friction (5.8), go up and left. Aid leads to a ledge at the base of a groove, and a pitch of mixed climbing goes up the groove. This is followed by chickenheads, a traverse left, and chimneys to the summit.

"The Cleaver"
(4079 m; 13,355 ft; 0.7 mi SE of Tunnabora Peak)

Northwest Ridge. Class 3. First ascent July 16, 1931, by Norman Clyde, who described it as being "a good rubber-soled shoe climb." Climb easy class 3 ledges to the summit.

Southwest Ridge. II, 5.6. First ascent July 1973 by Galen Rowell, Dennis Hennek, and Dave Lomba. Most of this ridge from Cleaver Col is class 4.

South Face. III, 5.9. First ascent June 1980 by Bill St. Jean, Allan Pietrasanta, and Alan Bartlett. This route climbs just left of the center of the south face. The first pitch is a strenuous off-width, and four more pitches lead to the lower left end of a gold-colored band high on the face. One pitch along the band leads to the summit pitch, going up cracks and over a roof.

"Tunnabora Pinnacles"
(3900 m+/-; 12,800 ft+/-; 0.8 mi NW of Tunnabora Peak)

These pinnacles are on the Sierra crest between Mt. Carl Heller and Tunnabora Peak. Tulainyo Tower is one of these pinnacles. These pinnacles were traversed on August 9, 1970, by Charles Bell from northwest to southeast. Class 3–4.

"Tulainyo Tower"
(3920 m+; 12,800 ft+; 0.6 mi SE of Vacation Pass)

This is the most prominent crag among the Tunnabora Pinnacles. The exact location is UTM 841521.

East Face. IV, 5.9. First ascent October 1972 by Galen Rowell and Marek Glogoczowski. This climb starts on the right side of the east face. Climb a wide chimney for two pitches to an area of red, broken rock. Traverse left to the main crack system of the face. Three pitches of 5.9 lead to an off-width crack. Traverse right onto easier climbing, and scramble up to the summit.

East Face Direct. IV, 5.8, A3. First ascent September 1973 by Bill Stronge and Arold Green. This route follows the 1,000-foot crack on the east face. This crack leads directly to the summit. Aid is needed on small portions of the upper section of this excellent route.

Tunnabora Peak   *(4134 m; 13,565 ft)*

South Slope. Class 2. First ascent August 1905 by George R. Davis. This is a talus hop from Tulainyo Lake.

Northwest Face. Class 2. First ascent 1958 by Bud Bingham, Barbara Lilley, and Fred Bressel. From George Creek, hike cross-country to the base of the northwest face. Ascend a chute to the summit.

"Mt. Carl Heller"

(4031 m; 13,211 ft; 0.2 mi SE of Vacation Pass)

This peak has been unofficially known as "Vacation Peak." The name "Mt. Carl Heller" has been proposed to the U.S. Board of Geographic Names in memory of the late founder of the China Lake Mountain Rescue Group. The southeast peak is the high point. It is a magnificent piece of granitic sculpture.

West Face. Class 3. Climb a broad chute on the southern side of the west face. The lower portion of this chute consists of smooth granite slabs.

Northwest Ridge. Class 4. First ascent August 14, 1966, by Andy Smatko, Bill Schuler, Tom Ross, and Ellen Siegal. Climb a narrow and steep gully that leads to the northwest ridge from the western side of the peak. The knife-edge ridge requires belays in three places: one to climb over a block sitting astride the ridge, another at a 20-foot vertical chimney, and the third along the ridge just below the summit.

East Ridge. Class 3. First ascent August 14, 1966, by Carl Heller and other members of the China Lake Mountain Rescue Group. This is a fine climb, once the approach up George Creek is completed.

Peak 3880m+

(12,723 ft; 1.5 mi NE of Vacation Pass)

South Slope. Class 2. Climb talus from the eastern approach to Vacation Pass.

North Face. Class 4. First ascent July 1963 by Arkel Erb and Sy Ossofsky. This peak is an impressive sight from the upper reaches of George Creek.

Mt. Barnard   *(4264 m; 13,990 ft)*

Southwest Slopes. Class 1. First ascent September 25, 1892, by John Hunter, William Hunter, and C. Mulholland. Hike up scree slopes from Wallace Creek.

Traverse from Trojan Peak. Class 2.

From George Creek. Class 2. From the head of the south branch of George Creek, climb the broad couloir to the gentle slope northeast of the summit.

East Face. III, 5.9. First ascent April 1972 by Tim Auger and Galen Rowell. This climbs the impressive face of the lower, eastern summit of Mt. Barnard, Peak 4180m+ (13,680+). This is an excellent but seldom-done route. The arduous approach and bighorn sheep restrictions of George Creek keep most climbers from doing this climb.

Two pitches (5.6) lead up the center of the lower face to a prominent ledge, which may be covered with snow. Continue up to a ceiling, where a 50-foot horizontal traverse across a smooth wall leads to the base of a dihedral. Climb the dihedral directly to the summit. The fifth pitch follows the corner over a roof, followed by a jam crack on the left. The next lead ends at a nice ledge. Two more steep pitches lead to the base of a right-facing dihedral. One more pitch leads to the summit. Most of the pitches of this route are 5.7 to 5.8, with the last pitch having a short 5.9 section.

Shaw Spire. III, 5.8. First ascent March 1971 by Galen Rowell and Jerry Gregg. This is the freestanding pinnacle beneath the east face of Mt. Barnard. Seven pitches on the southeast arete lead to the summit.

Trojan Peak   *(4251 m; 13,950 ft)*

From George Creek. Class 2. Climb the broad couloir that leads to the basin between Trojan Peak and Mt. Barnard.

Traverse from Mt. Barnard. Class 2.

West Face. Class 3. First ascent June 26, 1926, by Norman Clyde. Ascend the face to the southwest ridge from the Wright Creek Basin. Follow the ridge to the summit.

North Ridge. Class 2. Follow the ridge from the saddle south of Mt. Williamson.

Mt. Versteeg *(4100 m+; 13,470 ft)*

North Slope. Class 2–3. Descended 1964 by John Robinson and Andy Smatko. Ascend directly to the summit from Lake 3733m (12,160+) in Williamson Bowl.

Northeast Ridge. Class 2–3. First ascent 1964 by John Robinson and Andy Smatko. From Williamson Bowl, head to the saddle just north of Lake Helen of Troy. From the saddle, follow the northeast ridge to the summit.

Southwest Slope. Class 2. Climb a talus-filled chute that leads to the ridge south of the peak from the upper portion of Wright Creek. About 300 feet below the ridge crest, a steep, sandy chute with several chockstones leads to the crest just north of the summit. Climb the chute and scramble to the summit.

Northwest Ridge. Class 3. Follow the ridge from Tyndall Col.

Mt. Williamson *(4380 m+; 14,375 ft)*

California's second highest peak is an impressive sight from the Owens Valley. It has three summits: the high point on the southwestern side of the summit plateau, and two lower peaks high along the northeast ridge, which are known as the East Horn (4280 m+; 14,125 ft) and the West Horn (4300 m+; 14,160 ft+). Mt. Williamson is surrounded by the California Bighorn Sheep Zoological Area. The southeastern side of the peak (i.e., George Creek and the southeast ridge) is open only from December 15 to January 1 and from April 15 to May 15. The north and west sides of the peak are only open from December 15 to July 15. Further reading: *Summit,* October 1970, pp. 6–9.

Southeast Ridge from George Creek. Class 2. First ascent 1884 by W. L. Hunter and C. Mulholland. First winter ascent December 22, 1954, by Leigh Ortenburger and Bill Buckingham. After the long and arduous approach up George Creek, leave the stream at approximately 11,200 feet near a small meadow. Go north up the slope to the basin southeast of the summit plateau. A landmark for this slope is a large rock pinnacle sticking out of the slope about two-thirds of the way up. From the basin, either climb the ridge immediately to the left, or go north past a small lake to the ridge on the right, and climb to the summit plateau. *Variation: Bairs Creek.* Class 3. First ascent 1958 by Rick Jali, John Harding, and Dick Cowley. Follow the south

fork of Bairs Creek to the cirque at its head. Climb out of the cirque via a chute, and follow one of the ridges above it to the summit plateau.

Northeast Ridge. Class 4. First ascent by Norman Clyde. This route ascends the northeast ridge from the mouth of the canyon of Shepherd Creek. This 8,000-foot, waterless ascent is one hell of a hard climb. Over 2,000 feet of sand, brush, and loose rock lead to talus and blocks along the crest of the ridge. Obstacles along the ridge are passed on their southern sides before regaining the ridge crest beyond some gendarmes. This ridge leads to the broad northeast slope of the East Horn. Climb to the top of the East Horn, and descend to the saddle between it and the West Horn. Climb to the top of the West Horn via a shallow gully on its northeast side (class 3). Descend the northwest side of the West Horn for 200 feet, then ascend diagonally toward the summit plateau of Mt. Williamson to a small notch. Descend a short distance to another notch located between the West Horn and the summit plateau (class 4). Descend the southern side of this notch about 200 feet, and then traverse across the east side of the summit plateau to where it is possible to gain the summit plateau easily.

Northeast Ridge from Williamson Creek. Class 4. First ascent 1925 by Homer Erwin. First winter ascent December 29, 1954–January 2, 1955, by John Ohrenschall and Warren Harding. Hike up Shepherd Creek and then Williamson Creek to approximately 9,700 feet. The extreme eastern end of the north side of Mt. Williamson features two waterfalls, one above the other. There is a red buttress to the left of these waterfalls. This buttress comes all the way down to the canyon floor. Climb this buttress (class 3) to a steep wall, and bypass this wall via a chute to the left. Regain the buttress above the wall, and continue up to another obvious chute on the left. Climb this chute for a short distance and leave it on its left side and climb onto a loose, red slope. Ascend this slope to the crest of the main northeast ridge. The crest is gained at a small saddle that is to the left of a small, sharp peak. Continue up the northeast ridge, over the East Horn and West Horn to the summit plateau of Mt. Williamson.

North Rib. IV, 5.7. First ascent July 1972 by Edgar Boyles and Lito Tejada-Flores. There are two ribs on the eastern side of Mt.

Mt. Williamson, North Face (photo by R. J. Secor)

Williamson's north face. One leads to the West Horn and the other leads to the northeastern end of the summit plateau. From Williamson Creek, ascend the latter (right-hand) rib. The upper third of this rib consists of ten pitches of 5.5 to 5.7 climbing.

North Face. III, Class 4–5. First ascent July 6, 1957, by John Mendenhall and Ruth Mendenhall. This is one of the more imposing north faces of the Sierra. From approximately 11,100 feet on Williamson Creek, ascend the chute that leads directly to the northeastern end of the summit plateau. There is a short, difficult chimney in the lower portion of this chute, followed by easier climbing to about 500 feet below the summit plateau. At this point the chute begins to steepen. A short traverse over an ice couloir within the chute is followed by three pitches over steep, loose rock. The last pitch ends atop the summit plateau. *Variation:* First ascent August 23, 1970, by Steve Rogero and Wally Henry. The short, difficult chimney in the lower portion of the chute can be bypassed by climbing the buttress to the right.

North Couloir. IV, 5.4, A1. First ascent May 30–31, 1976, by John Mendenhall, Tim Ryan, and Fred Wing. This route climbs the snow couloir that slants up the right side of the north face. Climb the couloir to its head and ascend the rocks to the summit plateau. A short pitch of aid is encountered above the top of the couloir.

Northwest Buttress. Class 5. First ascent October 1970, by Galen Rowell. From the west face of Mt. Williamson, traverse up and left to a prominent notch behind a pinnacle at approximately 13,000 feet. Follow the buttress to the summit.

Bolton Brown Route. Class 3. First ascent July 1896 by Bolton Brown and Lucy Brown. The west face of Mt. Williamson is a confusing maze of chutes, many of which lead to dead ends. The following route description may not be of much help. Nevertheless ...

Go southeast from Shepherd Pass to the saddle leading to Williamson Bowl. Descend to the bowl, but stay on top of the ridge in the middle of the bowl, with two lakes on both sides of the ridge. Stay slightly to the right on top of the ridge to avoid a small cliff, and go to the second of the two lakes right of the ridge (Lake 3733m; 12,160 ft+). Head toward Mt. Williamson from this lake. Climb talus to the largest, most prominent black stains on rock (there are some smaller black stains farther south on the west face; avoid these). Above the larger black stains, enter the chute that leads up and slightly left (north). (Avoid a smaller chute that goes up and slightly right.) Follow this chute almost all of the way to the crest of the northwest buttress. Traverse right (south) about 100 feet to a 60-foot class 3 crack, which leads to the summit plateau. The true summit is a short distance to the south. *Variation:* Class 3. First ascent July 19, 1929, by Walter A. Starr, Jr. Near the top of the main chute on the west face, instead of traversing right (south), go left and up a small crack that appears to go nowhere. This crack turns into a chimney with a chockstone in it. Climb under the chockstone and emerge out onto the summit plateau.

Southwest Arete and South Face. Class 3. From Williamson Bowl, head toward red talus at the southern portion of the west face of Mt. Williamson. Above this talus, climb the southernmost of the chutes to a notch on the southwest arete. Cross onto the south face, and enter a broad chute in its upper portion. Climb ledges in a zigzag route to the summit plateau.

Direct South Arete. IV, 5.8. First ascent June 14, 1989, by Steve Porcella and Cameron Burns. This route ascends the most prominent arete on the south face. The route starts on the right-hand side of a large, triangular tower in the middle of the south face. Climb a dihedral for three pitches (5.8, 5.6, and 5.5) to where it disappears. Move left and climb the wildly exposed arete for three pitches of moderate class 5 climbing to the Sun Deck, a wide, sloping ledge. Climb a short, right-facing dihedral above the Sun Deck (5.8). Another pitch traverses around a wall (class 4) to a notch. Continue up the arete above for many class 4 pitches (with a few class 5 moves). This route ends close to the true summit of Mt. Williamson.

West Horn (Peak 4300m+; 14,160 ft+). Class 3–4. First ascent by Leroy Jeffers. This peak can be climbed via Mt. Williamson's northeast ridge (see the Northeast Ridge route, above) or directly from the summit plateau. Descend about 150 feet on the east side of the summit plateau, and traverse north to the chute leading up to the notch between the West Horn and the summit plateau. From the notch, go up and left (north) 40 feet to another notch. Descend diagonally across the north side of the West Horn for 120 feet, and then climb up to the summit.

East Horn (Peak 4280m+; 14,125 ft). Class 3–4. Descend a shallow gully on the northeast side of the West Horn to the saddle between the two horns. Traverse a short distance across the west face and then climb the face to the summit.

East Horn, South Face. Class 4. First ascent June 8, 1978, by Carl Heller, Dennis Burge, Arold Green, Dianne Lucas, Terry Moore, Bob Rockwell, and Bob Westbrook. Descend from the summit plateau to the chute that leads to the notch located west of the West Horn. Descend this chute approximately 400 feet to where it joins the chute leading to the notch between the West Horn and East Horn. Ascend this chute 100 feet and climb another chute, which leads up the south face of the East Horn. Easy class 4 rock across the south face leads to a buttress on the right side of the face. Climb the buttress (class 3) to the summit of the East Horn.

Mt. Tyndall   (4273 m; 14,018 ft)

Northwest Ridge. Class 2. This is the obvious ridge to the right of the north face, as viewed from Shepherd Pass.

North Rib. Class 3. First ascent July 6, 1864, by Clarence King and Richard Cotter. A shallow rib can be seen on the north face of Mt. Tyndall. Climb the rib to the summit ridge, and go left (east) along the ridge to the summit. This is a good climb.

East Face. Class 4. First ascent August 13, 1935, by Marjory Farquhar and William F. Loomis. The name of this route may be a misnomer; the climb could be considered as a variation of the north rib. Climb the prominent, open chute on the extreme right-hand side of the east face. A short class 4 pitch in the chute leads to easier climbing. The chute ends on the lower portion of the north face. Climb the north face or the north rib to the summit ridge.

Northeast Arete. III, 5.9. First ascent June 12, 1989, by Cameron Burns and Steve Porcella. There is a large broken crack that ascends vertically and splits, forming a large y at the base of this arete. Climb broken class

3 rocks to a small ledge at the base of this crack. The crack narrows, with an overhang about 35 feet above the ledge. This is immediately followed by a 5.9 face move onto a sloping triangular block on the left side of the crack. Another pitch leads up to a broken, snow-filled chimney (5.7). Increasingly easier pitches follow the left crack, and pass the remains of a small deer. The upper part of the route ascends class 4–5 slabs.

The Climbing Art. II, 5.7. First ascent June 1977 by David Mazel. This route climbs the second rib north of the rib of the Direct East Face route. About 800 feet of climbing leads to the north face of Mt. Tyndall.

Direct East Face. V, 5.10, A2. First ascent September 1983 by Steve Brewer, David Wilson, and Galen Rowell. This route ascends the east face directly beneath the summit. Difficult, vertical climbing (free and aid) for the first few pitches leads to moderate difficulties in the middle portion of the face. The final headwall has 5.8 to 5.10 cracks before reaching the summit.

East Couloir. III, 5.8. First ascent May 31, 1970, by Charles Raymond and Fred Beckey. This route climbs the deep couloir that splits the east face. The final, rotten headwall is the crux of the climb. It ends just south of the summit.

East Chimney. IV, 5.8. First ascent August 1972 by Michael Heath and Bill Sumner. This route climbs the subtle chimney system to the left of the east couloir. Overhangs in

Mt. Williamson, West Face (photo by R. J. Secor)

MT. TYNDALL

Northwest
Ridge

East
Couloir

North
Rib

Direct
East Face

Northeast
Arete

East
Face

The
Climbing
Art

Mt. Tyndall from northeast (photo by R. J. Secor)

the bottom of the chimney are bypassed to the right, and then the chimney is followed to the summit ridge.

Southeast Ridge. Class 4. First ascent August 11, 1939, by Ted Waller and Fritz Lippmann. Climb the third large chute south of Mt. Tyndall's great east face. Five hundred feet of class 4 climbing leads to the southeast ridge. Follow the ridge to the summit.

Southwest Slopes. Class 2. Descended July 6, 1864, by Richard Cotter and Clarence King. First winter ascent 1950 by Norman Goldstein, Al Steck, Jim Wilson, and Bill Dunmire. This is a simple talus hop from the Wright Lakes basin.

Peak 4120m+

(13,540 ft+; 0.8 mi WSW of Mt. Tyndall)

The northwest face of this peak presents

an interesting work of sculpture to those viewing it from the Shepherd Pass Trail. The southern slopes are class 2 from Wright Lakes.

Tawny Point   *(3740 m; 12,332 ft)*

First ascent July 12, 1946, by A. J. Reyman. Class 1 from the Bighorn Plateau.

Wrinkles

Alternatives to the Mt. Whitney Trail. The Mt. Whitney Trail is one of the most heavily used trails in this area. It has a strict quota, and many people have been turned away from the summit by the lack of a reservation. An alternative approach is to start an extended hiking trip from Horseshoe Meadows, across Cottonwood Pass to the Pacific

Crest Trail. This trail is followed down lovely Rock Creek, and then north to where it meets the John Muir Trail near Crabtree Meadow. The John Muir Trail is then followed to the summit of Mt. Whitney. This alternative is much longer than the standard Whitney approach, but it has the advantage of fewer people, tremendous scenic vistas of the west side of the Sierra crest, and access to lakes that can offer fantastic fishing.

Another alternative is to cross spectacular New Army Pass before joining the Pacific Crest Trail along Rock Creek. The approach to New Army Pass goes by way of Cottonwood Lakes, however, and this area also suffers from overuse.

Other alternatives are hiking to the west side of Mt. Whitney from Shepherd Pass, Kearsarge Pass, or Giant Forest, but as the old joke goes, every place is within walking distance if you have enough time.

Perhaps the best option is to get into excellent physical condition and hike up Mt. Whitney in a day from Whitney Portal. There is no quota on day hikes, and some people have done the 22-mile round trip (with 6,100 feet of gain) in remarkably fast time—although others have become altitude-sick just sleeping at Whitney Portal.

The East Face of Mt. Whitney. This has become a "classic" climb, and now suffers from overcrowding. A large part of this route is class 3, with a few intervening roped pitches. There is also quite a bit of loose rock.

The East Buttress of Mt. Whitney is a far better climb. The roped climbing is continuous, yet not difficult, but exposed, and the setting on the crest of the buttress is awe inspiring (far preferable to the alcoves on the East Face route). Glen Dawson participated on the first ascents of both the East Face and the East Buttress, and after fifty years the East Buttress is still his favorite climb, one that he has repeated many times.

A one-day (from Whitney Portal) ascent of the East Face or East Buttress is not a realistic possibility for most rock climbers. The climbing begins after 4,500 feet of gain in a mostly trailless approach. I know a handful of individuals who have done this successfully, but they had an intimate knowledge of the approach and climbing routes. Even so, for them it was a predawn to post-dusk affair.

The Kaweahs and
The Great Western Divide

THIS PROMINENT SUBRANGE IS EVERY BIT AS impressive as the Sierra crest itself. Located west of the Kern River, it follows the Great Western Divide south from Table Mountain to Vandever Mountain and is bounded on the north by Sentinel Ridge (the southern rim of Kings Canyon). The Kaweah Peaks Ridge branches off from the Great Western Divide at Triple Divide Peak. The Kaweahs are high, consist of very loose rock, and feature the walk-up of Mt. Kaweah and the sinister Black Kaweah.

History

Shepherds drove their flocks high into the Kern River and Kaweah River basins in the 1860s. They were the first to explore the high passes and the cirques at timberline, always searching for the perfect meadow. A prominent early explorer was William B. Wallace. Wallace was a judge, but he was also a prospector who searched for gold, silver, and copper following the 1879 mining excitement in Mineral King. In 1881 he crossed the Kern River and made an early ascent of Mt. Whitney. Returning to the west, he and James A. Wright and the Reverend Frederick H. Wales climbed Mt. Kaweah.

For many years it was thought that the Kaweah River originated near the Kaweah Peaks. In 1896 William R. Dudley climbed Sawtooth Peak and could readily see that the Kaweahs were not on the crest of the Great Western Divide, but instead were far into the Kern River watershed. The next year he climbed Mt. Kaweah and named Kern–Kaweah River, Milestone Bowl, Red Spur, and Picket Guard Peak.

The first significant mountaineering for sport occurred in 1912. Charles Michael climbed Michael's Pinnacle in the Kaweahs, and farther north, Robert Price, William

Colby, and Francis Farquhar climbed Milestone Mountain and Midway Mountain during the same summer.

The greatest prize of all was the first ascent of the Black Kaweah. This happened in 1920, when James Hutchinson, Duncan McDuffie, and the horse packer Onis Imis Brown reached the summit via the long west ridge.

Maps

United States Geological Survey: 7.5-minute series: Chagoopa Falls, Mineral King, Silver City, Mt. Kaweah, Triple Divide Peak, Lodgepole, Giant Forest, Mt. Brewer, Sphinx Lakes, Mt. Silliman, Muir Grove; 15-minute series: Mount Whitney, Kern Peak, Mineral King, Triple Divide Peak, Giant Forest, Tehipite Dome. National park maps: Sequoia and Kings Canyon National Parks and Vicinity (1:125,000).

United States Forest Service: John Muir Wilderness and the Sequoia–Kings Canyon National Parks Backcountry (1:63,360).

Wilderness Permits

For west-side entry into the Sequoia and Kings Canyon national parks backcountry: Sequoia and Kings Canyon National Parks, Three Rivers, CA 93271.

For southern entry via the Golden Trout Wilderness: Sequoia National Forest, Tule River Ranger District, Porterville, CA 93257.

Roads

Mineral King Road

The Mineral King Road leaves Highway 198 3.9 miles east of the community of Three Rivers. It is a narrow and steep road with many curves, paved for the most part, and reaches the summer-home community of

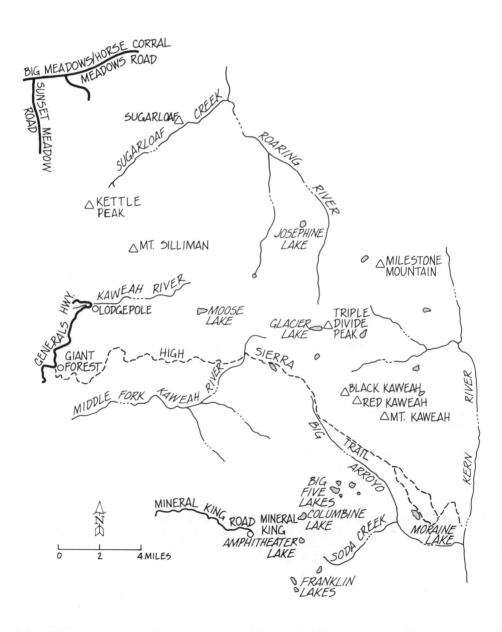

Cabin Cove after 20.4 miles. Silver City is 0.7 mile farther, and Mineral King itself is 2.7 miles beyond Silver City. Facilities at Mineral King are minimal: a pack station and a hiker parking lot. The town of Mineral King disappeared many years ago, the victim of fires and avalanches. Mineral King is now a beautiful, unspoiled, tranquil valley.

Warning: The marmots of Mineral King like to chew on automobile radiator hoses and fan belts. Be sure to bring spares and tools for replacement, along with enough water to fill the vehicle's cooling system. This is not a joke—after one weekend, a friend of mine drove back to L.A. with a live marmot under the hood of her car!

The Generals Highway

The Generals Highway (Highway 198) leads from Lake Kaweah to Giant Forest and Grant Grove in Sequoia and Kings Canyon National Parks. At 6.2 miles east of Three Rivers, the road enters Sequoia National Park, and at 12.0 miles it meets another road leading to Buckeye Flat Campground; the trailhead for the Middle Fork Trail is 1.9 miles down this road, and the Paradise Creek Trailhead is at nearby Buckeye Flat Campground. The highway goes on, passing Hospital Rock, and at 10.4 miles from the turnoff, it reaches Giant Forest. The Crescent Meadow Road leads south and then east from Giant Forest for 2.4 miles to the trailhead for the High Sierra Trail. The Generals Highway continues from Giant Forest another 1.7 miles to the junction with the road leading to Wolverton; the trailheads for the trails leading to Pear Lake and Alta Peak are along the loop at the end of this road, 1.4 miles from the highway. The Generals Highway continues another 1.6 miles beyond the junction with the Wolverton Road to Lodgepole. The trailhead for the J.O. Pass Trail is in this area.

From Lodgepole, the Generals Highway goes 18.7 miles farther to the junction with the Big Meadows/Horse Corral Meadow Road. The Generals Highway continues toward Grant Grove, and it meets Highway 180 6.8 miles beyond the Big Meadow/Horse Corral Meadows Road junction.

Big Meadows/ Horse Corral Meadow Road

The Big Meadows/Horse Corral Meadow Road starts along the Generals Highway 18.7 miles from Lodgepole (or 6.8 miles from the junction with State Highway 180 near Grant Grove). It goes east (past Big Meadows) for 9.4 miles to a junction with the road leading to Sunset Meadow; the trailhead for the Scaffold Meadow Trail is 2.2 miles beyond the junction, along the Sunset Meadow Road. The Horse Corral Meadow Road continues east from the junction another 1.3 miles to Horse Corral Meadow, where it meets a road that goes south, leading to the trailhead for the Marvin Pass Trail; the trailhead is 4.2 miles beyond this junction. From this junction, the Horse Corral Meadow road continues another 3.8 miles to Summit Meadow. This is the upper trailhead for the Don Cecil

Trail, which comes up from Kings Canyon. There is also a trail that leads from this trailhead to the summit of Lookout Peak, where an outstanding view of Kings Canyon can be had for only $1/2$ mile of hiking with approximately 500 feet of gain.

Trails

Farewell Gap Trail   (4 miles)

From Mineral King, the Farewell Gap Trail goes south up the valley, passing the trail leading to Franklin Pass, to the summit of Farewell Gap, 4 miles from Mineral King. The trail continues south from Farewell Gap to the headwaters of the Little Kern River.

Franklin Pass Trail and Soda Creek Trail   (14 miles)

This trail follows the east side of the valley of Mineral King and climbs Franklin Creek to Franklin Lakes, $4^{1}/2$ miles from Mineral King. One and a half miles farther, it crosses the Great Western Divide at Franklin Pass. It descends the east side of the pass for 1 mile to the junction with the Rattlesnake Creek Trail. The Soda Creek Trail heads northeast from here for $1^{1}/2$ miles to Little Clare Lake, and descends Soda Creek another $5^{1}/2$ miles to a junction with the Big Arroyo Trail.

Rattlesnake Creek Trail and the Kern River Trail   ($10^{3}/4$ miles)

This trail begins at its junction with the Soda Creek Trail, 7 miles from Mineral King via Franklin Pass. It descends Rattlesnake Creek for $6^{3}/4$ miles to a junction with the Big Arroyo Trail. A steep $1^{1}/2$-mile descent follows, ending with a junction along the Kern River Trail. Upper Funston Meadow and the junction with the High Sierra Trail are $2^{1}/2$ miles to the north.

Sawtooth Pass Trail   (11 miles)

This trail goes east out of Mineral King and climbs Monarch Creek basin. At an elevation of 8,757 feet (UTM 580355), the trail encounters "Groundhog Meadow," where cross-country hikers can leave the trail and climb directly uphill toward the Sawtooth Pass Trail, which crosses the basin 1,500 feet above. From Groundhog Meadow the proper Sawtooth Pass Trail switchbacks up the slope to the south and traverses east just below Monarch Lakes. It then goes north across sandy slopes and switchbacks to the southeast before climbing over Sawtooth Pass (4 miles from Mineral King). The trail descends the east side of the pass for 1 mile to Columbine Lake. After a short climb out of this basin, it descends Lost Canyon and joins the Soda Creek Trail before both trails descend to the Big Arroyo Trail, 6 miles from Columbine Lake.

Timber Gap Trail *(9 miles)*

This trail starts approximately ½ mile above Mineral King along the Sawtooth Pass Trail. It climbs for 2 miles to the north to Timber Gap before descending to its junction with the Black Rock Pass Trail, 3½ miles from Timber Gap. The trail continues down Cliff Creek another 3½ miles to Redwood Meadow.

Black Rock Pass Trail *(11½ miles)*

This trail begins along the Big Arroyo Trail about ¼ mile below the junction of the High Sierra Trail and the Big Arroyo Trail. After crossing the Big Arroyo, the Black Rock Pass Trail climbs to a bench on the southwest wall of the canyon, and makes a gentle ascent to Little Five Lakes (3 miles from the Big Arroyo Trail). The trail climbs another 2 miles to Black Rock Pass, and features splendid views of the Kaweah Peaks Ridge. A long, rough descent with many switchbacks follows, along Cliff Creek, past Pinto Lake, and between the walls of the canyon, to the junction with the Timber Gap Trail, 6½ miles below Black Rock Pass.

Big Five Lakes Trail *(5 miles)*

This trail connects Little Five Lakes with the Sawtooth Pass Trail in Lost Canyon by way of Big Five Lakes. It starts in the Little Five Lakes basin at its junction with the Black Rock Pass Trail, 3 miles from the junction with the Big Arroyo Trail junction. It traverses around a spur of the Great Western Divide before descending to Big Five Lakes, 2 miles from its start in Little Five Lakes. It then climbs a steep wall to the southeast before circling around to the southwest and meeting the Sawtooth Pass Trail in Lost Canyon, 3 miles from Big Five Lakes.

Redwood Meadow Trail *(9 miles)*

The Redwood Meadow Trail starts at the Atwell Mill Ranger Station, at 19.5 miles

along the Mineral King Road from Highway 198, and climbs to the north to the ridge that divides the East and Middle Forks of the Kaweah River. (A trail traverses the ridge to the west, ending near the summit of Paradise Peak.) It then descends to Redwood Meadow, 9 miles from Atwell Mill Ranger Station.

This trail involves slightly more elevation gain than the Timber Gap Trail. But the Redwood Meadow Trail passes through the Atwell Grove of sequoias, and it has more shade, giving relief on a hot day.

Paradise Creek Trail *(3¼ miles)*

The trailhead for this trail is at Buckeye Flat Campground, across from site No. 23. It crosses the Middle Fork of the Kaweah River on a bridge about ¼ mile beyond the campground. The trail continues up Paradise Creek for 3 miles. At one time the trail went all the way to the upper reaches of Paradise Creek, but the upper portion of the trail has not been maintained for many years and is very faint.

This trail starts and ends at a low elevation. It is a great day hike in the spring, with fields of wild flowers and splendid views of Moro Rock.

Middle Fork Trail *(15 miles)*

At a point near Hospital Rock along the Generals Highway, 5.8 miles beyond the Sequoia National Park boundary, a road to Buckeye Flat Campground branches to the right. The road forks 0.6 mile from the Generals Highway; take the left fork 1.3 miles to the trailhead for the Middle Fork Trail. The trail follows the drainage of the Middle Fork of the Kaweah River on the north side of the canyon 15 miles to Redwood Meadow. A trail descends to the river near Mehrten Creek, and side trails branch off from the main trail at Sevenmile Hill, Buck Creek, and Bearpaw Meadow to join the High Sierra Trail, which traverses the canyon high on its northern side.

An alternate route to Redwood Meadow leaves the Middle Fork Trail just beyond the crossing of the Middle Fork of the Kaweah River. This trail continues upstream before turning to the south, crossing Eagle Scout and Granite creeks before descending to Redwood Meadow, adding 2 miles to the hiking distance and about 600 feet of elevation gain.

The Middle Fork Trail begins at an elevation of approximately 3,300 feet and ends at Redwood Meadow, about 6,000 feet above sea level. Accordingly, it could be a viable option for an early-season hike in the High Sierra while snow is still choking the higher elevations of the mountains. Caution must be exercised, however, while crossing Moro, Panther, Mehrten, and Buck creeks during the spring. The Middle Fork itself must be crossed just below Redwood Meadow. This may be impassable during the early season of a heavy snow year.

High Sierra Trail (50 miles)

The High Sierra Trail starts in Crescent Meadow at Giant Forest, crosses the Great Western Divide at Kaweah Gap, and descends to the Kern River before meeting the John Muir Trail at Wallace Creek. This trail can be considered the trans-Sierra equivalent of the John Muir Trail. It crosses a beautiful region of the Sierra Nevada.

The trailhead is at the end of the Crescent Meadow Road in Giant Forest. Six miles from the trailhead the High Sierra Trail meets the Sevenmile Hill Trail, which descends to the Middle Fork Trail, 3,000 feet below. The High Sierra Trail continues east another 5 miles to Bearpaw Meadow. Two miles farther the trail meets the Elizabeth Pass Trail, and another 3 miles lead to Hamilton Lake, a magnificent amphitheater surrounded by big walls; this is a miniature Yosemite Valley. There is a two-night camp limit in the Hamilton Lakes basin, and wood fires are prohibited. Kaweah Gap is reached after 4 miles and the High Sierra Trail goes south, down the Big Arroyo to a three-way junction, 2¼ miles beyond Kaweah Gap. From the junction, a trail goes a short distance to the stream, where the Big Arroyo Trail goes southeast, and the Black Rock Pass Trail heads southwest. The High Sierra Trail climbs slightly from the junction for 5 miles to the junction with the Moraine Lake Trail. Moraine Lake is 2½ miles from this junction, and the trail meets the High Sierra Trail about 1¼ miles beyond Moraine Lake. (Alternatively, you can remain on the High Sierra Trail for 3½ miles, meeting the eastern end of the Moraine Lake Trail just above Funston Creek, but you should not miss a visit to beautiful Moraine Lake just to save ¼ mile of hiking.) The High Sierra Trail makes a steep descent for 4 miles to the Kern

River canyon, ending just above the level of Upper Funston Meadow.

The junction with the Big Arroyo Trail and the Rattlesnake Creek Trail is 2½ miles to the south, but the High Sierra Trail continues north for 9 miles to Junction Meadow, passing through the giant Kern River canyon along the way. At Junction Meadow the Colby Pass Trail comes in from the west, and the High Sierra Trail goes north for 1 mile before leaving the upper Kern River trail and going east, ascending Wallace Creek to the John Muir Trail, 5 miles from the point where it left the Kern River.

Big Arroyo Trail (10 miles)

From the three-way junction in the Big Arroyo (High Sierra Trail, Black Rock Pass Trail, and the Big Arroyo Trail), this trail goes downstream, first on the north side and then on the south side, for 6 miles to the junction with the Soda Creek Trail. It continues downstream about ¾ mile before climbing to the southeast and meeting the Rattlesnake Creek Trail 3¼ miles farther.

Cross-country hikers may be tempted to descend the Big Arroyo directly to the Kern River canyon, but this involves many steep drops and waterfalls; the Big Arroyo turns into a hanging valley in this area. It is possible to ascend the north side of the canyon from the lower reaches of the Big Arroyo to Sky Parlor Meadow and Moraine Lake.

Alta Peak Trail and the Moose Lake Trail (11 miles)

From Wolverton this trail follows Wolverton Creek for 2 miles to a junction with the Pear Lake Trail. After another 1 mile it reaches Panther Gap, and the trail goes east to Mehrten Meadow, 2½ miles from Panther Gap. From Mehrten Meadow, the Alta Peak Trail goes to the summit of the peak; there is a splendid view of the Great Western Divide from the summit. The Moose Lake Trail goes to the east from Mehrten Meadow to Alta Meadow, and then the trail heads north, over the ridge to desolate Moose Lake.

Camping is prohibited along Wolverton Creek from the parking area to 8,000 feet. Wood fires are prohibited above 9,000 feet.

Pear Lake Trail (5 miles)

This trail follows Wolverton Creek for 2 miles from Wolverton, where it leaves the

Alta Peak Trail. The Pear Lake Trail goes north and then east, passing Heather Lake, Emerald Lake, and Aster Lake to arrive at Pear Lake, nestled in a bowl beneath the steep cliffs north of Alta Peak. An alternate route goes farther to the north along the southern rim of Tokopah Valley before turning to the southeast and meeting the main Pear Lake Trail west of Heather Lake.

The Pear Lake Hut serves as a backcountry ranger station in the summer, and during the winter months it is a popular destination for cross-country skiers. It was constructed in the 1930s by the Civilian Conservation Corps. Reservations are required to use the hut; contact Sequoia National Park for more information.

Camping is prohibited along Wolverton Creek from the parking area to 8,000 feet. Wood fires are prohibited above 9,000 feet.

Silliman Pass Trail (15 miles)

The Silliman Pass Trail leaves the Lodgepole Campground along the Generals Highway and goes north 6 miles to a junction with the J.O. Pass Trail. The Silliman Pass Trail goes east, past Twin Lakes and over Silliman Pass, to Ranger Lakes, which are 3 miles from the junction with the J.O. Pass Trail. From Ranger Lakes the trail goes north, with side trails to Lost Lake and Seville Lake, for 6 miles to Comanche Meadow. From Comanche Meadow you can follow trails to either Horse Corral Meadow or Scaffold Meadow.

Marvin Pass Trail and J.O. Pass Trail (7 miles)

From Horse Corral Meadow, a road winds south for 4.2 miles to the trailhead for the Marvin Pass Trail. In 2 miles the trail crosses Marvin Pass and descends to a junction with the Scaffold Meadow Trail at Rowell Meadow. The J.O. Pass Trail continues south for 5 miles, over J.O. Pass to the junction with the Silliman Pass Trail on the East Fork of Clover Creek.

Scaffold Meadow Trail (14¹/₂ miles)

This trail starts near the end of the Sunset Meadow Road, which is off of the Horse Corral Meadow Road. After a 2¹/₂-mile gentle climb it crosses Rowell Meadow and meets the Marvin Pass Trail and J.O. Pass Trail junction. The Scaffold Meadow Trail continues east over a small pass and into Kings

Canyon National Park. Three miles from Rowell Meadow it comes to a junction with the Silliman Pass Trail near Comanche Meadow along Sugarloaf Creek. The trail goes east for 9 miles through rolling terrain to Scaffold Meadow along Roaring River.

Three trails lead from Scaffold Meadow: the Elizabeth Pass Trail, the Colby Pass Trail, and the Sphinx Creek Trail. The Sphinx Creek Trail is described in Chapter 4: The Kings–Kern Divide.

Colby Pass Trail (22 miles)

From Scaffold Meadow the Colby Pass Trail ascends beautiful Cloud Canyon (with impressive views of Whaleback), goes past Big Wet Meadow (also known as "Big West Meadow"), and continues for 9 miles to a junction with a side trail, which goes up Cloud Canyon. (This side trail, approximately 3 miles long, serves as the approach for ascents of Glacier Ridge and Whaleback, and is used for crossing Triple Divide Pass, Lion Lake Pass, and Coppermine Pass.) The Colby Pass Trail starts to climb toward the southeast, past Colby Lake, and up to Colby Pass, 4 miles from the junction with the side trail. The upper portion of this trail is very rough and steep. From the pass, the trail descends 3 miles to the Kern–Kaweah River at Gallats Lake, another beautiful canyon. The trail goes downstream another 6 miles to Junction Meadow, where it meets the High Sierra Trail.

Elizabeth Pass Trail (17 miles)

The Elizabeth Pass Trail goes south from Scaffold Meadow and up Deadman Canyon (a shepherd was killed here in the 1800s). This is an easy, gradual ascent through forests and meadows. Big Bird Lake (which has also been called "Dollar Lake") can be reached by scrambling up its outlet stream. In the upper reaches of the canyon the trail becomes steep and rough, and Elizabeth Pass is finally attained, about 10 miles from Scaffold Meadow. The 4-mile descent on the southern side of the pass is easy. The trail comes to a three-way junction above Lone Pine Creek. (One trail goes east, up to Tamarack Lake and Lion Lake, and another descends about 2¹/₂ miles to meet the High Sierra Trail.) The Elizabeth Pass Trail (the middle trail at the junction) at first climbs to the southeast and then ascends to Bearpaw Meadow, 3 miles from the junction.

Cross-Country Routes

Glacier Pass

(11,080 ft+; 11,080 ft+; 0.6 mi ESE of Empire Mtn.)

Class 3. This route connects the Sawtooth Pass Trail with the Black Rock Pass Trail via Spring Lake. It is the easiest and fastest one-day route for experienced cross-country hikers traveling from Mineral King to the Big Arroyo. From "Groundhog Meadow" along the Sawtooth Pass Trail (at an elevation of 8,757 ft; UTM 580355), leave the trail and hike directly up the slope above. (Alternatively, you can remain on the Sawtooth Pass Trail beyond Monarch Lake.) You eventually regain the Sawtooth Pass Trail below Sawtooth Pass. At the point where the trail switchbacks to Sawtooth Pass, leave the trail and head for the saddle to the north. The north side of Glacier Pass is a short, steep cliff, which usually has a small snowfield until late in the summer; in the spring there may be a cornice blocking the way. Descend on the north side of the pass and go down to Spring Lake, circling it on its north side. Remain above the 10,000-foot contour and make a level traverse to the Black Rock Pass Trail.

When approaching Glacier Pass from the north, follow the north side of the stream that feeds Spring Lake to the tarns in the meadows below the pass. During low snow years it may be possible to skirt the snow on the right (west) side of the pass by climbing steep talus.

"Crystal Pass"

(11,400 ft+; 11,360 ft+; 0.7 mi S of Sawtooth Pk.)

Class 3. This pass leads between Crystal Lake and Amphitheater Lake. It is class 2 from the west, and class 3 from the east on huge granite slabs and benches.

"Cyclamen Lake Pass"

(11,145 ft; 11,040 ft+; 0.5 mi NE of Cyclamen Lake)

Class 3. This difficult cross-country route leads from Columbine Lake to Big Five Lakes. (It is the author's experience that it is easier and faster to hike down the Sawtooth Pass Trail through Lost Canyon and then take the Big Five Lakes Trail.) From Columbine Lake, cross the shallow pass to the north and descend steep slabs and talus to the east

shore of Cyclamen Lake. Make an ascending traverse from the lake to Cyclamen Lake Pass; this involves more steep slabs and talus. From the top of the pass either descend to Big Five Lakes or traverse north around the east ridge of Peak 11,680+ (11,600 ft+) to the Black Rock Pass Trail above Little Five Lakes.

"Bilko Pass"

(11,480 ft+; 11,360 ft+; 1.1 mi NNW of Needham Mtn.)

Class 3. This name commemorates Bill Croxson, Bill Schuler, and Andy Smatko, who crossed this pass on August 26, 1969. This is the pass just to the east of Peak 11,760+ (11,772 ft). It is a variation of the Cyclamen Lake Pass route. From Columbine Lake, make an ascending traverse to the pass and descend to Big Five Lakes. Only the very top portion of this pass is class 3.

"Kaweah Pass"

(3760 m+; 12,320 ft+; 0.5 mi NE of Mt. Kaweah)

Class 2. This pass leads from the High Sierra Trail to Chagoopa Plateau, across beautiful Kaweah Basin, and down the west side of Picket Creek to the Colby Pass Trail along the Kern–Kaweah River. This is a very nice cross-country route through magnificent scenery. From the High Sierra Trail follow Chagoopa Creek to the basin northeast of Mt. Kaweah. Cross Kaweah Pass at its low point, and descend (loose rock!) to Kaweah Basin. Go north through Kaweah Basin to the low point of the shallow ridge dividing Kaweah Basin and Picket Creek (Pass 3300m+; 10,800 ft+; 1.1 mi SE of Picket Guard Peak; UTM 693473). Descend Picket Creek to Lake 3320m+ (10,560 ft+; 1.0 mi ESE of Picket Guard Peak; UTM 699483). At this point, leave Picket Creek and descend class 2 terrain to the north down to the Colby Pass Trail. Don't follow Picket Creek down to the Colby Pass Trail; there are some waterfalls along the lower end of Picket Creek that bar the way. *Variation:* Class 3. An unnamed creek is about 1/2 mile to the southeast of Picket Creek. It is possible to ascend or descend the west side of the creek. Two short sections of class 3 are encountered.

"Pyra–Queen Col"

(12,840 ft+; 12,800 ft+; 0.2 mi S of Kaweah Queen)

Class 2. This pass provides access to Kaweah Basin from Nine Lakes Basin in the upper part of the Big Arroyo. Pass Lake 11,705 (11,680 ft+; the lake at the base of the north face of the Black Kaweah) on its north shore. Climb a chute that leads up diagonally from right to left to the easier, southernmost saddle, the one closest to Pyramidal Pinnacle.

"Pants Pass"

(11,960 ft+; 12,000 ft+; 1.4 mi S of Triple Divide Peak; UTM 634484)

Class 2. This is a difficult cross-country pass that provides access between Nine Lake Basin and the Kern–Kaweah River. It is also known as "Kern–Kaweah Col," but anyone who has crossed it will appreciate the name Pants Pass. From Nine Lakes Basin, climb loose scree and talus to the pass. There are actually two notches atop the pass. The correct notch is the higher one to the north; the southern, lower notch is class 3 on its western side.

From the Kern–Kaweah River proceed to the tarn just north of Lake 11,360+ (11,380 ft+), and climb the steep chute leading to the easier northern notch atop the pass.

You may be tempted to take the next pass to the north, Pass 11,775 (11,760 ft+). This pass has a vertical cliff on its eastern side. Pants Pass is the best route.

"Lion Rock Pass"

(11,760 ft+; 11,680 ft+; 0.5 mi E of Lion Rock)

Class 2. Lion Rock Pass, in combination with Lion Lake Pass, provides a direct route between Nine Lakes Basin and Cloud Canyon. Actually, there are two passes used for Lion Rock Pass: the lower pass, and the higher pass 0.2 mile to the west at 11,840 feet+ (11,760 ft+). Both passes are class 2.

"Lion Lake Pass"

(11,600 ft+; 11,520 ft; 0.4 mi W of Triple Divide Peak)

Class 2. This is the route between Cloud Canyon and Lion Lake. When traversing from Triple Divide Pass to Lion Lake Pass it is necessary to drop below the level of Glacier Lake to avoid a cliff to the east of Lion Lake Pass.

Triple Divide Pass

(12,200 ft+; 12,160 ft+; 0.4 mi NE of Triple Divide Peak)

Class 2. This is the route between upper Cloud Canyon and the Kern–Kaweah River. From Glacier Lake go across the small bowl

immediately north of Triple Divide Peak to the pass. From here there are two routes. You cross the basin east of the pass to the south shoulder of Peak 12,560+ (12,600 ft+). Cross the shoulder at the 12,000-foot contour and descend to the Colby Pass Trail. The other route from Triple Divide Pass traverses around the east side of Triple Divide Peak to the southeast side of the peak. A steep descent, heading almost due south, leads to a break in the steep wall surrounding this side of Triple Divide Peak. From here it is easy to follow the Kern–Kaweah River downstream.

Coppermine Pass

(11,960 ft+; 11,920 ft+; 1.4 mi NW of Triple Divide Peak)

Class 2. This pass crosses Glacier Ridge just north of the divide that separates the Kings River watershed from the Kaweah River. This is a steep and difficult route, but it has spectacular views of the Kaweahs and Palisades, and this makes the route worthwhile.

This is one of the passes of the Sierra High Route, a trans-Sierra ski tour going from Shepherd Pass to Wolverton. Depending on the snowfall and winds during the previous winter, this pass can be either easy or extremely difficult, with floating cornices and steep, icy slopes on its western side. Some ski mountaineers have referred to this pass as "Deadman Pass."

The name Coppermine Pass commemorates a mine that was located along the ridge east of Elizabeth Pass. At one time a trail went from upper Cloud Canyon and along the east and west ridges of Peak 12,345 (12,340 ft+) to the Elizabeth Pass Trail. The trail has been abandoned for a long time, and the mine has been abandoned even longer than that.

"Horn Col"

(11,280 ft+; 11,280 ft+; 0.5 mi NW of Elizabeth Pass)

Class 1. This is the small pass just to the north of The Fin. It is one of the passes used on the Sierra High Route trans-Sierra ski tour.

"Pterodactyl Pass"

(10,880 ft+; 10,880 ft+; 1.1 mi SW of Big Bird Lake)

Class 2. This is technically not a pass, but a crossing of the south ridge of Big Bird Peak. This is one of the passes used on the Sierra High Route.

"The Right Pass"

(9,680 ft+; 9,680 ft+; 0.3 mi E of Pear Lake Hut)

Class 1. This is the small pass which must be crossed before dropping down to the Pear Lake Ranger Station on the Sierra High Route. With religious use of the map, compass, and altimeter, it is possible to ski "down" (i.e., no stopping to put on climbing skins) to this pass from Table Meadows.

Milestone Creek

At one time a trail ascended Milestone Creek to Lake 3620m+ (11,480 ft+), but it has been abandoned. You may still find traces of it, however. The trail began at an elevation of 3240 meters+ (10,640 ft+; UTM 719563) along the Lake South America Trail. After crossing the Kern River, it contoured to meet Milestone Creek. It continued up this drainage to approximately 11,100 feet, where it turned up the main stream of Milestone Creek. The best route for cross-country hikers is to follow the north branch of the creek in a west-northwesterly direction past a small lake, and proceed directly to Lake 3620m+ (11,480 ft+), in the cirque between Table Mountain and Midway Mountain.

"Milestone Pass"

(3980 m+; 12,960 ft+; 0.2 mi SE of Milestone Mtn.; UTM 676550)

Class 2. This is actually a crossing of the southeast ridge of Milestone Mountain; the low point of the saddle has a cliff on its northeastern side. From Milestone Creek, approach the pass on its far right (north) side, and traverse to the left (south) down into the pass.

From Milestone Bowl, climb to the low point of the saddle and follow the ridge on the left (north) until it is possible to easily descend to Milestone Creek.

"Midway Col"

(3920 m+; 12,880 ft+; 0.3 mi S of Midway Mtn.)

Class 2. This is a direct route between Cloud Canyon and Milestone Creek. Leave the Colby Pass Trail at Colby Lake and climb to Lake 3512m (11,523 ft), southwest of Midway Mountain. Climb directly to the col from the lake over talus. The east side of the col is gentler than the west.

Peaks

Vandever Mountain

(11,947 ft; 11,047 ft)

From Farewell Gap. Class 1.

Northwest Couloir. II, 5.0. First ascent September 1971 by Bruce Rogers. Climb the couloir that leads to the saddle just north of the summit. There is much loose rock on this route.

Northwest Ridge. Class 3. This is the ridge immediately right of the couloir.

Florence Peak   *(12,432 ft; 12,432 ft)*

Northeast Ridge. Class 2. This is a straightforward climb from Franklin Pass.

The Ramp. II, 5.1. First ascent August 1972 by Bruce Rogers and Carl Boro. Climb the prominent, right-ascending ramp on the northwest face of Florence Peak. At one point it is necessary to leave the ramp and climb to the top of the ridge above.

Direct Northwest Face. III, 5.8. First ascent August 1972 by Gary Kirk and Craig Thorn. This route begins in the middle of the face, directly above Franklin Lakes. Go to the left of a small tower. A huge ledge is reached after four pitches. Two more pitches lead to another ledge. Go right on this for about 100 feet and climb a right-leaning diagonal crack to the summit ridge.

Rampant. II, 5.7. First ascent August 22, 1976, by Bob Olson and Doug Meyer. Climb a 5.7 pitch to a large ledge below a broad ramp. Climb up and right to a ledge on the right margin of this ramp. A long pitch up some blocks ends on a ledge system, which is followed up and right to the broad gully above the Great Chimney.

The Great Chimney. III, 5.6. First ascent September 1968 by Jack Delk and Bill Sorenson. There is an obvious chimney on the northwest face. Climb the right wall of the chimney for three pitches, then move right onto easier terrain when difficulties increase. A bit of scrambling leads to a headwall, and two pitches on this lead to the summit ridge.

Southwest Slope. Class 3. From Bullfrog Lakes, south of the peak, ascend the slope to the west ridge of Florence Peak. Climb over large blocks along the ridge to the summit. Some may be tempted to make a direct ascent along the west ridge from Farewell Gap. There are many false summits along the way, resulting in an unnecessarily large amount of elevation gain and loss.

East Side. Class 3. Ascend directly to the summit from the upper reaches of Rattlesnake Creek. Large blocks are encountered near the summit; careful route finding is required. The Northeast Ridge is the preferred route.

Rainbow Mountain

(12,043 ft; 12,000 ft+)
Class 2 from the Franklin Pass Trail.

Peak 12,019

(12,045 ft; 1.4 mi S of Sawtooth Pk.)
Class 2 from either the Franklin Pass Trail or Crystal Lake.

Mineral Peak *(11,615 ft; 11,550 ft)*

Class 2 from Crystal Lake, on the south, or from Monarch Lake, to the north. The summit rocks are best approached from the south.

Sawtooth Peak *(12,343 ft; 12,343 ft)*

Northwest Ridge from Sawtooth Pass. Class 2. First ascent 1871 by Joseph Lovelace. Follow the ridge to the summit. The magnificent view from the summit makes it a worthwhile detour for hikers on the Sawtooth Pass Trail.

North Face. III, 5.8, A1. First ascent June 1970 by Ben Dewell, Dale Kruse, and Gary Goodson. There is a shallow rib on the face above Columbine Lake. Either climb the rib or the face to the right of the rib. When difficulties increase, traverse to the left and then go straight up to the summit.

Sawtooth Peak, North Face (photo by Pete Yamagata)

Traverse from Needham Mountain. Class 2–3 along the ridge connecting the two peaks. It is necessary to stay on the south side of this ridge beneath the pinnacles while traversing. Those doing this traverse who must return to Sawtooth Pass will have to reclimb Sawtooth Peak.

South Slope. Class 3. First ascent July 12, 1929, by Walter A. Starr, Jr. From Monarch Lakes climb the steep ridge leading to the saddle between Amphitheater Lake and Monarch Lakes. Go up the south slope of Sawtooth Peak to the summit. *Variation:* Class 2. The south slope can also be reached from the Soda Creek drainage.

Needham Mountain

(12,520 ft+; 12,467 ft)

South Slope. Class 2. First ascent July 1916 by Marion Randall Parsons, Agnes Vaile, H. C. Graham, and Edmund Chamberlin. This is usually done from the upper reaches of Soda Creek.

Traverse from Sawtooth Peak. Class 2–3. The pinnacles on this ridge can be avoided by traversing just below them on their southern sides.

North Slope. Class 3. First ascent July 28, 1949, by R. R. Breckenfeld, Emily Frazer, and Donald Scanlon. From Lost Canyon, climb to the notch on the ridge between Sawtooth Peak and Needham Mountain. Follow the ridge to the summit of Needham Mountain.

Northwest Face. IV, 5.7. First ascent November 1968 by Gary Kirk and Bernard Hallet. The route is reportedly somewhere on this face.

North Face. Class 3. First ascent July 28, 1949, by Howard Parker and Helen Parker. Climb the couloir that leads to the east ridge. Follow the ridge to the summit.

Southeast Slope. Class 2. First ascent August 8, 1951, by A. J. Reyman on a traverse from Peak 12,360+ (12,320 ft+).

Peak 12,360+

(12,320 ft+; 0.8 mi ESE of Needham Mtn.)

South Ridge. Class 3. First ascent August 8, 1951, by A. J. Reyman on a traverse from Peak 12,168 (12,172 ft).

Southwest Slope. Class 2. There is a lot of scree on this slope.

North Buttress. III, 5.9. First ascent June 1973 by Vern Clevenger and Jon Ross. This buttress ends about ½ mile from the peak along the northwest ridge. Make a left-ascending traverse to the crest of the buttress and follow it to the top.

Peak 11,880+

(11,861 ft; 1.5 mi NE of Needham Mtn.)

Northeast Ridge. Class 3. First ascent 1966 by W. K. Jennings and friend.

"Two Fingers Peak"

(11,760 ft+; 11,680 ft+; 1.3 mi NE of Needham Mtn.)

The summit blocks of this peak are composed of semisolid scree, and are class 3. The peak has a class 1 scree slope on its south side; the north face is class 3.

Peak 11,760+

(11,772 ft; 1.2 mi NE of Sawtooth Pk.)

The south slopes are class 2, and the summit rocks are class 3.

Peak 11,480+

(11,440 ft+; 1.0 mi E of Empire Mtn.)

This little peak has a 1,000-foot sheer north face that drops down to Spring Lake. The south side of the peak is class 2.

"That's a Sheer Cliff" Route. IV, 5.9. First ascent 1975 by Vern Clevenger and Galen Rowell. This route ascends the dihedral to the right of center on the north face. Four pitches of 5.9 are followed by five pitches of 5.7 to 5.8.

North Face, Left Side. III, 5.6. First ascent July 14, 1974, by Rob Dellinger, Debbie Winters, and Fred Beckey. This route follows a crack and dihedral system directly to the summit.

Empire Mountain

(11,550 ft+; 11,509 ft)

Class 2 from Glacier Pass. The east face is class 2–3.

Mt. Eisen

(12,160 ft+; 12,160 ft+; UTM 596402)

Southeast Ridge. Class 2. This is a long, tedious hike from Black Rock Pass. It features loose scree, a lot of side-hilling, a false summit, and a shallow angle so that it isn't any fun coming down.

From Little Five Lakes. Class 3. First ascent August 23, 1984, by Dale Van Dalsem, Jim Murphy, and Scott Sullivan. A use trail branches off of the Black Rock Pass Trail just north of where the trail crosses the stream draining Lake 10,410 (10,410 ft). Follow the use trail to Lake 10,410, circle it on its south shore, and go to the cirque on the peak's southeast side. Go up and left of a water-stained headwall and make a diagonal, right-ascending traverse to the south ridge of the peak. The southernmost summit is the high point.

Northeast Face. Class 3. First ascent July 15, 1949, by Howard Parker, Mildred Jentsch, Ralph Youngberg, and Martha Ann McDuffie. There is a lake immediately northeast of Mt. Eisen with a small island in it. From this lake, climb the higher of two notches to the southwest, and then up to the summit.

Peak 11,680+

(11,760 ft+; 0.8 mi S of Lippincott Mtn.)

Northeast Ridge. Class 4. First ascent August 30, 1969, by Andy Smatko and Bill Schuler. Most of this ridge is class 3; only the last 50 feet below the (higher) southwest peak is class 4.

Peak 11,800+

(11,830 ft; 0.5 mi SE of Lippincott Mtn.)

Southwest Ridge. Class 2. First ascent August 30, 1969, by Carl Heller and Bill Stein.

North-Northwest Ridge. Class 2. First ascent 20 minutes later on August 30, 1969, by Andy Smatko and Bill Schuler.

Lippincott Mountain

(12,265 ft; 12,260 ft)

Southeast Slope. Class 2. First ascent July 1936 by Jules Eichorn and party. Leave the Black Rock Pass Trail at an elevation of approximately 10,400 feet, just north of Little Five Lakes. Contour north and northwest into the basin southeast of the peak.

East Ridge. Class 2. First ascent 1922 by Norman Clyde. Attain the ridge from the basin immediately north of Lippincott Mountain.

Northwest Ridge. First ascent August 30, 1969, by Bill Schuler and Andy Smatko. This was climbed during a traverse from Peak 12,200+ (12,250 ft). They traversed the west side of both peaks well below the saddle connecting Lippincott Mountain with Peak 12,200+ (12,250 ft) and then gained the northwest ridge.

Peak 12,200+

(12,250 ft; 0.6 mi N of Lippincott Mtn.)

East Ridge. Class 2. The ridge can be attained either from the Big Arroyo or from the lake basin north of the peak.

South-Southwest Ridge. Class 2 from the saddle to the south of the peak.

West Face. Class 2. Descended August 30, 1969, by Andy Smatko and Bill Schuler. A steep chute on the face provides the key to this route.

Eagle Scout Peak *(12,000 ft+; 12,040 ft)*

Class 2 from the Big Arroyo. It is best to head for the saddle just south of the peak, and then go directly to the summit. First ascent July 15, 1926, by Francis P. Farquhar and Eagle Scouts Frederick Armstrong, Eugene Howell, and Coe Swift. There is a wonderful view of the Hamilton Lakes area from the summit.

"Eagle Scout Towers"

(9,330–9,720 ft+; 9,550–9,840 ft+)

These towers are on the south side of the canyon containing Eagle Scout Creek. Some of these were climbed by the Rock Climbing Section, Loma Prieta Chapter, Sierra Club, in 1953.

"Hamilton Towers"

(9,680 ft+–10,040 ft+; 9,680 ft+–10,000 ft+)

These towers are on the ridge between Hamilton Creek and Eagle Scout Creek. There are nine towers in all, and their difficulty ranges from class 4 to 5.8. Some of the towers were first climbed by the Rock Climbing Section, Loma Prieta Chapter, Sierra Club, in 1953. The most difficult tower was first climbed in September 1970 by Greg Henzie, Chris Jones, and Galen Rowell.

"Hamilton Dome"

(9,745 ft; 9,770 ft; 1.9 mi WNW of Eagle Scout Pk.)

This is the beautiful dome at the western end of Hamilton Towers.

East Gully. I, 5.6. First ascent 1936 by Dick Johnson and party. Second ascent June 1969 by Curt Chadwick, Chuck Kroger, and Norm Weeden.

North Arete. II, 5.7. First ascent 1971 by Don Lauria and TM Herbert. Seven pitches directly up the arete provide a fine climb.

"Angel Wings"

(10,360 ft+; 10,252 ft; 1.6 mi W of Mt. Stewart; UTM 585485)

The south face of this peak is the biggest rock wall in Sequoia National Park; and, unlike Yosemite walls, it is 16 miles from the nearest road.

North Side. Class 3–4. First ascent August 1980 by Bob Ayers and party. Leave the trail leading to Tamarack Lake at around 8,000 feet, and climb gullies leading through the huge cirque on the north side of Angel Wings. Leave the cirque via an easy chute that goes through its headwall. (A landmark for this chute is two large pine trees growing at its head in a small notch; don't go to the larger western notch in the headwall.) From the top of the headwall, cross over large talus blocks to the lower northern summit, drop down a bit, then climb some large talus blocks to the summit. The very last section has two class 4 moves.

West Side. Class 3–4. Descended June 1971 by Galen Rowell and Chris Jones. Climb slabs from Lone Pine Creek to the summit area.

South Face, Left Side. Grade V. First ascent May 1977 by Fred Beckey, Alan Neilfel, Bill

Angel Wings, South Face (photo by Howard Stagner, Sequoia and Kings Canyon National Parks)

Lahr, and Craig Martinson. This route climbs the rounded buttress on the left side of the face. Difficult aid and free climbing was required on the first ascent.

South Face, Right Side. V, 5.8, A4. First ascent July 28–August 2, 1967, by Les Wilson, Jim Wilson, Dick Long, and Allen Steck. This route ascends the most massive part of the south face. High on this face is a huge dihedral; the route starts directly underneath this feature. Begin by climbing a rounded buttress, and then go up the right side of a sickle-shaped ledge to a large crack. Climb the crack; it eventually turns into a chimney. From the top of the chimney, traverse right to some broken rock, then to a sandy alcove at the bottom of a deep chimney. The chimney features a huge, detached finger of rock, which is gradually separating from the right-hand wall. From the tip of the finger, climb an open book that gradually slants back to a horizontal system of ledges that leads to Upper Bearpaw Meadow, a 45-degree patch of wet grass that slopes up to an alcove filled with ferns and dripping water. Instead of climbing the chimney above, climb the face to a flake and move right 40 feet to a flaring chimney, which leads to the base of a tower of vertical slabs known as the House of Cards. One pitch goes up from here, and another diagonals left back into the chimney. Continue climbing the chimney to the top.

Hell on Wings. V, 5.10, A3. First ascent July 1989 by Edwin C. Joe, Richard Leversee, and Kim Grandfield. This route ascends an obvious crack system to the left of the south arete. This ten-pitch route involves some nailing, nutting, and hooking at the ends of the third and fifth pitches. The route ends atop the arete, a long way from the summit.

South Arete. IV, 5.10. First ascent June 1971 by Galen Rowell and Chris Jones. First free ascent 1984 by the Hope Valley Fun Hogs. This route climbs the curving arete that leads to the summit of Angel Wings. Scramble up talus and slabs (some class 4) to the wall at the base of the arete. Two pitches end atop a strenuous jam crack. Easier climbing leads to the 10 feet overhanging Black Ceiling. Climb over the ceiling (5.10) to a point above it. Traverse to the right and then climb to the base of a chimney. Follow this chimney to the summit. Talus then leads to the summit.

Mt. Stewart *(12,200 ft+; 12,205 ft)*

There is an outstanding view of the Black Kaweah from the summit.

From Nine Lakes Basin. Class 2. From the north end of Lake 10,440+ (10,400 ft+) climb a grassy gully to the slabs and ramps of the summit area. The high point of the peak is at the far western end of the high ridge atop the peak.

North Face. III, 5.6. First ascent August 19, 1973, by Michael Graber, Jack Roberts, and Hooman Aprin. Two buttresses drop down the north face, directly beneath the summit. From the large bench at the base of the north face, climb to the left of the eastern buttress, directly up to a point just east of the summit.

Dawn Pillar. III, 5.10. First ascent June 17, 1986, by David Wilson and Michael Graber. This route climbs the western buttress on Mt. Stewart's north face. The route begins by climbing jam cracks on the left side (east) of the buttress. Nine pitches lead to the west summit of the peak.

Lion Rock *(12,360 ft+; 12,320 ft+)*

West Ridge. Class 3. First ascent July 7, 1927, by Dave Winkley, William Curlett, and Earl S. Wallace. From approximately 10,500 feet, between Tamarack Lake and Lion Lake, traverse southeast and diagonally upward across a talus slope into the bowl between the two west ridges of Lion Rock. Aim for the obvious ledge system, which allows ascent of the southern west ridge. Follow the top of the ridge to the summit. The pitch just below the summit is loose, exposed class 3. The north peak is the high point.

South-Southwest Slope. Class 2–3. First ascent September 9, 1968, by John Fredlund. From Tamarack Lake ascend the slopes leading to the bowl south of the peak; this involves tedious route finding through brush around small cliffs. From the bowl, climb the broad slope to the summit. *Variation:* It is also possible to reach this bowl from Nine Lakes Basin by crossing the south ridge of the peak.

South Ridge. Class 4. First ascent August 20, 1984, by Ron Hudson, R. J. Secor, and Jim Murphy. From Nine Lakes Basin, follow the south ridge to the summit of Lion Rock. Two class 4 moves are encountered on this ridge.

East Chute. Class 4. From the western Lion Rock Pass climb the first chute north of the pass and then ascend the rock rib on its right (north) to the summit.

Northeast Chute. Class 3. This is the next chute north of the east chute. It leads to the saddle between the two peaks of Lion Rock. From a point about halfway up this chute, climb the southeast face of the north peak to the summit of Lion Rock. Snow and ice remain in these chutes for most of the summer; ice axes may be required.

Lawson Peak
(13,120 ft+; 13,140 ft; 1 mi N of Black Kaweah)
First ascent July 11, 1924, by Gerald A. Gaines, C. A. Gaines, and H. H. Bliss. The southwest slope and the northeast ridge are class 2.

Kaweah Queen   *(13,382 ft; 13,360 ft+)*
Northwest Ridge. Class 3. First ascent July 11, 1924, by Gerald Gaines, C. A. Gaines, and H. H. Bliss, on a traverse from Lawson Peak. This traverse is accomplished by remaining about 50 feet below the ridge crest on its western side. There is a lot of loose rock on this traverse.

Southwest Slope. Class 2. Loose rock is encountered while climbing the peak from the western approach of Pyra–Queen Col.

North Slope. Class 2. Some extraordinarily loose rock is encountered while climbing this peak from the upper reaches of Picket Creek.

Peak 4033m
(13,232 ft; 0.5 mi E of Kaweah Queen; UTM 658464)
South Face. Class 3. First ascent July 2, 1967, by Andy Smatko, Bill Schuler, and Ellen Siegal. Climb a chute on the south face that leads to a point approximately 150 feet west of the summit. The upper portion of the chute is loose class 3.

The northeast ridge is reportedly easy class 3.

Black Kaweah   *(13,680 ft+; 13,765 ft)*
The Black Kaweah is one of the great peaks of the High Sierra. It is high and remote, looks good from a distance, and is in a scenic area. Plus, even its easy routes are challenging. But it is perhaps the least known of the more difficult peaks in the range. During the sixty years after its first ascent, fewer than one hundred parties visited the summit. It deserves more attention.

The Black Kaweah has a well-deserved reputation for loose rock, as do the rest of the

Kaweah Peaks Ridge from the southwest (photo by F. E. Matthes, #1096, USGS Photographic Library, Denver, CO)

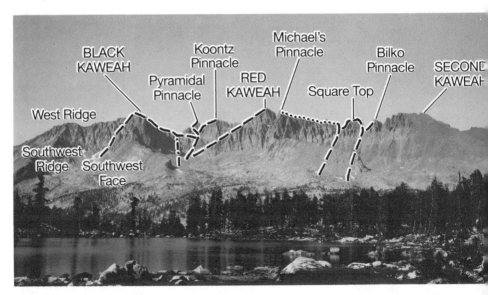

Kaweah peaks. But the rock is not as loose as that encountered on some other peaks, such as the Devil's Crags or Mt. Morrison. Nevertheless, caution is advised. The party attempting this ascent should be small (no more than six climbers) and constantly vigilant. As my friend Dave Dykeman once said:

"This peak demands intelligent risk management."

West Ridge. Class 3. First ascent August 11, 1920, by Duncan McDuffie, Onis I. Brown, and James Hutchinson. From the Big Arroyo, climb to the top of the west ridge, and follow it toward the summit. At approxi-

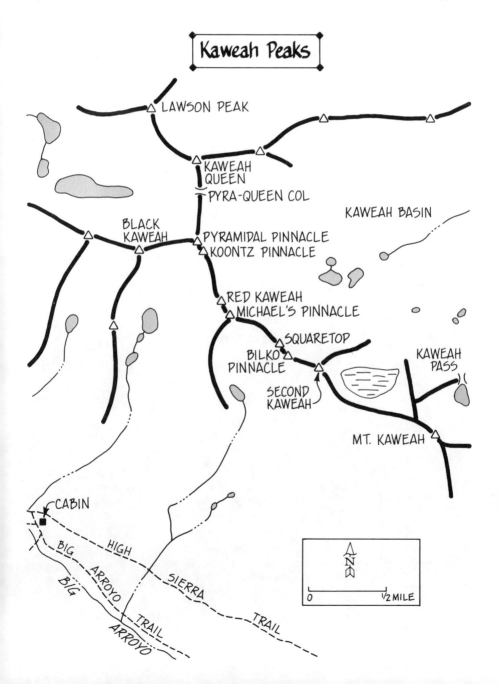

mately 13,200 feet a deep notch bars further progress. Descend about 100 or 200 feet on the south side of the ridge and traverse to the chute of the Southwest Face route. Climb the chute to where it joins the west ridge, approximately 100 feet beneath the summit. Scramble up the remaining class 3 to the top. *Variation: Southwest Ridge.* Class 3. First ascent August 1928 by Albert Ellingwood and Carl Blaurock. Ascend the southwest ridge from the Big Arroyo to where it meets the west ridge. Follow the West Ridge route to the summit.

Southwest Face. Class 3. First ascent July 26, 1921, by Philip E. Smith, Marian Simpson, and Irene Smith. First winter ascent January 4, 1970, by Eric Adelberger, Paul Emerson, and Lowell Smith. This is the most direct route to the summit of the Black Kaweah. Although it is not as technically easy as the West Ridge route, this seems to be the pre-ferred route of ascent for most climbers. From the Big Arroyo, hike to the cirque immediately southwest of the peak. Pass over some loose talus to the base of the southwest face, and head for the right-hand chute. Climb the chute for about 100 feet, and then cross over to the left-hand chute via a ledge that goes diagonally up and to the left. A landmark for the crossover point is a black waterfall in the right-hand chute; the crossover point is 50 feet below this. Climb the left-hand chute to the summit. Most of this climb is moderate class 3, consisting of reaching across delicately perched rocks. In early season both of these chutes are likely to be filled with hard snow and/or ice. Should this be the case, full ice-climbing regalia may be necessary. The angle averages 40 degrees.

South Face. IV, 5.7. First ascent 1968 by David Beck, Nick Hartzell, and Gary Kirk. Head toward a prominent dihedral on the

The Black Kaweah from the southeast (photo by F. E. Matthes, #1427, USGS Photographic Library, Denver, CO)

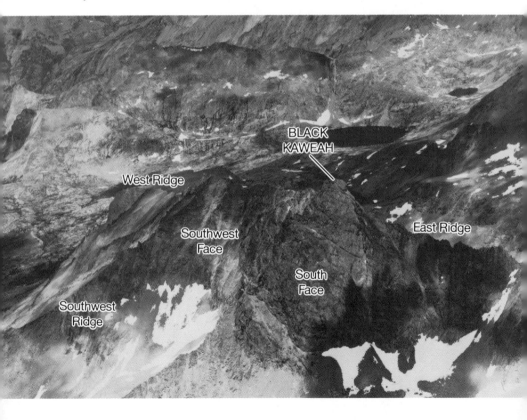

On the East Ridge of Black Kaweah (photo by R. J. Secor)

south face of the peak from the cirque between the Black Kaweah and Red Kaweah. Climb to the left of the dihedral and continue up and left for fourteen pitches to the summit. Protection is hard to come by on the loose rock.

East Ridge. Class 4. First ascent June 1935 by Neil Ruge and James Smith. From the lake basin south of the Black Kaweah climb the small chute that leads to the notch between Pyramidal Pinnacle and Koontz Pinnacle. Before reaching the notch, traverse diagonally up and to the left along a convenient, broad ledge to the low point of the ridge connecting the Black Kaweah with Pyramidal Pinnacle. Follow the arete westward to where a yellow gendarme blocks progress. Traverse left via a ledge, and regain the east ridge by climbing a short, loose chimney. Head for a sloping ledge that goes around the south side of the peak. From the end of the ledge, either climb a chimney or an outside corner (easier but more exposed than the chimney) to the top. *Variation:* Class 4. First ascent August 1, 1968, by John Mendenhall and Ruth Mendenhall. This is the preferred variation. Ascend the chute that leads directly to the low point of the east ridge of the Black Kaweah from the lake basin south of the peak. Leave this chute about 250 feet below its top and climb a class 4 chute to the left to the crest of the east ridge of the Black Kaweah. (The upper portion of the chute, which leads to the low point of the east ridge, consists of loose, dangerous class 3+ crud; it is only safe when the chute is full of snow.) *Variation:* Class 4. First ascent August 1955 by Carl Heller and Robert Stein. The east ridge can also be reached from Lake 11,682 (11,705 ft), which is just north of the Black Kaweah. Head for the low point of the ridge connecting the Black Kaweah with Pyramidal Pinnacle.

"Pyramidal Pinnacle"

(13,665 ft; 13,600 ft+; 0.4 mi E of Black Kaweah)

West Face. Class 4. First ascent August 1, 1932, by Glen Dawson and Jules Eichorn. From the cirque between Red Kaweah and the Black Kaweah, climb the small couloir (loose rock!) that leads to the notch between Pyramidal Pinnacle and Koontz Pinnacle. Before reaching the notch, traverse up and left to the ridge connecting Pyramidal Pinnacle with the Black Kaweah. From the top of the ridge climb the west face (three pitches of class 4) to the summit of Pyramidal Pinnacle. *Variation:* Class 4. First ascent August 1955 by Carl Heller and Robert Stein. The west face of Pyramidal Pinnacle can also be reached from Lake 11,682 (11,705 ft), which is north of the Black Kaweah.

"Koontz Pinnacle"

(13,600 ft+; 0.5 mi E of Black Kaweah; UTM 652452)

For some reason, this pinnacle does not appear in the contours of the Triple Divide Peak 7.5-minute map.

West Face. Class 4. First ascent August 26, 1953, by Jim Koontz, Pete Murphy, and Fred Peters. From the cirque between Red Kaweah and the Black Kaweah, climb the chute leading to the notch between Pyramidal Pinnacle and Koontz Pinnacle. The upper part of this chute is very loose, and it may be best to climb it on the right side. From the notch, climb the northern side of the west face to the summit. The first pitch from the notch is extraordinarily loose.

Red Kaweah   *(13,720 ft+; 13,760 ft+)*

West Face. Class 3. First ascent 1912 by Charles W. Michael. From the Big Arroyo hike cross-country to the basin west of Red Kaweah. Pass Lake 11,795 (11,825 ft) on its east side on a bench, and go through small rocks and talus to a prominent chute (big, loose rocks!), which leads to a ramp just beneath the summit. Follow the ramp left (north) up to the ridge and follow the ridge to the summit.

"Michael's Pinnacle"

(13,680 ft+; 13,680 ft+; 0.1 mi SE of Red Kaweah; UTM 654446)

Charles W. Michael made the first ascent of this pinnacle in 1912, via an unknown route.

Southeast Ridge. Class 4. First ascent August 28, 1953, by Jim Koontz, Pete Murphy, and Fred Peters. Climb to the saddle between Michael's Pinnacle and Squaretop. From the saddle, follow the ridge to the fourth major pinnacle from the saddle. Descend the southeast side of this pinnacle, then traverse across its west face along a ledge that ends in a steep chute. Descend this chute about 30 feet to where it joins another chute. Climb this next chute to the ledge at its top. Follow the ledge to the saddle immediately southeast of Michael's Pinnacle. From the saddle climb a broad ledge on the northern side of the ridge to some easy rock that leads to the summit.

"Squaretop"

(4120 m+; 13,520 ft+; 1.3 mi NW of Mt. Kaweah; UTM 659442)

The rock on this peak is rather solid, at least when compared to the other Kaweah peaks.

Southeast Face. Class 4. First ascent June 26, 1935, by Jim Smith and Neil Ruge. From Lake 11,840+ (11,885 ft) climb loose scree and talus to the saddle between Squaretop and Bilko Pinnacle. Go straight up the southeast face (far to the left of a huge chute) to a wide ledge that ascends diagonally to the right. The ledge ends in a shallow chute. Climb the chute a short distance, to where it is possible to traverse left on some ledges which end on the summit ridge. *Variation:* It is also possible to reach the saddle southeast of Squaretop from Kaweah Basin.

Southeast Ridge. I, 5.7. First ascent August 13, 1981, by Vern Clevenger. This route climbs the ridge to the right of the huge chute rising from the saddle southeast of the peak.

Northwest Face. Class 4. First ascent July 7, 1970, by Dick Beach and Barbara Lilley. From Lake 11,840+ (11,885 ft) ascend to the notch just northwest of Squaretop. Just before reaching the notch, leave the chute at a large chockstone and climb two class 4 pitches to the summit.

"Bilko Pinnacle"

(4080 m+; 13,360 ft+; 1.2 mi NW of Mt. Kaweah; UTM 661441)

The second-ascent party named this peak after themselves.

Northwest Face. Class 3. First ascent August 27, 1953, by Jim Koontz, Fred Peters, and Pete Murphy. This is supposed to go class 3 directly from the saddle between Squaretop and Bilko Pinnacle.

Southwest Ridge. Class 4. First ascent August 28, 1969, by Andy Smatko and Bill Schuler. From the saddle between Bilko Pinnacle and Squaretop, descend 40 feet to the southwest and go around a sharp buttress. Ascend a steep chute to the southwest ridge; one 30-foot class 4 pitch is encountered. Follow the southwest ridge to the top.

"Second Kaweah"

(4146 m; 13,680 ft+; 1.0 mi NW of Mt. Kaweah)

This peak is also known as "Gray Kaweah." First ascent 1922 by Norman Clyde. The south slope from the High Sierra Trail is class

2, as is the traverse from Mt. Kaweah. The high point is the southeastern summit.

The three pinnacles on the northwest ridge are loose class 3; they were first climbed on August 29, 1953, by Jim Koontz, Fred Peters, and Pete Murphy.

Mt. Kaweah *(4207 m+; 13,802 ft)*

This mountain has also been called "Big Kaweah" and "Great Kaweah." It is the highest point in the southwestern High Sierra.

South Slopes. Class 1. First ascent September 1881 by Judge William B. Wallace, Captain James Albert Wright, and the Reverend Frederick H. Wales. This is a simple cross-country hike from the High Sierra Trail.

East Ridge. Class 3. First ascent August 17, 1966, by Bill Schuler. This is a direct route to the summit of Mt. Kaweah from the southern approach to Kaweah Pass. Don't climb the ridge leading directly up from Kaweah Pass. Instead, approach the east ridge from the southern end of the lake near the top of the pass. As with other routes in the Kaweahs, caution must be exercised due to loose rock.

North Ridge. Class 4. First ascent September 1964 by Eduardo Garcia and Carlos Puente, two guys from Chile. Climb the ridge leading directly from Kaweah Basin.

Peak 4049m

(13,285 ft; 1.4 mi NE of Mt. Kaweah)

First ascent July 17, 1936, by Jules Eichorn, Virginia Adams, Jane Younger, and Carl P. Jensen. The south slope from Chagoopa Plateau is class 2.

Red Spur *(4019 m; 13,183 ft)*

Southwest Ridge. Class 3. First ascent July 17, 1936, by Jules Eichorn, Virginia Adams, Jane Younger, and Carl P. Jensen, on a traverse from Peak 4049m (13,285 ft). Stay below the crest of the ridge on its southern side.

Picket Guard Peak *(3750 m; 12,302 ft)*

First ascent August 1, 1936, by C. Dohlman, H. Manheim, and B. Breeding. The east ridge is class 2 and the north ridge is class 3.

Kern Point *(3880 m; 12,789 ft)*

First ascent July 25, 1924, by William Horsfall and C. Lauglin. The southwest slope is class 2, as is the traverse from Kern Ridge.

Triple Divide Peak *(12,634 ft; 12,634 ft)*

This peak divides the Kern, Kaweah, and Kings rivers.

East Ridge. Class 2. First ascent 1920 by James Hutchinson and Charles A. Noble. Follow the ridge from Triple Divide Pass to the summit.

North Ridge. Class 3. First ascent August 31, 1975, by Walton Kabler, Betty Kabler, and R. J. Secor. From Glacier Lake ascend steep talus directly to the summit of the peak.

West Ridge. Class 3. First ascent 1963 by John Wedberg, Bill Engs, and party. Follow the crest of the ridge from Lion Lake Pass, with an occasional detour from Lion Lake.

Southwest Face. Class 2–3. Climb any of several chutes and gullies to the summit from Lion Lake.

South Ridge. Class 3. First ascent by Don Clarke. Follow the ridge to where progress is impeded by a gendarme. Detour and lose 200 feet of gain on the ridge's eastern side. Traverse across the peak's eastern side to the east ridge, and follow this to the top.

Peak 12,640+

(12,640 ft+; 0.7 mi NE of Triple Divide Peak)

First ascent July 21, 1926, by George R. Bunn and R. C. Lewis. The southwest slope is class 3.

Peak 12,560+

(12,600 ft; 0.4 mi SW of Colby Pass)

Southwest Ridge. Class 2. First ascent 1936 by Howard Gates and Carl P. Jensen.

Northeast Ridge. Class 3. First ascent 1936 by Jules Eichorn, Kenneth May, and A. Tagliapietra.

Peak 4129m

(13,520 ft+; 0.6 mi SE of Milestone Mtn.)

This peak has been referred to as "Milestone Mesa." First ascent August 3, 1897, by W. F. Dean, Otis B. Wright, Harry C. Dudley, and W. R. Dudley. The south slope is class 2; the northwest ridge from Milestone Pass is class 3.

Centennial Peak

(4032 m; 13,255 ft; 0.6 mi SW of Milestone Mtn.)

This peak was named in honor of Sequoia

National Park's 100th anniversary in 1990.

Southwest Slope. Class 1. First ascent 1912 by Francis Farquhar, William E. Colby, and Robert M. Price.

East Face of the South Ridge. Class 3. First ascent September 12, 1967, by Bill Schuler and Andy Smatko. From the highest lakes of Milestone Bowl, gain the south ridge via a gully. From the ridge, head west to the plateau and then to the summit.

Milestone Mountain

(4157 m; 13,641 ft)

The summit pinnacle of this peak is an impressive sight from the upper Kern River Basin. The view of the Kern River and Kings River basins from the summit is equally impressive.

East Side. Class 3. First ascent July 28, 1927, by Norman Clyde. From the upper reaches of Milestone Creek climb the steep, scree-filled gully that leads to the notch just north of the summit pinnacle. Cross over the notch, descend about 75 feet on the western side of the peak, go south across the west face around a buttress, and climb the west face and ridge to the summit.

Southeast Arete. II, 5.6. First ascent August 1964 by Steve Thompson and Jeff Dozier. Climb over and around gendarmes along the arete from Milestone Pass.

Southwest Ridge. Class 3. First ascent July 14, 1912, by Francis P. Farquhar, William E. Colby, and Robert M. Price. From Milestone Bowl traverse across the south face of the peak toward the southwest ridge. Much loose rock is encountered just before reaching the ridge. Follow the ridge to the summit.

Northwest Face. Class 3. First ascent September 19, 1931, by Walter A. Starr, Jr. The northwest face of Milestone Mountain consists of many chutes. From Lake 3512m (11,523 ft) climb the second chute west of the summit; this chute appears to be s-shaped when viewed from the lake. Leave the chute on the left side near its top, just beyond a large buttress that separates the first chute west of the summit from the second chute. Traverse left to the west face of the summit pinnacle.

Northwest Ridge. II, 5.7. First ascent August 3, 1987, by Jean Baptiste Raqeeoir. This route begins from the notch just north of the summit of Milestone Mountain. Drop down and to the right 40 feet from the notch, and then climb back to the left (5.6). Continue up the buttress that is 150 feet to the left of the west ridge (5.7).

Midway Mountain

(4165 m; 13,666 ft)

West Slope. Class 2. First ascent July 1912 by Francis P. Farquhar, William E. Colby, Robert M. Price, and four others. Climb the west slope of the peak from Lake 3512m (11,523 ft). Approach the summit from the northwest.

East Ridge. Class 2. First ascent July 30, 1927, by Norman Clyde. Climb the north side of the east ridge from Milestone Creek. The crest of the east ridge can also be reached from Milestone Mountain by means of a deep notch in the east ridge.

South Face of the East Ridge. I, 5.7. First ascent July 1987 by Robin Ingraham, Jr., Mark Hoffman, and Mark Tuttle. This route starts 30 feet to the right of a prominent, right-facing dihedral. Stemming and jam cracks lead to a belay slab, and two more pitches lead to the east ridge of the peak, at an elevation of 13,000 feet.

South Ridge and Southeast Face. Class 4. First ascent August 18, 1978, by Bill T. Russell and party on a traverse from Milestone Mountain. Climb the south ridge to where difficulties increase, and traverse out onto the southeast face. One class 4 pitch is encountered just below the summit.

South Ridge. Descended August 3, 1987, by Jean Baptiste Raqeeoir. This ridge has been reported as being 5.7 in places.

Peak 4149m

(13,600 ft+; 0.7 mi SE of Table Mtn.)

First ascent August 18, 1949, by Jim Koontz and Jim Griffin. The east slope is class 3. Begin climbing from the brown ledge on the south side of Table Mountain.

Table Mountain   *(4155 m; 13,630 ft)*

This flat-topped mountain is a popular ascent by . . . helicopters.

Northeast Couloir. Class 4. First ascent July 26, 1927, by Norman Clyde, Glen Dawson, and party.

East Face. Class 3. First ascent 1932 by Norman Clyde, Alice Carter, Dorothy Baird, Emily A. Lillie, William Duley, and Rose M. Pischel. From the small lake due east of the summit plateau (at UTM 688575), climb the broken face to the top. There is a lot of loose rock on this route.

South Side. Class 3. First ascent July 29, 1927, by Norman Clyde. Even though this is listed as a class 3 route, a rope should be carried, because many parties have had difficulty locating the easiest route on the broad face on this side of the peak. From Lake 3620m+ (11,480 ft+) along the main drainage of Milestone Creek, climb to a ledge just left (west) of the two highest scree fans. From this ledge, zigzag up to a point above a distinctive brown ledge. Traverse downward to the right (east) to and then along the brown ledge, passing a vertical face, to where it is possible to scramble to the summit plateau. Just below the rim of the plateau, crawl through a hole under a big rock.

West Ridge, South Side. Class 3. First ascent August 25, 1908, by Paul Shoup, Fred Shoup, and Gilbert Hassel. From the cirque southwest of Table Mountain, ascend the easternmost chute on the southern side of Table Mountain's west ridge. Approximately 100 feet below the crest of the ridge, traverse up and right a short distance to another chute. Follow this chute to the summit plateau.

West Ridge, North Side. Class 3–4. First ascent August 1978 by David Vandervoet, Geof Glassner, Bob Hozelton, and Ella Hozelton. From the cirque northwest of Table Mountain, climb the easternmost chute on the northern side of the Table Mountain's west ridge. This chute, which may be filled with snow, is marked by a short rock cliff in the middle. Once atop the ridge, descend about 100 feet on the southern side of the ridge, and traverse east to another chute. Follow this chute to the summit plateau.

Whaleback *(11,717 ft; 11,726 ft)*

This is the beautiful peak rising above Big Wet Meadow in Cloud Canyon.

Southwest Face. Class 3. First ascent August 5, 1936, by May Pridham and Adel Von Lobensels. From Cloud Canyon, climb through a prominent patch of grass and brush to a point about ¼ mile south of the summit along the peak's south ridge. Traverse north across the west side of the peak on some ledges to a broad chute. Climb the chute to the south ridge, and follow the ridge to the summit. (The south ridge can be followed directly to the summit, but this is

class 4 in places.)

North Ridge. Class 4. First ascent 1951 by Fred Davenport and others. One piton was used on the first ascent.

East Face. Class 3. First ascent August 1971 by Frank Meyers and Jack Wolfe. Leave the Colby Pass Trail at approximately 10,000 feet and hike up the valley east of Whaleback. Climb onto the east face of the peak and gain a ledge system which diagonally ascends across the southern part of the face from the right to the left. The ledges lead to a notch on the south ridge of the peak. Cross the ridge, and traverse north across the west side of the peak on ledges to a broad chute. Climb the chute to the south ridge, and follow the ridge to the summit. *Variation:* Class 3. First ascent 1978 by David Vandervoet. It is possible to zigzag up the east face via a series of connecting ledges which leads to the summit.

Glacier Ridge

(12,360 ft+; 12,416 ft; 1.8 mi SW of Whaleback)

Glacier Ridge is about 4 miles long. This description refers to the high point of the ridge.

South Side. Class 2, with a class 4 summit block. From Cloud Canyon ascend slabs and talus to the summit block. The summit block is about 15 feet high and is easy class 4.

North Face. II, 5.7. First ascent September 1971 by Galen Rowell and Jeanne Neale. Climb a diagonal crack system for five pitches to the summit.

There are two routes on the "Grave Site Wall," which is located on the east side of Deadman Canyon (UTM 603590). *Once Upon a Time in the West* is rated II, 5.11. *We Jammin* is II, 5.10b. Two ropes are needed to rappel these routes. These were climbed by Randy Judycki and Eric Fogel in 1986.

Peak 11,760+

(11,830 ft; 0.6 mi NW of Elizabeth Pass)

This peak has been called "Horn Peak," "The Horn," or "The Fin" by skiers on the Sierra High Route trans-Sierra ski tour.

Southeast Ridge. Class 2. First ascent 1936 by May Pridham and party. Follow the ridge from the top of Elizabeth Pass.

North Arete. III, 5.8. First ascent September 1970 by Greg Henzie, Galen Rowell, and Chris Jones. Four pitches on the arete lead to the summit.

Peak 11,600+
(11,602 ft; 1.0 mi SE of Big Bird Lake)

First ascent 1936 by May Pridham and party. The southwest slope is class 2, and it is a good ski run.

"Big Bird Peak"
(11,600 ft+; 11,598 ft; 1.0 mi SW of Big Bird Lake)

This peak has also been called "Bird Peak" and "Ghost Mountain." First ascent 1936 by May Pridham and party. It is class 2 from the west.

Northeast Face. III, 5.8. First ascent September 1970 by Chris Jones, Greg Henzie, and Galen Rowell. Relatively easy climbing leads to a dihedral system left of the center portion of the face. Climb the dihedrals to the summit.

Sugarloaf   *(7,995 ft; 8,002 ft)*

South Face. Class 3. First ascent October 18, 1975, by two Basic Mountaineering Training Course students. This route is on the left side of the south face.

Great West Chimney. Class 4. First ascent August 5, 1936, by Carl Jensen, Howard Gates, and John Poindexter. Leave the Scaffold Meadow Trail and cross over the low, southwest ridge of the peak. Traverse north and climb into the chimney that splits the peak. When the difficulties in the chimney increase, crawl under a chockstone. Two more chockstones follow through narrow, cavelike passages. These secret passages lead to a large dark room. A chimney within the Great West Chimney leads up and out of the room to the south. Scramble north to the high point of the peak. Headlamps are recommended!

West Face. III, 5.8. First ascent October 1979 by Alan Roberts and Fred Beckey. This climb involves thin crack problems, a committing overhang, and challenging friction climbing.

Ball Dome   *(9,435 ft; 9,357 ft)*

The southwest buttress is class 4.

Mt. Silliman   *(11,188 ft; 11,188 ft)*

First ascent June 28, 1864, by Clarence King, James Gardiner, Richard Cotter, and William Brewer. There is a swell view from the summit. The south slope is class 2. It is also class 2 from Silliman Pass: traverse to the east ridge from the pass and follow the ridge to the summit.

There are two rock-climbing routes on the southern side of the west ridge of Mt. Silliman. One consists of five pitches of 5.7, and the other is seven pitches of 5.8. These were climbed in June 1981 by Guy McClure and Peter Cummings.

"Winter Alta"
(11,328 ft; 11,200 ft+; 0.7 mi NE of Alta Pk.)

This is a popular destination for skiers touring out of the Pear Lake Hut. Beautiful ski runs can be done on the northern and southern sides of the this peak from January through May.

Alta Peak   *(11,204 ft; 11,204 ft)*

First ascent 1896 by William R. Dudley. The trail from Panther Gap is class 1.

"Castle Rock Spire"
(7,600 ft+; UTM 462415)

This incredible blade of rock, visible from Moro Rock and the Generals Highway, is the most spectacular rock spire in California outside of Yosemite Valley. In the thirty-eight years after its first ascent, it had been climbed only fourteen times. A long, difficult approach discourages most climbers from attempting an ascent. But the climbing is superb, and the setting is wild. Further reading: *Rock & Ice,* No. 28, November–December 1988, pp. 52–53.

There are two approaches to Castle Rocks. You leave the Mineral King Road at Atwell Mill Ranger Station and follow the trail to a point near Paradise Peak. At this point the trail disappears, and much tortuous bushwhacking is needed to reach the gully that leads to the notch between Castle Rock Spire and The Fin.

Most climbers have used the Paradise Creek approach. From the Buckeye Flat Campground near the Generals Highway, follow the Paradise Creek Trail for 1½ miles. At this point the trail starts to leave the stream, and a little farther along it meets the old, abandoned Castle Rocks Trail. Follow this faint trail east toward Dome Creek for about 4 miles. Leave this trail at the second rock gully encountered, and follow the gully to the notch between Castle Rock Spire and The

Fin. This 4,000-foot approach has poison oak and a lot of brush.

The Wilson Route. III, 5.9, A2 or 5.11b. First ascent April 27, 1950, by Jim Wilson, Allen Steck, Phil Bettler, Will Siri, and Bill Long. First free ascent September 7, 1983, by Rob Raker and Dick Leversee. From the notch, traverse out onto the east face; this

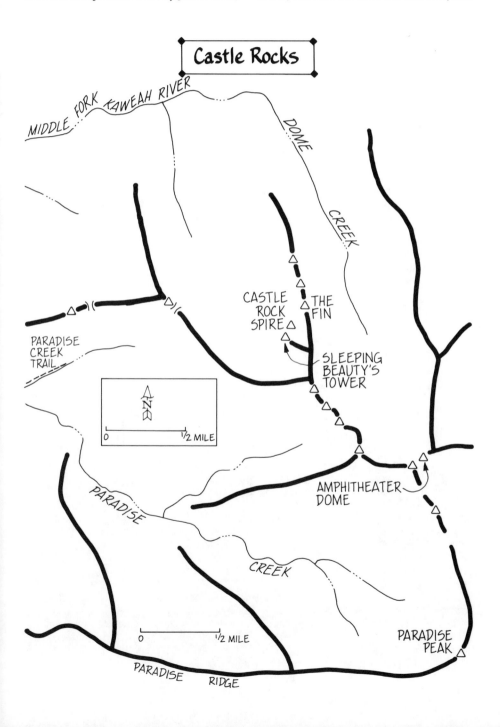

involves two horizontal class 4 pitches. These lead to a crack, which eventually turns into a gully (loose blocks!), which goes behind a large flake. Climb through a slot near the top of this flake, and descend about 50 feet to an outside corner. Climb the corner to an overhang, and pass this on the left side. Climb a crack to a cramped belay stance beneath an overhang. The next pitch is the crux: the Traverse Pitch. Climb up and right, across an exposed face to an indistinct corner, then traverse horizontally left to a left-slanting jam crack that leads to a belay alcove. After surmounting an overhang, climb an easy chimney. A long aid pitch goes up and to the left, and ends on some small ledges in a notch below a gendarme. The final pitch is easy, except for two aid placements in a steep corner. A typical rack for this climb would include two complete sets of tapered chocks, one complete set of spring-loaded camming devices, plus twelve runners and perhaps a bolt kit. *Variation:* First ascent May 15, 1988, by Miguel Carmona and Alois Smrz. The two horizontal class 4 pitches can be avoided by climbing directly to the flake from the approach gully. This involves one pitch of 5.10 and one pitch of 5.9. Further reading: *Summit,* June–July 1978, pp. 26–27; *Sierra Club Bulletin,* 1951, pp. 133–36.

Northeast Face. V, 5.8, A4. First ascent September 1967 by Tom Frost and TM Herbert. This route follows a crack system that eventually joins the Wilson Route behind the large flake. The first two pitches ascend a rotten corner that rises above the approach gully. The third, fourth, and fifth pitches go free, and the sixth pitch is mixed. Follow the rest of the Wilson Route to the summit.

West Face. IV, 5.9, A4. First ascent May 1969 by Mort Hempel, Ben Borson, Fred Beckey, and Galen Rowell. Some creative aid climbing is needed to reach the main crack system on the west face. At one point it is necessary to tie-off manzanita bushes for direct aid! This 200-foot section took the first-ascent party three days to climb. The remainder of the climb is pleasant crack and chimney climbing. Further reading: *Summit,* May 1970, pp. 8–13.

"The Fin" *(7,641 ft; UTM 464417)*

This is the next formation east of Castle Rock Spire. Some of the finest rock climbs in the High Sierra are on its west face. Further

Castle Rocks from the northwest

The Fin ▶   Castle Rock ▶
                      Spire

reading: *Rock & Ice,* No. 28, November–December 1988, p. 52.

Silver Lining. IV, 5.9. First ascent May 26, 1985, by Patrick Paul, Ron Carson, Eve Laeger, and Herb Laeger. This route starts at a pine tree at the lower edge of the apron at the base of the west face of The Fin. Nine pitches of beautiful face climbing on excellent rock (with a lot of runouts) lead to the summit. The route passes the prominent block on its right side during the seventh pitch. Some 5.9 climbing is found on every pitch, with some serious chimneys.

Aspire. IV, 5.9. First ascent May 1986 by Dick Leversee and Herb Laeger. This route starts about 150 feet above and right of the pine tree at the base of the preceding route. It goes up and slightly right for nine pitches, parallel to Silver Lining.

Charley Knapp Route. III, 5.9. First ascent May 23, 1984, by Ron Carson, Patrick Paul, and Herb Laeger. This route is across from Castle Rock Spire, on the southern side of the west face of The Fin. The route goes directly up for four pitches before moving up and left to the crest of The Fin.

Rappel Route. This begins near a manzanita bush at the top of the narrow summit ridge, near the top of Aspire. Two 165-foot ropes and twelve runners are needed to complete the rappels.

"Sleeping Beauty's Tower"
(7,680 ft+; UTM 461414)

This tower is high above and slightly southwest of Castle Rock Spire.

The Gargoyle Route. III, 5.9, A1. First ascent July 1983 by Herb Laeger, Eve Laeger,

Castle Rock Spire (photo by Sequoia and Kings Canyon National Parks)

and Rick Smith. This route starts low in a gully on the northwest side of the tower. It traverses right on a ramp system onto the vertical west face. It then follows a crack-and-corner system directly to the summit. These six pitches consist of beautiful climbing. A 10-foot tension traverse to the left on the second pitch is the only aid; it leads to a crack system. Descend to the southwest with a few rappels to gain the gully south of the tower.

"Amphitheater Dome"
(9,081 ft; 9,180 ft)

This dome is best approached from Paradise Peak.

Southeast Side. Class 3–4. First ascent 1946 by Ted Knowles, DeWitt Allen, and Anton Nelson.

North Buttress. II, 5.8, A2. First ascent June 23, 1968, by Fred Beckey, Roger Briggs, Jim Jones, and Dave Leen. The crux of this climb is an overhang (overcome with aid) followed by difficult free climbing.

Paradise Peak *(9,362 ft; 9,360 ft+)*

A side trail leads almost to the top of this peak from the trail between Atwell Mill Ranger Station and Redwood Meadow.

Wrinkles

Mineral King to the upper Big Arroyo. There are many options for this route, and many cross-country hikers have argued over which is the best approach. In my experience, the easiest route is to cross Glacier Pass (the only obstacle is a short class 3 cliff with seasonal snowfields) and descend to meet the Black Rock Pass Trail near the headwaters of Cliff Creek. Follow the Black Rock Pass Trail to the Big Arroyo. The other passes may be technically easier, but they also involve hiking across miles of talus, which is hardly a pleasant prospect, especially with a heavy pack.

High Sierra Trail. The vast majority of the trails in the High Sierra were placed by the Native Americans and the shepherds. In other words, they just happened. Many of these trails have been rerouted and graded by the National Park Service and the United States Forest Service, but the vast majority still maintain their original steep pitches. Exceptions to this include a few specifically built recreational trails. These include parts of the John Muir Trail, and the High Sierra Trail. The High Sierra Trail is a trans-Sierra trail, leading from Giant Forest to meet the John Muir Trail along Wallace Creek; the John Muir Trail then goes to the summit of Mt. Whitney. The High Sierra Trail traverses scenic terrain at a relatively gentle grade. There are tremendous views across the Middle Fork of the Kaweah River to Castle Rocks. It then passes through Valhalla, with its impressive cliffs. The High Sierra Trail then descends the Big Arroyo to the canyon of the Kern River; anyone hiking this section should not miss visiting Moraine Lake, which requires a slight detour. The High Sierra Trail then ascends the Kern River drainage to meet the John Muir Trail, with views to the west of terrain it has traversed.

Of all the High Sierra trails, the John Muir Trail receives the vast majority of attention in the public imagination. But its rival, the High Sierra Trail, should not be ignored.

Junction Meadow. There are two Junction Meadows in the High Sierra, located just close enough together to cause confusion. Prudent hikers should specify Junction Meadow (Kern River) or Junction Meadow (Bubbs Creek) when making ironclad arrangements for rendezvous or food drops.

Approaches to Triple Divide Peak, Whaleback, Glacier Ridge, Milestone Mountain, Midway Mountain, and other hard-to-reach places in this vicinity. Many people assume that the best approach to the northern portion of the Great Western Divide is from the east over Shepherd Pass and that Triple Divide Peak and points north should be approached via the High Sierra Trail or by a cross-country route from Mineral King. An often neglected alternative is to approach these places from the west via the Scaffold Meadow Trail from the Big Meadows/Horse Corral Meadow Road. Granted, this approach is long (25+ miles) but it has none of the severe ups and downs of the other alternatives. Besides, the view of Whaleback rising above Big Wet Meadow is worth the long hike. (Although it is outside the territory of this chapter, this is also a viable alternative to ascents of North Guard, Mt. Brewer, South Guard, and other peaks at the northern end of the Great Western Divide. After all, Mt. Brewer was first climbed by this approach and route.)

4

The Kings–Kern Divide

THE KINGS–KERN DIVIDE IS A MAJOR BAR-
rier of the southern High Sierra. This wall of
mountains extends for 6 miles west from
Junction Peak on the Sierra crest to Thunder
Mountain on the Great Western Divide.

This chapter covers the area bounded on
the north by Bubbs Creek and Kearsarge
Pass, on the south by Shepherd Pass and
Tyndall Creek, on the west by the Kern River
and Thunder Mountain, and on the east by
the Roaring River and Avalanche Pass.

For years, the only trail that crossed this
divide was the old sheep route over Harrison
Pass. One of the last sections of the John Muir
Trail to be constructed, Forester Pass, was
completed in 1932, making a crossing of the
Kings–Kern Divide possible for mere mortals. Prior to this, travelers had to bypass the
divide entirely, crossing Junction Pass and
Shepherd Pass. This compact area features
rugged terrain, awesome scenery, and beautiful lakes and streams.

History

Clarence King and Richard Cotter crossed
the Kings–Kern Divide twice during their
epic journey to Mt. Tyndall in 1864. King
described this adventure in his American
classic, *Mountaineering in the Sierra Nevada*.
In the dramatic style so popular in the nineteenth century, King tells of crossing the
divide somewhere between Thunder Mountain and Mt. Jordan, where they lassoed a
loose spike of rock and climbed the rope
hand over hand, and of rope-downs where
retreat was impossible and continued descent uncertain. On their return to their
camp along Roaring River, somewhere in the
vicinity of Lake Reflection, King attempted a
steep climb and failed. Cotter succeeded,
however, and called down to King that he

had a secure stance, and King shouldn't be
afraid to use the rope for tension. King's
pride insisted that he climb the pitch free,
and after having done so, he discovered that
Cotter was precariously balanced, where the
slightest tug on the rope would have caused
them both to catch big air.

John Muir visited the Kings–Kern Divide
in 1873 and, as was his practice, climbed
several peaks—but he neglected to record
which peaks he ascended. Sheepherders were
active in this region in the latter part of the
nineteenth century, particularly on the southern part of the divide. Mountaineers began to
climb some of the peaks in the late nineteenth and early twentieth centuries; these
individuals included Bolton Brown and Joseph LeConte.

Maps

United States Geological Survey: 7.5-
minute series: Mt. Williamson, Mt. Brewer,
Sphinx Lakes, Kearsarge Peak, Mt. Clarence
King, The Sphinx; 15-minute series: Mount
Whitney, Mt. Pinchot, Triple Divide Peak,
Marion Peak; national park maps: Sequoia
and Kings Canyon National Parks and Vicin-
ity (1:125,000).

United States Forest Service: John Muir
Wilderness and Sequoia–Kings Canyon National Parks Backcountry (1:63,360).

Wilderness Permits

For east-side entry into the John Muir
Wilderness: Inyo National Forest, Mt.
Whitney Ranger District, Lone Pine, CA
93545.

For west-side entry into the Sequoia or
Kings Canyon national parks backcountry:
Sequoia and Kings Canyon National Parks,
Three Rivers, CA 93271.

Roads

Onion Valley Road

The Onion Valley Road heads west from Independence for 14.1 miles to Onion Valley, one of the highest trailheads in the eastern High Sierra. Trails leading out of Onion Valley are the Kearsarge Pass Trail, the Robinson Lake Trail, and the Golden Trout Lake Trail. There is a campground, a pack station, and hiker parking at Onion Valley.

Pinyon Creek Road

The Pinyon Creek Road leaves the Onion Valley Road 4.7 miles from Independence. The road heads southwest 1.2 miles from the Onion Valley Road and ends in the desert, next to Pinyon Creek. This is the trailhead for the cross-country hike up Pinyon Creek and the eastern approach for Mt. Bradley and the Center Basin Crags.

Kings Canyon Highway (Highway 180)

This road and trailhead are described in Chapter 6: Monarch Divide and Cirque Crest. The Bubbs Creek Trail starts 2 miles from the end of Highway 180 in Kings Canyon.

Trails

Shepherd Pass Trail (12 miles)

This trail, along with either the John Muir Trail or the Lake South America Trail, provides access to the southern portion of the Kings–Kern Divide. The Shepherd Pass Trail is described in Chapter 2: The Whitney Region.

Tyndall Creek Trail (5 miles)

The Tyndall Creek Trail, which could be considered part of the Shepherd Pass Trail, begins about 1/4 mile south of where the John Muir Trail crosses Tyndall Creek. It follows a long, wet meadow, crossing Tyndall Creek along the way, and passes through a lodgepole forest before making a slight climb. This climb ends at the edge of the Kern River canyon, with excellent views of the Great Western Divide. The trail then makes a steep descent with many switchbacks before meeting the Lake South America Trail along the Kern River, 4 1/2 miles north of Junction Meadow.

John Muir Trail (15 miles)

After meeting the Shepherd Pass Trail on the south side of Tyndall Creek, the John

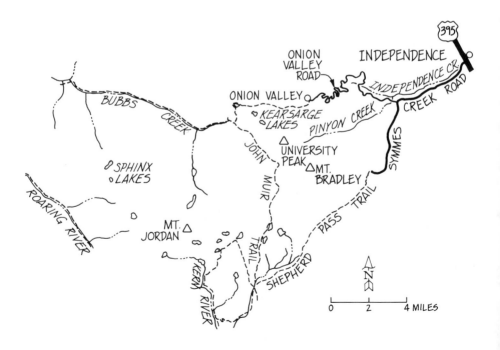

Muir Trail crosses the creek and heads north. After about ³/₄ mile, it meets the Lake South America Trail. The John Muir Trail continues north, passes some lakes, and switchbacks up the cliff on the south side of Forester Pass to its summit 5 miles from the Lake South America Trail junction. (The John Muir Trail and the Pacific Crest Trail are the same trail in this area; Forester Pass is the high point of the entire 2,400-mile Pacific Crest Trail.) The trail descends the gradual north side of the pass for 4 miles to the junction with the Center Basin Trail. The John Muir Trail continues descending Bubbs Creek, passing through beautiful forests and meadows, for another 3 miles to the junction with the Bubbs Creek Trail below Vidette Meadow. The John Muir Trail leaves Bubbs Creek here, climbs to the north, and meets the Bullfrog Lake Trail after 1¹/₂ miles. Three-quarters of a mile farther the John Muir Trail comes to the junction with the Kearsarge Pass Trail and the Charlotte Lake Trail.

Lake South America Trail   (11¹/₂ miles)

The Lake South America Trail starts along the John Muir Trail ³/₄ mile north of the John Muir Trail junction with the Shepherd Pass Trail, along Tyndall Creek. The Lake South America Trail climbs and goes west about ¹/₂ mile to a junction with a trail that continues west directly to the Kern River. From this junction, the Lake South America Trail turns to the north for 2 miles and ascends a basin with a short cliff at its head to the top of the ridge overlooking Lake South America. A short descent to the northwest leads to a use trail to the lake.

The trail continues southwest, down a lovely wooded and grassy basin that serves as the headwaters of the Kern River. After 4 miles, it meets the trail that leads back to Tyndall Creek. The trail continues down the Kern River canyon another 5 miles to a junction with the High Sierra Trail, 1 mile north of Junction Meadow.

Center Basin Trail   (3 miles)

The Center Basin Trail starts along the John Muir Trail 4 miles north of Forester Pass and 3 miles south of the John Muir Trail junction with the Bubbs Creek Trail. The trail climbs up into Center Basin and circles around Golden Bear Lake on its north shore

before disappearing in fields of talus.

This is one of the original routes of the John Muir Trail. It was used until the trail over Forester Pass was constructed in 1932. Traces of the trail may still be found in the upper reaches of Center Basin and over Junction Pass, but this is now more of a cross-country route than a trail. It is described under Junction Pass.

Bubbs Creek Trail   (10³/₄ miles)

The Bubbs Creek Trail begins 2 miles from the end of the Kings Canyon Highway along the Paradise Valley Trail. It crosses the South Fork of the Kings River on a bridge and switchbacks up the north bank of Bubbs Creek. Two miles from the bridge it meets the trail descending from Avalanche Pass via Sphinx Creek. The Bubbs Creek Trail continues up the north bank of the creek another 6¹/₂ miles to meet the East Lake Trail at Junction Meadow, then goes upstream another 2¹/₄ miles to meet the John Muir Trail near Vidette Meadow.

Sphinx Creek Trail   (14³/₄ miles)

The Sphinx Creek Trail starts along the Bubbs Creek Trail 4 miles from the end of the road in Kings Canyon. It switchbacks up the east side of Sphinx Creek for 3 miles before crossing to its west bank. (From this point, a use trail continues up the west side of the creek to Sphinx Lakes, from which Mt. Brewer can be climbed.) The Sphinx Creek Trail makes a gradual ascent to the west and leaves the drainage before reaching Avalanche Pass, which is 3 miles from the crossing of Sphinx Creek. The trail descends from the pass in 8³/₄ miles to Scaffold Meadow along Roaring River.

East Lake Trail   (5 miles)

The beautiful East Lake Trail passes through forests of aspen and pine and meadows with flowers and willows. The sound of East Creek adds to the ambiance, and the views of Mt. Brewer and the peaks of the Kings–Kern Divide are outstanding.

The East Lake Trail leaves the Bubbs Creek Trail at Junction Meadow and crosses Bubbs Creek before ascending East Creek. At first, the trail follows the western bank of the creek, but soon it crosses the stream and ascends the east side for 3 miles to East Lake. The trail continues up the east side of the creek another 2 miles to Lake Reflection, one of the most beautiful lakes in the High Sierra.

Kearsarge Pass Trail (7 miles)

The Kearsarge Pass Trail is one of the most heavily used trails in the High Sierra. Wood fires are prohibited in the basin east of Kearsarge Pass, and above 10,000 feet in Kings Canyon National Park.

The trail goes west out of Onion Valley and switchbacks up to overused Gilbert Lake; just beyond Gilbert Lake a trail heads south to Matlock and Slim lakes, which offer more privacy. The Kearsarge Pass Trail continues climbing to the west and passes north of well-named Big Pothole Lake to reach the barren plateau just east of the pass. A gradual climb across the plateau brings you to the pass, 4 miles from the trailhead. The trail makes a steep descent on the western side of the pass for ³/₄ mile to the junction with the Bullfrog Lake Trail and Kearsarge Lakes Trail. The Kearsarge Pass Trail goes west from this junction, making a gradual descent, for 2¹/₄ miles to meet the John Muir Trail. About ¹/₄ mile before this junction, there is a y-shaped fork: Those heading north on the John Muir Trail toward Glen Pass go right; those bound for Charlotte Lake or Bubbs Creek go left. Either variation is about ¹/₄ mile in length.

Bullfrog Lake Trail (2 miles)

This is the original route of the Kearsarge Pass Trail, but Bullfrog Lake became so scarred and polluted from too many thoughtless campers that the National Park Service constructed a new trail to the north to help divert traffic away from this site. Bullfrog Lake is closed to all camping, and Kearsarge Lakes has a one-night limit on camps.

The Bullfrog Lake Trail starts approximately ³/₄ mile west of Kearsarge Pass. A short distance after it begins, it forks, and the left fork goes for ¹/₂ mile to the Kearsarge Lakes. The main trail continues to the west, passing north of Bullfrog Lake, with outstanding views of East Vidette, Deerhorn Mountain, and West Vidette. From Bullfrog Lake, the trail contours southwest to meet the John Muir Trail.

Robinson Lake Trail (2 miles)

This short hike leads to an extremely popular overnight camping destination.

Campfires are prohibited in the Robinson Lake basin.

From the eastern end of the Onion Valley Campground, a trail leads through aspen and climbs the steep hillside to the entrance of the hanging valley. The trail goes south and, after climbing a slight rise, leads to Robinson Lake.

Cross-Country Routes

Junction Pass

(4020 m+; 13,200 ft+; 0.4 mi NE of Junction Pk.; UTM 785617)

Class 2. This is the original route of the John Muir Trail. It has not been maintained since 1932, but traces of the old trail are still visible. From The Pothole on the eastern side of Shepherd Pass, head northwest and go across the meadow on the bench above. Ascend the west side of the stream that leads into the meadow and head into the valley between Junction Peak and Junction Pass. Stay on the north side of the valley, and ascend sand and scree to the plateau near the summit of Junction Pass. (The correct pass is 0.3 mile west of the name "Junction Pass" that appears on some editions of the Mt. Williamson 7.5-minute quadrangle.) The route on the north side of the pass descends into Center Basin, and remains west of the lakes in the upper portion of the basin. The Center Basin Trail is met southeast of Golden Bear Lake.

"Ski Mountaineers Pass"

(4000 m; 13,120 ft+; 0.3 mi ESE of Forester Pass)

Class 1–2. This pass consists of sand, scree, and talus, but during moderate to heavy snow years it provides a means for skiers to cross the Kings–Kern Divide without having to negotiate the cliffs on the south side of Forester Pass.

"Andy's Foot Pass"

(4160 m+; 13,600 ft+; 0.2 mi SSE of Gregory's Monument)

Class 2; ice axe required. This is a direct route between Lake South America and the upper regions of Bubbs Creek. From the top of Harrison Pass, hike to the top of Andy's Foot Pass, which is the first pass southsoutheast of Gregory's Monument. There is a permanent snowfield in the couloir on the northeast side of the pass, and the angle is quite steep. This pass goes best in the late spring or early summer, when the snow is consolidated but not too icy, and covers the huge talus northeast of the pass.

Harrison Pass *(3880 m+; 12,720 ft+)*

Class 2. Some maps show a trail over Harrison Pass. Be forewarned: This trail has not been maintained for many years, and the critical portion leading up the north side of the pass has all but disappeared. With snow, the north side of the pass is steep and icy; no snow reveals steep and loose rock.

From the East Lake Trail, climb into the basin north of Harrison Pass and the Ericsson Crags. The upper portion of this basin is composed of huge pieces of talus. From the highest lake, either climb ledges toward Mt. Ericsson that lead back to the top of the pass, or ascend a loose rock chute directly to the summit of the pass. The south side of the pass is easy.

"Ericsson Pass"

(3840 m+; 12,560 ft+; 0.4 mi NE of Mt. Ericsson)

Class 2–3. This is an alternative to Harrison Pass. Only the upper portion of the northern side of this pass is difficult.

"Deerhorn Saddle"

(3840 m+; 12,560 ft+; 0.4 mi SE of Deerhorn Mtn.)

Class 2. This pass is used to gain access between Vidette Creek and the basin north of Harrison Pass.

Lucy's Foot Pass

Class 2. This pass was first crossed by Lucy Brown and Bolton Brown in 1896 during their exploration of the Kings–Kern Divide. Difficult talus is encountered on the north side of the pass. A short cliff just below the top on the north side can be bypassed by moving 150 feet to the east. The south side of the pass is easy.

Milly's Foot Pass *(3740 m+; 12,240 ft+)*

Class 2. This is the most direct route between Lake Reflection and the upper Kern River Basin. This pass was first crossed in July 1953 by Mildred Jentsch and Sylvia Kershaw. Class 2 talus leads to the prominent slot that marks the pass on its northwestern side. Near the top, this slot narrows,

and the climbing becomes class 3 for about 100 feet. The southeast side of the pass is easy.

"Thunder Pass"

(3860 m+; 0.2 mi ESE of Thunder Mtn.)

Class 2; ice axe required. This pass was probably first crossed by Clarence King and Richard Cotter in their quest for Mt. Tyndall. The southern side is easy, but care must be taken when descending the northern slopes to ensure that the easiest route is followed. Some huge talus is encountered on the lower northern portion of the pass.

Longley Pass *(3780 m+; 12,400 ft+)*

Class 1. This is the first pass south of South Guard. The west side of the pass is easy, but the east side is a little more difficult. In early season, the east side of the pass may be blocked by a cornice. This can be bypassed on the north by means of a short class 3 section.

"Brewer Pass"

(3860 m+; 12,640 ft+; 0.5 mi SE of Mt. Brewer)

Class 2. This pass connects Brewer Creek with East Lake. The east side of this pass may be impassable due to steep snow. If this is the case, it can be bypassed by climbing the south ridge of Mt. Brewer and descending the peak's east ridge to East Lake. Ugh!

Vidette Creek

The chief difficulty in a trip up beautiful Vidette Creek is finding a safe crossing of Bubbs Creek. If you are lucky, there may be large logs that allow you to cross the creek with ease. It seems, however, that most hikers end up fording Bubbs Creek. From Bubbs Creek, ascend the east side of Vidette Creek to the vicinity of Vidette Lakes, where most hikers cross to the west side of the stream. Cross-country travel is easy in this basin until just beneath Deerhorn Saddle.

Pinyon Creek

Class 2. This serves as the eastern approach to Mt. Bradley and the Center Basin Crags. From the trailhead, a use trail ascends the north side of the stream to the base of the diamond-shaped hill in the middle of the valley, which is best passed on its dry, left side. Regain the stream above the hill, and follow it to the basin north of Mt. Bradley.

"University Pass"

(3840 m+; 12,640 ft+; 0.6 mi SE of University Peak)

Class 2. This is the most direct route from Onion Valley to Center Basin and the Kings–Kern Divide, but it is a rough, cross-country route. Only experienced cross-country hikers should attempt it. From Robinson Lake, hike up the creek to the lowest point between University Peak and Peak 3926m (12,910 ft). There is a steep snow gully here for most of the summer (an ice axe may be helpful), and huge boulders at the base of the pass can make the approach rather tedious. The southwest side of the pass is a long chute with loose rocks.

"University Shoulder"

(3700 m+; 12,160 ft+; 0.6 mi NW of University Peak; UTM 773678)

Class 2. This high-level route has been used by cross-country skiers to avoid losing altitude by way of Vidette Meadow or Onion Valley. Make an ascending traverse across the southwest side of University Peak to the northwest shoulder of the peak, which is southeast of Kearsarge Pinnacles. The north side of the shoulder is rather steep (with huge talus in the summer), but it leads directly to the Kearsarge Lakes basin.

Peaks

Thunder Mountain

(4120 m+; 13,588 ft)

East Ridge. Class 3 with a class 4 summit block. First ascent August 1905 by George Davis of the U.S. Geological Survey. Gain Thunder Pass from either Lake Reflection or the Kern River Basin. Follow the east ridge of the peak (or the talus slope to the southeast) to the south summit of the peak. Cross over the south summit and descend about 20 feet to the notch between the south and middle summits. Cross to the north side of the notch on an airy bridge and traverse across the east face of the middle summit to the notch between it and the north summit. The north summit, the high point, can be climbed via a crack with natural chockstones on the southern side of the block, or by means of a jam crack on its southwest side. Either way is class 4.

Peak 3840m+

(12560 ft+; 1.3 mi W of Thunder Mtn.)

South Slope. Class 2. First ascent 1940 by a Sierra Club party.

North Face and West Ridge. Class 3–4. First ascent July 1958 by Phil Arnot and party.

Peak 3980m+

(13,040 ft+; 0.5 mi NNW of Thunder Mtn.)

Southeast Face. Class 2–3. First ascent 1940 by Oliver Kehrlein and party.

Peak 3960m+

(12,960 ft+; 0.3 mi S of Longley Pass)

First ascent 1925 by Norman Clyde. The peak is class 2 from Longley Pass.

South Guard   *(4033 m; 13,224 ft)*

North Ridge. Class 2–3. First ascent 1864 by Clarence King and Richard Cotter. Follow the ridge from Brewer Pass.

South Slope. Class 2 from Longley Pass.

Peak 3940m+

(12,960 ft+; 0.9 mi SE of Mt. Brewer)

Northeast Ridge. Class 3. First ascent July 26, 1916, by Walter L. Huber, Florence Burrell, Inezetta Holt, and James Rennie. Climb the northeast ridge from the south fork of Ouzel Creek. This ridge is loose and knife-edged.

North Face. Class 3. The climb is made by following a series of ledges.

South Face. Class 2. Climb to the ridge west of the summit and follow it to the top.

Peak 3904m

(12,805 ft; 1.2 mi ESE of Mt. Brewer)

The west ridge is class 1–2.

Peak 12,640+

(12,683 ft; 1.1 mi W of South Guard)

South Slope. Class 2. First ascent July 1959 by Phil Arnot, Shel Arnot, Harry Pancoast, Dale Nelson, and Charlie Backus. The north summit is the high point of the peak.

Mt. Brewer   *(4136 m; 13,570 ft)*

Mt. Brewer is separate from the Sierra crest and the Kings–Kern Divide. It therefore has a wide, unobstructed view in all directions from its summit.

East Ridge. Class 2. First ascent 1895 by A.

Mt. Brewer from the east (photo by Sequoia and Kings Canyon National Parks)

B. Clark and Bolton Brown. First winter ascent February 15, 1971, by Paul Emerson, Rix Rieder, Mike Lee, and Tim Duffy. From East Lake, follow Ouzel Creek upstream to where it is possible to climb onto the ridge that leads directly up Mt. Brewer. Follow the ridge to where it ends against the south ridge of the peak; go left (south) through a small notch, and climb the south ridge to the summit.

South Ridge. Class 2. First ascent July 2, 1864, by William H. Brewer and Charles F. Hoffman. From Brewer Creek or South Guard Lake, ascend to Brewer Pass and follow the south ridge to the summit. The south ridge can also be ascended from East Lake, but the east ridge is an easier route.

Northwest Slopes. Class 2. Cross into the Brewer Creek basin from Sphinx Lakes via the notch northeast of Point 12,360+ (12,393 ft). Traverse and climb into the bowl between North Guard and Mt. Brewer and climb the northwest slope of Mt. Brewer.

Northeast Couloir. Class 2–3. First ascent August 4, 1940, by Oliver Kehrlein, August Fruge, Grete Fruge, E. Hanson, L. West, R. Leggett, and A. Mauley. Climb the prominent snow-and-ice couloir just north of the northeast face of Mt. Brewer. The couloir ends along the north ridge. Climb the north ridge to the summit.

Northeast Face. III, 5.7. First ascent September 1963 by Kenneth Boche and Russ McLean. This route begins by climbing the first chimney to the right of the rib that leads directly to the summit of the peak. Climb the chimney for about 200 feet to an overhang. Traverse right for 10 feet (5.7) into the next chimney. Climb this chimney, passing a chockstone on the left. Go up and right for about 40 feet to some class 4 slabs. Climb toward the higher of two notches that are to the right of the summit. The top of the climb is reached by climbing between the two notches.

Peak 3520m+

(11,520 ft+; 1.9 mi ENE of Mt. Brewer)

This is a long ridge that overlooks East Lake. This peak has been called "Peak Corbel" and "Peak Korbel."

South Face. Class 3. First ascent May 28, 1934, by David Brower and Hervey Voge. The first-ascent party described this as "an entertaining climb, just below the difficulty requiring a rope."

Southwest Ridge. Class 3. First ascent May 28, 1934, by Hervey Voge and David Brower. This traverse is among towers, blocks, and knife edges.

North Guard   *(4026 m; 13,327 ft)*

Mt. Brewer may have a swell view from its summit, but North Guard is the better climb, hands down.

South Face. Class 3. First ascent July 12, 1925, by Norman Clyde. There are two chutes on the southern side of North Guard. Climb the left-hand (western) chute to the west ridge of the peak. The traverse along the ridge to the summit involves some impressive scrambling and bouldering. Most impressive of all, however, is the large, sloping summit block, which overhangs the east face.

East Face. III, 5.8. First ascent June 1981 by Fred Beckey and Rick Nolting. Climb the center portion of the east face to an exposed edge. Make a difficult exit to the right and climb an outside corner, which lacks holds and protection. The rest of the climb has better holds and protection.

East and North Faces. Class 4. First ascent May 28, 1934, by Hervey Voge and David Brower. Climb to the col north-northeast of the summit from the Ouzel Creek drainage. From the col, climb a 30-foot, v-shaped crack on the north ridge to a ledge. Traverse right (west) across broken ledges on the north face to a crack, which leads to easier rocks and the summit.

North Peak of North Guard. First ascent August 10, 1948, by James Koontz and party.

Peak 3840m+

(12,600 ft; 0.5 mi NW of North Guard)

The northeast face is class 3; it was first climbed September 1973 by Andy Smatko and Bill Schuler.

Mt. Francis Farquhar

(3929 m; 12,893 ft; 1.0 mi NW of North Guard)

This is a beautiful peak, and all of its routes are splendid. Prior to its official naming, this peak was informally called "Notch Peak," due to the prominent notch seen in the northwest ridge of the peak when viewed from the east. The new, official name is appropriate to both the memory of the man and the stature of the peak.

South Ridge. Class 3. First ascent July 17, 1932, by Alice Carter, Julie Mortimer, Dorothy Baird, Patricia Goodhue, Katherine Lindforth, D. R. Brothers, Glen Dawson, Thomas Rawles, Lincoln O'Brien, Arthur Neld, Norman Clyde, William Dulley, John Schager, and Alfred Weiler. Climb to the saddle south of the peak from Sphinx Lakes, and follow the ridge to the summit.

Northwest Ridge. Class 3. From Sphinx Lakes, ascend the chute that leads to the notch on the northwest ridge. The chute divides just below the notch. Take the right branch, and follow it almost to the ridge crest. Go right onto a face and up to the summit. A nice climb.

Northeast Face. IV, 5.8. First ascent September 1971 by Jeanne Neale and Galen Rowell. This route begins by climbing a dihedral on the right side of the face, and follows it to a ledge system in the middle of the face. Traverse left for two pitches to a prow, which leads directly to the summit. The first-ascent party encountered much ice on this route.

Cross Mountain   *(12,160 ft+; 12,185 ft)*

This insignificant peak is class 2 from Sphinx Lakes.

Peak 3620m+

(11,920 ft+; 0.6 mi N of Cross Mtn.)

This peak was once known as "Cross Mountain," until that name was placed in its correct location on the map. It is even less significant than the real Cross Mountain, and is class 2 from the Sphinx Creek drainage.

The Sphinx   *(9,143 ft; 9,146 ft)*

This is the rock formation with two summits, as seen to the southeast from the end of the road in Kings Canyon. The easiest approach is to hike up the Sphinx Creek Trail until you are south of Peak 9,721 (9,721 ft). Leave the trail here and hike cross-country to the rock.

South Side. I, 5.2. First ascent July 26, 1940, by Art Argiewicz and Bob Jacobs. From the higher southern summit descend to the notch between the two summits. Descend to a ledge from the notch, and ascend a 20-foot vertical pitch at the far end of the ledge. This pitch ends near the ridge on the south side of the peak. Follow the ridge to the summit.

North Buttress. II, 5.7. First ascent October 18, 1970, by Greg Donaldson, Walt Vennum, and Fred Beckey. This climb ascends the slabs west of the north buttress. Two pitches across the slabs lead to the buttress itself. Follow the buttress to the north summit of The Sphinx.

Peak 4032m
(13,231 ft; 0.7 mi ENE of Thunder Mtn.)
The southwest face and the east face are both class 2.

Peak 3980m+
(13,090 ft; 0.4 mi SW of Mt. Jordan)
East Face. Class 4. First ascent September 9, 1967, by Andy Smatko, Dennis McAllister, and Tom Ross. Climb a left-ascending diagonal chute on the east face of the peak. Pass a big chockstone in this chute on the right. The chute ends on the south ridge. Two class 4 pitches along the ridge lead to the lower south summit. A short traverse leads to the higher north summit.

There are several interesting pinnacles between this peak and Mt. Jordan.

Peak 3813m
(12,513 ft; 1.0 mi SE of Mt. Jordan)
Class 3 from the south. First ascent August 1939 by Fritz Lippman, Dave Nelson, Don Woods, and Ed Koskinen.

Mt. Jordan *(4060 m+; 13,344 ft)*
East Slope. Class 3 with a class 4 summit block. First ascent July 1936 by parties led by Lewis Clark and Carl Jensen. Climb to the saddle between the north summit and the higher south summit. Easy class 3 leads to the summit block. It can be climbed either by friction on its east side, or by making a delicate step-across on its northern side. The step-across is more sporting, but either way is class 4.

North Face. Class 3 with a class 4 summit block. First ascent August 3, 1940, by Art Argiewicz and party. Gain the north face from the basin southeast of Lake Reflection and northwest of Milly's Foot Pass. Climb the north face and traverse south to the summit block.

West Slope. Class 3 with a class 4 summit block. Descended August 3, 1940, by Art

The Sphinx (photo by Norm Rohn)

Argiewicz and party. Most of this climb is class 2, except for the summit area.

Mt. Genevra *(3979 m; 13,055 ft)*

First ascent July 15, 1926, by Norman Clyde. An ascent of this peak from the west, south, or east consists of sand, talus, and class 2 summit rocks.

North Face. Class 3. First ascent July 19, 1951, by Barbara Lilley, Bill Bade, and Franklin Barnett. Climb a snow chute that leads to the ridge west of the summit. Follow the ridge to the summit.

Mt. Ericsson *(4120 m+; 13,608 ft)*

West Ridge. Class 2. First ascent August 1, 1896, by Bolton C. Brown and Lucy Brown. Follow the easy ridge from Lucy's Foot Pass to the summit.

South Ridge. Class 3. First ascent 1936 by Lewis Clark and Carl Jensen. This is a long climb around a lot of gendarmes and over many false summits.

Northeast Ridge. Class 3. Descended August 1, 1896, by Bolton Brown and Lucy Brown. Ascend the northeast ridge from Harrison Pass and gradually move into a chute that leads to a narrow notch near the summit. Pass through the notch to the west side of the peak, and traverse north to the summit.

Northwest Couloir. Class 4. First ascent July 1946 by Norman Clyde, Robert Breckenfeld, Jules Eichorn, Joe Brower, and Danny Kaplan. Climb the rocky chute between Mt. Ericsson and Ericsson Crag 1A; this chute is best approached from low on the north slope of Lucy's Foot Pass. Approximately 100 feet below the top of this chute, go right (south) and climb a steep, ice couloir. The couloir ends atop the west ridge of the peak. Follow the ridge to the summit.

Ericsson Crags

These are the crags to the north of Mt. Ericsson.

"Ericsson Crag No. 1A"

(3960 m; 13,040 ft+; UTM 736622)

Class 4. This is the smallest, but most spectacular of the Ericsson Crags. First ascent August 1939 by Hervey Voge, Ted Waller, and Don Woods. The ascent was made from the shoulder between Ericsson Crag 1A and Ericsson Crag 1.

Ericsson Crags from the northwest

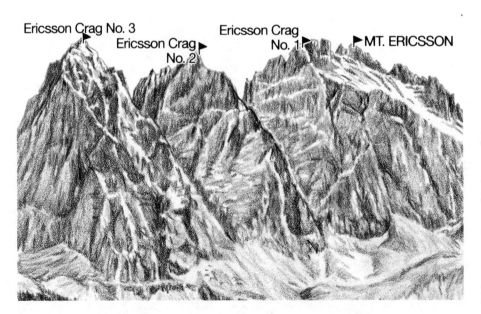

Ericsson Crag No. 3
Ericsson Crag No. 2
Ericsson Crag No. 1
MT. ERICSSON

"Ericsson Crag No. 1"

(4000 m; 13,120 ft+; UTM 735623)

West Chute and Southeast Face. Class 4. First ascent August 4, 1939, by Don Woods, Edward Koskinen, and DeWitt Allen. Ascend the chute between Mt. Ericsson and Ericsson Crag 1. About two-thirds of the way up, the chute branches; take the left (north) branch to the broad shoulder just south of Ericsson Crag 1. Climb a chimney on the southeast face of the crag. The overhanging portion of the chimney can be bypassed by making a downward traverse from a small rib just left of the chimney, and then climbing above the overhang into the chimney. Climb over several large steps in the chimney; the summit block is climbed on its northwest side.

"Ericsson Crag No. 1W"

This is the impressive crag on the west ridge of Ericsson Crag 1. Not much is known about this crag.

"Ericsson Crag No. 2"

(3980 m+; 13,120 ft+; UTM 735625)

West Chute. Class 4. First ascent August 3, 1939, by Hervey Voge and David Brower. From the west, ascend the main chute between crags 2 and 3. Climb the right-hand branch of the second-highest chute, which enters the main chute from the south. This next-to-highest chute leads to the northwest face of Ericsson Crag 2. Climb out of this chute just to the left of some caves by means of a class 4 pitch. Scramble to the top from here.

"Ericsson Crag No. 3"

(3940 m; 13,040 ft+; UTM 735629)

West Chute. Class 4. Ascend the major rocky chute that descends to the west between crags 2 and 3. When near the top of this chute, cross a rib to the left (north) by means of a chimney at the top of this chute. Follow the east side of this ridge to the arete that is east of the summit. Follow the arete to the top.

Brujo Dihedral. III, 5.9. First ascent August 18, 1980, by Ti Neff and David Wilson. This route ascends the prominent dihedral on the right side of the north face of Ericsson Crag 3. An off-width crack (5.7) leads to 300 feet of scrambling to the base of the dihedral.

Two pitches in the dihedral end at a ledge beneath an overhanging block. Go up and right from the ledge on a face (5.8) to a hanging belay on a sharp edge. Climb to the gentler summit slabs (class 4) and up to the summit.

Vinland. IV, 5.9. First ascent July 1987 by Alan Bartlett and Fred Beckey. This route is on the north face of the crag. The climb follows the obvious cracks and chimneys to the right of the prow that descends the north face. These lead to a ledge that goes left to the edge of the prow. The remaining portion of the climb is on the prow itself.

North Face. IV, 5.7. First ascent May 25, 1972, by Reed Cundiff and Fred Beckey. This route climbs the bowls and depressions to the left of the prow on the north face.

Deerhorn Mountain

(4048 m; 13,265 ft)

This fine-looking peak has some classic routes, none of which are trivial. The southeast summit is the high point.

Northeast Buttress. Class 3. First ascent July 8, 1927, by Norman Clyde. This is the buttress that rises directly from the Vidette Creek drainage to the lower northwest summit of the peak. Climb the buttress to a point approximately 100 feet below the northwest peak. Traverse left to the notch between the two peaks of Deerhorn Mountain. The higher southeast peak can be attained either by traversing across the southwest side of the peak over broken rock to the southeast ridge just below the summit, or by ascending the northwest arete or north face. The summit itself is very small; there is room for about four climbers on the very top.

Northeast Couloir. Class 3. First ascent July 4, 1980, by Bill T. Russell, Jim Erb, Gene Mauk, and party. This couloir leads from Vidette Creek to the notch between the peaks of Deerhorn Mountain. It has much loose rock, and it is only safe from rockfall when the couloir is full of snow. Ice axes and crampons will be needed in this case.

Northeast Ridge. Class 3–4. First ascent by Arkel Erb, Andy Smatko, Frede Jensen, Tom Ross, David Oyler, and Mike McNicholas. This ridge leads directly to the higher southeast peak from Vidette Creek. Gain the ridge from the base of the northeast couloir, climbing rock left (south) of the snow, and reach

Deerhorn Mountain from the northeast (photo by Norm Rohn)

the crest of the ridge about halfway up. Follow the ridge to the summit. A class 3–4 pitch is encountered just below the top. Some parties have found easier climbing by traversing left (south) at this point and climbing the upper southeast ridge to the summit.

Southwest Chute. Class 4. First ascent August 3, 1939, by DeWitt Allen and Fritz Lippmann. This chute leads to the notch between the two peaks of Deerhorn Mountain. Only the very bottom and very top of this chute are difficult. *Variation:* First ascent July 2, 1989, by Don Borad. The lower difficult portion of the chute can be avoided by climbing the next chute to the left before entering the main chute.

Southwest Face. Class 3–4. First ascent July 1946 by Norman Clyde, Jules Eichorn, Robert Breckenfeld, and party. Climb the southwest face of the mountain, aiming for a point just west of, and about 300 feet below, the northwest peak. Climb the northwest peak by traversing across the north side of the northwest ridge and climb to the top by means of some ledges.

West Ridge. Class 3. First ascent August 6, 1939, by Ted Waller, David Brower, and Norman Clyde. Gain the saddle between Deerhorn Mountain and The Minster from either the north or south; a southern approach to this saddle is easier if it is approached from the left (west). From the saddle proceed up a wide scree chute, then move right into another scree chute and climb up to the ridge, meeting it to the right of a small peak. Climb the ridge until progress is stopped by a gendarme. Drop down about 60 feet on the northeast side of the ridge and traverse southeast before climbing up to the notch behind the gendarme. Go to the left of the pillars in this notch to reach the ridge crest. Continue up the ridge to the northwest peak, which is climbed by means of ledges on its north side. Descend to the notch between the peaks, and climb the southeast peak. *Variation:* First ascent July 2, 1989, by Don Borad. The northwest peak can be easily bypassed on its southwest side via some rock slabs. This is followed by a horizontal traverse to the notch between the two peaks.

Subsidiary Peaks of Deerhorn Mountain. There are two small peaks on the southeast ridge. The southeast peak was first climbed August 3, 1939, by DeWitt Allen and Fritz Lippman via a chute/chimney on its southeast side. Class 4.

The Minster (3740 m+; 12,240 ft+)

This ridge of pinnacles was traversed from east to west on August 3, 1939, by Ted Waller, Don Woods, and Edward Koskinen.

West Spur (3817 m; 12,640 ft+)

First ascent August 8, 1940, by William Morrison, Richard Kauffman, and Norman Roth, from East Lake.

From Vidette Creek. Class 2. First ascent by Arkel Erb, Andy Smatko, Tom Ross, Frede Jensen, David Oyler, and Mike McNicholas. Climb to the saddle north of the peak, and follow the ridge to the summit.

West Vidette *(3820 m+; 12,560 ft+)*

East Slopes and South Ridge. Class 2. First ascent 1926 by Norman Clyde. Climb to the saddle south of the peak and follow the ridge to the summit.

Northeast Chute. Class 2. Climb the chute to the saddle north of the summit and follow the ridge to the top.

East Vidette *(3766 m; 12,350 ft)*

East Ridge. Class 3. First ascent 1910 by a Sierra Club party. Hike to the basin southeast

of the peak from the John Muir Trail and climb the east ridge. This is a nice class 3 climb.

North Side. Class 3–4 routes can be found on this side of the peak.

West Chute. Class 4. First ascent by Arkel Erb and Mike McNicholas. Climb a steep, shallow chute (loose rock!) that ends about 300 yards south of the summit on the south ridge. Follow the ridge to the summit.

Southeast Chute. Class 1–2. A scree chute leads from the basin southeast of the peak to the summit. This is a good descent route.

East Spur *(3886 m; 12,735 ft)*

First ascent July 14, 1940, by Jim Harkins and Pat Goldsworthy.

East Vidette from Bullfrog Lake (photo by Walter L. Huber, Sequoia and Kings Canyon National Parks)

Mt. Stanford   *(4259 m; 13,963 ft)*

This is the "shyest" major peak in the High Sierra. Most of the other major peaks can be seen from great distances. In contrast, Mt. Stanford is prominent only from Vidette Creek and from the top of Gregory's Monument. The peak can be seen from the John Muir Trail north of Forester Pass; it is the tall, dark cliff to the west. It makes up for its lack of prominence by the quality of its climbing.

The south peak is Gregory's Monument, and the higher north peak is Mt. Stanford.

South Ridge. Class 3. First ascent August 1, 1896, by Bolton Brown. Gregory's Monument is reached by going east from Harrison Pass over easy slopes. Descend the north side of Gregory's Monument by making a delicate class 3 move over a chockstone. Descend to a ledge on the east side of the south ridge; the ledge is about 100 feet below the ridge crest. Traverse the ledge to a point east of the summit and scramble to the top. (This is much easier than it looks from the summit of Gregory's Monument.)

West Face. Class 3. Descended August 1, 1896, by Bolton Brown. From the north side of Harrison Pass climb the first chute north of Gregory's Monument. This follows a steep ramp, which goes up and left to a small waterfall. Follow this upward for about 500 feet to a narrow chute filled with talus. This chute ends on the south ridge of Mt. Stanford.

West Face and North Ridge. Class 3. First ascent August 1940 by Art Argiewicz and party. The northern portion of the west face can be ascended to the north ridge. Follow the north ridge to the summit.

North Ridge. Class 3. First ascent August 4, 1939, by David Brower and Norman Clyde. Climb to the ridge north of Mt. Stanford from Deerhorn Saddle. The most difficult portion of the north ridge is the upper part. The north ridge can also be reached from Bubbs Creek.

East Face. Class 3. First ascent August 1947 by James Harkins and others. A steep chute descends directly from the summit just south of the east arete. Climb either the chute or the face to the left.

Peak 4200m+

(13,760 ft+; 0,8 mi SE of Mt. Stanford; UTM 755621)

West Ridge. Class 3. First ascent June 3, 1934, by Hervey Voge and David Brower.

Attain the west ridge of this peak from the south and follow the west ridge to the summit.

Southeast Face. Class 4. Descended June 3, 1934, by David Brower and Hervey Voge. This follows the shallow chute which descends from the east ridge at a point near the summit. There is a 20-foot class 4 pitch in this chute.

Caltech Peak   *(4216 m; 13,832 ft)*

Southeast Slopes. Class 2. First ascent June 22, 1926, by Norman Clyde.

East Ridge. Class 3. First ascent June 8, 1963, by Arkel Erb, Gordon MacCleod, Tom Ross, and Andy Smatko.

West Face. Class 3 via any of the many chutes.

Junction Peak   *(4220 m+; 13,888 ft)*

West Ridge. Class 3. Follow the ridge from Forester Pass, either crossing over or traversing south of the peak that separates Forester Pass from Ski Mountaineers Pass. Once on the main peak, stay south of the ridge and climb any combination of chutes or gullies to the summit.

North Buttress. III, 5.7. First ascent June 17, 1972, by John Rupley and Fred Beckey. Climb just to the right (west) of the crest of the buttress. There is some extremely loose rock on this route.

East Couloir. Class 3–4. Descended 1956 by Carl Heller, Kermit Ross, and Bob Stein. Climb the northernmost of the two couloirs on the east side of the peak.

Southeast Ridge. Class 4. First ascent August 21, 1929, by Albert Ellingwood. Follow the ridge from Shepherd Pass to the summit.

South Face. Class 3. First ascent July 17, 1982, by Nancy Gordon, Dave Dykeman, Ruth Armentrout, and David Lesikar. From Lake 3806m (12,460 ft) ascend toward a u-shaped notch on the southeast ridge of the peak. Follow the southeast ridge to the summit.

South Ridge. Class 3. First ascent August 8, 1889, by E. B. Shepherd and E. N. Anderson. Follow the knife-edged ridge from Diamond Mesa to the summit of Junction Peak. The easiest route onto Diamond Mesa is at its extreme southern end. It is necessary to drop down approximately 100 feet on the west side of the south ridge just before reaching the summit.

Mt. Keith *(4260 m; 13,977 ft)*

Northwest Face. Class 2. First ascent July 6, 1898, by Robert Price, C. B. Bradley, Jennie Price, and J. C. Shinn. Climb loose boulders and scree from the upper lakes of Center Basin.

Southwest Ridge. Class 3. First ascent 1916 by a Sierra Club party. This ridge rising from Junction Pass is a nice climb.

South Face. Class 2. First ascent 1922 by Norman Clyde. A chute descends the south face of Mt. Keith from a point just west of the summit. The chute is full of loose scree, and it makes a nice descent route. In the early season, when the chute is full of snow, it is a fine climb.

Northeast Slopes. Class 2.

"Courte-Echelle"

(4020 m+; 0.7 mi NE of Mt. Keith)

This peak has also been called "Bat Pinnacle." It is quite prominent from the Shepherd Pass Trailhead. It can be reached by traversing from the summit of Mt. Keith, or by ascending directly from Center Basin or the upper part of the Shepherd Pass Trail. The summit block was first climbed August 10, 1963, by Arkel Erb and Sy Ossofsky, who used aid (a shoulder-stand) and a piton to overcome a slight overhang.

Center Peak *(3880 m+; 12,760 ft)*

East Face. Class 2. First ascent July 5, 1898, by C. G. Bradley. This is a straightforward climb from Center Basin.

North Face. Class 3. First ascent May 22, 1934, by David Brower and Hervey Voge. There are three talus chutes on the north side of Center Peak. Climb the center chute and leave it via the chute that leads up to the northwest buttress of the peak. Follow the buttress to a saddle. From the saddle, stay on the west side of the northwest buttress to a point about 200 feet below the summit. Zigzag to the summit from here.

Northwest Face. Class 3. First ascent July 26, 1952, by Phillip Berry and Frank Tarver. This climb begins about 100 yards south of the steepest part of the north face. Climb the northwest face to a tunnel at its top. From the tunnel, ledges lead to the summit.

Mt. Bradley *(4043 m; 13,289 ft)*

West Face. Class 2. First ascent July 5, 1898, by Robert Price, Jennie Price, J. Shinn,

and Lalla Harris. This climb follows the talus chute that descends directly from the summit, as seen from Center Basin. The chute forks about three-fourths of the way up. Take the right branch, which leads to the saddle between the two summits of Mt. Bradley. The high point is the northern summit; it is reached by climbing a narrow chute on its southeast side.

South Ridge. Class 2. First ascent 1966 by Steve Rogero, Gary Bowen, and Dick Beach. Follow the ridge from Courte-Echelle.

East Ridge. Class 3. First ascent October 27, 1948, by Fred L. Jones. This long climb begins along Symmes Creek in the Owens Valley. Stay on the southern side of the ridge, passing many saddles and pinnacles, for 8,000 feet of gain to the summit. There is a remarkable amount of brush on this ridge.

North Slope. Class 2. Climb the long, barren north slope from the head of Pinyon Creek.

Northwest Ridge. Class 2–3. First ascent August 31, 1948, by Fred L. Jones. Follow the ridge from Center Basin Crag No. 5.

Center Basin Crags

(3820 m+–3840 m+; 12,480 ft+)

The Center Basin Crags are on the Sierra crest north of Mt. Bradley. There are five crags, and they are numbered from north to south. They are composed of loose rock. The notch north of crag No. 2 has been reached by traversing across the western side of the ridge south of crag No. 1. The notch between crags No. 3 and No. 4 is reached by traversing to it from the large scree gully that leads from Center Basin to the saddle north of crag No. 5.

"Center Basin Crag No. 1"

(3820 m+; UTM 797664)

South Ridge. Class 5. First ascent August 29, 1953, by Phillip Berry and party.

North Ridge. Class 4. First ascent September 1, 1984, by Dick Beach and Bob Good. Traverse the west side of the ridge from Peak 3926m (12,910 ft).

"Center Basin Crag No. 2"

(3820 m+; UTM 799661)

South Ridge. Class 4. First ascent July 1940 by David Brower and Bruce Meyer.

North Face. II, 5.6. First ascent September

1, 1984, by Dick Beach and Bob Good. Climb the crack that leads directly to the summit.

"Center Basin Crag No. 3"

(3820 m+; UTM 799661)

North Ridge. I, 5.8. First ascent July 1940 by David Brower and Bruce Meyer. One steep, exposed pitch leads to the summit from the notch between crags No. 2 and No. 3.

South Ridge. I, 5.6. First ascent August 1953 by David Brower and Phil Berry. A 50-foot 5.6 pitch is encountered; climb from the notch between crags No. 3 and No. 4.

"Center Basin Crag No. 4"

(3840 m+; UTM 799660)

North Ridge. I, 5.6. First ascent July 1940 by David Brower and Bruce Meyer. Two pitches over some big, loose rocks lead to the summit from the notch between crags No. 3 and No. 4.

"Center Basin Crag No. 5"

(3840 m+; UTM 800659)

This is a class 2 scramble from the north.

University Peak   *(4142 m; 13,632 ft)*

Southeast Ridge. Class 2. Follow the southern side of the ridge from University Pass.

South Slopes. Class 1. First ascent July 12, 1896, by Joseph LeConte, Helen M. Gompertz, Estelle Miller, and Belle Miller. Follow the easy southern slopes from Center Basin.

Northwest Side. Class 2. First ascent 1899 by Vernon L. Kellogg and others. Climb to the top of University Shoulder from Kearsarge

Center Basin Crags from the east (photo by R. J. Secor)

University Peak from the northwest (photo by Walter L. Huber, Sequoia and Kings Canyon National Parks)

University Peak and vicinity

KEARSARGE PASS
BIG POTHOLE LAKE
ONION VALLEY ROAD
GILBERT LAKE
BULLFROG LK.
NAMELESS PYRAMID
LITTLE POTHOLE LK.
KEARSARGE LAKES
HEART LAKE
KEARSARGE PINNACLES
BENCH LAKE
SLIM LAKE
ROBINSON LAKE
VIDETTE MEADOW
MATLOCK LAKE
UNIVERSITY SHOULDER
UNIVERSITY PEAK
BUBBS CREEK
JOHN MUIR TRAIL
EAST VIDETTE
VIDETTE LAKES
UNIVERSITY PASS
CENTER BASIN CRAGS
MT. BRADLEY
CENTER BASIN

N

0   ½ MILE

Lakes. Traverse southeast and follow the easy southwest or south slopes to the top. *Variation:* Class 3. First ascent August 14, 1932, by Walter A. Starr, Jr. Climb the northwest ridge from University Shoulder.

North Face. Class 3. First ascent by Norman Clyde. From Slim Lake climb a steep talus slope to the eastern end of a knife-edged ridge. Follow the ridge to the summit.

Northeast Face. III, 5.7. First ascent July 1968 by Fred Beckey, Joe Brown, and Dan Clements. This route climbs the prominent wall above Slim Lake. Class 3 gullies lead to the massive part of the face. Six hundred feet of moderate rock climbing lead to the upper part of the northeast ridge.

Northeast Ridge. Class 4. The best approach for this ridge is from Robinson Lake.

East Slopes. Class 3. This climb begins in the basin just north of University Pass.

Independence Peak *(3579 m; 11,744 ft)*

This is a nice climb from Onion Valley. The north ridge is class 3, as is the south ridge, which is reached from Robinson Lake.

"Nameless Pyramid"

(3669 m; 11,920 ft+; 0.2 mi S of Big Pothole Lake)

This is a contradictory name for a small peak that is easily seen from the Owens Valley; its summit fin is class 5.

North Ridge. Class 3. First ascent July 1952 by Ted Matthes, Frank Tarver, and Phillip Berry. Follow the ridge from Kearsarge Pass.

East Face. III, 5.8. First ascent May 1968 by Burt Turney and Chuck Ray. This route follows the prominent crack system that diagonals up the face from left to right. The crack system ends at a notch high on the north ridge of the peak. Further reading: *Summit,* October 1975, pp. 10–13.

Kearsarge Pinnacles

(3560 m+–3660 m+; 11,680 ft+–12,000 ft+)

These interesting pinnacles are located south of Kearsarge Lakes. The quality of rock varies from excellent to extremely rotten. On July 6, 1981, Dick Beach and Dave King traversed every single bump on this ridge from northwest to southeast. Many more pinnacles in the vicinity are more interesting and beautiful than the "official" twelve listed here.

"Kearsarge Pinnacle No. 1"

(3640 m+; 12,000 ft+; UTM 769682)

Northwest Ridge. Class 3. First ascent July 28, 1935, by May Pridham, Niles Werner, and Pam Coffin. Approach this ridge from the top of the chute between pinnacles No. 1 and No. 2, or traverse from the top of the chute between pinnacles No. 3 and No. 4.

"Kearsarge Pinnacle No. 2"

(3640 m+; 12,000 ft+; UTM 768683)

Northwest Ridge. Class 3. First ascent July 28, 1935, by May Pridham, Niles Werner, and Pam Coffin. Ascend the ridge from the top of the gully between pinnacles No. 3 and No. 4.

"Kearsarge Pinnacle No. 3"

(3640 m+; 11,920 ft+; UTM 767684)

Northwest Ridge. Class 4. First ascent August 1, 1939, by Ted Waller, Don Woods, David Nelson, and Edward Koskinen. Climb the ridge from the top of the notch between pinnacles No. 3 and No. 4.

"Kearsarge Pinnacle No. 4"

(3660 m+; 12,000 ft+; UTM 766686)

Southeast Ridge. Class 3. First ascent August 1, 1939, by Ted Waller, Don Woods, David Nelson, and Edward Koskinen. Climb the ridge from the notch between pinnacles No. 3 and No. 4.

"Kearsarge Pinnacle No. 5"

(3580 m; 11,760 ft+; UTM 763687)

This pinnacle can be climbed from the notch between pinnacles No. 5 and No. 6.

"Kearsarge Pinnacle No. 6"

(3580 m+; 11,760 ft+; UTM 762688)

Southeast Ridge. Class 3. First ascent August 18, 1954, by Dwight Ericsson from the notch between pinnacles No. 5 and No. 6.

West Face. II, 5.6. First ascent July 1970 by Liesl Day and Richard Hechtel. From the top of the gully between pinnacles No. 6 and No. 7, traverse east into a gully and climb over an overhang and up ledges and cracks to the base of a prominent open book. Ascend this book about halfway and traverse right on a small ledge until another, higher ledge can be reached via a shallow crack. Follow the ledge to a large shoulder south of the summit. Steep rock then leads to the top of the pinnacle.

Kearsarge Pinnacles (photo by Sequoia and Kings Canyon National Parks)

"Kearsarge Pinnacle No. 7"

(3620 m+; 11,840 ft+; UTM 761690)

This pinnacle is class 2 from the notch between pinnacles No. 6 and No. 7.

Northeast Face. II, 5.4. First ascent June 13, 1971, by Scott Evans and Doug Kinzy. There is a prominent gully on this face that is visible from Kearsarge Lakes. Begin by climbing the less prominent gully 30 feet to the east of this main gully. The first pitch (5.4) follows this gully and passes an overhang on the right. After about 200 feet the route crosses the main gully and continues up on the right for several class 4 pitches. Aim for the chute that separates the two summits of pinnacle No. 7. A class 4 pitch on the right side of this chute leads to a point directly beneath the western summit. A short traverse left leads to the notch between the two summits. Either summit is class 3 from here.

"Kearsarge Pinnacle No. 8"

(3620 m+; 11,920 ft+; UTM 759690)

In the words of Dick Beach, "This pinnacle stops the traffic!"

Southeast Face. Class 5. First ascent July 1932 by Glen Dawson, Thomas Rawles, and Hans Leschke. Climb the steep face rising above the notch between No. 7 and No. 8.

Northwest Face. II, 5.8. First ascent July 6, 1981, by Dave King and Dick Beach. Climb a crack system above the notch between pinnacles No. 8 and No. 9. Most of this climb is easy class 5; there is one 30-foot 5.8 pitch.

"Kearsarge Pinnacle No. 9"

(3620 m+; 11,920 ft+; UTM 759691)

Northwest Ridge. Class 2 from the notch between pinnacles No. 9 and No. 10.

Southeast Ridge. Class 4. First ascent July 25, 1924, by R. Howard. From the top of the chute between pinnacles No. 8 and No. 9, climb the south side of the small pinnacle rising above the notch. It is an easy scramble from the top of the pinnacle to the top of pinnacle No. 9.

"Kearsarge Pinnacle No. 10"

(3645 m; 11,680 ft+; UTM 757693)

First ascent 1932 by Hans Leschke, Glen Dawson, and Owen Ward. Class 2 from the notch between pinnacles No. 9 and No. 10, or by traversing from pinnacles No. 11 and No. 12.

Kearsarge Pinnacles Nos. 8 and 9 (photo by Sequoia and Kings Canyon National Parks)

"Kearsarge Pinnacle No. 11"

(3560 m+; 11,680 ft+; UTM 754695)

First ascent 1932 by Hans Leschke, Glen Dawson, and Owen Ward. Class 2 from either pinnacle No. 10 or No. 12.

"Kearsarge Pinnacle No. 12"

(3560 m+; 11,680 ft+; UTM 753695)

First ascent 1932 by Owen Ward, Glen Dawson, and Hans Leschke. Class 2 from pinnacle No. 11 or via the northwest slopes from Bullfrog Lake.

Wrinkles

Junction Meadow. Or perhaps I should say Junction *Meadows.* There are two Junction Meadows in the High Sierra, just close enough together to cause confusion. If you are making arrangements to meet someone, or pick up a cache of food, it is prudent to specify either Junction Meadow (Bubbs Creek) or Junction Meadow (Kern River).

Skiing across the Kings–Kern Divide. Those skiing from Mt. Whitney to Yosemite will find this to be either a minor inconvenience or an impassable barrier. This depends on the amount of snowfall over the previous winter. Light snow years may leave the south side completely bare, but a heavy snow year can build up cornices atop the passes. On the other hand, a friend of mine skied across the Kings–Kern Divide during a light snow year, and went through a few minutes of stark terror of an intensity not experienced before in his thirty-year mountaineering career. The "snow" slope turned out to be a huge sheet of ice!

Ski Mountaineers Pass has scree on both of its sides during the summer, but the angle is moderate, and it may be passable in the winter or spring; a cornice has formed here, however, so exercise caution. Forester Pass has a trail over it, but the south side of the pass is a cliff; the north side is rather gentle. Andy's Foot Pass is dramatically steep on its north side, but it has been skied. Harrison Pass is very steep and icy on its north side. Ericsson Pass is not as steep as Harrison Pass, and this combined with Deerhorn Saddle may be a good alternative route. Lucy's Foot Pass and Milly's Foot Pass, both class 3, are dramatically steep for skiers. Thunder Pass will probably be passable, but it is far away from the Sierra crest.

The best alternative may be to bypass the entire Kings–Kern Divide by crossing Shepherd Pass and then Junction Pass.

University Pass. This route appears to offer a one-day direct route from Onion Valley to Center Basin, but this is only the case for experienced cross-country hikers. All others will find it much quicker and easier to approach Center Basin via the Kearsarge Pass and John Muir trails.

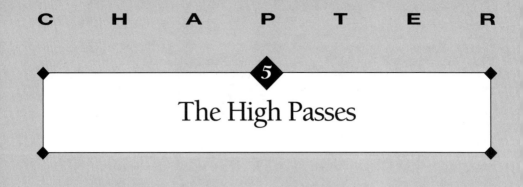

The High Passes

THIS REGION COVERS THE SIERRA CREST FROM Kearsarge Pass to Taboose Pass; it is bounded on the west by the South Fork of the Kings River.

The title of this chapter refers to Baxter Pass, Sawmill Pass, and Taboose Pass. These passes are not the highest in the Sierra, but they seem to be the highest, because each requires gaining over 6,000 feet of elevation to reach the summits from the trailheads. The Sierra crest divides the Great Basin from the Pacific Ocean watersheds, and a hike up one of these passes moves the hiker from desert to Arctic conditions. Early in the morning a hiker can walk across a plain of brush and sand, then follow the trail through barren talus fields. But at the summit of a high pass, the world comes alive again, with meadows and wonderful vistas.

History

Indians had crossed Kearsarge Pass and descended Bubbs Creek long before a party of prospectors, including a man named Bubbs, followed this route in 1863. The following year the California Geological Survey crossed the Sierra crest via this route after their exploration of Kings Canyon. John Muir visited this region in 1873, and the shepherds overran the area over the next twenty years. Taboose and Sawmill passes were used to move sheep between the Owens Valley and High Sierra meadows. Bolton Brown descended the South Fork of the Kings River in 1895, and climbed Mt. Clarence King and explored Rae Lakes in the following years.

It seems logical that a region which features passes with 6,000 feet of gain must have some mountain ridges with 8,000 feet to 9,000 feet of gain—and it does. These ridges are east of the Sierra crest, face the desert, and are therefore dry. They were first explored by

Fred L. Jones in the late 1940s and early 1950s during his studies of the Sierra Nevada bighorn sheep. These routes are seldom repeated, but the few individuals who have climbed these ridges have the utmost respect and admiration for Fred L. Jones.

Maps

United States Geological Survey: 7.5-minute series: Kearsarge Peak, Mt. Clarence King, The Sphinx, Aberdeen, Mt. Pinchot, Marion Peak, Fish Springs; 15-minute series: Mt. Pinchot, Marion Peak, Big Pine; national park maps: Sequoia and Kings Canyon National Parks and Vicinity (1:125,000).

United States Forest Service: John Muir Wilderness and the Sequoia–Kings Canyon National Parks Backcountry (1:63,360).

Wilderness Permits

For east-side entry to the John Muir Wilderness: Inyo National Forest, Mt. Whitney Ranger District, Lone Pine, CA 93545.

For west-side entry to the Kings Canyon National Park backcountry: Sequoia and Kings Canyon National Parks, Three Rivers, CA 93271.

Roads

Onion Valley Road

The Onion Valley Road provides access to the Kearsarge Pass Trail and the Golden Trout Lake Trail. It is described in Chapter 4: The Kings–Kern Divide.

Oak Creek Road

The Oak Creek Road leads to the trailhead for the Baxter Pass Trail. Leave Highway 395 2.4 miles north of Independence or 23.7 miles south of Big Pine. The road goes west past the Mt. Whitney Fish Hatchery for 1.2

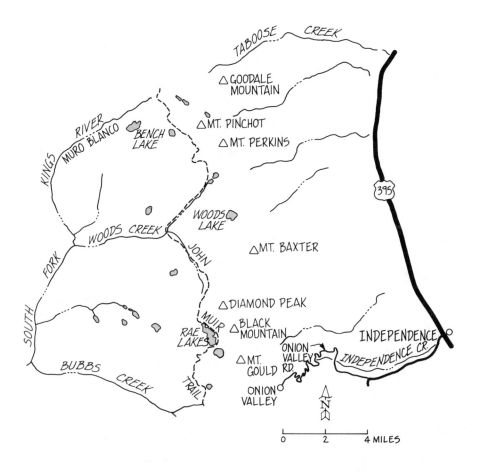

miles to a fork. Go right, passing Oak Creek Campground, for another 4.5 miles to the end of the road near the North Fork of Oak Creek.

Division Creek Powerhouse and Scotty Spring Road

This maze of roads leads to the trailheads for Sawmill Pass and Armstrong Canyon. Leave Highway 395 8.6 miles north of Independence or 18.0 miles south of Big Pine. Go west on the Black Rock Springs Road for 0.8 mile to its junction with the Tinemaha Road. Turn right and go north on the Tinemaha Road for 1.2 miles to the junction with the Division Creek Powerhouse Road. Go left onto the road leading to the Division Creek Powerhouse and, after 1.5 miles, you come to the powerhouse and the hikers' trailhead for the Sawmill Pass Trail.

There is also a stock trailhead for the Sawmill Pass Trail. Leave the Tinemaha Road 0.7 mile north of its junction with the Sawmill Creek Road. The road goes left for 2.0 miles to the trailhead along Sawmill Creek.

The trailhead for Armstrong Canyon is beyond the Division Creek Powerhouse. Continue up the road for another 2.0 miles to a fork. Go right another 0.5 mile to Scotty Spring. This is the limit for most cars. There is a difficult four-wheel-drive road that climbs up into Armstrong Canyon from this point.

Taboose Creek Road

The Taboose Creek Road is the driving approach to the trailhead for the Taboose Pass Trail. Leave Highway 395 13.7 miles north of Independence or 12.1 miles south of Big Pine. Take the Taboose Creek Road west to a four-way junction 0.4 mile from Highway 395. Go straight through this junction another 0.8 mile to another four-way junction. Go straight through this second junction another 0.5 mile to a fork, passing Taboose Campground along the way. Go right at the fork, through a gate (be sure to leave it as you found it, either open or closed) to another fork 2.1 miles beyond the previous fork. Take the right fork 1.9 miles to the trailhead for Taboose Pass. This last section of the road is rough, but most two-wheel-drive vehicles should be able to reach the trailhead with little trouble.

Kings Canyon Highway (Highway 180)

The Paradise Valley Trail starts from the end of Highway 180 in Kings Canyon. This trailhead is described in Chapter 6: Monarch Divide and the Cirque Crest.

Trails

Kearsarge Pass Trail (7 miles)

The Kearsarge Pass Trail leads from Onion Valley over Kearsarge Pass to meet the John Muir Trail between Charlotte Lake and Bullfrog Lake. It is described in Chapter 4: The Kings–Kern Divide.

Golden Trout Lake Trail (2¹/₄ miles)

This is a popular day hike from Onion Valley. Golden Trout Lake is a heavily used camping area. Wood campfires are prohibited anywhere in this drainage.

The trail goes north out of Onion Valley, starting next to the ruins of the old store. A wide, rocky path goes up to the base of the waterfall. The trail fords the creek and climbs the slope east of the waterfall; this part is steep and loose and it is easy to miss the trail. At the top of the cliff the trail crosses the stream again before climbing a small ridge south of the stream. The trail eventually descends to the stream and follows it to a wet meadow. Skirt the meadow on the south side and head up a small canyon to Golden Trout Lake.

From the meadow, a trail goes north to the two unnamed lakes in the basin north of Golden Trout Lake. This trail, which is approximately 1³/₄ miles long, is the approach for North Dragon Pass.

John Muir Trail (23 miles)

The John Muir Trail goes north from its junction with the Kearsarge Pass Trail and the Charlotte Lake Trail. (Charlotte Lake is 1 mile west of this junction.) The John Muir Trail climbs 2¹/₄ miles to the top of Glen Pass. The trail descends the rough and difficult northern side of the pass for 2 miles to a junction with the Sixty Lake Basin Trail near the highest of the Rae Lakes. (Rae Lakes is a beautiful but heavily used area. There is a one-night camp limit along the John Muir Trail between Glen Pass and Woods Creek, and at Dragon Lake; wood fires are prohibited anywhere in Kings Canyon National Park above 10,000 feet.) The trail crosses to the eastern side of Rae Lakes and gradually descends the South Fork of Woods Creek approximately 2³/₄ miles to the junction with the Baxter Pass Trail. In this area the John Muir Trail crosses to the west bank of Woods Creek and descends 4 miles to meet the Paradise Valley Trail as it comes up Woods Creek.

The John Muir Trail fords Woods Creek and goes upstream 3¹/₂ miles to the junction with the Sawmill Pass Trail. The trail climbs another 1 mile to a use trail that leads down to beautiful Twin Lakes, beneath Mt. Cedric Wright. The John Muir Trail climbs to a high, rocky basin, with occasional small meadows, and then to the top of Pinchot Pass, 3 miles from Twin Lakes. The trail descends the north side of the pass, with many steep switchbacks, 1¹/₂ miles to Lake Marjorie, which is located in the middle of a scenic basin with many smaller lakes. The trail descends another 1¹/₂ miles to the junction with the Bench Lake Trail, fords the stream, and meets the Taboose Pass Trail ¹/₄ mile from the Bench Lake Trail junction. The John Muir Trail then makes a steep descent to the South Fork of the Kings River for 1³/₄ miles to meet what is left of the Cartridge Pass Trail.

Sixty Lake Basin Trail (4 miles)

Sixty Lake Basin is one of the most beautiful places in the High Sierra. It is heavily used, however. The National Park Service has a one-night camp limit in the basin, and wood fires are prohibited.

The Sixty Lake Basin Trail leaves the John

Muir Trail at the northwest shore of the highest lake of the Rae Lakes, climbs over the ridge just south of Fin Dome, and drops into Sixty Lake Basin. The trail gradually descends the basin and eventually disappears along the eastern shore of the northernmost lake.

Bench Lake Trail (2 miles)

The Bench Lake Trail leaves the John Muir Trail just south of the Taboose Pass Trail junction. The trail crosses a meadow, descends slightly, and then contours across the bench from which the lake gets its name. The trail makes two easy stream crossings before reaching the north shore of Bench Lake. The view of Arrow Peak from the lake is one of the classic views in the Sierra. The trail ends at the western shore of the lake, 2 miles from the John Muir Trail.

Paradise Valley Trail (15 miles)

The Paradise Valley Trail follows the South Fork of the Kings River to the mouth of Woods Creek, and then follows Woods Creek to the John Muir Trail.

The trail starts at the end of Highway 180 in Kings Canyon. It goes upstream for 2 miles to meet the Bubbs Creek Trail. The Paradise Valley Trail continues up the South Fork of the Kings River for 8 miles, goes past Mist Falls and through Paradise Valley itself, and crosses the river upstream from Woods Creek. The trail ascends the north side of the Woods Creek drainage for 5 miles to meet the John Muir Trail.

Baxter Pass Trail (13 miles)

This is a long, hard hike. Fortunately, the first part of the trail is in the shade, and this makes this trail unique among the trails that lead over the Sierra crest from the floor of Owens Valley. The Baxter Pass Trail starts at the end of the Oak Creek Road and follows an old road on the north side of Oak Creek. After a short distance the road forks; the trail goes right and makes a steep ascent. It soon crosses to the south side of the creek, switchbacks up the canyon floor, goes around a rocky rib, and crosses to the north side of the creek. The trail continues to climb, and reaches the alpine basin of Summit Meadow at approximately 10,800 feet (Summit Meadow is incorrectly placed on some maps). The last part of the ascent goes through a area of red, green, and black metamorphic rock to the summit of Baxter Pass, 8 miles from the trailhead.

The trail steeply descends the north side of the pass before skirting the north shore of the largest of the Baxter Lakes. The trail continues down the rocky basin, crosses a small stream and later, fords Baxter Creek before turning south and contouring far above the South Fork of Woods Creek. The Baxter Pass Trail meets the John Muir Trail 5 miles from the top of Baxter Pass, at an unsigned junction just below Dollar Lake.

Sawmill Pass Trail (13$^1\!/_2$ miles)

This is another long, hard hike. The hikers' trail begins near Division Creek Powerhouse and climbs for 1$^3\!/_4$ miles before meeting the stock trail that rises steeply from Sawmill Creek, 1$^1\!/_4$ miles below. The trail then climbs a steep, brush-covered slope before contouring into the Sawmill Creek drainage. (You can see the remains of the old sawmill at the lower end of The Hogsback.) The trail crosses the small stream north of The Hogsback and goes south over The Hogsback to Sawmill Meadow. The trail zigzags up a headwall, crosses the bench of Mule Lake, and makes two stream crossings while climbing up to beautiful Sawmill Lake, 6$^1\!/_2$ miles from where the hikers' trail meets the stock trail. Above the lake, the trail crosses a timberline basin and makes a steep ascent to the top of Sawmill Pass, 1$^3\!/_4$ miles from Sawmill Lake. The trail makes a gentle descent from the pass across fields of talus and sand before leading to the alpine basin of the headwaters of Woods Creek. At the lower end of this basin, the trail turns north and meets the John Muir Trail 3$^1\!/_2$ miles from the summit of Sawmill Pass.

Armstrong Canyon (5 miles)

Armstrong Canyon is used as the approach for climbing Mt. Perkins and Colosseum Mountain and for crossing Armstrong Col. It is a dry canyon, i.e., there is no running water in the canyon. Most visits to the canyon are during the spring, when snow can be melted for water. This "trail" is actually a former road. Over the years, the elements have combined forces to make the road impassable, even for four-wheel-drive vehicles.

The trailhead is beyond the Division Creek Powerhouse at Scotty Spring, the limit for most automobiles. The road makes one big zig and another big zag before climbing and contouring to the abandoned mines in Armstrong Canyon. A fork is encountered along the way; take the right fork. The road ends once it reaches the canyon itself, but it is an easy cross-country hike to the upper reaches of the canyon and from there to the base of Mt. Perkins.

Taboose Pass Trail (8¹/₄ miles)

The long, hard hike up Taboose Pass starts in the desert, and it passes through a seeming wasteland of talus with only the occasional bit of vegetation. But then you reach the summit of the pass, which has a breathtaking view of the headwaters of the South Fork of the Kings River, Bench Lake, and Arrow Peak. You enter another world atop Taboose Pass.

From the end of the Taboose Creek Road, the trail crosses the sandy desert floor before going left into the Taboose Creek drainage. The trail remains on the north side of the creek for a considerable distance, and then crosses the stream before climbing onto a bench. The trail then traverses west before crossing the creek just below a small waterfall. It continues to ascend the canyon, and passes through some small meadows with tarns just before reaching the summit of the pass, 5¹/₂ miles from the trailhead.

The trail gently descends the west side of the pass, through meadows with wild flowers in early season, for 1¹/₄ miles to a junction. The left fork goes 1¹/₂ miles farther to meet the John Muir Trail at its junction with the Bench Lake Trail. The right fork goes 1¹/₂ miles to meet the John Muir Trail along the South Fork of the Kings River before it makes its climb into Upper Basin.

Cross-Country Routes

Gardiner Pass (3429 m; 11,200 ft+)

Class 2. At one time there was a trail over Gardiner Pass, but it has been abandoned for a long time. Traces of it may still be seen, however.

The route begins at the western end of Charlotte Lake. Cross the outlet stream, skirt a small meadow on its southern side, and then cross the stream again to its northern side. Make a gradual descent through this basin, leaving Charlotte Creek far below. At approximately 10,000 feet go right, and cross the northern tributary stream of Charlotte Creek before making the zigzag climb to Gardiner Pass. It is ironic that you cross barren scree and talus in order to reach the forested summit of this pass. The route descends the steep, northern side of the pass and leads from ledge to ledge in the basin below. From the large lake at the bottom of this basin, climb a small rise and then make a steep descent to Gardiner Creek.

To reach Gardiner Basin, follow Gardiner Creek upstream. Cliffs are avoided by first climbing to the south and then traversing east to cross to the north side of Gardiner Creek at UTM 684763. It is best to approach Gardiner Basin from this point, staying high on the northern side of the basin to avoid many small cliffs.

"King Col"

(3540 m; 11,600 ft+; 1.0 mi W of Mt. Clarence King; UTM 695744)

Class 2. This has also been referred to as "Moulthrop Pass" after Paul Moulthrop, who crossed it in 1940. King Col provides direct access between Gardiner Basin and Woods Creek. From the lower end of Gardiner Basin, climb steep slopes to the gentle sandy slope leading northeast to the top of King Col. Descend the northeast side of the pass on steep, loose rock and sand. Descend the basin below by keeping west of the three lakes and stream. The big difficulty is crossing Woods Creek. If the water level is low, you may be able to ford the creek near the meadow opposite Castle Domes. If the water is high, then remain on the south side of Woods Creek and hike 1¹/₂ miles upstream to where the John Muir Trail crosses Woods Creek.

"Sixty Lake Col"

(3560 m+; 11,680 ft+; 1.0 mi S of Mt. Cotter)

Class 2. This pass provides access to Gardiner Basin from Sixty Lake Basin. Leave the Sixty Lake Basin Trail where the trail makes an abrupt turn to the north (at UTM 729751). Follow a use trail to the western side of a long, unnamed lake. From the lake, climb over talus and slabs to the low gap in the ridge south of Mt. Cotter. Just below this gap, follow ledges to cross the divide just north of the low point. Make a careful descent from the top of the ridge, picking your way through talus and ledges to skirt the east and north shores of Lake 3477m (11,394 ft). Before reaching the outlet of this lake, climb over the low ridge to the north and descend to the bowl just west of Mt. Cotter. Keep to the west of the lakes in this bowl. A direct descent of Gardiner Basin is best accomplished by keeping to the north and above the lakes in the basin, to avoid the many small cliffs. Of course, you can descend to any of the lakes in the basin by careful route finding.

"Basin Notch"

(3260 m+; 10,720 ft+; 0.9 mi NNW of Fin Dome)

Class 1. This is an easy cross-country route between Arrowhead Lake and Sixty Lake Basin. Leave the John Muir Trail at the outlet of Arrowhead Lake and go southwest to the little pass on the ridge north of Fin Dome. Cross-country travel is easy in Sixty Lake Basin.

"Rae Col"

(3560 m+; 11,680 ft+; 0.7 mi NNW of Glen Pass)

Class 2. This is a direct route from the basin north of Glen Pass to Sixty Lake Basin.

"Gould Pass"

(3820 m+; 12,800 ft+; 0.5 mi N of Gould Peak)

Class 2. Also known as "Dragon Pass," Gould Pass provides a direct route between Onion Valley and Rae Lakes. From Golden Trout Lake climb west and then north to the small notch on the ridge between Mt. Gould and Dragon Peak. (Alternatively, you can approach the top of the pass from the summit of Kearsarge Pass by skirting the summit of Mt. Gould and descending the ridge to the pass.) The west side of the pass is descended by means of a steep chute over loose rock to the lakes in the basin west of Dragon Peak. Boulder hop north to Dragon Lake to meet a use trail on its north shore that leads down to the Rae Lakes.

When approaching this pass from the west, make the final approach via the southern of two talus slopes.

"North Dragon Pass"

(3640 m+; 11,920 ft+; 0.7 mi N of Dragon Peak; UTM 775733)

Class 3. This pass is typically approached from Onion Valley via the unnamed lakes east of and below Dragon Peak. With this approach, it is necessary to first climb to 12,400 feet on the Sierra crest and then descend to North Dragon Pass. From the unnamed lakes, head for the v-shaped notch just north of Dragon Peak. Before reaching this notch, go right (north) toward a square-shaped peak. Pass this peak to the right (east) and remain on the eastern side of the crest while moving north to the actual pass. Pass another minor peak on its right (east) side, and then descend on scree down to Dragon Lake. A use trail on the north side of the lake leads to the John Muir Trail at Rae Lakes.

Both Gould Pass and North Dragon Pass are difficult cross-country routes, and should only be undertaken by experienced hikers. Many who have crossed these passes prefer the trails over Kearsarge Pass and Glen Pass as the easiest one-day route to Rae Lakes from Onion Valley.

North Dragon Pass is only open from December 15 to July 1 each year due to bighorn sheep restrictions.

"Lilley Pass"

(3660 m+; 11,920 ft+; 0.5 mi W of Kearsarge Peak)

Class 2. Named in honor of Barbara Lilley, this pass is typically used by skiers who wish to ski Sardine Canyon with the minimum amount of climbing and the maximum amount of vertical feet skied. Leave the Golden Trout Lake Trail below the unnamed lakes east of Dragon Peak and climb to the lowest saddle west of Kearsarge Peak. A chute leads to the saddle; it is filled with disagreeable loose rock and dirt during the height of the summer.

Sardine Canyon

Sardine Canyon is a barren, desolate place during the height of the summer, but in the spring it is a fantastic ski run. It is approached by leaving the Onion Valley Road approximately 8 miles from Independence, where a dirt road leads north, blocked by a locked gate. Hike up the road to where it forks. Take the left fork, which soon turns into a long-abandoned trail that gets fainter as it approaches Sardine Lake. (This lake, despite its name, has no fish.)

Parker Lakes

These lakes are within the California Bighorn Sheep Zoological Area, which is open only from December 15 to July 1 each year. The approach is the same as for Sardine Canyon, except that you continue hiking north where the gated road forks. This leads to Little Onion Valley and, after crossing the South Fork of Oak Creek, the route goes up

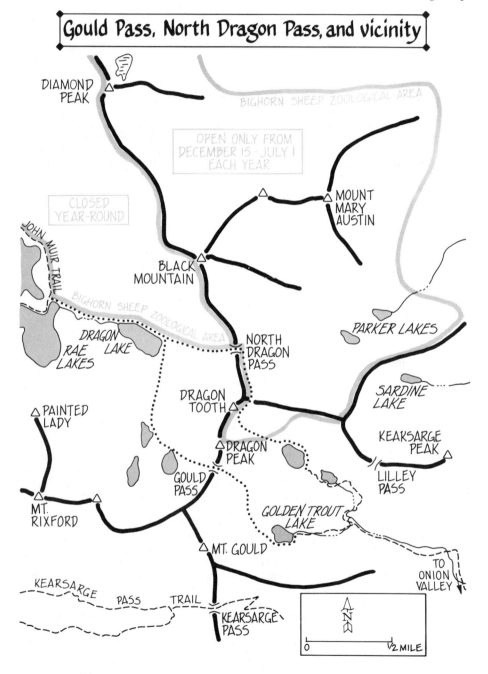

Gould Pass, North Dragon Pass, and vicinity

DIAMOND PEAK

BIGHORN SHEEP ZOOLOGICAL AREA

OPEN ONLY FROM DECEMBER 15 - JULY 1 EACH YEAR

CLOSED YEAR-ROUND

JOHN MUIR TRAIL

MOUNT MARY AUSTIN

BLACK MOUNTAIN

BIGHORN SHEEP ZOOLOGICAL AREA

PARKER LAKES

DRAGON RAE LAKES LAKE

NORTH DRAGON PASS

DRAGON TOOTH

SARDINE LAKE

PAINTED LADY

KEARSARGE PEAK

DRAGON PEAK

GOULD PASS

LILLEY PASS

MT. RIXFORD

GOLDEN TROUT LAKE

MT. GOULD

TO ONION VALLEY

KEARSARGE   PASS   TRAIL

KEARSARGE PASS

N

0   ½ MILE

the canyon to the lowest of the Parker Lakes. The upper lake is reached via ½ mile of talus hopping.

"Grasshopper Pass"

(3900 m+; 12,480 ft+; 0.3 mi E of Acrodectes Peak)

Class 3. This pass has also been named "Baxter Col," but Grasshopper Pass is used here to avoid confusion with Baxter Pass. If open to cross-country travel, it would provide direct access between Woods Lake and the Baxter Lakes. The pass is class 3 on its northern side (loose rock!) and class 2 on the south.

This pass is included only for the record, since it is in an area of Kings Canyon National Park that has been closed to all cross-country travel due to bighorn sheep restrictions.

"Arrow Pass"

(3540 m+; 11,600 ft+; 0.7 mi SE of Arrow Peak; UTM 684874)

Class 2. This is the direct route between Bench Lake and Paradise Valley. From Bench Lake head for the *second* saddle southeast of Arrow Peak (the first saddle has a cliff on its northern side). From the top of the pass, traverse west above the lake at the head of Arrow Creek before descending the creek to the lowest lake in the basin. Climb over the southwest spur of Pyramid Peak and descend the east side of the unnamed creek that leads down to Woods Creek.

An alternate route is to descend the east side of Arrow Creek to where it meets the South Fork of the Kings River and Woods Creek, in the upper part of Paradise Valley. A short pitch of class 3 is encountered at the waterfalls at the lower part of Arrow Creek.

"Explorer Pass"

(3720 m+; 12,240 ft+; 0.9 mi NE of Pyramid Peak)

Class 3; ice axe required. This route leads to upper Woods Creek from Bench Lake. From Bench Lake traverse southwest to the valley east of Arrow Pass. Ascend the valley to its head, and climb to the saddle immediately southwest of Peak 3891m (12,773 ft). The route involves ascending a steep chute, which usually contains hard snow well into the summer; the easiest route ascends the

slope to the east of the chute and ends about 100 feet east of the low point of the pass. Descend the basin, staying east of the stream and lakes, to the large lake east of Window Peak. Go southeast, passing a small lake on its south shore and cross its outlet. Descend the east side of the creek, through a lot of brush, to the John Muir Trail along Woods Creek.

The first pass southwest of Explorer Pass is class 2.

"Armstrong Col"

(3660 m+; 12,000 ft+; 0.8 mi N of Colosseum Mtn.)

Class 2. This is the approach for climbing Colosseum Mountain, Mt. Cedric Wright, Mt. Wynne, and Mt. Pinchot from Armstrong Canyon. Climb the chute at the head of Armstrong Canyon to the east shoulder of Peak 3705m (12,080 ft+), which leads to the plateau north of Colosseum Mountain. Descend from the plateau to the southwest before turning northwest to the John Muir Trail near Twin Lakes.

Muro Blanco

Class 2. To be precise, the Muro Blanco actually refers to the great white wall that descends from Arrow Ridge to the South Fork of the Kings River. The description here refers to a descent of the canyon. This trailless descent involves numerous varieties of brush, talus, and rock slabs—but also some small, beautiful meadows and forests, along with superb scenery. This is one of the classic bushwhacks of the High Sierra.

The entire route remains on the northwest side of the South Fork of the Kings River. From the John Muir Trail north of the river, follow the trail downstream past the Cartridge Pass Trail junction. The trail disappears when it passes through some boulders, but reappears in a grove of trees on the other side of the boulders. The trail soon disappears for good in a small meadow. The rest of the route is impossible to describe. General comments: Above the crossing of Kid Creek you have a choice of beating through brush near the river or traversing across talus high above. And the worst brush of the entire route is encountered 1½ miles before reaching the Paradise Valley Trail, near the mouth of Woods Creek.

Peaks

Mt. Bago (3618 m; 11,868 ft)

East Slope. Class 1 from Charlotte Lake. First ascent July 11, 1896, by Joseph LeConte and W. S. Gould. The south summit is the high point.

South Arete. IV, 5.7. First ascent September 1, 1974, by David Boyd and Paul Hurd. This route climbs the right-hand skyline (as seen from Junction Meadow) of an orange dihedral. One thousand feet of excellent rock is found on this climb.

The Parapet. III, 5.8. First ascent May 1982 by Rick Nolting and Fred Beckey. This climb is on the central portion of the south face of Mt. Bago. Begin by climbing a long chimney-and-gully system to a vertical, overhanging headwall which consists of flakes. This headwall leads to a long, easy ramp to an outside corner. Zigzag up another headwall, then traverse left across small holds to a shallow crack system. Easier climbing follows.

"Bubbs Creek Wall"

(3237 m; 10,617 ft; 1.4 mi NW of Mt. Bago)

This massive wall is about ½ mile southwest of Peak 3237m (10,617 ft).

Aquaman. III, 5.10+. First ascent July 1983 by Bill McConachie and Dick Leversee. The east side of the Bubbs Creek Wall has two obvious crack systems. This route climbs the right crack. Eight pitches of 5.7 and 5.8 lead to a 5.10 off-width inside corner, which ends 200 feet below the top.

The left crack was first climbed June 8–9, 1974, by Fred Beckey, Mike McGooey, and Mark Losleben.

Crystal Banzai. VI, 5.11, A3. First ascent August 1986 by Dick Leversee and Eddie Joe. One of the few grade VI routes in the High Sierra, this climbs the highest section of the Bubbs Creek Wall just to the left of center, following a band of white crystal from bottom to top. The route begins at a large pine tree about 100 yards up and right of a huge left-facing dihedral which marks the beginning of the crystal band. Climb up and left to a ramp that leads to Crystal Palace ledge. Climb the dihedral to its top and follow the Crystal Corner up and left, using bat hooks and bolts, to a small stance with two bolts. Climb up and slightly right to the main crack-and-corner system, which is followed

for five pitches to Zero Point Ledge. Two pitches of cracks lead up and left to a good ledge. A pitch to the right leads to a right-facing dihedral. Instead of climbing the dihedral, face climb to the left for 20 feet to a large flake; climb this and a thin crack to Dead Tree Ledge. Climb diagonally left to a blank, right-facing corner. From the corner, traverse left to easy knobs, which lead to the top. This seventeen-pitch route requires two complete sets of nuts (from tiny to 4-inch), skyhooks, bat hooks, and hammocks.

Charlotte Dome (3253 m; 10,690 ft)

This beautiful piece of rock was one of the earliest Sierra domes to be discovered outside of Yosemite Valley. In 1864, the California Geological Survey camped along Charlotte Creek, and Charles Hoffman sketched this dome. It was first climbed 102 years later, and in 1970, one of the world's finest rock climbs was discovered on its south face.

Charlotte Dome can be approached from either the west (the end of Highway 180 in Kings Canyon) or the east (from Onion Valley over Kearsarge Pass via Charlotte Lake). The consensus of most climbers is that the eastern approach is easier, but longer. Those approaching from the west should note that a use trail has appeared about 100 to 200 feet to the northwest of, and parallel to, Charlotte Creek. Bears have been known to raid food caches in this area.

North Ridge. Class 3. First ascent August 1966 by Ed Lane from Gardiner Pass. This is the usual descent route for climbs on the south face. Many parties make the mistake of descending too directly from the summit. It is better to go well north, beyond the small saddle behind the dome, before turning right and descending to the unnamed tributary of Charlotte Creek.

Neutron Dance. IV, 5.10d. First ascent 1985 by Jack Wenzel and Elizabeth Ammon. This ten-pitch route starts at a prominent orange dike on the southeast face. The first pitch is the crux. The rest of the climb is moderate, except for the summit pitch, which is 5.10a.

E. B. White. IV, 5.9. First ascent August 1979 by Allan Pietrasanta and Alan Bartlett. This route is on the eastern side of the south face of Charlotte Dome. There are two parallel water groves on this side of the face. Follow the left-hand groove, passing two

Charlotte Dome, South Face

bolts and one bolt-anchor belay, for several pitches. Go left and continue up cracks to where the angle lessens. Climb the headwall to the summit.

Classic South Face. III, 5.7. First ascent October 1970 by Galen Rowell, Chris Jones, and Fred Beckey. This justifiably popular route climbs the highest part of the south face. Start climbing from the top of the large recess at the lowest portion of the face. Two class 4 pitches up and right lead to a steep section, which is climbed by the most prominent crack to a big belay ledge. This is followed by some easy knobs to the Slot Pitch. Climb to the very top of the slot and belay from a small ledge on its left side. Climb a knobby face above the Slot Pitch to a wide ramp that leads to the right. Follow the ramp around an outside corner to the Furrow Pitch. The Furrow Pitch ends on a steep headwall, with a belay in a little nook. A long pitch in a left-facing corner is followed by a pitch up a steep, left-leaning crack, which ends on a huge ledge with a dead tree. One more easy pitch up and left leads to the top. A common mistake made on this route is not taking enough runners; six is not enough, and a dozen (with some doubles and triples) is not too many. And there are many possible variations on this climb; it seems that many parties end up too far to the right. But the quality of the rock and

magnificent surroundings usually make up for any route-finding errors. Further reading: Allen Steck and Steve Roper, *Fifty Classic Climbs of North America,* Sierra Club Books, San Francisco, 1979, pp. 294–99.

Charlotte's Web. IV, 5.8. First ascent August 1976 by Bart O'Brien and Dave Harden. This route is left of the Classic South Face route. Start climbing from near a solitary pine tree between a small recess on the south face and the larger recess of the Classic South Face route. About 100 feet of class 3 climbing ends on a flat ledge. Four pitches up and right lead to the base of a steep, shallow crack. Two long (165-foot) pitches are needed to climb the crack. The route continues straight up over beautiful knobs and chickenheads for several hundred feet to a large, sandy ledge with a dead tree. Climb the knob-covered face directly above the ledge. One more pitch of easy climbing leads to the summit. Further reading: *Summit,* June–July 1978, pp. 28–32.

Southwest Arete. IV, 5.9. First ascent May 1973 by Dave Lomba and Galen Rowell. This climb consists of eleven pitches on excellent rock along the narrow ridge.

Charlito Dome, The Artesian Route. III, 5.9. First ascent June 1986 by E. C. Joe and Dick Leversee. This is a large slab facing southwest, just south of Charlotte Dome. This route climbs the right-facing corner on the upper half of the slab. There is a spring about halfway up this route.

Glacier Monument *(11,154 ft; 11,165 ft)*

First ascent September 1972 by Andy Smatko, Tom Ross, and Bill Schuler, on a traverse from Gardiner Pass.

Mt. Gardiner *(3934 m; 12,907 ft)*

This would be one of the classic peaks of the High Sierra, except for all of that darned climbing! (This peak requires a long slog up an scree-and-talus slope to reach a classic knife-edge.)

South Slope. Class 4. First ascent July 1896 by Bolton Brown and Joseph LeConte, who met by chance on the south summit of the peak. Climb almost interminable scree-and-talus slopes from the Charlotte Creek drainage to the south summit of the peak. From the south summit, a 300-foot class 4 knife-edge leads to the higher north summit. As a variation, you can also climb the southeast ridge to the south summit.

Northeast Chute. Class 4. First ascent July 9, 1940, by a party led by Norman Clyde. Climb the shallow class 2 chute just south of Mt. Gardiner's northeast ridge from Gardiner Basin. This chute leads to the southeast ridge and the south summit. Climb the class 4 knife-edged ridge to the north summit.

Mt. Cotter   *(3875 m; 12,721 ft)*

The south peak is the high point.

Southeast Slope. Class 2–3. First ascent August 6, 1922, by Bob Fitzsimons. Climb the slope rising from Sixty Lake Basin. Only the summit rocks are difficult.

South Ridge. Class 3. Follow the ridge rising from Sixty Lake Col.

Southwest Slope. Class 2–3. Climb the slope from Lake 3477m (11,394 ft) in Gardiner Basin.

North Ridge. First ascent July 8, 1940, by a party led by David Brower. This has been reported as having only one difficult section, a 20-foot class 4 wall. (I don't believe it—this ridge appears to be much more difficult than that!)

North Cotter, Northeast Buttress. Class 4–5. First ascent June 23, 1984, by Dick Beach and Steve Rogero. This exceptionally fine climb leads to the lower, north summit of Mt. Cotter. Approach the buttress from Sixty Lake Basin by staying on ledges on the north (right) side of the lower part of the buttress. Climb to a notch that is on the crest of the buttress. Climb the buttress from the notch, keeping to its north (right) side, to the summit of the north peak. Protection is scarce on many of the leads, but this is balanced by incredible hand- and footholds.

North Cotter, East Face. IV, 5.9, A1. First ascent June 1972 by Tony Qamar, Marek Glogoczowski, and Galen Rowell. This route begins just right of the center portion of the east face. The second pitch includes a gigantic pendulum traverse to the left. On the first ascent, one piton was used for aid at the beginning of a 5.9 jam crack higher on the wall. This route ends atop the north summit of Mt. Cotter.

Mt. Clarence King   *(3943 m; 12,905 ft)*

This beautiful peak dominates the entire Woods Creek drainage. Its first ascent was the hardest rock climb in nineteenth-century America.

South Face. I, 5.4. First ascent August 1896 by Bolton Brown. From either Gardiner Basin or Sixty Lake Basin, climb to the saddle on the south ridge of the peak. The final approach to the saddle from Sixty Lake Basin uses either a ledge in the cliff on the eastern side of the saddle, or a scree-and-talus slope farther south. Climb talus and sand from the saddle to the highest rocks, which are near the eastern cliff. A jam crack and squeeze chimney are climbed to gain access to the final summit block. The summit block is climbed via a crack on its eastern side, and then by standing on the edge of a subsidiary block before making the delicate move onto the highest rock. Alternatively, you can climb the southern face of the summit block (with the aid of a shoulder stand) before making the delicate move. *Starr's Variation:* First ascent July 27, 1929, by Walter A. Starr, Jr. There is a prominent overhang around the corner to the right of the jam crack and squeeze chimney. Climb up a *very small* hole under the overhang to the summit block. This hole is in line with the summit of Mt. Clarence King, Mt. Cotter, and Mt. Stanford.

Northwest Face, Right Side. III, 5.4. First ascent August 25, 1975, by Bill Stronge, Scott Charlton, and Mike Walters. Ascend the west ridge of Mt. Clarence King to approximately halfway up the ridge. Traverse left onto the northwest face via a talus ledge. Climb directly to the summit via cracks and chimneys that begin in a broken area on the right side of the center of the face. This is a six-pitch climb.

Northwest Face, Left Side. IV, 5.7. First ascent September 1971 by Gilles Corcos and Graeme Wilson. This climb starts on the left side of the face. Ascend a 200-foot class 4 ramp to a shallow spur on the face. Climb the inside corner of the spur (5.7) for one pitch, then climb up and right for another lead. Continue climbing up and right, with alternate horizontal traverses, to a point about 300 feet west of the summit, where it is possible to climb up to the west ridge. Follow the west ridge to the summit block.

North Ridge. I, 5.4. First ascent September 3, 1972, by George Oetzel, Dick Brown, Stu Langdoc, and Pat Buchanan. This climb begins from near the top of Peak 3760m+ (12,356 ft). From this point, the ridge appears to be more of a face, with some small

Mt. Clarence King from the southeast (photo by Sequoia and Kings Canyon National Parks)

aretes to the east. Climb the face, keeping within 50 to 100 feet of its junction with the northwest face. Some steep slabs near the top can be bypassed by going to the left of a 20-foot sloping ledge at their base. A 50-foot class 4 pitch, up cracks at the top of the slabs, leads to a bowl where the north ridge joins the east ridge. From the bowl, an easy but exposed scramble along the top of the northwest face leads to the summit block (5.4).

East Ridge. I, 5.4. First ascent August 1948 by Fred Davenport and Standish Mitchell. Follow the ridge from Sixty Lake Basin to the summit block. A difficult section on the lower part of the ridge is bypassed on its south side, via a series of narrow cracks and ledges. The upper part of the ridge features a "large wafer," or thin block of rock. This is bypassed (5.2) on the northern side of the ridge. The summit block is 5.4.

Southeast Face. III, 5.8. First ascent August 1970 by Greg Henzies and Galen Rowell. This route climbs cracks to the left of the prominent chimney system on this face. The route follows a line that drops directly from the summit. There is a class 3 section in the middle of the route.

Peak 3620m+

(11,870 ft; 0.7 mi W of Mt. Clarence King)

South Face and East Ridge. Class 3. First ascent September 11, 1972, by Bill Schuler,

Mt. Clarence King, Southeast Face (photo by Pete Yamagata)

Tom Ross, and Andy Smatko. Climb a chute on the south face and follow the east ridge to the summit.

Peak 3722m
(12,160 ft+; 1.1 mi N of Mt. Clarence King)
First ascent July 6, 1940, by Jim Harkins, Bob Jacobs, Art Argiewicz, and Bruce Meyer. The two summit blocks are class 4.

Fin Dome *(3558 m; 11,693 ft)*
West Face. Class 3. First ascent 1910 by James Rennie. From the top of the talus fan on the southwest side of the dome, contour left (west) and slightly upward on the west face. The route zigzags on sandy ledges and over boulders between large slabs. It is easy to get off route and onto class 4 terrain.

South Ridge. Class 4. First ascent July 7, 1940, by David Brower and party.

East Face. I, 5.7. First ascent June 1972 by Marek Glogoczowski and Galen Rowell. Two pitches lead to the summit.

North Buttress. Class 4. First ascent June 16, 1966, by Arkel Erb, Ken McNutt, and Dick Beach. Approach this ridge from the west, and keep to the right side of the buttress for five pitches to the summit.

Painted Lady *(3694 m; 12,126 ft)*
First ascent 1931 by Robert Owen. Class 2 from the John Muir Trail north of Glen Pass.

Mt. Rixford *(3928 m; 12,890 ft)*
First ascent 1897 by Emmet Rixford and two others, via an unknown route. This peak is class 1 from Bullfrog Lake. It is class 2 from Mt. Gould, as long as you remain low on the southern side of the ridge connecting the two peaks. The northeast side of this peak has loose rock.

Peak 3912m
(12,800 ft+; 0.4 mi E of Mt. Rixford)
This peak is class 3 via its southwest face, southeast ridge, or east face.

Mt. Gould *(3964 m; 13,005 ft)*
The summit rocks of this peak are class 3.
From Kearsarge Pass. Class 1. First ascent July 2, 1890, by Joseph N. LeConte, Hubert P. Dyer, Fred S. Pheby, and C. B. Lakeman.

The south ridge is an easy talus hop.

Southeast Ridge. Class 1. Ascend the southeast slope from the eastern side of Kearsarge Pass to the southeast ridge. Stay south of the crest of the ridge while climbing to the summit to keep the difficulties to a minimum.

North Side. Class 2. The plateau north of Mt. Gould can be reached from Golden Trout Lake, Dragon Peak, or from the Kearsarge Lakes basin.

Kearsarge Peak *(3846 m; 12,598 ft)*

This peak is class 1 from Sardine Canyon and from the old mining trails that climb the southeastern side of the peak from the Onion Valley Road. This peak has also been climbed from Golden Trout Lake via Lilley Pass: class 2.

Bighorn Sheep

The following eleven peaks are in areas that have restricted access due to bighorn sheep habitat. These sheep once roamed throughout the High Sierra, but the herds were decimated with the introduction of domestic sheep in the nineteenth century. Domestic sheep haven't grazed in the High Sierra since the 1940s, but the remaining herds of bighorn sheep are so small that it is still considered an endangered species. Long-range plans call for bighorn sheep to repopulate the entire High Sierra, so these areas of restricted access should be completely open to the public again, someday. In the meantime, please respect these closed areas, and give the bighorn sheep a fighting chance at a comeback.

The eleven peaks are Dragon Peak, Dragon Tooth, Mt. Mary Austin, Black Mountain, Diamond Peak, Peak 3984m (13,070 ft), Mt. Baxter, Acrodectes Peak, Peak 3914m (12,852 ft), Peak 3903m (12,804 ft), and Indian Rock.

All cross-country travel above 11,000 feet is prohibited east of the John Muir Trail and west of the Sierra crest from North Dragon Pass on the south to the Sawmill Pass Trail on the north. And cross-country travel is prohibited east of the Sierra crest between Dragon Peak and Sawmill Pass from December 15 to July 1 every year.

Dragon Peak *(3940 m+; 12,955)*

South Ridge. Class 3. First ascent 1920 by Fred Parker and J. E. Rother. This ridge can be approached from either Mt. Gould or from the unnamed lakes north of Golden Trout Lake. From the col immediately south of the peak, traverse the western side of the south ridge over many minor ribs and buttresses to the summit gendarme. This is climbed on its west side via a ledge that lacks handholds. The ledge is class 3, with a lot of exposure. This is a nice climb that can be done easily in a day from Onion Valley.

Southwest Slope. Class 3. First ascent 1920 by Norman Clyde. The summit gendarme can be approached directly from the western approach to Gould Pass.

Northwest Ridge. II, 5.8. First ascent June 1985 by Vern Clevenger and Claude Fiddler. This route climbs the left of two aretes on the northwest side of the peak. This climb consists of six pitches.

"Dragon Tooth"

(3803 m; 12,480 ft+; 0.3 mi N of Dragon Peak)

This is the large square-topped peak that is passed during the eastern approach to North Dragon Pass.

North Face. II, 5.6, A1. First ascent July 26, 1944, by Parker Severson. Second ascent June 22, 1984, by Dick Beach and Steve Rogero. This route is open from December 15 to July 1 each year. The climb begins on the northern side of the east face. The first pitch is followed by a 15-foot aid crack. The route then goes through a prominent notch to the north face; this features a large flake, with a narrow walkway. Descend the walkway and traverse onto the north face. At the far side of the north face a series of cracks is climbed to the summit.

Mt. Mary Austin *(3978 m; 13,040 ft+)*

First ascent May 3, 1965, by Andy Smatko, Tom Ross, Ellen Siegal, and Eric Schumacher. The southeast slope is class 2. The entire peak is open only from December 15 to July 1 each year.

Black Mountain *(4051 m; 13,289 ft)*

South Slope. Class 2. First ascent 1905 by George R. Davis. This route is now closed year-round.

North Slope. Class 2. First ascent August 20, 1948, by Fred L. Jones. This route is open only from December 15 to July 1 each year. Climb the slope from the Baxter Pass Trail. A short, steep section is encountered when approaching the basin immediately north of the summit. (It is easier to climb Black Mountain first, and then climb Diamond Peak via the southeast slope from the 11,800-foot level.)

East Ridge. Class 2. Descended August 19, 1948, by Fred L. Jones. This route is open only from December 15 to July 1 each year. The large blocks just below the summit are class 2. This ridge can be approached from the Baxter Pass Trail, from the summit of Mt. Mary Austin, or from Parker Lakes.

South Ridge. Class 2. The Sierra crest can be followed from North Dragon Pass to the summit of Black Mountain. This route is open only from December 15 to July 1 each year.

Diamond Peak *(4001 m; 13,126 ft)*

Black Diamond Traverse. Class 2. First ascent August 20, 1948, by Fred L. Jones. This route is open only from December 15 to July 1 each year. The southeast slope of Diamond Peak is a splendid snow climb in the spring. Those traversing from Black Mountain should drop down to the 11,800-foot contour before climbing Diamond Peak.

Northeast Couloir. Class 3. Descended May 30, 1960, by Henry Mandolf, Charles Bell, and Rowland Radcliffe. This route is open only from December 15 to July 1 each year. The route ascends the left-hand (eastern) snow couloir on the north side of the peak.

West Slope. Class 2. First ascent August 1922 by Norman Clyde. This route is now closed year-round.

Peak 3984m

(13,070 ft; 0.6 mi N of Diamond Peak)

First ascent 1925 by Norman Clyde. The southeast slope is class 2. This route is open only from December 15 to July 1 each year.

East Ridge. Class 3. First ascent August 6, 1948, by Fred L. Jones. This route is open only from December 15 to July 1 each year. Follow the ridge from Baxter Pass. Traverse the chutes and ribs on the south side of the ridge until beneath the summit.

Mt. Baxter

(4004 m; 13,125 ft; 0.5 mi E of Acrodectes Peak)

For some reason, this peak is unnamed on

some copies of the Kearsarge Peak 7.5-minute quadrangle. The west peak is the high point.

South Ridge. Class 3. Descended August 5, 1948, by Fred L. Jones. This route is now closed year-round.

Southwest Slope. Class 2. This route is now closed year-round.

From the Northwest. Class 3. This route is now closed year-round.

Northwest Face. Class 4–5. First ascent July 1986 by Dave Scheven and Steve Porcella. This route is now closed year-round.

North Ridge. Class 2. First ascent 1905 by George R. Davis. This route is now closed year-round.

North Face. Class 3. Ascend a wide chute that ends near the top of the lower eastern peak of Mt. Baxter. This route is open only from December 15 to July 1 each year.

Northeast Ridge. Class 3. Descended July 25, 1948, by Fred L. Jones. This route is open only from December 15 to July 1 each year. This traverse begins atop Peak 3795m (12,400 ft+), about 1 mile northeast of Mt. Baxter. This peak can be reached from the Sawmill Pass Trail. From this peak, make a direct traverse on the northwest side of the ridge to the base of two pinnacles on the ridge crest. Continue traversing to a small col, and cross the col to the southeast side of the ridge. Climb the southeast side of the ridge to the ridge crest, climb over a small peak, and descend to a notch. Traverse the northwestern side of the ridge across large talus blocks to the lower, eastern peak of Mt. Baxter.

The entire northeast ridge of Mt. Baxter, from Sawmill Creek to the summit, was climbed by Dick Beach and Bob Good on June 11, 1988. (This route is now open only from December 15 to July 1 each year.) The ridge rises 9,500 feet from the floor of Owens Valley to the summit of Mt. Baxter. Dick Beach said after completing this ascent, "It is important not to become overwhelmed by the length of this ridge or the complexity of the route finding. This ridge above all others puts all the ingredients of challenging mountaineering into play. That's why doing a ridge like this becomes an element of high adventure and not one of an arduous slog."

Southeast Slope. Class 2. Climb to the basin southeast of Mt. Baxter from the Baxter Pass Trail and ascend the southeast slope of the peak to the summit. This route is open only from December 15 to July 1 each year.

Acrodectes Peak *(4018 m; 13,183 ft)*

First ascent July 1935 by a party led by Norman Clyde on a traverse from Mt. Baxter. This entire peak is closed year-round.

North Buttress of West Peak. III, 5.10a. First ascent 1988 by Galen Rowell and Vern Clevenger.

Peak 3914m

(12,852 ft; 0.9 mi W of Acrodectes Peak)

North Ridge. Class 2. First ascent July 1935 by a party led by Norman Clyde, on a traverse from Acrodectes Peak. This entire peak is closed year-round.

Peak 3903m

(12,804 ft; 1.0 mi NW of Acrodectes Peak)

This is the prominent peak seen to the south of Woods Lake. It has been referred to as "Woods Peak." This entire peak is closed year-round.

Northeast Ridge. Class 3. First ascent July 6, 1929, by Vance Hopkins, Tom Bundy, R. L. Worden, W. F. Angbauer, Bill Widney, Earl Wallace, and Toni Freeman.

From the Northwest. Class 2. First ascent July 21, 1948, by Fred L. Jones.

Southeast Ridge. Class 3. First ascent July 1935 by a party led by Norman Clyde on a traverse from Peak 3914m (12,852 ft).

Indian Rock

(3712 m; 12,160 ft+; 1.5 mi NE of Mt. Baxter)

This is the prominent spire seen from Highway 395 between Big Pine and Independence.

Southwest Arete. Class 3. First ascent October 16, 1948, by Fred L. Jones. This entire peak is open only from December 15 to July 1 each year. Ascend the canyon of Thibaut Creek to its head, and climb a talus chute to the saddle on the northwestern side of Indian Rock. Climb over a series of rubble-covered ledges and ascend a 50-foot section of class 3 to the southwest arete. Follow the southwest arete to the flat summit.

West Face. Class 4. First ascent June 11, 1988, by Dick Beach. Approximately 200 feet of class 4 climbing over solid rock leads to the summit.

Castle Domes *(3200 m+; 11,360 ft+)*

These are class 1 from Woods Creek via the east slope and northeast ridge.

Window Peak *(3684 m; 12,085 ft)*

First ascent July 5, 1940, by Art Argiewicz and Bob Jacobs, via an unknown route. The east face is class 3. The north and south ridges have been climbed, but their difficulty is unknown. The "window" on this peak measures 5 by 7 feet.

Peak 3764m

(12,350 ft; 1.1 mi SE of Pyramid Peak)

First ascent June 27, 1940, by Jed Garthwaite, Jim Quick, and Howard Leach. The west slope and the south ridge are class 2–3.

Pyramid Peak *(3895 m; 12,777 ft)*

South Ridge. Class 3. First ascent July 21, 1942, by Art Reyman. Climb to the first notch south of the peak from either the west or the east, and follow the knife-edge to the summit. A possible alternative route is a traverse from Window Peak, but Peak 3721m (12,160 ft+) is an obstacle which must be bypassed.

West Ridge. Class 2. From the upper part of Arrow Creek, head southeast to where a scree-and-talus gully breaks through the cliffs along the west ridge of the peak. This gully leads to the ridge at an elevation of approximately 11,500 feet, or 3500m. Follow the west ridge to the summit.

Northeast Ridge. Class 3. Gain this ridge from the basin south of Explorer Pass and follow the knife-edged ridge to the summit.

Arrow Ridge *(12,188 ft; 12,188 ft)*

First ascent August 8, 1945, by Art Reyman. Class 1 from Arrow Peak.

Arrow Peak *(3950 m; 12,958 ft)*

The view of Arrow Peak from Bench Lake is one of the finest in the High Sierra. And the view from the summit isn't bad either.

Southeast Slope. Class 2. First ascent August 20, 1930, by Walter A. Starr, Jr. This is an easy climb over talus from the head of Arrow Creek, or from the top of Arrow Pass. Be sure to head for the higher, northeastern summit.

Southwest Ridge. Class 3. First ascent June 1902 by Joseph LeConte, Tracey Kelley, and Robert Pike. Ascend the south slope from Arrow Creek to the top of the ridge. There is a knife-edged ridge between the false summit (Peak 3921m; 12,800 ft+) and the true summit, which is bypassed on its southern side.

Northeast Spur. Class 3. First ascent August 8, 1895, by Bolton C. Brown from the South Fork of the Kings River. This spur has some narrow knife-edges.

Peak 3681m

(12,000 ft+; 0.5 mi SE of Bench Lake)

First ascent August 12, 1922, by W. and J. Sloane.

Bench Lake Boogie. III, 5.9. First ascent July 1973 by Vern Clevenger and Jon Ross. Climb a left-facing dihedral for two pitches; a few more pitches lead to the top of the climb.

Mt. Ickes   *(3942 m; 12,968 ft)*

First ascent July 25, 1939, by a party led by Art Argiewicz, via the west ridge. The west ridge and the northeast ridge are class 2.

Peak 3891m

(12,773 ft; 1.1 mi NE of Pyramid Peak)

First ascent July 13, 1970, by Doug Sabastion, Jack Dozier, Eric Ratner, and Steve Ratner, via the class 2 northeast ridge. The southwest ridge is class 1.

Crater Mountain   *(3924 m; 12,874 ft)*

Class 2 from the east and northeast. First ascent July 19, 1922, by W. H. Ink, Meyers Butte, and Captain Wallace.

Mt. Cedric Wright   *(3761 m; 12,372 ft)*

First ascent August 25, 1935, by Norman Clyde. The southeast slope is class 1. The peak is class 3 from the saddle between it and Colosseum Mountain.

Colosseum Mountain

(3794 m; 12,473 ft)

Southwest Slope. Class 1. First ascent August 5, 1922, by Chester Versteeg. Leave the Sawmill Pass Trail in the vicinity of Woods Lake and hike up sand to the summit.

West Ridge. Class 1. The saddle between Colosseum Mountain and Mt. Cedric Wright can be reached from either the north or south. From the saddle, ascend the west ridge to the summit.

Northwest Chute. Class 2. There are many gullies and chutes on the northwest side of the peak. Ascend the chute that leads to the north ridge just north of the summit. Cross over the north ridge and climb a small bowl to the summit plateau of Colosseum Mountain.

North Ridge. Class 3. Follow the Sierra crest south from Armstrong Col. There are many knife-edges on this ridge, and care must be used to ensure that the easiest route is followed. The final part of the climb leaves the north ridge on its east side and ascends a small bowl to the summit plateau.

Mt. Perkins   *(3830 m; 12,591 ft)*

South Ridge. Class 2. Follow the Sierra crest north from Armstrong Col.

West Slope. Class 2 from the John Muir Trail north of Twin Lakes.

North Ridge. Class 2. First ascent 1972 by Dave King. Gain the north ridge from Armstrong Canyon, and follow the ridge to the summit.

Mt. Wynne   *(4017 m; 13,179 ft)*

First ascent 1935 by a Sierra Club party. The west ridge from Pinchot Pass is class 2, as is the southeast slope.

East Ridge. Class 2. First ascent August 15, 1972, by Natalie Smith, Dick Beach, Elton Fletcher, Gordon MacLeod, and Jerry Keating. This was done in one day round trip from the end of the road in Armstrong Canyon.

North Ridge. Class 3. The traverse from Mt. Pinchot goes best by staying on top of the ridge that connects both peaks.

Mt. Pinchot   *(4113 m; 13,495 ft)*

South Ridge. Class 3. The traverse from Mt. Wynne involves some loose rock. It is best to stay on top of the ridge crest.

East Ridge. Class 2.

Northwest Face. Class 2. This is commonly used as a descent route after climbing the south ridge. Numerous ribs and gullies lead to small cliffs, which are easily bypassed.

Peak 4043m

(13,259 ft; 0.6 mi S of Striped Mountain)

First ascent September 26, 1965, by Ed Lane and Gary Lewis, via the class 3 north face. The class 2 east ridge from Goodale Creek was climbed June 9, 1968, by Tom

Ross, Ellen Siegal, Bill Schuler, and Andy Smatko.

Peak 3905m
(12,720 ft+; 0.9 mi SW of Striped Mountain)
First ascent July 23, 1939, by Madi Bacon and Tom Noble, via an unknown route. The northwest ridge is class 3. The class 3 east face was climbed by Tom Ross, Bill Schuler, and Andy Smatko on September 13, 1970.

Striped Mountain *(4017 m; 13,120 ft+)*
From Taboose Pass. Class 2. First ascent July 1905 by George R. Davis. Head southeast from Taboose Pass to the cirque between Striped Mountain and Goodale Mountain. Climb the northeast slope to the summit.

West Ridge. Class 2. First ascent August 1, 1948, by Fred L. Jones. This ridge is most easily climbed on its northern side.

From Goodale Creek. Class 2. First ascent August 11, 1948, by Fred L. Jones. Climb to the saddle between Striped Mountain and Goodale Mountain from Goodale Creek. Ascend the east slope of the peak to the summit. This route was originally climbed from the Woods Creek drainage, crossing the Sierra crest east of Peak 4043m (13,259 ft); this variation is class 3.

Goodale Mountain *(3893 m; 12,790 ft)*
West Slope. Class 2. First ascent July 23, 1939, by Norman Clyde, Allan A. MacRae, and Albion J. Whitney. Climb to the saddle between Goodale Mountain and Striped Mountain from either Taboose Pass or Goodale Creek. The summit block is class 3.

East Slope. Class 2. This is a long climb from the Owens Valley. The starting point is between Taboose Creek and Goodale Creek.

Peak 3744m
(12,285 ft; 0.8 mi NW of Goodale Mountain)
The class 3 west face of this peak was climbed on September 18, 1970, by Andy Smatko, Bill Schuler, and Tom Ross.

Wrinkles

Alternatives to Kearsarge Pass. Kearsarge Pass is the easiest crossing of the Sierra crest in this region, and it receives the bulk of the traffic. Baxter Pass is the most pleasant of the other three high passes, with water over most of its 8 miles (to the summit) and 6,160 feet of gain; this trail also has the most shade. Sawmill Pass starts in the desert, and climbs a long way before reaching water; but Sawmill Meadow and Sawmill Lake may balance out the discomfort suffered during the start of the hike. Taboose Pass is the shortest of the three trails leading to the Sierra crest, but it seems to be in the desert all the way to the summit of the pass; on the other hand, the view from the summit is outstanding, and it will rejuvenate any hiker who has just ascended its barren east side.

Onion Valley to Rae Lakes. Despite having discouraged hikers from using Kearsarge Pass, I do encourage them to use Kearsarge Pass and Glen Pass to get to Rae Lakes from Onion Valley. Gould Pass and North Dragon Pass are hard cross-country routes featuring difficult route finding and loose rock. Using either of these routes usually turns out to be an all-day affair. Anyone who has the skill and strength to cross the Sierra crest via North Dragon Pass or Gould Pass certainly has the strength to cross Kearsarge and Glen Passes over trails. This is much more pleasant and much safer.

6

The Monarch Divide and The Cirque Crest

THE WORDS "KINGS CANYON" MAY BRING TO mind images of the great valley along the South Fork of the Kings River, the village of Cedar Grove, and the hordes of car campers who traveled there by driving along Highway 180. But there is another great valley to the north that few people ever see. This is the Middle Fork of the Kings River, a wild, roadless area, with difficult access. If Kings Canyon is the rival of Yosemite Valley, then the Middle Fork of the Kings River is the rival of Kings Canyon. The Middle and South forks are separated by a great ridge that extends westward from the Sierra crest at Mt. Bolton Brown and Mather Pass. This is known as the Monarch Divide and the Cirque Crest.

This region is bounded by Sentinel Ridge on the south, the South Fork of the Kings River on the east, Palisade Creek on the north, and the Middle Fork of the Kings River on the west.

History

The Monarch Divide proved to be an impassable barrier to the California Geological Survey in 1864. After their adventures on Mt. Brewer and Mt. Tyndall, the survey moved north in an attempt to climb Mt. Goddard. Their pack animals were unable to descend the north side of the divide to the Middle Fork of the Kings River, however, so they moved east, up Bubbs Creek, to temporarily leave the High Sierra via Kearsarge Pass.

The shepherds moved into this area in the 1870s and created the Granite Pass Trail across the Monarch Divide to reach the ample pasturage available in the vast Middle Fork drainage. Bolton Brown followed this trail in 1895, and ascended Mt. Ruskin and crossed Cartridge Pass before returning to Kings Canyon via the South Fork of the Kings River.

The rock towers of the Grand Dike and in the Gorge of Despair were first climbed in the early 1950s. Few parties visit these areas, and there has been comparatively little exploratory climbing in this region. There are still unclimbed spires and pinnacles in the gorges branching away from the crest of the Monarch Divide.

Maps

United States Geological Survey: 7.5-minute series: The Sphinx, Cedar Grove, Wren Peak, Tehipite Dome, Slide Bluffs, Marion Peak, Mt. Pinchot, Split Mtn., North Palisade; 15-minute series: Marion Peak, Tehipite Dome, Mt. Goddard, Big Pine, Mt. Pinchot.

United States Forest Service: John Muir Wilderness and the Sequoia–Kings Canyon National Parks Backcountry (1:63,360).

Wilderness Permits

For entry to the Kings Canyon National Park backcountry: Sequoia and Kings Canyon National Parks, Three Rivers, CA 93271.

For entry to the Monarch Wilderness: Sequoia National Forest, Hume Lake Ranger District, Miramonte, CA 93641.

Roads

The Kings Canyon Highway (Highway 180)

The Kings Canyon Highway goes east from Fresno and enters Kings Canyon National Park near Wilsonia and Grant Grove. From the junction with the Generals Highway, the Kings Canyon Highway turns north, passes by Wilsonia, passes through Grant Grove Village, and then leaves Kings Canyon National Park. The road is open year-round as far as the turnoff to Hume Lake, 7.5 miles

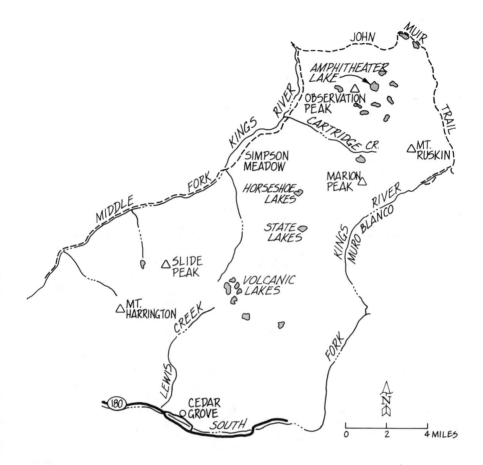

Trails

Deer Cove and
Wildman Meadow Trail (5 miles)

from its junction with the Generals Highway. Beyond this point, the road is closed from late October or early November to approximately the first week of May.

The Kings Canyon Highway descends into Kings Canyon and goes east, following the South Fork of the Kings River to reenter Kings Canyon National Park 36.1 miles from the junction with the Generals Highway. The road continues another 1.1 miles to Cedar Grove, which features campgrounds, a ranger station, a lodge, a grocery store, and a gas station. The Kings Canyon Highway continues another 5.8 miles to Road's End, the trailhead for the Paradise Valley Trail and the Granite Pass Trail.

The trailhead for this trail is 35.1 miles from the Generals Highway on Highway 180, approximately 1 mile west of the national park boundary. The trail climbs the north side of Kings Canyon and, after 1½ miles, crosses Deer Cove Creek. After another 1½ miles it comes to a junction. The trail to the right climbs (with excellent views) for 2 miles to above the level of Wildman Meadow. The trail on the left descends a short distance to another junction, and goes right (north) up the East Fork of Grizzly

Creek for 2 miles to Wildman Meadow. This latter trail has some shade, and is preferable on a hot day. These two trails meet on top of the ridge serving as the Kings Canyon National Park boundary; two side trails lead from there to Frypan Meadow and the Kennedy Pass Trail.

Also deserving mention are two side trails leading to the west from the Wildman Meadow Trail. From the lower portion of the East Fork of Grizzly Creek, a trail goes 1½ miles to a dead end beyond Wren Creek. This trail serves as an approach to the lower end of the Grand Dike. The other trail heads west from Wildman Meadow to its end just beyond Happy Gap. This trail serves as the approach to the upper end of the Grand Dike.

Don Cecil Trail (6 miles)

The Don Cecil Trail leads from the floor of Kings Canyon to the saddle just south of Lookout Peak on the south rim of the canyon. (A splendid view of Kings Canyon is available from the top of Lookout Peak.) This hike is mostly downhill when started from Summit Meadow at the end of the Big Meadow/Horse Corral Meadow Road, which is described in Chapter 3: The Kaweahs and the Great Western Divide. The following description starts on the floor of Kings Canyon at Cedar Grove.

Head south from the Cedar Grove Ranger Station and cross the Kings Canyon Highway. The trail climbs through the forest and soon crosses a dirt road, and then continues its ascent to Sheep Creek. It crosses the creek on a bridge and climbs to the west fork of Sheep Creek. In this area the trail passes through some beautiful flower gardens with views across the canyon to the Monarch Divide; Mt. Clarence King dominates the up-canyon view. The trail climbs to a ridge before turning south across the east side of Lookout Peak to the saddle south of the peak. At the saddle, the trail meets the Big Meadows/Horse Corral Meadow Road. A trail leads from here to the top of Lookout Peak, which has an outstanding view of Kings Canyon. The trail to the top of the peak is another ½ mile.

Kennedy Pass Trail (15 miles)

This long, hard hike is made bearable by the sound of Lewis Creek, ample forest cover, wild flowers in meadows, and changing views of the High Sierra as you gain elevation from the floor of Kings Canyon.

The preferred starting point for this trail is where Lewis Creek crosses the Kings Canyon Highway, approximately 1½ miles west of Cedar Grove. (The alternate route is the Hotel Creek Trail, which starts at Cedar Grove, makes a steep ascent up the north wall of Kings Canyon, and then descends to meet the Lewis Creek Trail.) The trail makes a steep ascent of the west bank of Lewis Creek for 1½ miles to meet the Hotel Creek Trail. The trail continues climbing to the north another 2½ miles to Frypan Meadow. The Kennedy Pass Trail goes east from Frypan Meadow and gradually turns northeast and then north on the final climb to the top of Kennedy Pass, where there is an outstanding view. The trail descends the north side of the pass to Kennedy Canyon, passing through its meadows for 3½ miles before crossing to the east bank of the creek and climbing onto Dead Pine Ridge. The trail traverses south along the ridge before turning east and descending to Volcanic Lakes, 2½ miles from Kennedy Canyon. It leaves this basin on the eastern side and descends to the middle fork of Dougherty Creek, where it meets the Granite Pass and Simpson Meadow Trail approximately 2 miles north of Granite Pass.

Granite Pass Trail (23 miles)

The Granite Pass Trail goes from the floor of Kings Canyon over the Monarch Divide to beautiful Simpson Meadow. The strenuousness of this hike is made up for by the rewarding views available from both sides of the Monarch Divide.

The trailhead is at Road's End of the Kings Canyon Highway. The trail goes north on the western side of Copper Creek, and climbs and climbs 5,000 feet in 8 miles to the first level terrain, at Granite Basin. The trail goes north for 2 miles to Granite Pass and descends the north side of the pass another 3 miles to meet the Kennedy Pass Trail, which provides access to Volcanic Lakes. A half-mile farther, a trail branches off to the west, to the Lake of the Fallen Moon. Another ½ mile from this junction, the State Lakes Trail goes east. The trail to Simpson Meadow descends toward the north and leads to Dougherty Meadow, along the east fork of Dougherty Creek, followed by a short ascent to meet the Horseshoe Lakes Trail after 1 mile. The trail to Simpson Meadow goes north from this junction and descends the crest of the ridge between Dougherty Creek and Horseshoe Creek for 7 miles to Simpson Meadow, along the Middle Fork of the Kings River.

State Lakes Trail and
Horseshoe Lakes Trail (6 miles)

This trail leaves the Granite Pass Trail 4 miles north of Granite Pass. It goes east 2 miles to State Lakes. The trail goes beyond the lakes another 2 miles to a junction. From here, the Horseshoe Lakes Trail goes north 1 mile to Horseshoe Lakes; the other trail goes west for 2 miles to meet the Granite Pass Trail, 7 miles above Simpson Meadow.

The Middle Fork Trail (8¹/₂ miles)

The description of this trail from Crown Valley to Simpson Meadow is given in Chapter 7: Kettle Ridge and The LeConte Divide. From Simpson Meadow the trail ascends the Middle Fork of the Kings River on the south bank for 4¹/₄ miles to meet the last traces of the Cartridge Pass Trail, just north of where it crosses Cartridge Creek. The trail continues north, passing through the narrow canyon with many small waterfalls, to meet the John Muir Trail after another 4¹/₄ miles, on the north side of Palisade Creek.

Cross-Country Routes

"Harrington Pass"

(10,680 ft+; 10,640 ft+; 0.5 mi NE of Mt. Harrington; UTM 459824)

Class 2. This is the approach to the Gorge of Despair. After reaching Frypan Meadow via the Kennedy Pass Trail, take the west branch of the trail to Grizzly Lakes. Head northwest from the lakes to the high pass immediately northeast of Mt. Harrington. The Gorge of Despair is descended on the northeastern side of the stream as far as possible. (It is impossible to travel the Gorge of Despair its entire distance to the Middle Fork of the Kings River due to some huge cliffs and waterfalls.) *Variation:* The Gorge of Despair has also been reached by crossing the Monarch Divide just west of Hogback Peak. Traverse west across the northern side of the divide to the upper part of the Gorge of Despair. Further reading: H. Warren Lewis,

You're Standing on My Fingers!, Howell-North Books, Berkeley, California, 1969, pp. 188–202.

"Gimme Pass"

(10,440 ft+; 10,400 ft+; 0.6 mi S of Slide Peak)

This class 2 pass leads between Lost and Slide canyons north of the Monarch Divide.

"Grouse Lake Pass"

(11,040 ft+; 11,040 ft+; 0.5 mi N of Grouse Lake)

Class 2. This pass, immediately northeast of Peak 11,320+ (11,354 ft), is the first pass crossed as part of a cross-country route between upper Copper Creek and State Lakes. The south side of the pass is easy, but there are talus blocks on the north side of the pass. Further reading: Steve Roper, *Timberline Country*, Sierra Club Books, San Francisco, 1982, pp. 116–17.

"Goat Crest Saddle"

(11,440 ft+; 11,440 ft+; 1.5 mi NE of Granite Pass)

Class 1. This pass is between Peaks 11,822 and 12,000+ (11,797 and 12,059 ft). The south side of the pass is easy, but careful route finding is needed on the upper portion of the northern portion of the pass. It is best to begin the descent to Glacier Valley well to the west of the lowest Glacier Lake. Further reading: Steve Roper, *Timberline Country*, Sierra Club Books, San Francisco, 1982, pp. 117–18.

"Gray Pass"

(10,760 ft+; 10,000 ft+; 2.8 mi ESE of Windy Peak)

Class 1. Gray Pass, White Pass, and Red Pass are the three passes used on the cross-country route between Horseshoe Lakes and Marion Lake. From Horseshoe Lakes hike north, past the largest Horseshoe Lake, to the steep slope that drops into Windy Canyon. Go northeast from this point, across the crest of Windy Ridge, and descend to the small lake at UTM 605918. Traverse east along a small bench from the pond to Gray Pass, which overlooks the south fork of Cartridge Creek. Descend the southeast side of the pass by means of a shallow, grassy gully to the stream at the bottom of this canyon. Further reading: Steve Roper, *Timberline Country*, Sierra Club Books, San Francisco, 1982, pp. 119–21.

"White Pass"

(11,680 ft+; 11,680 ft+; 0.7 mi NW of Marion Peak)

Class 2. The western approach to this pass starts where the description for Gray Pass ends. Continue up the stream a short distance to a round lake. Head east-northeast from the lake to the basin immediately northwest of Marion Peak. White Pass is the almost-level saddle low on Marion Peak's northwest ridge, characterized by the white talus. From the top of the pass, climb the ridge leading toward Marion Peak a very short distance in order to bypass a small cliff on the north side of the pass. Make a level traverse to the east across talus before making a gradual descent through some loose chutes until you are immediately west of and below Red Pass. Further reading: Steve Roper, *Timberline Country,* Sierra Club Books, San Francisco, 1982, pp. 121–22.

"Red Pass"

(11,560 ft+; 11,600 ft+; 0.2 mi S of Red Point)

Class 2. After traversing and descending from White Pass climb the easy but loose western side of Red Pass to its summit. Descend the eastern side of the pass and head toward Marion Lake. There is a cliff above the southwestern side of Marion Lake; this is bypassed by means of a gully on its northern side. Further reading: Steve Roper, *Timberline Country,* Sierra Club Books, San Francisco, 1982, pp. 122–23.

"Pete's Col"

(3520 m+; 11,520 ft+; 0.7 mi SW of Cartridge Pass; UTM 669922)

Class 3. This pass, named here in honor of Pete Yamagata, is a shortcut across the Cirque Crest from the basin south of Cartridge Pass to Marion Lake. It has been used while making the Ruskin–Marion traverse. The east side of the pass is easy; the west side features loose class 3 rock and sand.

Cartridge Pass *(3560 m+; 11,680 ft+)*

Some maps may show a trail leading up Cartridge Creek, over Cartridge Pass, and descending to the South Fork of the Kings River, but this trail has not been maintained for more than fifty years—if it was ever maintained at all. This is an old sheep route which was once the route for the John Muir Trail, until the trail was constructed up Palisade Creek and over Mather Pass in 1938. The Cartridge Pass "Trail" is for all intents and purposes a difficult cross-country route. On a more positive note, this route takes the hiker to beautiful Marion Lake, Lake Basin, and the unnamed lakes on the bench south of Cartridge Pass.

Leave the Middle Fork Trail at the mouth of Cartridge Creek and ascend the brushy north side of the stream. Ascend a steep, broken cliff to the north of Triple Falls, and then cross to the south side of Cartridge Creek. Stay on the south side for about ¼ mile and cross to the north side for about 1 mile before crossing back to the south side again. Difficult cross-country travel leads you across the outlet stream of Marion Lake and up to the lower part of Lake Basin. For the easiest approach to beautiful Marion Lake, traverse south across the lowest bench in Lake Basin to the lake. Anyone who is in this area should not miss a visit to this beautiful lake.

After the ascent through the brush, dust, and loose talus of Cartridge Creek, the meadows and lakes of Lake Basin may at first appear to be mirages. The route remains on the north shores of the lakes to the highest lake in the basin, located north of Cartridge Pass. From the eastern shore of this lake, go south and ascend a steep cliff with loose rock, followed by an easier talus slope, to the top of Cartridge Pass. Descend the south side of the pass over talus past a small lake to the larger lake at the south end of the bench below. Skirt the eastern shore of this lake and descend to the South Fork of the Kings River, keeping to the east of the outlet stream. You can either ascend the South Fork to the John Muir Trail (easier) or descend the Muro Blanco (harder). (See the description of the Muro Blanco in Chapter 5: The High Passes.)

"Vennacher Col"

(3780 m+; 12,320 ft+; 0.2 mi S of Vennacher Needle)

Class 3. This pass has also been referred to as "Upper Basin Pass." It provides access between Lake Basin and the John Muir Trail south of Upper Basin. From the lake north of Cartridge Pass in Lake Basin, ascend the stream that leads to the cirque southwest of Vennacher Needle. Ascend a steep, loose chute to a point about 100 feet below the top of the pass. The class 3 section that follows is best climbed via a left-ascending traverse so that you cross the pass just north of the actual low point. Descend the east side of the pass and follow the stream southeastward to meet the John Muir Trail east of Mt. Ruskin and The Saddlehorn.

"Frozen Lake Pass"

(3760 m+; 12,320 ft+; 2.1 mi SW of Mather Pass; UTM 682964)

Class 2–3; ice axe required. This pass has also been called "Lake Basin Pass." This is the direct cross-country route between Lake Basin

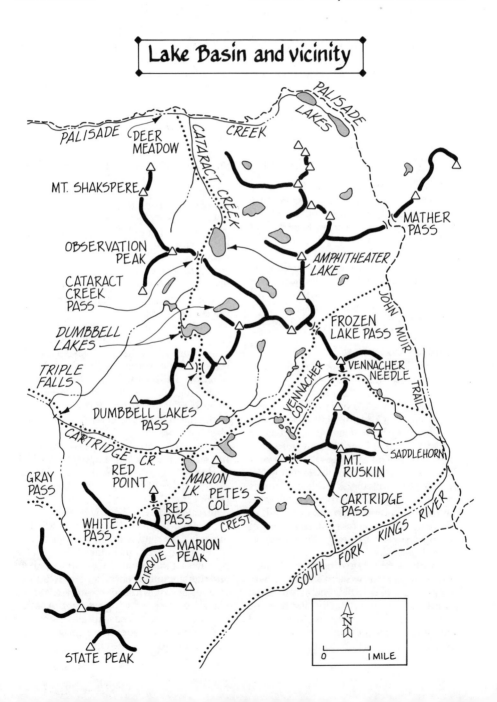

Lake Basin and vicinity

and Upper Basin. From Lake Basin, ascend to Lake 3540m+ (11,600 ft+) in the cirque northwest of Vennacher Needle. Climb steep talus to the left-hand notch visible to the northeast. Descend the steep, loose northeast side of the pass to the permanent snowfield below. Pass the frozen lake and then make a diagonal descent through a steep talus slope to the round lake at 3500 meters+ (11,520 ft+) in Upper Basin. Easy cross-country travel east across Upper Basin leads to the John Muir Trail south of Mather Pass. Further reading: Steve Roper, *Timberline Country,* Sierra Club Books, San Francisco, 1982, pp. 124–27.

"Dumbbell Lakes Pass"

(11,640 ft+; 11,680 ft+; 1.5 mi N of Marion Lake; UTM 652954)

Class 2. Also called "Dumbbell Pass" and "Sheep Pass," this is the direct cross-country route between Lake Basin and Dumbbell Lakes. It is necessary to pass Lake 11,108 (11,120 ft+) on its west shore.

The Dumbbell Lakes basin can also be reached from Cartridge Creek by following the stream that drains Dumbbell Lakes. Leave Cartridge Creek downstream from Triple Falls and remain on the southeast side of the stream all of the way up.

"Cataract Creek Pass"

(11,520 ft+; 11,520 ft+; 0.4 mi ESE of Observation Pk.; UTM 652982)

Class 2. This pass has also been called "Observation Pass." At one time there was a trail up Cataract Creek to Amphitheater Lake, but it has long been abandoned. Leave the John Muir Trail at Deer Meadow, ford Palisade Creek, and hike through the forest west of Cataract Creek. The route eventually follows the west bank of the creek and crosses a tributary stream uphill from a small lake. The route then crosses to the east bank of Cataract Creek. Easy cross-country hiking in the upper part of Cataract Creek leads to Amphitheater Lake.

From the north side of Amphitheater Lake, hop over talus on its western shore to where it is possible to make a diagonal ascent to the southwest. Cataract Creek Pass may be blocked by a snow cornice; this can be passed by climbing above the level of the pass on its northern side.

Peaks

"Scarlet Slipstream"

IV, 5.11. First ascent July 1986 by Eric Richard, Vaino Kodas, and Herb Laeger. This rock climb is on the south wall of Kings Canyon, to the east of the Grand Sentinel. From Road's End, cross the South Fork of the Kings River on the footbridge, and hike upstream along the south bank for 1½ miles. The route climbs a red streak on a low-angle slab for six pitches. Start climbing to the right of the streak, going up a series of steps to the left of the corner to the first bolt. Then follow bolts, small cracks, and corners to the top. Four of the pitches are 5.10 and two are 5.11. Two 165-foot ropes should be taken to rappel the route; RURPs, along with small- to medium-sized chocks, are needed for protection.

Grand Sentinel   *(8,518 ft; 8,504 ft)*

South Side. Class 1 from the Sphinx Creek Trail. First ascent 1896 by Joseph N. LeConte, Helen M. Gompertz, Mr. and Mrs. Gould, and party.

Y Gully. Class 4. First ascent 1967 by Dick Blankenbecler, W. Thompson, and G. Nelson. Climb the right branch of the talus near the upper part of the west face.

Northwest Buttress. Class 5. First ascent July 7, 1951, by Roy Gorin and Jerry Ganapole. This route climbs the two steps seen to the right of the north face when viewed from Road's End. From the floor of Kings Canyon, ascend the stream west of the Grand Sentinel to the base of the buttress immediately right of the north face. One class 4 and two easy class 5 pitches along the buttress lead to the top of the first step. Walk across the top of the first step to the base of the upper face, which is climbed via several moderately difficult class 5 pitches. The climb ends on top of the second step.

Invisible Nebulae. V, 5.10, A4. First ascent September 1985 by Craig Peer and Mike Stewart. This route is on the right side of the north face. It starts on a hidden ramp near the northwest buttress and follows the ramp up and right for four pitches. Hard free climbing leads up and right to an overhang and a knifeblade aid crack, which goes right. Another difficult aid pitch leads up and right to a pendulum, which goes into a corner. Climb the inside corner to the top.

Robbins-Chouinard Route. V, 5.10, A2. First ascent June 1967 by Yvon Chouinard and Royal Robbins. This route has also been called "The Green Dihedral." It climbs the prominent open book on the north face. The climb starts in a gully which features a seasonal waterfall. The gully climbs up and left to an overhanging chockstone near its top. After attaining some good ledges above the chockstone, climb an overhanging trough, then some cracks to a small ledge. Leave this ledge via a crack on the left, then wander up the face above. Climb to the left to a large sloping ledge, and then climb toward the green dihedral. Five difficult, mixed pitches in the dihedral lead to a chockstone. The rest of the climb follows cracks to the left of the main corner of the dihedral. Further reading: *American Alpine Journal,* 1968, pp. 77–80; *Summit,* May–June 1986, pp. 12–13, 34.

Cosmopolis. V, 5.10, A3. First ascent July 1985 by Craig Peer and Bruce Bourassa. This route climbs the steep wall left of the Robbins-Chouinard Route. Start climbing on a right-ascending system of ramps and ledges to a large ledge beneath a huge rectangular block. Climb a crack and a dihedral on the left side of the block for two pitches. Zigzag up cracks, past a large flake and over a roof, to a ramp, which leads to the top. Many thin pins are needed on this nine-pitch route.

"Red Blade"

(7,646 ft; 7,600 ft+; 0.5 mi SE of North Dome)
This formation is southeast of North Dome, and is approached from the Copper Creek Trail. Leave the trail 2 miles from Road's End and hike cross-country to the northeastern end of the rock.

Southeast Face. III, 5.8, A2. First ascent May 1979 by Fred Beckey, Mike Scherer, and Michael Warburton. Climb a crack system in a recess to reach the roof that diagonals across the face. From the left end of this roof, climb cracks to the top.

North Dome *(8,800 ft+; 8,717 ft)*

First ascent June 30, 1940, by Neil Ruge and Florence Rata, from Copper Creek.

North of Eden. V, 5.10+. First ascent July 1986 by Roy Swafford, Todd Vogeland, and E. C. Joe. This eleven-pitch route ascends the east buttress of North Dome. Follow a prominent corner system of wide cracks. Where

the cracks end, climb the face to the left around a headwall. Brushy ledges and face climbing lead to the top.

A Tall Cool One. V, 5.11. First ascent 1986 by Eddie Joe and Dick Leversee. This route ascends a crack system to the right of the prominent dihedral on the south face. This eleven-pitch route involves climbing on less than perfect rock, with eight pitches being 5.10 or harder. It is best to do this climb in the late season because the third pitch can be wet and slimy. Your rack should include three chocks to 4 inches and one to 5 inches.

Herbert-Frost Route. IV, 5.8, A4. First ascent 1968 by TM Herbert and Tom Frost. Ascend the left-leaning dihedral in the center of the south face. The overhangs in the dihedral are passed on their right sides.

North to the Bone. V, 5,9, A3. First ascent August 1986 by Dick Leversee, Mike Meng, and E. C. Joe. This route ascends the south face just to the left of the Herbert-Frost Route. The climb starts in some vertical left-facing corners and ascends thin cracks near the left corner of the dihedral of the Herbert-Frost Route. Two sets of roofs are passed before joining the Herbert-Frost Route just below the top.

Freak Show. V, 5.10, A3+. First ascent July 4, 1986, by Craig Peer, Gary Hinton, and Blaine Neely. This route is mostly free climbing, with aid consisting of hooking thin flakes.

Dolphin Dreams. V, 5.10, A3. First ascent 1985 by Bruce Bourassa, Mike Stewart, and Craig Peer. This route starts with 5.9 face climbing to the base of a ramp. From the ramp's end, four pitches of mixed climbing lead to two easier free pitches and the top.

Roaring River Falls

Three short routes were established in the early 1970s by Dick Blankenbecler and J. Botke.

The Apron. II, 5.6. This climb begins from a small, solitary pine on the apron east of the falls. Ascend the face to a large block, and pass it on its right side. Continue straight up the apron to a tree and traverse left, passing an overhang on its left side, and go up to another tree. Traverse left from here to easier climbing.

The Black Bowl. II, 5.6. There is a right-facing open book several hundred feet west of the preceding route. Start climbing just right of this open book and climb two pitches to an obvious ledge system. From the highest ledge, traverse left, and then climb directly over an overhang. Continue up, aiming for a black bowl. Leave the bowl on the right side, and climb up to the top.

Right Side. II, 5.4. This route is approximately 500 feet west of the falls. There is a large gully with a white block halfway up its right side. Climb the obvious line 100 feet *to the left* of this gully.

North Mountain (8,640 ft+; 8,632 ft)

Nowhere to Run. III, 5.11. First ascent May 1986 by E. C. Joe, Bill McConachie, and Barry Fowlie. This route climbs the prominent south buttress rising from the floor of Kings Canyon. It is approached via the Motor Nature Trail and a park service residential area. Five outstanding pitches of crack climbing (from fingers to off-width) lead to a point far from the true summit of North Mountain. The crux is the fourth pitch.

"Spook Spire"

This pinnacle is almost impossible to see; it helps if the sun is low on the horizon so that its shadow is visible. There is a viewpoint on the Kings Canyon Highway about ¼ mile east of Moraine Campground. Look southwest from this viewpoint; a square cliff can be seen high on the south rim of the canyon. This square cliff extends out from the rim much farther than the other cliffs. Spook Spire is the thin, 200-foot-high pinnacle at the left end of this cliff.

East Face. II, 5.6, A2. First ascent May 17, 1958, by Merle Alley, Jerry Dixon, and George Sessions. Class 4 and 5 climbing lead to the notch behind the pinnacle. Climb out onto a ledge on the east face, and make a long reach to a crack. The crack goes up and diagonally left; nail the crack to the summit.

"Hathaway's Delight"

This rock and Bulldog Rock can be seen from the bridge across Lewis Creek on the Kings Canyon Highway. They are on the south side of the canyon, on a rock ridge. Hathaway's Delight is higher than Bulldog Rock.

Cruddy Gully. II, 5.5, A?. First ascent June 13, 1957, by Merle Alley and George Sessions. Leave the Kings Canyon Highway at the bridge that crosses the South Fork of the

Kings River west of Cedar Grove. Approach the pinnacle from the west to a steep, loose gully that leads to the upper southern notch. This gully involves about 500 feet of class 5 climbing, with an aid move around an overhanging chockstone about halfway up. From the notch, traverse east to a platform, and ascend the high-angle trough leading to the summit. The southern point of the summit is the high point. Descend the west face via rappel, passing an oddly shaped pinnacle which marks the start of the climb of Bulldog Rock.

"Bulldog Rock"

North Face. II, 5.6, A1. First ascent June 13, 1957, by George Sessions and Merle Alley. From the oddly shaped pinnacle on the west face of Hathaway's Delight, traverse into the notch south of Bulldog Rock. From the notch an easy ledge leads east around to the north face, which overlooks the river. From the top of a block, use direct aid to reach a narrow ledge that leads up and right. At the end of this ledge, more direct aid is needed to reach the steep west face. Friction climbing up the face leads to the summit. Rappel the north face to the easy ledge.

Grand Dike

(8,600 ft+ –7,440 ft+)

This impressive ridge contains many jagged towers. The Grand Dike is on the north side of Kings Canyon, and the best approach is from the Deer Cove Trail. The towers are numbered starting from the lower, southeastern end of the ridge.

"Tower No. ½"

(7,440 ft+; 7,520 ft+; UTM 450772)

This small pinnacle is on the south side of Tower No. 1.

Northwest Face. I, 5.3. First ascent November 26, 1954, by Kim Malville, John Ohrenschall, and Richard Smyth. From the notch immediately south of Tower No. 1, descend to the southwest and go through a keyhole formed by a chockstone. Climb a small ledge on the face of Tower No. 1 and climb to the top of the chockstone. Cross over to the northeast side of Tower No. ½ and traverse a ledge on the northwest face to the base of a small chimney. Rope up here, and climb the chimney to the summit, passing a chockstone on its right side. Descend via rappel over the southeast corner of the tower.

East Face. Class 5. First ascent August 11, 1956, by John Ohrenschall and Russ Hoopes. From the notch between Tower No. 1 and Tower No. ¹/₂, traverse onto the east face, and climb it to the summit.

"Tower No. 1"

(7,560 ft+; 7,680 ft+; UTM 449772)

First ascent July 28, 1951, by David Hammack and Anton Nelson. Climb the east face of Tower No. 2 for about 70 feet to a broad, horizontal ledge (avoid the diagonal ledge). The broad, horizontal ledge leads to the notch between Towers No. 1 and No. 2. Traverse out onto the west face from the notch, and climb the class 4 west face to the summit. The broad, horizontal ledge can also be reached from the notch between Towers No. 2 and No. 3 by following a wide ledge.

"Tower No. 2"

(7,480 ft+; 7,680 ft+; UTM 449773)

East Face. Class 4. First ascent July 28, 1951, by David Hammack and Anton Nelson. Climb a class 4 chimney from the broad ledge that leads across the east face of the tower.

Northwest Face. Class 4. First ascent August 12, 1956, by John Ohrenschall and Russ Hoopes. From the notch between Towers No. 2 and No. 3, climb a chimney on the northwest face to the summit.

"Tower No. 3"

(7,760 ft+; 7,760 ft+; UTM 448774)

Southeast Face. I, 5.5. First ascent July 28, 1951, by Anton Nelson and David Hammack. From the notch between Towers No. 2 and No. 3, traverse across the southeast face. When difficulties increase, go up and back to the right on a steep face with good holds to a large ledge. Go left and climb the northwest corner of the tower. This leads to the crux of the climb: a 70-degree face with few holds. Climb this on its right side to an undercling. The next pitch, which leads to the summit, is easy. *Variation:* I, 5.4. First ascent November 27, 1954, by Kim Malville, John Ohrenschall, and Richard Smyth. Traverse across the southeast face to a ledge with a tree on it. Climb the tree to get started, and go

toward some bushes. Traverse to the right around a corner and climb to the summit.

"Tower No. 4"

(7,720 ft; 7,680 ft; UTM 448775)

Northeast Face. I, 5.3. First ascent June 15, 1952, by David Hammack, Bob Smith, George Larimore, and Bob Purington. Ascend a large chimney on the northeast face for 30 feet. Traverse to the right onto the face and climb to some small ledges. Continue straight up and then traverse slightly left to a large, detached flake. Climb the flake and the face above it on good holds. Ascend a tight chimney to a ledge with a tree. Continue climbing the face to the north shoulder. A class 3 pitch leads to the summit from here. The best descent route is a 110-foot rappel from the shoulder to the notch between Towers No. 4 and No. 5.

"Tower No. 5"

(7,760 ft+; 7,760 ft+; UTM 447776)

Southeast Face. Class 4. First ascent July 28, 1951, by Anton Nelson and David Hammack. Climb the broken southeast face from the notch between Towers No. 4 and No. 5. The only difficult section of the face is about halfway up, where a short, slightly overhanging wall must be climbed to get out of an alcove. Follow the main arete to the summit.

North Face. Class 3. First ascent November 27, 1954, by Kim Malville, John Ohrenschall, and Richard Smyth.

"Tower No. 6" *(7,928 ft; 7,929 ft)*

First ascent July 28, 1951, by Anton Nelson and David Hammack. The face above the notch between Towers No. 5 and No. 6 is blocked by an overhang, which is overcome by descending the west side of the notch for about 30 feet and climbing a small tree. Traverse across the wall to easier climbing. Continue up the face to the summit.

The north side of this tower is class 3.

"Tower No. 7"

(8,560 ft+; 8,400 ft+; UTM 442784)

"Tower No. 8"

(8,600 ft+; 8,400 ft+; UTM 442785)

Both of these towers were first climbed July 28, 1951, by Anton Nelson and David

Hammack. They are easily climbed by class 2 and class 3 routes.

Mt. Harrington   (11,009 ft; 11,005 ft)

North Ridge. Class 3. First ascent July 27, 1951, by David Hammack and Anton Nelson. This short, yet steep climb has many excellent holds. And there is a great view from the summit.

The south arete is class 4, and was first climbed by Arkel Erb and friend. There is also a class 3 route on the west face.

The Gorge of Despair

This outstanding rock-climbing area is hard to get to, so solitude is easy to find in the gorge. The rock on these towers, which features many knobs, horns, and chickenheads, is similar to that found on the south face of Charlotte Dome. Some of the finest rock climbs of the High Sierra are found here, and their remoteness only adds to the ambiance. Further reading: H. Warren Lewis, *You're Standing on My Fingers!*, Howell-North Books, Berkeley, California, 1969, pp. 188–202.

"Bushmaster"

This pinnacle is above the Python, along the Silver Spur.

Northwest Ridge. I, 5.4. First ascent June 1991 by Bart O'Brien and Peter Cummings. Follow the ridge from the Python for two pitches.

"The Python"

(9,936 ft; 9,840 ft+; UTM 439831)

Class 2 from Fang Turret; class 4 from the south. First ascent June 1955 by Fred Martin, Kim Malville, and Robert Tambling.

"Silver Turret"

(9,880 ft+; 9,913 ft; UTM 435832)

This is the most impressive rock formation on the Silver Spur, the ridge serving as the southern boundary of the Gorge of Despair.

Southeast Ridge. Class 4. First ascent July 27, 1951, by David Hammack and Anton Nelson. This is an enjoyable and straightforward climb from the notch southeast of the rock.

West Face. Class 3. First ascent September 1973 by Gary Valle and Phil Warrender. This is a very devious, yet enjoyable route on the west face that leads to the northwest arete near the summit. Careful route finding is needed to keep the difficulty down to a class 3 level.

North Buttress. III, 5.8, A1. First ascent July 1972 by Mike Cohen and Mort Hempel. This route starts on a slab that gradually steepens. After a few pitches, climb a chimney to the top of an inconspicuous green wall. Climb up and left to some more chimneys, which lead to an overhang. Ascend the overhang directly and climb several class 4 pitches to the summit. A tension traverse low on the route is the only direct aid on this climb.

"Fang Turret"

This 75-foot rock spire is just south of Silver Turret.

Southeast Notch. I, 5.7. First ascent July 27, 1951, by Anton Nelson and David Hammack. First free ascent September 1955 by John Ohrenschall and Russ Hoopes. Ascend vertical cracks on the southeast corner past a bolt and two fixed pitons.

"Silver Maiden"

(9,280 ft+; UTM 436828)

This formation is in the Silver Creek drainage, about 500 feet below the notch between Fang Turret and Silver Turret.

Northeast Arete. Class 5 and A. First ascent August 3, 1962, by Bruce Edwards, Howard Lewis, Bob Smith, James Smith, and Ed Sutton. Ascend the broken wall to the edge of the northeast arete. A traverse on the exposed left side of the arete leads to a ledge. The next pitch traverses 50 feet to the south to the base of a prominent rib. Ascend the rib to an alcove under a large block. Ascend the chimney directly above the alcove. This chimney eventually turns into a classic layback, and a bolt and some aid climbing is needed to reach the shoulder just below the summit. A class 4 pitch on large knobs leads to the summit. Further reading: H. Warren Lewis, *You're Standing on My Fingers!*, Howell-North Books, Berkeley, California, 1969, p. 201.

"Friday's Folly"

(9,411 ft; 9,388 ft; UTM 431832)

This is the large, wedge-shaped formation west of Silver Turret.

East Face. I, 5.3. First ascent July 8, 1955, by Felix Knauth, Harold Sipperly, and John

Whitmer. Climb the overlapping flakes in the middle of the east face.

"Tenderfoot Peak"

(10,600 ft+; 10,621 ft; UTM 452836)

This gray peak dominates the view from the lake near the head of the Gorge of Despair. First ascent June 1955 by Fred Martin, Kim Malville, and Robert Tambling. The right-hand ridge above the lake is class 2.

Southwest Face. II, 5.6. First ascent 1971 by Steve Devoto and party. This route ascends the large open book on the face. Climb the book for 80 feet, then traverse right into a gully. Ascend the gully for about 200 feet, traverse left, and climb to the top.

"Crystal Turret"

(9,608 ft; 9,520 ft+; UTM 442848)

This is the highest crag on the north rim of the Gorge of Despair.

South Face. I, 5.4. First ascent July 25, 1951, by David Hammack and Anton Nelson. From the Gorge of Despair, hike through brush to the notch southeast of Crystal Turret. Before reaching the notch, ascend a layback crack on the south face. (This crack is about 50 feet left of a "window" below some huge overhanging blocks.) Traverse to the right from the top of the crack to another jam crack. Pass through the window and turn right and climb an arete to a huge ledge. Go to the far, southern edge of the ledge, and climb the southeast edge of the summit block.

East Buttress. I, 5.7. First ascent August 1971 by Steve DeVoto and Bill Oldfield. This route starts at the notch southeast of Crystal Turret. Climb a dike of dark rock to its end, and then traverse to the prow of the buttress. Climb the buttress to the huge ledge just below the summit.

Southwest Face. I, 5.8. First ascent July 1972 by Steve Roper and Tom Gerughty. Climb the obvious chimney that ascends the

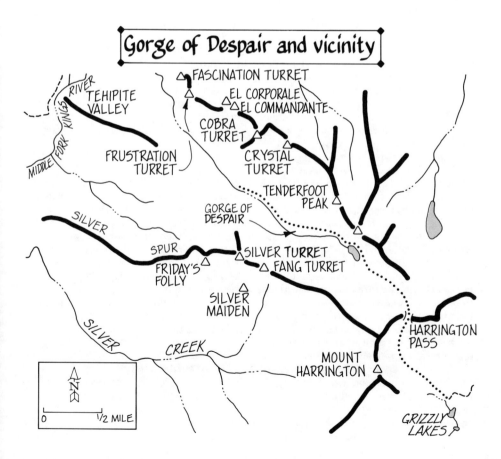

Gorge of Despair and vicinity

face diagonally. Most of this route is class 4. A short, difficult section is found in a flared chimney immediately above a big ledge.

"Cobra Turret"

(9,097 ft; 9,040 ft; UTM 438849)

This is the bulky tower down the ridge from Crystal Turret.

Northwest Face. I, 5.8. First ascent July 26, 1951, by David Hammack and Anton Nelson. Start climbing from the highest point of the forest on the northwest side of the rock. Approximately 75 feet of class 3 climbing leads to a large tree. Go right for 25 feet, and ascend a left-facing corner, which leads into the obvious right-facing ramp. Follow the ramp for a rope length past two fixed pins to a belay at two bolts. Continue up the crack, or the knobby face on the left, to the summit.

Direct Northwest Face. I, 5.9. First ascent September 1973 by Phil Warrender and Gary Valle. This route climbs a thin, vertical crack that is about 100 feet to the left of the Northwest Face route. Follow the crack to the summit cairn for three pitches of crack and face climbing on large knobs.

Prow of Cobra. III, 5.9. First ascent 1979 by Gary Valle and Phil Warrender. This route ascends the prow of the west buttress of Cobra Turret, passing between the left- and right-facing arches in the middle of the face. A 165-foot rope is needed for this climb. Approach the route by scrambling to the left edge of the prow at its base. Climb up and left to a notch in the first overhang, followed by friction (5.6) up and right to a huge ledge and a belay bolt. Climb a 30-foot-long jam crack and traverse left or right and then up to an obvious knobby area with a rib (5.5) to a two-bolt belay. Go up from this belay to a depression, traverse right and up (5.8) to another knobby area, followed by 80 feet of easy but unprotected climbing to another bolt belay among some knobs. Continue up on knobs to a large ledge, and then move right to a large flake with a fixed pin. Climb over the flake (5.9) to a tiny ledge and step to the right onto the knobby face to a two-bolt belay. The fifth pitch goes up and right at first, then back left to a depression with shallow potholes. Easy climbing leads up for 70 feet (unprotected) to another two-bolt belay at the right edge of the overhang. Overcome the roof on knobs and then go up and right to the Wanderland, an area of huge solution tubs. This pitch ends along the left side of the Wanderland at a

single-bolt belay at a large pothole or ledge. Class 4 climbing goes left to a trough that gradually turns into a low-angle cleft, followed by the broken summit arete, which features a few class 5 moves.

Descent Route. Walk west 50 feet to two fixed pitons. A 165-foot rappel leads to two bolts. Another 165-foot rappel ends at class 3 rock just above the large tree at the start of the Northwest Face route.

"El Comandante Turret"

(8,640 ft+; 8,530 ft; UTM 434854)

Hammack-Nelson Route. I, 5.7. First ascent July 25, 1951, by David Hammack and Anton Nelson. There is a large chimney on the south side of the turret which leads to a large ledge. Ascend the chimney for about 30 feet, then traverse left and climb knobs to the large ledge. Follow the ledge up to where it ends, overlooking the north face. Zigzag up the steep face to just below the summit block. A 5.7 friction traverse across the face of the block leads to the southwest corner. Ascend the corner to the summit.

South Chimney. I, 5.6. First ascent July 19, 1952, by a Sierra Club party of nine. Follow the chimney on the south side of the peak to where it ends on the large ledge. Go right to a steep chimney and climb it to its top. Traverse right, and climb a steep layback crack to a ledge just below the summit. A narrow, steep ledge leads to the summit block.

Southwest Face. II, 5.7. First ascent July 1972 by Mort Hempel, Steve Roper, and George Sessions. This route begins on the lower right side of the face at a small, orange dike. Ascend the dike and the face to its left to a slot. Ascend up and left from the top of the slot and follow a left-ascending crack and ledge underneath an overhang. Go to the right above the overhang, and traverse up and right to a sloping belay ledge. A long but easy pitch over many fine knobs leads to a ledge; follow the ledge to where it ends, overlooking the north face. Continue to the summit as described under the Hammack-Nelson Route.

"El Corporale Turret"

(8,480 ft+; 8,400 ft; UTM 433854)

This small turret is on the north side of El Comandante Turret.

South Face. Class 4. First ascent July 25, 1951, by David Hammack and Anton Nelson.

Climb the gully or the ridge to its left to the summit.

"Frustration Turret"

(7,480 ft+; 7,280 ft+; UTM 428855)

This turret is about ½ mile from El Comandante Turret.

East Face. II, 5.7, A1. First ascent June 18, 1952, by David Hammack, Jules Eichorn, Clinton Kelley, and Bob Smith. This climb starts from below the notch that separates the turret from the hillside. Go straight up the face for 100 feet to a small tree. Ascend another 15 feet to a small ledge. Traverse across the face to the right, passing underneath an overhanging slab, to a broken shoulder on the northeastern side of the turret. Ascend the shoulder to a large friction ledge above. From the upper end of the ledge ascend a crack/chimney and go right, up a steep slab on the northwest corner of the turret. Climb a vertical jam crack from the slab, and then go up and right to a small ledge. Either go left and ascend small holds, or go right and climb a steep trough (using friction) to a narrow ledge under a vertical face about 100 feet below the summit. One or two aid placements in a small crack are needed to overcome a short wall. Continue up and to the left, using hidden holds with long arm pulls. This leads to the northeast shoulder at the summit block. Traverse around the block to its south side and climb to the top.

Two rappels are needed to descend the north face to the large friction ledge. Downclimb the route from the ledge to the small tree. One more rappel is needed from the tree.

"Gendarme Turret"

This is the small needle on the ridge between Frustration Turret and Fascination Turret. First ascent June 1955 by Kim Malville, Fred Martin, and Robert Tambling. Descend the steep talus gully leading north from the base of the east face of Frustration Turret. Ascend the first gully rising to the left toward the gendarme. A few aid placements are needed to reach the top.

"Fascination Turret"

(7,120 ft+; 7,120 ft+; UTM 427858)

This is the last turret on the ridge north of the Gorge of Despair. Its north face drops 3,000 feet to Tehipite Valley.

East Face. Class 3. First ascent June 16, 1955, by Kim Malville, Fred Martin, and Robert Tambling. Descend the steep talus gully leading north from the base of the east face of Frustration Turret. After dropping about 300 vertical feet, contour north to the second gully. Climb over loose rock to the base of the turret. Ascend the east face to the summit.

Hogback Peak   *(11,080 ft+; 11,077 ft)*

Class 2 over huge talus blocks from the saddle to the west. First ascent September 10, 1955, by John Ohrenschall and James M. Carl.

Slide Peak   *(10,915 ft; 10,915 ft)*

First ascent May 29, 1960, by George Whitmore. The east slope is class 1.

Kennedy Mountain   *(11,433 ft; 11,433 ft)*

This peak is class 1–2 from Kennedy Pass.

Comb Spur   *(11,618 ft; 11,618 ft)*

Class 2. This was traversed by Robert A. Owen in July 1931.

Mt. Hutchings   *(10,785 ft; 10,785 ft)*

Class 2 via the north ridge from the Granite Pass Trail. First ascent April 1, 1933, by Norman Clyde and friend.

Goat Mountain   *(12,207 ft; 12,207 ft)*

First ascent July 22, 1864, by James T. Gardiner and Charles F. Hoffman. The northwest ridge is class 2. The south ridge is class 2–3.

Munger Peak

(12,040 ft+; 12,076 ft; 0.5 mi NW of Goat Mtn.)

The northeast ridge is class 2.

Kid Peak   *(11,458 ft; 11,458 ft)*

First ascent July 2, 1940, by a party led by Norman Clyde and David Brower, from Paradise Valley.

This peak can be climbed from Kid Lakes by ascending one of the chutes that lead to a point just west of the summit.

Dougherty Peak   *(12,241 ft; 12,244 ft)*

Class 2 from State Lakes. First ascent 1935 by a Sierra Club party.

State Peak   *(12,620 ft; 12,620 ft)*

Class 2 from State Lakes. The best route

goes up the obvious, broad, shallow chute on the southwest side of the peak. The peak is also class 2 from the south and east.

"Windy Point"
(11,200 ft+; 11,150 ft; 1.5 mi N of Horseshoe Lakes)

This is not a peak, but rather a point where there is a fantastic view of the Middle Fork of the Kings River. It can be easily reached during the approach to Gray Pass by following the crest of Windy Ridge out to the point. The National Park Service also recognizes this as a great viewpoint: A line-of-sight radio repeater has been installed on the summit!

Marion Peak *(12,719 ft; 12,719 ft)*

The northeast ridge is class 2 and was first climbed from Marion Lake on July 22, 1902, by Joseph N. LeConte and Curtis Lindley.

The northwest ridge, rising from White Pass, is class 3. First ascent August 11, 1945, by Art Reyman.

Marion Peak has been descended on its southern side, with a direct descent to the South Fork of the Kings River. This is class 2, with a lot of nasty brush along the floor of the canyon.

Red Point *(11,884 ft; 11,840 ft+)*

First ascent August 11, 1945, by Art Reyman. Class 1 from Red Pass.

Peak 11,440+
(11,553 ft; 0.4 mi E of Marion Lake)

There is an excellent view from the top of this small peak. First ascent August 6, 1895, by Bolton C. Brown. It is class 2 from Marion Lake. Ascend to the basin southeast of Marion Lake, and climb talus and slabs toward the northeast to the summit.

Mt. Ruskin *(3938 m; 12,920 ft)*

All of the routes on this peak are classic climbs, and there is an outstanding view from the summit.

From Cartridge Pass. Class 3. First ascent August 7, 1895, by Bolton C. Brown. Follow the ridge from the pass to the northwest arete. Either continue along the arete to the summit, or traverse across the west face to the south ridge, and then climb to the top.

Southwest Face. Class 3. First ascent Au-

gust 13, 1945, by Art Reyman. From the basin south of Cartridge Pass, ascend the southwest face via a rock chute to a point on the south ridge just below the summit. A gendarme along the south ridge is passed on its left (west) side.

East Ridge. Class 3. First ascent 1961 by Andy Smatko, Tom Ross, and Arkel Erb. The best approach to the east ridge is from the south. Once on the ridge, follow it to the summit, passing a block near the top on its north side.

"Saddlehorn"
(3722 m; 12,080 ft+; 0.5 mi NE of Mt. Ruskin)

This is the first peak to catch a rock climber's eye from the summit of Taboose Pass. It is frequently mistaken for Vennacher Needle.

East Ridge. Class 4. First ascent July 22, 1939, by Bruce Meyer, Charlotte Mauk, and David Brower. From the base of the east ridge, traverse across the south side of the ridge for about 200 feet. This traverse ends in an area of broken rock. Climb up and over the crest of the east ridge, and ascend a system of ledges to the summit.

South Face. II, 5.8. First ascent May 1972 by Galen Rowell and Steve Roper. Three steep pitches of crack climbing lead to the summit. A shallow crack above an overhang is the crux.

Vennacher Needle *(3961 m; 12,996 ft)*

This poorly named peak is class 2 from the southeast.

North Arete. III, 5.8. First ascent July 12, 1988, by Galen Rowell. This route begins above a dark, holelike overhang near the base of the wall.

Peak 12,882
(12,860 ft; 1.6 mi SE of Observation Pk.)

Southeast Face. Class 3. First ascent August 12, 1945, by Art Reyman. Ascend a chute with loose rocks from the lake southeast of the mountain.

Cyclorama Wall. V, 5.10, A1. First ascent September 1979 by Claude Fiddler, Vern Clevenger, and Galen Rowell. This route climbs the impressive north face of this peak. Start by climbing a difficult crack system. Four 5.10 pitches with some aid and tension traverses lead to a steep dihedral. Follow the dihedral directly to the summit.

Observation Peak *(12,362 ft; 12,322 ft)*

There is a swell view of the Palisades from the summit of Observation Peak. The south slopes from Dumbbell Lakes or Cataract Creek Pass are class 2; first ascent July 25, 1902, by Joseph N. LeConte and Curtis Lindley. The northwest ridge is class 2 and was climbed by Marjory Hurd in 1926. The class 2 northeast ridge can be reached from the west branch of Cataract Creek.

Mt. Shakspere *(12,174 ft; 12,151 ft)*

First ascent July 20, 1930, by Francis P. Farquhar, Mary Lou Michaels, Doris Drust, Lorna Kilgariff, and Robert Lipman. Class 2 from Observation Peak. The northwest slopes from Palisade Creek are also class 2.

Windy Cliff *(11,151 ft; 11,132 ft)*

The class 2 east ridge was climbed by Douglas Dooley on August 29, 1970.

Peak 11,998

(11,948 ft; 0.7 mi ESE of Windy Cliff)

The north ridge is class 2–3. First ascent August 29, 1970, by Douglas Dooley.

Wrinkles

Cross-country routes from the Monarch Divide to the Middle Fork of the Kings River. There aren't any. All of the canyons that lead north from the Monarch Divide turn into hanging valleys before dropping precipitously into the Middle Fork. The only reasonable route is the Granite Pass Trail.

Marion Peak to State Peak. This traverse is typically done at the 11,500-foot level on the southeast side of the Cirque Crest. A saddle northeast of State Peak is crossed before climbing over the peak and descending to State Lakes.

Mt. Ruskin to Marion Peak. Although these peaks are on two different maps, they are only 2 miles apart as the Clark's nutcracker flies. This traverse is typically done by ascending the east ridge of Mt. Ruskin, descending the southwest face to the basin south of Cartridge Pass, and then ascending the Cirque Crest to Pete's Col. From this point either follow the Cirque Crest, or cross Pete's Col and traverse the basin north of the Cirque Crest, to Marion Peak's northeast ridge. The south side of Marion Peak is descended to the South Fork of the Kings River, which is followed upstream to return to the starting point of the traverse.

Kettle Ridge and The LeConte Divide

AT FIRST GLANCE, THIS REGION MAY APPEAR to be rather dull to the experienced hiker or climber. There is little of the great relief seen in the other areas of the High Sierra, glaciers are absent, and you have to walk a long way to reach timberline. A journey in this area would seem to be better suited for stock users than for self-propelled individuals. The long walk to Kettle Ridge and the LeConte Divide is worthwhile, however. There are outstanding views of the High Sierra from the crest. Those who prefer a close-up view of the timberline country will be delighted with Blackcap Basin, and moving farther south, Blue Canyon is a sight to behold. Blue Canyon Creek drops into the Middle Fork of the Kings River, which turns downstream to Tehipite Valley, a miniature Yosemite Valley that features the largest dome in the entire Sierra Nevada, Tehipite Dome. Rock climbers can find excellent climbing in complete solitude on Kettle Dome and the Obelisk.

This region is bounded by Rodgers Ridge, Tombstone Ridge, and the Middle Fork of the Kings River on the south; by Goddard Creek and Goddard Canyon on the east; by the South Fork of the San Joaquin River on the north; and by Florence Lake, Courtright Reservoir, and Wishon Reservoir on the west.

History

Frank Dusy and Bill Helm set up a partnership in sheep raising at Dinkey Creek in 1869. Later in that same year Dusy wounded a grizzly bear during a hunting trip near Crown Creek. He followed it down to the Middle Fork of the Kings River, where he discovered Tehipite Valley and Tehipite Dome. He continued upstream and found a huge amount of forage at Simpson Meadow. In the next few years Dusy and Helm built the Dinkey Trail to Crown Valley, and the Tunemah Trail to Simpson Meadow.

Comparatively little mountaineering was done in this area. Tehipite Dome's first recorded ascent was in 1896, and Kettle Dome was climbed by Hermann Ulrichs in 1920. The Obelisk was first climbed in 1947, and some of the peaks along Kettle Ridge and the LeConte Divide were first climbed as late as the 1950s.

Maps

United States Geological Survey: 7.5-minute series: Ward Mountain, Mt. Henry, Blackcap Mtn., Courtright Reservoir, Mt. Goddard, Slide Bluffs, Tehipite Dome, Rough Spur; 15-minute series: Marion Peak, Tehipite Dome, Blackcap Mtn., Mt. Goddard; national park maps: Sequoia and Kings Canyon National Parks and Vicinity (1:125,000).

United States Forest Service: John Muir Wilderness and the Sequoia–Kings Canyon National Parks Backcountry (1:63,360).

Wilderness Permits

For west-side entry to the John Muir Wilderness and Kings Canyon National Park backcountry: Sierra National Forest, Pineridge Ranger District, Shaver Lake, CA 93271.

Roads
Dinkey Creek Road and McKinley Grove Road

Dinkey Creek Road leaves Highway 168 at Shaver Lake. It goes east for about 12 miles to just short of Dinkey Creek; turn right onto the McKinley Grove Road. After approximately 15 miles the road ends at the beginning of the Wishon Road and the Courtright Road.

The Wishon Road

The Wishon Road heads east from a three-way junction with the McKinley Grove and Courtright roads. It crosses the dam that forms Wishon Reservoir after 3.3 miles, and passes the Woodchuck Trailhead at 4.1 miles. At 6.6 miles, it comes to the junction with the road leading to the Crown Valley Trailhead; go left if headed for the Rancheria Trailhead.

Another junction is encountered 1.8 miles farther up the Wishon Road. Turn left, and the Rancheria Trailhead is 0.7 mile beyond.

To reach the Crown Valley Trailhead, turn right at the junction of the Wishon Road 2.5 miles beyond the dam (6.6 miles from the junction with the McKinley Grove and Courtright roads). The Crown Valley Trailhead is 1.1 miles farther.

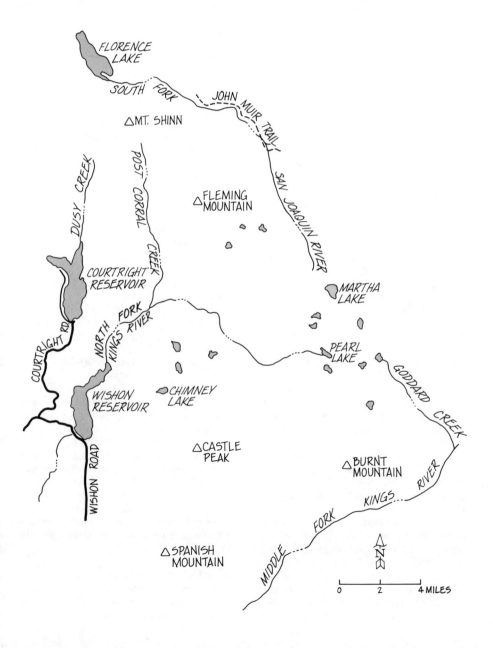

Courtright Road

The Courtright Road goes left from the three-way junction of the McKinley Grove and Wishon roads. There is a junction just before Courtright Reservoir after 7.9 miles; go right. Drive across the spillway and the dam 0.4 mile farther; the Maxson Trailhead is 0.9 mile beyond the dam.

Florence Lake Road

This road is described in Chapter 10: The Mono Recesses.

Trails

Spanish Lake Trail and Geraldine Lakes Trail   (7 miles)

This trail starts at the Crown Valley Trailhead, and goes east for ³/₄ mile to where it branches south from the Crown Valley Trail. The trail to Spanish Lake descends to and crosses Rancheria Creek and, after 2¹/₂ miles, comes to Statum Meadow. Instead of crossing the meadow, the trail climbs the ridge to the north for ¹/₄ mile to a junction. The left branch leads to Crown Valley; the right or southern branch continues for 1 mile to Spanish Meadow. A quarter-mile after the meadow, the trail meets the old four-wheel-drive track that leads to Spanish Lake and Little Spanish Lake. The trail to Geraldine Lakes goes east, across the four-wheel-drive track, for about ¹/₂ mile to the meadow. A trail leads north from here to Wet Meadow and Crown Valley; the Geraldine Lakes Trail goes south, along the western edge of the meadow, and eventually into the forest. The trail climbs slightly, and crosses a small pass before descending to Geraldine Lakes. (Just beyond the pass another trail branches off of the main trail and heads southwest to the top of Spanish Mountain.) The trail eventually comes to the eastern shore of the lower Geraldine Lake approximately 2 miles from Spanish Lake. From Geraldine Lake a trail goes northeast to Crown Valley; another trail goes southeast and ends north of the Obelisk.

There is also a four-wheel-drive track that climbs to the top of Rodgers Ridge from Rancheria Creek. At one time the track went by Spanish Lake and almost to Chain Lakes, but the road has been blocked at the point where it leaves Rodgers Ridge and descends to Spanish Lakes. (This was done because of an enlargement of the John Muir Wilder-

ness in 1984.) The four-wheel-drive route has many ups and downs, and most hikers will find it tedious walking. The Spanish Lake Trail is preferable.

Crown Valley Trail   (7¹/₂ miles)

This trail leaves the Crown Valley Trailhead and goes east for ³/₄ mile to the junction with the trail to Spanish Lake. The Crown Valley Trail goes left, climbs past Three Springs, and, after 1¹/₂ miles, meets a trail that leads north to the Rancheria Trail. The Crown Valley Trail continues east another 2¹/₂ miles to where it meets the old four-wheel-drive track between Spanish Lake and Chain Lakes; a short distance beyond this the trail goes southeast over a small pass and down to another trail junction near Cow Meadow. The trail leading west meets the Spanish Lake Trail above Statum Meadow. The Crown Valley Trail continues east, passing Wet Meadow, two side trails leading south to Spanish and Geraldine lakes, and the Crown Valley Ranger Station before descending to Crown Valley.

Tehipite Valley Trail and the Middle Fork Trail   (21 miles)

These trails descend to and travel along the floor of the canyon of the Middle Fork of the Kings River. This is one of the great canyons of the Sierra Nevada, rivaling in grandeur Kings Canyon (South Fork of the Kings River) and Yosemite Valley. But what makes this canyon unique is that no roads approach it. It is as wild today as when Frank Dusy, a shepherd, first traveled this route in 1869.

This trail leaves Crown Valley and goes south, past a side trail that heads southwest to Geraldine Lakes, and passes through the forest to Gnat Meadow in about 5 miles. From Gnat Meadow the trail climbs to the top of a ridge and makes a gradual descent before starting down the canyon over many switchbacks for 4 miles to Tehipite Valley. The Middle Fork Trail ascends the canyon floor on the north side of the stream for 12 miles to Simpson Meadow, where it crosses the Middle Fork and meets the Granite Pass Trail.

Blue Canyon Trail   (12 miles)

Although this trail has not been maintained for many years, it is still serviceable for a visit to beautiful Blue Canyon.

The trail goes east from Crown Valley for 3½ miles to Crown Creek, which is a dangerous crossing at high water. Across the stream, the trail climbs around the south side of Kettle Dome before descending to Blue Canyon after 5 miles. The trail follows the west bank of Blue Canyon Creek for 3 miles, and then crosses the stream and ascends its east bank to where the trail ends in the lake basin above. Cross-country travel is easy among the lakes.

Rancheria Trail *(5¾ miles)*

This trail goes east from the Rancheria Trailhead (see the description for the Wishon Road, above). At first it climbs slightly and then contours before meeting a side trail that leads south to the Crown Valley Trail (this junction is 1¾ miles from the trailhead). The Rancheria Trail then climbs slightly for 2 miles before meeting another trail junction east of Finger Rock. One trail branches south from here and leads to Crown Valley; another trail goes east to Duck Lake. The Rancheria Trail continues north 1½ miles to meet the Chuck Pass Trail. The Rancheria Trail goes north another ½ mile to meet the Woodchuck Trail.

Chuck Pass Trail *(5½ miles)*

The Chuck Pass Trail starts along the Rancheria Trail about ½ mile from the Woodchuck Trail. It goes east past Indian Springs and over Chuck Pass to meet the Crown Pass Trail approximately 3½ miles north of Crown Valley.

Crown Pass Trail *(9 miles)*

The Crown Pass Trail connects Crown Valley with the summit of Crown Pass. From Crown Valley, follow the Blue Canyon Trail approximately ½ mile to meet the Crown Pass Trail. The trail goes north, and after ½ mile it meets a trail that leads northeast to Mountain Meadow and Coyote Pass. The Crown Pass Trail continues north, passes Elizabeth Lake, and meets the Chuck Pass Trail after 3 miles. The trail continues north another 5½ miles to the top of Crown Pass, passing Scepter Lake and Crown Lake along the way.

Woodchuck Trail *(14 miles)*

This trail leaves the Woodchuck Trailhead and goes south, then north, and finally to the east up the Woodchuck Creek drainage to cross the Rancheria Trail after 5 miles. The Woodchuck Trail climbs to the north for ½ mile and meets the side trail leading to Woodchuck Lake. The Woodchuck Trail continues east, passing a side trail to March Lake and the end of the Woodchuck Lake Trail, for 5 miles to Crown Pass (which, strictly speaking, is not a pass, but a crossing of the shoulder of an unnamed peak). The Crown Pass Trail descends the south side of the pass to Crown Valley; the Woodchuck Trail continues north, down past Halfmoon Lake to where the trail branches. The north branch descends for 2½ miles to meet the Blackcap Basin Trail near Big Maxson Meadow. The east branch goes east, across the outlet to Halfmoon Lake, for 3 miles to meet the Blackcap Basin Trail approximately 3½ miles upstream from Big Maxson Meadow.

Woodchuck Lake Trail *(3½ miles)*

This side trail leaves the Woodchuck Trail about ½ mile from the Rancheria Trail junction. After 2½ miles it reaches Woodchuck Lake, and after rounding the lake on its eastern shore, the trail goes south 1 mile to meet the Woodchuck Trail again.

Blackcap Basin Trail *(22½ miles)*

The Blackcap Basin Trail starts from the Maxson Trailhead near Courtright Reservoir. The trail, a dirt road at first, turns into a proper trail before reaching Maxson Meadows. It then crosses a small pass and descends to meet the Burnt Corral Meadow Trail, 4½ miles from the trailhead. The Blackcap Basin Trail goes east, and after 1½ miles it meets another branch of the Burnt Corral Meadow Trail. The Blackcap Basin Trail gradually descends Post Corral Creek to meet the Hell-For-Sure Pass Trail after 3½ miles. The Blackcap Basin Trail goes south for 5 miles to the junction with the Meadow Brook Trail, along the North Fork of the Kings River. The Blackcap Basin Trail remains on the north bank of the river, and continues upstream for 2 miles to meet the branch of the Woodchuck Trail that descends from Halfmoon Lake. After going another 1 mile upstream, the trail meets the Bench Valley Trail; after another 1½ miles it leads to a crossing of the river, and a junction with the other branch of the Woodchuck Trail. The Blackcap Basin Trail remains on the south side of the river and gradually climbs for 3 miles to where the trail forks. The east branch leads for ½ mile to Portal Lake; the west branch goes over a small pass to Crown Basin.

Bench Valley Trail (7 miles)

At one time a trail ascended the south branch of Fall Creek, but it has not been maintained for many years. The best route ascends a trail that leaves the Blackcap Basin Trail about 1 mile east of Big Maxson Meadow. The trail makes a steep ascent before gradually climbing around and up to the hanging valley that holds McGuire Lake. The trail goes around the north and east sides of the lake and makes a short climb to Guest Lake. It then goes north over a small pass to Horsehead Lake. There are many use trails that lead to the small lakes in this basin.

Meadow Brook Trail (7 miles)

This trail leaves the Blackcap Basin Trail about 5 miles downstream from Big Maxson Meadow. It makes a steep ascent to the east of Meadow Brook to Devil's Punchbowl. It continues another mile north to meet the Hell-For-Sure Pass Trail.

Hell-For-Sure Pass Trail (12½ miles)

This trail leaves the Blackcap Basin Trail 9½ miles from the trailhead near Courtright Reservoir. The Hell-For-Sure Pass Trail goes east, climbs over a small ridge, and passes south of Fleming Lake to meet the Indian Lakes Trail 5½ miles from the Blackcap Basin Trail. The trail makes a gradual ascent to the east for 1½ miles to meet the Meadow Brook Trail coming from Devil's Punchbowl, then continues climbing to the east to the summit of Hell-For-Sure Pass (named by Joseph LeConte and Karl Grove Gilbert when they crossed it in 1904, after they had failed to find a route for pack animals across the Goddard Divide). The trail makes a steep descent down the northeast side of the pass and comes to a fork. One branch makes a direct descent to Goddard Canyon; the other follows a bench southeast across the wall of Goddard Canyon, making a gradual descent to the Goddard Canyon Trail.

Indian Lakes Trail (2½ miles)

The Indian Lakes Trail leaves the Hell-For-Sure Pass Trail just east of Fleming Lake.

It goes north, and after a short distance it meets a branch trail leading to Rae Lake. The main trail continues north to the west shore of Lower Indian Lake, becoming rather faint north of the lake, but travel is easy through the meadows and sand flats upstream to Upper Indian Lake.

Burnt Corral Meadow Trail (11 miles)

This trail leaves the Blackcap Basin Trail 4½ miles from the Maxson Trailhead (or from a point 1½ miles farther along the trail at Long Meadow). It goes north, past Hobler Lake, to meet the trail's other branch near Burnt Corral Creek. The trail goes up the west bank of the creek and crosses to the east side before reaching Burnt Corral Meadow. It then continues upstream and crosses an unnamed pass before descending to Thompson Lake. The trail goes north from the lake and gradually descends to meet the Blayney Meadows Trail south of Florence Lake.

Blayney Meadows Trail (9¼ miles)

The Blayney Meadows Trail provides access to the northern portion of the LeConte Divide. It is described in Chapter 10: The Mono Recesses.

Cross-Country Routes

The Tunemah Trail

This is an old sheep and cattle route that led from Crown Valley to Simpson Meadow. The trail has not been used for many years, and it is now an adventurous and historic cross-country route.

Leave Blue Canyon at the 8,000-foot level and ascend to the saddle north of Burnt Mountain. Descend and traverse east to cross Alpine Creek, and reach Bunchgrass Flat on a level traverse from Alpine Creek. Make a steep ascent to the northeast, climbing over Peak 10,987 (10,985 ft), which is the real Tunemah "Pass." (Some maps place the name on the saddle 0.4 mile northwest of the peak.) From the top of the "pass" you can see Simpson Meadow far below. The word "Tunemah" is a Chinese obscenity, and this is the Tunemah part of the cross-country route: Descend (i.e., slide down) the east side of the pass to a point along Goddard Creek approximately ½ mile upstream from its junction with the Middle Fork of the Kings

River. After finding a safe place to cross the river, you have access to the Middle Fork Trail or the Granite Pass Trail.

Coyote Pass *(10,071 ft; 10,000 ft+)*

At one time a trail went over this pass, providing access between Crown Valley and the upper part of Blue Canyon. Only traces of the trail may still be seen, however.

From Crown Valley take the Crown Pass Trail north for ½ mile to a trail junction. The trail goes east and then northeast across many small creeks and big Crown Creek to Mountain Meadow. Alternatively, it is possible and perhaps easier to hike up Crown Creek to the meadow. From Mountain Meadow, go east to the summit of the pass atop Kettle Ridge. The descent of the east side of the pass is steep in places; the route eventually breaks out of the forest and into the beautiful meadows of Blue Canyon.

"Dykeman Pass"

(11,040 ft+; 11,046 ft; 2.0 mi SSW of Blue Canyon Pk.)

Class 2. Dykeman Pass, named here in honor of Dave Dykeman, provides access between the upper reaches of Blue Canyon Creek and Alpine Creek.

"Alpine Pass"

(11,160 ft+; 11,120 ft+; 0.1 mi S of Tunemah Lake)

Class 2. This pass is at the head of the Alpine Creek drainage; it provides access to Tunemah Lake.

"Mantle Pass"

(10,960 ft+; 10,880 ft+; 1.2 mi WSW of Finger Pk.)

Class 2. Mantle Pass, named here in honor of Doug Mantle, crosses Kettle Ridge and provides access between Crown Basin and the upper part of Blue Canyon. It is best to round the lake east of the pass, on its northern shore.

"Midway Pass"

(11,640 ft+; 11,600 ft+; 0.7 mi WNW of Finger Pk.; UTM 451997)

Class 2. This pass crosses Kettle Ridge and leads between Blue Canyon Creek and Midway Lake. Strictly speaking, it is not a pass but rather a ridge crossing. Climb steep slabs interspersed with sand on the south side of the pass. From the top of the pass, follow the ridge crest northwest from Kettle Ridge, which overlooks Cathedral Lake and Midway Lake to the north. Descend the southeast side of this small ridge over rock and sand, and gradually contour around to the north to meet Midway Lake.

"Blue Canyon Pass"

(11,480 ft+; 11,440 ft+; 0.5 mi E of Finger Pk.)

Class 2. Blue Canyon Pass leads between Blue Canyon Creek and the upper part of Goddard Creek. The southern approach to the pass is made from the southwest by ascending a series of chutes to the top of the pass. The north side of the pass consists of large talus, and it is best to traverse across the north side of Finger Peak before going north and then northeast to Goddard Creek.

"Finger Col"

(11,560 ft+; 11,520 ft+; 0.4 mi NNW of Finger Pk.; UTM 459000)

Class 2. This pass provides access between the headwaters of the North Fork of the Kings River and Goddard Creek. Ascend the south side of the stream between Portal Lake and Midway Lake; this is over steep slabs and talus. Pass Midway Lake on its northern side and head for the north shore of Cathedral Lake. Ascend northeast, away from Cathedral Lake, on slabs and talus, and then traverse south, gradually ascending to the first, small col north of Finger Peak. Descend the east side of the pass by following a ledge that leads south, and then descend slabs to a gully that descends northeast. Stay south of the small lake east of the pass, and continue descending to Goddard Creek.

North Fork of the Kings River

This is a difficult descent of the gorge of the North Fork between the Blackcap Basin Trail and Wishon Reservoir. It is for experienced cross-country hikers only.

Leave the Blackcap Basin Trail at the point where the trail descends from Post Corral Meadows and meets the North Fork. Descend the north bank of the river for ¼ mile, and then go right to avoid a precipitous, yet beautiful, series of cascades. After this the route remains near the north side of the river, with occasional, small detours to avoid small cliffs and domes. You eventually come to some more cascades, which end in a large pool. Contour west from here to Post Corral Creek and follow it downstream to where it meets the North Fork. Cross over to the south bank of the river at this point, and make a level traverse across the southeast side of the gorge, above the steep cliffs. Continue southwest and downstream, gradually moving away from the North Fork drainage to the drainage north of Cape Horn. Follow this creek downstream to where it meets the North Fork. Follow the North Fork downstream, through loose rock and brush, to where Wishon Reservoir (or its mud flats, if the water level is low) becomes visible. Shortly after this you come to a small creek. Descend the south side of the creek, staying south and west of its steep sections, to the boat campsite on the northeast shore of Wishon Reservoir.

The easiest way from here is by boat. Failing that, it is necessary to go south, climb over a ridge, and descend to the Woodchuck Trail. During the winter and early spring, it may be possible to hike along the dry bottom of the reservoir to the road leading to Shaver Lake—but watch out for deep mud!

Nichols Canyon

The trail that once descended this canyon is long gone. For the cross-country route, descend the north slope of Crown Pass and keep to the east of the stream in the canyon. There is a meadow where the stream from Old Pipe Lake meets the main stream of Nichols Canyon. Continue downstream, keeping to the east of the creek, to where the canyon drops off above the North Fork of the Kings River. Continue down to the North Fork, and cross on any of the many fallen logs.

"Blackcap Pass"

(11,160 ft+; 11,120 ft+; 0.5 mi NE of Blackcap Mtn.)

Class 2. This pass is between Blackcap Basin and Guest Lake, in Bench Valley. The ascent of the pass from Blackcap Basin is easy. From the top of the pass, make a steep, rocky descent on its west side to a sandy bench. Descend the north side of the stream to Guest Lake.

"Reinstein Pass"

(11,880 ft+; 11,840 ft+; 0.2 mi NE of Mt. Reinstein)

Class 2. Although this pass crosses the Goddard Divide and connects Goddard Creek with Goddard Canyon, it has come to be known as Reinstein Pass by cross-country hikers.

From Goddard Creek climb into the basin southeast of Mt. Reinstein, and go north over ledges and boulders to the summit of the pass. Descend the north side of the pass, over talus and slabs, to Martha Lake.

"Valor Pass"

(11,760 ft+; 11,760 ft+; 1.0 mi NNW of Mt. Reinstein)

Class 2–3. This pass, which connects Blackcap Basin with the lake at the head of Goddard Canyon (Martha Lake), is commonly used by climbers on their way to Mt. Goddard. From Blackcap Basin ascend to Ambition Lake, and make the steep ascent to the cirque that holds Valor Lake. Steep talus leads to the surprisingly flat summit of the pass. Descend the northeast side of the pass by first going east and then north to Martha Lake.

"Confusion Pass"

(11,360 ft+; 11,360 ft+; 2.5 mi NE of Blackcap Mtn.)

Class 2. This pass crosses the LeConte Divide between Blackcap Basin and Goddard Canyon. The name of the pass comes from the lake almost atop the crest of the LeConte Divide. This eastern shore of the lake is actually a huge cliff overlooking Goddard Canyon; the north, west, and south shores of this lake are composed of gigantic blocks of talus. Valor Pass is a preferable route.

Ascend to Rainbow Lake in Blackcap Basin, and continue northward to a broken granite bench. Enter a shallow chute or gorge, hopping from block to block to where the chute ends at the southwest corner of "Confusion Lake." Follow the western shore of the lake northward over much broken talus to Confusion Pass, which is located at the northwest corner of the lake. The descent into Goddard Canyon consists of much steep, loose talus.

"Gunsight Pass"

(11,600 ft+; 11,600 ft+; 1.0 mi E of Bullet Lake)

Class 2. This pass leads from the lakes in the upper reaches of Bench Valley, over the LeConte Divide, and into Goddard Canyon. A direct ascent to the pass from Bullet Lake encounters much talus. It is better to begin the ascent from the north and east shore of Holster Lake. Go east, between the rocky canyon on the right (south) and the long recesses on the left; avoid the recesses themselves. At the last recess, go left (east) and ascend some slabs to the top of the pass. A lot of loose, steep talus is encountered while descending the east side of the pass to Goddard Canyon.

"Two Passes"

(11,000 ft+ and 11,120 ft+; 10,960 ft+ and 11,120 ft+; 1.0 and 1.2 mi SE of Devil's Punchbowl)

Class 2. These two passes connect Red Mountain Basin with the lakes in Bench Valley. Head southeast from the north shore of Devil's Punchbowl, passing the two unnamed lakes southeast of Devil's Punchbowl on their northern shores. Go north a short distance to a small meadow. Leave this meadow from its southern side, and climb a granite face of slabs and blocks toward a low notch visible above and to the left, eventually reaching a chute that leads away from the notch, to the right. Follow this chute to the top of the ridge and cross the sand flat, keeping to its right, to a meadow. Leave the meadow at its eastern side, next to the stream, and climb up and right to another face of granite slabs. Climb this face to the top of the first pass.

From here the second pass, to the east, is an easy climb. From the top of the second pass you can either traverse north and then east to Schoolmarm Lake, or descend directly east on sand, and then traverse south down the Falls Creek drainage.

"Fleming Pass"

(10,560 ft+; 10,560 ft+; 0.4 mi N of Fleming Mtn.)

Class 1. Fleming Pass is an easy climb from Lower Indian Lake. It is best to descend the western side of the pass by first going north and then west.

"Post Corral Pass"

(10,240 ft+; 10,240 ft+; 2.5 mi NNE of Post Corral Meadows; UTM 327166)

Class 1. This pass leads to the upper reaches of Post Corral Creek from the meadows northwest of Fleming Mountain. It is commonly used by packers and cowboys to move stock that graze in these meadows over the summer.

Mosquito Pass *(10,440 ft+; 10,400 ft+)*

Class 2. This route leads from Upper Indian Lake to the South Fork of the San Joaquin River. Follow the eastern shore of Upper Indian Lake northward and ascend a short chute. At its top, traverse left (west) to the top of Mosquito Pass. Descend the north side of the pass by traversing west across sandy chutes and broken granite to a small stream choked with willows. An area of huge boulders is bypassed by going to the east. Descend through the forest to the stream that drains the lake north of Mosquito Pass. Continue hiking downstream by any number of routes to the river. The Blayney Meadows Trail is easily reached once the South Fork of the San Joaquin River is crossed.

Peaks

Finger Rock *(9,606 ft; 9,606 ft)*

The north side is class 3.

South Face. III, 5.8, A3. First ascent 1981 by Rick Nolting and Fred Beckey. Begin by climbing the chimney that splits the center of the pillar on the south face. Two pitches in the chimney lead to a ledge that angles right and ends at a blank wall. This wall is overcome by climbing from an isolated ledge using tiny holds and cracks, and one aid move. Continue up cracks and then traverse left across a steep, friction slab. This is followed by ascending a rib, and then climbing slabs to the summit.

Spanish Mountain *(10,051 ft; 10,051 ft)*

First ascent 1921 by Hermann F. Ulrichs. A trail leaves the Geraldine Lakes Trail and leads almost to the very top. Class 1.

A more interesting (class 2) route ascends the southeast ridge from the highest of the Geraldine Lakes. Many small cliffs and boulders must be overcome, but this route offers the most outstanding view of Kings Canyon.

Obelisk *(9,705 ft; 9,700 ft)*

This landmark peak serves as the extreme western boundary of Kings Canyon National Park. It has excellent rock (reminiscent of Charlotte Dome), but the long approach keeps it from being overwhelmed by climbers. From Geraldine Lakes, the best approach is on top of the ridge between the Obelisk and Spanish Mountain. The final approach is made from near the top of Peak 9,628 (9,600 ft+; 0.2 mi NE of the Obelisk). A direct approach from the west results in much bushwhacking. Routes on the east and south faces are best approached from the small peak northeast of the Obelisk. Further reading: *Rock & Ice,* No. 30, p. 54.

South Face. II, 5.6. First ascent 1947 by Jim Wilson and Allen Steck. This route goes up a long, broken chimney on the south face. The chimney ends at the foot of a steep wall, the crux of the climb. This pitch is about 100 feet long, and it is sustained. The route to the summit is easy from the top of this pitch.

Los Pollos Locos. II, 5.8. First ascent August 13, 1989, by Greg Vernon, Mike Baca, and R. J. Secor. This route climbs the southwest recess of the Obelisk. A crack splits the face (which is covered with knobs and chickenheads), passes through a small roof, and ascends a vertical headwall. Bushwhack up a chimney (class 4) and go up and left over almost unbelievable knobs and chickenheads to the crack. Climb the face left of the crack to a point above the roof, move right across the crack, and then left across the crack again to a tiny belay stance. Go straight up from the stance, keeping to the right of a black watermark and left of the crack. The top of this headwall is blank, and the crack assumes a wicked overhanging flare at this point (5.8). The last pitch is easier, followed by 300 feet of class 3 to the top.

WasabiMan. II, 5.8. First ascent July 1990 by Barry Chambers and Leni Reeves. This route is on the southwest side of the Obelisk, and climbs between two dihedrals that form an arch. (This is not the system that leads to a deep cleft, but the next one to the right.) Scramble up the blocky right dihedral to a ledge. Climb the dihedral for about 30 feet, then move left out onto the face and up over good holds to a ledge in the middle of the face. Continue up from the ledge to where climbing gets harder. An undercling to the left is followed by a small flake, and then more face climbing leads up to the roof at the apex of the two dihedrals. Climb the big crack that splits the roof, and continue up and slightly right for four more pitches to the summit.

West Face. II, 5.7. First ascent April 1971 by Fred Beckey and Hooman Aprin. Climb a chimney on the left side of the face before moving to the right onto the face. This is followed by six pitches of excellent climbing on knobs and chickenheads to the summit.

Rock Solid. II, 5.8. First ascent September 2, 1990, by Bart O'Brien, Richard Swayze, and Mike Jaurequi. This route follows the crack system that is 40 feet to the left of the chimney on the West Face route. The route starts from a narrow ledge at the base of the crack system, about 50 feet above the talus. A nice pitch with one 5.8 move leads to a belay alcove in a chimney. Step to the right and climb a full rope-length of outstanding 5.8 face climbing. Three more pitches on big knobs lead to the summit.

Handle With Care. III, 5.8. First ascent June 1990 by David Harden, Jack Bedell, and Don Palmer. This route is close to the northwest corner of the Obelisk, and consists of seven pitches of excellent face climbing. Begin by climbing the left side of the west face for four pitches of face climbing (5.5 to 5.7). These pitches lead to a notch behind an obvious pillar on the northwest corner. A beautiful hand crack goes up and slightly left on the north face for 200 feet. Sustained, steep face climbing (5.8) leads along the crack over some eroded and friable knobs. Traverse to the right from the top of the crack onto a steep prow. Follow the prow to easier climbing.

The Flake Route. II, 5.9. First ascent September 1983 by Herb Laeger, Eve Laeger, and Rick Smith. This route ascends the overhanging flakes on the right side of the north face. The climb continues up the left-facing corner system above the cracks.

North Face and West Face. II, 5.7. First ascent June 1951 by Anton Nelson, David Hammack, John Salathe, and Alice Ann Dayton. The north face has a 45-degree ridge near its center. Either climb the ridge for 100 feet to its end (class 4), or climb to the left of the ridge (5.3). From the top of this ridge, traverse right on a small, exposed ledge. This traverse ends at two short dihedrals. The one on the left is off-width, the right is a hand jam, and they both are 5.7. After this, go up and right to climb a tight chimney (5.4) to the west face. It is class 3 from the upper west face to the summit.

The Bacanal. II, 5.9, A1. First ascent August 1988 by Mike Baca and Greg Vernon. This route climbs the dihedral directly above the 45-degree ridge on the north face. A couple of aid placements are needed at the start of the dihedral. Go up and left just below the top of the dihedral to the summit.

Hands of Fate. II, 5.10. First ascent September 1976 by Alan Bartlett and Robb Dellinger. This route follows the obvious crack system that is to the left of The Bacanal. An easy pitch leads to the base of the crack, where two small overhangs bar the way. Bypass the first by traversing right, then follow a difficult arch up and left. Surmounting the second overhang is the crux of the climb.

East Face. II, 5.5. First ascent March 1972 by Chuck Kroger and Ben Dewell. Descend about 200 feet from the small peak northeast of the Obelisk. Walk through some brush, and climb class 3 ledges to the bottom of a large chimney on the east face. The route goes up 100 feet on the poorly protected face left of the chimney to a ledge system. Traverse left 100 feet on easy ledges, and climb to the summit from these ledges.

Descent Route. The south face requires six rappels to reach the ground. The northeast shoulder requires two rappels: a short one from the summit to a ledge above the great overhang, and a 165-foot free rappel from above the overhang to the notch northeast of the Obelisk. Care should be taken when

The Obelisk, North Face (photo by Mike Baca)

The Obelisk from the northeast (photo by R. J. Secor)

rappel

Hands
of Fate

The
Bacanal

West
Face

North
Face

Flake
Route

Rock
Solid

The Obelisk, Southeast Face (photo by Mike Baca)

placing the rappel to prevent rope jams. (There are at least two ropes tangled among the horns above the great overhang; the 3/8-inch twisted nylon rope has been there since September 1975.) From the notch, it is class 3 over the small peak northeast of the Obelisk to the ground.

Kettle Dome   (9,451 ft; 9,446 ft)

Northeast Face. Class 4. First ascent July 20, 1920, by Hermann Ulrichs. A short class 4 move is followed by a traverse across slabs to two class 4 pitches, which lead directly to the flat summit.

West Face. II, 5.7. First ascent October 20, 1974, by Phil Warrender, Walt Vennum, and Fred Beckey. Climb a long, poorly protected crack to the center of a shallow bowl on the west face. Two pitches of friction in the bowl are followed by a traverse right for 100 feet to a flared outside corner. Climb the corner to the crest of the southwest ridge, and follow the ridge to the summit.

Tehipite Dome   (7,708 ft; 7,708 ft)

This is the largest dome in the Sierra Nevada. There is an outstanding view from its summit.

North Ridge. Class 3. First ascent July 31, 1896, by Allan L. Chickering and Walter A. Starr, Sr. Many parties make the mistake of leaving the Blue Canyon Trail too early, and end up traversing across duff and brush to Tehipite Dome. It is better to follow the Blue Canyon Trail to where it starts its descent to Blue Canyon at UTM 420896, at an elevation of 8,600 feet. Head south-southeast to Point 8,401 (8,369 ft), where there is a fantastic view of the Middle Fork of the Kings River. Head south and then southwest, over the top of Point 7,719 (7,680 ft+), to the north base of the dome. Stay on the east side of the ridge a short distance below its crest before making the short class 3 move onto the ridge. An easy scramble leads to the summit of the dome. The spectacular view of the Middle Fork canyon during the approach and on the summit is ample reward for the modest effort expended to reach the summit.

The Time Warp. IV, 5.9. First ascent June 1963 by Fred Beckey, Herb Swedlund, John Ahern, and Ken Weeks. First free ascent June 1983 by Bob Harrington, Dale Bard, and Dick Leversee. The crux of this climb is the approach. An approach from the floor of the Middle Fork canyon is not recommended due to the difficulty of crossing the river. The best approach is from the base of the north ridge of the dome and down the dome's east side, through trees, brush, rappels from hanging trees, and some creative down-climbing.

The approach ends on a tree- and brush-covered ledge directly beneath the nose in the center of the south face of the dome. Ascend a crack behind a pillar that leans against the wall, then follow a crack system that is to the right of the nose. Traverse left and climb a long, difficult flaring chimney and off-width crack. One pitch on the very nose leads to another traverse left into a chimney. Climb an unprotected sloping ramp that leads to a shallow chimney. One more pitch leads to the huge ledge that traverses across the southwest face of the dome. (This ledge can be used as an escape route, if needed.)

From the huge ledge, climb the overhanging, brush-filled crack left of a wide tower that leans against the dome. This pitch ends with some wide stemming. Climb flakes and cracks on the main part of the dome; this leads to a dihedral system, which is followed to just below the summit. The route ends with pleasurable climbing on knobs and solution pockets. Further reading: *Summit,* September 1963, pp. 1, 31; *Summit,* November 1963, pp. 14–19.

Southwest Face. VI, 5.9, A4. First ascent July 1970 by Chuck Kroger, Curt Chadwick, and Norm Weeden. This climb begins several hundred feet below and left of The Time Warp. Climb some ramps (some are difficult, but short) to a gigantic hollow flake. Ascend the left edge of this to a terrace just left of the start of The Time Warp. Above the terrace, climb a left-facing dihedral, which leads to a difficult, narrow chimney. This chimney ends on the huge ledge that crosses the southwest face of the dome. Follow The Time Warp to the summit from here.

Wilderness Serenity. II, 5.10b. First ascent August 1990 by Barry Chambers and Leni Reeves. This route is on the apron on the lower portion of Tehipite Dome. Begin by climbing a right-facing dihedral, followed by a crack (5.10a) to a belay from a tree; a minor variation here is to climb the crack about halfway up, and face climb up and right (5.9) to another crack, which leads back to the tree. Continue up a groove from the tree, where an undercling leads left to a left-facing dihedral. Belay from two trees on top of the dihedral. Climb another groove from the two trees, at first leading left (5.8), bypassing a small roof on its right side, and continuing to the right to a belay beneath a large roof. The last part of this pitch is the crux: some 5.10b face moves beneath the roof. Surmount the roof (5.10a) and continue up and right over a combination of face and crack climbing (5.8) to a large ledge.

Tehipite Dome from the southwest (photo by Walter L. Huber, Sequoia and Kings Canyon National Parks)

Climb diagonally right from the ledge and overcome another roof (5.8), followed by 5.6 face climbing to a tree. The tree is the end of the climb.

Burnt Mountain *(10,608 ft; 10,608 ft)*
Class 1 from the saddle north of the peak.

Tunemah Peak *(11,894 ft; 11,894 ft)*
The west and southwest slopes of this peak are loose class 2. The south ridge from Tunemah Pass is class 2.

Blue Canyon Peak *(11,860 ft; 11,849 ft)*
First ascent August 27, 1959, by Robin J. McKeown and Frank Orme. This peak is class 2 from all directions.

Finger Peak *(12,404 ft; 12,404 ft)*
The northwest ridge of this peak is class 3. From Cathedral Lake, climb either the obvious chute or the buttress (on its left side) to the crest of the northwest ridge. Stay on the southern side of the northwest ridge while traversing to the summit.
The southwest slope is class 3; the southeast slope and east ridge are class 2.

Mt. Reinstein *(12,586 ft; 12,604 ft)*
The northeast ridge from Reinstein Pass is class 3. The southeast ridge is also class 3; the south slope from Blackcap Basin is class 2.

Blackcap Mountain
(11,600 ft+; 11,559 ft)
The northeast slope from Blackcap Pass is class 1; the west ridge of this peak is class 2.

Peak 12,200+
(12,265 ft; 2.8 mi NE of Blackcap Mtn.)
First ascent July 13, 1951, by Art Reyman, via the class 3, knife-edged west ridge.

Mt. Hutton
(11,990 ft; 11,998 ft; 1.4 mi S of Hell-For-Sure Pass)
The south slope is class 1 and was first climbed by Art Reyman on July 12, 1951.
The Cooked Walnut. II, 5.7, A2. First ascent August 31, 1973, by Walt Vennum, Curt Chadwick, and Rick Boyce. This 600-foot climb is on the north face of this peak. Climb a crack system immediately to the right of a pillar that splits the center of the north face. Most of this climb goes free, on excellent rock.

Red Mountain *(11,963 ft; 11,951 ft)*
First ascent July 12, 1898, by J. N. LeConte and C. L. Cory. Class 1 from all directions.

Peak 12,120+
(12,154 ft; 1.0 mi SSE of Mt. Henry)
The northeast ridge of this peak is an awesome sight from Mt. Henry. First ascent July 10, 1951, by A. J. Reyman, via the class 2 northeast ridge.

Mt. Henry *(12,196 ft; 12,106 ft)*
North Ridge. Class 3. First ascent July 10, 1951, by A. J. Reyman. Follow the ridge from Peak 11,600+ (11.600 ft), keeping to its east side to pass blocks and notches.
Northeast Ridge. Class 2. First ascent July 7, 1939, by David Brower and party. This is a straightforward climb from Goddard Canyon.
The south ridge is class 2 and the southwest and west slopes are class 2.

Zingheim Heights
(11,138 ft; 11,148 ft; 0.2 mi SW of Mosquito Pass)
First ascent July 10, 1951, by A. J. Reyman. The south slope is class 1.

Fleming Mountain *(10,796 ft; 10,796 ft)*
Class 2 from Fleming Pass.

Ward Mountain *(10,840 ft+; 10,682 ft)*
The west slope is class 2.

Mt. Shinn *(10,960 ft+; 11,020 ft)*
This peak dominates Florence Lake. First ascent August 8, 1925, by Francis A. Corey. The steep west slope from Mt. Shinn Lake is class 2.

Wrinkles

Cross-Country Routes to the Middle Fork of the Kings River. The only route that goes is the Tunemah Trail, which isn't really a trail, but a cross-country route. The Middle Fork has steep cliffs on both sides, and the only other alternative is the Tehipite Trail from Crown Valley to Tehipite Valley.

The Palisades

THIS IS THE MOST ALPINE REGION OF THE High Sierra. These peaks are high—five summits exceed 14,000 feet in elevation. The Palisade Glacier is the largest glacier in the range, and most of the peaks in this region are steep on all sides, not just on one or two. The glaciers on the northeast sides of the Palisades are fed by some steep ice couloirs, which can complicate an ascent for a typical California climber who is at home on rock, but not on ice. A climber on the summit of North Palisade may have used all of his or her skills on snow, ice, and rock to get there, and will look out upon a tremendous panorama of tundra, cliff, glacier, forest, and desert.

This region covers the Sierra crest from Taboose Pass to Bishop Pass, and is bounded on the west by Palisade Creek and the Middle Fork of the Kings River.

Further reading: *Summit,* September–October 1981, pp. 16–20; *Climbing,* No. 87, December 1984, pp. 32–41; *Off Belay,* No. 21, June 1975, pp. 8–29.

History

The Palisades were discovered and named in 1864 by the California Geological Survey. Frank Dusy explored the entire Middle Fork of the Kings River in the 1870s, searching for the perfect meadow for his sheep. He was probably the first white man to see the Palisade Glacier, from somewhere near Dusy Basin. During this same time, the Wheeler Survey triangulated Split Mountain and North Palisade from the east, and in 1879 Lil A. Winchell visited the region and named Mt. Winchell (after his father's cousin, geologist Alexander Winchell) and Mt. Agassiz (at the time named "Agassiz Needle"). Winchell gave the name "Dusy Peak" to North Palisade, in honor of Frank Dusy, who had shown him the approaches to this region

from the west. In 1895 Bolton Brown named it "Mt. Jordan," after David Starr Jordan, the president of Stanford University, where Brown was a professor. (I assume that Brown's tenure decision was imminent at that time.) Eventually Joseph LeConte's admirably descriptive name was accepted as official, after his first ascent of the peak in 1903.

Middle Palisade was attempted in 1919, but the climbers selected the wrong route and ended up atop Disappointment Peak. Two years later, Ansel F. Hall and Francis P. Farquhar repeated the mistake, but then descended and climbed another 2,000 feet to the true summit on the same day.

Norman Clyde moved to Independence in the 1920s, and proceeded to explore the eastern approaches to the Palisades. In 1930, on June 7, he climbed the east face of Middle Palisade, which he reported as being "one of the best climbs in the Sierra." Two days later, he climbed what was to become known as Norman Clyde Peak via the north face. He moved to the other side of the Sierra crest later in the month and climbed Middle Palisade again on June 18 via the Farquhar Route, and the south face of Norman Clyde Peak the next day. On June 20 he climbed Disappointment Peak from the northeast. On July 5 he climbed the northeast face of Mt. Agassiz and said that it was "one of the finest rock climbs in the Sierra." The next day he climbed the Clyde Couloir of North Palisade and called it "one of the very best climbs in the Sierra." On July 9 he repeated part of this climb, ascending Starlight Peak instead, and called it "a superb climb." He also made nine ascents of Temple Crag that year, in addition to ascents of The Thumb, Mt. Winchell, and Mt. Bolton Brown. All of these climbs were done solo. As his friend Jules Eichorn once said, "For me there can

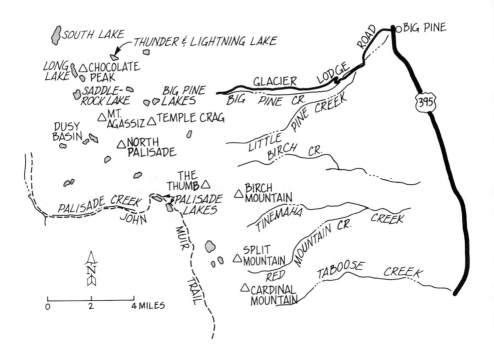

never be another human being so completely in tune with his chosen environment—mountains—as Norman Clyde."

Robert L. M. Underhill of the Appalachian Mountain Club visited the High Sierra in 1931 at the invitation of Francis Farquhar, at the time vice president of the Sierra Club. Underhill taught selected members of the Sierra Club proper management of the rope for safe rock climbing during the High Trip that year, and a grand tour of the High Sierra was arranged afterwards. This tour included a visit to the Palisades, where the northwest face of Temple Crag was climbed, and the first ascent of the last 14,000-foot unclimbed peak in the High Sierra, Thunderbolt Peak. In the decade of the 1930s, many routes were established on the high peaks of the Palisades by members of the Sierra Club's Rock Climbing Sections from various cities in California.

Larry Williams opened the Mountaineering Guide Service in 1959, operating under a permit from the Inyo National Forest. This was the first mountain-based climbing school

in California. It was a popular school, and its guides and instructors (and a few students) soon put up many difficult routes in the Palisades. For many years, the school had its base camp at Third Lake, beneath Temple Crag, and Don Jensen established many fine routes on this peak's massive north face. After Larry Williams' untimely death in an airplane crash in 1968, the Mountaineering Guide Service changed owners and its name to the Palisade School of Mountaineering, under the direction of John Fischer. Unfortunately, PSOM (pronounced "possum") stopped operation in 1989, the victim of rogue guides who operated without permits. PSOM's presence in the Palisades will be missed.

Maps

United States Geological Survey: 7.5-minute series: Fish Springs, Aberdeen, Mt. Pinchot, Split Mtn., North Palisade, Mt. Thompson, Coyote Flat; 15-minute series: Mt. Pinchot, Big Pine, Mt. Goddard; national park maps: Sequoia and Kings Canyon National Parks and Vicinity (1:125,000).

United States Forest Service: John Muir Wilderness and the Sequoia–Kings Canyon National Parks Backcountry (1:63,360).

Wilderness Permits

For east-side entry to the John Muir Wilderness via Taboose Pass: Inyo National Forest, Mount Whitney Ranger District, Lone Pine, CA 93545.

For east-side entry to the John Muir Wilderness from the Red Lake Trail to the Bishop Pass Trail: Inyo National Forest, White Mountain Ranger District, Bishop, CA 93514.

Roads

Taboose Creek Road

This is the road leading to the trailhead for the Taboose Pass Trail. It is described in Chapter 5: The High Passes.

Tinemaha Creek Road

The Tinemaha Creek Road leads to the trailhead for the Red Lake Trail. This could serve as the eastern approach for climbing Split Mountain; however, the road passes through private property and is not open to the public. The McMurry Meadow Road is the current approach to the Red Lake Trailhead.

McMurry Meadow Road

The McMurry Meadow Road leads to the trailhead for Birch Lake and to the Red Lake Trailhead. From Big Pine, go west up the Glacier Lodge Road for 2.4 miles to the McMurry Meadow Road. Turn left onto the road and take the left fork (the lower road). A short distance later the road forks again; take the right fork. Continue up the road another 6 miles to a junction; those headed for the Birch Lake Trailhead turn right. High-clearance vehicles are recommended beyond this point.

If headed for the Red Lake Trailhead, go left at the junction and, after a couple of difficult fords (four-wheel-drive recommended), you come to a road marked "10S01-A." Go right at the first fork, then go left on the road marked "10S01." Continue to the second fork and turn right. You eventually come to the last fork. The right branch leads to Tinemaha Creek; the left fork leads to the Red Lake Trailhead.

Glacier Lodge Road

The Glacier Lodge Road leads from Big Pine to the trailheads for trails leading up the North and South Forks of Big Pine Creek. The road goes west from Big Pine and passes the McMurry Meadow Road after 2.4 miles. It continues west, with much climbing, to the "Hiker Parking" area at 13.9 miles. This is the trailhead for trails leading up the North and South Forks. The road ends near Glacier Lodge, another 0.5 mile farther.

At one time this road continued up the canyon to a point along the North Fork of Big Pine Creek between the First Falls and Second Falls. This section of the road was wiped out by a flood in 1982.

South Lake Road

This road is described in Chapter 9: The Evolution Region.

Trails

Taboose Pass Trail *(8¹/₄ miles)*

This trail provides access to the southern part of the Palisades. It is described in Chapter 5: The High Passes.

Red Lake Trail *(6 miles)*

The Red Lake Trail leads to Red Lake, and serves as the eastern approach to Split Mountain. Contrary to what many maps may indicate, the trail is on the north side of Red Mountain Creek. From the trailhead, the trail ascends over 600 feet to a prominent rock outcrop high on the northern side of the canyon. The trail then traverses before climbing many short switchbacks to Red Lake. This trail hasn't been maintained for many years, and care must be taken to ensure that you are on the correct path.

John Muir Trail *(20 miles)*

This section of the John Muir Trail begins along the South Fork of the Kings River at its junction with the remains of the Cartridge Pass Trail. The John Muir Trail goes north and passes a side trail leading to the Taboose Pass Trail. The John Muir Trail continues north and eventually climbs to Upper Basin, one of the most beautiful lake basins in the Sierra Nevada. At the northern end of the basin, the trail has some switchbacks that lead to the top of Mather Pass, 5¹/₄ miles from the South Fork of the Kings River. The north side of the pass has some rough talus, and the trail zigzags through it before descending across slabs to the upper Palisade Lake. The trail traverses across the top of the cliffs north of the Palisade Lakes to the lower lake, 4 miles from Mather Pass. For the next 3 miles the trail descends a steep cliff (this was the last portion of the John Muir Trail to be completed) to Deer Meadow, which seems to consist more of timber than grass. The trail continues down the north bank of Palisade Creek for 3 1/2 miles to meet the Middle Fork Trail, which comes upstream from Simpson Meadow. The John Muir Trail goes west a short distance to the mouth of Palisade Creek, where it turns north and leads to Grouse Meadows, 1 mile from the junction with the Middle Fork Trail. The John Muir Trail goes north through LeConte Canyon for 3 1/4 miles to meet the Bishop Pass Trail descending from Dusy Basin. The LeConte Canyon Ranger Station is west of this junction.

Birch Lake Trail   (5 miles)

This trail starts by following an old jeep road that heads west from the trailhead near McMurry Meadows. This road leads to a gully, where the road turns into a trail, and then goes to the crest of the ridge on the north side of the gully. The trail continues west, across two more gullies and ridges, before turning south and following Birch Creek upstream in a broad valley. Cross the stream and contour up through talus to a meadow just below Birch Lake.

South Fork Trail   (5 miles)

The South Fork Trail has also been called the Brainard Lake Trail. From the hikers' parking lot along Big Pine Creek, follow the road past Glacier Lodge to its end. Follow the trail along the north bank of the stream, below some cabins. The trail crosses a bridge beneath First Falls, and crosses the old dirt road a short distance before entering a brush-covered plain. The trail eventually crosses the South Fork of Big Pine Creek and begins to switchback up beneath a steep cliff. It then makes a slight descent to Willow Lake. Those headed for Willow Lake and the cross-country route to Elinore Lake and Glacier Notch go right at the first stream past Willow Lake. The main trail goes left and climbs up to Brainard Lake.

Finger Lake is 1/4 mile west of Brainard Lake. Follow a good use trail around the north shore of Brainard Lake, climb a steep talus slope, and then traverse across granite slabs to the northern end of Finger Lake. There is a splendid view of Middle Palisade from the lake.

North Fork Trail   (8 miles)

The North Fork Trail passes through the most alpine scenery of the High Sierra. There are outstanding views of Temple Crag and the northern Palisade peaks. This trail ends at Seventh Lake—it does not cross the Sierra crest, contrary to the opinion of many misinformed yet enthusiastic trans-Sierra hikers.

From the hikers' parking area follow the trail west (past a fork leading to Brainard Lake), and then north into the canyon of the North Fork of Big Pine Creek. After 1 3/4 miles the trail meets the old trail coming up from the old trailhead (wiped out by a flood in 1982) and another trail, which leads uphill to Baker Lakes. The North Fork Trail continues upstream and passes the cataract of Second Falls to the remarkably flat terrain above. The trail then passes Cienaga Mirth; the abandoned stone cabin south of the trail was built by actor Lon Chaney in 1925. The North Fork Trail meets the Black Lake Trail 3 miles from the Baker Lakes Trail. The North Fork Trail turns southwest for 1 1/2 miles, passing First Lake, Second Lake, and Third Lake, then climbs to the junction with the Sam Mack Meadow Trail. The North Fork Trail continues north another 1/2 mile to a four-way junction. The Black Lake Trail comes in from the east, and another trail leads to Fifth Lake, 1/4 mile to the west. The North Fork Trail passes the west shore of Fourth Lake and then gradually turns west over a small rise, passing Sixth Lake before arriving at Seventh Lake.

Wood fires are prohibited in the drainage of the North Fork of Big Pine Creek above Cienaga Mirth.

Black Lake Trail   (1 1/2 miles)

This trail leaves the North Fork Trail 3 miles from the junction of the Baker Lakes Trail and the old trail leading to the former trailhead in the canyon of the North Fork of Big Pine Creek. It gradually switchbacks up the northern slope of the canyon and turns west, passing the southern shore of Black Lake before rejoining the North Fork Trail.

There are some outstanding views of North Palisade, Mt. Sill, and Thunderbolt Peak along this trail. Wood fires are prohibited in this basin.

Sam Mack Meadow Trail   (2¹/₂ miles)

This trail has also been called the Glacier Trail because its upper portion leads to the Palisade Glacier. Leave the North Fork Trail approximately 1 mile beyond Third Lake. The trail descends to a small meadow, crosses the stream, and ascends a forested boulder field to Sam Mack Meadow. Wood campfires are prohibited in the vicinity of Sam Mack Meadow.

From Sam Mack Meadow the Glacier Trail crosses the creek, goes south, and ascends benches to the ridge above the meadow. The trail turns south and traverses under and just east of the terminal moraine of the Palisade Glacier, then turns southwest across a short stretch of loose boulders to some slabs. Follow the slabs to the toe of the northwest ridge

of Mt. Gayley, where there is an outstanding view of the Palisade Glacier.

Bishop Pass Trail   (12 miles)

The Bishop Pass Trail provides access from South Lake to the western approaches of the Palisades. It is described in Chapter 9: The Evolution Region.

Cross-Country Routes

"Red Lake Pass"

(3940 m+; 12,960 ft+; 0.4 mi N of Split Mtn.)

Class 2. This is not really a pass, but instead a traverse across the north slope of Split Mountain between Red Lake and Upper Basin. Head northwest from Red Lake, but stay low and go to the far left side of the snowfield before climbing a chute that leads to the top of the ridge between Peak 3832m (12,627 ft) and the Sierra crest. A short traverse along this ridge leads to the "pass" at the base of the north slope of Split Mountain.

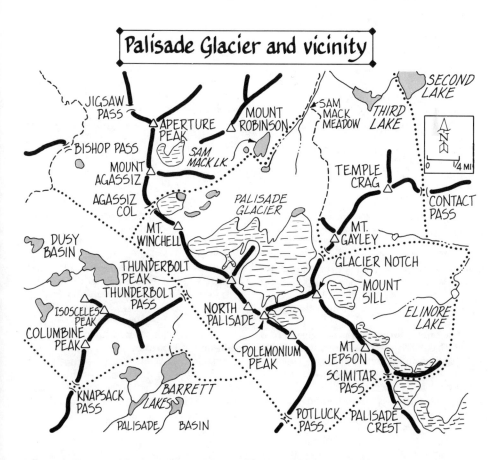

Palisade Glacier and vicinity

The west side of the pass is easy; horses climbed it from Upper Basin in 1943.

Tinemaha Creek

The Tinemaha Creek canyon has been used as an early-season approach for climbs of Mt. Prater and Mt. Bolton Brown. Take the McMurry Meadows Road or the Tinemaha Creek Road to a point approximately 1 mile below the start of the Red Lake Trail. Climb onto the ridge just south of the creek and follow it upstream, bypassing some willows on the south side.

"Lane Pass"

(3980 m+; 13,120 ft+; 0.6 mi NE of Mt. Bolton Brown)

Class 2. This pass has been used to climb Mt. Bolton Brown from Birch Lake; it also provides access to the upper part of the Palisade Creek drainage. The name commemorates Ed Lane.

From Birch Lake, go south to the saddle southwest of Birch Mountain. Traverse west from the saddle across the plateau to the pass along the Sierra crest. The west side of the pass is class 2.

"Birch Creek Pass"

(3900 m+; 12,800 ft+; 0.4 mi S of The Thumb)

Class 3. This pass provides access between Birch Lake and the upper portion of the Palisade Creek drainage. From Birch Lake, ascend the class 3 cliff that is southeast of The Thumb. Turn south at the top of the cliff and cross the pass, located along The Thumb's southeast ridge. The southwestern side of the pass is class 2.

Southfork Pass   *(3800 m+; 12,560 ft+)*

Class 3. Southfork Pass is used to gain access to the Palisade Creek drainage from the South Fork of Big Pine Creek. This is a difficult cross-country route, and should only be undertaken by experienced mountaineers. An ice axe and perhaps crampons and a rope may be needed, depending on the previous winter's snowfall and the time of year.

The easiest northern approach to the pass starts from the south side of Finger Lake. Follow the inlet stream uphill to where it forks. Take the left (southeast) fork, and pass two small lakes while traversing over a sea of talus and small cliffs to Pass 3660m+ (12,000 ft+; UTM 707037). Descend the east side of the pass to the small glacier beneath the north side of Southfork Pass.

From this point, the best route is virtually impossible to describe. Two passes are visible, each with a chute/couloir that leads to the top of Southfork Pass. "East Southfork Pass" (UTM 709032) usually has a passable bergschrund, but its lower portion is usually a steep, narrow ice funnel; the middle portion of the chute is gentler and broader, but it has loose rock, unless it is covered with snow or ice. "West Southfork Pass" (UTM 708032) is not quite as steep, and may be the best route. Pass the bergschrund on its right side, climb through the moat, and climb the chute to its top. But the bergschrund may be impassable, and the middle and upper portions of this chute consist of scree and loose rock, unless there is sufficient snow cover. Both chutes must be examined beforehand, preferably from the north.

The south side of the pass consists of easy scree and talus down to Lake 3589m (11,767 ft).

"Chimney Pass"

(3840 m+; 12,560 ft+; 0.5 mi S of Palisade Crest; UTM 676041)

Class 2. This pass has been used by climbers exploring the western side of Palisade Crest. Hikers will find Chimney Pass a preferable route between the Palisade Lakes and the Glacier Creek drainage. There are no steep slabs and the route is more obvious than Cirque Pass.

"Cirque Pass"

(3680 m+; 12,000 ft+; 0.9 mi SW of Palisade Crest; UTM 667036)

Class 3. This pass, in combination with Potluck Pass and Knapsack Pass, is a popular cross-country route between Mather Pass and Bishop Pass. Leave the John Muir Trail just below the lowest of the Palisade Lakes and make a gradual ascent to the west to bypass a cliff in the cirque above the level of the trail. Ascend the western edge of the cliff on a series of ledges. Beyond this barrier, pass a tarn on its western side, and ascend rock slabs and gullies to the broad saddle to the north. Descend a few feet on the north side of Cirque Pass and then traverse northwest across ledges to the outlet stream of Lake 3559m (11,672 ft) in the Glacier Creek drainage.

Potluck Pass *(12,120 ft+; 12,080 ft+)*

Class 2. From Glacier Creek, either traverse or ascend to the cliff that marks the southeastern side of Potluck Pass. This cliff is bypassed by ascending a scree slope southwest of the cliff, and then climbing a series of rock ledges, which lead diagonally upward to the summit of the pass. Make a very gradual descending traverse from Potluck Pass, at first going north, and then west to a flat saddle just northwest of Point 12,005 (12,000 ft+; UTM 654051). Descend from here to the largest of the Barrett Lakes (Lake 11,523; 11,440 ft+), and circle the lake on its eastern and northern shores.

"Scimitar Pass"

(4100 m+; 0.4 mi SE of Mt. Jepson; UTM 675052)

Class 3. This pass provides access between the South Fork of Big Pine Creek and the Glacier Creek drainage. It crosses the Sierra crest north of Palisade Crest. Technically, it is not a pass but a ridge crossing. Leave the cross-country route to Glacier Notch at UTM 689069, where the stream from Elinore Lake meets the stream descending from the cirque between Temple Crag and Mt. Gayley. Hike up the open chute west of the stream that descends from Elinore Lake; the easiest route is on the eastern side of the chute. Continue south from Elinore Lake, aiming for the flat spot on the ridge leading west up to the Sierra crest. Follow the ridge up to the "pass," skirting the permanent snowfield northeast of Palisade Crest.

From the west, climb to the northeast from Lake 3559m (11,672 ft). Instead of going to the low point immediately southeast of Mt. Jepson, climb onto the northwest shoulder of Palisade Crest. The correct crossing is approximately 200 feet above the saddle; it can be easily identified once the ridge leading down to the east is seen.

"Glacier Notch"

(13,080 ft+; 13,120 ft+; 0.3 mi N of Mt. Sill)

Class 3; ice axe required. This pass is between Mt. Sill and Mt. Gayley. From Willow Lake along the South Fork of Big Pine Creek, cross the meadow upstream from the lake and follow the south side of the stream descending from the cirque between Mt. Gayley and Temple Crag. Cross to the north side of the stream at the outlet of a meadow, and continue west through talus to the junction with the stream descending from Elinore Lake. Continue following the stream west to the cirque between Temple Crag and Mt. Gayley. Skirt Mt. Gayley on its south side, and head directly to Glacier Notch.

From the eastern side of the Palisade Glacier, cross the bergschrund (difficulty varies with the season and snow year) and climb a chute with much loose rock to the top of Glacier Notch.

Contact Pass *(3580 m+; 11,760 ft+)*

Class 2. This pass provides access between the North and South Forks of Big Pine Creek. Follow the contact zone of light and dark rock south from Second Lake to the top of the pass east of Temple Crag. Descend the south side of the pass to a small tarn on a bench; descend the southeast side of the bench to the stream that descends to Willow Lake. This section of the route is described above under Glacier Notch.

"The U Notch"

(13,880 ft+; 13,920 ft+; 0.1 mi SE of North Palisade)

Class 4; ice axe and perhaps crampons required. This is a climbers' route, and it is not suitable for cross-country hikers without climbing equipment and experience. It has been used by climbers to gain the southwest side of the North Palisade massif from the Palisade Glacier. For details, see the climbing descriptions of the U Notch and LeConte routes for North Palisade, later in this chapter.

Knapsack Pass *(11,680 ft+; 11,673 ft)*

Class 1. Knapsack Pass leads from Dusy Basin to the Barrett Lakes in Palisade Basin. Leave the Bishop Pass Trail near the lowest lakes in Dusy Basin and head southeast to the saddle south of Columbine Peak, which is Knapsack Pass. Rock slabs and shallow gullies lead to the summit of the pass. Traverse east beneath the southern cliffs of Columbine Peak to where it is possible to make a short, easy descent to the Barrett Lakes.

If you are headed toward Deer Meadow along Palisade Creek, make a direct descent from the summit of Knapsack Pass over many tedious class 2 cliffs. It is best to remain on the western bank of the stream for most of the time during the descent to the John Muir Trail.

"Isosceles Pass"

(12,080 ft+; 12,000 ft+; 0.1 mi S of Isosceles Peak)

Class 3. This pass has been used as an alternative to Knapsack Pass. It is class 3 on the Dusy Basin side and class 2 on the Barrett Lakes side. Knapsack Pass is much easier and is preferable.

"Thunderbolt Pass"

(12,360 ft+; 12,320 ft+; 0.4 mi WSW of Thunderbolt Peak)

Class 2. This is another route between Dusy Basin and Palisade Basin. Leave the Bishop Pass Trail south of Bishop Pass and contour southeast above the level of Lake 11,400+ (11,393 ft) to the obvious saddle southwest of Thunderbolt Peak. Much tedious talus is encountered before reaching the summit of the pass. From the top of the pass, either descend to the south over talus and many small cliffs to the largest of the Barrett Lakes, or traverse southeast across talus beneath North Palisade to Potluck Pass.

"Winchell Col"

(13,040 ft+; 12,960 ft+; 0.2 mi S of Mt. Winchell)

Class 4, A1. This col is to the south of the pinnacle ("Dolphin Fin") near the saddle between Thunderbolt Peak and Mt. Winchell. This pass has been used by climbers to approach the west sides of Mt. Winchell and Thunderbolt Peak from the Thunderbolt Glacier. This involves a 100-foot rappel when going from east to west, so it is a route used by climbers only.

Agassiz Col   *(13,080 ft+; 13,040 ft+)*

Class 3. This pass leads between Sam Mack Meadow and Dusy Basin. Leave Sam Mack Meadow at its western end and go north (the snow chute at the western end of Sam Mack Meadow is frequently too icy to climb, especially with heavy packs). Follow a good use trail up and right to a point approximately 100 feet below a waterfall, the outlet of Sam Mack Lake. Traverse right (east) and then go up sandy ledges to the ridge above. Go west across boulders to Sam Mack Lake. From the western shore of the lake go west to the cirque and glacier between Mt. Winchell and Mt. Agassiz. Cross

the glacier and approach the col from the northeast, making a diagonally ascending traverse across the base of the south face of Mt. Agassiz to the top of the col. Descend the west side of the col over scree and talus to Dusy Basin.

When crossing Agassiz Col from the west to east, ascend the largest chute between Mt. Winchell and Mt. Agassiz to the top of the col.

Jigsaw Pass

(12,720 ft+; 12,720 ft+; 0.1 mi NW of Aperture Peak; UTM 639090)

Class 3. Jigsaw Pass is between Fifth Lake (in the drainage of the North Fork of Big Pine Creek) and the Bishop Creek basin (just north of Bishop Pass). From the south shore of Fifth Lake, ascend talus and slabs south of the inlet stream that flows from Mt. Agassiz. Take the north branch from where the stream forks and then go left over easy terrain to Jigsaw Pass, which is south of the lowest point on the crest of the ridge leading northwest from Aperture Peak. Descend the west side of the pass via an easy chute and cross boulders to meet the Bishop Pass Trail.

It is difficult to identify the correct chute leading to Jigsaw Pass when crossing the pass from west to east. Jigsaw Pass is south of the lowest point northwest from Aperture Peak, and is separated from the low point by a small peak. Ascend the southern of two chutes, over scree, grass, and broken rock. The ascent is easier than it appears from below.

Peaks

Peak 3917m

(12,851 ft; 1.0 mi SW of Cardinal Mtn.)

First ascent August 5, 1945, by A. J. Reyman, via the class 1 southeast ridge.

Cardinal Mountain   *(4083 m; 13,397 ft)*

First ascent August 11, 1922, by George Downing, Jr. Ascend a chute on the south side of the mountain from the vicinity of Taboose Pass. The chute is class 2, and it is filled with disagreeably loose rock.

Peak 4180m+

(13,803 ft; 0.6 mi SSW of Split Mtn.)

Southeast Couloir. Class 4. First ascent October 3, 1965, by Gary Lewis and Ed Lane.

Hike up the south branch of Red Mountain Creek and head for a huge pillar on the southeast side of the peak. Ascend the couloir just west of this pillar. The couloir is blocked at one point; this obstacle is easily bypassed by a short class 4 move on its right side. The couloir then goes west and then southwest to the summit rocks.

Northwest Ridge. Class 4. First ascent August 28, 1989, by Steve Porcella and Cameron Burns. Most of this ridge is class 3, but a few class 4 sections are encountered where the ridge gradually turns to the east.

The southwest ridge of this peak is blocked by an overhanging cliff.

Split Mountain *(4280 m+; 14,058 ft)*

This mountain was once known as "South Palisade." It is easily identified from the Owens Valley by the chute on its east side, which leads to the notch between its two summits. The north summit is the high point. After Mt. Whitney, this is the easiest 14,000-foot peak in the Sierra. First ascent July 1887 by Frank Saulque and party, via an unknown route.

North Slope. Class 2. First ascent July 23, 1902, by Joseph LeConte, Helen LeConte, and Curtis Lindley. Ascend to the saddle between Mt. Prater and Split Mountain from Upper Basin and climb the easy talus slopes to the summit.

North Slope from the East. Class 2. The north slope can be easily reached from Red Lake by crossing Red Lake Pass.

Northeast Arete of North Summit. III, 5.8. First ascent October 1976 by Galen Rowell. Climb this arete from Red Lake. A 5.8 squeeze chimney is encountered before the angle of the arete eases. Continue following the arete to where it is blocked by some large gendarmes. An impossible-appearing gendarme is climbed on its left side from a small ledge via a 5.8 layback. Follow the crest of the gendarmes to where the arete ends just north of the north summit.

Split Mountain Gully. This is the eastern gully that descends to Red Lake from the notch between the two summits of Split Mountain. This 1,300-foot gully has been reported as being one of the better ice climbs in the High Sierra, with an 80-degree crux section.

Northeast Arete of South Summit. IV, 5.9. First ascent February 1976 by David Belden and Galen Rowell. Ascend easy rock from Red Lake to the base of a sheer wall. Some 5.9 climbing is needed to climb the wall. The route eventually leads to the crest of the arete. Follow the crest to a small headwall, which is overcome by some 5.8 climbing. The arete ends atop the lower south summit.

East Arete. IV, 5.9. First ascent September 1984 by Dean Hobbs and Gary Slate. This route climbs the farthest left arete on the east side of Split Mountain, as viewed from Red Lake. More than twenty pitches of varied climbing lead to the south summit.

Southeast Slopes. Class 3. Ascend the broad slope between Peak 4180m+ (13,803 ft) and Split Mountain to the south summit. A class 3 traverse is made between the south and north summits of Split Mountain.

South Ridge. II, 5.6. First ascent 1932 by Jules Eichorn and Glen Dawson. Follow the ridge north from Peak 4180m+ (13,803 ft), bypassing gendarmes to the left and right as needed. This ridge is dangerously loose, and the crux is at the notch beneath Peak 4180m+; climb straight up the opposite wall of loose bricks.

West Face. Class 3. Descended by Norman Clyde. The west side of Split Mountain is marked by ribs and chutes. It is better to ascend the ribs, as there are many small cliffs in the chutes. This climb can become class 4 if the best route isn't chosen.

Mt. Tinemaha *(3186 m; 12,561 ft)*

West Ridge. Class 2. First ascent July 1, 1937, by Chester Versteeg. From Tinemaha Creek ascend to the west ridge of the peak, and follow the ridge to the summit. This ridge can also be followed from Red Lake Pass. Follow the south side of the ridge over many class 3 ribs and chutes.

South Slope. Class 1. This is an easy ascent from Red Lake.

The south and east ridges are class 3.

Mt. Prater *(4106 m; 13,329 ft)*

Southeast Ridge. Class 1. Gain the southeast ridge from Upper Basin and follow the ridge to the summit. A short knife-edge is easy but scary.

Hidden Couloir. II, 5.2. First ascent September 1980 by Del Johns and Wayne N. Sawka. This 800-foot, 45-degree ice couloir leads to the southeast ridge of Mt. Prater from Tinemaha Creek.

Split Mountain from Red Lake (photo by R. J. Secor)

Obvious Chute. Class 3. First ascent March 19, 1972, by Ed Treacy, Karl Bennett, Dave Gladstone, Vi Grasso, Dave King, and Doug Mantle. From Tinemaha Lake, climb the chute leading to the plateau between Mt. Bolton Brown and Mt. Prater. Turn south to the deep notch north of Mt. Prater, where a 100-foot class 3 pitch leads to the summit.

North Ridge. Class 3. First ascent October 6, 1948, by Fred L. Jones. Ascend to the plateau north of Mt. Prater from the northernmost part of Upper Basin. It is best to ascend the largest chute south of the pinnacles that are south of Mt. Bolton Brown. Traverse south from the top to the deep notch north of Mt. Prater. It is class 3 to the summit from there.

Mt. Bolton Brown *(4112 m; 13,538 ft)*

South Ridge. Class 3. First ascent March 19, 1972, by Ed Treacy, Karl Bennett, Dave Gladstone, Vi Grasso, Dave King, and Doug Mantle. Follow the ridge from the plateau southeast of Mt. Bolton Brown. Drop down on the west side of the ridge before reaching the lower, southeast summit, and climb to the true summit via the northwest ridge.

North Slope. Class 2. First ascent October 6, 1948, by Fred L. Jones. It is best to ascend the slope to the northwest ridge and follow the ridge to the summit.

Southwest Slope. Class 3. Descended August 14, 1922, by Chester Versteeg and Rudolph Berls. The slope directly beneath the summit has much loose rock.

Birch Mountain *(4146 m; 13,665 ft)*

First ascent 1887 by J. W. Bledsoe. The southwest ridge is class 2 from the saddle between Birch Creek and Tinemaha Creek. The south slope is class 2 from Tinemaha Creek. Ribs and gullies on the west and northwest sides of the peak are class 2–3.

Peak 4138m

(13,520 ft+; 1.0 mi N of Mt. Bolton Brown)

This peak has been referred to as "Ed Lane Peak."

North Ridge. Class 3. First ascent June 14, 1930, by Norman Clyde. Climb to the saddle south of The Thumb from either the east or west and ascend the western side of the north ridge to the summit. Only the last portion of this climb is class 3.

West Chute. Class 3. First ascent by Don Clarke. Ascend a chute or gully on the west side of the peak to a point on the north ridge just north of the summit.

North Couloir. Class 4. First ascent June 1979 by Peter von Gaza and Lars Mollor. Ascend a snow couloir on the north face to the north ridge of the peak, then follow the western side of the north ridge to the summit.

The Thumb *(4146 m; 13,665 ft)*

Southeast Slope. Class 2–3. First ascent December 12, 1921, by W. B. Putnam. This is a straightforward climb from Birch Lake. A small cliff low on the slope is bypassed on its southwest side by climbing a ramp with some loose class 3 moves. The rest of the climb is easy.

From Southfork Pass. Class 2. This climb begins from the top of "East Southfork Pass." Contour toward the east to a broad, scree-filled chute. Ascend it to where it narrows and then cross into the next chute right. Follow this chute to the gentle slopes southeast of the summit.

Northwest Face. Class 4. First ascent June 5, 1930, by Norman Clyde. Climb the large, recessed couloir at the far right-hand side of the northwest face of The Thumb. The couloir gradually narrows and is blocked by a large chockstone, which is bypassed by climbing the wall on the right. You eventually reach the crest of the rib between the couloir and the next chute south. Enter the next chute south, and follow it to the gentle slope south of The Thumb.

Northwest Corner. III, 5.7. First ascent June 1965 by Hank Abrons, Peter Carman, and C. Bickel. This route ascends an outside corner high on the northwest side of The Thumb. This corner is flanked by two faces marked by prominent black dikes.

Black Dike. IV, 5.9. First ascent 1983 by Karl McConachie and Charlie Jenkewitz. This route ascends a conspicuous vein of black diorite on the northwest face.

North-Northeast Ridge. Class 5. First ascent September 12, 1957, by Leigh Ortenburger and Irene Ortenburger. Climb the deep couloir (loose rock!) on the west side of The Thumb that ends closest to the summit along the north-northeast ridge. Three chockstones in the couloir are easily bypassed. Leave the couloir near the top on its right side. Ascend an arete to the main

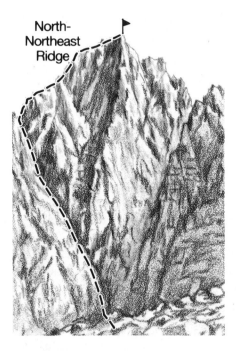

North-Northeast Ridge

The Thumb, Northwest Face

north-northeast ridge. Follow the north-northeast ridge to the summit. Turn the last obstacle just below the top on its left side, and climb a series of class 5 ledges to a point near the summit.

"Balcony Peak"

(4220 m+; 13,840 ft+; 0.1 mi SE of Disappointment Peak)

This small peak is a landmark for those ascending Disappointment Peak. The east ridge and the southeast slope are class 2.

Disappointment Peak

(4242 m; 13,917 ft)

This is the second peak south of Middle Palisade, and the first peak north of Balcony Peak. Its name commemorates the feelings of the first-ascent party in 1919, who thought they were climbing Middle Palisade only to find themselves separated from it by class 4 cliffs. There is much loose rock on this peak, and extreme caution is advised.

Northeast Couloir. Class 4. First ascent June 20, 1930, by Norman Clyde. There are two couloirs on the northeast side of Disap-

pointment Peak. Climb the right-hand (north) couloir, which leads to the notch north of the peak. Ascend the couloir part way, then traverse to the notch south of the peak. The summit is an easy scramble from here.

Doug's Chute. Class 4. First ascent August 1971 by Don Anderson, Dave King, and Ed Treacy. This route follows the left-hand (south) of the two couloirs on the northeast side of Disappointment Peak; this couloir leads to the notch south of the summit. Climb the chute to the right of a band of red rock which is intruded into the cliffs beneath the peak. This class 4 chute has some extraordinarily loose rock; it is more akin to climbing vertical seashells than rock. At the top of the chute, go right and climb the couloir to the notch south of the summit. The summit is easily reached from the notch.

East Ridge. Class 4. First ascent September 1953 by Bill Dunmire and Allen Steck, who in reality bypassed the summit of Disappointment Peak on their way to the summit of Middle Palisade. The name of this route actually refers to the east ridge of Balcony Peak. From the Middle Palisade Glacier, climb one of the snow or ice couloirs to the crest of the east ridge. Ascend the crest of the ridge to the point where the ridge crest appreciably steepens, which is about 300 feet below the summit of Balcony Peak. Traverse down and across the north face of Balcony Peak to a small notch in a rib. Traverse horizontally from the notch across three loose chutes to the couloir between Balcony Peak and Disappointment Peak. Climb the couloir to the notch, and then on to the summit.

Traverse from Balcony Peak. Class 4. This traverse starts by going *south* from the summit of Balcony Peak for approximately 150 (horizontal) feet. Descend a narrow chute, which is blocked by a chockstone, to the main southwest chute of Disappointment Peak. Ascend the southwest chute to the notch south of the summit, and follow the ridge north to the top of Disappointment Peak.

Southwest Chute. Class 4. First ascent July 20, 1919, by J. M. Davies, A. L. Jordan, and H. H. Bliss. There is a large buttress that descends southwest from the summit of Balcony Peak toward the Palisade Lakes. Ascend the first chute left (north) of this buttress to the notch south of Disappointment Peak. The summit is class 3 from the notch.

West Face. IV, 5.10, A2. First ascent September 1986 by Galen Rowell and Dan Frankl. This route begins by climbing the arete to the left (north) of the Southwest Chute route. Leave the arete to the left via a crack that leads to the main west face of Disappointment Peak. Continue up the face to the summit.

Traverse from Middle Palisade. Class 4. This route does not follow the ridge south from Middle Palisade, but rather descends from the summit of Middle Palisade, moving gradually southeast to a point approximately 200 vertical feet below the first peak south of Middle Palisade (known locally as "Excitement Peak"). Traverse horizontally from this point, across two small chutes and ribs to the couloir leading to the notch north of Disappointment Peak. Either ascend the couloir to the notch, or leave the couloir and traverse beneath Disappointment Peak to the notch south of the peak. *Variation:* 5.6, with rappels. You can also traverse along the crest of the ridge (or very close to it) from the summit of Middle Palisade.

Middle Palisade *(4271 m; 14,040 ft)*

The top of Middle Pal is a knife-edged fin, approximately 300 feet long.

Middle Palisade from the northeast, August 24, 1972 (photo by Austin Post, #72R2-156, USGS Ice and Climate Project, Tacoma, WA)

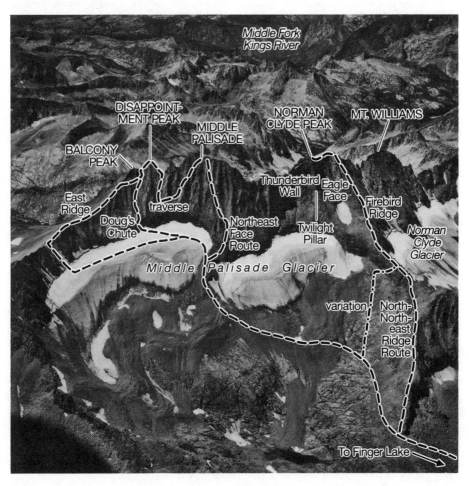

Northeast Face. Class 3. First ascent June 7, 1930, by Norman Clyde. First winter ascent January 5, 1960, by John Mendenhall and Tom Condon. You can approach the start of this route either from the top of the moraine that divides the Middle Palisade Glacier, or by climbing the southern half of the glacier. Gain a ledge that climbs diagonally up and right. This leads to a wide couloir, which is followed to where it is possible to traverse into the next couloir to the right (this point is marked by a patch of white or lightly colored reddish brown rock, depending on one's mood, it seems). Follow the left branch of this couloir to the summit. Further reading: *Summit,* July–August 1987, p. 12. *Variation:* From reading Clyde's account of the climb (*Touring Topics,* August 1931, p. 32) it appears that he climbed directly to the first couloir from the northern half of the Middle Palisade Glacier.

East Face. III, 5.4. First ascent August 31, 1975, by Tim Ryan and John Mendenhall. This climb begins at the highest point of the south Middle Palisade Glacier. Climb straight up to a 60-foot horizontal ledge. Move to the left end of the ledge and ascend a chimney. Go left from the top of the chimney, and ascend to a belay ledge beneath an overhang. Continue up for another pitch, and then traverse left into the broad chute that leads to the notch immediately south of the summit. From the notch, traverse right, across the east side of the peak, before climbing to the summit.

Traverse from Disappointment Peak. Class 4. First ascent July 20, 1939, by David Brower, Bruce Meyer, and Keith Taylor. Descend the north side of the summit of Disappointment Peak to the first notch. Descend the eastern side of the peak, down the chute approximately 300 feet, and traverse left (north) across two ribs and chutes. Make a diagonal ascent up and across the east side of Middle Palisade to the summit. *Variation:* 5.6, with rappels. You can traverse close to the ridge crest on its eastern side at first, then on its western side near the summit of Middle Palisade.

Farquhar Route. Class 3. First ascent August 26, 1921, by Francis P. Farquhar and Ansel F. Hall. When viewing Middle Palisade and Disappointment Peak from the Palisade Lakes, you see a chute leading to the notch between Disappointment Peak and Balcony Peak. There is another chute north of this one, followed by yet another, which leads to Middle Palisade. The correct chute is this third chute, which is north of the buttress that descends southwest from the summit of Balcony Peak. If the wrong chute is chosen, then this will result in . . . Disappointment.

Ascend this steep, loose chute to about three-fourths of the way up, where it becomes more difficult. Traverse left and climb up ledges and chutes to meet the summit ridge of the peak just south of the summit.

This route is exposed and has much loose rock, and it is easy to get off-route. A rope should be carried. Only experienced climbers should attempt this climb.

Direct West Buttress. IV, 5.9, with a rappel. First ascent July 10, 1990, by Steve Porcella and Cameron Burns. The first-ascent party also called this "The Smoke Blanchard Memorial Route." The route climbs the steep buttress in the center of Middle Palisade's west face. Many pitches of easy class 5 climbing lead to a steep headwall (5.9). Continue climbing the buttress to its top, where a rappel is necessary. Climb a class 3 ridge to a chimney on the right, and climb the chimney to the summit ridge. Climb the summit ridge to the top of the peak.

Northwest Ridge. 5.6, with rappels. First ascent July 30, 1933, by Jules Eichorn and Glen Dawson. This traverse starts from the summit of Norman Clyde Peak.

Norman Clyde Peak
(4223 m; 13,920 ft+)

This is the impressive peak seen from Glacier Lodge along Big Pine Creek. The southeast summit is the high point.

North Face. Class 4. First ascent June 9, 1930, by Norman Clyde. Ascend the 40-degree, 700-foot snow/ice couloir that leads to the col between Norman Clyde Peak and Mt. Williams (Peak 4152m; 13,659 ft). Pass through the col to its south side. Traverse east across the south side of the peak to a chute that leads to the crest of the ridge; the crest is marked by a chockstone. Ascend this chute, but go right when another broad, easy chute appears to the right. This leads to a notch behind a low tower. Pass through the notch to another large chute that descends to the south. Climb to the bowl at the head of

Middle Palisade from the west (photo by Edward Nunez)

this chute via a class 4 ledge. Another class 4 pitch leads to the lower, northwestern summit of Norman Clyde Peak. Follow the ridge southeast to the high point.

North-Northeast Ridge. Class 3–4. First ascent July 22, 1961, by Arkel Erb and Mike McNicholas. This is the preferred route from the north, but the route finding is tricky, and many outstanding climbers have been defeated. From Finger Lake, ascend scree and talus west to the crest of the ridge that runs north and south from Peak 3862m (12,640 ft+). Follow the ridge south to the start of Norman Clyde Peak's north-northeast ridge. Cross onto the north face where the ridge begins to steepen, at two large boulders on the ridge crest. Zigzag on ledges on the north face, always remaining between 50 and 200 feet of the north-northeast ridge. Aim for a series of black, watermarked slabs about 300 feet below the apparent summit ridge. A narrow crack system to the right of these slabs leads to the top of the false summit. Scramble southeast to the true summit. *Variation, Lichen Chimney:* This chimney is very close to the crest of the north-northeast

ridge, approximately 300 feet below the false summit. Climb the chimney and the face above it to the false summit. *Variation:* The north-northeast ridge can also be reached from the east by ascending a ledge and chute that lead to the saddle between Peak 3862m (12,640 ft+). *Variation:* The north-northeast ridge has also been approached from the Norman Clyde Glacier. Ice axes and crampons may be needed to cross the glacier, and there is much loose rock on the lower portion of the north face. A better alternative may be to bypass the glacier on its northern side and climb to the north ridge of Peak 3862m (12,640 ft+) before turning south to the start of the north-northeast ridge of Norman Clyde Peak. Further reading: *Summit*, July–August 1987, p. 12.

Firebird Ridge. IV, 5.9. First ascent July 1975 by Fred Beckey, Mike Graber, and Dave Black. This route has also been referred to as the "Primrose Ridge." This climb is accomplished by religiously staying on the very crest of the north-northeast ridge. The route consists of thirteen pitches.

Eagle Face. II, 5.4. First ascent August

Norman Clyde Peak, North Face (photo by Pete Yamagata)

1961 by John Sharsmith, Larry Williams, and Allen Steck. From the point where the north-northeast ridge begins to steepen, traverse left across the northeast side of Norman Clyde Peak to the large, circular snow patch on the northeast face. Left of this snow patch is Twilight Pillar, the steep buttress that drops directly from the true summit of Norman Clyde Peak. From the upper left-hand edge of this snowfield, enter a chimney about 100 feet to the right of Twilight Pillar. Ascend the chimney for 80 feet, and then traverse right onto the face and ascend it for several pitches. Cross the face to the left over some loose rock to a small snow patch. Continue climbing up and left over the steep wall to the summit, taking care that the easiest and safest route is followed.

Twilight Pillar. III, 5.8. First ascent July 1966 by Don Jensen and Frank Sarnquist. First winter ascent February 1986 by David Wilson and Galen Rowell. This is the prominent, steep outside corner leading directly to the summit on Norman Clyde Peak's northeast side: a beautiful route.

The buttress can be reached directly from the Middle Palisade Glacier by climbing one 5.7 pitch, or from the circular snowfield described under the Eagle Face route, above. Climb the prow of the buttress for a few pitches. Then, ascend the face that is left of a right-facing open book for 80 feet of 5.8 face and crack climbing before traversing back into the open book to a comfortable belay ledge. The next pitch climbs 90 feet above the book on cracks, with a delicate move over a slight overhang. The remainder of the climb follows a shallow trough on the crest of the pillar to the summit.

Thunderbird Wall. III, 5.7. First ascent June 1965 by Hank Abrons and Peter Carman. This route climbs a prominent crack-and-chimney system on the wall to the left of Twilight Pillar. This system can be reached by traversing from Twilight Pillar, or from the north Middle Palisade Glacier by climbing ledges that are below and left of the crack system. Four pitches in the crack system lead to the southeast ridge of the peak, approximately 200 feet from the summit.

Southeast Ridge. 5.6, with rappels. First ascent July 30, 1933, by Jules Eichorn and

Glen Dawson. Traverse the ridge from Middle Palisade. The first small peak encountered on the traverse is locally known as "Dent du Dent," and the second as "Bivouac Peak."

South Face. Class 3–4. First ascent June 19, 1930, by Norman Clyde. A buttress curves down to the southwest from the ridge between Mt. Williams (Peak 4152m; 13,659 ft) and Norman Clyde Peak. Ascend the inside curve of this buttress to a chute that leads to the right to the crest of the ridge; this chute becomes a narrow cleft with a chockstone bridging it on the crest. Ascend this chute, but go right over easy terrain to a notch behind a low tower. Pass through the notch to another large chute, which drops off to the south. Ascend to the bowl at the head of this chute via a class 4 ledge. Another class 4 pitch leads to the lower, northwestern sum-

mit of Norman Clyde Peak. Follow the ridge southeast to the high point.

"Mt. Williams"

(4152 m; 13,659 ft; 0.3 mi WNW of Norman Clyde Peak)

This peak has been unofficially named after Larry Williams, the founder of the mountaineering school and guide service in the Palisades. There is a 40-degree, 700-foot ice couloir on the north face of the peak. Doug Adams and John Fischer traversed this peak from south to north, and gave it a 5.2 rating.

Palisade Crest *(4131 m; 13,520 ft+)*

This is the impressive row of twelve pinnacles rising above Elinore Lake. The pinnacles have been named after characters from J. R. R. Tolkien's book, *The Hobbit.* The

Palisade Crest from the east, August 24, 1972 (photo by Austin Post, #72R2-155, USGS Ice and Climate Project, Tacoma, WA)

high point, known as "Gandalf Peak," is the northwesternmost pinnacle.

Northwest Ridge. Class 4. First ascent 1969 by Don Jensen, Rex Post, and Joan Jensen. From the top of Scimitar Pass, traverse at first on the west side of the ridge, then between flakes on top of the ridge, and then descend the eastern side of the ridge to the notch immediately northwest of the summit pinnacle. This traverse is class 3, with diligent route finding. From the notch, climb a 160-foot class 4 slab to just below the summit. It is class 3 from the top of this pitch to the summit.

Traverse. III, 5.5. First ascent 1969 by Don Jensen, Rex Post, and Joan Jensen. This traverse has been described as not too difficult, with high-quality climbing.

Northeast Face. Class 4. First ascent 1967 by Don Jensen and Stu Dole. Climb a rib on the northeast face of Palisade Crest. This route ends atop one of the central pinnacles.

Southeastern Pinnacles. II, 5.7. First ascent July 4, 1954, by John Mendenhall and Ruth Mendenhall. From the western lobe of the Norman Clyde Glacier, climb the snow couloir leading to the notch southeast of Palisade Crest. The first pitch up from the top of the notch is 5.7, and the rest of the climb to the top of the southeast pinnacle has been described as having some interesting class 4 and class 5 pitches. The two pinnacles northwest from the southeast pinnacle are class 4 from the southeast pinnacle.

Mt. Jepson   *(4081 m; 13,390 ft)*

This peak was once unofficially known as "The Pine Marten."

From the South. Class 2. First ascent July 3, 1939, by Don McGeein, Chet Errett, and Evelyn Errett. This is an easy climb from the Glacier Creek drainage, or from the top of Scimitar Pass.

Northeast Face. III, 5.8. First ascent August 1970 by Doug Robinson and Don Jensen. There are two chimneys on the northeast face. Begin climbing 40 feet to the right of the left-hand chimney. After one pitch of 5.7, go left into the chimney. Continue climbing in the chimney into an immense cave. Difficult chimney climbing leads out under the lip of the cave. One more pitch leads to the summit.

The Steeple. II, 5.8. First ascent by Richard Doheman and John Fischer. This route climbs

the far left-hand side of the northeast face. Climb a prominent pillar that is split by a crack.

Giraud Peak   *(12,608 ft; 12,585 ft)*

First ascent September 1925 by Norman Clyde. The southeast slope is class 2. The southeast slope can be reached from Dusy Basin by following the north ridge of Peak 12,265 (12,240 ft+). This ridge steepens at approximately 11,400 feet, and it is best to traverse to the right into a gully and climb it to the top of the east ridge of Giraud Peak. Descend the south side of the ridge about 400 feet before ascending the southeast slope.

North Face. II, 5.4. First ascent July 1979 by David Mazel. Climb the prominent snow couloir on the north face. This consists of several hundred feet of 45-degree snow/ice climbing, followed by two pitches of rock climbing, which lead directly up to the summit.

There is also a chute on the far right side of the north face that is full of loose class 2 rock.

Columbine Peak   *(12,662 ft; 12,652 ft)*

This peak is class 2 from nearby Knapsack Pass; a scree chute on the west side of the peak provides a good descent route. The northeast ridge is class 2. There is an outstanding view of the Palisades (and other peaks) from the summit.

Isosceles Peak   *(12,321 ft; 12,240 ft+)*

Northeast Face. Class 3 with a class 4 summit block. First ascent July 1938 by Wear and Morse.

West Face. II, 5.9. First ascent August 1978 by Alan Bartlett and Allan Pietrasanta. Climb the central crack-and-chimney system in the middle of the face.

West Chute. II, 5.7. First ascent July 1991 by Don Palmer and David Harden. Climb the chute (5.5) that leads to the notch just south of the summit. Climb through a tunnel in the ridge and climb a steep crack (5.7) on the east side to gain the summit block.

Mt. Alice   *(3541 m; 11,360 ft)*

This is the biggest pile of rubble in the High Sierra. The south side is class 2.

"Church of the Poisoned Mind"

This 200-foot-high triangular tower is on

the southwest side of the amphitheater north of Contact Pass.

The Temple of Doom. I, 5.10. First ascent 1984 by Scott Ayers and Mike Strassman. This route ascends the left-facing dihedral that crosses the face diagonally from left to right.

Sustained Chapel. I, 5.10. First ascent 1984 by Scott Ayers and Howard Cohen. This route is to the right of the Temple of Doom. It climbs a right-facing corner that goes through an overhang to a crack. Sustained hand and fist jamming is encountered in places.

Temple Crag *(3955 m; 12,999 ft)*

This is the beautiful peak seen above the North Fork of Big Pine Creek. When viewed from Third Lake, its most impressive feature is the north buttress. This buttress has three summits: the top of the Lower Buttress, the North Peak, and the true summit of Temple Crag. The northeast face is cut by two deep, narrow chimneys with many thin aretes. The northwest face is marked by a broad couloir, a narrow chute farther right, and many indistinct ribs far out on the face. Some of the finest rock climbs in the High Sierra are on the northern side of the peak. Temple Crag has a summit cairn that is 1 foot high, to make it a 13,000-foot peak. Its new metric elevation, however, makes the summit 12,975

feet above sea level. It will be interesting to see how the summit cairn grows over the years!

Southeast Face. Class 3. First ascent 1909 by the United States Geological Survey. Climb the chute that leads up the southeastern side of the peak; the entrance to this chute is approximately 300 feet below the south side of Contact Pass. The chute leads to a large talus slope, which is followed to its top. A short section of class 3 follows, and a few hundred feet of scrambling lead to the top. There is a 50-foot section of class 3 just beneath the summit.

Contact Crack. Class 4. First ascent November 1926 by Norman Clyde. This crack is west of the very top of Contact Pass. Climb the 30-foot class 4 crack to the talus slope above. Continue following the southeast face route to the summit.

Eclipsed Arete. III, 5.3. First ascent 1970 by Bob Swift, Pete Kennedy, and Tom Thayer. There are five aretes to the left of the right-hand couloir on the northeast face. The first arete (Sun Ribbon Arete) rises vertically from the snowfield beneath the couloir. The second arete (Moon Goddess Arete) starts from the lowest portion of this face, and eventually joins the first arete. The other aretes start much higher on the face. The third arete is rather minor, and is not as prominent. The fourth arete (Venusian Blind Arete) is to the

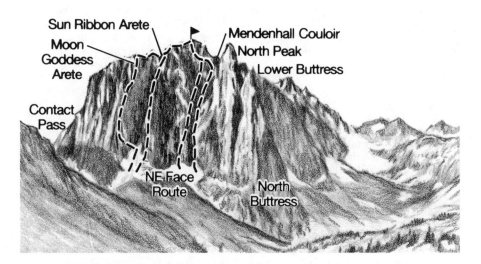

Temple Crag from the east

left of the minor arete, and starts with a large slab about 200 feet high. The fifth arete (Eclipsed Arete) is marked by a short, steep tower.

Climb onto a ledge from the snowfield below the left-hand couloir on the northeast face. This ledge leads horizontally left, out to the edge of the Moon Goddess Arete. Easy climbing up and left leads around the large slab marking the start of the Venusian Blind Arete. Traverse left to the start of the Eclipsed Arete, where about fifteen pitches lead to the talus slope on the southeast side of Temple Crag.

Venusian Blind Arete. III, 5.7. First ascent August 1969 by Don Jensen, S. Petroff, and A. Walker. From the snowfield beneath the left-hand couloir, climb out onto the horizontal ledge (class 3–4; locally known as "The Traverse of Death") that leads across the Moon Goddess Arete. Climb up and left over easy terrain to the large slab that is visibly farthest to the left, bypassing a minor slab to its right. Climb an open book on the left side of the slab, and remain on the left-hand edge of the slab to the prow of the arete above. Climb through a ceiling, followed by a class 4 pitch. Pass through a notch and climb a 100-foot tower on the right. (Escape route: From the top of the tower, go right into the class 4 gully between the Venusian Blind and Moon Goddess aretes.) From the top of the tower, go left and climb the major tower of the arete for three pitches. Climb over gendarmes to the base of the next tower on the arete. (This tower is 160 feet high.) Continue climbing the arete for several more pitches to the talus slopes on the southeast side of Temple Crag.

Moon Goddess Arete. III, 5.6. First ascent of lower part July 1969 by Don Jensen and J. Conners; first ascent of upper part September 1969 by Carl Dreisbach and Pat Armstrong. This is a fabulous climb, exposed, yet not continually difficult. Climb onto the horizontal ledge from the snowfield beneath the left-hand couloir on the northeast face. Climb up and left from the lower end of the arete for approximately 200 feet. Go right to the start of the Moon Goddess Arete and climb several class 4 and 5 pitches to a large gendarme. Bypass this by means of an exposed 5.4 traverse to the right to the notch behind the gendarme. Continue up another pitch to the flawless 200-foot-high

tower. (Escape route: You can move into a class 4 gully to the left when near the base of this tower.) Drop down and follow easy ledges to the right for about 120 feet to a belay stance. Climb steep cracks straight up for 150 feet to a chockstone behind the tower. Follow the arete for many more pitches upward to the talus slope on the southeast side of Temple Crag.

Sun Ribbon Arete. IV, 5.8, with a Tyrolean traverse. First ascent of lower part July 1969 by Don Jensen, W. Miller, and R. Schwartz; first ascent of upper part September 1969 by John Fischer and Don Jensen. First winter ascent February 1982 by George Lowe and Brock Wagstaff. This is a difficult climb that goes along the first arete to the right of the left-hand couloir on the northeast face. Climb the snowfield beneath the couloir, and traverse right over easy terrain to the base of a left-facing open book. Climb the book and scramble up 200 feet to the notch behind the small gendarme at the base of the arete above. Climb the edge of the arete for five pitches of 5.5 to 5.7 to the obvious alcove on top of the prow. There is a notch just beyond the alcove. This notch is most easily crossed by lassoing a block across the 15 foot gap. After the Tyrolean traverse, traverse across the left side of the arete to another notch. (Escape route: The gully on the left can be reached from this point.) Belay from a point 10 feet below the notch. Climb the left-facing crack above this point, either from its base (5.9) or by making a delicate traverse from the left (5.8). Continue climbing the arete to a notch; climb down into this and up the other side (5.4). Bypass a smooth, steep wall on its right side and regain the crest of the arete. This is followed by two more pitches, and scrambling leads to the talus slope.

Northeast Face. III, 5.4. First ascent June 9, 1957, by John Mendenhall and Ruth Mendenhall. This route starts from the snowfield beneath the right-hand couloir on the northeast side of Temple Crag. Climb a right-facing chimney from the left side of the snowfield. From the top of the chimney, climb up and right toward the notch behind the North Peak. Before reaching the notch, go left, encountering a few class 4 pitches before reaching the true summit.

Mendenhall Couloir. III, Class 4–5. First ascent July 7, 1940, by John Mendenhall and Ruth Mendenhall. This follows the right-

Temple Crag from the north (photo by Mike Baca)

hand couloir on the northeast face. Steep snow is encountered low, followed by a narrow slot choked with chockstones. Follow the couloir almost to the notch behind the North Peak, then go left toward the true summit.

26th of July Arete. III, 5.8. First ascent July 1970 by Don Jensen and Chuck Kroger. There are two aretes on the northeast side of the North Peak of Temple Crag. This route follows the right-hand arete. Begin by climbing the wall to the right of the arete for two pitches (5.8) to the base of the prominent gully. Go left onto the arete (5.8) and follow the crest (some 5.7) to the top of the arete. Go up and right through the small notch to the top of the lower buttress (one 5.5 move). The climb ends here, but it is possible to continue via the upper part of the Dark Star route or via the North Peak, Right Side route.

Communion Route. III, 5.8. First ascent 1966 by Tom Higgins and Bud Couch. Ascend the first two pitches of the 26th of July Arete to the base of the prominent gully. Climb the wall to the right of this gully to the notch just north of the Lower Buttress.

Dark Star. V, 5.10, A1. First ascent of lower part September 1970 by Don Jensen and John Fischer; first ascent of upper part July 1971 by Don Jensen and Keith Brueckner. First winter ascent by Jay Smith and Charlie Jenkewitz (date unknown). This is the longest technical route in the Palisades (thirty-three pitches). It ascends the north buttress of the peak. Climb the most prominent right-facing dihedral on the very prow of the buttress. One and a half pitches lead to a ledge left of the dihedral. Traverse left a short distance in order to pendulum left to a difficult crack. After this, ascend directly up over corners to some small ledges. Go slightly left and then up to a large flake. An easy pitch and then a moderate pitch lead to the base of a deep chimney. Ascend this chimney from deep inside to a ledge behind some chockstones. This is followed by scrambling and some easy class 5 moves to the top of the Lower Buttress. (Escape route: You can descend the North Peak, Right Side route from here.) Traverse left and up from the notch behind the Lower Buttress for 75 feet and then go straight up (5.7) for another 50 feet. Go right into a shallow gully and climb it a short way to a small ceiling, which is overcome by a 5.9 crack. This is followed by many pitches of free climbing with several significant gendarmes, and then a scramble to the top of the North Peak. Continue directly up the north ridge to the true summit of Temple Crag.

Barefoot Bynum. IV, 5.10, A1. First ascent September 1970 by Doug Robinson and Chuck Kroger. Climb the right-facing dihedral that is 40 feet to the right of the dihedral used for the start of Dark Star. Leave the dihedral on its right side part way up and aim for a large roof. An aid move over the roof is followed by a crack-and-chimney system, which is followed to its end after four pitches. Scrambling, with some technical moves, leads to the top of the lower buttress.

Planaria. IV, 5.10, A1. First ascent 1977 by Gordon Wiltsie and Jay Jensen. This route climbs the blank, steep face to the right of Dark Star and Barefoot Bynum. It leads into the shallow dihedral seen high on the face.

North Peak, Right Side. III, 5.4. First ascent August 18, 1963, by John Mendenhall, Vivian Mendenhall, Roy Coates, and Ed Lane. Begin by climbing the northwest couloir on Temple Crag. Leave the couloir on its left side on some easy ledges after a few hundred feet. Rope up and traverse left for two pitches (class 4–5) to easier ground. Scramble upward, and then go left and up (some class 4) to the top of the Lower Buttress. Traverse right on a ledge for 150 feet to a crack system that is to the left of the prominent open book on the northwest side of the North Peak. Climb the crack system (5.4) and then go right, scrambling to the top of the North Peak.

Northwest Chimney. III, 5.7. First ascent 1970 by Les Roberts and Joe Herbst. Ascend the northwest couloir for 500 feet to the prominent, right-facing dihedral on the western side of the North Peak. Five long pitches in a chimney in this dihedral lead almost to the top of the North Peak.

Northwest Couloir. Class 4. First ascent August 11, 1931, by Norman Clyde, Robert Underhill, Glen Dawson, and Jules Eichorn. Climb this prominent couloir, passing the chockstones on the right. Take the left branch of the couloir to the headwall beneath the summit. Go right to a prominent notch, and follow the arete to the true summit.

The Surgicle, East Side. II, 5.7. First ascent 1969 by Don Jensen and Joan Jensen. This is the pinnacle on the rib to the right of the northwest couloir. Climb the east face beneath the pinnacle, and then the east face of the pinnacle itself. Rappel the route to descend.

The Surgicle, North Rib. II, 5.8. Three pitches lead to the top of the Surgicle.

Northwest Face. Class 4. First ascent May 1930 by Norman Clyde. This route climbs the deep chute that is right (southwest) of the northwest couloir. Climb the left-ascending chute to where it joins the northwest couloir above the level of the chockstones. There is a 15-foot class 4 move approximately 200 feet above the base of the chute; the remainder of the climb is class 3.

Rabbit Ears. II, 5.5. First ascent 1968 by Chuck Pratt, Bob Swift, and friends. There is a sloping bench to the right of the chute used to ascend the Northwest Face route. There are three ribs above this bench. The Rabbit Ears is the large pinnacle on the central rib; its north face split by a large crack. From the bench, climb the gully that leads to the right side of the Rabbit Ears. The large crack on its north side is the crux. Rappel the route.

Red Eye Pillar. III, 5.9. First ascent August 1970 by Don Jensen and Chuck Kroger. This pillar is to the right (across a narrow chute) from the bench beneath the Rabbit Ears. There is a patch of red rock about three-fourths of the way up this pillar. The climb starts about 50 feet to the right of the narrow chute and goes up and to the left of a left-facing dihedral topped by a roof. Go right into the dihedral, and climb the roof via a 5.8 crack. Four pitches of easier climbing follow, and lead to the base of a large block with smooth, steep walls on both sides. Traverse right for 30 feet to a narrow crack, and climb this (5.9) to the top of the pillar. Continue to the crest of the ridge between Mt. Gayley and Temple Crag. To descend, continue along the crest of the ridge toward Mt. Gayley, then descend the northwest side of the ridge on ledges to the snowfields north of Mt. Gayley.

Cirith Anodyne. III, 5.10. First ascent by Doug Robinson, Jay Jensen, and Gordon Wiltsie. This climb consists of five pitches of difficult free climbing from the very bottom of the Red Eye Pillar.

Traverse from Mt. Gayley. Class 4–5. First ascent 1969 by Don Jensen and friend. This is a long traverse, with many exposed places.

Mt. Gayley   *(4118 m; 13,510 ft)*

There is a fine view of the peaks of the North and South Forks of Big Pine Creek from the summit.

Southwest Ridge. Class 3. First ascent June 10, 1927, by Norman Clyde. First winter ascent January 29, 1968, by Don Jensen and party. This route has also been called the "Yellow Brick Road." Follow the ridge from Glacier Notch.

West Face. Class 3. First ascent July 1949 by Norman Clyde and party. Climb the rib that is left (northeast) of the approach to Glacier Notch from the Palisade Glacier. Traverse left and up across some ledges from a point approximately 200 feet below the level of the notch. Go across the west face to the arete leading up to the summit, and follow the arete to the top.

Northwest Ridge. I, 5.2. First ascent July 10, 1971, by Wally Henry, Steve Rogero, and Jon Inskeep. The crest of the northwest ridge is followed most of the way, with occasional detours onto the north face.

North Face, Center Arete. III, 5.8. First ascent 1984 by James Eakin and Rick Todd. This route follows the curving arete in the center of the face, just right of a narrow gully. The crux is on the third pitch: Move down and right from a flake on the crest of the ridge to a crack system. Follow the cracks up and to the right to a left-facing corner with two cracks. Climb this corner to a small belay ledge. Continue up the arete, with short deviations to the right and left, until it is possible to traverse into the gully. Head left into the gully, climb it to its top, and go to the right through the notch that separates the lower and upper portions of the arete. This leads to a large bowl. Climb the left side of the bowl for two pitches to a belay beneath a short, wide chimney. Climb the chimney, followed by a hand traverse left to a ledge. Climb the short corner from the left end of the ledge to the crest of the upper arete. Class 3 and 4 climbing then leads to the north summit.

Northeast Ridge and East Face. I, 5.2. First ascent by Smoke Blanchard. Traverse left across the north face to a small notch on the northeast ridge. Pass through the notch and climb the east face to the summit.

South Side. Class 3. Descended September 28, 1931, by Walter A. Starr, Jr. This involves climbing over some huge boulders and small cliffs from the South Fork drainage.

Mt. Sill   *(14,153 ft; 14,162 ft)*

This peak has the best view from any summit in the Sierra.

Southwest Slope. Class 2–3. First ascent July 24, 1903, by Joseph N. LeConte, James K. Moffitt, James S. Hutchinson, and Robert D. Pike. Ascend the Glacier Creek drainage to where it is possible to go left (northwest) into the cirque between Mt. Sill and Polemonium Peak. Cross the snowfield at the head of the cirque, keeping to its right, and follow the west ridge of the peak to the summit. The upper part of the west ridge consists of large talus; this is the only difficulty. *Variation: South Headwall.* Class 4, with one rappel. First ascent July 15, 1975, by Woody Stark and Richard Webster. From the Glacier Creek drainage, instead of turning left toward the cirque southwest of Mt. Sill, climb the headwall that is visible from Lake 3559m (11,672 ft). The first-ascent party used one rappel to avoid aid. From the top of the headwall, follow the southeast ridge to the summit.

Traverse from the U Notch and Polemonium Peak. 5.4. First ascent August 2, 1933, by Lewis Clark, Ted Waller, Julie Mortimer, and Jack Riegelhuth. This route is described under Polemonium Peak. The ridge west of Mt. Sill to the gap before Polemonium Peak is class 2–3.

Northwest Face. Class 4. First ascent June 10, 1927, by Norman Clyde. There is a small pyramid-shaped peak (locally known as the "Apex Peak") just north of Mt. Sill (at UTM 664065). From the Palisade Glacier, climb the snow/ice couloir leading to the notch between this small peak and Mt. Sill, and continue up the North Couloir route to the summit. There is much loose rock on this side of Mt. Sill; the North Couloir route from Glacier Notch is the preferred route.

North Couloir. Class 4. First ascent September 25, 1931, by Walter A. Starr, Jr. From Glacier Notch ascend the L-shaped snow/ice couloir leading to the notch between Mt. Sill and the Apex Peak, on the north side of Mt. Sill. (Alternatively, you can ascend the class 3 rocks on the right side of the couloir.) Climb toward Mt. Sill from the notch for 80 feet and then traverse to the right across the northwest face. This leads to a small, scree-covered rib. Ascend the rib to the west ridge, and follow the ridge to the summit. *Variation:* 5.2. First ascent by George Wallerstein. Climb straight up from the start of the traverse for five short pitches. Some leader protection is needed on the third pitch. Further reading: *Summit*, July–August 1987, p. 10.

North Couloir, Descent Route. Class 4. This is commonly used as a descent route after climbs of the Swiss Arete, the east face, or the V Notch of Polemonium Peak. At an approximate elevation of 13,900 feet on the west ridge of Mt. Sill, descend the north side of the ridge about 200 feet. Traverse down and across the northwest face of Mt. Sill to a point just above the notch between Mt. Sill and the Apex Peak to the north. Descend to the notch and go down the 35-degree North Couloir (or the class 3 rocks on its north side) to Glacier Notch.

Swiss Arete. II, 5.5. First ascent July 3, 1938, by Spencer Austin, Ruth Dyar, Ray Ingwersen, Richard M. Jones, and Joe Momyer. This is one of the classic climbs of the High Sierra, ascending the north buttress of Mt. Sill. It is in a spectacular location, and it has little loose rock. From Glacier Notch, traverse up and left, across the North Couloir, to the north buttress of Mt. Sill. The climb begins at a point where the buttress flattens out a bit, at an approximate elevation of 13,500 feet. After two easy pitches, a 5.5 pitch leads to an impasse. Traverse to the right on ledges to an exposed outside corner (5.4). This is followed by 5.5 moves up an open book. The rest of the climb is mostly class 4, with a few class 5 moves over and around huge blocks to the summit. Further reading: *Summit*, September–October 1988, pp. 24–29; Allan Bard, *Swiss Arete of Mt. Sill*, Shooting Star Guides, Bishop, California, 1991 (a route card). *Variation:* Continue directly up the buttress from where the impasse is met; this is 5.9.

East Face. III, 5.7. First ascent September 1, 1963, by John Mendenhall, Rich Gnagy, Burt Turney, and Genevieve Turney. The glacier on the eastern side of Mt. Sill has been called the "Sill Glacier." This climb starts from the highest point of the glacier, just north of the middle portion of the east face. Climb a class 4 chimney to a large, overhanging chockstone. Climb a thin crack (5.7) behind the chockstone. This is followed by a 5.6 pitch, and then a 5.7 pitch. Easier climbing leads to a gully, which is ascended for four pitches on its right side. Head for a steep chimney and climb its right wall (5.4–5.7) to a point about 200 feet south of the summit. *Variation:* From the top of the gully, climb up and to the right around a small buttress to a chute. Ascend the chute and then follow a ramp system left to a point about 100 feet south of the summit.

Larry's Pillar, Center. III, 5.10. First ascent 1978 by Mike Farrell and Mike Graber. Ascend a left-leaning, overhanging crack before moving onto the center portion of the face.

Larry's Pillar, Left Side. III, 5.9. First ascent August 1986 by Ken Davenport, David Wilson, and Michael Graber. This prominent pillar is on the southern half of the east face of Mt. Sill. It was affectionately named by the guides of the Palisade School of Mountaineering after their late director, Larry Williams. Ascend a left-leaning, overhanging crack from the Sill Glacier. Go left and up the left side of the pillar.

East Couloir. Class 4. Descended June 16, 1934, by Norman Clyde, Hervey Voge, and David Brower. From the Sill Glacier ascend the left-hand snow/ice couloir to where the two couloirs join. Follow the main couloir to the notch on the southeast ridge, and ascend the ridge to the summit.

Polemonium Peak
(14,080 ft+; 14,000 ft+; 0.15 mi SE of North Palisade)

This is the small peak immediately southeast of the U Notch. On some maps, the name Polemonium Peak has been erroneously placed on Peak 13,962 (13,920 ft+), 0.3 mile southeast of the correct peak.

From the U Notch. I, 5.2. First ascent August 2, 1933, by Lewis Clark, Ted Waller, Julie Mortimer, and Jack Riegelhuth. The top of the U Notch is attained by ascending either the Southwest Chute or the U Notch Couloir on North Palisade. From the top of the U Notch, climb up and right onto a ledge on the northwest face of Polemonium Peak for 60 feet of easy class 4. Then traverse diagonally upward for about 100 feet toward the obvious notch that is just above the prominent gendarme on the southwest arete. Go up from the notch, and several class 5 moves are followed by class 4 climbing to the summit.

V Notch Couloir. Class 4. First ascent September 1957 by John Mathias and John Ohrenschall. This is one of the classic ice climbs of the High Sierra. The route ascends

Mt. Sill from the north (photo by Norm Rohn)

Climbing Polemonium Peak (photo by R. J. Secor)

Descending North Palisade (photo by R. J. Secor)

the left branch of the obvious couloir east of the U Notch, and features 50-degree snow/ice for 900 feet. The bergschrund is usually passable on its left side, and most parties belay from rock on the sides of the couloir. It is possible to climb the rocks in the upper part of the couloir, but this is seldom done in this age of modern ice-climbing equipment and *sangfroid*. Further reading: *Mountain*, No. 11, September 1970, pp. 24–26; *Summit*, April 1975, pp. 2–3, 16–19.

Southeast Side. Class 4. First ascent July 27, 1930, by Jules Eichorn, Glen Dawson, John Olmstead, and Charles Dodge. Ascend to the top of the snowfield southwest of Mt. Sill, or follow the west ridge of Mt. Sill west to the gap just before the true summit of Polemonium Peak. Down-climb into the gap, and follow the knife-edged ridge to the summit of the peak. This last section consists of two short pitches of easy class 4.

North Palisade *(14,242 ft; 14,242 ft)*

North Pal is *the* classic peak of the High Sierra. It is striking from a distance, and it has routes that will challenge climbers of all abilities and preferences. The true summit is the higher, southeast peak. The lower, northwest peak is known as "Starlight Peak."

U Notch Couloir. Class 4. First ascent June 1928 by Norman Clyde. First winter ascent March 17, 1940, by David Brower and Fred Kelley. This route climbs the couloir leading to the U Notch from the Palisade Glacier. The U Notch is unmistakable; it is the most prominent gap on the ridge between Mt. Sill and North Palisade. The couloir is a 700-foot, 40-degree, snow/ice climb. The bergschrund itself is frequently impassable, but can usually be bypassed by climbing an easy class 5 chimney on its right side. Keep to the far right side of the couloir when ascending to avoid being overexposed to the

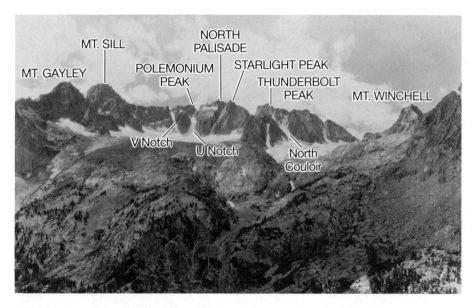

Palisade Glacier from the north (photo by F. E. Matthes, #1289, USGS Photographic Library, Denver, CO)

rockfall, which seems to prefer the lower right-center portion of the couloir; the first three to four pitches are the most exposed to rockfall. There is a peninsula of loose rocks about halfway up the couloir; pass this to its left and continue up snow/ice to easy scree, which leads to the top of the U Notch. From here you have two choices: the Chimney Variation and the Clyde Variation.

Chimney Variation: 5.4. Climb the steep chimney leading up the northwest wall of the U Notch for two pitches; the second pitch is especially strenuous. From the top of the chimney follow the southeast arete, at first keeping to its right side, and then moving to its left side. Traverse across the top of a large chute that drops toward the southwest, and follow a band of light-colored rock before heading directly for the huge boulders that make up the summit of the peak.

Clyde Variation: Class 4. Descend the southwest side of the U Notch 120 feet to a body-wedge crack that leads to a ledge. Climb the wall to the right of the crack (40 feet of easy class 4) to the ledge and follow the ledge left, around an arete, and into the next chute north. Climb the chute (class 3) to the southeast arete of North Pal, meeting it right next to the top of the Chimney Variation. Follow the southeast arete to the summit.

The U Notch Couloir with the Chimney Variation is the classic route, but most parties climb the Clyde Variation. Further reading: *Summit*, July–August 1987, p. 10.

Northeast Buttress. II, 5.6. First ascent July 1961 by Larry Williams, John Sharsmith, Burt Turney, and Genevieve Turney. Climb the obscure open book above and right of the bergschrund beneath the U Notch Couloir. The book consists of light-gray rock. Climb it for 300 feet to where the book becomes vertical. Traverse right over a slightly overhanging portion of the wall to broken, brown rock. Climb the buttress to the class 3 slabs on the upper portion of the north face. These slabs lead to the southeast arete, and the summit.

The Doors of Perception. II, 5.8. First ascent July 1970 by Allen Steck and Doug Robinson. This route ascends the obvious, gigantic dihedral to the right of the U Notch Couloir. Three pitches of crack and chimney climbing lead to the gentler upper portion of the north face of North Palisade.

North Buttress. II, 5.8, A2. First ascent July 12, 1970, by Ken Boche and Lee Panza. This route ascends the broad right-hand buttress of the three buttresses between the U Notch and Clyde couloirs. Begin by climbing the center of the buttress for a long pitch to a ledge. Go up to the right from the ledge, using some aid to pass some loose blocks, to a small ledge beneath a prominent overhang. Climb the overhang by means of a strenuous crack to a sloping ledge. Go up and left from the ledge (one 5.8 move) to the class 3 slabs beneath the summit snowfield.

Clyde Couloir. Class 4–5. First ascent July 6, 1930, by Norman Clyde. The Clyde Couloir is the narrow snow/ice couloir to the right (west) of the U Notch couloir; it leads to the notch between North Palisade and the lower, northwest summit, Starlight Peak. The bergschrund at the base of the couloir

may be impassable, except for the strongest and most skilled ice climbers. Once past the 'schrund, climb the right side of the couloir for 300 feet and traverse diagonally right onto the upper part of Starlight Buttress. Ascend the crest of the buttress (class 3 and 4) to a point about 200 feet below the summit of Starlight Peak. From this point, you can traverse across the distinctive snowfield high on North Pal's north face to the southeast ridge, head directly for the summit of North Pal (taking care to avoid cul-de-sacs), or climb the northwest ridge and follow it to either the summit of North Palisade or Starlight Peak; these options are listed in order of increasing difficulty. Norman Clyde de-

North Palisade from the northeast, August 24, 1972 (photo by Austin Post, #72R2-151, USGS Ice and Climate Project, Tacoma, WA)

Climbing Starlight Buttress on North Palisade (photo by R. J. Secor)

scribed this as being "one of the very best climbs in the Sierra." Very few climbers have disagreed. *Variation: The Narrows.* First ascent September 1955 by John Mendenhall and Dick Franklin. This party followed the couloir almost to its very top before moving right, out of the couloir. They experienced considerable rockfall, which is to be expected in the deteriorating ice conditions of late summer. (At one point, the belayer noticed that the leader was "wearing" his knapsack as if it were a helmet, as protection from falling rocks!) In early season, the Clyde Couloir can be a 900-foot snow climb, with an average angle of 55 degrees. Later in the summer it becomes a 300-foot ice climb, with some parts exceeding 60 degrees, surrounded by loose rocks. No matter what time of year you climb the Clyde Couloir, it is advisable to leave it for Starlight Buttress as soon as practical.

Starlight Buttress. II, 5.4. First ascent June 24, 1973, by Tom Naves, Ernie Spielher, Sheldon Moomaw, and R. J. Secor. This buttress is the first one right (west) of the Clyde Couloir. Cross the bergschrund of the Clyde Couloir, and traverse to the right onto the crest of the buttress. Follow it up for three pitches of exhilarating class 4 and 5 climbing. Class 3 and 4 ledges with a few class 5 moves lead to the notch on the northwest ridge between Starlight Peak and North Palisade. Follow the ridge to either summit.

Piper at the Gates of Dawn. III, 5.7. First ascent June 1968 by Doug Robinson and Carl Dreisbach. This is probably the most dangerous route in the Palisades. The lower portion of the northeast face of Starlight Peak has a large, smooth slab: the Flatiron. From the bergschrund to the right of the Flatiron, climb the dihedral formed by its right edge for one pitch of snow/ice climbing and one pitch of rock. Climb left out of the dihedral and onto the Flatiron. Climb cracks over two ceilings (5.7) for two pitches to the top of the Flatiron. Ascend the right margin of a right-leaning snow patch (class 4). This is followed by a class 3 pitch, which ends 70 feet below a prominent large chimney (full of dangerous loose blocks) that leads to the summit. Traverse left onto a small arete (5.6). Two increasingly easier pitches lead to the summit ridge, at a point about 50 feet west of the summit of Starlight Peak. *Variation:* First ascent August 1970 by W. Katra

and D. Summers. From the prominent large chimney, go right and ascend steep flakes and cracks (5.7). The last pitch traverses out onto the face and turns an overhang on the right.

The X. II, 5.7. First ascent July 1968 by John Clark, Jon Lonne, Dick James, and Steve Roper. This route is subject to the same dangerous rockfall as the preceding route. There are two diagonal crack systems on the right-hand side of the northeast face of Starlight Peak; these cracks form a huge x. Climb both right-hand segments of the x. The lower portion of this climb is 5.6 to 5.7, and the upper portion is easy class 5. There is much loose rock on this route.

Northwest Ridge. II, 5.5. First ascent June 29, 1934, by Norman Clyde, David Brower, and Hervey Voge. This is a spectacular climb, with great views, intricate route finding, and moderate difficulties. The climb begins from the notch between Thunderbolt Peak and Starlight Peak, which is reached from the top of either the Underhill Couloir or Southwest Chute No. 2 of Thunderbolt Peak. Ascend the western side of the northwest ridge (class 3 and 4), passing around gendarmes and into notches. A steep chimney (5.4) leads close to the summit block of Starlight Peak. A class 4 chimney leads down to the notch between Starlight Peak and North Palisade. From the notch, traverse on the southwest side of the ridge to another notch. Pass through it, and down-climb the northeast side of the ridge for about 30 feet (class 4). Traverse across this side of the ridge and climb up into another notch, with a flake on its south wall. Surmount the flake (easier said than done; some very experienced climbers have been embarrassed here). Next, traverse across the exposed northeast side of the ridge to a chimney. Ascend the chimney to the top of the northwest ridge; the second pitch on this ridge is especially difficult. From the top of the ridge descend about 15 feet on the southwest side to another chimney, which leads up the wall to the summit. *Variation:* The flake pitch has been bypassed by lowering the leader on tension to a point where it was possible for the leader to swing over the notch and flake to the large ledge on top of the flake. The rest of the party also followed on tension, with the help of protection placed by the leader.

Northwest Chute. Class 4. First ascent July

13, 1933, by James Wright. This is the first chute right (southwest) of the Southwest Chute No. 2 on Thunderbolt Peak; this chute leads to the summit of Starlight Peak. Ascend the chute to the headwall beneath Starlight Peak. Climb out onto the headwall and then to the base of the summit block of Starlight Peak.

Starlight Peak, West Rib. IV, 5.10b. First ascent July 4, 1990, by Steve Porcella and Cameron Burns. This rib connects the prows of two large, triangular buttresses on the west face of Starlight Peak. The lower triangular buttress is split by an enormous ledge. Start climbing just left of an obvious triangle of white quartzite. It goes up and slightly left for three leads (all about 5.8) to a large flake that is very obvious from the bottom. A beautiful pitch goes up behind this flake (5.9). This is followed by a ledge that leads through a small roof; this short, strenuous layback is the crux (5.10b). Follow the ledge up and left, following the line of least resistance. Another easy pitch goes up and around a corner and ends on the enormous ledge that splits the lower triangular buttress. Climb the White Dihedral pitch directly above the ledge for a long way. Continue up the rib above the dihedral, traverse right a few feet, and climb a shallow dihedral (5.8). One more lead (5.7) up blocks and cracks leads to the very prow of the first triangular buttress. Continue across a huge slab to a 40-foot 5.9 layback crack. This is followed by some unprotected mantles over blocks (5.8), and then an impasse. A rappel followed by two horizontal (more or less) class 4 pitches lead to the notch between the two triangular buttresses. A 5.8 pitch up the very crest of the upper buttress leads to the base of a loose chimney. Climb the chimney on its tight, right side (5.8). Three more pitches straight up flakes, dihedrals, and corners (5.7 to 5.8) lead to the top of the ridge. A short class 4 descent leads into a gully. From there it is a few hundred feet to the summit block, or "Milk Bottle." Further reading: *Mountain*, No. 135, pp. 36–41.

Starlight Chute. Class 5. Descended August 28, 1985, by Michael Feldman and Jim Shirley. This chute leads to the notch between North Pal and Starlight Peak from Palisade Basin. This chute contains a lot of dangerous loose rock, broken occasionally by polished slabs, and some difficult chimneys. The not very obvious start of the climb is marked by a black, watermarked stain 40 feet wide and 90 feet high, which is the chute outfall (the black watermarks for the west face route are hundreds of feet to the right, and are much higher and narrower). Ascend the wall and enter the chute. A vertical section is encountered and climbed by means of chimneys. This is followed by much class 3 and 4 to the notch south of Starlight Peak.

West Buttress. IV, 5.10. First ascent July 1982 by David Wilson and Galen Rowell. This route follows the buttress on the right (south) side of Starlight Chute. From the talus at the base of the west side of North Palisade, ascend three easy class 5 pitches to a smooth, slightly overhanging headwall. This headwall is overcome by means of four pitches of 5.9 and 5.10, followed by a steep arete, where a section of crackless towers forces you into a gully for a few hundred feet. The arete meets the northwest ridge between North Palisade and Starlight Peak. Follow the northwest ridge to the summit.

West Face. Class 5. First ascent August 1936 by Richard M. Jones and Mary Jane Edwards. This climb starts to the left of a long, narrow black watermark on the west side of the North Palisade. Ascend straight up to where progress is stopped by a large slab. Traverse right on a sloping ledge (across the watermark) and then go left into a wide chute. Ascend the right side of this chute to where it narrows. Traverse to the right on a horizontal white vein of rock into the next chute. Ascend this chute to the summit.

Es Lasst Sich Nicht Lesen. III, 5.10. First ascent July 3, 1989, by Cameron Burns and Steve Porcella. Climb the West Face route, but ascend the left side of the wide chute. From where the left side of this chute narrows, follow a horizontal band of light-colored rock for several hundred feet to the right. Drop down onto class 4 rock at one point to avoid a difficult, unprotected traverse. This detour leads to a steep, snow-filled couloir. Climb the face on the right side of the couloir (5.10), and go up and left over a loose face to the top of a huge buttress. Climb several left-facing dihedrals to an enormous flat area. Two easy class 5 pitches traverse around the ledge to the left and lead to an easy chimney system. One more pitch of easy class 5 leads to the summit ridge behind a tower. Drop down to the chute on the right and climb to the summit.

White Ship. II, 5.9. First ascent July 2, 1989, by Cameron Burns and Steve Porcella. There are three white cliffs along the base of the southwest face of North Palisade. Climb the northernmost cliff, starting to the left of a small, black watermark. Climb a dihedral with a difficult mantle (5.9). The second pitch climbs a series of blocks (5.8) and ends on a large ledge. Climb another dihedral, a strenuous and sustained 5.9 crux. This is followed by a chimney; then you move right, into a crack, and finish with easy face climbing. The last pitch climbs to a ledge, followed by a short dihedral to another ledge, and then moves left up a right-slanting flake.

Putterman Couloir. I, 5.5. First ascent July 2, 1989, by Cameron Burns and Steve Porcella. This couloir is on the southern side of the northernmost of the three white cliffs at the base of the southwest face of North Palisade. Climb loose talus to a steep section of crumbling mud and blocks. Climb the blocks and an orange headwall on the left (5.5). Follow a ledge to the left to the top of the cliff.

Southwest Buttress. IV, 5.11c. First ascent June 29, 1990, by Cameron Burns and Steve Porcella. This is the buttress that is left of the lower southwest chute, or LeConte Route. This route starts from the upper right-hand side of the large slab that is at the base of the middle cliff on the southwest face of North Palisade. A pitch up an easy crack system, followed by some ledges, leads to a steep headwall. This headwall features a choice of three steep off-width cracks. The next pitch above the headwall takes the off-width crack farthest right; this pitch is totally crazy, airy, and scary (5.11c). The next three pitches are class 3 and 4, and lead to the base of the proper southwest buttress. Four pitches up the buttress lead to a sustained fingertip crack (5.10). Stay close to the crest of the arete from here for another seven pitches (nothing harder than 5.8) to a notch. Either down-climb or rappel 20 feet into the notch and scramble up to the summit, which is nearby. Take off-width protection for this sixteen-pitch climb. Further reading: *Mountain,* No. 135, pp. 36–41.

The LeConte Route. Class 4. First ascent July 25, 1903, by Joseph LeConte, James Hutchinson, and James Moffitt. When viewing North Palisade from Barrett Lakes, you see three large white cliffs, which separate the entrances to two chutes. Ascend the talus slope above the largest of the lakes and climb the right-hand chute. This chute leads to the top of the U Notch. Approximately halfway up (at an elevation of 13,100 feet) this chute widens out in an area of slabs and rubble. The chute branches in this area, and a vague left branch goes almost due north, with a rock wall on its side. Climb this left branch for 100 feet to where a ledge appears on the rock wall. This narrow ledge leads left into the next chute to the north. Ascend this chute to where it narrows, at an elevation of 13,500

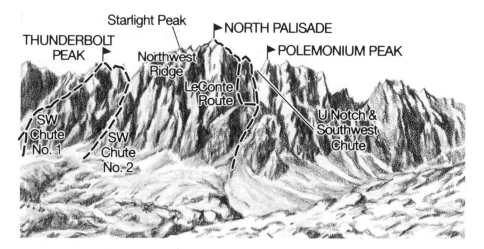

North Palisade from the southwest

feet. Traverse right into a narrow third chute on a horizontal white vein of rock; the chute may be filled with snow and hidden from below. This narrow third chute has two chockstones, which are both overcome by means of two class 4 moves; it is easier when it is filled with snow. Continue ascending this chute to the crest of the southeast ridge, just right of the summit. Class 3 climbing over blocks near the drop-off over the Palisade Glacier leads to the summit.

Southwest Chute. Class 4. First ascent July 19, 1921, by Hermann Ulrichs. Climb the chute for the LeConte Route to the top of the U Notch. There may be quite a bit of loose rock if there isn't any snow cover in the upper portion of this chute. From the top of the U Notch, climb either the Chimney Variation or the Clyde Variation to the summit. *Moore Variation:* Class 4. First ascent July 3, 1988, by Kathy Moore and R. J. Secor. Ascend the chute to an elevation of 13,700 ft; the floor of the chute is wall-to-wall scree at this point. Climb up and left via a narrow ledge to the next chute left, and ascend this chute to the summit.

Starlight Peak. First ascent July 9, 1930, by Norman Clyde, during his second ascent of the Clyde Couloir (his first was three days before; this is a fine testament to the character of the route and the man). The easiest route to the summit of the northwest peak of North Palisade is probably a traverse to the northwest ridge of North Palisade from the summit of North Pal. The summit block, known as the "Milk Bottle," is climbed by means of a delicate mantle. It is the best-looking summit block in the Palisades, and it is situated in the best location for dramatic photographs.

Thunderbolt Peak

(14,003 ft; 14,000 ft+)

This is another classic peak of the High Sierra, the last 14,000-foot peak to be climbed in the range. The summit block (on the higher, south peak) is difficult, and has defeated many climbers. Some really creative rope tricks are needed to pass a rope over it for aid or an upper belay; it goes free at 5.9. The lower, north peak (locally known as "The Lightning Rod") is class 5 from the notch between it and the south peak. The name "Thunderbolt Peak" commemorates an incident during the first ascent, when a nearby lightning strike temporarily broke Jules Eichorn's stride.

The Underhill Couloir. Class 4. First ascent August 13, 1931, by Robert Underhill, Norman Clyde, Bestor Robinson, Francis Farquhar, Glen Dawson, Lewis Clark, and Jules Eichorn. There are two couloirs that lead from the Palisade Glacier to the notch south of Thunderbolt Peak. Ascend the right-hand couloir to where progress is blocked by a chockstone. Bypass this by climbing the wall to its right before returning to the couloir and climbing it to the notch. Go north from the notch and ascend slabs to a chimney. There are two options from the top of the chimney. Either follow a ledge left to an exposed mantle, or continue up the face and chimney to the small notch next to the flat-topped pinnacle at the southern edge of the summit ridge. Follow the ridge to the summit. *Variation:* Class 4. The left couloir is full of loose rocks, unless there is sufficient snow cover—then it may be the preferable route. Ascend the left couloir approximately halfway up, and then move right and ascend the crest of the arete to the notch south of Thunderbolt Peak. *Variation:* 5.4. The arete between the two couloirs can also be followed from the bottom. Further reading: *Summit,* July–August 1987, p. 10.

East Face. III, 5.5. First ascent August 1965 by Charles Ray and Ulrich Brosch. Traverse right on scree-covered ledges from the base of the Underhill Couloir for approximately 200 feet. Ascend diagonally left to a shallow open book. Ascend this for many pitches to the summit ridge. This has been described as an enjoyable climb on relatively good rock.

East Couloir. Class 5. First ascent July 4, 1959, by Ellen Wilts and Rich Gnagy. This narrow couloir ascends the east face of Thunderbolt Peak from the Palisade Glacier. Ascend the couloir, and go up and right, toward the crest of the upper northeast buttress. At one point there is a choice of two cracks to climb; the crack on the right is the correct choice. Ascend the headwall to the crest of the buttress, and follow the crest around the west side of the Lightning Rod to the notch between the two summits of Thunderbolt Peak.

The Prow. III, 5.6. First ascent August 1970 by W. Katra and D. Sommers. This route ascends the great northeast buttress that almost divides the Palisade Glacier; the glacier north and west of this point has been called the "Thunderbolt Glacier." The route begins 50 feet to the left of the lowest tip of the buttress. Ascend a short, steep chimney to where class 4 and 5 climbing leads to the top of the long upper part of the northeast buttress.

Northeast Couloir. III, 5.6. First ascent August 1968 by Bob Lindgren and Brad Fowler. Ascend the first small couloir west of the prow of the northeast buttress. Keep to the left side of the couloir and climb onto a broken-rock ledge. Climb straight up from the ledge for one pitch (5.6). Continue up gentler rock for a few pitches (mostly class 4) to the top of the buttress. Follow the crest of the buttress around the west side of the north peak to the notch between the two summits of Thunderbolt Peak.

North Couloir. 5.0. First ascent by Norman Clyde. This route climbs the large, y-shaped snow and ice couloir west of the great northeast buttress of the peak. Cross the Thunderbolt Glacier (the western lobe of the Palisade Glacier, north of Thunderbolt Peak) to the bergschrund at the base of the couloir. Cross the bergschrund on its left side, and head for ledges on the left side of the couloir.

(Alternatively, you can directly ascend the 35-degree, 1,000-foot couloir; this may be preferable in early season.) Ascend the left side of the couloir, and its left branch where it divides, to the crest of the upper northeast buttress. Follow the northeast buttress around the north side of the Lightning Rod to the crest of the northwest ridge. Drop down and traverse across the west side of the peak on a series of ledges to a chute that leads up to the notch between the higher, south peak and the north peak. Pass through the notch, and a short, easy class 5 move to the left (much shorter than the class 4 leads via the Underhill Couloir) leads to less exposed climbing and the summit block.

Northwest Ridge. Class 5. First ascent August 11, 1938, by W. K. Davis and Jack Riegelhuth. Follow the ridge from Winchell Col to the summit. The first one-third of this route is class 3, and the rest is class 4 and 5.

West Face. Class 5. First ascent September 3, 1949, by Oscar Cook, Sylvia Kershaw, Mildred Jentsch, Hunter Morrison, and Isabella Morrison. Ascend the first chute north (left) of Thunderbolt Pass from Dusy Basin. Follow the right branch of this chute to where it ends in an ice-filled chimney. Traverse to the right to an arete. Climb the

North Palisade and Thunderbolt Peak from the north (photo by R. J. Secor)

arete for a while, and then leave it at a vein of rotten quartz by traversing to the right into a chute. A chockstone in this chute is passed on its left side (class 4). Ascend the chute to the southwest buttress of Thunderbolt Peak, which ends on the northwest ridge. Follow the ridge to the base of the Lightning Rod and drop down and traverse across its west side to the notch between the two summits of Thunderbolt Peak. Pass through the notch, and a short but easy class 5 pitch leads up and left to the base of the summit block.

Southwest Buttress. Class 5. First ascent August 28, 1964, by Kim Tucker, Sten Hedberg, and Alan Jedlicka. Follow the crest of the buttress upward from Thunderbolt Pass. Traverse left near the top and follow a chute to bypass some gendarmes to where it is possible to regain the buttress. The buttress ends atop the northwest ridge, which is followed to the southeast, to the notch between the two summits of Thunderbolt Peak. A class 5 move from the notch leads to the summit block of the higher, south peak.

Southwest Chute No. 1. Class 5. Descended September 3, 1949, by Oscar Cook, Sylvia Kershaw, Mildred Jentsch, Hunter Morrison, and Isabella Morrison. Ascend the first chute to the right (south) from Thunderbolt Pass. Approximately one-third of the way up, the chute narrows and is filled with chockstones. This section is bypassed by traversing right on a 3-foot-wide, scree-covered ledge. Continue up the chute to where it divides repeatedly; always take the right fork. These lead to the notch between the north and south summit of Thunderbolt Peak. An easy class 5 move leads up and left from the notch to the flat ridge on the eastern side of the south summit. A large crack is followed to the summit block.

Southwest Chute No. 2. Class 4. First ascent August 3, 1933, by Norman Clyde, John Poindexter, and Philip Von Lubken. This is the largest chute that climbs from Palisade Basin to the notch south of Thunderbolt Peak. The main obstacle in this chute is a large chockstone. It may be possible to crawl underneath it; otherwise, a short class 4 pitch on its right side is used. It is possible to continue up the chute to the notch south of Thunderbolt Peak, but a better route is to take a steep, loose, short chute leading left into the next major chute, and follow this to the slabs above the notch. Ascend the slabs to a chimney, and from its top either follow a ledge left to an exposed mantle, or continue up the face and chimney to the small notch next to the flat-topped pinnacle at the southern edge of the summit ridge.

The Lightning Rod. Class 5. This is the lower, north summit of Thunderbolt Peak. The route starts from the notch between the two summits of Thunderbolt Peak. Climb to a wide, sloping ledge on the east side of the north summit. At the far end of this ledge, go right to a notch in the ridge with a chockstone in it. Pass through the notch to a narrow ledge with a lot of exposure. Ascend straight up from the ledge over small ledges to a 2-inch-wide crack, which leads to the summit.

Mt. Winchell   (13,775 ft; 13,768 ft)

East Arete. Class 3. First ascent June 10, 1923, by W. B. Putnam, J. N. Newell, and H. C. Mansfield. First winter ascent January 10, 1938, by Norman Clyde, Morgan Harris, and David Brower. When viewing the southern side of the east arete from the Thunderbolt Glacier, you can see two chutes leading up to the arete. Climb the right-hand chute to the crest of the arete. Follow the arete to where it becomes a knife-edge, and then traverse left into a steep chute which leads to the summit. This route is not especially difficult, and the summit is spectacular, with an impressive view down the magnificent sculptures on the west face. *Variation:* Class 3. First ascent September 1953 by George Bloom, Kay Bloom, and Glenn Cushman. The east arete can also be approached from the north. Go to the north of a large buttress at the end of the east arete and climb a broken face to the crest of the arete. Follow the arete to the knife-edge just below the summit.

North Face. Class 4. First ascent August 14, 1955, by Robert Stebbins, Bill Rogers, and G. Ledyard Stebbins. Climb to the top of the glacier on the north side of Mt. Winchell and continue upward between the northeast buttress and the north couloir. At one point there is a long diagonal traverse. The route ends on the east arete just below the summit.

Northwest Ridge. IV, 5.8. First ascent August 1971 by Chris Fredericks and Tim

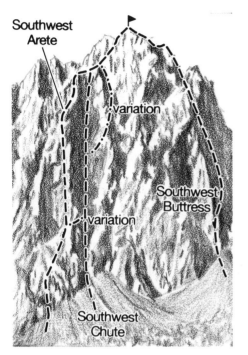

Southwest
Arete

variation

variation

Southwest
Buttress

Southwest
Chute

Mt. Winchell, West Face

Harrison. Climb onto the ridge at a point just south of Agassiz Col and follow the ridge to the summit. A long rappel is needed to descend into the major notch in the ridge. This is followed by a steep headwall, the crux of the climb.

West Chute. Class 4–5. First ascent July 29, 1930, by Jules Eichorn, Glen Dawson, and John Olmstead. From Dusy Basin, climb a chute that leads to a notch high on the northwest ridge. Some difficult chimneys are encountered in this chute.

Southwest Arete. III, 5.8. First ascent May 1976 by Galen Rowell and Warren Harding. Climb the broad face that is to the left of the two chutes in the center of the southwest face of Mt. Winchell. Gradually move right onto the crest of the arete, and follow the arete to where it ends on the northwest ridge, about 100 feet from the summit. Most of this route is moderate class 5.

Southwest Chute. Class 4–5. First ascent August 11, 1938, by W. K. Davis and Jack

Riegelhuth. Climb the left-hand chute of the two chutes on the southwest face of Mt. Winchell. Ascend the chute to its top, and traverse left to the top of the southwest arete. Follow the arete to the northwest ridge, and follow the ridge to the summit. *Variation:* Class 4. First ascent 1966 by Steve Roper and Gordon Waddle. Climb the face that is several hundred feet left of the left-hand chute. Ascend this face for approximately 400 feet, and traverse to the right across the southwest arete and into the southwest chute. *Variation:* Class 4. First ascent 1962 by Tom Mathes and Jim Eder. Ascend the chute to where it narrows. After climbing over a large boulder, a steep, yellow gully is seen on the right wall. Climb the class 4 gully to the crest of the arete that separates the two chutes on the southwest side of Mt. Winchell. Four more class 4 pitches lead to the summit.

Southwest Buttress. III, 5.7, A2. First ascent September 1977 by David Mazel. This is the first major buttress to the left (northwest) of Winchell Col. Climb two pitches in a left-facing dihedral and then move right (A2) and climb a prominent chimney. Move right again from the top of the chimney over class 3–4 rock, followed by some more technical climbing that leads to a shallow notch at the top of the buttress. Several hundred feet of class 3–4 climbing along the south arete leads to the summit.

Southeast Face. Class 5. First ascent June 21, 1959, by Don Dohrmann and Don Harmon. Class 3 climbing from Winchell Col leads to a prominent chute. Three class 4 pitches over loose rock in the chute end on a broad ledge. A long class 5 pitch leads over a small overhang and up a crack to a ledge beneath a second overhang. Turn this overhang on its right side, and climb out onto the east face of the peak. Some class 4 then leads to the top of the south arete a short distance from the summit.

Mt. Agassiz *(13,893 ft; 13,891 ft)*

This is the easiest major peak of the Palisades, and the ascent from Bishop Pass is very popular. There is a splendid view of the peaks surrounding the Palisade Glacier from the summit.

West Slope. Class 2. First ascent August 30, 1925, by Norman Clyde. First winter ascent

March 20, 1967, by Rich Gregersen and Gary Vogt. Ascend a spur that rises above Bishop Pass to the summit.

Southeast Face and South Ridge. Class 2. First ascent June 13, 1927, by Norman Clyde. From the northern moraine of the glacier east of Agassiz Col, climb a scree chute to the crest of the south ridge of Mt. Agassiz. Follow the ridge to the summit. The east side of the south ridge can also be followed from Agassiz Col; this is mostly talus, and may be preferable to the loose scree in the chute.

East Ridge. Class 4. Climb the left-hand couloir of the two couloirs that lead onto the east ridge from the glacier northeast of Mt. Agassiz. Ascend the east ridge to the summit.

Northeast Face. 5.2. First ascent July 5, 1930, by Norman Clyde. Cross the glacier northeast of Mt. Agassiz and ascend the y-shaped couloir that leads onto the north ridge of the peak. Ascend halfway up the y, and then traverse left onto the rocks. Climb the face diagonally; when about halfway up the face, traverse right onto an arete which overlooks the y-shaped couloir. Ascend the arete and either continue up the east face to the summit, or cross the arete to the gentler slopes to the right.

Mt. Robinson   *(12,967 ft; 12,800 ft)*

Northeast Face. Class 3. First ascent July 4, 1930, by Norman Clyde. Pass numerous pinnacles on the face and climb the long northeast ridge to the summit.

The Lichen Arete. II, 5.7. First ascent August 1969 by Don Jensen, D. Kennedy, and R. Davis. There are three couloirs on the right-hand side of the northeast face of Mt. Robinson. The two right-hand couloirs join halfway up, and there is an arete between these two couloirs and the left-hand couloir. Climb the broad face, with increasingly difficult climbing, to the start of the arete. Ascend an easy chimney and traverse right to a ledge on the prow of the arete. Climb a vertical 5.7 open book to a small ledge left of the prow, and continue climbing to a good belay ledge a few feet higher. Climb several pitches to a notch with a steep, red tower on its opposite side. Make a delicate ascending traverse on its left side. One more pitch leads to the summit of the arete. The true summit of Mt. Robinson is a long scramble along the northeast ridge.

West Ridge. Class 3. First ascent June 14, 1934, by David Brower and Hervey Voge. Follow the jagged ridge from the broad saddle between Mt. Robinson and Mt. Agassiz.

South Face. II, 5.7. First ascent July 1968 by Steve Roper, John Clark, Jon Lonne, and Dick James. Ascend the second arete from the right-hand arete on the south side of Mt. Robinson.

Southeast Face. Class 3. Descended June 14, 1934, by David Brower and Hervey Voge. Ascend any of the many chutes above Sam Mack Lake.

Aperture Peak   *(13,265 ft; 13,200 ft+)*

First ascent June 1934 by David Brower and Hervey Voge. This peak is class 3 from Jigsaw Pass or from the glacier northeast of Mt. Agassiz.

Gendarme Peak   *(13,252 ft; 13,241 ft)*

First ascent August 13, 1967, by Bill Schuler and Andy Smatko, via the southwest ridge. They descended a snow couloir on the southeast face. The summit rocks are easy class 3. There are four spectacular gendarmes on the northeast ridge.

Two Eagle Peak   *(12,966 ft; 12,880 ft+)*

This peak is actually a spur extending northeast from Gendarme Peak. It rises above Fifth Lake.

East Ridge. Class 3. First ascent July 6, 1929, by Norman Clyde. Follow the north side of the east ridge from Fifth Lake. The summit block is a smooth slab.

South Buttress. II, 5.6. First ascent July 1972 by Grant Hoag and Don Jensen. There are many small aretes and gullies to the right of a smooth face on the south side of this peak. Begin by climbing a class 4 chimney just right of the face. Climb the left wall of the chimney for four pitches to the top of the buttress. Traverse across the flat ridge atop the buttress to a large, red tower. This is climbed via a chimney on its right side. Follow a sharp arete to the summit.

The Diamond. III, 5.6. This excellent route consists of ten pitches with wild exposure. Go a few hundred feet up and left from the very bottom of the south face and follow an improbable ledge/crack system up and right. Then climb a pitch left to the crest of the south buttress, above the flat ridge.

Picture Puzzle *(13,280 ft+; 13,278 ft)*

North Slope. Class 3. First ascent 1937 by Norman Clyde from Ruwau Lake.

Northeast Couloir. Class 3. First ascent August 13, 1967, by Andy Smatko, Bill Schuler, Frank Yates, and Tom Ross. Ascend the 40-degree snow couloir on the northeast face to easy class 3 rock.

Southwest Face. Class 4. First ascent 1962 by Mike Loughman.

Cloudripper *(13,525 ft; 13,501 ft)*

First ascent June 15, 1926, by Norman Clyde. This peak is class 1 from Seventh Lake via the east ridge. The north slope is class 2 from Green Lake. The west slope from Chocolate Lakes is class 3 and was climbed by Ted Waller in 1932. The summit rocks are easy class 3.

Chocolate Peak *(11,682 ft; 11,658 ft)*

The class 2 southeast side was climbed by Don McGeein on July 4, 1932.

Wrinkles

The Palisade Glacier and its couloirs. The Palisade Glacier is the largest in the High Sierra, but it should not be confused with the sort of glaciers found in the Cascade Range. There are crevasses in the Palisade Glacier, but these are not the same obstacles that are encountered on Mt. Rainier, for example. During a typical snow year, the crevasses are small, narrow cracks that do not impede progress. During drought years, however, the crevasses may be 10 feet wide and perhaps 100 feet deep. But under these conditions, the Palisade Glacier is a "dry" glacier (i.e., no nevé, only bare ice) and the crevasses can be easily spotted and avoided, or crossed at convenient places. Climbers seldom rope up while crossing the Palisade Glacier.

The bergschrunds at the bottoms of the V Notch, U Notch, and Clyde couloirs are another matter. These are always wide and deep, and their snow bridges (if present) seem to be only a few inches thick, and climbers usually rope up. By mid-July these bridges may have collapsed, making the bergschrunds impassable unless the climber is skilled at climbing vertical ice. Sometimes these bridges collapse into a series of interconnected ramps, and remain that way until the next winter.

All of the couloirs above the Palisade Glacier can receive a phenomenal amount of rockfall. This can happen anytime, but in my experience it has been most frequent in the first half-hour after sunrise in the spring and early summer. On the other hand, in Norman Clyde's experience, rockfall was most frequent in the afternoon during the middle of the summer. It is best to be out of these couloirs (either at their tops or on the buttresses on their sides) before sunrise. Next best is to delay the start of the climb at least until 1 hour after sunrise, but not much later, and not dawdle in the couloir. The snow or ice in the couloirs will be soft in the spring and early summer after midmorning, and a party cannot help but knock off some big pieces of ice. It is foolish to climb behind another party under these conditions.

These couloirs don't really get into shape until late September to October. During this time the ice is hard (in terms of both density and difficulty), and a long, cold morning keeps most of the rock from falling.

But all of this is a generalization, and the only way to find out exactly what conditions are in the couloirs is to climb them and see for yourself. One summer weekend my partner and I didn't get to the base of the U Notch until midmorning, when other climbers were retreating because the bergschrund appeared to be impassable. The 'schrund was indeed impassable, but it had melted in such a way that we could find a way over the rock on the side of the couloir. It was a low snow year, and we expected the snow/ice in the couloir to be brick-hard. Instead, it was perfect Styrofoam, and we kicked steps to the top of the couloir. Yet, two months earlier, another partner and I attempted the Clyde Couloir only to find ourselves exposed to falling cannonades of rock and rime ice—the exact opposite of what would normally be expected at that time of year.

The "East Face" of North Palisade. North Palisade does not actually have an east face. The Sierra crest generally runs northwest–

southeast, but between North Palisade and Mt. Sill the crest runs west–east. The U Notch faces north, not east. Thunderbolt Peak does have an east face, however.

Traverses. Traversing peaks in the Palisades has a long tradition. It could be said that this began on August 11, 1938, when Ken Davis and Jack Riegelhuth made the first ascents of the Southwest Chute of Mt. Winchell and the Northwest Ridge of Thunderbolt Peak on their way to the summit of North Palisade (in 13 hours!). Another notable traverse went from Bishop Pass to Southfork Pass along the entire Sierra crest. This traverse is 8 miles long, with 1½ miles of moderate class 5 and 3 miles of class 4, along with snow and mixed pitches, and acres of scrambling. It was first completed in July 1979 by Gerry Adams and John Fischer, in seven days.

A popular traverse goes from Thunderbolt Peak to Mt. Sill; seasonal snowfields high on the southwest face of North Palisade can provide running water at a bivouac. The pinnacles that comprise Palisade Crest have been traversed in a day. Traverses between Norman Clyde Peak and Middle Palisade or Disappointment Peak have also been done.

Approach from Bishop Pass. The vast majority of climbers approach North Palisade and vicinity via the North Fork of Big Pine Creek. This is certainly aesthetically pleasant, with the approach passing lakes, forests, and approaches to climbs on the peaks looming over the Palisade Glacier. It seems that few climbers approach the peaks from the west, via Bishop Pass. It takes about the same amount of time to hike from South Lake to Palisade Basin as it does to hike from Glacier Lodge to a bivouac near the Palisade Glacier. The biggest rock faces are on the southwest sides of these peaks, and the easiest routes on North Palisade and Thunderbolt Peak are on their southwest sides. There is also a larger wilderness permit quota for the route from South Lake than for the route from the North Fork of Big Pine Creek. A western approach is not that difficult, and this side of the Palisades deserves more attention.

The Evolution Region

IF THE WILDERNESS OF THE HIGH SIERRA HAS a "destination resort," then Evolution Basin may be it. The John Muir Trail passes through this popular, lake-lined basin, but you only have to move a couple of miles to the west or south from the trail to find solitude. One of the wildest parts of the High Sierra is the area south of Muir Pass, which was not accurately charted until the 1950s. This remote area features rugged, trailless terrain, and place names that stir the imagination of all Sierra wanderers: Scylla, Charybdis, Disappearing Creek, the Enchanted Gorge, the Black Divide, and the Devil's Crags.

This region covers the Sierra crest from Bishop Pass to Piute Pass. Its northern boundary is marked by Piute Creek, and it is bounded on the west by the South Fork of the San Joaquin River and Goddard Creek. The Middle Fork of the Kings River and the Dusy Branch serve as the southern border.

History

The California Geological Survey first attempted to climb Mt. Goddard in 1864 from the south, from Kings Canyon via the Monarch Divide. This proved to be an impassable barrier for their pack animals, so they temporarily left the High Sierra via Kearsarge Pass, moved north through the Owens Valley, and reentered the range at Mono Pass (south). From their camp along Mono Creek they made a bold attempt to climb the mountain, 20 miles distant. Richard Cotter and a soldier by the name of Spratt got to within 300 feet of the summit before being turned back by hunger and exhaustion. John Muir visited the region in 1873, and may have climbed Mt. Darwin. Lil A. Winchell explored the Middle Fork of the Kings River in the 1870s; in 1879, with Louis W. Davis, he made the first ascent of Mt. Goddard.

It could be said that this area was "discovered" in 1895 by Theodore S. Solomons and Ernest C. Bonner. They shouldered heavy knapsacks at Florence Lake and hiked up the South Fork of the San Joaquin River, turned left at the mouth of Goddard Canyon, and ascended Evolution Creek, named by Solomons on the spot. They continued upstream and bestowed place names honoring the evolutionists. They returned to Goddard Canyon and ascended it to its head, and climbed Mt. Goddard. They then moved east through the Ionian Basin and descended the Enchanted Gorge. The purpose of Solomons' explorations was to discover a high mountain route between Yosemite Valley and Kings Canyon. He succeeded in finding one, but his route has seldom been repeated.

For years, early Sierra explorers tried in vain to cross the Goddard Divide with their pack animals. George Davis of the United States Geological Survey finally succeeded in crossing the Goddard Divide via Muir Pass in 1907, probably thanks to the heavy snowpack of that year, which made the talus on the east side of the pass passable. This feat was repeated in 1908 by Joseph LeConte, James Hutchinson, and Duncan McDuffie, but their mules just barely made it down into what is now called LeConte Canyon. Construction began on the John Muir Trail in 1915, and a humane route over Muir Pass was soon blasted through the talus.

There has been relatively little roped climbing practiced in this region. Exceptions to this are the ice couloirs on the north sides of Mt. Mendel and Mt. Darwin, and the rock faces and aretes of the Devil's Crags. Devil's Crag No. 1 was first climbed by Charles Michael in 1913, a bold solo climb. The crag was not climbed again until 1930, when Jules Eichorn, Glen Dawson, and John Olmstead

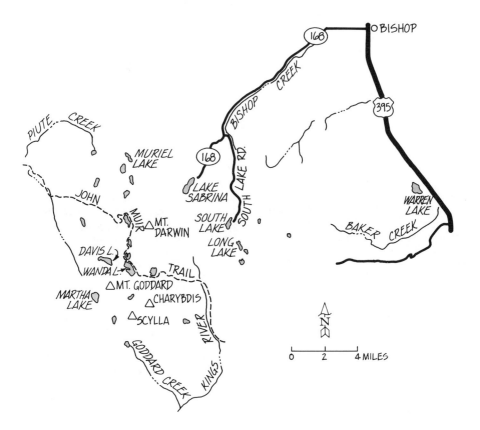

repeated Michael's route. Ascents of the other crags took place in 1933 and 1934, but they have been seldom visited since then, and each of them probably has only a handful of ascents. Devil's Crag No. 1 has received most of the traffic, and in the 1960s and 1970s it averaged one ascent a year. With the increase of interest in climbing in the 1980s it now averages two ascents per year.

Maps

United States Geological Survey: 7.5-minute series: Slide Bluffs, Marion Peak, North Palisade, Mt. Goddard, Blackcap Mountain, Mt. Thompson, Mt. Darwin, Mt. Henry; 15-minute series: Marion Peak, Mt. Goddard, Blackcap Mountain; national park maps: Sequoia and Kings Canyon National Parks and Vicinity (1:125,000).

United States Forest Service: John Muir Wilderness and the Sequoia–Kings Canyon National Parks Backcountry (1:63,360).

Wilderness Permits

For east-side entry to the John Muir Wilderness: Inyo National Forest, White Mountain Ranger District, Bishop, CA 93514.

For west-side entry to the John Muir Wilderness and Sequoia and Kings Canyon national parks backcountry: Sierra National Forest, Pineridge Ranger District, Shaver Lake, CA 93664.

Roads

South Lake Road

The South Lake Road leaves Highway 168 approximately 15 miles from Bishop. The South Lake Road goes up the South Fork of Bishop Creek, past some lodges and resorts, for 5.8 miles to South Lake and the trailhead for the Bishop Pass Trail and the Treasure Lakes Trail. Overnight parking is limited, and overflow parking is inconvenient for hikers to say the least: it's 1½ miles back down the road.

Lake Sabrina Road
(Highway 168)

The Lake Sabrina Road leads to Lake Sabrina at 18.7 miles from Bishop. Hiker parking is at the junction with the North Lake Road, 17.8 miles from Bishop, and 0.7 mile from the trailhead for the Sabrina Basin Trails.

North Lake Road

The North Lake Road leads to the trailhead for the Piute Pass Trail and the Lamarck Lakes Trail. It leaves Highway 168 at 17.8 miles from Bishop. The partly paved and partly dirt road makes a steep climb up and past North Lake to the trailhead after 2.0 miles. Hiker parking is on the north side of North Lake, 0.8 mile from the trailhead.

Trails

Bishop Pass Trail (12 miles)

The Bishop Pass Trail is one of the most popular trails in the High Sierra. It provides relatively quick and easy access to the backcountry of Kings Canyon National Park, and the views along it are terrific. And this is one of the few "downhill" trails—the start is at a higher elevation than the end. Wood campfires are prohibited within 300 feet of any lakes or streams along this trail.

The trail leaves the parking area at South Lake and climbs gently for 1 mile to meet the junction with the Treasure Lakes Trail. The Bishop Pass Trail goes left and continues to climb for another 1 mile to the junction with the short side trail leading to Bull Lake and Chocolate Lake. A short distance above this junction, the Bishop Pass Trail follows the eastern shore of beautiful Long Lake and meets the side trail leading to Ruwau Lake. The Bishop Pass Trail continues another 3 miles, past Saddlerock Lake and Bishop Lake, and makes a steep ascent with many switchbacks to the summit of Bishop Pass. The trail descends into and eventually wanders out of Dusy Basin. Wood campfires are prohibited above 10,000 feet anywhere in Kings Canyon National Park, and this includes Dusy Basin; overnight camping with pack stock is also prohibited in Dusy Basin. The trail makes a steep descent into LeConte Canyon and meets the John Muir Trail 6 miles from Bishop Pass.

Treasure Lakes Trail (3 miles)

This trail leads to beautiful Treasure Lakes, a favorite spot for anglers, above South Lake. The trail leaves the Bishop Pass Trail approximately 1 mile from South Lake. The Treasure Lakes Trail goes southwest and descends slightly before climbing to the largest of the Treasure Lakes after 3 miles. The main trail ends here, but a faint path leads upward to the higher lakes above.

John Muir Trail   (25 miles)

The John Muir Trail goes north from the junction with the Bishop Pass Trail in LeConte Canyon, and after ½ mile it comes to Little Pete Meadow, a heavily used campsite. (Big Pete Meadow doesn't receive as much use, and is only another ½ mile farther north along the trail.) The John Muir Trail gradually turns to the west and climbs along the Middle Fork of the Kings River. After 5¼ miles from Big Pete Meadow it comes to Helen Lake. The trail skirts the southeast shore of the lake and climbs 1 mile through talus and many small cliffs to the summit of Muir Pass. There is a hut atop Muir Pass, but it should only be used in case of emergency.

The John Muir Trail descends the western side of the pass and enters beautiful Evolu-tion Basin. The trail skirts the eastern shore of Wanda Lake and crosses its outlet before passing the western shore of Sapphire Lake and crossing the stream again just above Evolution Lake, 4½ miles from Muir Pass. The trail goes around the eastern shore of Evolution Lake for 1¼ miles. This lake is one of the finest in the High Sierra, but it has suffered from overuse due to many thought-less campers. From the northern shore of Evolution Lake, the John Muir Trail makes a steep descent into Evolution Valley and comes to Colby Meadow after 3½ miles. The trail continues to descend the valley, passes McClure Meadow and its ranger station after 1 mile, and arrives at Evolution Meadow 2 miles farther. After crossing Evolution Creek the trail makes a steep descent out of the valley for 2 miles to the bridge across the South Fork of the San Joaquin River, where it meets the Goddard Canyon Trail. The John

Hut on top of Muir Pass (photo by R. J. Secor)

Muir Trail continues down the South Fork of the San Joaquin River and crosses it on another bridge after ³/₄ mile. The trail goes downstream another 3 miles, where it crosses Piute Creek on a bridge and meets the Piute Pass Trail just beyond.

Sabrina Basin Trails (4–6 miles)

These trails lead to the scenic lakes above Lake Sabrina. The trailhead is just below the dam for Lake Sabrina. The trail traverses around and up above Lake Sabrina for 1¹/₄ miles to the junction with the trail leading to George and Tyee lakes. The trail continues another 1¹/₂ miles to Blue Lake, where wood campfires are prohibited within 300 feet of its shore. The trail branches here. The south branch goes another 1¹/₂ miles to Donkey Lake and Baboon Lakes. The other branch goes west past Dingleberry Lake to a fork after 2¹/₄ miles. The right-hand fork goes for another ¹/₂ mile to Midnight Lake; the left-hand fork continues another mile to Hungry Packer Lake and Moonlight Lake.

Lamarck Lakes Trail (2 miles)

This short trail not only provides access to Upper and Lower Lamarck lakes, but also serves as the approach for the Lamarck Col cross-country route. The trail starts at the North Lake Campground, next to the Piute Pass Trailhead. After crossing the stream the trail climbs ³/₄ mile to a junction with a side trail leading to Grass Lake. The right fork continues uphill to Lower Lamarck Lake. The main trail crosses the outlet stream, ascends a small canyon with trees, and crosses and recrosses a small stream (the route to Lamarck Col goes south in this area) before reaching Upper Lamarck Lake.

Piute Pass Trail (17 miles)

From the trailhead at the North Lake Campground, this trail gradually climbs into the scenic basin east of Piute Pass. The trail passes Loch Leven and Piute Lake. Wood campfires are prohibited within 300 feet of the shores of these lakes. After 5 miles the trail crosses Piute Pass, where there is a splendid view of Humphreys Basin. The trail descends into the basin and goes past Lower Golden Trout Lake, where camping is prohibited. The trail eventually meets Piute Creek, and descends into a steep canyon before meeting the Pine Creek Pass Trail at

Hutchinson Meadow, 6 miles from Piute Pass. The Piute Pass Trail continues another 6 miles down Piute Canyon, where it climbs above and descends to the creek many times before meeting the John Muir Trail just west of the bridge across Piute Creek.

Goddard Canyon Trail (6 miles)

The Goddard Canyon Trail leaves the John Muir Trail at the bridge across South Fork of the San Joaquin River, approximately 3³/₄ miles upstream from Piute Creek. It ascends the western bank of the South Fork of the San Joaquin River for 5 miles to meet the Hell-For-Sure-Pass Trail. The Goddard Canyon Trail continues upstream and gradually disappears in the upper reaches of the canyon. Cross-country travel is easy to Martha Lake.

Cross-Country Routes

"Rambaud Pass"

(11,560 ft+; 11,553 ft; 0.6 mi W of Devil's Crags)

Class 2. This is an old sheep route between Grouse Meadow and Simpson Meadow. The Middle Fork of the Kings River can be a difficult crossing in times of high water. The lower part of Rambaud Creek is choked with brush and manzanita close to the stream, so it is best to ascend from the southern end of Grouse Meadow and angle up to the 10,000-foot level of Rambaud Creek. Loose scree and talus lead to the saddle southeast of Wheel Mountain; the Devil's Crags and Mt. Woodworth are accessible from the saddle. Descend the southwest side of the pass to Goddard Creek.

The Enchanted Gorge

Class 2. The only thing "enchanted" about the Enchanted Gorge is its name. This is a difficult cross-country route that descends Disappearing Creek almost 4,000 feet in 7 miles. (The creek gets its name when it disappears beneath some huge talus.) This route features gigantic boulders, cliffs, and icy snowbanks; it is for experienced cross-country hikers only.

From the Ionian Basin, traverse the eastern side of Chasm Lake on either snow or talus. Descend steep, loose talus south from Chasm Lake to the amphitheater at the head of the gorge. Continue downstream, and beyond some small tarns, the creek disappears. The creek reappears, disappears, and reappears yet again before it enters a small lake. At this point the gorge narrows, and the route enters its most difficult section. It is impossible to give an accurate description of the rest of the route. In general, it is necessary to climb up and down giant talus, bypass cliffs next to the creek, and cross the creek on seasonal snow bridges. The lower reaches of the gorge are choked with brush. The route eventually joins Goddard Creek. Further reading: *Sierra Club Bulletin,* 1924, pp. 7–20.

Goddard Creek

Class 2. This is another difficult cross-country route, but it is not as difficult as the Enchanted Gorge. Goddard Creek is also a more pleasant area, with a few meadows and lakes, and trees and flowers. But these early features are followed by almost impenetrable brush and talus farther along the route.

From Simpson Meadow along the Middle Fork of the Kings River, go north along the east bank of Goddard Creek for 3¹/₂ miles through some thick brush. This is followed by a lovely area of grass, trees, and flowers where Disappearing Creek meets Goddard Creek. Continue ascending the east bank of Goddard Creek, and where the walls of the canyon close in, you are forced to cross much talus interspersed with thick willows. Eventually the canyon turns west, and beyond a fountainlike waterfall, the canyon opens up into a broad valley. Continue up the valley to Lake 10,232 (10,212 ft). After walking around the western shore of the lake, cross Reinstein Pass, cross Goddard Creek Pass, or head northeast into the Ionian Basin. Further reading: *Sierra Club Bulletin,* 1924, pp. 7–20.

"Goddard Creek Pass"

(12,240 ft+; 12,240 ft+; 0.7 mi S of Mt. Goddard)
Class 2. This route leads from Martha Lake to the Ionian Basin. From the South Fork of the San Joaquin River, skirt the north shore of Martha Lake and head for the lower, right-hand (south) saddle that is south of Mt. Goddard. Go left (northwest) from the top of the saddle, skirting the north shore of a small lake, and then descend southeast to Lake 11,818 (11,804 ft). Cross the lake over the two peninsulas that almost touch. From the southern shore of this lake,

you can either turn southwest toward Goddard Creek, or northeast into the Ionian Basin.

"Wanda Pass"

(12,440 ft+; 12,400 ft+; 0.4 mi S of Wanda Lake)
Class 2. This route leads from Evolution Basin into the Ionian Basin. Leave the John Muir Trail at the outlet of Wanda Lake, and follow the western shore of Wanda Lake. Go south up a gradually steepening slope to the obvious saddle on the Goddard Divide. Descend the south side of the pass to the eastern shore of Lake 11,592 (11,520 ft+). Those headed for Goddard Creek should pass Lake 11,837 (11,824 ft) on its southern shore. Those headed for the Enchanted Gorge should proceed southeast, making sure that Chasm Lake is passed on its eastern shore.

"Solomons Pass"

(12,440 ft+; 12,400 ft+; 0.3 mi NW of Mt. Solomons)
Class 2. This pass leads to the Ionian Basin from the vicinity of Muir Pass. Head southwest from Muir Pass, gradually ascending to the obvious saddle west of Mt. Solomons. The north side of the pass is frequently covered with snow. Descend the south side of the pass to the eastern shore of Lake 11,592 (11,520 ft+).

"Black Giant Pass"

(12,200 ft+; 12,160 ft+; 0.5 mi W of Black Giant)
Class 2. This pass serves as the eastern access to the Ionian Basin. Leave the John Muir Trail anywhere between Helen Lake and Muir Pass and head south to the obvious saddle west of the Black Giant. Cross the pass and descend to the western shore of the lake that is south of the pass. Go west and, after a short, steep descent, pass between many small lakes to the northern side of Chasm Lake.

"Treasure Col"

(12,000 ft+; 11,760 ft+; 0.3 mi NNW of Mt. Johnson)
Class 2; ice axe required. This pass leads between Treasure Lakes and Big Pete Meadow in LeConte Canyon. Head southwest from Treasure Lakes to the cirque north of Mt. Johnson. Climb a snow/ice chute (bordered

Mt. Solomons from Muir Pass (photo by R. J. Secor)

by loose rocks) on the southern side of the broad saddle north of Mt. Johnson. The western side of the pass is a steep and loose class 2 chute. Stay on the southeastern side of the stream that descends from the western basin between Mt. Gilbert and Mt. Johnson. When the cliffs above Big Pete Meadow appear, traverse left (south) along the base of a small cliff for approximately 100 feet, and then gain the crest of the blunt ridge above the cliff. Descend the crest of the ridge to where an obvious route to the stream is seen to the right (southwest). Cross the stream and bushwhack down its western bank for about 300 feet. Cross the stream again and descend through talus and some small patches of manzanita to Big Pete Meadow.

"Echo Pass"

(12,400 ft+; 12,400 ft+; 1.0 mi SE of Mt. Wallace; UTM 541112)

Class 3; ice axe required. This pass has also been referred to as "Echo Col" and "Black Notch." This is the direct route between Lake Sabrina and Muir Pass. Hike cross-country from the western shore of Moonlight Lake to the eastern shore of Echo Lake. Gradually contour up and onto the bench above and south of Echo Lake. The correct pass is to the right (west) of the saddle, atop a chimney marked by black rock; it is *not* the easier-appearing pass to the left (east). Ascend straight up to the top of the pass and descend a short chute on its southern side. Go slightly left (east) and pass Lake 11,428 (11,360 ft+) on its western shore. Go south over a low ridge before turning west. Descend a talus-filled chute to bypass a small cliff and meet the John Muir Trail where it crosses a small stream descending from the northwest.

"Wallace Col"

(12,960 ft+; 12,960 ft+; 0.2 mi SSE of Mt. Wallace)

Class 2. This is a loose class 2 route across the Sierra crest between Moonlight Lake and Sapphire Lake in Evolution Basin. From Moonlight Lake hike toward Echo Lake but make an ascending traverse southwest to the bench high above the western shore of Echo Lake. Go west from the bench to the low point of the broad saddle south of Mt. Wallace. Descend the west side of the pass over loose scree and talus. Go northwest and west, past benches, small meadows, and tarns, to the John Muir Trail near Sapphire Lake.

"Haeckel Col"

(12,680 ft+; 12,640 ft+; 0.3 mi NW of Mt. Haeckel)

Class 3. This pass is north of Mt. Haeckel and leads to Evolution Basin from the Sabrina Basin. Climb onto the long ridge between Midnight Lake and Hungry Packer Lake from near Topsy Turvy Lake. Follow the ridge to the cirque north of Mt. Haeckel. Pass north of Lake 12,345 (12,320 ft+) and head for a point to the right of a small, round peak on the crest; this point is about 300 feet northwest of the lowest point of the saddle. Traverse west from the top of the pass to a scree chute, and descend the chute to the northeast corner of Lake 11,808 (11,822 ft). Follow the north shore of the lake around to its outlet, and then descend directly to Sapphire Lake.

The long ridge between Midnight Lake and Hungry Packer Lake has also been reached directly from the northwest shore of Hungry Packer Lake.

"Davis Lake Pass"

(11,640 ft+; 11,600 ft+; 1.6 mi NE of Mt. Goddard)

Class 2. This pass leads from Evolution Basin to Goddard Canyon. Go southwest from the outlet of Wanda Lake to the obvious saddle to the west of the peninsula in the lake. Easy cross-country hiking leads over the saddle and down to Davis Lake. Circle around Davis Lake on its south shore, but cross to its north shore on the eastern peninsula; there is no crossing on the western peninsula. Head for the low saddle that is north of the outlet portion of the lake (at UTM 458107). Pass through the saddle and make a steep descent along North Goddard Creek to the floor of Goddard Canyon.

It is also possible to reach McGee Lakes from Davis Lake by crossing Pass 11,720+ (11,760 ft+; 1.3 mi ESE of Mt. McGee). Class 2.

"McGee Lakes Pass"

(11,560 ft+; 11,520 ft+; 1.5 mi SE of The Hermit)

Class 2. This route leads from Sapphire Lake in Evolution Basin, past McGee Lakes, and down to McClure Meadow in Evolution Valley. Leave the John Muir Trail near Sapphire Lake and make a steep ascent to the obvious saddle southeast of Peak 12,245

(12,260 ft). Descend the west side of the pass, keeping to the south of two small tarns and to the north of a small lake, to the northern shores of McGee Lakes. Continue down the outlet stream into McGee Canyon. Cross the stream immediately downstream of the fork that drains Lake 11,140 (11,137 ft). Continue downstream to meet a trail that comes up from Evolution Valley. Follow the trail down, and make a difficult crossing of Evolution Creek at the eastern end of McClure Meadow.

Another approach to McGee Lakes is via Pass 11,800+ (11,840 ft+; 1.2 mi W of Mt. Huxley). Leave the John Muir Trail north of Wanda Lake and ascend over talus to the saddle between Peaks 12,040+ and 12,262 (12,086 and 12,290 ft). Descend west and then north past two lakes to the eastern shore of the easternmost of the McGee Lakes.

Lamarck Col   *(12,960 ft+; 12,880 ft+)*

Class 2. This is probably the most popular cross-country route across the Sierra crest between Bishop Pass and Piute Pass. It has none of the loose rock found on the other passes, and the talus is not as severe. But this is still a long, arduous pass, and it should only be attempted by hikers in good condition.

Leave the Lamarck Lakes Trail between Lower Lamarck Lake and Upper Lamarck Lake. The correct place to leave the trail is near where the trail crosses the stream (at UTM 542196). Head southwest along a faint path, past a small meadow with a tarn, and climb the steep slope above. From the top of this slope, the route goes southwest up a broad, sandy valley with some boulders to the small lake immediately beneath Lamarck Col. Cross the snowfields beyond the lake, and pass through the first notch to the right of a small, sharp peak (the most easterly of several notches on the crest). Descend the southwest side of Lamarck Col approximately 200 feet and follow sandy ledges down into upper Darwin Canyon. Descend the canyon on the northern side of the lakes, passing over a few talus fields, and drop down to Darwin Bench. From the southern side of Lake 11,160+ (11,200 ft+) descend east of the outlet stream on a good use trail to meet the John Muir Trail northwest of Evolution Lake.

When crossing Lamarck Col from west to east, it is important to head toward the higher pass to the left (north) of the low pass at the head of Darwin Canyon; the lower pass leads to the lakes above Lake Sabrina. And be sure to go left (northeast) at the end of the long, sandy valley on the east side of Lamarck Col to reach the Lamarck Lakes Trail. The area beneath the long, sandy valley is a superb ski tour in the spring.

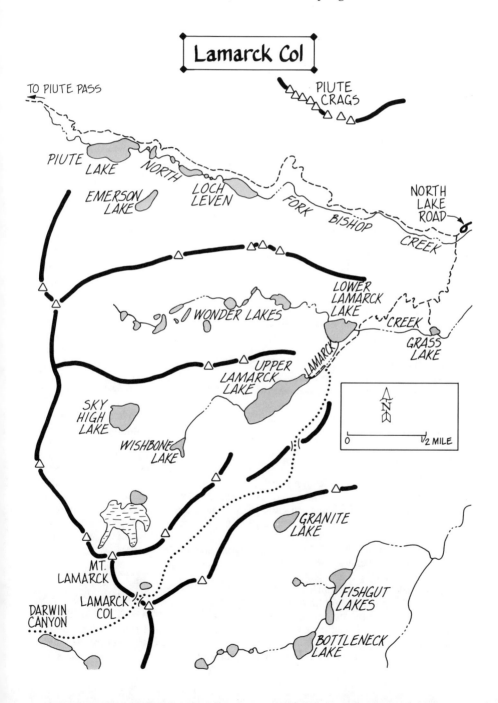

Lamarck Col

TO PIUTE PASS

PIUTE CRAGS

PIUTE LAKE

NORTH

EMERSON LAKE

LOCH LEVEN

FORK

NORTH LAKE ROAD

BISHOP

CREEK

LOWER LAMARCK LAKE

WONDER LAKES

CREEK

GRASS LAKE

UPPER LAMARCK LAKE

LAMARCK

N

0   ½ MILE

SKY HIGH LAKE

WISHBONE LAKE

GRANITE LAKE

MT. LAMARCK

LAMARCK COL

DARWIN CANYON

FISHGUT LAKES

BOTTLENECK LAKE

The Keyhole *(12,520 ft+; 12,560 ft+)*

Class 3. This pass is so named because you can pass through it, rather than over it. It leads between Humphreys Basin and Darwin Bench, and involves a lot of talus hopping. Climb southeast from Muriel Lake to the highest of the Lost Lakes. Climb toward a small notch that is southeast of Muriel Peak, skirting the western edge of a small glacier along the way. The Keyhole is a 4-foot triangular gap in the talus atop the notch. A short class 3 pitch is encountered just below the southwestern side of The Keyhole. Descend steep talus to the eastern shore of the lake below, and stay above its eastern shore while hiking to its south end. Pass between Lake 11,540 and Lake 11,546 (11,520 ft+) and head toward Darwin Bench to meet the Lamarck Col route, which heads down to the John Muir Trail.

Alpine Col *(12,320 ft+; 12,320 ft+)*

Class 2. Like The Keyhole, this pass also crosses the Glacier Divide between Darwin Bench and Humphreys Basin, and it also has a lot of unpleasant talus. From Darwin Bench pass between Lakes 11,540 and 11,546 (11,520 ft+ and 11,520 ft+) to the western shore of Lake 11,910 (11,840 ft+). Follow granite ledges above the lake to its northwest side. Ascend steep talus to the saddle southwest of Muriel Peak. The northwest side of Alpine Col consists of a wide chute filled with some huge boulders, which leads down to the eastern shore of Goethe Lake. Pass the lower lake on its western shore and descend to Muriel Lake.

"Snow-Tongue Pass"

(12,200 ft+; 12,160 ft+; 1.5 mi NW of Mt. Goethe)

Class 2–3. This pass crosses the Glacier Divide between Peaks 12,477 and 13,040+ (12,400 ft+ and 12,971 ft). Make a gradually ascending traverse northwest from the 10,680-foot level of the John Muir Trail northwest of Evolution Lake. This leads to the basin that holds Lake 11,092 (11,106 ft). Bypass the lake and ascend the stream that enters the lake from the northeast. After heading north, go to the right to the summit of the pass. Instead of descending directly down the northwest side of the pass, climb up the ridge leading south for about 50 feet to a small notch, and make a right diagonal

descent over loose rock. You can then descend either a snow couloir to the right (east) or the rocks on the side of the couloir. Descend talus to the Wahoo Lakes and hike cross-country to the Piute Pass Trail. Further reading: Steve Roper, *Timberline Country*, pp. 158–61.

"Packsaddle Pass"

(12,440 ft+; 12,400 ft+; 2.7 mi ESE of Pavilion Dome)

Class 2. This pass crosses the Glacier Divide between Packsaddle Lake and Evolution Meadow. Head southwest from Packsaddle Lake to the saddle southeast of Peak 12,900 (12,900 ft). The last 300 feet just below the pass is steep class 2. The southwest side of the pass is easy. Head down to the stream, and follow it downhill to Evolution Meadow.

"Lobe Pass"

(12,320 ft+; 12,320 ft+; 2.2 mi ENE of Pavilion Dome; UTM 432220)

Class 2. This pass also crosses the Glacier Divide between Lobe Lakes and Evolution Meadow. Go southwest from Lobe Lakes to the saddle southeast of Peak 12,560+ (12,591 ft). The northeast side of the pass is quite steep, but remains class 2. Go west from the summit of the pass before turning south to the large lake. Follow the outlet stream of this lake downstream to Evolution Meadow.

Lower Honeymoon Lake and Ramona Lake

Class 2. These two lakes are above Piute Creek, nestled in hanging valleys. Leave the Piute Pass Trail at the 9,760-foot level. Go south, across Piute Creek, and follow a good use trail upstream to Lower Honeymoon Lake. Go south around the western shore of the lake and turn to the northwest. Ascend granite slabs to the top of the rounded ridge to the west of Lower Honeymoon Lake. Go southwest to a small notch, which leads to the steep talus slope that leads down to Ramona Lake.

Peaks

Mt. Woodworth *(12,219 ft; 12,219 ft)*

First ascent August 1, 1895, by Bolton Brown, via the class 2 southwest spur. The traverse from Rambaud Pass is class 3.

Devil's Crags

(12,400 ft+ –11,440 ft+)

These impressive peaks are seldom visited. They deserve far more attention than they have received in the past, despite their remoteness and extremely abundant loose rock. Devil's Crag No. 5 received its second ascent thirty-seven years after its first ascent, which gave the author (then fourteen years of age) quite a thrill.

The Devil's Crags are numbered from the northwest to southeast, starting at the highest crag. But there are several different numbers in the registers atop the crags. For example, the small crag between Devil's Crag No. 1 and Devil's Crag No. 2 has been called "Devil's Crag No. 2." Jules Eichorn and Glen Dawson reported the first ascent of "Devil's Crag No. 11" in 1933; this turned out to be Devil's Crag No. 9 according to the system of numbers used here.

Most ascents of the Devil's Crags have utilized the chutes between the crags. The chutes that are relatively easy (class 4) to climb from the northeast are those between crags 2–3, 4–5, and 8–9. From the southwest, only the chute between crags No. 4 and No. 5 is difficult. The easiest chutes that cross the Devil's Crags are the northeast and southwest chutes between crags No. 8 and No. 9 (class 2–3). Further reading: *Sierra Club Bulletin,* 1934, pp. 19–23.

"White Top"

(12,262 ft; 12,240 ft+; 1.1 mi W of Rambaud Peak)

First ascent August 18, 1924, by Rollin E. Ecke and Jack B. Rhodes. This small peak northwest of Devil's Crag No. 1 is class 3 from the saddle to the southwest. The white rock atop this peak contrasts with the prevailing black rock of the Black Divide.

"Devil's Crag No. 1"

(12,400 ft+; 12,560 ft+; UTM 567001)

Michael's Chimney. Class 4. First ascent

Devil's Crag No. 1 from the north

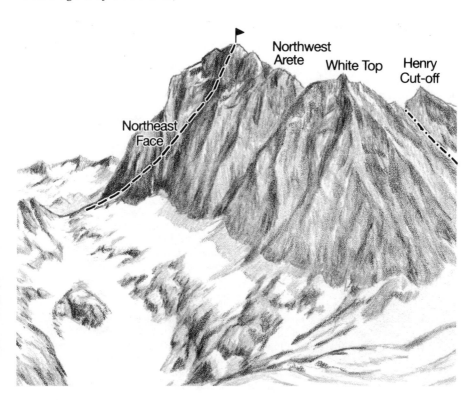

Northwest Arete

White Top

Henry Cut-off

Northeast Face

Devil's Crags Nos. 1–4 from the east (photo by R. J. Secor)

July 21, 1913, by Charles W. Michael. Go southeast from the top of Rambaud Pass to the first saddle west of the White Top. Descend a loose scree slope into the basin southwest of the Devil's Crags. On the southwest face of Devil's Crag No. 1 there are two great chutes or chimneys that form a huge x. Climb the lower left-hand branch of the x, and after passing a small chockstone, you come to the junction of the two chutes. Ascend the right-hand chimney to near the top. Then go left onto the crest of the northwest arete, and follow the arete to the summit.

Diagonal Chute. Class 4. First ascent July 25, 1933, by Hans Leschke, John Poindexter, and Ted Waller. Ascend the lower left-hand branch of the x on the southwest face to the junction of the two chutes. Ascend the upper left-hand branch of the x to the northwest arete of Devil's Crag No. 1. Follow the arete to the summit. This route is technically easier than Michael's Chimney.

Northwest Arete. Class 4. First ascent July 25, 1933, by Jules Eichorn, Helen LeConte, and Alfred Weiler. This is a classic climb, with much exposure. Not as much loose rock is encountered on this route compared to other routes on Devil's Crag No. 1. Reach the saddle west of the White Top from Rambaud Pass. Traverse across the south-west side of the northwest ridge for about 300 yards, gradually dropping 100 feet to the entry point of a prominent chute. Ascend the chute about 150 feet, and then climb 100 feet of class 3–4 on the buttress to the right of the chute to the crest of the arete. Ascend the arete, passing between a pair of black rocks ("Black Rabbit Ears") to a notch, where the Diagonal Chute meets the arete. A 60-foot class 4 pitch up from the notch is followed by class 3 to a dramatically exposed knife-edge notch; this is where Michael's Chimney joins the northwest arete. The knife-edge notch is crossed on the northeastern side of the arete. Much exposed class 3 then leads to the summit. *Variation:* Class 4. First ascent September 1, 1985, by Dave Dykeman, George Toby, Nancy Gordon, Bob Hartunian, and R. J. Secor. Instead of ascending the prominent chute and buttress to the crest of the arete, remain on the southwest side of the arete, passing a minor rib to a more prominent buttress farther south. Ascend this buttress to a point along the crest of the arete that is left (northwest) of where the Diagonal Chute joins the northwest arete. *Variation: Henry Cut-Off.* Instead of climbing to the top of Rambaud Pass, it is possible to turn left about 500 feet beneath the northeastern side of the pass and climb a loose class 2–3 couloir to the saddle west of the White Top. This is an

Devil's Crags Nos. 3–8 from the east (photo by R. J. Secor)

excellent descent route.

Northeast Face. Class 4. First ascent August 5, 1938, by Raffi Bedayan, Kenneth Davis, and Jack Riegelhuth. This route has ample exposure, good belay stances, and relatively sound rock. From the head of Rambaud Creek climb to the saddle northeast of Devil's Crag No. 1. This saddle is immediately southwest of Peak 11,408 (11,360 ft+). Rope up at the saddle, and traverse up and right over loose rock to the chute in the middle of the northeast face. (This traverse should be planned so that it ends above the lower, overhanging portion of the chute.) Ascend the chute to a point about 35 feet beneath the summit. Go right, where a short, steep pitch leads to the northwest arete. Follow the arete to the summit.

"Devil's Crag No. 2"
(12,280 ft+; 12,320 ft+)

Northeast Chimney. Class 4. First ascent July 26, 1933, by Jules Eichorn, Ted Waller, and Glen Dawson. Climb the narrow chimney south of Devil's Crag No. 1 and north of the intermediate crag between crags No. 1 and No. 2. This chimney is rather narrow and steep; proper chimney technique ("back and feet") is needed in some places. Ascend the chimney to its top, then traverse over the small crag on the ridge to the true summit of Devil's Crag No. 2.

Southwest Chute. Class 3–4. Descended July 26, 1933, by Jules Eichorn, Ted Waller, and Glen Dawson. Climb the southwest chute between Devil's Crag No. 2 and the small crag to the north. Further reading: *Sierra Club Bulletin*, 1934, pp. 21–22.

"Devil's Crag No. 3"
(12,240 ft+; 12,320 ft+)

North to South Traverse. Class 4 with rappels. First ascent June 24, 1934, by David Brower, Hervey Voge, and Norman Clyde. Ascend the northeast chute between crags No. 2 and No. 3. Remain on the floor of the chute, and pass under a huge chockstone to the notch at the top of the chute. From the notch, climb the left side of a broken face and then contour out and up a broad, sloping ledge on the north face to the north arete. Climb the left side of the arete to the northwest arete and follow this arete to the summit. Descend a sloping, broken ledge on the east side of the crag. Follow this around to the south, but traverse left and down (east) to a wide ledge along the way. This ledge leads around and beyond the southeast arete to its west side. Climb down another 60 feet. Rappel down overhangs to the notch between crags No. 3 and No. 4. Descend the southwest chute (class 3) or northeast chute (class 4) from this notch.

To climb Devil's Crag No. 3 from the notch between crags No. 3 and No. 4, you must overcome some vertical to overhanging rock.

Southwest Chute. Class 3. Climb the southwest chute between crags No. 2 and No. 3 to the notch, and ascend to the summit from the notch.

"Devil's Crag No. 4" *(12,240 ft+)*

Southwest Chute. Class 3. First ascent June 24, 1934, by Hervey Voge, David Brower, and Norman Clyde. Climb to the notch between crags No. 3 and No. 4 from the southwest, and ascend the southwest side of the northwest arete to the summit.

Northeast Chute. Class 4. First ascent August 1971 by Connie Eaton and Wally Henry. Climb the chute leading to the notch between crags No. 3 and No. 4 from the northeast, and follow the southwestern side of the northwest arete to the top.

The southeast face of Devil's Crag No. 4 is quite precipitous.

"Devil's Crag No. 5" *(12,240 ft+)*

North to South Traverse. Class 4. First ascent June 25, 1934, by Norman Clyde, David Brower, and Hervey Voge. Climb the northeast chute that leads to the notch between crags No. 4 and No. 5, passing a chockstone on its left side along the way. Climb a short chimney on the left-hand side near the top of the chute. Traverse and slightly descend across the western side of the crag and ascend the right side of the northwest arete to a point about 25 feet beneath the summit block. Go right, and walk up the south side to the summit. Descend the southeast arete to the notch between crags No. 5 and No. 6.

"Devil's Crag No. 6" *(12,240 ft+)*

North to South Traverse. Class 4. First ascent June 25, 1934, by David Brower, Norman Clyde, and Hervey Voge. Traverse from Devil's Crag No. 5 to the notch between crags No. 5 and No. 6, and ascend the west side of the northwest arete to the top.

"Devil's Crag No. 7" *(12,160 ft+)*

Southwest Chute and Northwest Ridge. First ascent June 25, 1934, by Hervey Voge, David Brower, and Norman Clyde. Climb the south-

Devil's Crags Nos. 6–11 from the east (photo by R. J. Secor)

west chute to the notch between crags No. 6 and No. 7. Alternatively, you may descend the southeast ridge from crag No. 6 to the notch. Ascend the northwest ridge to the summit of crag No. 7.

"Devil's Crag No. 8" *(12,000 ft+)*

Southwest Chute. Class 3. First ascent June 25, 1934, by Norman Clyde, Hervey Voge, and David Brower. Climb the southwest chute between crags No. 7 and No. 8 and follow the northwest slope (one short class 3 section) to the summit.

"Devil's Crag No. 9" *(11,720 ft+)*

Northwest Arete, Right Side. Class 4. First ascent August 1, 1933, by Jules Eichorn and Glen Dawson. Gain the notch between crags No. 8 and No. 9 from either the southwest or northeast. Ascend the right side of the northwest arete to the summit.

Northwest Arete, Left Side. Class 4. First ascent August 1988 by Mark Hoffman and Robin Ingraham, Jr. Ascend the left side of the arete to the summit.

"Devil's Crag No. 10" *(11,640 ft+)*

Traverse from Crag No. 9. Class 4 with two rappels. First ascent June 23, 1934, by David Brower, Hervey Voge, and Norman Clyde. Down-climb the southeast ridge of crag No. 9 to the notch between crags No. 9 and No. 10 and ascend the west side of the northwest ridge of crag No. 10.

Southeast Arete. Class 2. Climb the northeast chute between crags No. 10 and No. 11 and ascend the southeast ridge of crag No. 10, passing over a smaller crag along the ridge.

"Devil's Crag No. 11" *(11,440 ft+)*

Northeast Chute. Class 4. First ascent June 23, 1934, by David Brower, Hervey Voge, and Norman Clyde. Ascend the northeast chute to the notch between crags No. 10 and No. 11. Climb to the summit of crag No. 11 over exposed, broken rock.

Rambaud Peak *(11,044 ft; 10,960 ft+)*

First ascent 1925 by Ruth Prager and Albert Tachet. This peak is class 2 from Rambaud Creek to the northwest. The northwest buttress is a short class 4 climb, and was first done in August 1971 by Marc Leon and Ed Rose.

Wheel Mountain *(12,774 ft; 12,781 ft)*

Northwest Slopes. Class 3. First ascent July 26, 1933, by Marjory Bridge, Lewis F. Clark, John Cahill, and John Poindexter. From the summit of Rambaud Pass traverse around the southwest and west sides of the mountain to the bench northwest of the peak. Ascend the northwest slope to the east ridge, and climb the east ridge to the summit.

Southeast Ridge. Class 3. First ascent August 1963 by Phil Clayton, Jess Logan, Tom Ross, and Andy Smatko. This is the preferred route. Ascend the southeast ridge rising from Rambaud Pass. There is a short detour off of the ridge to the west just below the summit.

The Citadel *(11,738 ft; 11,744 ft)*

West Ridge. Class 2. First ascent June 24, 1951, by Richard Searle and William Wirt. Ascend the ridge from Ladder Lake.

Northwest Chute. Class 4. First ascent 1952 by Charles Bay Locker, R. J. McKenna, S. Hall, D. E. Albright, and Karl G. Hufbauer. Ascend the chute rising from the eastern end of Ladder Lake to the ridge west of the summit.

Northwest Buttress. Class 5. First ascent August 1971 by Dave Gladstone and Marc Leon. Climb the broad buttress to the left (northeast) of the chute on the northwest side of the peak.

North Face. IV, 5.7, A3. First ascent 1968 by TM Herbert, Don Lauria, and Dennis Hennek. Ascend a dihedral with several overhangs. The crux is about 600 feet above the ground, where an overhang is turned via difficult aid climbing. The remainder of the route is easier.

Northeast Face. Class 4. First ascent June 24, 1951, by Donald Goodrich and Robert Means, who arrived at the summit several hours after the first ascent of the west ridge. Climb the northeast face via several gullies and chutes to the ridge east of the peak. Follow the ridge to the summit, passing over the lower eastern summit.

Mt. McDuffie *(13,282 ft; 13,271 ft)*

North Ridge. Class 3. First ascent July 23, 1951, by Charles Bays Locker, Karl Hufbauer, and Alfred Elkin. Climb from the west to the saddle between Mt. McDuffie and Peak 13,041 (13,046 ft). Just below the saddle, traverse south toward Mt. McDuffie, keeping 150 to 200 feet below the crest of the north ridge.

About 600 feet from the summit, ascend a shallow, broad chute to the crest of the north ridge, and follow the ridge to the summit.

Southeast Ridge. Class 2. First ascent July 15, 1952, by Charles Bays Locker, Don Albright, Gary Hufbauer, and Karl Hufbauer. Head west-southwest from Ladder Lake to Lake 12,040+ (12,000 ft+; 0.8 mi SE of Mt. McDuffie). Climb to the southeast ridge of the peak from the lake, and ascend the ridge to the summit, keeping to its west side.

Southwest Ridge. Class 2. First ascent August 10, 1989, by Dave Helphrey, Ron Robson, and Reiner Stenzel. Follow the ridge from the Enchanted Gorge.

Northwest Slope and West Ridge. Class 3. First ascent August 1971 by Dave Gladstone. Climb the slope to the right of the prominent

The Citadel (photo by R. J. Secor)

snow couloir on the northwest side of Mt. McDuffie to the broad west ridge, and follow the ridge to the summit.

Langille Peak   *(12,018 ft; 11,991 ft)*

West Ridge. Class 3. First ascent August 1926 by Nathaniel Goodrich, Marjory Hurd, and Dean Peabody. This ridge is best approached from Hester Lake.

Southeast Face. Class 4. First ascent Norman Brown, Susanne Marcus, John Pearson, and Paul Axinn. Ascend slabs on the southeast face, over the lower, southeast peak and on to the true summit.

East Buttress. Class 4–5. First ascent July 2, 1970, by Chris Jones and Fred Beckey. The east face of Langille Peak is marked by many deep gullies and spurs. This route ascends close to the crest of the east buttress that drops from the lower, southeastern peak. The climb starts over talus and ascends gradually steepening slabs.

East Buttress Direct. IV, 5.10b. First ascent July 14, 1988, by Galen Rowell and David Wilson. This route climbs the very prominent arete that leads to the lower, southeastern summit.

Black Giant   *(13,330 ft; 13,330 ft)*

West Slope. Class 1. First ascent 1905 by George R. Davis. This is a simple climb from Black Giant Pass with a swell view from the summit.

South Slope. Class 2. This slope is usually climbed during a traverse to or from the north ridge of Mt. McDuffie.

Southeast Ridge. Class 3. First ascent August 19, 1971, by Wally Henry, R. J. Secor, and Jim Cervenka. Ascend the class 3 east ridge of Peak 12,800+ (12,804 ft) and follow the gentle southeast ridge to the summit.

Northeast Face. Class 4. First ascent August 1966 by Steve Roper. There are four small glaciers on the northeast side of Black Giant. Climb the northernmost glacier to its top, and ascend a loose chute for 100 feet. Follow a diagonal ledge system to the summit ridge.

Charybdis   *(13,096 ft; 13,091 ft)*

Northeast Ridge. Class 3. First ascent July 7, 1931, by Anna Dempster and John Dempster. Follow the southern side of the northeast ridge to the summit.

Southeast Ridge. Class 3. Descended August 1971 by Dave Gladstone. This route has been used to traverse to Mt. McDuffie, but it involves much elevation gain and loss. It is better to descend the northeast ridge of Charybdis and then cross Pass 12,360+ (12,400 ft+; 1.0 mi S of Black Giant) to approach the north ridge of Mt. McDuffie.

The Three Sirens
(12,640 ft+; 12,640 ft+)

These three pinnacles are east of Scylla. The snowfields and couloirs north of the Three Sirens last long into the summer. Ice axes will probably be needed.

"West Siren"   *(12,520 ft+; 12,480 ft+)*

West Chimney. Class 4. First ascent August 4, 1962, by George Wallerstein, Don Wilson, and Mike Raudenbush. Ascend a snowfield to the notch between Scylla and the West Siren. Go to a platform from the saddle and climb a class 4 chimney to the summit of the West Siren.

"Central Siren"   *(12,640 ft+; 12,640 ft+)*

West Ridge. Class 4. First ascent August 4, 1962, by George Wallerstein, Don Wilson, and Mike Raudenbush. This climb begins from the notch between the Central and West Sirens. This notch can be reached by two rappels from the summit of the West Siren, or by climbing the snow chute on the northern side of the notch. An alternate approach is done by going around the southern side of the West Siren. From the platform on the West Chimney route, follow a ledge around the West Siren to where it ends. Rappel 45 feet and then climb to the notch from the south.

Ascend a system of ledges up and right from the notch to the summit of the Central Siren.

East Siren   *(12,560 ft+; 12,480 ft+)*

West Ridge. Class 4. First ascent August 2, 1978, by Carl Heller, Dave Brown, and Peter Woodman. A short walk from the Central Siren is followed by a short class 4 pitch to the summit.

Scylla   *(12,956 ft; 12,939 ft)*

First ascent July 3, 1934, by David Brower and Hervey Voge, via the class 2 northwest slope.

Ragged Spur   *(12,843 ft; 12,841 ft)*

This entire ridge is class 1–2. The high point was first climbed by Robin McKeown and Frank Orme on August 17, 1954.

Mt. Solomons   *(13,034 ft; 13,016 ft)*

First ascent August 12, 1929, by M. H. Pramme and F. F. Harms, via the class 2 northeast shoulder from Muir Pass. The snow chute on the north face is also class 2. The west and south ridges are class 2 from the Ionian Basin.

Mt. Goddard   *(13,568 ft; 13,568 ft)*

Southwest Ridge. Class 2–3. First ascent September 23, 1879, by Lilbourne A. Winchell and Louis W. Davis. Go east from Martha Lake to a small lake that is surrounded by a cirque. Turn northeast to the next larger lake above and ascend a chute to the southwest ridge. The north summit is the high point, and a small bit of class 3 is encountered between the two summits.

East Slope. Class 2. Follow the Goddard Divide west from the summit of Wanda Pass.

The Goddard Divide and the southeast slope of Mt. Goddard can be reached from almost anywhere in the Ionian Basin.

Starr's Route. Class 2. First ascent August 1928 by Walter A. Starr, Jr. and companion. This is an interesting route on an otherwise dull mountain. Climb the north ridge of Peak 13,040+ (12,980 ft+) above Davis Lake (this is the first peak east of Mt. Goddard along the Goddard Divide). The ridge becomes steep just below the crest; follow a ledge around the left side of the ridge to the top of the Goddard Divide. Ascend tedious talus slopes to the summit of Mt. Goddard. *Variation:* Class 3. First ascent by Charles Bell. Instead of taking the ledge, cross a gully and continue straight up to the crest on good holds. *Variation:* The glacier to the right (west) of the ridge can be ascended before moving left onto the ridge.

Northeast Face. 5.8. First ascent June 1986 by Steve Porcella and Kevin Sugar. There is a tremendous amount of loose rock on this route. Cross the glacier to the right of Starr's Route and climb the steep, loose rock to the

The Three Sirens and Scylla from the north (photo by R. J. Secor)

Mt. Goddard, Northeast Face (photo by R. J. Secor)

crest of the Goddard Divide. Follow the ridge to the summit.

This same party descended the chute above the glacier, and found the conditions far worse than on the northeast face.

Peak 12,964

(12,913 ft; 0.9 mi N of Mt. Goddard)

North-Northwest Ridge. Class 2–3. First ascent July 27, 1941, by R. S. Fink. This ridge is best approached from the west, avoiding cliffs on the northern and northwestern sides of the ridge. A chute leads onto the crest of the ridge. Follow the ridge to the summit.

Southeast Ridge. Class 3–4. First ascent September 2, 1942, by August Fruge, William A. Sherrill, and Neal Harlow. Climb the steep, blunt buttress that leads to the top of the ridge that connects this peak with Mt. Goddard. Follow the ridge, passing a pinnacle to its right. Climb the left side of the ridge and then traverse out onto the south face of the peak. A narrow chimney leads up to several chutes, any of which can be followed to the top.

Hurd Peak   *(12,237 ft; 12,219 ft)*

First ascent 1906 by H. C. Hurd. The west face is class 3 from Treasure Lakes; the south ridge is class 4.

Mt. Goode   *(13,085 ft; 13,092 ft)*

Southeast Slope. Class 2. First ascent July 16, 1939, by Chester Versteeg. This is an easy climb from Bishop Lake.

South Ridge. Class 2. First ascent August 12, 1939, by Jack Sturgeon. Follow the ridge north from Peak 12,916 (12,916 ft).

North Buttress. II, 5.8. First ascent 1974 by John Fischer, Dennis Hennek, Jay Jensen, and TM Herbert. Begin by climbing an open book on the right side of the buttress. Two traverses left onto the crest of the buttress lead to the summit over a beautiful, blocky ridge.

Peak 12,916

(12,916 ft; 0.5 mi S of Mt. Goode)

This peak is frequently climbed by parties with the mistaken belief that they are climbing Mt. Goode. This peak has come to be informally named "Mt. No Goode." The peak is class 2 from the southeast, and was first climbed by Chester Versteeg on July 12, 1939.

Peak 13,040+

(12,960 ft+; 0.4 mi W of Mt. Goode)

West Ridge. Class 3. First ascent 1968 by Ed Lane. This is a straightforward climb from Mt. Johnson.

Northwest Face. Class 3. First ascent July 19, 1969, by Andy Smatko, Bill Schuler, Dave Wallace, and Tom Ross. Climb a snow couloir on the northwest face from the cirque southeast of Mt. Johnson. From the top of the couloir an easy class 3 wall leads to a short area of loose rock, which is followed by the sloping summit plateau and the summit block.

North Ridge. Class 3–4. First ascent July 1962 by a Sierra Club party. This is the long ridge that curves toward the east as it extends north from the summit. Gain the ridge from the east and follow it to the summit. Most of this route is class 3, with a few class 4 moves.

Mt. Johnson *(12,871 ft; 12,868 ft)*

North Ridge. Class 3 from Treasure Col.

Southeast Slope. Class 2 from Treasure Lakes.

West Ridge. Class 2. First ascent August 14, 1939, by Jack Sturgeon.

Mt. Gilbert *(13,106 ft; 13,103 ft)*

Southeast Slope. Class 2. First ascent September 15, 1928, by Norman Clyde. This route is usually climbed from Treasure Lakes. After climbing to the top of Treasure Col (ice axe required) ascend the easy southeast slope to the summit. This slope can also be reached from Big Pete Meadow.

Northeast Couloir. III, 5.6. First ascent September 3, 1972, by Al Fowler, Dan Eaton, and Ron Cale. The angle of ice in this 900-foot couloir varies between 50 and 65 degrees. From the notch atop the couloir drop down 40 feet, then climb up and left to the summit ridge. Further reading: *Summit*, March–April 1984, pp. 34–35.

Peak 13,120+

(12,993 ft; 1.6 mi NNE of Mt. Thompson)

First ascent November 7, 1931, by Norman Clyde. The summit block is class 4.

Peak 12,640+

(12,560 ft+; 1.1 mi NE of Mt. Thompson)

West Ridge. Class 4. First ascent June 24, 1973, by Barbara Lilley, Ed Treacy, Tom Ross, Bill Schuler, and Andy Smatko. Gain the saddle on the west ridge from the south. Follow the west ridge to the impressive summit block, which is climbed via a monstrous flake.

Peak 13,000+

(12,880 ft+; 1.0 mi NNE of Mt. Thompson)

First ascent August 25, 1968, by Andy Smatko and party. Gain the plateau north of Mt. Thompson via a class 2 chute on its southeastern side. The southwest summit is class 2. The northeast summit, a sliver of granite about 20 feet high, is rated 5.6.

"Ski Mountaineers Peak"

(13,280 ft+; 13,323 ft; 0.4 mi NNE of Mt. Thompson)

This is the high point of Thompson Ridge. This peak has been unofficially named after the Ski Mountaineers Section of the Sierra Club, who have skied off of its summit for many years. (Dissident members of the Ski Mountaineers Section call it "Motocross Peak.") The east slope is class 2 and was first climbed by Norman Clyde on September 6, 1931.

Mt. Thompson *(13,494 ft; 13,440 ft+)*

Southwest Face. Class 2. First ascent August 14, 1939, by Jack Sturgeon. A narrow chute north of Lake 12,120+ (12,132 ft) leads up to the small plateau south of the summit of Mt. Thompson. *Variation:* Class 2. The southwest face can also be reached from Sunset Lake. There are two chutes which lead to the col between Mt. Powell and Mt. Thompson from the north. Climb the right-hand chute to the col, and descend its south side about 200 feet. Traverse east from here along the bottom of the cliffs on the southern side of the west ridge of Mt. Thompson to a chute, which leads to the summit plateau.

West Ridge. Class 3. Climb to the saddle between Mt. Thompson and Mt. Powell; those approaching from the north may need ice axes to cross the glacier northwest of Mt. Thompson. Follow the west ridge to the summit.

Northwest Face. Class 3. First ascent June

30, 1931, by Norman Clyde. Ascend the glacier northwest of Mt. Thompson from Sunset Lake to the base of a steep chute close to where the northwest face meets Thompson Ridge. This chute rises diagonally from right to left and ends at a notch high on Thompson Ridge. Ascend the chute, bypassing an obstruction to its left, to a notch on the ridge. Keep to the left side of the ridge while climbing to the summit.

Thompson Ridge. Class 3. First ascent September 1959 by Henry Mandolf, Charles Bell, and Stuart Ferguson. Follow the ridge south from Peak 13,240+ (13,323 ft) to the deep notch between it and Mt. Thompson. Climb over broken benches on the east side of the ridge to the summit. *Variation:* Class 4. First ascent July 16, 1986, by Vern Clevenger. The ridge can also be climbed directly along its crest.

Northeast Couloir. Class 4. First ascent September 16, 1984, by Bruce Knudtson and Larry Cobb. This 800-foot couloir is the far left-hand (southeast) one, which rises to the crest from the glacier northeast of Mt. Thompson. It varies between 45 and 70 degrees in angle, and ends at a point about ¹/₂ mile southeast of the summit of Mt. Thompson.

Southeast Face. Class 3–4. Descended September 16, 1984, by Larry Cobb and Bruce Knudtson. There are many ledges and small cliffs on this side of the peak.

Peak 12,486

(12,440 ft+; 1.1 mi NNW of Mt. Thompson)
First ascent July 15, 1961, by Kenneth Taylor and party. The summit rocks are class 3.

Peak 13,040+

(13,040 ft+; 0.6 mi WNW of Mt. Thompson)
First ascent August 14, 1971, by Dave King. A crack on the southeast face is class 4.

Mt. Powell

(13,360 ft+; 13,360 ft+; UTM 557115)
The name of this peak has been misplaced on some maps. The true summit is 0.4 mile northeast of the lower, southwest summit, Peak 13,356 (13,360 ft+).

Northeast Chute. Class 2–3. First ascent June 1961 by a Sierra Club party. Climb a steep, loose chute to the left of the east face of Mt. Powell. (This chute starts from the west-

ern edge of the glacier between Mt. Powell and Mt. Thompson.) This is a fine snow climb in the spring; later in the year it may be icy, with loose rock.

Northeast Ridge. Class 3. First ascent by Norman Clyde. Ascend the ridge from the saddle between Mt. Powell and Mt. Thompson.

Southeast Chute. Class 2. This prominent chute leads to the plateau south of the summit of Mt. Powell. Climb the chute from the cirque south of the saddle between Mt. Thompson and Mt. Powell.

South Side. Class 2. First ascent August 1, 1925, by Walter L. Huber and James Rennie. This side of Mt. Powell is best approached from the 10,800-foot level of the John Muir Trail, east of Helen Lake. Hike cross-country to the east, contouring around the southern side of Peak 12,400+ (12,415 ft), to Lake 11,725 (11,710 ft). Climb talus to the plateau south of the summit.

West Ridge. Class 3. Cross the glacier northwest of Mt. Powell and climb the obvious chute that leads to a notch on the west ridge. Follow the west ridge to the lower southwest summit of Mt. Powell.

Northwest Chute. Class 3. First ascent June 29, 1931, by Norman Clyde. Climb the right-hand (south) chute of the two on the northwestern side of Mt. Powell. This chute ends atop the plateau, between the higher, northeast summit and the southwest summit.

East Face. III, 5.8, A2. First ascent June 1969 by Fred Beckey, Galen Rowell, and Dan McHale. The first pitch involves 5.8 crack climbing in a steep dihedral; the rest of the climb is in easier corners. The first-ascent party used aid to avoid an icy squeeze chimney.

Armless Fun. III, 5.9. First ascent August 1990 by David Harden and Glenn Harden. Climb two pitches (5.8) in the left-facing corner on the East Face route. Then go up and left for three pitches of 5.9. The first pitch out of the dihedral is steep, devious, and poorly protected. The quality of climbing improves above.

Broken Rainbow. III, 5.10. First ascent 1978 by Kim Walker and Alan Bartlett. This route is also on the east face. Climb a crack to an obvious orange bulge about halfway up the face. Traverse left and ascend the crack that forms the left side of the bulge. Some 4-inch to 6-inch chocks are advisable.

Peak 13,364

(13,360 ft+; 1.4 mi SE of Mt. Wallace)
The north-northwest face is class 3.

Peak 13,000+

(12,960 ft+; 1.3 mi ESE of Mt. Wallace)
The northwest ridge rising from Echo Lake is class 3–4, and was first climbed by Norman Clyde; careful route finding is needed to keep the difficulties to a minimum. The east face is class 4, and was first climbed in 1958 by Jay Holliday and Mike Loughman. The southernmost peak is the high point.

Clyde Spires

(13,240 ft+; 13,267 ft; UTM 535115)
The name of these spires has been misplaced on some maps. The correct location is 0.6 mile southeast of Mt. Wallace, atop the Sierra crest.

Southwest Side. Class 4. First ascent July 22, 1933, by Norman Clyde, Jules Eichorn, Theodore Waller, Helen LeConte, Julie Mortimer, Dorothy Baird, and John D. Forbes. Ascend a chute on the southwest side of the spires and traverse around the higher spire on its north side to the ridge leading east from its summit. Climb the ridge to the top.

The east spire, a difficult slab climb, was first climbed by Norman Clyde, Jules Eichorn, and Ted Waller July 22, 1933.

West Ridge. Class 4. Traversed June 20, 1959, by Ernest Bower and Carl Heller. The ridge between Clyde Spires and Mt. Wallace has a lot of loose rock. A spire along this ridge is class 4 via a chimney on its southwest side. A notch west of this spire is bypassed on its north side. The peak at the west end of this ridge (Peak 13,240+; 13,200 ft+) has become known as "Crumbly Spire," and was first climbed June 23, 1937, by Smoke Blanchard, Hubert North, and Gary Leech.

North Couloir. III, 5.7. First ascent 1978 by Marty Ross and Al Stone. Ascend the main couloir on the north face of Clyde Spires for several hundred feet, then traverse left to a small couloir on the left wall of the main couloir. Climb the small couloir to the summit ridge between the two spires.

North Arete. III, 5.10a. First ascent 1984 by Alan Swanson and Steve Schneider. This route ascends the arete left of the north couloir. The climb consists of seven pitches, the crux being a 1¼-inch crack on a blank slab, which is capped by an awkward, bulging slot.

Northeast Ridge. Class 4. First ascent October 9, 1966, by Gary Lewis and Ed Lane. Ascend the ridge rising from Echo Lake. Leave the ridge where you encounter loose, black rock, and traverse left and climb a couloir to the summit of a black spire. Follow the ridge west over and around some smaller spires to the highest of the Clyde Spires. The final approach to the higher spire is made from the south, and then up the east ridge to the summit. *Direct Variation:* Class 5 with one aid pitch. First ascent July 27, 1967, by Roy Bishop, Curt Chadwick, and Ed Keller. This variation is achieved by staying atop the very crest of the northeast ridge.

South Ridge. Class 4. First ascent August 27, 1967, by Andy Smatko and a (Sierra Club) Sierra Peaks Section party. Approach the base of the south ridge from Echo Pass, and ascend the ridge to a point about 50 feet below the summit. Go right and up to the small east arete that descends from the summit. Most of this route is class 2.

Mt. Wallace   *(13,377 ft; 13,377 ft)*

Southwest Chute. Class 2. First ascent July 16, 1895, by Theodore S. Solomons. Climb a rock-filled chute on the southwest face to a point near the summit.

Northwest Ridge. Class 3. The traverse between Mt. Haeckel and Mt. Wallace is done by keeping about 100 feet beneath the ridge on its northeastern side. Only the descent of Mt. Haeckel is class 3.

North Slope. Class 2. Climb to the cirque between Mt. Wallace and Mt. Haeckel by making a gradual ascending traverse from Moonlight Lake to the bench that is high above Echo Lake. Turn northwest and climb into the cirque, which features a small tarn. The ascent of Mt. Wallace is accomplished by climbing over talus blocks to the summit.

Southeast Slope. Class 2. Loose scree makes this a good descent route. Caution is needed when crossing loose blocks near the top.

South Ridge. Class 2. Climb over loose rock from the top of Wallace Col.

"Picture Peak"

(13,120 ft+; 13,120 ft+; 0.6 mi E of Mt. Haeckel)
This is one of the most beautiful Sierra peaks and, as its name implies, it is frequently photographed.

Clyde Spires, North Face (photo by R. J. Secor)

Southwest Side. Class 3. First ascent 1931 by Norman Clyde. There are three chutes on the southwest side of this peak. Climb the middle chute to within 100 feet of the summit, where easy class 3 leads to the top.

North Face. Class 4. First ascent 1960 by a Sierra Club party. Ascend scree on the north side of the peak for about two-thirds of the way up to the notch on the northeast buttress. Ascend diagonally right across a broken face with much loose rock to a chute, which goes to the summit.

Elphinston Buttress. IV, 5.10. First ascent August 1976 by Rick Mosher, Paul Landrum, and Chuck Fitch. This route climbs the prominent northeast buttress. Approach the toe of the buttress from the south shore of Hungry Packer Lake. Follow the buttress to the summit. The crux is about halfway up, where a thin crack leads to a slight overhang.

Northeast Rib. IV, 5.10. First ascent 1977 by Rick Wheeler and Tony Jennings. This rib is to the left of the preceding route, and forms the right-hand edge of the east face. Begin by climbing a hand-and-fist crack that runs parallel to a chimney for about 200 feet. A 5.9 roof is passed on the left. Continue up the rib

to a notch. This is followed by an awkward corner which requires some wide stemming.

East Face. IV, 5.9. First ascent July 1977 by Gary Colliver and Steve Thompson. Class 3 and 4 chimneys on the lower part of the face lead to a smooth wall. There are two flakes above the wall, separated by a squeeze chimney. Difficult climbing leads to a point about 75 feet below the flakes. Climb between the flakes (5.7) and ascend a face with a steep corner (5.9). Go up and right to a 5.9 move onto the corner of a buttress. Climb left along a steep ramp followed by a series of ramps and open books. Class 4 climbing leads to the top.

East Side. Class 5. First ascent 1958 by Mike Loughman, Bob Orser, Dick Grunebaum, and Rick Polsdorfer. Climb to the notch high on the northeast buttress from the east. Continue along the top of the northeast buttress to the summit. Several hundred feet of class 5 climbing were reported.

Mt. Haeckel *(13,418 ft; 13,435 ft)*

South Ridge. Class 3. First ascent July 14, 1920, by Edward O. Allen, Francis E.

Crofts, and Olcott Haskell, a few minutes after the first ascent of the west shoulder. They were quite surprised to find that they had been beaten to the summit. An even greater surprise was that they were not on the summit of Mt. Darwin, which was that day's objective!

The first-ascent party gained the ridge by climbing to the saddle between Mt. Haeckel and Mt. Wallace from the southwest. Most parties approach this ridge from the northeast, or by traversing from Mt. Wallace. Keep about 100 feet below the crest of the ridge on its northeastern side to a point close to the summit of Mt. Haeckel. A system of easy class 3 ledges leads to the summit block.

West Shoulder. Class 3. First ascent July 14, 1920, by Walter L. Huber and party. This climb begins from the eastern shore of Lake 11,808 (11,822 ft), which is west of the mountain. (This lake is best approached from the northern side of the basin between Mt. Spencer and Mt. Huxley in order to avoid loose scree in the middle of the basin.) Circle the lake on its southern shore to its extreme eastern shore. Climb the second chute from the left; this chute leads to the crest just south of the summit. A vertical face of 30 to 40 feet (with excellent handholds) is surmounted before arriving at the summit block.

Northwest Arete. Class 4. First ascent 1933 by Jack Riegelhuth. This beautiful arete is one of the classic climbs of the High Sierra. Ascend the crest of the arete from the first notch northwest of Mt. Haeckel. There may be steep snow on the northeastern side of this notch. *Variation:* First ascent August 4, 1984, by Jim Erb, Theresa Rutherford, Bill Gray, and Steve Nelson. The crest can also be followed from the top of Haeckel Col. This involves traversing a knife-edged ridge and a rappel into the notch. It is better to ascend directly to the notch. *Variation:* It is easier to climb the chute left (northeast) of the arete. But the climbing is excellent on the arete itself, with solid rock and excellent views. It is much better to ascend the crest.

North Face. Class 4. First ascent 1958 by Mike Loughman and Jay Holliday. Climb directly up steep snow and rock slabs from Lake 12,345 (12,320 ft+). Traverse to the right through a notch in a rib to the chute that is left of the northwest arete.

North Couloir. Class 4. First ascent November 5, 1971, by Choong-Ok Sunwoo and Yvon Chouinard. This 50-degree snow/ice couloir provides about 800 feet of climbing.

East Ridge. Class 3. First ascent 1935 by Merton Brown, Angus Taylor, and O. H. Taylor. Climb to the first saddle east of Mt. Haeckel from the north over loose scree slopes. Traverse across the southeast face of the peak to class 3 ledges near the south ridge, which lead to the base of the summit block.

Mt. Fiske (13,503 ft; 13,524 ft)

The west summit is the high point.

Southeast Ridge. Class 2. First ascent August 10, 1922, by Charles Norman Fiske, John N. Fiske, Stephen B. Fiske, and Frederick Kellet. Go north from Helen Lake to the southeast ridge. Ascend the southeast ridge over the lower, eastern summit to the true summit.

Southwest Ridge. First ascent August 18, 1939, by Jack Sturgeon. Ascend the ridge from the saddle between Mt. Fiske and Mt. Warlow. As a variation, you can climb the broad class 1 slope to the right (east) of this ridge.

North Ridge. Class 4. First ascent July 4, 1971, by Dick Irvin, Dave Madison, Jim Peterson, and Kirt Catanese.

Northeast Ridge. Class 2–3. First ascent August 20, 1958, by Andy Smatko, Peter Hunt, and John Robinson. Ascend the ridge from the basin west of Mt. Wallace to the east peak of Mt. Fiske. An easy walk leads to the higher, west summit.

Mt. Warlow (13,206 ft; 13,231 ft)

South Ridge. Class 1. First ascent 1926 by Nathaniel Goodrich and Marjory Hurd. This is an easy traverse along the ridge from Muir Pass.

Northwest Ridge. Class 3. Descended 1966 by Gordon Waddell. The ridge from the saddle south of Mt. Huxley is class 2–3. This saddle can be reached via the class 3 south ridge of Mt. Huxley, or via the class 4 rocks from the northeast.

Northeast Ridge. Class 4. First ascent 1966 by Gordon Waddell, during a 12-hour traverse from Mt. Spencer to Mt. Huxley. Follow the crest of the ridge from the saddle between Mt. Fiske and Mt. Warlow.

Mt. Huxley (13,086 ft; 13,117 ft)

West Shoulder. Class 3. First ascent July

15, 1920, by Norman Clyde. Leave the John Muir Trail at the northern end of the bench between Sapphire Lake and Wanda Lake and climb the left side of the west face. Head for a chute that leads to the summit ridge about 150 feet north of the summit. Most of this route is class 2, but a headwall just below the summit is class 3, with excellent handholds.

Southwest Chute. Class 3–4. This route is frequently climbed in error by those seeking the easier West Shoulder route. This left-ascending chute climbs the right side of the west face of Mt. Huxley, and leads to a point south of the summit along the summit ridge.

South Ridge. Class 3. First ascent August 22, 1963, by Arkel Erb. Traverse the ridge from Mt. Warlow. The saddle between Mt. Warlow and Mt. Huxley is class 3 from the southwest, or class 4 from the northeast.

Northeast Ridge. Class 3. First ascent May 30, 1970, by Wally Henry and Steve Rogero. There are two ridges or buttresses on the north side of Mt. Huxley, separated by a small cirque. Approach the left ridge from the east and follow it to the summit.

Northwest Ridge. Class 3. First ascent August 9, 1942, by A. J. Reyman. Approach the right buttress via the talus slope to the north, and go to the right onto the crest of the ridge. Follow the ridge to the summit.

Mt. McGee *(12,944 ft; 12,969 ft)*

This is the dark, impressive peak seen to the northwest from Muir Pass. There are three summits, running east to west. The central summit is the high point.

South Chute. Class 2–3. First ascent July 11, 1923, by Roger N. Burnham, Robert E. Brownlee, Ralph H. Brandt, and Leonard Keeler. Climb the westernmost of two chutes on the south side of the peak. The correct chute leads to the notch between the west and central peaks. This chute is composed mostly of disagreeably loose scree, and some climbers have preferred climbing the class 3 rock on the sides of the chute. From the top of the chute, go right and follow the ridge to the summit.

West Face. Class 4. First ascent July 17, 1933, by Glen Dawson, Neil Ruge, and Bala Ballantine. Go northwest from the outlet of lower Davis Lake to the small lake—Lake 11,800+ (11,760 ft+), at UTM 447117—west of Mt. McGee and southwest of Peter Peak. From the lake, climb talus to the north summit of the west peak. Descend northeast from the summit over class 2 rock until you are approximately 40 feet north of the notch between the west and central peaks of Mt. McGee. Climb up and to the south (class 2–3) and cross the main rib that runs into the notch from the west peak. Descend south and then east over class 3–4 rock into the notch atop the south chute. Follow the class 2 ridge to the central peak.

North Chute. Class 4. First ascent July 16, 1930, by Glen Dawson, Charles Dodge, Jules Eichorn, and John Olmstead. This chute climbs to the notch between the west and central peaks of Mt. McGee from the north. Head toward the chute on the right-hand side of the north face of the peak from upper McGee Canyon. Enter the chute from the right (west). There is usually snow in this chute, but it may be possible to climb along its edge, where the snow has melted away. The last 800-foot section of this chute is class 4. From the notch atop the chute, traverse east to the central peak.

Northeast Spur. Class 4. First ascent August 30, 1970, by Wally Henry. Climb the northeast spur of the east peak from McGee Lakes. Climb over the east peak and traverse to the notch between it and the central peak. Climb a dihedral and a wide crack on the east face of the central peak. This is followed by easier climbing over loose rock to the summit.

Peter Peak *(12,490 ft; 12,543 ft)*

Northeast Ridge. Class 2. First ascent July 11, 1936, by Peter Grubb and Richard G. Johnson. Climb to the notch in the northeast ridge from the east. The chute leading to this notch is loose, and you must, "hold the mountain together with one hand while climbing it with the other." Follow the crest of the ridge to the summit.

South Slope. Class 2. This is a long talus walk from the lake southwest of the peak.

Emerald Peak *(12,546 ft; 12,543 ft)*

Northwest Ridge. Class 2. First ascent August 8, 1925, by Norman Clyde, Julie Mortimer, and Eleanor Bartlett. Follow the northwest ridge from Peak 11,786 (11,778 ft). There is a lot of loose, unstable talus along this ridge.

West Slope. Class 2. This side of Emerald Peak has been approached from Evolution

Meadow and Goddard Canyon. It is generally preferred over the Northwest Ridge route.

South Ridge. Class 3. First ascent June 30, 1968, by Barbara Lilley, Jess Logan, and Dick Beach. Gain the south ridge by climbing to the saddle south of Emerald Peak from the east. A class 3 diagonal ledge leads across the east side of the saddle to the south ridge of the peak. Keep to the west side of the south ridge to the summit.

Northeast Ridge. Class 3. First ascent July 4, 1971, by Jerry Keating and Elton Fletcher. Climb a shallow chute for approximately 50 feet and then ascend ledges southward to the crest of the northeast ridge. Follow the crest of the ridge to the summit.

North Chute. Class 2. Descended June 30, 1968, by Barbara Lilley, Jess Logan, and Dick Beach. This gully rises from the basin between Emerald Peak and Peak 11,786 (11,778 ft). Climb the gully to the crest of the northwest ridge, and follow the ridge to the summit.

The Hermit   *(12,328 ft; 12,360 ft)*

This is the impressive peak seen from the upper reaches of Evolution Valley. The summit block is class 4 friction from the south; a jam crack on its east side is rated 5.6. Further reading: *National Geographic,* April 1989, pp. 484–85.

From Evolution Lake. Class 3. Cross the outlet of Evolution Lake and ascend rock slabs to the south to the first prominent notch on the ridge that is southwest of the lake. Pass through the notch and descend about 300 feet before traversing southwest to the meadow that is due east of The Hermit. Ascend a grassy chute southwest from the meadow to a bench directly beneath the peak. A diagonal chute leads across the east face and ends in a loose gully. Climb the diagonal chute, cross the loose gully, and ascend ledges to the summit. *Variation:* It is also feasible to climb to the saddle between The Hermit and Peak 12,343 (12,350 ft). Follow the ridge north from the saddle to the summit of The Hermit. *Variation:* You can also climb to the notch immediately south of The Hermit. From the notch, climb the east side of the ridge to the summit.

From McGee Canyon. Class 2. First ascent July 2, 1924, by Leonard Keeler, Ralph Brandt, Margaret Avery, and Marion Avery. Hike up to the lake that is southwest of The Hermit from McGee Canyon. Climb a loose chute that leads to the first notch south of the summit of The Hermit, and follow the east side of the ridge to the summit block.

Northwest Face. Class 3. First ascent July 9, 1939, by Harriet Parsons, Madi Bacon, and Maxine Cushing. From Evolution Valley, climb to a ledge on the north shoulder of the peak. (This ledge usually has a snowbank.) Follow a broad ledge to the right, up and around the west face. This leads to a chute that goes up and left to a point on the north face that overlooks the cliffs that shelter the snowbank. Proceed over rock slabs to the summit block of The Hermit.

North Face. Class 3. First ascent July 9, 1936, by Richard G. Johnson and Peter Grubb. This climb starts from the snowbank ledge on the north shoulder of the peak, as described under the Northwest Face route. Go left from the ledge, under the cliffs that shelter the snowbank, to where it is possible to climb up and right over rock slabs to the summit block.

East Face. I, 5.8. First ascent July 1988 by Galen Avery Rowell (whose mother, Margaret, was a member of the first-ascent party—see above). This route climbs the steepest part of the east face. Three short hand cracks form the cruxes of this route.

Peak 12,342

(12,350 ft; 0.5 mi SE of The Hermit)

This peak is frequently confused with The Hermit. In fact, some editions of the 1912 Mt. Goddard 30-minute quadrangle erroneously labeled this peak as The Hermit. It was first climbed by Dr. Grove Karl Gilbert and Mr. Kanawyer (the packer) in July 1904. The southeast ridge and northwest ridge are both class 2.

Mt. Spencer   *(12,431 ft; 12,400 ft+)*

First ascent August 20, 1921, by Robert M. Price, George J. Young, H. W. Hill, and Peter Frandsen. This peak has a swell view from its summit. It is class 2 from the saddle to the east.

Peak 13,322

(13,280 ft+; 0.5 mi SE of Mt. Darwin)

First ascent July 19, 1933, by Glen Dawson, Neil Ruge, and Bala Ballantine, via the class 3 south ridge. The southeast slopes are class 2.

Mt. Darwin *(13,831 ft; 13,830 ft)*

Mt. Darwin is the monarch of the Evolution region. All of its routes are challenging, and its flat-topped shape is easily recognizable from great distances. The true summit, however, is a pinnacle detached from the southeast side of the summit plateau. The pinnacle may be ascended by climbing down off of the plateau and traversing around to the east side of the pinnacle. Climb either of two cracks that lead to a narrow ledge that is about 6 feet below the top of the pinnacle on its southeast side. The final move can be either strong-armed or finessed, and most climbers will require a belay. Further reading: *Summit,* May 1971, pp. 6–9.

Darwin Glacier and West Ridge. Class 3. First ascent August 21, 1921, by Robert M. Price and Peter Frandsen. There is a large notch on the ridge between Mt. Darwin and Mt. Mendel, and a smaller notch about 300 feet to the east of the larger notch. Climb the Darwin Glacier and cross the bergschrund (ice axes and crampons may be required). Climb up to the smaller eastern notch and follow the ridge to the summit plateau. As a variation, you can bypass the glacier on its western side and make a diagonally ascending traverse from right to left to the smaller notch; this variation may be preferable during icy conditions and/or with an impassable bergschrund.

North Face. Class 3–4. Descended July 14, 1930, by Jules Eichorn, John Olmstead, and Glen Dawson. Ascended July 5, 1934, by David Brower and Hervey Voge. There are two ribs on the north face of Mt. Darwin. Climb the left rib, keeping just to the left of the crest of the rib. A boulder blocks progress about halfway up; bypass this by dropping down a little and moving left. This rib eventually merges into the north face. Climb a crack to the left and reach the summit plateau via a chimney. *Variation:* The broad couloir to the left of the left rib can be climbed to the summit plateau. This 900-foot snow/ice couloir averages 45 degrees in angle, and it is the preferred route in early season. In late season it is a fine ice climb.

Northeast Ridge. Class 4. First ascent 1945 by Spencer Austin, Bill Pabst, and Chuck Wilts. This ridge is most easily reached from Darwin Canyon. An approach from Blue

Mt. Darwin, North Face (photo by R. J. Secor)

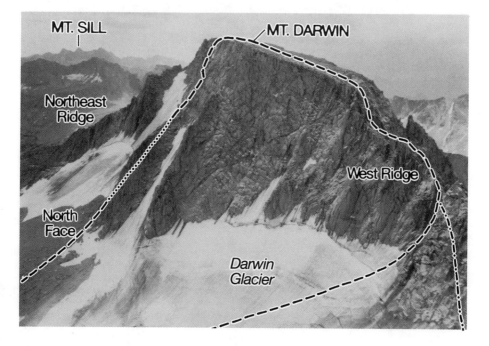

MT. SILL

MT. DARWIN

Northeast Ridge

West Ridge

North Face

Darwin Glacier

The summit block of Mt. Darwin (photo by Norm Rohn)

Heaven Lake involves climbing a scree gully to the left of Peak 13,048 (12,960 ft+); alternatively, you can climb class 4 rock to the flat saddle to the left of the scree gully. Follow the crest of the northeast ridge to the summit. It is possible to traverse off of the ridge to the left and climb the easier upper section of the east face.

East Face, Right Side. Class 3–4. First ascent July 1960 by a Sierra Club party. Follow the crest of the lower northeast ridge and climb a 60-foot class 4 pitch in a chimney. Traverse left on easy ledges across two sharp ribs to the main chute in the middle of the east face. Climb the right side of the chute and come out on the summit plateau near the top of the northeast ridge.

Direct East Face. II, 5.5. First ascent October 6, 1968, by Ed Lane, Barbara Lilley, and Dave McCoard. This route begins by climbing a dark watermark that descends from the main chute on the east face of Mt. Darwin. Ascend the watermark directly, and traverse left under an overhang (5.5) before climbing to a large ledge. Climb class 4–5 cracks for 100 feet, then traverse right into the broad main chute above. Ascend this chute to the summit plateau.

East Face, Left Side. Class 4. First ascent September 9, 1955, by Morrough O'Brien and Dick Leigh. This route starts below the

Mt. Darwin, East Face (photo by Austin Post, #72R2-125, USGS Ice and Climate Project, Tacoma, WA)

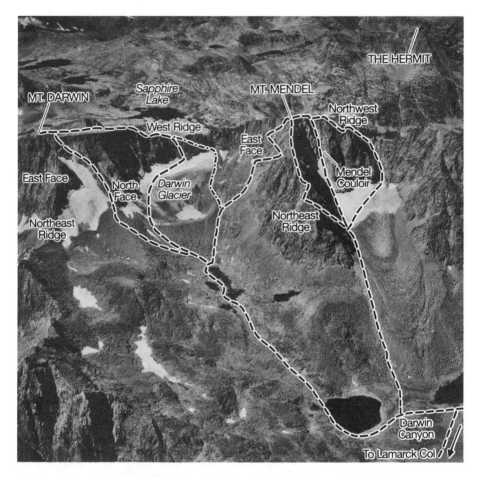

Mt. Darwin and Mt. Mendel from the north, August 24, 1972 (photo by Austin Post, #72R2-124, USGS Ice and Climate Project, Tacoma, WA)

left-hand rib of the main chute on the east face. Traverse up and left over a discontinuous ledge system for four pitches of class 4; the second pitch is the most difficult because the ledge system disappears. This traverse ends in a wide, ill-defined chute at the far left-hand side of the east face. Climb this chute to its head and traverse right on a wide ledge of dark rock over two ribs to the main chute. Climb the left side of the main chute to the notch between the summit plateau and summit pinnacle.

Southeast Ridge. Class 5. First ascent September 6, 1964, by Fred Martin, George Wallerstein, Herbert Weidner, Don Wilson, and Robert Wyman. From the southern end of Blue Heaven Lake climb class 4 rock to a

notch in this ridge near a band of yellow rock. Follow the ridge to a gendarme. Ascend a 75-foot crack on the face of the gendarme to a ledge. Go left and climb an exposed crack on the west face of the gendarme. Continue climbing the class 3 southeast ridge to the summit plateau.

West Face. Class 3. First ascent August 12, 1908, by E. C. Andrews of the Geological Survey of New South Wales (Australia!) and Willard D. Johnson of the United States Geological Survey. This side of Mt. Darwin in confusing, to say the least. The following route description may confuse many climbers, nevertheless . . .

Go east from the southern end of Evolution Lake and hike to the base of the west

Mt. Darwin and Mt. Mendel from the north (photo by Norm Rohn)

face, avoiding the cirque between Mt. Spencer and Mt. Darwin. There are three chutes with talus fans on the west face of Mt. Darwin. Climb the right-hand chute (this chute is best entered by climbing ledges on its left side). Ascend this chute about halfway to where it branches. Take the right branch through the gap just above a pinnacle and descend ledges to the middle of the second chute. Ascend the right side of this broad second chute almost to its head. Climb a shallow gully to a narrow, knife-edged ridge, which leads to the flat summit plateau of Mt. Darwin. The high point of the plateau is at its southeastern end, next to the detached summit pinnacle, the true high point of the peak.

Mt. Mendel *(13,710 ft; 13,691 ft)*

Although this peak is overshadowed by nearby Mt. Darwin, it is a worthwhile objective in its own right. None of its routes are trivial, and the hardest ice climbs in the High Sierra are found on its north face.

East Face. Class 3. From the western edge of the Darwin Glacier, climb a ledge that rises diagonally to the right. Then go left onto another ledge, which rises diagonally to the left. This leads to a chute filled with loose rocks, with a chockstone at its head, just below the rim of the summit plateau of Mt. Mendel. Climb the chute and surmount the

chockstone, and walk north to the summit.

Northeast Ridge. Class 3. First ascent 1956 by Bud Bingham and Don Clarke. There is a deep chute on the lower western side of the northeast ridge. Climb the ridge on the left side of this chute. This leads to a shallow chute, which ends on the crest of the northeast ridge. Follow the ridge to the summit. This is a much more pleasant climb than the East Face route.

Left Mendel Couloir. III, 5. First ascent July 1967 by Mike Cohen and Roy Bishop. This couloir is much more difficult than the couloir on the right side of the north face of Mt. Mendel. It is over 1,000 feet long and averages 50 to 60 degrees in angle, with some vertical sections. Further reading: *Summit,* March–April 1982, pp. 30–32.

Ice Nine. III, 5. First ascent June 1976 by Dale Bard and Doug Robinson. This ice climb is on the rock face to the right of the left Mendel Couloir. This is an ephemeral ice climb: The ice may be there one day but not the next. You can expect vertical, mixed climbing. Further reading: *Outside,* December 1977, pp. 26–29.

The Mendel Couloir. III, 5.2. First ascent June 21, 1958, by Felix Knauth and John Whitmer. This is the right-hand couloir on the north face of Mt. Mendel, and a highly coveted climb. It is well over 1,000 feet long,

Mt. Mendel and Mt. Darwin from the south (photo by F. E. Matthes, #571, USGS Photographic Library, Denver, CO)

with some bulges exceeding 60 degrees in angle. The first-ascent party climbed to the toe of the buttress that divides the two couloirs and climbed class 4 rock before entering the couloir itself. Today almost all parties climb the ice on the lower section of the couloir and belay from the rocks. The upper part of the couloir may be bare rock in late season, and a short rock pitch must be overcome in order to reach the crest of the northwest ridge. Follow the ridge to the summit. Further reading: Yvon Chouinard, *Climbing Ice,* Sierra Club Books, San Francisco, 1978, pp. 82–83, 104–5; Jeff Lowe, *The Ice Experience,* Contemporary Books, Chicago, 1979, pp. 169–70; *Summit,* April 1975, p. 17; *Summit,* June 1975, p. 34; *Summit,* March–April 1982, pp. 30–32.

Central Chute. Class 4. Descended 1966 by Mike Waddell and Steve Roper. There are many ribs and chutes on the southwest face of Mt. Mendel above Evolution Lake. Climb the central chute, which leads directly to the summit from the lower end of Evolution Lake. Many short class 4 sections are encountered in this chute.

Southwest Face. Class 3. First ascent July 18, 1930, by Jules Eichorn, Glen Dawson,

and John Olmstead. Leave the John Muir Trail about ¼ mile south from where the peninsula enters Evolution Lake from its eastern shore. Climb onto a buttress of glaciated granite surrounded by talus on its north and south sides. Ascend the buttress for approximately 1,500 feet onto broken rock. Go right to a talus fan, and ascend the left branch of the chute above it to the crest of the ridge. Follow the ridge to the summit.

Peak 13,360+

(13,385 ft; 0.5 mi NW of Mt. Mendel)

Not much is known about this striking peak. First ascent August 23, 1964, by R. G. Dunn. A chute on the west side is class 2. The north side is class 3–4.

Peak 13,253

(13,248 ft; 1.0 mi NE of Mt. Darwin)

First ascent 1925 by Norman Clyde. The southeast slope is class 2; the north ridge is class 3.

Mt. Lamarck *(13,417 ft; 13,417 ft)*

The southeast slope, the southern slope, and the ridge from Lamarck Col are all class 2.

North Couloir. Class 4. First ascent 1974 by John Fischer and Jay Jensen. There are several gullies on the right side of the north face. Climb the gully farthest to the left. This provides about 1,000 feet of 40-degree snow/ice climbing.

Peak 13,404
(13,400 ft+; 1.8 mi NW of Mt. Lamarck)

First ascent 1925 by Norman Clyde, via the class 1 north slope. The west slope is class 2 and was climbed July 8, 1933, by Hervey Voge.

Muriel Peak *(12,937 ft; 12,942 ft)*

The north summit is the high point. The southwest ridge from Alpine Col is class 2, and was first climbed July 8, 1933, by Hervey Voge. The southeast ridge from The Keyhole is class 2–3, over and around large blocks. Class 3 ledges above Lost Lakes lead to the summit plateau from the east.

Mt. Goethe *(13,264 ft; 13,200 ft+)*

First ascent July 6, 1933, by David R. Brower and George Rockwood. The south slope from the isthmus between Lakes 11,540 and 11,546 (11,520 ft+ and 11,520 ft+) is class 1. The northwest ridge is class 1. The northeast ridge from Alpine Col is class 3–4. A class 5 route has been done on the north face; climb from the highest reach of the glacier.

Mt. Lamarck from the north (photo by Austin Post, #72R2-123, USGS Ice and Climate Project, Tacoma, WA)

Peak 12,920+

(12,971 ft; 1.1 mi NW of Mt. Goethe)

North Ridge. Class 2. First ascent July 25, 1942, by R. S. Fink. Ascend large blocks from the top of Snow-Tongue Pass.

Southeast Ridge. Class 1. First ascent August 29, 1942, by August Fruge, Neal Harlow, and William A. Sherrill. This is an easy climb from the saddle southeast of the peak.

East Couloir. Class 3. First ascent September 16, 1967, by Wayne Inman, Alan Leeds, John Williams, and Ron Hudson. Climb the far left-hand snow/ice couloir on the northeast face and follow the southeast ridge to the summit.

Peak 12,477

(12,440 ft+; 1.8 mi NW of Mt. Goethe)

First ascent September 12, 1968, by Andy Smatko, Bill Schuler, Tom Ross, and Frank Yates. The southeast ridge is class 3; the southwest ridge is class 2.

Peak 12,488

(12,498 ft; 0.8 mi S of Lower Golden Trout Lake)

First ascent July 11, 1933, by Glen Dawson and Neil Ruge. The northwest ridge is class 3.

Peak 12,480+

(12,873 ft; 0.9 mi SSE of Packsaddle Lake)

The north ridge is class 4.

Peak 12,900

(12,900 ft; 1.2 mi S of Lobe Lakes)

The southeast ridge is class 2–3 and was first climbed September 11, 1968, by Andy Smatko, Bill Schuler, Tom Ross, and Frank Yates.

Peak 12,560+

(12,591 ft; 0.7 mi S of Upper Honeymoon Lake)

First ascent July 14, 1933, by Hans Helmut Leschke, Dr. Hans Leschke, and Helen LeConte, via the class 2 south ridge.

Pavilion Dome   *(11,856 ft; 11,846 ft)*

The south slope is class 2.

Wrinkles

Charybdis to Mt. McDuffie to Black Giant. A loop trip or traverse of these three peaks is a reasonable day trip from the vicinity of Helen Lake. This is typically done by first climbing Charybdis and then climbing the northwest slope of Mt. McDuffie. The north ridge of Mt. McDuffie is then descended before climbing the south slope of Black Giant.

Mt. Darwin to Mt. Mendel. The ridge connecting these two peaks is difficult. Most parties who have traversed between these two peaks have had to drop off of the ridge and onto the Darwin Glacier or the west side of Mt. Darwin/south side of Mt. Mendel.

Lamarck Col vs. The Keyhole or Alpine Col. Lamarck Col is high, and some cross-country hikers may assume that it may be easier to approach Darwin Canyon via Piute Pass and Alpine Col or The Keyhole, as this would involve less elevation gain. Alpine Col and The Keyhole are difficult cross-country routes, however, with a lot of unstable talus. Lamarck Col is much easier, and is a preferred route.

The Mono Recesses

THE MONO RECESSES ARE THE FOUR VALLEYS that drop precipitously into the Mono Creek valley from the south. This is one of the most scenic regions of the High Sierra, and south of the Mono Divide are the headwaters of Bear Creek, a fisherman's paradise. Northeast of Bear Creek is Rock Creek, with Mt. Abbot and Bear Creek Spire dominating the skyline. Southeast of this area is Humphreys Basin, a desolate region dominated by the isolated Mt. Humphreys.

This region follows the Sierra crest from Piute Pass to Mono Pass (south), and is bounded on the north by Mono Creek. Its western boundary is the South Fork of the San Joaquin River, and it is marked on the south by Piute Creek.

History

Native Americans had used Mono Pass (south) as a trading route for centuries, and in 1864 the California Geological Survey followed the Indian trail up and over the pass to a camp along Mono Creek. The party attempted to climb Mt. Goddard from here, but the peak was too distant, and the party left the region, moving west and northwest toward Yosemite.

Theodore Solomons explored the Mono Creek and Bear Creek regions in 1894 and 1895 during his search for a high mountain route from Yosemite to Kings Canyon. Solomons and Leigh Bierce climbed Seven Gables in 1894, and Solomons probably explored the entire upper Bear Creek drainage in June 1895 while waiting for the snow to diminish before moving south with Ernest Bonner on their epic journey to Kings Canyon.

James Hutchinson had an enviable collection of first ascents in the High Sierra, and some of his greatest trophies were collected in the Mono Recesses region. In 1904, he and his brother Edward made the first ascent of Mt. Humphreys. Four years later, accompanied by Joseph LeConte and Duncan McDuffie, James traveled from Tuolumne Meadows to Kings Canyon, and the trio bagged Mt. Mills and Mt. Abbot along the way.

Norman Clyde was active throughout the Sierra from the 1920s, but special mention should be made of his fondness for the Rock Creek region for backcountry skiing. This was his favorite area during the spring for ski tours, with a combination of perfect snow, breathtaking scenery, and easy access.

Maps

United States Geological Survey: 7.5-minute series: Tungsten Hills, Mt. Darwin, Mount Tom, Mt. Hilgard, Mt. Henry, Ward Mountain, Florence Lake, Graveyard Peak, Mt. Abbot, Mt. Morgan; 15-minute series: Mt. Goddard, Blackcap Mtn., Mt. Abbot, Mt. Tom.

United States Forest Service: John Muir Wilderness and the Sequoia–Kings Canyon National Parks Backcountry (1:63,360).

Wilderness Permits

For east-side entry to the John Muir Wilderness: Inyo National Forest, White Mountain Ranger District, Bishop, CA 93514.

For west-side entry to the John Muir Wilderness: Sierra National Forest, Pineridge Ranger District, Shaver Lake, CA 93664.

Roads

Florence Lake Road

Highway 168 leaves Fresno, climbs into the Sierra foothills, and goes past Shaver Lake to end at a three-way road junction east

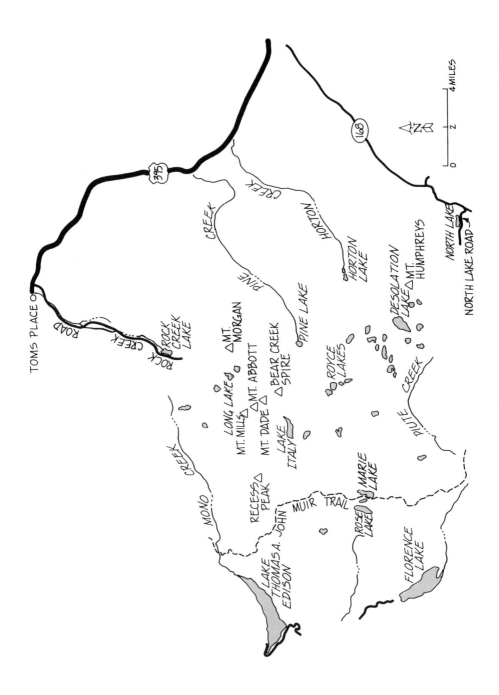

of Huntington Lake. Go right onto the Kaiser Pass Road, and after approximately 15 miles you come to a fork. The right fork leads to Florence Lake and the trailhead for the Blayney Meadows Trail in 7 miles. There may be a water taxi service across the lake, depending on the water level.

Lake Thomas A. Edison Road

The Lake Thomas A. Edison Road takes the left fork that is approximately 15 miles from Huntington Lake along the Kaiser Pass Road (the right fork goes to Florence Lake; see the Florence Lake Road descripton, above). The road descends to the South Fork of the San Joaquin River and goes past Mono Hot Springs and the Bear Creek Trailhead to Lake Thomas A. Edison. The road turns west, goes across the dam, and ends at the trailheads near the far western shore of the lake. It is approximately 6 miles from the Kaiser Pass Road to the trailheads.

North Lake Road

The North Lake Road leads to the Piute Pass Trailhead; it is described in Chapter 9: The Evolution Region.

Buttermilk Road

The Buttermilk Road leads to the Horton Lake Trailhead and the McGee Creek Trailhead, both located west of Bishop. Go west on Highway 168 from Bishop, and after 7 miles go right onto the Buttermilk Road. The road leads through a major cattle-grazing area, and there are many side roads and trails; always follow the most heavily traveled road. After 1.7 miles a major fork is encountered; go right. Another major fork is encountered at 3.7 miles; go left. At 6.0 miles the last major fork is met. Turn right, and after another 0.5 mile over a rough road there is parking for a few cars in a nice wooded area. The Horton Lake Trailhead is 0.3 mile farther.

Those headed to the McGee Creek Trailhead turn left at the last major fork. A rough road goes south for 2.3 miles across McGee Creek to a fork. Turn right, go straight at a junction 0.2 mile farther, and continue up the road another 0.6 mile to the trailhead.

An alternate approach to the McGee Creek Trailhead leaves Highway 168 approximately 10 miles west of Bishop. Turn right onto the Dutch Johns Meadow Road, and follow the rough road for 6.2 miles. Go left at the fork, and after 0.1 mile go left again. The trailhead is another 0.6 mile up the road.

Pine Creek Road

The Pine Creek Road leaves Highway 395 approximately 10 miles north of Bishop. Go west from Highway 395 for about 10 miles to the Pine Creek Pass Trailhead. Those headed to the Morgan Pass Trail continue up the road to the tungsten mine. Park along the side of the road outside of the mine's boundary.

Rock Creek Road

The Rock Creek Road leaves Highway 395 at Tom's Place. It goes south, past Tom's Place, and climbs up the canyon of Rock Creek approximately 9 miles to Rock Creek Lake. Those headed for the Tamarack Lake Trailhead turn left and drive to the trailhead on the eastern shore of this lake. The Davis Lake Trailhead is 0.6 mile farther up the Rock Creek Road. The Rock Creek Road goes up the canyon another 1.2 miles to Mosquito Flat, the trailhead for the Morgan Pass/Little Lakes Valley Trail and the Mono Pass Trail.

Trails

Piute Pass Trail (11 miles)

The Piute Pass Trail leads from the vicinity of North Lake over Piute Pass to Hutchinson Meadow, where it meets the Pine Creek Pass Trail. Wood campfires are prohibited within 300 feet of the lakes east of Piute Pass, and camping is prohibited at Lower Golden Trout Lake. This trail is described in Chapter 9: The Evolution Region.

Blayney Meadows Trail (9¹/₄ miles)

The Blayney Meadows Trail starts from Florence Lake, goes past Blayney Meadows, and meets the John Muir Trail. The trail leaves the end of the road at the Florence Lake dam and traverses high above the southwestern shore of the lake to meet the Burnt Corral Meadow Trail after 1³/₄ miles. The trail gradually descends, crosses the South Fork of the San Joaquin River, and meets the side trail coming up from the southeastern shore of Florence Lake after another 2¹/₂ miles. (Hikers who take advantage of the ferry service across Florence Lake save 4¹/₄ miles of walking.) After 3¹/₂ miles the cabins of the Muir Trail Ranch (a resort) will be seen to the south. Just beyond this point, across the river, are Blayney Meadows Hot Springs, a primitive site where hikers can soak for free. The Blayney Meadows Trail continues upstream another 1¹/₂ miles to meet the John Muir Trail.

There is an unmaintained and little-used trail that leaves the Blayney Meadows Trail approximately 1 mile west of the Muir Trail Ranch and the hot springs. The trail makes a steep ascent of the northeast side of the canyon to meet the John Muir Trail just south of Sallie Keyes Lakes. Those headed for Sallie Keyes Lakes and Selden Pass will save a lot of hiking by using this trail.

Horton Lakes Trail (4 miles)

This "trail" is actually an abandoned road that once provided motor access to what is now a wilderness area. From the locked gate at the end of the Buttermilk Road, hike up the road past some abandoned mining prospects to Horton Lake, 4 miles from the locked gate. A trail continues upstream to Upper Horton Lakes. Another trail (really a road) ascends the north slope of the canyon to the hanging valley southwest of Mt. Tom.

Gable Lakes Trail (3¹/₂ miles)

This steep, unmaintained trail leads to an abandoned mine near Gable Lakes. The trail starts from the Pine Creek Trailhead along the Pine Creek Road. The trail goes southeast before turning southwest and making some switchbacks. It eventually traverses upward along the west bank of Gable Creek, and crosses Gable Creek just below the lowest lake. A good use trail leads up to the upper lakes to the southeast.

Pine Creek Pass Trail (14 miles)

This trail leaves the Pine Creek Road and makes a steep climb, with many switchbacks, for 3¹/₂ miles to Pine Lake. The trail passes Pine Lake on its northern shore and, after a gentle climb of 1¹/₂ miles, it meets the Italy Pass Trail. The Pine Creek Pass Trail turns south from the fork and crosses Pine Creek Pass after 2 miles. The trail descends the southern side of the pass and meets a side trail leading to Moon Lake and L Lake 1 mile from the pass. The Pine Creek Pass Trail continues down French Canyon, with a spec-

tacular view of the falls draining the Royce Lakes on the northwest wall of the canyon, and after another 6 miles it meets the Piute Pass Trail at Hutchinson Meadow.

Italy Pass Trail (12¹/₂ miles)

This trail has not been maintained for many years. The section leading over Italy Pass itself is in the worst shape, but many parts are still visible, and cross-country travel is relatively easy over this section. The trail starts along the Pine Creek Pass Trail at 5 miles from the Pine Creek Road. The trail goes west into Granite Park, and passes north of the highest lake in this basin before traversing across the southern side of Mt. Julius Caesar and climbing up to Italy Pass. Italy Pass is 4 miles from the junction with the Pine Creek Pass Trail. The trail descends the western side of the pass, goes by the northern shore of Jumble Lake, and arrives at the southern shore of Lake Italy after 1¹/₂ miles. Follow the shore westward for 1 mile to the lake's outlet. The trail descends the Hilgard Branch of Bear Creek and meets the John Muir Trail 6 miles from Lake Italy. This lower section of the Italy Pass Trail is delightful, with a rushing stream, meadows, and trees.

John Muir Trail (22³/₄ miles)

From its junction with the Piute Pass Trail, the John Muir Trail descends the South Fork of the San Joaquin River for 1³/₄ miles to meet the Blayney Meadows Trail. The John Muir Trail takes the right fork, and climbs many switchbacks for 5¹/₂ miles to Sallie Keyes Lakes, passing a side trail that descends to Blayney Meadows, and crossing Senger Creek along the way. The trail continues north another 1 mile to the top of Selden Pass, with a beautiful view of Bear Creek from its summit. The trail descends the north side of the pass, and crosses the outlet of Marie Lake after 2 miles. The trail descends the eastern side of the West Fork of Bear Creek for 1¹/₄ miles to meet the junction with the Rose Lake Trail. The junction with the South Fork Trail is ¹/₄ mile farther north, and the John Muir Trail continues downstream, crossing the West Fork of Bear Creek and the main fork of Bear Creek itself before meeting the East Fork Trail after ³/₄ mile. The trail continues down the east bank of Bear Creek for 1¹/₄ miles to meet the Italy Pass Trail just beyond the crossing of the Hilgard Branch of Bear Creek. The trail continues down Bear Creek another 2¼ miles to meet the Bear Creek Trail. The John Muir Trail goes north from this junction and makes a steep ascent with many switchbacks for 2 miles to the top of Bear Ridge, where it meets the Bear Ridge Trail. The John Muir Trail goes northwest from the junction and at first makes a gradual descent before making a steep descent with many switchbacks to Mono Creek, 4¾ miles from the junction with the Bear Ridge Trail.

Rose Lake Trail *(1 mile)*

The Rose Lake Trail leaves the John Muir Trail about 1½ miles north of Marie Lake. The Rose Lake Trail goes west across the West Fork of Bear Creek and turns southwest before arriving at the northwestern shore of Rose Lake.

South Fork Trail *(2 miles)*

The South Fork Trail leads to Sandpiper Lake from the section of the John Muir Trail along Bear Creek. Leave the John Muir Trail about ¾ mile upstream from the East Fork Trail junction (see the East Fork Trail description, below). The trail goes southeast before turning east around the southern shore of Lou Beverly Lake. It then continues southeast to the eastern shore of Sandpiper Lake. Cross-country travel is easy to the lakes in the basin above.

East Fork Trail *(3 miles)*

This trail leaves the John Muir Trail from Bear Creek and ascends the East Fork of Bear Creek to lovely Seven Gables Lakes and Bear Lakes Basin. Leave the John Muir Trail where the John Muir Trail crosses Bear Creek, approximately 1¼ miles south of its junction with the Italy Pass Trail, or 2½ miles north of Marie Lake. The East Fork Trail goes south before turning east and ascending the north bank of the stream. The trail crosses to the south side of the East Fork below the lowest of the Seven Gables Lakes. The trail ends at this lake, but cross-country travel is easy in the basin above.

Bear Creek Trail *(6¼ miles)*

The trailhead for this trail is near the Bear Creek Diversion Dam; it can be reached by leaving the road leading to Lake Thomas A. Edison approximately 1 mile north of Mono Hot Springs. A steep, difficult road (four-wheel-drive recommended) goes east for 2½ miles to the trailhead; many hikers park their cars along the road leading to Lake Thomas A. Edison and hike along this road to the actual trailhead.

The Bear Creek Trail follows the north bank of Bear Creek for 6¾ miles to meet the John Muir Trail south of Bear Ridge.

Bear Ridge Trail *(5 miles)*

The trailhead for this trail is at the eastern end of the dam of Lake Thomas A. Edison. After an initial steep ascent, a moderate climb leads east through forests to meet the John Muir Trail after 5 miles.

Little Lakes Valley and Morgan Pass Trail *(9¼ miles)*

The portion of the this trail that passes through Little Lakes Valley features beautiful lakes and is surrounded by impressive peaks. The trailhead is at Mosquito Flat, at the end of the Rock Creek Road. The trail goes south, past the fork leading to Ruby Lake and Mono Pass, and goes by Long Lake on its eastern shore. It then leaves Little Lakes Valley, crosses Morgan Pass, and gradually widens and turns into an abandoned mining road, which leads down Morgan Creek to the tungsten mine along Pine Creek; the section between Morgan Pass and Pine Creek is rather dull, compared to the Little Lakes Valley section.

Another abandoned mining road leaves the Morgan Pass Trail approximately 4 miles from the tungsten mine and leads north into the basin between Mt. Morgan and Broken Finger Peak.

Mono Pass Trail *(15 miles)*

This trail leaves Mosquito Flat at the end of the Rock Creek Road and soon branches to the right, away from the Little Lakes Valley Trail. It makes a gradual ascent and, after 1½ miles, it meets a side trail leading to Ruby Lake. The Mono Pass Trail goes to the right, up many switchbacks, to the summit of Mono Pass, 1½ miles beyond Ruby Lake. The trail descends the north side of the pass, and after many zigzags it crosses Golden Creek after 2½ miles. A side trail leads east to Golden Lake from here; the main trail continues downstream another ¼ mile to meet a side trail that goes south to Fourth

Little Lakes Valley and vicinity

Recess Lake. A short distance downstream, another side trail leaves the Mono Pass Trail and goes north into lovely Pioneer Basin. The Mono Pass Trail continues downstream another 1½ miles to meet a rough side trail, which ascends the Third Recess to the lake at its head. Approximately ¾ mile beyond this junction, another side trail leads north to Lower Hopkins Lake and Hopkins Creek. The Mono Pass Trail continues down the northern bank of Mono Creek another 2¼ miles to where a trail leads north along Laurel Creek to Grinnell Lake. A half-mile farther down Mono Creek, the Mono Pass Trail meets the trail that ascends Second

Recess. The Mono Pass Trail continues down beautiful Mono Creek another 4¼ miles before climbing out of the main drainage to meet the John Muir Trail along the North Fork of Mono Creek.

Tamarack Lakes Trail (4½ miles)

The trailhead for this trail is on the eastern shore of Rock Creek Lake. The trail climbs to the east and eventually enters a forested basin with many small lakes. A side trail leaves the main trail near Kenneth Lake and leads to Francis Lake. The trail continues upstream along the East Fork of Rock Creek to Tamarack Lakes.

Little Lakes Valley (photo by F. E. Matthes, #543, USGS Photographic Library, Denver, CO)

Cross-Country Routes

McGee Creek

The title refers to the creek that drains into Buttermilk Country west of Bishop, not the creek of the same name that drains into Lake Crowley farther north. An abandoned road leaves the McGee Creek Trailhead (see the Buttermilk Road description, above) and ascends along the southern bank of the creek for about ¹/₂ mile before crossing the creek. It then makes a steep ascent before arriving at Longley Reservoir, beneath the north face of Mt. Humphreys.

"Carol Col"

(11,800 ft+; 11,760 ft+; 0.6 mi SE of Puppet Lake)

Class 2. This pass has also been called "Puppet Pass," but the name honoring Carol Cole is used here. This pass connects Humphreys Basin with the bench lakes above the upper reaches of French Canyon. Easy hiking leads northwest from the outlet of Desolation Lake to the pass, which overlooks Puppet Lake. A steep slope with huge talus leads down the northwest side of the pass to the eastern shore of Puppet Lake. Easy cross-country travel leads east from here to Star Lake. A descent to the north then leads to L Lake and Moon Lake, where a good use trail provides access to the Pine Creek Pass Trail.

"Steelhead Pass"

(12,080 ft+; 12,000 ft+; 0.6 mi SE of Steelhead Lake)

Class 2. This pass connects Steelhead Lake with Desolation Lake. Climb onto the bench southeast of Steelhead Lake, and continue to ascend, passing two small lakes on the next bench above before climbing the steep slope leading to the pass. Cross the pass, and gradually descend to the east before traversing south, aiming for a small bench northeast of Desolation Lake (the bench is located at UTM 496269). Descend the gully that goes south from this point to the southeastern shore of Desolation Lake.

Peak 11,840+

(11,840 ft+; 0.7 mi SE of Three Island Lake)

Class 2. This route provides access to the lakes at the head of West Pinnacles Creek. The "pass route" actually crosses over the top of a broad peak along the way from Three Island Lake to Wampum Lake in the West Pinnacles Creek drainage. Easy cross-country hiking leads from the end of the South Fork Trail near Sandpiper Lake to the outlet of Three Island Lake. Gradually ascend above the west shore of Three Island Lake to the saddle that is northeast of Mt. Senger. Turn east from the saddle and hike across tedious slopes over the top of Peak 11,840+ (11,840 ft+). Descend the eastern slope of the peak to a point north of Wampum Lake. Go downstream along the Wampum Lake outlet as far as Spearpoint Lake. This basin is a hanging valley, and a descent of lower West Pinnacles Creek is not recommended. The lakes of upper East Pinnacles Creek can be reached by going east from the outlet of Spearpoint Lake to Pemmican Lake before climbing the shallow ridge to the east and traversing northeast to the basin.

"Seven Gables Pass"
(12,040 ft+; 12,000 ft+; 0.8 mi SE of Seven Gables)

Class 2. This pass is used for ascents of Seven Gables and Gemini, and it can also be used as an alternative approach to the lakes in the upper portion of West Pinnacles Creek. Easy cross-country hiking leads from the end of the East Fork Trail to the largest of the Seven Gables Lakes. Some steep and rough terrain leads up and southwest to the pass between Seven Gables and Gemini.

Those headed for West Pinnacles Creek must traverse up and across the west side of Gemini to the prominent shoulder before descending to Wampum Lake.

"Merriam Pass"
(12,000 ft+; 11,920 ft+; 0.5 mi NW of Merriam Lake)

Class 2. This pass leads from Merriam Lake to Seven Gables Lake. Ascend the steep slopes above the northwestern shore of Merriam Lake to the small basin just below the pass, which contains two small lakes. Climb to the summit of the pass from the western lake. The northern side of the pass consists of steep, loose rock, and snow or ice may be present.

"Feather Pass"
(12,360 ft+; 13,320 ft+; 0.6 mi WNW of Royce Peak)

Class 2. This pass provides access to the Bear Lakes Basin from Merriam Lake. Ascend the north inlet stream of Merriam Lake and keep to the eastern shores of the lakes in the sandy valley above. Go left at the highest lake in the basin and climb to the broad saddle southwest of Feather Peak (13,280 ft+; 13,242 ft). A short, steep section of talus is encountered just below the top of the pass on its northwest side, and this is followed by sandy slopes down to Bearpaw Lake in Bear Lakes Basin. Further reading: Steve Roper, *Timberline Country,* Sierra Club Books, San Francisco, 1982, pp. 165–66.

"Royce Pass"
(11,760 ft+; 11,680 ft+; 1.0 mi NE of Royce Peak)

Class 1. This pass leads from Honeymoon Lake along the Italy Pass Trail to the Royce Lakes. Leave the Italy Pass Trail at the bench west of Honeymoon Lake, where the trail crosses a stream. Follow the stream uphill to where it disappears, and ascend easy terrain southwest to the top of the pass. Cross-country travel is easy from Royce Lakes southeast to Pine Creek Pass.

The next pass northwest of Royce Pass (Pass 11,840+; 11,760 ft+) has been used as a direct route between Royce Lakes and Granite Park. It is a tricky pass, however, with many small cliffs on its southwestern side that impede progress. It is best to by-pass this pass by climbing above it, over the southwest shoulder of Peak 12,470 (12,400 ft+).

"Ursula Pass"
(11,840 ft+; 11,760 ft+; 0.4 mi S of Beartrap Lake)

Class 2. This pass, named here for Ursula Slager, provides access to Bear Lakes Basin from the Hilgard Branch of Bear Creek. Leave the Italy Pass Trail downstream from Lake Italy and ascend to the south, past Beartrap Lake and a smaller lake, to the broad saddle above. Descend the south side of the pass by going east to Coronet Lake.

"White Bear Pass"
(11,880 ft+; 11,760 ft+; 0.1 mi NW of White Bear Lake)

Class 2. This pass leads to White Bear Lake, and also to Bear Lakes Basin, from the Hilgard Branch of Bear Creek. Leave the Italy Pass Trail at the point where it crosses the Hilgard Branch downstream from Lake Italy. Contour south on the eastern bank of the stream before traversing up to the northern and eastern sides, and climb steep terrain to the broad saddle above; the final approach to the pass is made from the left (northeast). White Bear Lake is on the southeast side of the pass. Black Bear Lake can be reached by crossing a sandy saddle to the southeast of White Bear Lake.

"Dancing Bear Pass"
(12,120 ft+; 12,080 ft+; 1.0 mi SW of Italy Pass)

Class 2. This pass leads to Bear Lakes Basin from the western side of Italy Pass. The easiest route traverses south from the western side of Italy Pass before turning west and meeting the northeastern side of Dancing Bear Pass. (An alternate route leaves the eastern shore of Jumble Lake and ascends steep talus to the entrance of the pass.) The pass consists of a long gravel corridor. Descend the southwestern side of the pass by aiming for the sandy saddle between White Bear Lake and Black Bear Lake.

"Peppermint Pass"
(12,360 ft+; 12,320 ft+; 0.4 mi NE of Bear Creek Spire)

Class 2. This pass is used in combination with Spire Pass to go from the Rock Creek drainage to the Pine Creek drainage. From Dade Lake in Little Lakes Valley climb to the pass between Pyramid Peak and Bear Creek Spire. The southeast side of the pass can be descended directly to Spire Lake; those headed for Peppermint Pass make a slightly descending traverse to the southeast before climbing to the top of Peppermint Pass.

"Spire Pass"
(12,400 ft+; 12,320 ft+; 0.5 mi E of Bear Creek Spire)

Class 5. The easiest crossing of this pass is at the eastern side of the low point of the saddle between Bear Creek Spire and Peppermint Peak. A steep, 50-foot moderate class 5 chute (5.6) leads up from the north to the top of the pass. An exposed class 3 ledge system on the south side of the pass leads down to the Pine Creek drainage.

"Cox Col"
(13,040 ft+; 12,960 ft+; 0.2 mi NW of Bear Creek Spire)

Class 2. This is the only reasonable route from Rock Creek across the Sierra crest to Lake Italy. From the western shore of Dade Lake climb steep and loose slopes to the first saddle northwest of Bear Creek Spire. This saddle is marked by several notches on its eastern side; the first notch south of the lowest notch is preferred. The descent of the western side of the pass is easy. It is necessary to head northwest before turning southwest and heading directly for Toe Lake and Lake Italy. Circle Lake Italy on its northern shore.

This pass has been named here in honor of Chris Cox, one of the pioneers of the Redline ski tour.

Gabbot Pass
(12,240 ft+; 12,240 ft+; 0.6 mi SW of Mt. Abbot)

Class 2. Gabbot Pass is the easiest route across the Mono Divide between the Second Recess and Lake Italy. Leave the Mono Pass Trail, cross Mono Creek, and ascend the trail that leads up the Second Recess. The trail remains on the northern bank of Mills Creek (it is hard to follow in places) to Lower Mills Creek Lake. A use trail continues upstream from here to the lovely meadows beneath Upper Mills Creek Lake. Bypass Upper Mills Creek Lake by heading east from the lake, then turning south-southeast to a small lake at the entrance of the valley leading up to Gabbot Pass. Ascend the valley over sand and talus to the top of the pass between Mt. Gabb and Mt. Abbot. The south side of the pass is easy, and the easiest route around Lake Italy is on its northern shore.

"Hilgard Pass"
(12,480 ft+; 12,400 ft+; 0.6 mi NNE of Mt. Hilgard; UTM 385371)

Class 2. This route is much more difficult than Gabbot Pass. Leave the trail that ascends Mills Creek in the Second Recess. Cross Mills Creek and directly ascend the Second Recess. The headwall at the head of the recess is bypassed on its right (west) side on sloping ledges to the hanging valley above. Go to Lake 11,320+ (11,280 ft+; UTM 388378) and ascend the steep slope to the south, crossing over a small permanent snowfield to the top of the pass. Descend the south side of the pass to the outlet of Lake Italy and the Italy Pass Trail.

"Recess Pass"
(11,920 ft+; 11,920 ft+; 0.5 mi NW of Recess Peak)

Class 2. This route crosses the Mono Divide between the First Recess and the section of the John Muir Trail north of Bear Creek. Ascend the First Recess from the Mono Pass Trail to the highest of the First Recess Lakes. Go southwest to the saddle between Recess Peak and Peak 12,188 (12,205 ft); the saddle has some steep sections on its northeastern side, so take care to ensure that the easiest route is selected. The southwestern side of the pass is easy. A gentle descent over meadows leads west to the John Muir Trail atop Bear Ridge.

Fourth Recess

This cross-country route goes from Fourth Recess Lake to Snow Lakes, near the head of the Fourth Recess. Take the trail that leads to Fourth Recess Lake from the Mono Pass Trail. Cross the outlet of the lake and traverse high above the western shore of the lake to the hanging valley that marks the upper part of the Fourth Recess. Cross-country hiking is easy in the valley above.

Peaks
Piute Crags

The Piute Crags, the series of pinnacles southeast of Mt. Emerson, are easily approached from the south via the Piute Pass Trail. These crags have abundant loose rock. The numbering system used here may or may not agree with the numbers in the summit registers.

"Piute Crag No. 1"

South Couloir and North Face. Class 5. First ascent September 2, 1950, by Charles Wilts and George Harr. Ascend the couloir leading to the notch between crags No. 1 and No. 2. Approach crag No. 1 from the northeast, and traverse diagonally upward across the 70-degree north face on excellent holds to the summit ridge. Follow the ridge to the summit.

"Piute Crag No. 2"

Northeast Face. Class 4. Descended September 3, 1950, by George Harr and Charles Wilts. Climb onto the northeast face from the notch between crags No. 2 and No. 3. Loose, high-angle rock leads to the summit.

South Face. Class 5. First ascent September 3, 1950, by George Harr and Charles Wilts. Traverse onto the south face from a point below the notch between crags No. 1 and No. 2. Some interesting but easy class 5 pitches lead to the summit.

West Face. Class 5. First ascent August 27, 1949, by Ray Van Aken, George Harr, and Ray Osoling. Ascend the lower west face

Piute Crags from the south

(class 4) to a belay ledge at the junction of the west face and the west arete. Climb up and right on a smooth slab for one class 5 pitch. Climb onto the west arete and ascend it to the summit.

"The White Tower"

This is the prominent point of white rock on the southern side of Piute Crag No. 2. It is a class 2 talus hop from the west, and was first climbed on August 27, 1949, by Ray Osoling, George Harr, and Ray Van Aken.

"Piute Crag No. 3"

West Arete. Class 4. Descended July 7, 1951, by Ray Van Aken, Wallace Hayes, and Lou Hayes. Ascend the arete rising from the notch between crags No. 2 and No. 3.

East and North Faces. Class 4. First ascent July 7, 1951, by Ray Van Aken, Wallace Hayes, and Lou Hayes. There is a small crag to the west of the deep notch between crags No. 3 and No. 4. Climb to the notch between this small crag and Piute Crag No. 3. Climb over loose class 3 rock to the base of the east face. Traverse around the corner onto the north face. Go up and right across the north face to the summit ridge and follow it to the top.

"Piute Crag No. 4"

North Face. Class 5. First ascent September 1949 by Charles Wilts, Ellen Wilts, and George Harr. There is a small crag to the east of the deep notch between crags No. 3 and No. 4; this crag is high above the notch, closer to Piute Crag No. 4. Climb to the notch between this small crag and Piute Crag No. 4. From the notch, traverse across the north face to a large belay ledge. One class 5 pitch leads straight up from the ledge to the crest of the east ridge. Another one and a half pitches along the east ridge lead to the summit.

"Piute Crag No. 5"

South Ridge. Class 3. First ascent 1927 by Norman Clyde. Climb onto the south ridge from the notch between crags No. 5 and No. 6. Follow the south ridge to the summit.

There is a minor crag between crags No. 5 and No. 6. It is class 4 and can be traversed from either the east or west. This route was first climbed on June 17, 1950, by George Harr and Ray Van Aken.

"Piute Crag No. 6"

East Ridge. Class 2. Descended June 17, 1950, by George Harr and Ray Van Aken. Ascend the talus and ledges from the notch between crags No. 6 and No. 7.

West Ridge. Class 4. First ascent June 17, 1950, by George Harr and Ray Van Aken. Climb up and to the right from the notch between crags No. 5 and No. 6.

"Piute Crag No. 7"

Class 3. This crag was traversed on October 12, 1974, by Dick Beach and Dave King.

"Piute Crag No. 8"

This is the prominent red pinnacle on the south face of Piute Crag No. 7.

Northeast Face. Class 3. First ascent July 21, 1951, by Ray Van Aken, George Harr, Charles Wilts, and Ellen Wilts. Climb the couloir to the east of crag No. 7 and head for the notch north of crag No. 8. Climb sound class 3 rock up the northeast face to the summit.

"Piute Crag No. 9"

This is the higher of the two pinnacles east of crag No. 8.

North Arete. Class 3. Descended July 21, 1951, by Charles Wilts, Ellen Wilts, George Harr, and Ray Van Aken. Climb to the notch south of crag No. 9 from the broad couloir to the east of the crag. Follow the arete from the notch to the summit.

South Ridge. Class 5. First ascent July 21, 1951, by Charles Wilts, Ellen Wilts, George Harr, and Ray Van Aken. Ascend the south ridge from the notch between crags No. 9 and No. 10. This route is on solid rock.

"Piute Crag No. 10"

This is the lower of the two pinnacles east of crag No. 8.

North Face. Class 3. First ascent July 21, 1951, by George Harr, Charles Wilts, Ellen Wilts, and Ray Van Aken. Ascend the south-facing gully between crags No. 9 and No. 10 to the notch between the two crags. Loose rock on the north face leads to the summit.

"Piute Crag No. 11"

Southeast Buttress and North Face. Class 4–5. Climb the broken southeast buttress from the couloir east of the crag. This leads to a chute that goes up and left to a notch behind the crag. An easy pitch from the notch leads to the summit.

Mt. Emerson   *(13,204 ft; 13,225 ft)*

The name of this peak has been misplaced on some maps. The true summit is on Peak 13,204 (13,255 ft; UTM 534229), 0.4 mile southeast of the false summit.

West Ridge. Class 3. Head northeast from the summit of Piute Pass to the bench with many small lakes to the west of Mt. Emerson. Scramble up to the lower, northwestern summit of the peak and traverse the south side of the ridge to the true summit.

South Slope. Class 3. Leave the Piute Pass Trail about $^1/_4$ mile west of Loch Leven and ascend a rib that goes up the southern side of Mt. Emerson. The summit is two small bumps on the skyline, left of the apparent high point. Head for the summit ridge, aiming for a point left (west) of a prominent overhang that is just below the crest. The rib eventually turns into ledges, and then turns into a couloir, which leads onto the summit ridge a few hundred feet west of the summit.

A common mistake made on this route is to begin the ascent too far to the west; this leads onto the lower, northwestern summit of the peak. By the way, there is a fine view from this lower summit, but it is not the true summit.

Southeast Face. Class 4. First ascent August 1955 by G. Ledyard Stebbins and Robert Stebbins. This appealing route is on beautiful rock. Leave the Piute Pass Trail below Loch Leven and climb to the base of the southeast face. There are two prominent cracks on this face, which is left (southwest) of the couloir that separates the Piute Crags from Mt. Emerson. Climb the left-hand crack; the first pitch is the hardest. Continue up class 4 slabs to the right of the crack, followed by 100 feet of class 3. Reenter the crack for another class 4 pitch. This leads to a broad chute, which is climbed for about 500 feet. Cross a rib to the left into another chute, which leads to a notch in the ridge above. Climb to the summit from the notch, passing the first gendarme on its right over class 4 ledges into another notch. Follow the class 3 ridge, passing over several gendarmes, to the summit.

Southwest Ridge. Class 3. First ascent October 12, 1974, by Dick Beach and Dave King. The first ascent of this route was accomplished after traversing the Piute Crags. This ridge can be reached from the Piute Pass Trail by climbing the couloir that separates the Piute Crags from Mt. Emerson. Follow the ridge from the top of the couloir to the summit of Mt. Emerson.

North Face. Class 4. First ascent July 1, 1926, by Norman Clyde. This route ascends a 1,400-foot snow/ice couloir with an average angle of 40 degrees. This couloir is surrounded by loose rocks.

"Checkered Demon"

(13,121 ft; 13,112 ft; 1.1 mi SE of Mt. Humphreys)

First ascent July 7, 1926, by Norman Clyde. The western side of this peak and south ridge is class 2–3. The southeast slope is class 2. There are two snow/ice couloirs on its northeastern side. The right-hand couloir involves 800 feet of 50-degree snow/ice climbing. It was first climbed by Doug Robinson and friend in 1970.

Mt. Humphreys *(13,986 ft; 13,986 ft)*

This is an impressive peak when viewed from either the east or west. The easy routes are challenging, the summit is high, and the scenery is outstanding.

Southwest Slope and Northwest Face. Class 4. First ascent August 3, 1919, by George R. Bunn and party. First winter ascent December 28, 1956, by Dick Long, Jim Wilson, Gary Hemming, Steve Roper, Fred Martin, and Terry Tarver. This has become the regular route on the peak. Most of this route is class 2, with a 100-foot easy class 4 section just below the summit. Climb onto the loose southwest slope from the highest of the Humphreys Lakes. Gain a scree-covered ledge

that goes left (north) to the wide gully, which leads to the notch northwest of the summit. Ascend a trough from the notch (class 3) toward the summit of Mt. Humphreys. A vertical wall is encountered after 200 feet. A short class 4 pitch to the right leads to the crest of the arete on the west side of the trough. Another short class 4 pitch (with excellent holds) up the crest of the arete leads to a short scramble to the summit. *Variation:* 5.5. First ascent July 1958 by John Dorsey, Jim Koontz, and Leif Thorne-Thomsen. Leave the gully leading to the notch and climb the southwest face via chimneys and broken ledges, crossing a sharp wedge beneath an overhang. Rejoin the regular route about halfway between the notch and the summit. *Variation:* 5.9. First ascent August 1988 by Mark Hoffman and Robin Ingraham, Jr. Climb the regular route to the crest of the arete just below the summit. Go right and ascend a vertical-to-overhanging inside corner with a thin finger crack. Small nuts are needed to protect the crux.

Southwest Face. Class 5. First ascent July 29, 1938, by Jack Riegelhuth, Dick Cahill, George Wilkins, Bill Leovy, and Bruce Meyer. This route starts near a prominent pointed spire at the base of the southwest face of Mt. Humphreys. Climb the face up and diagonally left to the summit. The last pitch is class 5.

Hutchinson Route. I, 5.4. First ascent July 18, 1904, by Edward C. Hutchinson and James S. Hutchinson. This route climbs the south couloir, which is high on the southwest face of Mt. Humphreys. Climb the gully that leads to the deep notch southeast of the summit of Mt. Humphreys. Leave this gully before reaching the notch and turn left (north) into the deep, south couloir. (This couloir passes between two black formations, and it may contain snow or ice.) The south couloir leads to a notch that is just to the right of the summit. Some responsible members of the first-ascent party named this notch "Married Men's Point" and remained there while the Hutchinson brothers went on to bag the peak. Go left a few feet from Married Men's Point and climb a 50-foot 5.4 pitch up a ladderlike series of small ledges. The rest of the climb is a scramble to the summit.

Triangle Face. II, 5.8. First ascent August 15, 1970, by Al Fowler, Mike Levine, and Jerry Snyder. This face rises above the south

Mt. Humphreys from the southwest (photo by Norm Rohn)

couloir; the top of the face is the southeast buttress. Climb the deep, south couloir of the Hutchinson Route to an area of light-colored rock. The route ascends a crack/ledge system directly up the face, climbing the left side of the triangle. Follow the Southeast Buttress route from the top of the face.

Southeast Buttress. II, 5.4. First ascent July 7, 1933, by Hervey Voge. Ascend the gully from Humphreys Lakes that leads to the deep notch southeast of the summit of Mt. Humphreys. Climb four roped pitches on the left (southwest) side of the buttress before moving right onto the crest of the buttress. Follow the ridge to the notch just below the summit, Married Men's Point. Go left from this notch, climb a 50-foot 5.4 pitch, and then scramble onto the summit. *Variation:* Descended June 29, 1935, by Norman Clyde. The deep notch southeast of Mt. Humphreys can be reached from the

south fork of McGee Creek by climbing a loose class 3–4 gully.

South Pillar of the Southeast Face. III, 5.8. First ascent December 30, 1975, by Galen Rowell and Jay Jensen. This pillar is on the left side of the southeast face, above the south fork of McGee Creek. The pillar leads to the southeast ridge, which is followed to the summit.

East Arete. II, 5.4. First ascent June 29, 1935, by Norman Clyde. This is the most enjoyable route on Mt. Humphreys. Ascend the south fork of McGee Creek and skirt the east side of a permanent snowfield on the southeastern side of Mt. Humphreys. Climb the chute that is closest to the southeast face to the crest of the east arete. Follow the crest of the arete upward to a steep section, which is passed on its left side via a class 4 crack system for one pitch. Another 100 feet of climbing over and around the arete leads to the surprisingly flat plateau where the east arete and southeast ridge join. Follow the southeast ridge to Married Men's Point. Move left from the notch, where a short 5.4 pitch leads to easier climbing and the summit. *Variation:* The crest of the east arete can also be reached from the glacier north of Mt. Humphreys. Start climbing from the left (east) side of the glacier by keeping to the left of a couloir that leads to the crest of the east arete. Cross the couloir and follow a ledge which goes up and right. Leave the ridge after a few hundred yards and climb the face above to the crest of the east arete. With careful route finding, this variation never exceeds class 4 to the crest of the arete.

North Face. III, 5.7. First ascent May 1970 by Joe Faint and Galen Rowell. A snow/ice couloir ascends the right side of the north face. Go up and left from the bottom of this couloir over broken rock for about 500 feet. Then traverse up and right, following a ledge and eventually passing around a rib. Go straight up from here, and then go up and right to a dihedral, which leads to the summit ridge at a point about 40 feet east of the summit. The first-ascent party encountered much frozen snow on this route and needed ice axes and crampons.

North Couloir. Class 4. First ascent August 8, 1929, by Walter A. Starr, Jr. Ascend the snow/ice couloir on the right side of the north face. After about 300 feet the couloir forks. Take the right fork (or the rocks to the

Mt. Humphreys from the northeast, August 24, 1972 (photo by Austin Post, #72R2-110, USGS Ice and Climate Project, Tacoma, WA)

right) to the crest at a point northwest of the first small peak northwest of Mt. Humphreys. Climb around this small peak on its southern side to the notch northwest of the summit. Ascend the class 3 trough leading up the northwest face to a vertical wall. Climb up and right over a short class 4 pitch to the crest of the arete, where another short, easy class 4 pitch leads to scrambling and the summit.

Northwest Ridge. Class 4. First ascent July 18, 1920, by C. H. Rhudy, L. C. Bogue, and J. L. Findlay. This long ridge can be gained from either McGee Creek or Desolation Lake. Follow the ridge from the large, flat area to the notch northwest of the summit. Climb the trough and right-hand arete on the northwest face.

Southeast Pinnacle. First ascent July 20, 1933, by Jules Eichorn and Marjory Bridge. This is the pinnacle that rises above the deep notch southeast of Mt. Humphreys. The first-ascent party climbed its southwest face and descended its northwest ridge. The northwest ridge is class 3 from the notch.

Peak 12,241

(12,160 ft+; 1.2 mi NE of Mt. Humphreys)

First ascent 1940s by Smoke Blanchard, via the class 2 south slope. The summit rocks are class 4. The west face from Longley Reservoir is class 3.

Peaklet Wall. III, 5.7. First ascent August 1975 by Galen Rowell, Jay Jensen, Gordon Wiltsie, and Helmut Kiene. This route climbs the north-northeast face of the peak. This route has been described as being slightly longer and more difficult than the East Face route of Mt. Whitney. It includes some long class 4 sections. The crux is a 200-foot vertical dihedral with a bulge near its top, about halfway up the face.

Basin Mountain *(13,181 ft; 13,240 ft)*

The east summit is the high point.

North Slope. Class 2. First ascent September 15, 1937, by Norman Clyde. This is a simple climb from Horton Lake.

East Chute. Class 4. First ascent October 1974 by Dick Beach and Dave King. This route climbs the large chute or basin that is visible from Owens Valley. A dirt road leaves the Horton Lakes Trail (which is actually a road) and switchbacks into the basin, ending at an abandoned mine. Climb the chute to the rock slabs beneath the summit. Approxi-

mately 400 feet of clean class 4 rock lead to the summit. *Variation:* Climb the chute to the small saddle that is just to the southeast of the summit. A large couloir leads to the summit from the saddle.

Four Gables

(12,720 ft+; 12,720 ft+; UTM 499299)

South Slope. Class 1. First ascent 1931 by Norman Clyde.

South Ridge. Class 2. First ascent August 27, 1978, by a party led by Bill Bradley. Climb from Upper Horton Lakes to the next basin to the south. Bypass the glacier in this cirque and climb a steep talus slope to the south, eventually reaching a saddle at 12,600 feet+ (12,640 ft+). Follow the south ridge from the saddle to the summit.

East Face. III, 5.8. First ascent June 1971 by Jeanne Neale and Galen Rowell. This refers to the wall that is above the cirque to the west of Upper Horton Lakes. Climb a prominent buttress that is on the right side of the east face. Ten pitches in cracks and chimneys lead directly to the summit.

East Ridge. Class 3. First ascent 1963 by Rick Jali. Ascend the southern side of the east ridge from Upper Horton Lakes. A chute appears on the extreme right-hand side of the east face when you are within 100 feet of the headwall in the cirque. Climb the chute to another wall, then go left into another chute, which leads to the plateau just below the summit.

Northeast Buttress. II, 5.6. First ascent June 15, 1974, by Fred Beckey and Mike Levine. This buttress is on the face to the north of the east ridge of Four Gables. Ascend the prominent, sharp buttress to a point about 500 feet below the summit, where much loose rock is encountered. Traverse left into a steep snow gully, which leads to the summit plateau.

Northeast Face, Right Side. IV, 5.9. First ascent 1978 by Sibylle Hechtel and David Evans. This route follows the crack system on the right side of the large pillar in the center of the face. Twelve pitches lead to the top.

North Ridge. Class 2. First ascent May 27, 1973, by John Ripley, Fred Clements, John Halcomb, John Isaac, and Bruce Masson. Follow the ridge from the saddle north of Four Gables. This saddle can be reached by traversing over Peak 12,808 (12,825 ft), or from the west. The east side of the saddle is blocked by cliffs.

Mt. Tom   (13,652 ft; 13,652 ft)

This is the enormous mountain west of Bishop.

From Horton Lake. Class 1. An abandoned mining road leads north from Horton Lake to the old Tungstar Mine. The easiest route leaves the road where it crosses the southwest ridge, and follows the ridge to the summit. The peak can also be climbed from the Tungstar Mine.

From Gable Creek. Class 2. This is a long, hard hike. Leave the Gable Lakes Trail at approximately 8,000 feet and follow the path of an abandoned tramway across Gable Creek and up the northwest slope of Mt. Tom. Ugh!

North Ridge. Class 2. First ascent October 1971 by Steve Rogero and Dick Beach. This ridge is best approached from the Pine Creek Road. Follow the crest of the ridge to the summit, with a lot of 20-foot bumps that must be climbed up and down. Ugh! Ugh!

Elderberry Canyon. Class 2. This is a popular ski tour in the spring. Leave the Pine Creek Road at Rovana. Go south on this road for approximately 0.5 mile to a junction. Go south from this junction and follow a rough dirt road to the trailhead for Elderberry Canyon. A trail ascends the canyon to the abandoned Lambert Mine. Continue ascending the canyon to the north ridge of Mt. Tom. Follow the ridge south to the summit. Elderberry Canyon is a dry canyon (i.e., there is no running water) during the summer and fall. But in the spring it is a great ski tour. Some parties arrange a car shuttle in order climb the peak from Horton Lake and descend Elderberry Canyon—a ski descent with perhaps a 7,000-foot vertical drop. The upper part of the canyon is dramatically steep. If this were a ski area it would be rated with double diamonds.

Pilot Knob   (12,245 ft; 12,245 ft)

This peak is class 2 from the saddle to the east of the peak. There is an outstanding view from the summit.

Turret Peak   (12,091 ft; 12,000 ft+)

A north or south traverse of this peak is easy.

Mt. Senger   (12,286 ft; 12,271 ft)

First ascent 1907–09 by George R. Davis, T. G. Gerdine, C. F. Uruquhart, and L. F. Briggs of the United States Geological Survey. This peak is class 1 from Sallie Keyes Lakes. It is also class 1 from Selden Pass; traverse southeast from the northern side of the pass, and climb rock slabs and sand to the high saddle northeast of Peak 12,068 (12,000 ft+), at UTM 348273. Go south of the intermediate peak and ascend the northwest ridge to the summit of Mt. Senger. Mt. Senger is class 2 from the east.

Peak 12,000+

(12,014 ft; 0.9 mi SE of Mt. Hooper)

The southeast slope is class 1 from Sallie Keyes Lakes.

Northeast Ridge. Class 2–3. First ascent July 15, 1954, by Oliver Kehrlein and Jim Koontz. Ascend the southern side of the northeast ridge to the small plateau beneath the summit. Go west across the plateau to a knife-edged ridge and follow this to the summit.

Peak 12,080+

(12,080 ft; 0.4 mi SE of Mt. Hooper)

The west slope and south ridge are class 3.

Mt. Hooper   (12,349 ft; 12,349 ft)

First ascent 1929 by Glen Dawson, William A. Horsfall, and John Nixon. This peak is class 2 from Selden Pass. Traverse west from the northern side of Selden Pass to the flat saddle southeast of Mt. Hooper. Descend slightly while traversing westward from the saddle and climb the easy southern slope to the summit block. The block is climbed by crossing its west side to the north face before reaching the top (class 4). A crack on the southern side of the block can also be climbed.

The Pinnacles

(12,320 ft+–12,080 ft+; 12,240 ft+–12,080 ft+)

Not much is known about this ridge, which extends south from Gemini. Generally speaking, the northern pinnacles seem more difficult than those on the southern side of the ridge, and ascents seem to be easier on their eastern sides than on their western sides. The highest pinnacle (Peak 12,320+; 12,240 ft+; 1.0 mi S of Gemini) was first climbed July 14, 1933, by Glen Dawson,

Neil Ruge, and Alfred Weiler. The two southernmost pinnacles (12,120 ft+ and 12,122 ft; 0.5 mi E of Big Chief Lake) were first climbed July 5, 1939, by L. Bruce Meyer and Jim Harkins, from Hutchinson Meadow.

Gemini   *(12,880 ft+; 12,866 ft)*

The northwest summit is the high point. First ascent July 30, 1953, by Jim Koontz and Rosemarie Lenel. Class 2 from Seven Gables Pass. Go south from the saddle on the western slope of the north ridge. Gain the west spur of the northwest summit and ascend talus to the summit. This peak is also class 2 from Aweetsal Lake via the east slope and south ridge.

Seven Gables   *(13,080 ft+; 13,075 ft)*

The south summit is the high point.

South Slope. Class 3. Traverse west and northwest from Seven Gables Pass onto the south slope of Seven Gables. Most of this is class 2, with a short class 3 chute passing through some cliffs. Descend the north side of the knife-edged ridge just below the summit and climb a chimney/wide crack for 100 feet until you are 20 feet below the summit. Go to the left around and under an overhanging block and then go right to the summit.

West Ridge. Class 2. First ascent September 20, 1894, by Theodore S. Solomons and Leigh Bierce. Go east from Sandpiper Lake, passing through some barely penetrable brush, to the rocky bowl northwest of Seven Gables. Make a left-diagonal ascent of the northern slope of the west ridge, passing a permanent snowfield on its left side, to the crest of the ridge. Follow the ridge to the summit.

North Ridge. Class 2–3. This ridge can be reached from the approach to the west ridge, or from Seven Gables Lakes to the east. Go west from the oblong lake at 10,720 feet+ (10,720 ft+) in the Seven Gables Lakes basin to the saddle north of Seven Gables. The saddle is best approached from the north. The ridge above the saddle ascends talus, ledges, and chimneys to the summit.

East Face. Class 4. First ascent August 1, 1970, by Steve Roper and Jani Roper. This route climbs the northern part of the east face, where a steep, broken wall leads to a point about 200 feet north of the north summit. The lower section of the route is

class 4; the middle section consists of 700 feet of class 3, and the last section is class 4.

East Face, Right Wall. IV, 5.9. First ascent August 18, 1988, by Dick Duane and Sebastian Letemendia. This route climbs the central portion of the true (i.e., huge) east face of Seven Gables.

East Face, Chimney Route. IV, 5.9. First ascent August 18, 1988, by Galen Rowell and Kevin Worral. As the name says, this route climbs the chimney on the true east face of Seven Gables.

Merriam Peak   *(13,103 ft; 13,077 ft)*

First ascent July 14, 1933, by Lewis Clark, Julie Mortimer, and Ted Waller. This peak is class 2 from the saddle between Royce Peak and Merriam Peak. The east face is class 3 and was first climbed July 3, 1939, by Alan Bryant and Bob Helliwell. The south slope and southwest ridge are both class 3.

Royce Peak   *(13,280 ft+; 13,253 ft)*

The southeast ridge rising from the saddle between Merriam Peak and Royce Peak is class 2; first ascent June 23, 1931, by Nathan Clark and Roy Crites. The southwest ridge is also class 2. The class 3 east face was first climbed in 1936 by Ellis Porter, Herbert Welch, and Frank Richardson.

Feather Peak   *(13,240 ft+; 13,242 ft)*

Southwest Ridge. Class 3. First ascent July 13, 1933, by David Brower. Climb the ridge rising from the top of Feather Pass, keeping to its southern side to keep the difficulty down to class 3.

Southeast Slope. Class 2–3. Descended July 13, 1933, by David Brower. Ascend sand and talus from the saddle between Royce Peak and Feather Peak to the easy class 3 summit rocks.

Northeast Face. III, 5.8. First ascent August 1966 by Gary Colliver, Edward Keller, Mark Waller, and Andy Lichtman. Scramble up the lower part of the face to a large, sloping ledge beneath a large crack. Make a right-ascending traverse to where easier climbing leads to the base of a headwall. The 300-foot headwall is overcome by an inside corner to a belay stance beneath a ceiling. Go left into a jam crack (5.8) and climb this to the summit area.

Feather Couloir. Class 4. First ascent December 1976 by Alan Bartlett and Michael Graber. This 700-foot snow/ice couloir never exceeds 60 degrees in angle.

Peak 12,470+

(12,400 ft+; 1.0 mi NNE of Royce Peak)

First ascent August 3, 1969, by Andy Smatko and Bill Schuler, via a loose chute on the south-southwest face. The summit block is class 4 on its north side.

Peak 12,563

(12,563 ft; 1.1 mi NE of Royce Peak)

West Slope. Class 3. First ascent 1938 by Norman Clyde. The spectacular summit block is climbed on its south side.

Northwest Face, Right Side. II, 5.7. First ascent August 1966 by Gary Colliver, Andy Lichtman, and Mark Waller. Climb an open book that ends in a bowl.

Northwest Face, Left Side. II, 5.8, A2. First ascent August 1966 by Andy Lichtman and Mike Cohen. Aid climbing on the face leads up a crack past an overhang. This is followed by free climbing to the top of a pinnacle high on the face.

Northeast Ridge. II, 5.6. First ascent July 1982 by Galen Rowell. Follow the ridge to the summit.

Peak 12,320+

(12,287 ft; 0.5 mi SE of Beartrap Lake)

First ascent July 1947 by W. J. Losh, via the class 2–3 west ridge.

Peak 12,760+

(12,756 ft; 1.0 mi SW of Italy Pass)

First ascent July 13, 1933, by George Rockwood and David Brower, who described the southeast slope as being one of the better sand climbs in the High Sierra. The northwest ridge is class 3.

Mt. Julius Caesar   *(13,200 ft+; 13,196 ft)*

First ascent August 12, 1928, by A. H. Prater and Myrtle Prater. First winter ascent March 18, 1965, by Tom Ross and Peter Lewis. The west ridge is a classic class 3 climb; the southwest slope and south ridge are class 2.

This peak has been climbed from the cirque between it and Bear Creek Spire. Climb south from the cirque up a class 2 slope to the top of the Sierra crest, and follow the crest (class 3) to the summit of Mt. Julius Caesar. This was first done August 9, 1953, by Jim Koontz, Pete Murphy, Al Wolf, and Ed Toby.

Peak 13,160+

(13,120 ft+; 0.6 mi S of Bear Creek Spire)

South Slope. Class 2. First ascent August 2, 1969, by a party led by Andy Smatko. Climb the south slope to the summit of the east peak. The higher, west peak is easy from there. A convenient descent route goes south, down a chute between the two summits.

West Ridge. Class 3. Descended July 8, 1954, by Jim Koontz, Mike Loughman, Dan Popper, and Roger Popper. Climb a chute on the southern side of the cirque that is west of the peak. This chute leads to the the Sierra crest. Follow the crest eastward to a point just below the summit. Climb onto a ledge that crosses the west point about 200 feet below the summit. The ledge ends about 100 feet north of the summit.

West Face. Class 4. First ascent July 8, 1954, by Jim Koontz, Mike Loughman, Dan Popper, and Roger Popper. Climb up and right across the west face from the cirque west of the peak. Climb past the low point of the north ridge, and then climb up and left onto the north ridge. Follow the north ridge to the summit.

"Peppermint Peak"

(12,680 ft+; 12,640 ft+; 0.6 mi ESE of Bear Creek Spire)

West Ridge. Class 3. First ascent August 20, 1972, by Andy Smatko, Barbara Lilley, Bill Schuler, and Tom Ross. From the eastern end of Spire Pass, climb around a large chockstone in a narrow chute. Climb up and across the southern side of the peak, crossing some gullies and ribs, to the base of the eastern summit pinnacle. The high point is the summit of the east pinnacle, an easy scramble from its base.

Bear Creek Spire   *(13,720 ft+; 13,713 ft)*

This is the impressive peak at the head of Little Lakes Valley.

Ulrichs Route. Class 3–4. First ascent August 16, 1923, by Hermann F. Ulrichs. This route ascends the northwest slope of Bear Creek Spire; it can be approached from Lake Italy, or from Little Lakes Valley via Cox Col. Ascend the slope to the base of the final summit spire, which is climbed by a diagonal crack that is left of the high point. The crack leads to a squeeze chimney, followed by an exposed boulder move onto the high point.

North Arete. III, 5.8. First ascent August 1971 by Galen Rowell and Jeanne Neale. First winter ascent February 1987 by Greg Orton and Robert J. Parker. This is an enjoyable climb, consisting of about a dozen pitches of moderate technical climbing with spectacular surroundings. There is about 20 feet of 5.8, and two pitches of 5.7 on this climb; the remainder is easy class 5.

Start climbing from the very lowest point of the arete, where a 100-foot section of 5.6 leads to a large ledge. Go about 15 feet left of a large, left-facing dihedral, and climb a thin, steep crack with small flakes (5.7). Climb down and left and ascend a crack that eventually widens into a chimney; 5.8 climbing leads out of the chimney and up a thin crack. The fourth pitch goes slightly left and ascends over many steps before returning to the crest of the arete. Continue climbing along the arete, moving right to bypass some short, steep walls, to the base of a gendarme. Go left across the gendarme, passing two difficult-looking cracks, to the third crack; this crack is steep, with sharp flakes in it

(5.7). Walk about 10 feet to the right from the top of this pitch and squeeze through a triangular hole in the base of a wall to the other side of the arete. The rest of the route diagonals slightly left and ascends the left side of the arete before crossing to its right (west) side, where a class 4 ramp leads to the base of the summit rocks.

Northeast Buttress. Class 4. First ascent May 27, 1932, by Norman Clyde. This is a very enjoyable route. This buttress is left (east) of the north arete; the buttress is marked by a tower on its lower section. Approach the buttress from the east and follow it to the summit. Some class 4 (approximately 200 feet) is encountered just below the summit.

Northeast Face. Class 3–4. First ascent October 7, 1931, by Norman Clyde. Climb the wide face between the northeast buttress and east ridge of Bear Creek Spire. Many variations are possible.

Killer Pace. III, 5.9. First ascent August 1978 by Sibylle Hechtel and David Evans. This route is on the buttress on the far left side of the northeast face. Climb a crack system in the middle of the buttress.

East Ridge. IV, 5.8 with rappels. First ascent July 1981 by Jim Lucke and David Stevenson. Follow the crest of the ridge

Bear Creek Spire from the northeast (photo by Pete Yamagata)

(more or less) from the top of Spire Pass. This route is more than twenty pitches long.

South Face. IV, 5.9. First ascent August 1971 by Galen Rowell. The right side of the south face has two cracks that are separated by a steep, serrated fin. Climb the wall to the right of the right-hand crack, over steep, rough granite. The crux is located below the crest of the east ridge, where a short overhang with a discontinuous crack system must be overcome. This is followed by a traverse on a long ledge to a dihedral, which leads to the crest of the east ridge. Further reading: Galen Rowell, *High and Wild*, Lexicos, San Francisco, 1983, pp. 15–21.

British Chimney Route. IV, 5.9, with a pendulum. First ascent July 5, 1978, by Nigel Gifford and Galen Rowell. This route ascends the prominent chimney on the west side of the south face. Continue up the chimney to a steep headwall, which is bypassed by a short pendulum. Climb to the crest of the east ridge, meeting it near the summit.

South Face Direct. IV, 5.9. First ascent February 1988 by Bill Kerwin and Robert J. Parker. This climb begins from rock slabs at a point directly beneath the summit of Bear Creek Spire. The route ends 10 feet left of the summit block.

"Pyramid Peak"

(12,840 ft+; 12,866 ft; 0.7 mi NE of Bear Creek Spire; UTM 445377)

First ascent 1927 by Norman Clyde. The southeast ridge is class 2 from the top of Peppermint Pass. The northwest face is class 2–3, and was first climbed March 28, 1966, by Tom Ross. The north ridge is class 3.

"Pip-squeak Spire"

(13,268 ft; 13,200 ft+; 0.6 mi SE of Mt. Dade)

First ascent 1957 by Andy Smatko, John Robinson, and Peter Hunt, via the class 2–3 southeast ridge. The north ridge from the top of The Hourglass on Mt. Dade is class 3. The northwest ridge is class 2.

"Rosy Finch Peak"

(12,744 ft; 12,744 ft; 0.5 mi SSW of Upper Morgan Lake)

The southeast slopes are class 2, the east ridge is class 3, and the north ridge from Morgan Pass is class 4.

Mt. Dade *(13,600 ft+; 13,600 ft+)*

The Hourglass. Class 2. This route has also been called the "Dade Couloir" and "East Couloir." This broad couloir leads from Treasure Lakes to the cirque south of Mt. Dade. In early season it is filled with snow, and it is a fine 1,000-foot climb, but the angle approaches 40 degrees in places. Later in the summer it has patches of ice surrounded by much loose scree. *Variation:* It is possible to bypass the couloir by climbing rock ribs to the right of the couloir. There is a lot of loose rock on these ribs.

East Face. Class 4. First ascent August 20, 1960, by Frederick Roy Suppe. Climb the second chute from the northern end of the east face. Ascend the chute about two-thirds of the way up, go left a short distance, and climb toward a depression in the crest. Follow the crest to the summit. There is some extraordinarily loose rock in this chute.

Northeast Face. Class 4. First ascent September 1956 by Ray Van Aken and Kim Malville. Ascend a steep snow couloir that is to the left of a large rock face. Follow a ledge to the right to bypass some vertical sections. This leads to easier terrain and the summit. There is a lot of loose rock on this route.

North Face. Class 4. First ascent 1972 by Al Green, Dave Brown, and Bill Stronge. Ascend steep snow from the glacier north of Mt. Dade to a rock rib which forks at the top of a broad couloir. Class 4 rock on the left side of the rib leads to the summit.

North Couloir. Class 4. This is a moderate snow/ice couloir. The couloir leads to the notch between the Cat's Ears and Mt. Dade. Follow the northwest ridge to the summit.

Northwest Chute. Class 3. First ascent August 24, 1951, by Lloyd Chorley and Don Chorley. This chute leads from the basin southeast of Gabbot Pass to the northwest ridge of Mt. Dade. Follow the northwest ridge to the summit.

West Chute. Class 2. First ascent August 19, 1911, by Liston and McKeen. This chute leads almost directly to the summit of Mt. Dade from the basin southeast of Gabbot Pass. The rock rib immediately south of this chute is class 3.

South Slope. Class 2. This slope can be reached from the west side of the Sierra crest, or from the top of The Hourglass.

Climbing Mt. Dade (photo by R. J. Secor)

Mt. Dade and Mt. Abbot from the east, September 2, 1965 (photo by Austin Post, #F655-192, USGS Ice and Climate Project, Tacoma, WA)

Mt. Abbot   *(13,704 ft; 13,715 ft)*

North Couloir. Class 3. First ascent July 11, 1934, by David Brower, Hervey Voge, and Norman Clyde. First winter ascent December 30, 1967, by George Barnes, Lowell Smith, Margaret Young, Pat Buchanan, Bob Summers, and Dave Duff. This is the easiest route up Mt. Abbot from Little Lakes Valley. Climb the prominent snow couloir that is north of the northeast buttress. Class 3 rock leads right from a point about halfway up the couloir. Go up and right to the north ridge, and follow the ridge to the summit. *Variation:* Class 5. The north couloir can be followed all the way to the summit. This 1,000-foot couloir has angles up to 50 degrees, followed by a short rock wall.

Northeast Buttress. Class 4. This buttress is left of the north couloir, and has much loose rock.

East Side. Class 3–4. Descended August 19, 1932, by Samuel W. French. The best approach for this route is from near the saddle between Mt. Abbot and Treasure Peak (12,920 ft+; 12,975 ft). Cross the glacier east of Mt. Abbot and aim for a small, poorly defined ridge south of a prominent snow gully on the east side of the peak. (This snow gully is south of the northeast buttress.) Climb up and over ledges to the south of this small ridge. These lead to the plateau beneath the summit. There is a lot of loose rock on this route. *Variation:* In early season it may be preferable to climb the snow gully to

Mt. Abbot, Southwest Face

where it is possible to go left onto ledges to the north of the small ridge. This reduces, but does not entirely eliminate, exposure to rockfall.

Southeast Buttress. Class 3. First ascent August 19, 1932, by Samuel W. French. This route ascends the buttress at the left side of the east face of Mt. Abbot. Climb the southern side of the buttress, with occasional detours onto its northern side. There is a lot of loose rock on this route.

Southwest Chute. Class 3. First ascent July 13, 1908, by James Hutchinson, Joseph LeConte, and Duncan McDuffie. Follow a talus slope from Gabbot Pass and climb to the top of the talus, beneath the summit of Mt. Abbot. Three chutes are visible from this point. Climb the central chute; the entrance to this chute is just to the left of the top of the talus fan and close to the rock wall that descends directly from the summit. Ascend the right side of the chute to the class 3 headwall, which is much easier than it looks. The headwall ends at the summit plateau,

and the true summit is a short talus walk to the left (north).

West Chimney. Class 4. First ascent July 22, 1953, by C. N. LaVene and Hervey Voge. This route ascends the farthest left of the three chutes that are visible from the top of the talus fan along the Southwest Chute route. A chockstone in this chute is passed on its left side, and the chute (or chimney) leads to a notch between Mt. Abbot and an overhanging spire on the west ridge. Climb up and left from the notch to the summit plateau.

West Ridge. Class 4. First ascent August 30, 1927, by Robert Yatman and Maurice L. Higgins. Ascend the west ridge of Mt. Abbot from Gabbot Pass. Some deviations from the crest of the ridge are needed to keep the difficulty within a class 4 range.

"Treasure Peak"

(Peak 12,920+; 12,975 ft; 0.6 mi NE of Mt. Abbot)

West Face and North Ridge. Class 3. First

Mt. Abbot and Mt. Mills from the northeast, September 2, 1965 (photo by Austin Post, #F655-191, USGS Ice and Climate Project, Tacoma, WA)

ascent August 19, 1972, by Andy Smatko, Barbara Lilley, Bill Schuler, and Tom Ross. Climb the west face on its northern side, and ascend easy class 3 rock on the face and ridge to the summit.

"Petite Griffon"

(13,040 ft+; 0.3 mi NNW of Mt. Abbot; UTM 419395)

This spire is between Mt. Mills and Mt. Abbot. The southeast side is class 4, and was first climbed by John Moynier in 1984.

The couloir that leads to the saddle between Mt. Mills and Mt. Abbot is 1,000 feet long and 40 degrees steep.

Mt. Mills *(13,451 ft; 13,468 ft)*

East Couloir. Class 3. First ascent August 1921 by Norman Clyde. First winter ascent February 14, 1971, by Dick Beach, Bernard Hallet, Dave MacCoard, Charles Morfin, Frank Risely, and Mike Risely. This route ascends a large couloir which appears to be blocked by a large chockstone. The main

difficulty is climbing over the chockstone; in early season the chockstone may be covered with verglas, and in late season it may be covered with sand. Continue up the loose couloir to the summit plateau. Move south over the plateau to the summit. *Variation:* Class 3. First ascent September 5, 1981, by Jackie Van Dalsem and Dave Heany. Go right (north) from the chockstone to an alcove. Climb up and right from the alcove onto some ledges, and climb up and over the ledges to the top of the couloir. Cross the plateau to the summit. This variation avoids much of the loose rock found in the main couloir. *Variation:* Class 3. First ascent June 21, 1980, by Cuno Ranschau and Larry Machleder. Climb a chute located about 100 feet south of the chockstone. Continue up the chute, and climb from below and left of a large rock outcrop to gain the summit plateau.

South Notch. Class 4, A1. First ascent July 1960 by Rich Gnagy, Barbara Lilley, and Sy Ossofsky. Climb to the notch between Mt.

Abbot and Mt. Mills from the east. Some aid climbing is needed to climb out of the notch and onto the ridge. Follow the ridge to the summit.

Southwest Face. Class 4. First ascent July 23, 1953, by Jim Koontz, Marian Steineke, Louis Christian, and Jim Carl. Climb avalanche chutes on the right side of the face. The last 200-foot section is class 4.

North Face. Class 3; ice axe needed. First ascent July 10, 1908, by James S. Hutchinson, Joseph N. LeConte, and Duncan McDuffie. From the Fourth Recess, climb onto the glacier that is north of Mt. Mills. Ascend the couloir between the central and western rock ribs on the north face, then climb onto the central rock rib. Traverse to the right near the top of the central rib, and ascend the western rock rib to the summit plateau.

North Ridge. Class 3 with a rappel; a class 4 down-climb. Follow the north ridge and either down-climb or rappel to the top of the east couloir. Ascend the couloir a short distance to the summit plateau.

"Ruby Peak"

(13,188 ft; 13,198 ft; 0.7 mi SW of Ruby Lake)
"Ruby Wall" is the east face of the ridge between Peak 13,188 (13,198 ft) and Peak 13,125 (12,960 ft+).

The Gendarmes. Class 5. First ascent 1963 by Mike Loughman and Jay Waller. Traverse the gendarmes along the Sierra crest between Mt. Mills and Ruby Peak.

West Couloir. Class 3. First ascent July 24, 1946, by Fritz Gerstaker and Virginia Whitacre. Climb the couloir and its side buttress, which is located immediately beneath the highest pinnacle.

West Wall and North Ridge. Class 5. First ascent August 17, 1953, by Jim Koontz, Ralph Perry, and Fred Peters. From Snow Lakes in the Fourth Recess, climb the chockstone-filled chimney that leads to the large col on the north ridge of Ruby Peak. Leave the chimney partway up, and climb the face to the col. Traverse south along the north ridge, on its right (west) side for the most part, to the summit.

North Arete. Class 5. Traverse the ridge from Mono Pass.

Pteradon. III, 5.10, A1. First ascent October 1986 by Robert J. Parker and Bill Kerwin. This route is on the wall that is to the right

(north) of the main Ruby Wall (this wall is hidden when viewed from Ruby Lake). Climb the left side of the wall via a prominent system of corners with an ever-widening crack, for five pitches.

Wide Sargasso Sea. IV, 5.10b. First ascent September 1988 by Robert J. Parker and Malcolm Ives. This route makes a direct ascent of the Ruby Wall. Six pitches lead to a traverse left into the summit dihedral below the top.

Northeast Face. IV, 5.10. First ascent July 10, 1982, by Galen Rowell and Mike White. Climb the middle of the face via a chimney system that is not obvious from Ruby Lake. The route continues upward to where a scary ramp slants left and leads into the easy summit dihedral. Follow the dihedral for two pitches to the summit.

Technical Knockout. IV, 5.11. First ascent July 1989 by Richard Leversee, Kim Miller, and Roanne Miller. This route climbs the farthest left outside corner of the four dihedrals on the Ruby Wall. This corner has a large roof halfway up on its left side, followed by a 3-inch to 8-inch crack. Take a double set of protection, from 1/2-inch to 5-inch.

East and South Aretes. IV, 5.10. First ascent August 1984 by David Wilson and Galen Rowell. This route starts along the east ridge of Ruby Peak. Cross a permanent snowfield and begin by climbing over fluted overhangs. Eight long, steep pitches of fine climbing (5.7 to 5.9, with a couple of 5.10 spots) over steep rock lead to the summit.

East Couloirs. Class 3. First ascent August 1, 1946, by Lester Lavelle and Malcolm Smith. These couloirs are south of the east ridge, and have an angle of about 35 degrees.

"Lookout Peak"

(11,902 ft; 11,898 ft; 0.3 mi SE of Ruby Lake)
This peak has also been called "Tempest Peak" and "Ruby Peak." The northeast ridge and east slope are class 2.

"Little Lakes Peak"

(12,782 ft; 12,808 ft; 0.8 mi SW of Mt. Morgan)
First ascent October 2, 1947, by A. J. Reyman, via the class 2 scree slope on the south side of the peak.

The traverse from Mt. Morgan is class 3, and the northwest ridge is an enjoyable class

4 route. The southwest side of the peak consists of class 5 slabs, which have been climbed from Morgan Pass. The west couloir consists of 35-degree snow in winter and early spring.

Mt. Morgan *(13,748 ft; 13,748 ft)*

First ascent 1870 by the Wheeler Survey. This peak is class 1 from Francis Lake; keep to the far right-hand (north) side of the northeast slope for the easiest route. Class 2 from both forks of Morgan Creek. The west slope from Little Lakes Valley is a loose, tedious class 2 climb. The southwest ridge is class 3 from Little Lakes Peak. There is a splendid view of Bear Creek Spire, Mt. Dade, Mt. Abbot, and Mt. Mills from the summit.

Broken Finger Peak

(13,280 ft+; 13,120 ft+)

Northeast Couloir and Northwest Ridge. Class 3. First ascent October 28, 1967, by Frank Yates, Bill Schuler, and Andy Smatko (who broke a finger during an attempt on the southeast ridge earlier that year). Ascend steep snow and loose class 3 rock in the couloir that leads to the col northwest of the summit. From the col, traverse across the west side of the peak, climb over two ribs, and then ascend a gully, which leads up to a false summit. Traverse southeast over another false summit to the true summit.

"Wheeler Peak"

(13,000 ft+; 12,966 ft; 1.4 mi NE of Broken Finger Peak)

This is the high point of Wheeler Ridge. The north summit is the true summit. The northeast and southwest ridges are class 2. First ascent August 14, 1945, by Don McGeein and Virgil Sisson.

Northwest Couloir. III, 5.4. First ascent December 1982 by Robert J. Parker. The angle in this couloir never exceeds 50 degrees.

Northwest Arete. III, 5.8. First ascent May 1984 by Susan Williams and Robert J. Parker. Follow the arete that is left of the northwest couloir.

Recess Peak *(12,813 ft; 12,836 ft)*

Southwest Arete. Class 3. This is a straightforward climb up steeply tilted flakes along the arete. The problem is approaching the arete. One approach leaves the Italy Pass Trail at the 9,600-foot level along the Hilgard Branch. Go north, pass northeast of Peak 11,416 (11,338 ft), and descend into the hanging valley to the southwest of the peak. Ascend the valley to the southwest arete, and follow the arete to the summit. This hanging valley can also be approached from the John Muir Trail at the 9,800-foot level atop Bear Ridge. Go east, using map and compass, to the foot of the arete and follow it to the summit.

Southeast Ridge. Class 3. First ascent June 26, 1985, by Ron Jones, Norm Rohn, Nathan Wong, and Joy Fagert. Leave the Italy Pass Trail at the 9,680-foot level and follow the east bank of the outlet stream of Hilgard Lake. Cross the stream before reaching Hilgard Lake and ascend the easy southern scree slope of Peak 12,680+ (12,692 ft). Descend the northeast side of this peak, and follow the southeast ridge to the summit of Recess Peak.

Northeast Arete. Class 3. Leave the upper reaches of the Second Recess and hike into the large cirque that is east of Recess Peak. Climb to the col on the northeast arete and follow it to the summit.

Peak 12,760+

(12,720 ft+; 0.7 mi NNW of Mt. Hilgard)

Northeast Arete. Class 4. First ascent August 11, 1953, by Jim Koontz, Al Schmitz, George Wallerstein, and Fred Peters.

West Face. Class 2. First ascent July 6, 1954, by a Sierra Club Base Camp party. Diagonally ascend the west face to the apparent high point, which is the summit.

Mt. Hilgard *(13,361 ft; 13,361 ft)*

First ascent July 10, 1905, by Charles F. Urquhart. The south slope is class 2. The southeast face from the outlet of Lake Italy is class 3: A narrow chute leads left high on this face and heads for a prominent gendarme. The right-hand rib of this chute is class 3. The east face is class 2 via a chute located south of the broad east ridge. The northeast ridge is class 3–4, and was climbed on September 8, 1963, by Arkel Erb, Ed Lane, and Barbara Lilley. Several gendarmes on this ridge are passed on one side of the ridge or the other.

The traverse from Mt. Hilgard to Mt. Gabb is typically done on the southern side of the Mono Divide by following benches from the eastern side of Mt. Hilgard to the southern side of Mt. Gabb, or vice versa. This is mostly class 2, but some class 3 is encountered along the benches.

Mt. Gabb (13,741 ft; 13,711 ft)

South Slope and Southwest Ridge. Class 2. First ascent June 17, 1917, by H. H. Bliss and A. L. Jordan. Go north from Lake Italy to a band of cliffs south of Mt. Gabb. Climb through these via chutes and gullies, and go left to the southwest ridge. Follow the ridge to the summit. It is possible to continue up the south slope to the summit, but this increases the difficulty to class 3, with broad, sandy chutes and a system of chimneys.

Northeast Ridge. Class 3. Keep to the southern side of this ridge while climbing it from Gabbot Pass.

North Face. Class 4. First ascent August 13, 1953, by Jim Koontz, Ralph Perry, Fred Peters, George Wallerstein, and Al Schmitz. Cross the glacier on the north side of Mt. Gabb to a point that is west of the prominent split on the north face. Ascend slabs to the split, and follow the split up and right to a large chockstone. Pass the chockstone via exposed ledges, a 25-foot crack, and a 20-foot chimney, and continue to the top of the west wall of the split. This leads to the northwest ridge. Follow the northwest ridge to the summit.

Glacier Route. Class 2. Head southwest from Upper Mills Creek Lake to the glacier beneath the saddle on Mt. Gabb's northwest ridge. Cross the glacier and climb the scree headwall to the saddle. Climb over large blocks along the northwest ridge to the summit.

Northwest Ridge, East Spur. Class 3. From Upper Mills Creek Lake ascend steep, unstable talus to the notch that is right (west) of the prominent gendarme on the east spur of the northwest ridge. Follow the ridge from the notch to the summit.

Peak 12,360+

(12,320 ft+; 0.5 mi W of Upper Mills Creek Lake)

Northeast Couloir. Class 3. First ascent September 8, 1927, by James Wright. Climb over talus from Upper Mills Creek Lake and ascend the snow-filled couloir to the north ridge. Follow the ridge to the summit.

Peak 12,692

(12,691 ft; 1.8 mi NW of Mt. Mills)

First ascent August 3, 1864, by William H. Brewer. The east slope is class 2 from the head of the Third Recess.

Peak 12,193

(12,160 ft+; 0.7 mi S of Frog Lake)

West Face. Class 3–4. First ascent July 23, 1953, by Hervey Voge, Jan Collard, and Mary Crothers. Ascend the west ridge and west face from the Second Recess to the top of Peak 12,160+ (12,145 ft). Follow the ridge south to the top of Peak 12,193 (12,160 ft+).

Mono Rock (11,554 ft; 11,555 ft)

East Slope. Class 2. First ascent July 18, 1934, by Norman Clyde and friend. Ascend the east slope from Fourth Recess Lake to the saddle south of Mono Rock. Follow the ridge from the saddle to the summit.

East Face. Class 4. First ascent August 17, 1953, by Bill Wallace. Ascend the east face up and right to a small bowl. Climb to the summit from the bowl.

North Face. Class 5. First ascent August 6, 1946, by Lester LaVelle, Paul Hunter, Willard Dean, Fred Foulon, Dan Sharp, Joe Sharp, and Homer Wellman. One difficult pitch is encountered.

Wrinkles

Peaks of Little Lakes Valley. Mt. Mills, Mt. Abbot, Mt. Dade, and Bear Creek Spire can be easily climbed in a day from Mosquito Flat during the quota period, eliminating the need for an overnight permit. Little Lakes Valley is a heavily used area, and day outings are preferable to overnight trips in this area.

Gabbot Pass vs. Hilgard Pass. The Mono Divide presents a formidable barrier west of the Sierra crest. Hilgard Pass is a more direct route between Mono Creek and Lake Italy, but Gabbot Pass is much easier, and involves less elevation gain.

Mono to Morgan Traverse. The ridge between these two passes has been traversed by Vern Clevenger, Claude Fiddler, and Rick Cashner. This multiday traverse rivals and in some places exceeds the Palisades Traverse, in terms of difficulty, exposure, commitment, and rock quality.

Mammoth Lakes and The Silver Divide

MANY PEOPLE GET THEIR FIRST INTRODUC-tion to the High Sierra at Mammoth Lakes. Mammoth Lakes is a popular resort year-round, featuring one of the largest ski areas in the country, and excellent summer fishing as well. But I doubt that many of the visitors to the Mammoth Lakes area realize that it is located on one of the great edges of North America: the division between the lush Pacific coast and the Great American Desert. Downhill skiers can ski down one run into the Pacific Ocean watershed, and the next into the Great Basin watershed. Typical winter storms move out of the west, and by April the snowpack at Mammoth Pass, atop the Sierra crest, has an average water content of 42.4 inches. Less than 2 miles to the east, the average April water content drops to 20.0 inches.

This region covers the Sierra crest from Mono Pass (south) to Minaret Summit, and its western limit is Silver Creek and the Middle Fork of the San Joaquin River.

History

The history of this region follows the pattern of the rest of the High Sierra. James T. Gardiner of the California Geological Survey climbed Red Slate Mountain in 1864, and mountaineers interested in sport visited the region in 1902, with the Hutchinson brothers and Charles Noble climbing Red and White Mountain.

By the 1920s this region had become known as a resort, and Convict Lake served the needs of city residents looking for rest and relaxation by providing sport fishing in the mountains. John Mendenhall visited Convict Lake annually with his family during this period, and gradually became interested in the sport of mountaineering, probably by gazing up at the impressive north face of Mt. Morrison from the lake. He wondered if Mt.

Morrison had ever been climbed, so he wrote the most experienced Sierra mountaineer of the day, Norman Clyde. Upon receiving this letter, Clyde hopped into his 1927 Chevrolet, drove to Convict Lake, and made the first ascent of Mt. Morrison. As John said to me many years later, "I kept my plans secret from then on." But it could be said that Mendenhall captured the greatest prize of all, by making the first proper roped climb in the Sierra, on the northeast gully of Laurel Mountain in 1930.

Maps

United States Geological Survey: 7.5-minute series: Mt. Morgan, Mt. Abbot, Graveyard Peak, Sharktooth Peak, Convict Lake, Bloody Mtn., Crystal Crag, Mammoth Mtn.; 15-minute series: Mt. Tom, Mt. Abbot, Casa Diablo Mtn., Mt. Morrison, Devils Postpile, Kaiser Peak.

United States Forest Service: John Muir Wilderness and the Sequoia–Kings Canyon National Parks Backcountry (1:63,360).

Wilderness Permits

For east-side entry to the John Muir Wilderness via Rock Creek and McGee Creek: Inyo National Forest, White Mountain Ranger District, Bishop, CA 93514.

For east-side entry to the John Muir Wilderness from Devil's Postpile to Convict Lake: Inyo National Forest, Mammoth Ranger District, Mammoth Lakes, CA 93546.

For west-side entry to the John Muir Wilderness: Sierra National Forest, Pineridge Ranger District, Shaver Lake, CA 93664.

Roads

Lake Thomas A. Edison Road

This road provides access to the southern

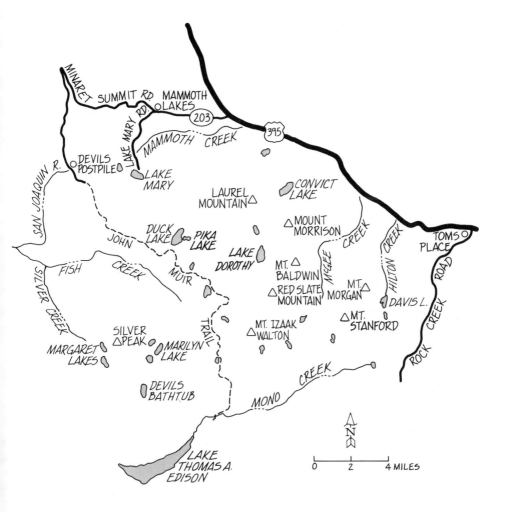

part of the Mammoth Region. It is described in Chapter 10: The Mono Recesses.

Rock Creek Road

The Rock Creek Road leads to the trailheads for the Davis Lake Trail and the Mono Pass Trail. It is described in Chapter 10: The Mono Recesses.

Hilton Creek Road

The Hilton Creek Road leads to the Hilton Creek Trailhead for the Davis Lake Trail. Leave Highway 395 at the major interchange approximately 4 miles north of Tom's Place, or about 11 miles south of the turnoff for the road leading to Mammoth Lakes. Go south-

west from Highway 395 to Crowley Lake Drive and turn right. Drive through the small community of Hilton Creek for 1.8 miles, and turn left onto a dirt road. The road goes past a campground and climbs for 2 miles before arriving at the hikers' trailhead.

The stock trailhead can be reached by turning left off of Crowley Lake Drive 1 mile from its junction with the road leading to Highway 395. The trailhead is 0.5 mile from Crowley Lake Drive.

McGee Creek Road

This road provides access to the trailhead for the McGee Pass Trail. (It should not be confused with the creek of the same name

which is located farther south, near Bishop.)
Leave Highway 395 about 6.4 miles north of
Tom's Place, or about 8.4 miles south of the
turnoff for Highway 203 and Mammoth
Lakes. Go southwest from Highway 395,
cross Crowley Lake Drive, and follow the
McGee Creek Road for 4 miles, past a camp-
ground, to the trailhead for the McGee Pass
Trail.

Convict Lake Road

The Convict Lake Road leads to the
trailhead for the Convict Creek Trail. It leaves
Highway 395 10.4 miles north of Tom's
Place, or 4.4 miles south of its junction with
the road leading to Mammoth Lakes, Highway 203. The road goes southwest, and after
2 miles it meets the trailhead for the Convict
Creek Trail. The road continues another 0.7
mile to Convict Lake.

Sherwin Creek Road

The Sherwin Creek Road provides access
to the trailheads serving the Sherwin Creek
Trail and the Laurel Creek Trail. The road
begins along the Old Mammoth Road in the
town of Mammoth Lakes. Go south along
the Old Mammoth Road from Main Street
(Highway 203) for 0.9 mile to where the
Sherwin Creek Road branches off to the left.
There is a fork 1.3 miles later; go left. The
road continues east another 1.9 miles, past a
campground, to another road, which
branches off to the south. Continue east on
the main road another 0.9 mile to another
road, which branches off to the south. (This
road goes up Laurel Creek.) The Sherwin
Creek Road goes east and then northeast
another 1.5 miles before meeting Highway
395.

Lake Mary Road

The Lake Mary Road provides access to
the trailheads serving the Duck Pass Trail,
the Mammoth Crest Trail, and the Mammoth Pass Trail. The road begins at the three-
way junction in Mammoth Lakes where Main
Street ends, the Minaret Road goes north,
and the Lake Mary Road goes west. The Lake
Mary Road goes past Twin Lakes and, after
3.4 miles, it meets the eastern terminus of a
road that goes around Lake Mary. This road
comes to a junction after 0.2 mile; go left
another 0.7 mile, past a campground, to the
Duck Pass Trail trailhead. Returning to the

Lake Mary Road, the road passes the northern shore of Lake Mary for 0.3 mile before
coming to another junction; this road goes
left and comes to a junction after 0.2 mile. Go
right another 0.5 mile to the trailhead for the
Mammoth Crest Trail on the northern shore
of Lake George. The Lake Mary Road continues another 0.9 mile to the Mammoth Pass
Trail trailhead on the northern shore of
Horseshoe Lake.

Minaret Summit Road

The Minaret Summit Road starts at the
junction of Main Street and the Lake Mary
Road in the town of Mammoth Lakes. The
Minaret Road goes north, and after 1 mile it
meets the junction with the Mammoth Scenic Loop, a euphemistic name that makes
names like "Freedom Highway," "Friend-
ship Road," and "Peace Road" seem pale (it
was actually constructed to serve as a year-
round escape route in case of volcanic activity). The Minaret Road continues past the
Mammoth Mountain Ski Area another 3.9
miles to Minaret Summit, the lowest pass
across the Sierra crest in the High Sierra.
Traffic is restricted beyond this point during
the summer; private vehicles may travel the
remaining portion of the road only during
certain hours. (A shuttle-bus service oper-
ates during the restricted hours.) The Minaret Summit Road descends the west side of
the pass for 2.6 miles to Agnew Meadows. It
then turns south and, after another 6.4 miles,
it meets the junction with the road leading to
Devil's Postpile. The right (west) fork travels
another 0.4 mile to Devil's Postpile National
Monument; the left (south) fork goes another 1.6 miles to Red's Meadow.

Trails

Mono Pass Trail (15 miles)

This trail is described in Chapter 10: The
Mono Recesses.

Golden Lake Trail (³/₄ mile)

The Golden Lake Trail leaves the Mono
Pass Trail approximately 2¹/₂ miles north of
Mono Pass, and follows the northern bank of
Golden Creek to Golden Lake.

Pioneer Basin Trail (2 miles)

This trail leaves the Mono Pass Trail a
short distance downstream from where the

trail to Fourth Recess Lake leaves the Mono Pass Trail. The Pioneer Basin Trail goes north, and after many switchbacks it reaches the lowest of the Pioneer Basin Lakes. A good use trail continues up into beautiful Pioneer Basin.

Hopkins Creek Trail *(3 miles)*

The Hopkins Creek Trail leaves the Mono Pass Trail ³/₄ mile downstream from its junction with the trail that ascends the Third Recess. The Hopkins Creek Trail goes north, and after many switchbacks it crosses Hopkins Creek. A short side trail leads up to Lower Hopkins Lake from here; the Hopkins Creek Trail continues upstream into the beautiful upper portion of Hopkins Creek. A good use trail leads to Upper Hopkins Lake.

Laurel Lake Trail *(3 miles)*

Please don't confuse this trail with the Laurel Creek Trail on the Mammoth side of the Sierra crest. The Laurel Lake Trail leaves the Mono Creek Trail 2¹/₄ miles downstream from the Hopkins Creek Trail. It ascends with many switchbacks up the west bank of Laurel Creek (not to be confused with the creek of the same name farther north) before crossing the creek and making a gentler climb to Laurel Lake. A good use trail leads farther upstream to Grinnell Lake. Further reading: Steve Roper, *Timberline Country,* Sierra Club Books, San Francisco, 1982, pp. 193–94.

Devil's Bathtub Trail *(4 miles)*

This trail starts from near the western shore of Lake Thomas A. Edison and follows an abandoned dirt road northeast, and then north past Twin Meadows to meet the side trail leading to Graveyard Meadows along Cold Creek. The Devil's Bathtub Trail continues north to the outlet of Devil's Bathtub.

Goodale Pass Trail *(8¹/₂ miles)*

The Goodale Pass Trail parallels the northwest shore of Lake Thomas A. Edison, crosses Cold Creek, and meets the Quail Meadows Trail after 1¹/₄ miles. It then goes left and climbs up to Graveyard Meadows after 2 miles. The trail meets a side trail here that leads to the Devil's Bathtub Trail. The Goodale Pass Trail continues upstream another 2 miles to Upper Graveyard Meadows, where it meets another side trail, which goes west to Graveyard Lakes. The Goodale Pass Trail continues up to Goodale Pass in another 2 miles and descends the north side of the pass for 1¹/₄ miles to meet the John Muir Trail north of Silver Pass.

Quail Meadows Trail *(4¹/₂ miles)*

This trail leaves the Goodale Pass Trail after 1¹/₄ miles from the trailhead near the western shore of Lake Thomas A. Edison. The Quail Meadows Trail goes parallel to the northwest shore of Lake Thomas A. Edison, then passes through Quail Meadows along the north bank of Mono Creek before meeting the John Muir Trail at the bridge that crosses Mono Creek.

John Muir Trail *(30 miles)*

After the John Muir Trail crosses Mono Creek on a bridge, it goes right and ascends the northern bank of Mono Creek before crossing the North Fork and meeting the Mono Pass Trail after 1¹/₂ miles. The John Muir Trail continues north and, after passing through Pocket Meadow, it crosses the North Fork of Mono Creek after another 1¹/₂ miles. A side trail leads to Mott Lake from here. The John Muir Trail goes west and makes a steep ascent before making a gradual climb into the beautiful basin south of Silver Pass. Silver Pass Lake is 3 miles from the North Fork of Mono Creek, and Silver Pass is ¹/₂ mile north of the lake. There is an outstanding view from the summit of Silver Pass, with views of Mt. Ritter and Banner Peak to the northwest, and Seven Gables to the south. The trail descends the north side of the pass and meets the Goodale Pass Trail after 1¹/₂ miles. The John Muir Trail goes northeast from this junction, crosses Fish Creek, and after 1¹/₄ miles it meets the McGee Pass Trail at Tully Hole. It then makes a steep climb to the north, crosses a small pass, and crosses the outlet of Lake Virginia 2 miles from Tully Hole. The trail continues northwest and crosses another small pass before dropping down to Purple Lake, 1³/₄ miles from Lake Virginia. Camping and wood fires are prohibited within 300 feet of the outlet of Purple Lake. The trail turns southwest from Purple Lake and traverses around a broad ridge for 2¹/₂ miles to meet the Duck Lake Trail.

From the Duck Lake Trail junction, the John Muir Trail traverses high above Fish Creek along the rim of its canyon for 5¹/₄ miles to where it meets the Deer Creek Trail (after crossing Deer Creek). The John Muir Trail makes a gradual descent from the junction, and slightly ascends to cross a small pass before meeting a side trail that leads to Mammoth Pass. A half-mile beyond this junction, the Pacific Crest Trail branches left and descends between the Red Cones to the Middle Fork of the San Joaquin River. The John Muir Trail goes right, and after ¼ mile it meets another side trail leading to Mammoth Pass. The John Muir Trail continues north, and gently descends for 1¼ miles to meet the Mammoth Pass Trail. The John Muir Trail continues downhill, turns left at a junction ½ mile from the Mammoth Pass Trail (the right fork leads to Sotcher Lake), and after another 1 mile it arrives at Red's Meadow. The trail follows a road, crosses the main road below Red's Meadow, and passes beneath Devil's Postpile after ¾ mile. The John Muir Trail continues north another ¼ mile to the bridge across the Middle Fork of the San Joaquin River. Devil's Postpile National Monument headquarters is ½ mile farther to the north on the east bank of the San Joaquin.

Mott Lake Trail (2 miles)

This trail leaves the John Muir Trail at its upper crossing of the North Fork of Mono Creek. At first, the Mott Lake Trail ascends along the south bank of the creek, and then crosses to its north bank before arriving at Mott Lake. Easy cross-country travel above Mott Lake leads to Bighorn Lake.

Davis Lake Trail (10 miles)

The description for this trail begins along the Rock Creek Road, 9.2 miles from Tom's Place. The trail goes north from the Rock Creek Road and traverses along the western rim of the canyon of Rock Creek for 1¼ miles to where it meets a side trail coming up from a lower portion of the Rock Creek Road. The Davis Lake Trail continues traversing along the bench and turns west and climbs, arriving at a trail junction after 2½ miles. A side trail heads southwest from here and leads to the upper Hilton Creek Lakes. The Davis Lake Trail continues downstream another 1¼ miles to the eastern shore of Davis Lake. The trail continues down Hilton Creek, at first on the east bank and later on the west, for 4 miles to a fork. The hikers' trail goes

west for 1 mile from this point to the hikers' trailhead. The stock trail continues downstream to the stock trailhead near the community of Hilton Creek.

McGee Pass Trail (11½ miles)

The McGee Pass Trail starts from the end of the McGee Creek Road near Crowley Lake. It ascends the canyon of McGee Creek and crosses the stream twice before coming to a four-way trail junction after 3 miles. One trail goes southeast from the junction to Steelhead Lake and another goes northwest to an abandoned mine on the southeast slopes of Mt. Baldwin. The McGee Pass Trail continues upstream another 2 miles to Big McGee Lake, a beautiful place. The trail passes north of the lake, climbs up to Little McGee Lake, and climbs farther into the spectacular basin east of McGee Pass. The trail approaches McGee Pass (which is 2 miles from Big McGee Lake) from the north and descends the western side over many grassy benches down to Fish Creek. The trail crosses Fish Creek several times before descending to Tully Hole, where it meets the John Muir Trail at 4½ miles from McGee Pass.

Fish Creek Trail (21½ miles)

The Fish Creek Trail starts near Red's Meadow, which is near Devil's Postpile. The trail goes south, crosses the Pacific Crest Trail, passes a fork leading to Rainbow Falls, and descends to Crater Creek. It follows the west bank of Crater Creek a considerable distance downstream before crossing the creek at 5 miles from Red's Meadow. The trail continues south and turns east on the rim of Fish Valley before descending into the valley. The trail crosses Fish Creek on a bridge and shortly after meets a trail that ascends Silver Creek to Margaret Lakes. The Fish Creek Trail continues east another 3 miles to Fish Creek Hot Springs (also known as Iva Belle Hot Springs), a delightful spot. The trail crosses Sharktooth Creek just beyond the hot springs and meets the Minnow Creek Trail. The Fish Creek Trail makes a short, steep climb and then briefly descends to the upper portion of Fish Creek. The trail follows the south bank before crossing over to the north bank and entering Cascade Valley. The Fish Creek Trail passes the junction with the Purple Lake Trail and then a side trail, which leads up Minnow Creek, and continues upstream to meet the John Muir Trail at the head of the valley.

Minnow Creek Trail (8¼ miles)

This trail leaves the Fish Creek Trail near Fish Creek Hot Springs. It follows the northeast bank of Sharktooth Creek and, after 1¼ miles, it meets the junction of a short side trail that leads to Lost Keys Lakes. The Minnow Creek Trail makes a slight climb and then gently descends for 1¾ miles to the junction with a side trail that ascends Long Canyon. The Minnow Creek Trail continues southeast, skirting the southwestern shore of Marsh Lake, for ½ mile to meet the junction of a side trail that descends to Cascade Valley. The Minnow Creek Trail then goes southeast from the junction, passes through Jackson Meadow, and after 2 miles it meets a side trail that leads to Olive Lake. It then leaves Minnow Creek, skirts the northern shore of Grassy Lake, and after 1¼ miles it meets a short side trail that goes to Wilbur May Lake. The Minnow Creek Trail continues another 1½ miles, and after crossing a small ridge, the trail rounds the southwestern shore of Lake of the Lone Indian and meets the Goodale Pass Trail just north of Chief Lake.

Purple Lake Trail (2½ miles)

This trail leaves the Fish Creek Trail in Cascade Valley and, after some incredibly long switchbacks, follows the northwestern bank of Purple Creek to meet the John Muir Trail north of the outlet of Purple Lake. Camping and wood campfires are prohibited within 300 feet of the outlet of Purple Lake.

Convict Creek Trail (7½ miles)

This trail leads from Convict Lake to Lake Dorothy and Lake Genevieve. From the hikers' parking area north of Convict Lake, the trail makes a slight climb and descent to meet the fishing trail that follows the northwestern shore of Convict Lake at ½ mile. The Convict Creek Trail follows the lakeshore and climbs along the western bank of Convict Creek to the remains of a bridge that crossed the creek, 3 miles from Convict Lake. The trail continues up the eastern bank of the creek, circles around Mildred Lake, and makes a brief ascent to meet a side trail that follows the eastern shore of Lake Dorothy and leads to Bighorn Lake. The Convict Creek Trail crosses the outlet of Lake Dorothy and, after ¾ mile, it meets the Laurel Creek Trail. It then passes the southern shore of Lake Genevieve and climbs to Edith Lake before ending after another 1 mile along the western shore of Cloverleaf Lake.

Bright Dot Lake, a popular fishing spot, is best reached by leaving the Convict Creek Trail earlier, at Mildred Lake. Easy cross-country hiking for approximately 1 mile to the south (to UTM 351555) leads to a relatively easy talus slope, which leads back toward the northeast to Bright Dot Lake. A direct ascent or descent between Bright Dot Lake and lower Convict Creek is not recommended.

Laurel Creek Trail (5¾ miles)

This trail should not be confused with the trail of a similar name that climbs out of Mono Creek. The Laurel Creek Trail actually follows an abandoned mining road. The road is in poor shape, however, and it is best traveled on foot. The trail begins along the Sherwin Creek Road, 1.5 miles from Highway 395, or 4.1 miles from Old Mammoth. It ascends the east bank of Laurel Creek for 3¼ miles to where a side trail branches off to the southwest to Laurel Lakes. The Laurel Creek Trail continues southeast over a saddle (which is to the southwest of Laurel Mountain) and descends to meet the Convict Creek Trail at Lake Genevieve.

Duck Lake Trail (7 miles)

The Duck Lake Trail leaves the road southeast of Lake Mary and passes by the lakes of upper Mammoth Creek on the way to the summit of a pass atop the Sierra crest. The trail descends the southern side of the pass to Duck Lake, a beautiful lake with fine views. The trail crosses the outlet of the lake and descends to meet the John Muir Trail.

Camping and campfires are prohibited within 300 feet of the outlet of Duck Lake.

Mammoth Crest and
Deer Lakes Trail (9 miles)

The trailhead for this trail is at the end of the road near Lake George. The trail makes a steep ascent to the top of the Mammoth Crest (with a side trail that goes by Crystal Lake). It continues southeast along the top of the Mammoth Crest, with spectacular views in all directions. The trail eventually turns south off of the crest and leads down to Deer Lakes. A rough trail descends Deer Creek to the John Muir Trail.

Mammoth Pass Trail (2½ miles)

This trail leaves the road near Horseshoe Lake and leads to McCloud Lake. The trail forks here, its left branch leading to the John Muir Trail near Red Cones, another branch meeting the John Muir Trail farther south along the upper portion of Crater Creek. The main right branch continues west and meets the John Muir Trail above Red's Meadow.

Pacific Crest Trail (4 miles)

After the Pacific Crest Trail crosses to the east bank of the Middle Fork of the San Joaquin River, it goes east for ¼ mile to where it crosses the Fish Creek Trail; Red's Meadow is ¼ mile to the north. The Pacific Crest Trail then climbs to the southeast for 3½ miles to meet the John Muir Trail near Red Cones.

Cross-Country Routes

"Half-Moon Pass"
(11,480 ft+; 11,440 ft+; 0.2 mi E of Golden Lake)

Class 3. This is a quick cross-country route across the Sierra crest from Rock Creek to Mono Creek. The route begins along the Rock Creek Road near the trailhead for the Davis Lake Trail, due west from Rock Creek Lake. Ascend a broad valley to the sharp notch of Half-Moon Pass. A short class 3 section is encountered on the west side of the pass, followed by a sandy use trail, which leads down to Golden Lake. It is best to go around Golden Lake on its northern side.

"Huntington Col"
(11,840 ft+; 11,760 ft+; 0.4 mi NW of Mt. Huntington)

Class 2–3. This is a direct route between Pioneer Basin and Hilton Creek Lakes.

"Stanford Col"
(11,560 ft+; 11,600 ft+; 0.7 mi WSW of Mt. Stanford)

Class 3. The south side of this pass is easy, but the north side is quite precipitous. It is a direct route between Pioneer Basin and Steelhead Lake in the McGee Creek drainage.

"Hopkins Pass"
(11,400 ft+; 11,360 ft+; 0.7 mi E of Red and White Mtn.)

Class 2. This pass is named on some maps, but not on others. The route leads between Upper Hopkins Lake and Big McGee Lake. Go east from Upper Hopkins Lake before turning north to ascend over gentle, grassy slopes to the low point of the pass. Go west over the north side of the ridge crest to where a class 2 descent to Big McGee Lake can be made.

"Grinnell Pass"
(11,600 ft+; 11,600 ft+; 0.4 mi W of Red and White Mtn.)

Class 2. This pass has also been called "Pace Col." It provides a direct route across the Silver Divide between the upper reaches of Laurel Creek and Fish Creek. Hike north past Grinnell Lake and Little Grinnell Lake to the pass. The north side of the pass consists of loose shale, interspersed with patches of snow. Circle around Red and White Lake on its eastern and northern sides.

"Bighorn Pass"
(11,240 ft+; 11,200 ft+; 1.1 mi SSW of Red and White Mtn.)

Class 2. This pass has also been called "Rosy Finch Pass," and it is used in combination with Shout of Relief Pass to cross the Silver Divide. It can be approached directly from either Laurel Lake or Grinnell Lake by following a grassy bench southwest to the base of the final slope leading up the eastern side of the pass. Large talus blocks are encountered on the west side of the pass. You can either head directly down to Rosy Finch Lake, or head northwest to Shout of Relief Pass. Further reading: Steve Roper, *Timberline Country*, Sierra Club Books, San Francisco, 1982, pp. 194–95.

"Shout of Relief Pass"
(11,400 ft+; 11,360 ft+; 1.0 mi SW of Red and White Mtn.)

Class 2. The southwest side of the pass consists of jumbled terrain with much tedious talus. The northwest side is much more pleasant, the route traversing many meadows and benches. Further reading: Steve Roper, *Timberline Country*, Sierra Club Books, San Francisco, 1982, pp. 195–97.

"Rohn Pass"
(11,240 ft+; 11,200 ft+; 0.6 mi NE of Mt. Izaak Walton)

Class 2. This pass has been named here in memory of Norm Rohn. It crosses the Silver Divide between Tully Lake and Bighorn Lake. The north side of the pass is easy, with the exception of one short, steep section; the south side consists of some stretches of talus.

"Corridor Pass"
(3580 m+; 11,760 ft+; 1.0 mi E of Red Slate Mtn.)

Class 2. This pass provides a direct route between McGee Creek and Convict Creek.

The next pass to the west (Pass 3640 m+; 11,920 ft+) is dramatically steep, with much loose rock on its northern side.

"Gemini Pass"
(3660 m+; 12,080 ft+; 0.7 mi ENE of Cecil Lake)

Class 2. This pass leads from Convict Creek to the upper portion of the Fish Creek drainage. Leave the Convict Creek Trail at Mildred Lake and ascend the gentle valley to the south to where the stream forks. Ascend the right-hand stream southwest to Lake Wit-so-nah-pah and continue south over talus and snowfields to the first broad saddle that is west of Red Slate Mountain. Descend the south side of the saddle to the first small lake and continue downstream to Lee Lake. A good use trail leads from Lee Lake down to the McGee Pass Trail along Fish Creek.

Pass 3800m+
(12,160 ft+; 0.6 mi NE of Cecil Lake; UTM 338532)

Class 2. This pass has been used during high-level ski tours between Rock Creek and Mammoth Lakes. It is best not to descend the west side of the pass, but rather to make a slightly descending traverse to the northwest in order to reach Bard Pass.

"Bard Pass"
(3660 m+; 12,000 ft+; 0.7 mi NNE of Cecil Lake; UTM 333534)

Class 2. This pass is used in combination with Pass 3800m+. It has been named here in honor of Allan Bard, one of the pioneers of the Redline ski traverse of the Sierra crest. Instead of crossing over the summit of the

pass, it is better to make a slightly ascending traverse to the southeast, aiming for the low point of Pass 3800m+ (12,160 ft+).

"Franklin Pass"
(3580 m+; 11,760 ft+; 0.5 mi SE of Franklin Lake; UTM 315549)

Class 2–3. This is another pass that has been used during high-level ski tours. The headwall on the north side of this pass is dramatically steep, at least for a skier. Instead of descending the southern side of the pass, continue climbing to the southeast, and go over the southwest shoulder of Mt. Mendenhall (Peak 3737m; 12,277 ft) to approach Bard Pass.

"Pretty Pass"
(3620 m+; 11,840 ft+; 1.0 mi SW of Lake Dorothy)

Class 2. This pass crosses the Sierra crest between Lake Dorothy and Franklin Lake. Climb into the basin southwest of Lake Dorothy and then to the summit of the pass, just north of Mt. Mendenhall (Peak 3737m; 12,277 ft). The west side is a straightforward descent to Franklin Lake and Purple Creek.

"Pika Pass"
(3520 m+; 11,520 ft+; 0.7 mi ENE of Pika Lake; UTM 288578)

Class 2. Also used during high-level ski tours between Mammoth Lakes and Rock Creek, this route does not cross the Sierra crest, but instead traverses the west side of the crest by going over the pass northeast of Peak 3632m (11,894 ft). The southeastern side of this pass is really steep!

"Deer Pass"
(3420 m+; 11,200 ft+; 0.6 mi SW of Barney Lake; UTM 256585)

Class 1. This pass leads between the Duck Lake Trail and Deer Lakes. Leave the Duck Lake Trail just beneath the southern side of the pass. Go west, up the gentle southern side of the Sierra crest, to the broad saddle northeast of Peak 3560m+ (11,647 ft). Go over the pass and cross the sandy basin beyond to the gap at its western end. A good use trail leads through talus and on to Deer Lakes. Further reading: Steve Roper, *Timberline Country,* Sierra Club Books, San Francisco, 1982, pp. 200–1.

Peaks

Mt. Starr (12,835 ft; 12,870 ft)

West Slope. Class 2. First ascent July 16, 1896, by Walter A. Starr and Allen L. Chickering. Climb loose talus east from Mono Pass to the broad, sandy false summit. The true summit is 200 yards to the north.

East Slope. Class 2. From Mosquito Flat along Rock Creek, climb a chute on the northeast side of the peak to the north ridge. Follow the ridge to the summit.

"Pointless Peak"

(12,256 ft; 12,252 ft; 1.4 mi SE of Mt. Huntington)

This peak, which has also been called "Mono Mesa," is easy class 3 from the summit of Half-Moon Pass. The southeast slope is class 1 from Rock Creek Lake. The peak is class 2 from Golden Lake; climb the sides of a steep chute on the southwest side of the peak. The east couloirs of Pointless Peak are about 2,500 feet long, and have angles from 25 to 40 degrees. Some technical routes have been done on the north face; the north arete is III, 5.10. The north ridge is class 3 on a traverse from Patricia Peak.

Mt. Huntington (12,394 ft; 12,405 ft)

Southwest Ridge. Class 2. First ascent July 14, 1934, by David Brower, Norman Clyde, and Hervey Voge. Ascend the ridge from Pioneer Basin.

Northwest Ridge. Class 3. Descended July 14, 1934, by David Brower, Norman Clyde, and Hervey Voge. Traverse the Sierra crest from Mt. Stanford.

North Face and Northwest Ridge. Class 2. First ascent August 22, 1987, by Jerry Keating, Dick Agnos, and Elton Fletcher. Ascend the far right-hand (western) side of the north face almost to the crest of the northwest ridge. Traverse beneath the northwest ridge across the top of several loose chutes on the north face to the summit.

Northeast Ridge. Class 2–3. First ascent June 23, 1973, by Bill Schuler, Bill Sanders, and Ed Treacy. Climb a steep chute on the north side of the northeast ridge and follow the ridge to the summit.

"Patricia Peak"

(11,962 ft; 11,962 ft; 1.3 mi NE of Mt. Huntington)

The northwest ridge is class 3 from Hilton Lakes. There are also many one- and two-pitch climbs on the pinnacles southeast of the south summit, which have been called the "Patricia Spires."

E-Ticket. I, 5.10b. First ascent 1989 by Richard Leversee, Todd Vogel, and Pat Kent. This route climbs the south side of the large, rectangular spire on the left side of the bowl south of Patricia Peak. Follow the obvious crack system for two pitches.

Templo del Sol. II, 5.12. First ascent 1989 by Pat Kent, Todd Vogel, and Richard Leversee. This route climbs the formation that, halfway up, resembles a temple with vertical pillars on each side. Climb the obvious crack/corner system to the left side of a ledge, followed by a thin finger crack on the wall above the ledge. This four-pitch route requires a double set of protection, from tiny to 3½-inch. Two rappels lead down to the bottom.

Diamond Star Tower. I, 5.10. First ascent 1989 by Todd Vogel, Pat Kent, and Richard Leversee. This route climbs the south side of the beautiful tower on the right side of the bowl southeast of Patricia Peak.

Mt. Stanford (12,838 ft; 12,851 ft)

First ascent 1907–09 by George R. Davis, C. F. Urquhart, R. B. Marshall, and L. F. Biggs, during the survey of the 30-minute Mt. Goddard quadrangle. This peak is class 2 from Pioneer Basin via the west ridge or the gullies on its southern side. A traverse of the Sierra crest from Mt. Huntington is class 3.

The east slope is class 2; from Hilton Creek, ascend a stream the goes west-north-west to the saddle that is south of Stanford Lake. The low point of the saddle is best bypassed; instead, head for the far western edge of the saddle, climbing it via a chute. Go north and ascend the final northeast slope over a false summit to the true summit of Mt. Stanford.

The north-northeast ridge is class 3 in places, and is commonly used during traverses to Mt. Morgan.

Mt. Morgan (3963 m; 13,005 ft)

First ascent July 9, 1934, by David Brower and Norman Clyde, via the class 3 ridge from Mt. Stanford. The southeast slope from Davis Lake is class 2. This is commonly used as a descent route following a traverse of Mt. Stanford and Mt. Morgan. Care must be taken to ensure that the correct chute is selected. Some chutes drain into cliffs near the bottom, and a party could find itself stranded.

Mt. Hopkins *(12,304 ft; 12,302 ft)*

First ascent July 16, 1934, by David Brower, Norman Clyde, and Hervey Voge. This is a class 1 sand climb from the east. The peak is class 2 from Hopkins Creek.

Peak 12,404

(12,408 ft; 0.8 mi NNW of Mt. Hopkins)

First ascent July 5, 1950, by T. H. Hasheim, Elly Hinreiner, and Jean Campbell. The traverse from Mt. Hopkins is class 2, as are the western and southwestern slopes. The traverse from Mt. Crocker is class 2–3. There is a class 3 chute on the northeast side of the mountain.

Mt. Crocker *(12,458 ft; 12,457 ft)*

First ascent August 29, 1929, by Nazario Sparrea, a Basque shepherd. The class 1 south slope leads to the class 3 summit rocks. The south slope can be reached from Pioneer Basin by crossing the saddle between Mt. Crocker and Peak 12,404 (12,408 ft). There are some loose class 2–3 chutes on the northwest face, and the last part of the northeast ridge is class 3, after an approach over sand.

Red and White Mountain

(12,816 ft; 12,850 ft)

Southwest Face. Class 2. Descended July 18, 1902, by James S. Hutchinson, Lincoln Hutchinson, and Charles A. Noble. Climb the large chute rising above Little Grinnell Lake. There is quite a bit of loose rock in this chute.

West Ridge. Class 3. First ascent July 18, 1902, by James S. Hutchinson, Lincoln Hutchinson, and Charles A. Noble. Ascend talus from the summit of Grinnell Pass to the knife-edged ridge that leads to a false summit. Traverse around the north side of the false summit, and continue on to the true summit. This is an exposed route with much loose rock.

North Face. The north side of Red and White Mountain features a rare sight in the High Sierra: a permanent, 900-foot, 40-degree snow/ice face.

Northeast Ridge. Class 3. First ascent July 3, 1928, by Norman Clyde. This is probably the best route on Red and White Mountain

because it doesn't have as much loose rock as the other routes that are commonly used. Head southwest from Little McGee Lake and ascend the northeast slope of Peak 12,360+ (12,320 ft+; 0.5 mi N of Red and White Mountain). Descend to the saddle to the south and follow the ridge to the summit of Red and White Mountain, bypassing a false summit on its western side. Keep to the southeast side of the ridge just below the summit. *Variation:* Descended July 13, 1985, by Norm Rohn and Lloyd Brown. Climb from Red and White Lake into the cirque north of the peak. Skirt the northeast side of the snowfield, climbing to the first small saddle northeast of the true summit of Red and White Mountain. Follow the northeast ridge to the top.

Southeast Face. Class 2–3. Climb into the cirque southeast of the peak from Big McGee Lake. Ascend the left-hand (southwest) side of the face via a chute filled with loose rocks. It is best to keep to the rocks on the side of the chute. Go right (northeast) a short distance from the top of the chute to the summit. There is a great deal of loose rock on this route, and it is not suitable for large parties.

Peak 12,238

(12,238 ft; 0.7 mi SW of Red and White Mtn.)

North Slope. Class 2. First ascent August 14, 1952, by G. A. Daum, G. F. Hurley, and J. M. Schnitzler. This is an easy climb from either Grinnell Pass or Red and White Lake.

Southwest Face. Class 5. First ascent August 1972 by Tom Flynn and Ken Cardwell. Ascend a shallow chute, which ends atop the northwest ridge at a point about 50 feet from the summit.

Mt. Izaak Walton *(12,077 ft; 12,099 ft)*

Southwest Slope. Class 2. First ascent July 5, 1971, by Andy Smatko, Bill Schuler, and Ed Treacy. Ascend talus and scree up this slope to the summit. The slope can be approached via the small saddle southeast of the peak.

Northeast Ridge. Class 3. Descended July 5, 1971, by Andy Smatko, Bill Schuler, and Ed Treacy. This is a good climb along the ridge rising from the saddle northeast of the peak.

East Face. Class 3. First ascent June 13, 1985, by Lloyd Brown, Norm Rohn, and R. J. Secor. Ascend the left side of the east face to the southeast ridge, and follow the ridge to the summit. There is quite a bit of loose rock on the east face.

Peak 12,221
(12,221 ft; 0.7 mi E of Silver Pass)

The southwest and southeast sides consist of class 2 scree and boulders.

"Old Izaak Walton"
(11,880 ft+; 11,840 ft+; 0.9 mi NE of Silver Pass)

This peak was referred to as "Mt. Izaak Walton" in old guidebooks. First ascent July 20, 1938, by Jim Harkins and Norman Clyde. The last 50 feet of the northwest ridge is class 4. The south side is class 2, except for the last 100 feet to the summit, where it is class 4.

"Piscator Peak"
(11,343 ft; 11,280 ft+; 1.4 mi N of Silver Pass)

North Buttress. II, 5.8. First ascent August 15, 1988, by Galen Rowell and Kevin Worral. Ascend the buttress over excellent knobs and solid plates to the summit.

North Dihedral. II, 5.8. First ascent August 15, 1988, by Dick Duane and Sebastian Letemendia. This route climbs the large dihedral that is right of the north buttress. This route eventually leaves the dihedral and joins the north buttress.

Peak 11,424
(11,428 ft; 0.3 mi W of Silver Pass)

The middle summit is the high point. The three summits were traversed on August 17, 1937, by Owen Williams.

Double Barrel Right. II, 5.9. First ascent August 16, 1988, by Dick Duane and Galen Rowell. This 600-foot route is on the right-center side of the east face.

Double Barrel Left. II, 5.8. First ascent August 16, 1988, by Sebastian Letemendia and Kevin Worral. Climb the left-center side of the east face.

Graveyard Peak *(11,494 ft; 11,520 ft+)*

First ascent September 8, 1935, by William Stewart and David Parish. The northeast ridge is easy class 3. Benchmark 3503m (11,494 ft) is not the high point.

Silver Peak *(11,878 ft; 11,878 ft)*

The west and south slopes are class 2. This peak is frequently climbed from Devil's Bathtub. Head north from the lake to the cirque at the head of the valley above the lake. Continue north and cross Pass 11,240+ (11,200 ft+; UTM 225475), which is southwest of Peak 11,520+ (11,476 ft). Continue down to the tarn northwest of the saddle and climb onto the long southeast ridge. Follow the ridge to the summit.

Sharktooth Peak *(11,640 ft+; 11,639 ft)*

This peak is class 2 from Margaret Lakes.

Red Slate Mountain
(4000 m+; 13,163 ft)

First ascent 1864 by James T. Gardiner. Believe it or not, this is the highest peak in the High Sierra north of Mt. Abbot. This peak is a big pile of rubble, and is class 1 or 2 from McGee Pass, Fish Creek, or Gemini Pass. There is a short class 3 pitch along the northwest ridge. On the positive side, there is a swell view from the summit. The couloir on the north side provides about 1,000 feet of 40-degree snow and ice climbing.

Peak 3797m
(12,400 ft+; 0.9 mi SE of Red Slate Mtn.)

First ascent August 29, 1952, by A. J. Reyman. This peak is composed of loose slate, and is class 3 from the northwest.

Peak 3776m
(12,320 ft+; 1.0 mi E of Red Slate Mtn.)

First ascent July 17, 1934, by David Brower and Hervey Voge. Class 2 from Corridor Pass.

Mt. Baldwin *(3845 m; 12,614 ft)*

First ascent July 2, 1928, by Norman Clyde. The northwest slope is class 2 from Bright Dot Lake. The upper west slope of the peak is remarkably smooth. The north ridge is class 3.

East Face and South Ridge. Class 4. First ascent May 1972 by Gary Valle, Tom Oetzell, and Bill McIntosh. Leave McGee Creek just south of Horsetail Falls and climb into the cirque southeast of the peak. Contour west to the last of three prominent chutes. Climb this steep chute to its head and then follow a shattered ridge to the base of a steep wall. The wall, which has some class 4 moves, leads to Mt. Baldwin's south ridge. Follow the ridge to the summit.

Peak 3735m
(12,240 ft+; 0.6 mi N of Mt. Baldwin)

First ascent April 1968 by Galen Rowell, Charles Raymond, and Pat Callis, via the class 3 northwest chute.

Mt. Aggie *(3525 m; 11,561 ft)*

First ascent September 1, 1952, by A. J. Reyman. Class 2 via the southwest ridge.

Mt. Morrison *(3742 m; 12,268 ft)*

This is the spectacular peak that is seen south of Highway 395 near the Mammoth Lakes airport. The rock is extremely loose, and caution must be exercised on any of its routes. The north side of this peak has earned the nickname, "The Eiger of the Sierra."

East Slope. Class 2. First ascent 1928 by John D. Mendenhall. Go south from near the campground at Convict Lake and climb up into the hanging valley that is east of Peak 3321m (10,858 ft). Continue up the valley to a small tarn, then turn right (west) and ascend a bowl-shaped valley. This valley eventually turns into a chute, and it may be easier to climb the right rib of the chute. Follow the chute or its rib to the summit. *Variation:* Another approach uses the hanging valley that is north of Mt. Morrison from the inlet side of Convict Lake. This is more scenic, but much more tiring than the eastern hanging valley.

Northeast Wall and Buttress. IV, 5.7. First ascent September 7, 1946, by Charles Wilts and Harry Sutherland. First winter ascent January 22, 1968, by Reggie Donatelli, Alvin McLane, and Brian Bartlett, who wrote in the summit register, "Never again." Ascend the hanging valley north of Mt. Morrison to the toe of the north buttress. Begin by climbing the northeast face just left of the north buttress via two prominent chutes. Go up and slightly right over high angle rock for almost 1,000 feet to the crest of the buttress, meeting it at a point where its angle declines abruptly. Follow the crest of the buttress for some distance, passing an outside corner on its left. Climb a prominent red chimney on the right side of the buttress. (This chimney has a 5.8 overhanging chockstone near its top.)

Mt. Morrison from the north (photo by F. E. Matthes, #595 USGS Photographic Library, Denver, CO)

Rappel 50 feet down the other side of the chimney to a class 2 talus chute, which leads to the summit.

North Buttress. IV, 5.8, A2. First ascent July 5, 1960, by Jim Wilson, Ron Hayes, and Allen Steck. Start by climbing the northeast wall, then make a 200-foot traverse up and to the right to the base of a crack system on the crest of the north buttress. Ascend directly up the buttress for 500 feet (5.7) to the base of a 60-foot headwall. Climb the wall (5.7, A3) and continue up the crest of the buttress. Pass an outside corner on its left; a prominent red chimney with an overhanging chockstone follows. Rappel from the top of the chockstone down the other side to a class 2 talus slope, which leads to the summit.

North Face. IV, 5.8. First ascent May 28, 1967, by Tom Higgins and Charlie Raymond. Begin by climbing a squat, black rock about 200 feet to the right of the toe of the north buttress. This first pitch is devious and difficult, and the route generally goes straight up, but goes to the right where the black rock turns gray. Traverse down and left (5.8) past a clean, sharp dihedral to a broken area. Continue up broken rock to the base of a large, white rock (shaped like the state of California), which is visible from the hanging valley below. A friction traverse left leads to an exposed corner, and the corner leads to the crest of the north buttress. Continue up the crest of the buttress to a gold-colored chute. This chute leads to a steep headwall, followed by a thin ridge, which leads to the summit. After the first four pitches, the climbing is never more difficult than 5.6.

Northwest Couloir. Class 3. First ascent 1931 by John D. Mendenhall. Go to the right past the north buttress from the hanging valley north of Mt. Morrison and climb the prominent, steep chute on the northwest side of the peak. Ice axes and crampons may be needed to ascend this chute.

Northwest Ridge. Class 3. First ascent June 22, 1928, by Norman Clyde. Leave the Convict Creek Trail at the southwestern shore of Convict Lake and climb a prominent talus slope toward a saddle with some clumps of trees. Just below this saddle, traverse left (east) past a couple of notches and ascend a class 3 rib to the crest of the northwest ridge. Continue up the ridge to the summit.

South Summit from the West. Class 2. First ascent 1928 by John D. Mendenhall. The actual high point of Mt. Morrison is the south summit (3765 m; 12,320 ft+). Hike up the Convict Creek Trail past the bridge and climb a long talus slope to the summit.

South Summit from Mt. Morrison. Class 3–4. First ascent May 21, 1966, by Dick Beach, Mike McNicholas, and John Thornton. Follow the very crest of the arete between the two summits.

South Summit from the East. Class 2. First ascent September 9, 1930, by James Van Patten and John D. Mendenhall. Climb to the eastern hanging valley south of Convict Lake, then to the eastern base of the south peak. A steep, loose chute leads to the summit. It may be better to ascend the rocks south of this chute.

Laurel Mountain *(3600 m+; 11,812 ft)*

North Ridge. Class 1. First ascent September 25, 1926, by Norman Clyde. This ridge can be approached from either Laurel Creek or Convict Lake.

Northeast Trough. Class 2. First ascent 1925 by John D. Mendenhall. This trough is to the right of the cliffs on the east face of Laurel Mountain. The bottom of the trough can be easily reached from the Convict Creek Trail.

Northeast Gully. Class 4. First ascent September 7, 1930, by John D. Mendenhall and James M. Van Patten. This historic climb marked the first time that a proper (i.e., belayed) roped climb occurred in the High Sierra. This steep gully is halfway between the northeast trough and the arete that splits the cliffs on the east face of the peak. Ascend the trough to the upper part of the arete, turn right, and head directly for the summit. *Variation:* Class 4. First ascent July 4, 1990, by Chris Keith and Pete Lowery. This variation is achieved by continuing straight up a huge gray slab instead of turning right.

Bloody Mountain *(3826 m; 12,544 ft)*

First ascent July 3, 1928, by Norman Clyde. The northeast ridge is class 2, as are the south and southwest slopes. A snow/ice couloir on its north side provides 1,500 feet of climbing, up to an angle of 40 degrees.

Peak 3770m
(12,320 ft+; 0.7 mi NE of Cecil Lake)

First ascent July 7, 1971, by Bill Schuler,

Andy Smatko, and Ed Treacy. The south ridge is class 2.

"Mt. Mendenhall"

(3737 m; 12,277 ft; 1.0 mi SW of Lake Dorothy)

This peak has been named here after the late John Mendenhall. First ascent July 17, 1934, by David Brower, via the class 2 north ridge.

"Virginia Pass Crag"

(3403 m; 11,147 ft; 0.5 mi NW of Lake Virginia)

"Virginia Pass" is crossed by the John Muir Trail between Lake Virginia and Purple Lake. This peak is southwest of this pass.

North-Northwest Chute. This steep chute was first climbed August 16, 1965, by Bob Syndor.

Left Crack. I, 5.10a. First ascent August 14, 1988, by Galen Rowell, Dick Duane, Sebastian Letemendia, and Kevin Worral. This is a 200-foot, overhanging hand crack on the face that faces the pass.

Peak 3762m

(12,354 ft; 1.1 mi NE of Lake Virginia)

First ascent 1963 by A. J. Reyman, via the class 2 north ridge.

Peak 3632m

(11,894; 0.5 mi E of Pika Lake)

The north-northeast ridge (class 3) was first climbed September 5, 1966, by Bob Herlihy, Bill Schuler, and Andy Smatko. This party descended via the steep southwest chute.

Peak 3580m+

(11,760;+; 1.6 mi SW of Bloody Mtn.)

The east face is class 3–4, and was first climbed September 4, 1966, by Andy Smatko, Ellen Siegal, Bill Schuler, and Bob Herlihy.

Peak 3681m

(12,052 ft; 1.7 mi W of Bloody Mtn.)

First ascent August 18, 1924, by E. S. Wallace, E. E. Wix, and Bill Dye. This peak is class 2 from the west. The steep chute at the southern end of the east face is class 3.

Crystal Crag   *(3163 m; 10,364 ft)*

There is a class 3 route along the west face. Go to the base of the west face from the outlet of Crystal Lake. Climb diagonally to the right and up the west face to within 60 feet of the top. Go to the right and up for about 20 feet to the top of an exposed rib. Follow the rib to the summit. Further reading: Alan Bartlett and Errett Allen, *Rock Climbs of the Sierra East Side,* Chockstone Press, Evergreen, Colorado, 1985, p. 118.

Mammoth Mountain

(3362 m; 11,053 ft)

This is a famous ski area; the easiest route to the top is via Gondola No. 2.

Wrinkles

Fish Creek Trail vs. the John Muir Trail. The John Muir Trail leaves the Fish Creek drainage north of Silver Pass. It then traverses high above Fish Creek and passes along the heavily used campsites at Lake Virginia, Purple Lake, and Duck Lake. An often overlooked alternative is to instead take the Fish Creek Trail down through Cascade Valley, Fish Creek Hot Springs, and Fish Valley, eventually reaching Devil's Postpile. Both trails lead to the same place, but the Fish Creek option is much more pleasant, and less visited.

Morgan–Stanford Traverse. Mt. Stanford and Mt. Morgan can be easily climbed in a day from Davis Lake; this has also been done in a long day from Rock Creek Lake. Mt. Stanford is usually climbed first, followed by a traverse along its long north ridge (class 3 in places) to the summit of Mt. Morgan. A descent of the east slopes of Mt. Morgan must be carefully selected to ensure that the party does not find itself stranded on some cliffs above Davis Lake.

Grinnell Pass vs. Bighorn Pass and Shout of Relief Pass. It is hard to cross the Silver Divide in this area. The most direct route is Grinnell Pass, but it has some loose rock on its northern side. On the other hand, Bighorn Pass and Shout of Relief Pass are more solid, but have some huge fields of talus that must be overcome.

Red and White–Izaak Walton Traverse. These two peaks have been done from the headwaters of Fish Creek. The best route descends the northeast ridge of Red and White Mountain down to the northern shore of Red and White Lake. It then crosses the Silver Divide at Rohn Pass and climbs Mt. Izaak Walton via the class 3 northeast arete.

The Minarets and June Lake

THE MINARETS ARE A STRIKING SIGHT FROM Mammoth Mountain. Most prominent is Clyde Minaret, but those with sharp eyes can make out the thin needle to its left, Michael Minaret. Banner Peak and Mt. Ritter dominate the skyline, but this row of peaks is not on the Sierra crest; this subrange is known as the Ritter Range, and while it is scenic, it is also well known among climbers for its loose rock, and the danger of rockfall is high.

This chapter covers the Sierra crest from Minaret Summit to Tioga Pass; its western limit is formed by the North Fork of the San Joaquin River and the Lyell Fork of the Tuolumne River. The western boundary has been adjusted in such a way that Rodgers Peak and Mt. Lyell are covered in Chapter 13: The Cathedral and Clark Ranges.

History

Mt. Ritter is perhaps the most prominent peak in the High Sierra, and can even be seen from certain summits in the southern portion of the range. Clarence King attempted to climb it in 1866, and John Muir succeeded in climbing it in 1872. After guiding a party of artists into Yosemite's wilderness, he set out for a week with his blanket, biscuits, and tea, and climbed the peak from the saddle between it and Banner Peak.

The first recorded climbing in the Minarets was in 1923, by Charles W. Michael, the assistant postmaster of Yosemite, and his wife, Enid, a seasonal Yosemite National Park naturalist. In September, the couple hiked from Tuolumne Meadows to a camp at Ediza Lake. They crossed North Notch, made their way along the west base of the Minarets, and started up the chimney which they believed led to the high point of the Minarets. They passed the two lower chockstones easily, but were momentarily halted by the third

huge boulder. Enid remained behind while Charles climbed past the "ladder with the lower rungs missing." He continued solo climbing to the Portal and surmounted the ledges leading to the top of what is now known as Michael Minaret. A few years later Norman Clyde climbed the highest of the Minarets, now known as Clyde Minaret, but Charles Michael was satisfied with his minaret. He later wrote, "Whether my peak was the highest or not does not matter to me so much, for I can recommend it as a grand and thrilling climb."

The Minarets were the scene of much climbing activity in August 1933, when Walter A. Starr, Jr. was reported overdue from a trip to the Ritter Range. A large search party composed of some of California's finest climbers spent a week in the area, climbing peaks and checking summit registers, continually looking for clues from the missing man. The search was called off on August 19, but Clyde remained, climbing Leonard Minaret and searching the shores of Cecile Lake that day. On August 21 he climbed Clyde Minaret, looking for signs of a fallen climber in the bergschrund along its north glacier. Two days later he searched the cliffs above Amphitheater Lake with binoculars, and continued the search from the summit of Kehrlein Minaret. On August 25 he put all of the clues together, and climbed Michael Minaret via Clyde's Ledge. During his descent a fly droned by, and then another. He moved north, away from the Portal, and turned to face the northwestern side of Michael Minaret. And then he saw the earthly remains of Walter A. Starr, Jr. A few days later, Clyde and Jules Eichorn interred the body on the ledge where it had come to rest, while Starr's father, Walter A. Starr, Sr., watched from below.

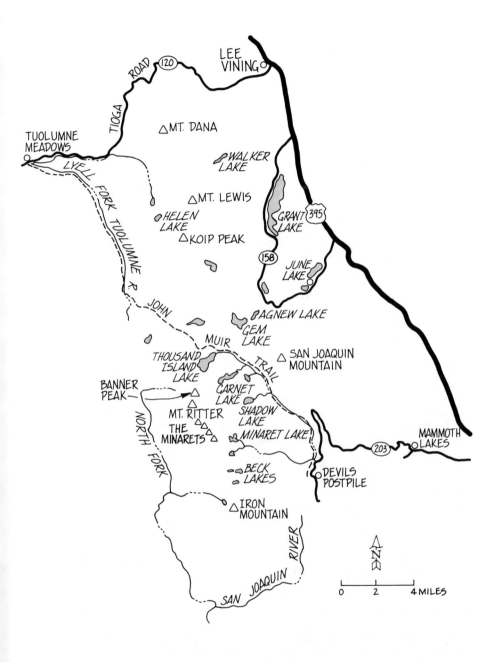

LEE VINING

TIOGA ROAD 120

TUOLUMNE MEADOWS

MT. DANA

WALKER LAKE

LYELL FORK TUOLUMNE R.

MT. LEWIS

HELEN LAKE

KOIP PEAK

GRANT LAKE 395

158

JUNE LAKE

JOHN

AGNEW LAKE

GEM LAKE

MUIR

THOUSAND ISLAND LAKE

SAN JOAQUIN MOUNTAIN

BANNER PEAK

GARNET LAKE

TRAIL

MT. RITTER

SHADOW LAKE

THE MINARETS

MINARET LAKE

NORTH FORK

MAMMOTH LAKES

203

BECK LAKES

DEVILS POSTPILE

IRON MOUNTAIN

SAN JOAQUIN RIVER

N

0   2   4 MILES

Maps

United States Geological Survey: 7.5-minute series: Cattle Mtn., Devils Postpile, Mammoth Mtn., Mt. Ritter, Koip Peak, Vogelsang Peak, Tioga Pass, Mt. Dana; 15-minute series: Devils Postpile, Mono Craters, Tuolumne Meadows; national park maps: Yosemite National Park and Vicinity (1:125,000).

United States Forest Service: Ansel Adams Wilderness (1:63,360).

Wilderness Permits

For east-side entry to the Ansel Adams Wilderness from Red's Meadow to Agnew Meadow: Inyo National Forest, Mammoth Ranger District, Mammoth Lakes, CA 93546.

For east-side entry to the Ansel Adams Wilderness from Silver Lake to Tioga Pass: Inyo National Forest, Mono Lake Ranger District, Lee Vining, CA 93541.

For west-side entry to the Ansel Adams Wilderness: Sierra National Forest, Minarets Ranger District, North Fork, CA 93541.

For entry to Yosemite National Park backcountry: Backcountry Office, P.O. Box 577, Yosemite National Park, CA 95389.

Roads

Minaret Summit Road

The Minaret Summit Road leads from the town of Mammoth Lakes to the trailheads near Devil's Postpile National Monument. It is described in Chapter 11: Mammoth Lakes and The Silver Divide.

Minarets Highway

The Minarets Highway can be used to approach the western trailhead for the Mammoth Trail. It is described in Chapter 13: The Clark and Cathedral Ranges.

Beasore Road

The Beasore Road serves as another approach to the western trailhead for the Mammoth Trail. It is described in Chapter 13: The Clark and Cathedral Ranges.

June Lake Loop (Highway 158)

This loop leaves Highway 395 approximately 15 miles north of the junction of Highways 395 and 203. The road goes west from Highway 395, passes through the town of June Lake and its ski area, then loops around to the north to the Rush Creek Trailhead near the western shore of Silver Lake. The road continues north, passes the west shore of Grant Lake, and rejoins Highway 395 approximately 4 miles south of Lee Vining.

Parker Creek Road

The Parker Creek Road leads to the Parker Lake Trailhead. It leaves the June Lake Loop 1.4 miles from its northern junction of Highway 395, north of Grant Lake. The road goes 0.5 mile to a four-way junction. Drive straight through the junction and, at 1.4 miles, take the left fork, and drive another 0.6 mile to the Parker Lake Trailhead.

Sawmill Canyon Road

The Sawmill Canyon Road leads to the eastern trailhead for the Mono Pass Trail. From the four-way junction along the Parker Creek Road, go north 0.5 mile to a junction. Take the right fork another 0.3 mile to another junction. Go left for another 2.1 miles to the trailhead, high above Walker Lake and Bloody Canyon.

Horse Meadow Road

The Horse Meadow Road leads to Upper Horse Meadow and the trailhead for the Gibbs Lake Trail. The road starts by going west from Highway 395 approximately 1.5 miles south of Lee Vining. The road comes to a junction after 0.3 mile. Go straight (or left) 0.7 mile to a four-way junction. Go straight to Lower Horse Meadow. This is the limit for most passenger cars; four-wheel-drive vehicles can continue up the road another 1.4 miles to the trailhead.

Tioga Road (Highway 120)

The Tioga Road leads from Lee Vining, up and over Tioga Pass, and on to Tuolumne Meadows after approximately 20 miles. The trailhead for the Glacier Canyon Trail is at a turnout along the road near the inlet of Tioga Lake. The western trailhead for the Mono Pass Trail is at Dana Meadows. The John Muir Trail runs the length of Tuolumne Meadows, but most hikes up Lyell Canyon start from the hikers' parking area along the side road leading to the Tuolumne Meadows Lodge.

Trails

The Mammoth Trail (17 *miles*)

This historic trail was used to supply the town of Mammoth Lakes during its first heyday, as a mining town. From Devil's Postpile, take the John Muir Trail across the Middle Fork of the San Joaquin River and up toward Johnston Meadow for 1/4 mile to where the trail forks. Take the fork heading southwest toward King Creek. The Mammoth Trail gradually climbs before descending to cross King Creek after 2 miles. The trail then climbs for 2 miles to meet the Beck Lakes Trail. The Mammoth Trail then climbs for 1/2 mile to the south to misnamed Summit Meadow, which is no longer a meadow, and which is not at the summit. The trail then goes west, climbs over a small ridge, and descends to Granite Stairway. It continues its descent to Cargyle Meadow, and then makes a short climb before descending to Corral Meadow, 5 3/4 miles from Summit Meadow. The North Fork Trail goes west from Corral Meadow; the Mammoth Trail descends to the southwest for 1 1/2 miles to Snake Meadow. A side trail goes north from here for 2 miles to meet the North Fork Trail at Earthquake Meadow. The Mammoth Trail continues to descend for another 2 miles to the North Fork of the San Joaquin River. The trail crosses the river on a bridge at Sheep Crossing, then climbs the western wall of the canyon for 3 1/4 miles to the trailhead, which is 1.2 miles east of the Granite Creek Campground.

North Fork Trail (11 1/2 *miles*)

This trail leads to the headwaters of the North Fork of the San Joaquin River. Start from either Snake Meadow or Corral Meadow along the Mammoth Trail—the two trails join after 2 miles, at Earthquake Meadow. The North Fork Trail continues north to cross Iron Creek after another 3 miles. It continues north, crosses Dike Creek, and comes to Hemlock Crossing after 2 miles. (In reality, there are *two* crossings of the North Fork of the San Joaquin River at Hemlock Crossing, but it is possible to traverse the east side of the stream to avoid crossing the river unnecessarily.) The trail then ascends the east bank of Slide Creek before crossing, and continues northward up the east bank of the San Joaquin River. The trail eventually disappears after passing through a long meadow and crossing the outlet stream that drains the lakes west of Mt. Ritter. Twin Island Lakes are an easy cross-country hike to the west; North Glacier Pass, a harder hike, is to the northeast.

An alternate route to Hemlock Crossing leaves the Isberg Pass Trail 2 1/2 miles from the Granite Creek Campground. The right fork from this junction leads northeast, passing a stock driveway and a side trail leading down Cora Creek, and comes to another fork after 1/2 mile. Take the right fork northeast, cross Cora Creek and Chetwood Creek, and then make a long climb to the north before turning northeast and descending to meet the main North Fork Trail at Hemlock Crossing. The length of this alternate route to Hemlock Crossing is 9 miles.

Beck Lakes Trail (6 *miles*)

This trail can be hiked as a loop trip that starts from Devil's Postpile via the John Muir Trail or the Mammoth Trail. The entire length of this loop is 11 1/2 miles. Follow the Mammoth Trail across King Creek to the trail junction north of Summit Meadow. The Beck Lakes Trail goes west from here and, after 1/2 mile, it meets the side trail that leads to Fern Lake. The Beck Lakes Trail goes north another 1 3/4 miles to the junction with the side trails to Holcomb Lake and Ashley Lake. The Beck Lakes Trail continues northeast another 1/4 mile to the junction with the side trail that leads to Beck Lakes, 1 1/2 miles from the last junction. The main Beck Lakes Trail continues east from this junction another 3 1/2 miles over soft, dusty trail to meet the John Muir Trail, 1 1/4 miles from Devil's Postpile.

John Muir Trail (32 *miles*)

The John Muir Trail crosses the San Joaquin River on a bridge and meets the Mammoth Trail after 1/4 mile. The John Muir Trail goes northwest from this junction, passes the junction with the Beck Lakes Trail, crosses Minaret Creek, and meets the Minaret Creek Trail on the northern side of Johnston Meadow after 1 3/4 miles. The John Muir Trail goes north from this junction, climbs to the top of a high plateau, passes Trinity Lakes, and meets a side trail leading to Emily Lake after 3 miles. The main trail continues north another ³/₄ mile to Gladys Lake, and meets Rosalie Lake another ³/₄ mile farther. The trail makes a short ascent beyond Rosalie Lake and then descends for 1¹/₂ miles to the upper end of Shadow Lake, where the trail meets the lower section of the Shadow Creek Trail. Camping and campfires are prohibited along the northern shore of Shadow Lake. The John Muir Trail turns north from this junction and makes a long, gentle climb before descending to the outlet of Garnet Lake after 3 miles. The Garnet Lake Trail meets the John Muir Trail just south of the outlet. Camping and campfires are prohibited along the eastern end of Garnet Lake. The trail follows the northern shore of Garnet Lake, climbs over a small pass, and descends to Ruby Lake after ³/₄ mile. The trail continues another ³/₄ mile to the outlet of Thousand Island Lake, where it meets the Pacific Crest Trail. Camping and campfires are prohibited along the northeastern end of Thousand Island Lake. The trail continues northwest for another 2 miles to the summit of Island Pass, and then descends to the northwest, passing a side trail to Davis Lakes, and meeting the Rush Creek Trail after another 1¹/₄ miles.

The John Muir Trail goes northwest from its junction with the Rush Creek Trail, passes a side trail leading to Marie Lakes, and continues on to the summit of Donahue Pass after 3 miles. The trail descends the northwest side of the pass for 4 miles and crosses the Lyell Fork of the Tuolumne River via a bridge. The trail continues down this beautiful, long, flat canyon another 3 miles and meets the Evelyn Lake Trail, which leads to the vicinity of Tuolumne Pass. The John Muir Trail follows the Lyell Fork downstream from this junction for 4¹/₄ miles to the junction with the Tuolumne Pass Trail. The John Muir Trail meets another trail junction ¹/₂ mile to the west. The left fork leads to the Tuolumne Meadows Campground; the John Muir Trail turns right, crosses the Lyell Fork and Dana Fork, and leads to the road serving the Tuolumne Meadows Lodge and the parking lot for hikers.

Pacific Crest Trail *(15¹/₄ miles)*

The Pacific Crest Trail crosses the Middle Fork of the San Joaquin river on a bridge near the eastern boundary of Devil's Postpile National Monument. It then goes north for 1 mile, crosses the Mammoth Trail, and continues north another ¹/₂ mile to where it crosses the John Muir Trail, which comes up from Devil's Postpile. The Pacific Crest Trail continues north, fords Minaret Creek, crosses the Middle Fork on a bridge, and, after 2 miles, comes to a trail junction near the Soda Springs Campground. It goes left from the fork and follows the east bank of the Middle Fork for 2¹/₄ miles to a trail junction. The left fork leads to the River Trail; the Pacific Crest Trail goes right and, after ¹/₂ mile of switchbacks, meets the River Trail near Agnew Meadows. The Pacific Crest Trail turns right (east) and passes through Agnew Meadows for 1 mile, at first on trail and finally by road.

From Agnew Meadows, the Pacific Crest Trail (also known as the "High Trail" from this point) makes a few switchbacks from the road and then climbs high above the eastern slope of the Middle Fork (with outstanding views of the Ritter Range) for 5¹/₄ miles to where it meets the Agnew Pass Trail. The Pacific Crest Trail continues northwest from the junction for ³/₄ mile to meet another side trail leading to Agnew Pass. It then goes another ³/₄ mile west to meet the upper terminus of the River Trail. The Pacific Crest Trail then heads northwest ¹/₄ mile to a junction with a side trail leading to Clark Lakes, and continues another 1 mile to meet the John Muir Trail at Thousand Island Lake.

Minaret Lake Trail *(5 miles)*

The Minaret Lake Trail leaves the John Muir Trail at Johnston Meadow and follows the northern bank of Minaret Creek. After the trail switchbacks up a bare granite slope, it meets a side trail that leads north to an abandoned mine that is south of Volcanic Pass. The Minaret Lake Trail continues up Minaret Creek to the outlet of Minaret Lake. Wood campfires are prohibited at Minaret Lake.

River Trail *(5¹/₄ miles)*

This trail ascends the east bank of the Middle Fork of the San Joaquin River from Agnew Meadows to meet the Pacific Crest Trail between Agnew Pass and Thousand Island Lake. Follow the Pacific Crest Trail from Agnew Meadows downhill toward the river. The River Trail starts from its junction with the Pacific Crest Trail, $1/2$ mile from Agnew Meadows. The River Trail passes a side trail, which leads south, after $1/2$ mile and continues upstream, past Olaine Lake, to the junction with the Shadow Creek Trail after $1^1/4$ miles. The River Trail continues upstream another 2 miles to the junction with the Agnew Pass Trail, and the River Trail meets the Garnet Lake Trail $1/2$ mile beyond this junction. The River Trail continues upstream another 1 mile from this junction to meet the Pacific Crest Trail west of Badger Lakes.

Shadow Creek Trail ($1^1/2$ and 2 miles)

This trail includes a 1-mile section of the John Muir Trail, so the total distance from the Middle Fork to Ediza Lake is $4^1/2$ miles. The Shadow Creek Trail leaves the River Trail, crosses the Middle Fork on a bridge, and makes a steep ascent near the falls of Shadow Creek. The trail emerges though a rocky gap with a spectacular view of Mt. Ritter and Banner Peak. The trail passes the northern shore of Shadow Lake, where camping and campfires are prohibited. After $1^1/2$ miles from the Middle Fork, the Shadow Creek Trail meets the John Muir Trail near the upper end of Shadow Lake.

The John Muir Trail goes up Shadow Creek for 1 mile to where the upper section of the Shadow Creek Trail branches off to the left. The Shadow Creek Trail goes upstream another 2 miles, passing though some beautiful forests and meadows (with fantastic views of the Minarets along the way) to Ediza Lake, a charming lake in the middle of one of the High Sierra's most scenic areas. Wood campfires are prohibited at Ediza Lake, and camping is prohibited along Ediza Lake's eastern and southern shores.

Garnet Lake Trail (1 mile)

The Garnet Lake Trail leaves the River Trail $1/2$ mile upstream from the junction of the Agnew Pass Trail and the River Trail. It makes a steep ascent of the southern bank of the outlet stream of Garnet Lake and meets the John Muir Trail at the lake. Camping and campfires are prohibited along the eastern side of Garnet Lake.

Rush Creek Trail ($9^1/4$ miles)

This trail starts from the northern end of Silver Lake, along the June Lake Loop (High-

way 158). The trail goes south, up and across the cliff above Silver Lake, for $2^1/4$ miles to the junction with the Agnew Pass Trail just below Agnew Lake. The Rush Creek Trail ascends from the north side of Agnew Lake and contours around the north shore of Gem Lake for another $2^1/2$ miles to the junction with the Parker Pass Trail at the northwest corner of Gem Lake. The Rush Creek Trail turns south, climbs over a small saddle, and meets the side trail leading to Clark Lakes after $3/4$ mile. The main trail remains on the north bank of Rush Creek for $1^1/4$ miles to meet a side trail that leads south, across the creek, to Weber Lake. The Rush Creek Trail continues upstream, goes around the northern shore of Waugh Lake, and arrives at the junction with the John Muir Trail after $2^1/2$ miles.

Clark Lakes Trail ($2^3/4$ miles)

The Clark Lakes Trail leaves the Rush Creek Trail above Gem Lake, along Rush Creek. The trail crosses Rush Creek and ascends to the southwest for $1^3/4$ miles to Clark Lakes. The Agnew Pass Trail is a short distance to the east; the Clark Lakes Trail goes south before turning southwest and crossing the Sierra crest west of Agnew Pass. The trail continues west to meet the Pacific Crest Trail, 1 mile from Clark Lakes.

Agnew Pass Trail ($4^1/2$ miles)

This trail leaves the Rush Creek Trail below Agnew Lake and crosses Rush Creek on a bridge. The trail zigzags up a steep slope to Spooky Meadow, a scenic spot surrounded by red and black volcanic cliffs. The trail continues southwest to Clark Lakes, $2^3/4$ miles from Agnew Lake. The Clark Lakes Trail is a short distance to the west. The Agnew Pass Trail goes south, up and over Agnew Pass, to picturesque Summit Lake, $1/2$ mile from Clark Lakes. A side trail heads southeast from here to join the Pacific Crest Trail (or High Trail). The Agnew Pass Trail descends another $1/4$ mile to where it crosses the Pacific Crest Trail and continues downhill another 1 mile to the River Trail.

Parker Pass Trail ($12^3/4$ miles)

The Parker Pass Trail leaves the Rush Creek Trail at the northwestern end of Gem Lake, climbs to the northwest over Gem Pass, and heads down to Alger Lakes after

3½ miles. The trail continues northwest from Alger Lakes, switchbacks up to the summit of Koip Peak Pass, traverses across the north side of Parker Peak, and descends to the small basin to the north. The trail then climbs to Parker Pass and descends to meet a side trail that leads north to the Mono Pass Trail, 7 miles from Alger Lakes. The Parker Pass Trail continues west from the junction to Parker Pass Creek, and turns north to meet the Mono Pass Trail after another 2 miles.

Parker Lake Trail (1¾ miles)

This trail leads from the trailhead at the end of Parker Creek Road to Parker Lake. It remains on the southeastern bank of the creek.

Mono Pass Trail (9 miles)

The trailhead for this trail is at Dana Meadows, along the Tioga Pass Road east of Tuolumne Meadows. The trail goes southwest across some lovely meadows for 2¾ miles to the junction with the Parker Pass Trail. The Mono Pass Trail begins a slight climb, passes a side trail that leads south to the Parker Pass Trail, and gains the summit of Mono Pass (north). The trail descends the east side of the pass, goes past Sardine Lakes, and enters Bloody Canyon. The trail forks just above Walker Lake; take the right fork and make a steep climb to the trailhead at Sawmill Canyon.

Gibbs Lake Trail (4 miles)

The Gibbs Lake Trail leads from the end of the Horse Meadow Road to Gibbs Lake. The upper portion of the Horse Meadow Road requires a four-wheel-drive vehicle. Ordinary passenger cars can go as far as Lower Horse Meadow; this adds about 1½ miles of hiking.

Glacier Canyon Trail (2½ miles)

The approach for this trail starts from a turnout west of Tioga Lake along the Tioga Pass Road. A good use trail leads down, across the inlet of Tioga Lake, and up the south bank of the stream draining Glacier Canyon. Continue up the canyon to Dana Lake. There is an impressive view of Mt. Dana and its glacier from the lake.

Cross-Country Routes

"Nancy Pass"

(3100 m+; 10,160 ft+; 0.4 mi N of Superior Lake)

Class 2. This pass leads between King Creek and Minaret Creek. Go north from Superior Lake to the low saddle east of Peak 3345m (10,640 ft+). Loose talus on the north side of the pass leads down to the Minaret Creek drainage. Further reading: Steve Roper, *Timberline Country,* Sierra Club Books, San Francisco, 1982, pp. 223–24.

"Deadhorse Pass"

(2960 m+; 9,760 ft+; 0.5 mi E of Deadhorse Lake)

Class 1. This pass is usually used in combination with Nancy Pass while traveling between Beck Lakes and Minaret Lake. Make a gradual descending traverse to the northwest from the summit of Nancy Pass to the base of the small saddle west of Peak 3004m (9,933 ft). Climb to the top of the pass and hike north across some beautiful meadows to Minaret Lake. Further reading: Steve Roper, *Timberline Country,* Sierra Club Books, San Francisco, 1982, pp. 223–24.

"Beck Lakes Pass"

(3280 m+; 10,800 ft+; 0.5 mi NW of upper Beck Lake)

Class 2. Talus and seasonal snow slopes lead from Beck Lakes to the summit of this pass. It is best to traverse north about 1 mile from the pass before descending the north fork of Iron Creek.

"McDonald Pass"

(3240 m+; 10,560 ft+; 0.5 mi NE of Shellenberger Lake)

Class 2. This pass leads between the upper north fork of Iron Creek and the upper portion of Dike Creek. It has been named here in honor of Rob Roy and Doug McDonald, who missed out on the first ascent of Pridham Minaret by a matter of days.

"South Notch"

(3440 m+; 11,280 ft+; 0.5 mi SW of Cecile Lake; UTM 086696)

Class 2; ice axe required. This pass is between Ken Minaret and Kehrlein Minaret. It is commonly used to approach the hard-to-get-to west side of the Minarets, and for climbs of Michael Minaret and Adams Minaret from Minaret Lake. Ascend snow and talus above the southern shore of Cecile Lake to the prominent pass that is to the left (southeast) of the east face of Ken Minaret. From the top of the pass, traverse into Minaret Amphitheater and climb over the notch between Michael Minaret and Adams Minaret. Descend the class 3 chute on the west side of the notch to the base of Michael Minaret. Another route is much longer but easier: Traverse around the southern and western sides of Adams Minaret to the base of Michael Minaret. Care must be taken when crossing the west spur of Adams Minaret to ensure that the easiest route is selected.

"North Notch"
(3480 m+; 11,520 ft+; 0.6 mi SW of Iceberg Lake; UTM 077708)

Class 3. This pass is used to approach the western side of the Minarets from Ediza Lake and Iceberg Lake. Climb onto the ridge that is northwest of Iceberg Lake and follow it to the chute that leads to the low point between Jensen Minaret and Dyer Minaret. There is a curving ledge that leads from the north into the chute. One small chockstone is encountered in the chute before reaching the notch. The west side of North Notch is composed of steep talus (as is the western side of the Minarets). Steep snow and ice may exist on North Notch until late in the season, and an ice axe may be needed.

"The Gap"
(3380 m+; 11,120 ft+; 0.7 mi W of Iceberg Lake; UTM 075711)

Class 2; ice axe required. This pass is between Waller Minaret and Leonard Minaret. Climb onto the small glacier north of the pass and cross it to the summit of the pass. The south side of the pass consists of steep talus.

Ritter Pass
(3380 m+; 11,120 ft+; 1.2 mi SSE of Mt. Ritter; UTM 068714)

Class 2. This is the easiest route across the Minarets. Head southwest from Ediza Lake and climb the small cliff to the base of the pass. The correct pass is to the right (north-

west); a gentle snowfield leads to its summit. Easy, rocky slopes are found on the southwest side of the pass.

"Volcanic Pass"
(3220 m+; 10,560 ft+; 0.9 mi SE of Ediza Lake)

Class 2. This pass leads between Minaret Creek and Shadow Creek. Leave the Minaret Lake Trail at the large meadow bench beneath Minaret Lake and ascend the side trail that leads north to the abandoned Minaret Mine. Continue hiking cross-country from the mine to the lowest pass atop Volcanic Ridge. Loose rock on the north side of the pass leads down to Cabin Lake; follow the outlet stream to the Shadow Creek Trail.

Minaret Lake to Ediza Lake

Class 2–3. This may be the most popular cross-country route in the High Sierra. It traverses interesting terrain, and has outstanding close-up views of the Minarets. A good use trail has formed over most of this route.

Circle around Minaret Lake on its northern shore and climb up along the north bank of the stream that enters the lake from the west. The stream makes a dogleg turn to the southwest; leave the stream at this point and ascend a steep, narrow slot (class 2–3) to the eastern shore of Cecile Lake. Circle around Cecile Lake on its east and north shores to its outlet. Descend diagonally to the northeast, aiming for the far shore of Iceberg Lake; a semipermanent snowfield is usually encountered along this section, and ice axes may be needed. Follow the east bank of the outlet stream of Iceberg Lake down to Ediza Lake. Wood campfires are prohibited all along this route, and camping is prohibited along the southern and eastern shores of Ediza Lake. Further reading: Steve Roper, *Timberline Country*, Sierra Club Books, San Francisco, 1982, pp. 225–26.

"Whitebark Pass"
(3200 m+; 10,480 ft+; 1.0 mi E of Banner Peak)

Class 2. This pass leads between Nydiver Lakes and Garnet Lake. The south side of the pass is easy, but the north side consists of steep, loose scree and talus, with seasonal snowfields. The easiest route on the north side generally goes northeast from the summit of the pass, bypassing snowfields. Further reading: Steve Roper, *Timberline Country*, Sierra Club Books, San Francisco, 1982, pp. 227–28.

"Ritter–Banner Saddle"
(3660 m+; 12,000 ft+; 0.3 mi NNE of Mt. Ritter)

Class 3; ice axe required. From Ediza Lake, climb to the base of the cliff that is east of the saddle. Climb the cliff, keeping to the right of the black watermarks by zigzagging up class 3 ledges. Ascend snow to the low point of the saddle, and descend the glacier on the northwest side of the saddle to Lake Catherine.

"Garnet Pass"
(3080 m+; 10,080 ft+; 0.9 mi NE of Banner Peak)

Class 1. This is an easy cross-country route between Thousand Island Lake and Garnet Lake.

North Glacier Pass
(3400 m+; 10,080 ft+; 0.9 mi NE of Banner Peak)

Class 2. This pass leads from Thousand Island Lake to Lake Catherine. Head southwest from Thousand Island Lake to the low saddle between Banner Peak and Mt. Davis. The final approach to the top of the pass is best made from the northwest. Lake Catherine is a short distance southwest of the pass. Circle Lake Catherine on its north and west shores and descend to the North Fork of the San Joaquin River by keeping on the north bank of the stream that drains Ritter Lakes.

"Clinch Pass"
(3500 m+; 11,520 ft+; 0.8 mi NW of Mt. Davis)

Class 2. This pass, named in honor of Nick Clinch, provides access between upper Rush Creek and the North Fork of the San Joaquin River. It is best to climb to the pass directly from Rodgers Lakes. The south side of the pass consists of steep talus.

"Lost Lakes Pass"
(11,440 ft+; 11,360 ft+; 0.8 mi W of Blacktop Peak)

Class 1. This pass provides access from Rush Creek to the unnamed lakes at the head of Kuna Creek. Gentle slopes lead from the vicinity of Waugh Lake to the basin that

contains Lost Lakes. Continue north in the basin to the summit of the pass, keeping to the east of the small dome on top of the pass. Sand and granite benches lead down the north side of the pass to the lakes that are west of Koip Crest.

"Kuna Crest Saddle"
(11,812 ft; 11,960 ft+; 1.5 mi NW of Kuna Peak)

Class 2. This pass leads from the Parker Pass Trail over Kuna Crest to the numerous small lakes in the upper reaches of Kuna Creek. Leave the Parker Pass Trail where a good use trail leads to Spillway Lake. From the southern shore of Spillway Lake, follow its inlet stream uphill to the eastern shore of Helen Lake. Head southwest from the lake toward the low saddle atop the Kuna Crest. Talus and sand are encountered on the north side of the saddle, and snowfields can be avoided by keeping to their right. Easier terrain on the southwest side of the pass eventually leads south around a small ridge to the lakes in the cirque at the head of Kuna Creek.

Peaks

Iron Mountain *(3318 m; 11,149 ft)*

South Slope. Class 1. A trail leads north from Corral Meadow (on the Mammoth Trail) to Iron Lake. Climb onto the ridge south of the lake and follow it to the summit.

East Slope. Class 2. First ascent July 17, 1988, by Vi Grasso, Delores Holladay, and Barbara Reber. Climb benches above Anona Lake to the prominent gap between two knobs on top of the face. Pass through the knobs and follow the southern side of the southeast ridge to the summit.

Northeast Couloir. Class 2; ice axe required. First ascent August 2, 1935, by Jules Eichorn. Pass Ashley Lake on its west shore and climb the couloir that gradually steepens near its top. Much of the snow can be avoided by keeping to the rocks on its right side. It is class 1 from the top of the couloir to the summit.

"The Watchtower"
(3420 m+; 11,200 ft+; 0.5 mi SW of Deadhorse Lake; UTM 091683)

This peak has also been called "Crown Prince Spire." The east face (II, 5.5) was climbed in August 1974 by Rupert

Kammerlander and John Schaffert. The north face (II, 5.6) was first climbed July 16, 1978, by Kim Grandfield and Amadeo Tagliapietra.

"Starr Minaret"
(3506 m; 11,512 ft; 0.4 mi W of Deadhorse Lake)

Northwest Slope. Class 2. First ascent July 14, 1937, by Walter A. Starr, Sr., Ansel Adams, and Rondal Partridge. This slope can be reached from South Notch.

Sleeping Beauty Chimney. III, 5.9. First ascent August 1974 by Rupert Kammerlander and John Schaffert. Ascend the 700-foot chimney on the south face.

East Face. Class 5. First ascent September 1960 by Chuck Wilts and Ray Van Aken. Climb to the cirque between Starr and Kehrlein minarets from Deadhorse Lake. Ascend the east face, which is mostly class 3 with a few class 4 pitches. The summit pitch is class 5.

"Riegelhuth Minaret"
(3260 m+; 10,560 ft+; 0.2 mi S of Minaret Lake; UTM 097694)

West Face. Class 4. First ascent July 13, 1938, by Jack Riegelhuth, Charlotte Mauk, Josephine Allen, and Bill Leovoy. Climb to the saddle between Riegelhuth and Pridham minarets from Minaret Lake, and ascend a class 4 trough up the west face to the summit.

North Prow. III, 5.7. First ascent August 15, 1980, by Adam Paul and Scott Martin. This prow drops down to Minaret Lake from the summit. The first pitch (5.7) is followed by 200 to 300 feet of class 3 to 4 climbing. The crux pitch steepens considerably from here, leading over poor-quality rock (5.7) to the base of the large dihedrals atop the prow. Bypass these dihedrals to their right and then climb up for two pitches over extremely loose rock (5.6). Approximately 200 feet of class 3–4 climbing then leads to the summit.

Northeast Face. Class 4. First ascent Au-

The Minarets from Volcanic Ridge (photo by Pete Yamagata)

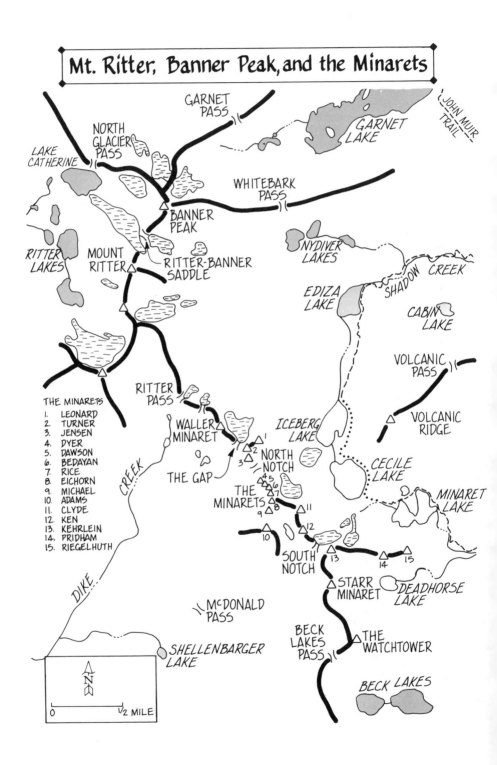

Mt. Ritter, Banner Peak, and the Minarets

GARNET PASS

JOHN MUIR TRAIL

GARNET LAKE

NORTH GLACIER PASS

LAKE CATHERINE

WHITEBARK PASS

BANNER PEAK

NYDIVER LAKES

SHADOW CREEK

RITTER LAKES

MOUNT RITTER

RITTER-BANNER SADDLE

EDIZA LAKE

CABIN LAKE

VOLCANIC PASS

RITTER PASS

THE MINARETS
1. LEONARD
2. TURNER
3. JENSEN
4. DYER
5. DAWSON
6. BEDAYAN
7. RICE
8. EICHORN
9. MICHAEL
10. ADAMS
11. CLYDE
12. KEN
13. KEHRLEIN
14. PRIDHAM
15. RIEGELHUTH

WALLER MINARET

ICEBERG LAKE

VOLCANIC RIDGE

THE GAP

NORTH NOTCH

THE MINARETS

CECILE LAKE

MINARET LAKE

CREEK

SOUTH NOTCH

STARR MINARET

DEADHORSE LAKE

DIKE

McDONALD PASS

BECK LAKES PASS

THE WATCHTOWER

SHELLENBARGER LAKE

N

BECK LAKES

0   ½ MILE

gust 6, 1955, by David Tonkin and Lito Tejada-Flores. Climb toward a prominent gully that leads up and to the left. Follow this gully to a notch on the east ridge, and follow the ridge to the summit. This is a ten-pitch climb. *Variation:* Leave the gully about 200 feet below the east ridge and climb a 5.5 wall directly to the summit.

East Face. I, 5.6. First ascent August 1973, by Gilles Corcos and Steve Roper. Wander up the broad east face, following the line of least resistance.

"Pridham Minaret"
(3340 m+; 10,960 ft+; 0.2 mi N of Deadhorse Lake; UTM 094695)

East Ridge. Class 2. First ascent July 4, 1938, by May Pridham and Mary Van Velsen. Follow the ridge from the saddle between Riegelhuth and Pridham minarets.

"Kehrlein Minaret"
(3540 m+; 11,440 ft+; 0.4 mi SSW of Cecile Lake; UTM 087696)

A party led by Oliver Kehrlein made the second ascent of this minaret, and it has been named after him to avoid confusion. The west summit is the high point.

West Ridge. Class 4. First ascent August 23, 1933, by Norman Clyde. Climb the southern side of the west ridge before crossing to the north. Traverse across a slab leading up onto the northwest face. Climb this face, and work left, staying on the north side of the west ridge to the summit.

North Face. Class 4. First ascent August 1941 by Fred Hudson and R. Olson. Climb over broken ledges on the north face to the summit.

East Ridge. Class 5 with rappels. First ascent September 3, 1961, by Chuck Wilts and Ray Van Aken. This climb starts from the notch between Kehrlein and Pridham minarets. This notch can be reached by climbing over Pridham Minaret or directly from the south; either way is class 2. This long ridge is class 2, 3, 4, 5, with some rappels. Generally, the route is class 4–5 on the faces of the many steps on the ridge, and some rappels are needed to descend the west side of towers along the ridge. Descend the northern side of the east summit and traverse across the north face below the small spire between the east

and west summits. Climb to the notch between the spire and the higher, west summit by means of a difficult class 5 pitch.

"South Notch Minaret"
This small spire is just north of South Notch. The northwest face is class 5, and was first climbed in 1959 by Ray Van Aken and Ernest Bauer.

"Ken Minaret"
(3620 m+; 11,760 ft+; 0.5 mi SW of Cecile Lake; UTM 084699)

The northwest peak is the high point.

Northeast Face. Class 4–5. First ascent September 5, 1938, by Kenneth Davis and Kenneth Adam. Ascend the left branch of the couloir between Ken and Clyde minarets for a few hundred feet. Climb onto the face that is left of the couloir and to the right of the crest of the large rib that descends from Ken Minaret's summit. Approach the summit rocks from the north and climb a short class 4–5 crack to reach the summit.

Southeast Ridge. Class 5. First ascent September 1958 by Chuck Wilts, Ellen Wilts, and Ray Van Aken. Climb the west side of the ridge rising from South Notch, aiming for the notch just north of a prominent tower. Bypass the notch, and continue climbing the west side of the ridge for several leads to the top of the wall above the notch. Turn this first step on its east side (class 5). Continue following the crest of the ridge to the tower beneath the next step, which is a big one. Rappel from the tower into another notch, and traverse and then climb (class 5) to the top of this big step. Continue up the ridge to the summit.

Southwest Face. Class 3–4. Descended September 5, 1938, by Kenneth Davis and Kenneth Adam. The summit rocks are difficult.

"Adams Minaret"
(3640 m+; 12,000 ft+; UTM 079699)

First ascent July 15, 1937, by Ansel Adams and Rondal C. Partridge. This peak is class 3 from the notch between it and Michael Minaret.

"Clyde Minaret"
(3738 m; 12,281 ft; UTM 083702)

Central Chute. I, 5.2. First ascent September 24, 1984, by Dale Van Dalsem, Elden Hughes, and J. C. Eckert. Climb to an area of red rock in the cirque above Cecile Lake. Move up and right over the red rock to a wide ledge that runs across the face of Clyde Minaret. On the face above this ledge there are two ribs that separate three chutes. Climb the central chute; this consists of class 3 followed by one technical pitch (5.2), a class 4 pitch, and class 3 to the summit.

Starr's Route. Class 4. First ascent August 8, 1932, by Walter A. Starr, Jr. This route climbs the right-hand chute on the northeast face of Clyde Minaret. Climb onto the ledge that runs across the northeast face of Clyde Minaret from the area of red rock to the east of the peak. Ascend the right-hand chute from the ledge, keeping to the left of a prominent gendarme. Climb above the level of the gendarme to the shallow rib and chute that lead to the crest of the ridge connecting Clyde Minaret with Eichorn Minaret. Follow the ridge left (southeast) to the summit of Clyde Minaret. A short class 4 move is encountered along this ridge.

Rock Route. Class 4. First ascent July 26, 1929, by Glen Dawson, John Nixon, and William Horsfall. This is the easiest route on Clyde Minaret, and is preferred by many over the other routes on the northeast face. Follow the ledge across the northeast face of Clyde Minaret to its western end, where it drops down to the glacier. Just before this drop-off, the ledge crosses a steep chute that goes up toward the summit. Climb this chute, keeping to the right of a prominent gendarme, and follow the face and rib to the crest of the ridge above. Follow the ridge left (southeast), and climb down a 10-foot class 4 move along the ridge before reaching the summit. *Variation:* The ledge that runs across the northeast face of Clyde Minaret can be reached from the base of the face. Climb up and left to gain the ledge about 300 feet to the left (southeast) of the chute for the Rock Route. *Variation:* The ledge described in the previous variation can also be reached from the glacier to the north of Clyde Minaret. Climb the far left side of the glacier and ascend the moat to the ledge. *Variation:* The chute of the Rock Route crosses the ledge, and it is possible to climb the chute directly from its very bottom. The lower portion of the chute is actually a steep, difficult (5.5) chimney, however, and it is better to approach the chute from the ledge.

Descent of the Rock Route. Follow the ridge toward Eichorn Minaret from the summit of Clyde Minaret, and make a 10-foot class 4 move along the ridge. Climb to the crest of the ridge, and look down the north side of Clyde Minaret. Descend the north side, aiming for the chute that is left of a prominent gendarme and right of a shallow rib, as seen looking downward. This chute leads to a ledge that runs across the northeast face of Clyde Minaret. The ledge ends in an area of red rock, which is descended to where it is possible to make a descending traverse to the right to the base of the east face and southeast face of Clyde Minaret.

Glacier Route. Class 4. First ascent June 27, 1928, by Norman Clyde. Climb to the highest left-hand edge of the glacier north of Clyde Minaret. Cross the bergschrund and make a left-diagonal ascent across some shallow ribs and chutes to the ridge between Eichorn and Clyde minarets. Follow the ridge toward Clyde Minaret. A short class 4 move is encountered just before the summit.

Traverse from Eichorn Minaret. Class 4. First ascent July 31, 1931, by Jules Eichorn, Walter Brem, and Glen Dawson. Descend approximately 50 feet southwest from the summit of Eichorn Minaret to a ledge that runs across the southern side of the ridge leading to Clyde Minaret. Follow the ledge and ridge to the summit of Clyde Minaret. Most of this traverse is class 3.

Southwest Face. Class 4. First ascent unknown; first winter ascent January 2, 1948, by Bill Long, Jim Wilson, and Allen Steck. Go east from the north end of Amphitheater Lake to a point that is near the notch between Clyde and Ken minarets. Ledges lead left (northwest) to a gully that goes up to the top of the ridge between Clyde and Eichorn minarets. Follow the ridge to the summit of Clyde Minaret. *Variation:* Class 4. First ascent July 22, 1973, by Doug DeWolf and Frank Meyers. Ascend an easy chute from near the notch between Clyde and Ken minarets. Traverse to the right at the point where this chute suddenly steepens into the next chute. This next chute drops out onto the southeast face of Clyde Minaret. Ascend this chute to the ridge between Clyde and Eichorn minarets, and follow the ridge to the summit of Clyde Minaret.

Clyde–Ken Couloir. Class 4–5. Descended August 16, 1933, by Jules Eichorn, Glen Dawson, and Richard Jones. A huge chockstone is encountered when this couloir is climbed from the east. Pass the chockstone on its right side. Continue up the couloir to the Clyde–Ken notch, and follow ledges on the southwest side of Clyde Minaret to a chute that leads up to the ridge between Eichorn and Clyde minarets. Follow the ridge to the summit of Clyde Minaret.

Clyde–Ken Couloir Descent Route. This is commonly used as a descent route following climbs of the southeast face of Clyde Minaret. Follow the ridge from Clyde Minaret toward Eichorn Minaret to the second gully that leads down to the south; this gully is close to the low point of the ridge between Clyde and Eichorn minarets. Descend the gully to some ledges that lead southeast to the Clyde–Ken notch. Descend the east side of the couloir to the chockstone. A short

rappel from the right side (looking down) of the chockstone leads to the base of the southeast face. If there is much snow present in the couloir, and if it is late in the day, you may need either ice axes and crampons, or bivouac gear.

Southeast Edge. IV, 5.9. First ascent June 28, 1986, by Joel Richnik and Mike Carville. This route follows the right side of the far left-hand outside corner of the southeast face. Climb a series of shallow corners followed by an off-width crack. Continue up a face on ledges, and move slightly right and then left to the bottom of a right-facing open book. From the top of the book, go up and follow the right side of the ridge to the summit.

Southeast Face. IV, 5.8. First ascent June 22, 1963, by John Evans, Dick Long, Allen Steck, and Chuck Wilts. First winter ascent

Clyde Minaret from the east, September 2, 1965 (photo by Austin Post, #F655-189, USGS Ice and Climate Project, Tacoma, WA)

February 1980 by Galen Rowell and Kim Schmitz. This route is justifiably popular. Ascend the Clyde–Ken Couloir until ap-proximately level with the toe of the large buttress that descends the northeast face of Ken Minaret. Make a horizontal 125-foot

Clyde Minaret, Northeast Face (photo by Pete Yamagata)

traverse (5.6) to the right to an obvious ledge that is visible on the right skyline from the correct start of this, the first, pitch. Climb up and slightly right for four pitches (nothing harder than 5.7) from this ledge, aiming for a large ledge that is left of the bottom of a shallow, left-facing dihedral. An easy, slightly descending traverse to the right with hidden holds leads to the bottom of the dihedral. Ascend the dihedral (5.8) to a small belay alcove. Climb up and slightly right from the alcove, passing a prominent white scar on its left side, and then climb up and slightly left, mantling over blocks (5.8) to a large ledge at the bottom of the most prominent dihedral on the face. Ascend 90 feet in the dihedral to a belay ledge. An improbable traverse left for 50 feet is followed by 100 feet of 5.6 straight up (with some loose blocks) to a ledge. Another 150-foot pitch of 5.7 leads to the top of the face. Traverse left over class 4 rock to the southeast edge, and follow the right side of the southeast edge to the summit. *Variation:* The improbable traverse can be avoided by continuing up the dihedral for one pitch (5.8) over some big, loose blocks. Further reading: Steve Roper and Allen Steck, *Fifty Classic Climbs of North America*, Sierra Club Books, San Francisco, 1979, pp. 288–93; *Summit,* January – February 1971, pp. 11–13; *Summit*, March–April 1987, p. 19.

East Ridge. III, 5.7. First ascent June 15, 1970, by Marek Glogoczowski and Bill Katra. This route apparently follows the crest of the ridge formed by the junction of the southeast face and northeast face.

"Michael Minaret"

(3736 m; 12,240 ft+; UTM 078701)

Michael's Chute. Class 4–5. First ascent September 6, 1923, by Charles W. Michael. This is the right-hand chute of the two chutes that lead up the west side of Michael Minaret to the notch just north of the minaret. The third chockstone in this chute is passed by climbing the wall to its right; start climbing about 30 feet below the chockstone and climb the wall to a ledge. Traverse left on the ledge back into the chute, and follow the chute to the notch, the Portal. Climb underneath the boulder that forms the Portal, traverse left (southeast), and then zigzag up over ledges. The final approach to the summit follows a ledge on the west side of the summit spire. *Variation: The Ladder With the Lower Rungs Missing*. Class 5. This small

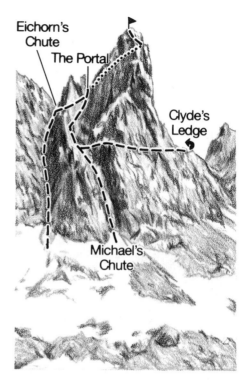

Michael Minaret from the west

variation climbs the wall immediately right of the third chockstone in Michael's Chute. Strenuous climbing leads up the wall and back into the chute above the chockstone. Further reading: *Sierra Club Bulletin*, 1924, pp. 28–33.

Eichorn's Chute. Class 4. First ascent August 16, 1933, by Jules Eichorn, Glen Dawson, and Richard Jones. This is the first chute north of Michael's Chute. Traverse right from the top of the chute over into Michael's Chute, under two small spires, and to the Portal. Continue to the top of Michael Minaret as described under Michael's Chute.

Starr's Chute. Class 4. First ascent August 3, 1933, by Walter A. Starr, Jr.; this was Starr's last climb. First winter ascent December 29, 1963, by Dick Long, Jim Wilson, George Bloom, and George Marks. This is probably the best route up Michael Minaret. Ascend the second chute north of Michael's Chute, and follow its right branch at a point about 300 feet beneath the ridge crest. This chute leads up the south side of Eichorn

Minaret. Traverse right near the top of the chute to the head of Eichorn's Chute, and continue to the summit of Michael Minaret as described under the Eichorn's Chute and Michael's Chute routes.

Amphitheater Chute. I, 5.4. First ascent August 31, 1958, by Mike Sherrick and Wally Tinsley. This is the prominent chute that leads to the notch between Michael and Eichorn minarets from Amphitheater Lake. The chute leads up from the north end of the lake, and the right side of the chute is followed to the top. The crux of this route is at the first chockstone; a poorly protected move goes around its right side. Higher, a second chockstone is passed by traversing out about 50 feet to the right. From the top of the notch work down and west to the Portal, and continue to the summit via the description for Michael's Chute.

South Face. III, 5.7, A1. First ascent August 13, 1962, by John Dorsey, George Steck, and Allen Steck. This route starts from the notch between Adams and Michael minarets. Ascend an obvious chimney system for three pitches, followed by two pitches up and right toward a small notch in the southeast ridge. Two class 4 pitches then lead to the summit. The first-ascent party used only one aid placement.

Clyde's Ledge. Class 4. First ascent August 25, 1933, by Norman Clyde. Ascend the west face of Michael Minaret to a sloping ledge that leads left (north) into Michael's Chute, above the level of the third chockstone in that chute. Continue up Michael's Chute to the Portal, and on to the summit as in the description for Michael's Chute.

"Eichorn Minaret"
(3120 m+; 12,255 ft; UTM 079703)

First ascent July 31, 1931, by Jules Eichorn, Glen Dawson, and Walter Brem. Eichorn Minaret is class 4 from Clyde Minaret: Follow the ridge from Clyde Minaret to where it is possible to descend the southern side of the ridge to a ledge that leads to a point about 50 feet southwest of Eichorn Minaret. A short class 4 pitch leads to the summit.

Eichorn Minaret can also be climbed from the Portal on Michael Minaret. Pass through the Portal, and climb to the notch between Michael and Eichorn minarets. Eichorn Minaret is class 3, with one short class 4 pitch from the notch.

The northeast face is class 4 and was first climbed in 1955 by Jim Gorin and party.

"Rice Minaret"
(3720 m+; 12,160 ft+; UTM 079704)

Starr's Chute. Class 4. First ascent August 11, 1936, by William Rice and Torcom Bedayan. Ascend Starr's Chute on Michael Minaret, but take the left branch instead of the right. Rice Minaret is north of the head of the left branch of the chute.

Traverse from Bedayan Minaret. Class 3. First ascent August 11, 1936, by William Rice and Torcom Bedayan. This traverse is made on the west side of Rice Minaret.

Eichorn–Rice Couloir. Class 5. First ascent September 1965 by Rich Gnagy and Barbara Lilley. Climb this couloir from the east; the hardest climbing is in the upper portion of the couloir, just below the notch. Climb the first chute left (west) from the notch to a small wall, which is climbed on its right side. This is followed by an open book, which leads to the summit ridge.

"Bedayan Minaret"
(3680 m+; 12,080 ft+; UTM 079705)

Northwest Chute. Class 4. First ascent August 25, 1950, by L. Bruce Meyer and Hervey Voge. This chute leads to the notch north of Bedayan Minaret. Enter the chute from its right (south) side on a ledge, and climb the chute until you are approximately 300 feet below its top. Traverse to the right into the next chute to the south, and climb the minaret via its south face.

East Couloir. This is the couloir that leads to the Bedayan–Dawson notch. This couloir of full of dangerous, loose blocks!

Northeast Face. Class 5. First ascent July 6, 1963, by Rich Gnagy and Barbara Lilley. This route starts from the high point of the glacier, left of the east couloir. Climb up and slightly left over a series of ledges. A short traverse left and up leads to a sloping ledge, which is followed left to a watercourse. Ascend the right side of the watercourse for two pitches to a steep, seasonal snowfield. Above the snowfield, 300 feet of class 3 and 4 lead to the summit ridge, which is followed west to the summit.

Traverse from Rice Minaret. Class 3. First ascent August 11, 1936, by Torcom Bedayan and William Rice. Most of this traverse is done on the west side of the ridge.

"Dawson Minaret"

(3540 m+; 11,920 ft+; UTM 078706)

From North Notch. Class 4. First ascent August 16, 1933, by Glen Dawson, Jules Eichorn, and Richard Jones. Traverse around Dyer Minaret on its west side from North Notch. Enter the next chute to the south. Climb directly toward the summit of Dawson Minaret over a broken face, working gradually to the right to a ledge on the ridge. Traverse around to the south side of the minaret, and climb an open chimney to the summit.

The south face of Dawson Minaret can also be reached from the west by climbing the chute directly under this broken face; bypass the chockstone in the chute on its left side.

Bedayan–Dawson Chute. Class 4. Climb to the Bedayan–Dawson notch from the west. A chockstone in this chute is bypassed on its left side. An open chimney on the face of Dawson Minaret leads to the summit.

"Dyer Minaret"

(3550 m+; 11,680 ft+; UTM 077707)

Northwest Face. I, 5.6. First ascent 1948 by John Dyer and William Horsfall. Climb to a small notch on the west side of this minaret from North Notch. One pitch up the northwest face leads to the summit.

East Face. I, 5.7. First ascent August 1962 by John Dorsey and Allen Steck. Traverse south from North Notch to the base of the east ridge. One pitch from a large sloping ledge leads to a belay ledge on the east face. One more pitch up the east face leads to the summit.

"North Notch Minaret"

This tiny pinnacle is just northeast of Dyer Minaret. It is class 5 from the notch between it and Dyer Minaret. First ascent 1937 by David Brower and Morgan Harris.

"Jensen Minaret"

(3540 m+; 11,760 ft+; UTM 077708)

From North Notch. Class 4. First ascent June 1937 by Carl Jensen and Howard Gates. There is much loose rock on this route.

Northeast Face. I, 5.4. First ascent July 27, 1943, by Chuck Wilts, Dan Bannerman, and Spencer Austin. Traverse beneath the east side of Jensen Minaret from North Notch. There are two chimneys on the northeast face. Climb the right-hand chimney to a

small notch between two small spires on the ridge between Jensen and Turner minarets. Follow the ridge to the top.

"Turner Minaret"

(3547 m; 11,600 ft+; UTM 076709)

Traverse from Jensen Minaret. Class 3. First ascent July 14, 1938, by Ed Turner and party.

East Side. II, 5.4. First ascent September 1972 by Rupert Kammerlander. This route actually starts on Leonard Minaret. Ascend a crack system that is left of a prominent chimney on the lower portion of Leonard Minaret's east face. Continue up and left to a large, curving open book, which leads to the notch that is to the right of Turner Minaret. This notch is marked by a large block; pass the block on its right side and climb up to the notch. Traverse out onto the west face of Turner Minaret from the notch, and climb a 5.4 pitch to the summit ridge.

"Leonard Minaret"

(3520 m+; 11,600 ft+; UTM 078711)

Southeast Rock Chimney. Class 4. First ascent August 4, 1932, by Richard Leonard and Herbert Blanks. There is a prominent chimney, which may be filled with snow, on the southeast side of Leonard Minaret. Climb the less prominent chimney that is to the left of the snow chimney. Climb to a wide ramp that leads to the right. Climb up and left from this ledge to the summit ridge.

South Face. Class 4. First ascent September 3, 1964, by Don Wilson and Bob Weyman. This route is to the left (west) of the southeast rock chimney.

West Ridge. Class 4. First ascent August 19, 1933, by Norman Clyde. Follow the ridge from The Gap (between Waller and Leonard minarets; see the section on cross-country routes earlier in this chapter).

"Waller Minaret"

(3557 m; 11,711 ft; UTM 073703)

West Side. Class 4. Climb the prominent chute on the west side of the minaret that leads to a point about 300 feet north of the summit. Follow the ridge south to the summit. An impasse on this ridge is turned on its right (west) side via a short, steep crack.

Eichorn Route. II, 5.4. First ascent August 1934 by Ted Waller and Jules Eichorn. First winter ascent December 29, 1963, by Dick

Long, Jim Wilson, Dave Beck, and George Bloom. Climb onto the southeast ridge of Waller Minaret from The Gap, and follow a ledge that goes out onto the east face. Follow this ledge for one pitch, and then climb the face, aiming for the arete that rises above the vertical wall of The Gap. Follow the arete north for about 150 feet to a large tower. Climb this by going directly up its center. Scramble over the top of this tower and descend 20 feet down its west side. Traverse around the top of a steep couloir and rib on its west face and climb another tower to the summit ridge.

East Face. III, 5.5. First ascent July 1961 by Dick Long and Bob Hill. This route begins directly beneath the summit, and seven or eight pitches lead to the ridge just south of the summit. A direct variation of this route (III, 5.8) was climbed in August 1971 by Craig Mackay and Rupert Kammerlander.

Volcanic Ridge
(3501 m; 11,501 ft; 0.4 mi E of Iceberg Lake)

First ascent August 13, 1933, by Craig Barbash and Howard Gates. There is an outstanding view from the summit. Go north from Minaret Lake and ascend a long, grassy slope to the saddle that is west of the summit. The north ridge from Ediza Lake is class 2, as is the long ridge from Volcanic Pass.

Peak 3734m
(12,344 ft; 0.9 mi SSW of Mt. Ritter)

This is the craggy peak that is on the long southwest ridge of Mt. Ritter. The first-ascent party named this peak "Neglected Peak," because it was probably one of the last major summits in the High Sierra to be climbed.

South Ridge. I, 5.7. First ascent 1964 by Mike Loughman and Steve Arnon. Follow the south ridge from Slide Creek to the top of a gendarme that overlooks a prominent, deep notch. Make a short, difficult (5.7) descent into a wide chimney on the west side of the gendarme and gain the notch. A steep pitch (5.2) out of the notch leads to the left onto the broken face that is west of the south ridge. Class 4 rock then leads to the top.

The deep notch has also been reached directly from Dike Creek.

"Ritter Pinnacles"
(3780 m+; 12,320 ft+; 0.5 mi SSE of Mt. Ritter)

The highest of these pinnacles is class 3 from the southeast glacier of Mt. Ritter, and

was first climbed August 4, 1936, by Richard M. Jones and William Rice.

Mt. Ritter   *(4006 m; 13,157 ft)*

Southeast Glacier. Class 3. Descended October 1872 by John Muir. Go west from Ediza Lake to the cliff beneath the snout of the glacier that is southeast of Mt. Ritter. Start by climbing slabs to the left of a gully before crossing the head of the gully to reach the left (south) end of a vegetation-covered ledge. This ledge leads diagonally right across the cliff; a few small waterfalls fall upon it from above. The ledge eventually splits. Go up a steep, narrow, grassy ledge before switchbacking up onto another ledge, which leads to the top of the cliff. Skirt the north side of the glacier, and climb a chute that leads to the broad talus slope beneath the summit. *Variation:* Class 3. First ascent June 28, 1928, by Norman Clyde. The cliff beneath the glacier can be passed on its far southern (left) side. Climb toward the lowest pinnacles to the south and pass through the gap above them onto the glacier. Ascend the southern side of the glacier, keeping to the left of an ice ridge, to where a crevasse bars further progress. Cross to the north side of the glacier, over the ice ridge, to the chute that leads to the talus slope and the summit. Ice axes and crampons are almost always needed on this variation.

East Face. Class 4–5. First ascent September 1961 by Nick Clinch and Tom Hornbein. This route is on the far left side of the east face. Ascend a ledge that diagonals right from the north side of the southeast glacier. This ledge leads to the left side of a prominent scar. Continue up the face to the summit.

Northeast Buttress. Class 4. First ascent August 7, 1941, by Art Argiewicz and Lorin Trubschenk. This is the prominent buttress that rises 2,000 feet above the east cirque between Mt. Ritter and Banner Peak. Climb toward the Ritter–Banner Saddle from the east to the top of the cliff that is beneath the saddle. Traverse left from the top of the cliff and climb onto the crest of the buttress. Follow the buttress to the summit.

North Face. Class 3. First ascent October 1872 by John Muir. Climb to the top of the Ritter–Banner Saddle from either the east or west. Ascend the far right (west) chute on the north face of Mt. Ritter. From the top of the right chute, traverse left to a wide ledge that leads up and left to an arete. Follow the arete to the summit. *Variation:* Class 3. First ascent July 3, 1932, by Walter A. Starr, Jr. Traverse right from the top of the right chute over a ridge, and drop down onto and cross the ledges on the northwest side of Mt. Ritter. Ascend the ledges to the summit. *Variation:* Class 3. First ascent July 20, 1986, by Igor Mamedalin, Jim Farkas, Marty Washburn, Tom Scott, Lisa Freundlich, Steve Crooks, Bruce Parker, Suzanne Thomas, and Jim Floyd. The left chute on the north face may be preferable if there is a lack of snow. Further reading: John Muir, *The Mountains of California,* New York, The Century Co., 1917, pp. 52–73.

West Slope. Class 2. First ascent August 20, 1892, by Theodore S. Solomons. First winter ascent February 1952 by George Bloom, Bob Swift, and Floyd Burnette. Go south from Lake Catherine to the southernmost lake of the Ritter Lakes. Follow the eastern shore of this lake toward the south, past the first talus

fan and around a low buttress, to the second talus fan. Ascend this fan (a real slog) to the upper bowl. Traverse right to a chute; be sure to enter the chute about halfway up, and not from its bottom. This chute leads to another talus fan, which leads to another chute. Climb this chute until about you are 50 to 75 feet below its top. Traverse left and up to the top of the summit ridge, which is followed to the summit of Mt. Ritter.

Banner Peak *(3943 m; 12,945 ft)*

From Ritter–Banner Saddle. Class 2. First ascent August 26, 1883, by Willard D. Johnson and John Miller. First winter ascent March 1, 1939, by Chester L. Errett, Bob Brinton, and Lloyd Warner. This route is class 2 from Lake Catherine; a class 3 section is encountered when approaching the saddle from the east. Banner Peak is a talus slog from the saddle.

Southeast Face. Class 5. First ascent July 6,

Mt. Ritter and Banner Peak from the southeast, August 24, 1972 (photo by Austin Post, #72R2-88, USGS Ice and Climate Project, Tacoma, WA)

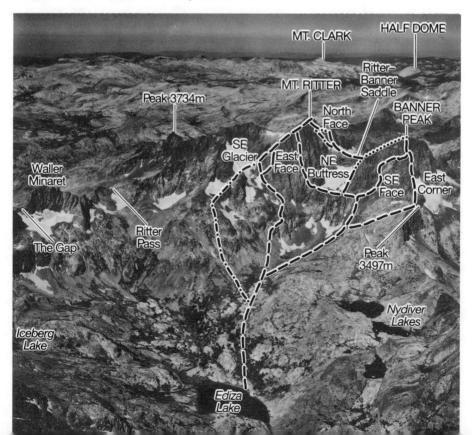

1946, by Charles Wilts and Harry Sutherland. This route, which ascends the middle of the southeast face, is most readily seen from the vicinity of Ediza Lake. Most of the route is class 4; however, two class 5 pitches are encountered. Start by climbing the first couloir to the right of a deep chimney. Ascend easy rock at first, then cross left into another couloir, which branches up from the deep chimney. Ascend diagonally right over almost vertical rock to a large ledge, which usually has a small snow patch. Traverse right about 200 feet from this ledge, then continue straight up to the summit ridge, aiming for a point about 300 feet from the summit. *Variation:* Class 5. First ascent August 17, 1989, by Chris Keith and Pete Lowery. Climb the couloir that branches up from the deep chimney. Climb another chimney to the left of the vertical rock. This second chimney leads to the ridge south of the summit.

East Corner. Class 4. First ascent August 3, 1931, by Jules Eichorn and Robert Underhill. This route starts from the saddle between Banner Peak and Peak 3497m (11,440 ft+; 0.4 mi E of Banner Peak). Ascend a chute (loose rock!) on the left side of the ridge rising from the saddle. It is eventually possible to climb onto the ridge crest and continue up the ridge or buttress until you are stopped by an overhang. Climb up and right for about 80 feet over smooth rock, and follow some broad, steep chutes to the summit.

East Face. III, 5.6. First ascent August 1961 by Allen Steck and Floyd Burnette. Cross the glacier that is northeast of Banner Peak to its highest point. (This high point is in a couloir to the right of a prominent buttress that almost touches the east corner.) Climb the wall about 40 feet to the right of this couloir. Two pitches of 5.6 over steep, blocky rock lead to easier climbing. Climb up and slightly right for three class 4 pitches, and continue climbing an obvious route to the summit ridge, about 200 feet north of the summit. *Variation:* 5.7. Traverse to the right around an arete after the three class 4 pitches. Climb the arete and the wall above to the summit ridge.

East Face, Right Side. III, 5.8. First ascent August 10, 1975, by Kim Grandfield and Arne Myrabo. This route climbs a rib that diagonally ascends from right to left across

and up the east face of Banner Peak. Start climbing about 200 feet to the right of the East Face route on the left side of the left-facing open books. Climb about 200 feet to the crest of a rib. Continue up the rib for ten pitches of class 4 and 5 until you are about 200 feet below the summit ridge. Traverse up and left for two easy pitches to some white watermarks on overhanging rock. A short, difficult pitch straight up leads to the summit ridge. Follow the ridge south to the summit.

Northeast Buttress. III, 5.6. First ascent August 28, 1973, by David Harden and Kevin Sutter. This climb starts from the shoulder that is north of the glacier northeast of Banner Peak. Climb onto the shoulder from the north via two class 4 pitches. Two 5.6 pitches lead up a prominent chute to the left from the shoulder. Approximately 200 feet of scrambling leads to a talus-filled notch on the buttress itself. Three very enjoyable pitches lead from here to the summit ridge.

Northwest Shoulder. Class 4. First ascent August 1950 by Sarah Haynes and Jim Koontz. Ascend the north side of the ridge from North Glacier Pass. The last part of this climb ascends the crest of the northwest ridge.

"Annie's Spire"
(3600 m+; 0.8 mi SE of Mt. Davis; UTM 053753)

First ascent July 12, 1966, by Ann Gibson, Dave Rossum, and Richard Clough. This pinnacle is on the eastern side of the southwest ridge of Mt. Davis. Ascend a snow couloir to the right (north) of the spire from Thousand Island Lake. Climb a 60-foot class 3 crack on the west side of the pinnacle to a ledge. One pitch up a jam crack (5.4) leads straight up to a large ledge on the southwest arete. Climb the arete (5.3) to the summit.

Mt. Davis *(3750 m; 12,311 ft)*
Southeast Slope. Class 2. First ascent August 28, 1891, by Milton F. Davis. Keep to the southwest side of the ridge while climbing the peak from North Glacier Pass.

North Buttress. Class 4. First ascent August 20, 1950, by Jim Koontz and Sarah Haynes. This buttress is between the two glaciers on the north side of Mt. Davis. Start by climbing the west side of the buttress at first, and later move onto the crest of the buttress to reach the summit.

Northeast Buttress. Class 4. First ascent

August 20, 1950, by Hervey Voge and Virginia Romain. This buttress is east of the north buttress, and leads to a lower summit that is southeast of the true summit of Mt. Davis. Ascend the east side of the northeast buttress and climb a chute to the crest of the buttress. Climb the crest of the buttress to the lower peak, and walk up the easy southeast slope to the true summit.

Peak 3597m

(11,627 ft; 0.7 mi NW of Mt. Davis)

    Northwest Arete. Class 4. First ascent September 1975 by Bill Schuler, Andy Smatko,

Banner Peak and Mt. Ritter from the northwest, September 2, 1965 (photo by Austin Post, #F655-188, USGS Ice and Climate Project, Tacoma, WA)

and Tom Ross. Climb the ridge rising from Clinch Pass. Two class 4 pitches along the top of this ridge lead to the summit.

Two Teats *(3460 m+; 11,387 ft)*
The summit rocks are class 3.

San Joaquin Mountain
(3535 m; 11,600 ft)
Class 1 from the northwest or southeast. There is an outstanding view of the Minarets, Mt. Ritter, and Banner Peak from the summit.

Carson Peak *(3325 m; 10,909 ft)*
The south slope is class 1. The left rib on the north face is rated III, 5.9, A1, and was first climbed June 11, 1974, by Pete Kilbourne and Loring Young. Start on the left side of the rib and continue up its center. The left side of the central rib is rated class 4+, and was climbed by Pete Lowery and Chris Keith on October 17, 1987. Climb about 1,000 feet of class 3 rock until you are level with the bottom of a major chimney on the rib. Climb the chimney, past chockstones, to its top. Traverse left across many chutes until it is possible to climb straight up to the summit. The central rib has been rated IV, 5.8, and was first climbed September 6, 1974, by Pete Kilbourne, Vern Clevenger, and Bill Dougherty. There is a good ski tour off of the summit to the north. Further reading: *Summit*, November–December 1987, pp. 8–11.

Donohue Peak *(12,023 ft; 12,023 ft)*
First ascent 1895 by Sergeant Donohue, U.S. Cavalry, on horseback. The northwest slope is class 1. The southwest ridge from Donohue Pass is class 2–3.

Peak 12,245
(12,223 ft; 0.6 mi ENE of Donohue Peak)
The southeast ridge is class 2.

Koip Crest *(12,651 ft; 12,668 ft)*
This is a ridge of pinnacles that extends south from Koip Peak and then southeast from Blacktop Peak. The nine pinnacles between Koip Peak and Peak 12,651 (12,668 ft) are class 4, and were traversed August 9, 1939, by George Templeton and Milton Hildebrand. Peak 12,651 (12,668 ft) is class 2 from Blacktop Peak, and the southeast

arete is class 3; the southwest chimney is class 5, and was first climbed August 1950 by Richard M. Leonard and Jim Koontz.

Not much is known about the six pinnacles that are southeast of Peak 12,651 (12,668 ft). The buttress on the "third from the left" pinnacle (as seen from northern Lost Lake) was first climbed July 1973 by Art Buck and Allen Fletcher; this six-pitch climb has a II, 5.6 rating.

Blacktop Peak *(12,720 ft+; 12,710 ft+)*
The southeast slope is class 2, as is the traverse from Peak 12,651 (12,688 ft).

Mt. Wood *(12,657 ft; 12,637 ft)*
Class 1 from Parker Peak. The east slope is class 2. Further reading: Hans Joachim Burhenne, *Sierra Spring Ski-Touring*, Mountain Press, San Francisco, 1971, pp. 80–81.

Parker Peak *(12,851 ft; 12,861 ft)*
First ascent 1914 by Norman Clyde. Class 1 from Koip Peak Pass.

Koip Peak *(12,962 ft; 12,979 ft)*
First ascent 1912 by Chester Versteeg. Class 1 from Koip Peak Pass.

Kuna Peak *(13,002 ft; 12,960 ft+)*
First ascent 1919 by Walter L. Huber. The northwest side is class 3, and the traverse from Koip Peak is class 2.

Kuna Crest *(12,202 ft; 12,207 ft)*
First ascent 1919 by Walter L. Huber. Class 3 from either the east or the west.

Mammoth Peak *(12,016 ft; 12,117 ft)*
First ascent 1902 by Walter L. Huber. The slabs on the north side of the peak are class 2–3. The west slope is class 2.

Mt. Lewis *(12,342 ft; 12,296 ft)*
Class 1 from either Mono Pass or Parker Pass.

"Bloody Canyon Crags"
These crags are less than 1 mile from Walker Lake. There is a II, 5.6 route on the easternmost pinnacle. Climb the face to the right of a black open book, and then the book itself for eight pitches to the top of the pinnacle. This was first climbed October 1972 by Art Buck and Allen Fletcher.

Mt. Gibbs *(12,773 ft; 12,764 ft)*

First ascent August 31, 1864, by William H. Brewer and F. L. Olmstead, by horseback. The north, west, and south slopes are class 1.

Mt. Dana *(13,057 ft; 13,053 ft)*

First ascent June 28, 1864, by Charles Hoffman and William Brewer. The northwest, west, and south slopes are class 1. A good use trail starts from the entrance station at Tioga Pass. Further reading: Hans Joachim Burhenne, *Sierra Spring Ski-Touring*, Mountain Press, San Francisco, 1971, pp. 78–79.

North Rib. III, 5.6. First ascent May 1982 by Harry Marinakis and Yorgos Marinakis. This is the far right-hand rib on the northeast face of Mt. Dana. Approach the base of this rib from the Dana Glacier, and follow the crest of the rib for twelve pitches or so. Most of this route is class 3 and 4, with a few class 5 moves. The crux is a 30-foot headwall about eight or nine pitches up the rib. The first-ascent party was forced off of the rib near its top by some snow cornices. They traversed left and up across a bowl to the northwest slopes of the peak.

Northeast Face. Class 3. First ascent 1949 by Frank Meyers and party. Start climbing this loose face from midway between Dana Lake and the glacier. Follow the northwest ridge to the summit.

Dana Glacier. Class 3. Cross the glacier and ascend the 40-degree snow/ice couloir to the southeast ridge. Follow the ridge to the summit. As an alternative, it is possible to climb the loose class 3 rocks on the side of the couloir.

Wrinkles

River Trail vs. High Trail. Those hiking from Agnew Meadows to Thousand Island Lake have the choice of these two trails. The River Trail is more direct, with less elevation gain, but the High Trail has outstanding views along almost its entire length.

How to cross the Minarets. North Notch is a climbers' route across the Minarets. Ritter Pass is a preferable route for hikers.

Koip, Gibbs, and Dana Traverse. These three peaks have been climbed in a long day from Dana Meadows along the Tioga Road.

The Clark and Cathedral Ranges

THESE TWO SUBRANGES ARE WEST OF THE Sierra crest, in one of the most scenic regions of the Sierra Nevada: the southern part of Yosemite National Park. The Clark Range is composed of colorful metamorphic rock, with the exception of Mt. Clark itself, which is composed of the firm granite that the High Sierra is known for throughout the world. The granite of the Cathedral Range has been eroded by glaciers into some surrealistic shapes; this, combined with the vast forests and meadows and its position atop the divide between the Merced and Tuolumne rivers gives it a commanding presence.

This region is bounded on the north by the Tioga Road, on the west by an imaginary line running from Snow Creek to Glacier Point to Chiquito Pass, and on the east by the North Fork of the San Joaquin River and the Lyell Fork of the Tuolumne River.

History

The first mountaineering in this region was in November 1864, when Clarence King and Richard Cotter attempted Mt. Clark, then known as the Obelisk. An early winter storm struck them at their camp between Mt. Clark and Gray Peak, and their retreat through 1½ feet of new snow has become an epic tale. Two years later King and James Gardiner attempted the peak again, during the month of July. King's tale of their ascent of the southeast ridge was even more thrilling than that of the winter retreat two years before. This adventure was followed by John Muir's more modest account of his solo climb of Cathedral Peak in 1869. Mt. Lyell was climbed in 1871, and the spires of the Cathedral Range were climbed by rock climbers after the 1930s. But, of course, all of this first-ascent speculation is moot when you consider the fact that a Native American bow (as

in bow and arrow) was found high on Parsons Peak by geologist Francois Matthes before 1920.

Maps

United States Geological Survey: 7.5-minute series: Cattle Mtn., Timber Knob, Sing Peak, Mariposa Grove, Half Dome, Merced Peak, Mount Lyell, Mt. Ritter, Vogelsang Peak, Tenaya Lake, Yosemite Falls; 15-minute series: Devils Postpile, Merced Peak, Yosemite, Tuolumne Meadows, Hetch Hetchy Reservoir; national park maps: Yosemite National Park and Vicinity (1:125,000).

United States Forest Service: Ansel Adams Wilderness (1:63,360).

Wilderness Permits

For west-side entry to the Ansel Adams Wilderness: Sierra National Forest, Minarets Ranger District, North Fork, CA 93643.

For entry to the Yosemite National Park backcountry: Backcountry Office, P.O. Box 577, Yosemite National Park, CA 95389.

Roads

Minarets Highway

This is the direct route to Clover Meadow and the Granite Creek Trailhead. It consists of approximately 50 miles of curving, paved road. The road leaves the town of North Fork and traverses high above the San Joaquin River, passing many side roads and campgrounds, before meeting the Beasore Road near Miller Meadow.

Beasore Road

The Beasore Road starts from near Bass Lake, and provides access to the Chiquito Pass, Jackass Lakes, Norris Lake, and

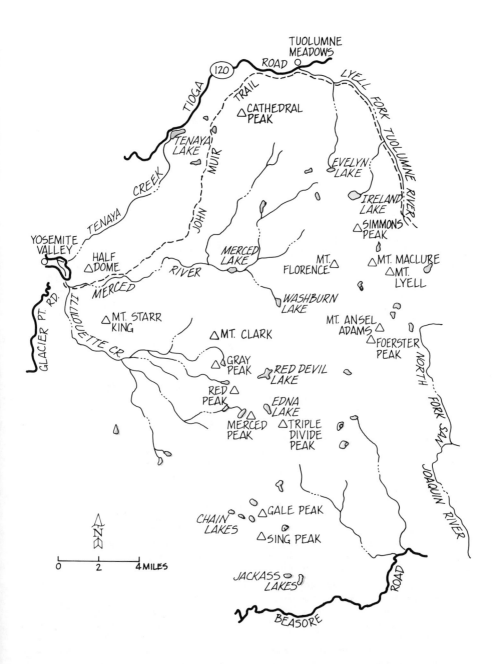

Fernandez Pass trailheads, and passes Clover Meadow on the way to the Cora Lakes and Granite Creek trailheads. The Beasore Road goes north from its junction with County Road 222, just north of the town of Bass Lake. After 14.2 miles, it comes to a major fork; go left toward Clover Meadow. At 20.3 miles it meets the road that goes left 2.4 miles to the Chiquito Pass Trailhead. The Beasore Road continues east, and passes many side roads and meets the Jackass Lakes Trailhead at 26.9 miles. A road goes left (north) at 27.6 miles; it leads 1.9 miles (rough road) to the Norris Lake Trailhead. The Beasore Road continues east to a side road at 27.7 miles that goes left (north) another 2.4 miles to the Fernandez Pass Trailhead. The Beasore Road continues east, passes a junction (go straight or left) at 29.7 miles, and meets the Minarets Highway 0.2 mile later.

Go left (north) from this junction another 1.7 miles to Clover Meadow. The road continues north another 1.5 miles to the Cora Lakes Trailhead, and then turns right (east) and goes 1.2 miles to the Granite Creek Trailhead.

Glacier Point Road

The Glacier Point Road leads from Chinquapin to Glacier Point. Leave Highway 41 approximately 12 miles north from Wawona, or 9 miles south from Yosemite Valley. The road goes east, past Badger Pass Ski Area and Bridalveil Creek Campground, and meets the trailhead for the Mono Meadow Trail 10.6 miles from Chinquapin. The road continues another 5.2 miles to Glacier Point.

Yosemite Valley

There are two trailheads within the scope of this book that are in The Valley: the John Muir Trail and the Snow Creek Trail. The John Muir Trail starts at Happy Isles at the far southeast corner of The Valley. You can only drive private vehicles as far as Upper Pines Campground; shuttle-bus service is available to the trailhead.

The traditional starting point of the John Muir Trail was from the LeConte Memorial Lodge of the Sierra Club when it was located at Curry Village. The lodge has been moved ¹/₂ mile to the west away from Curry Village. Starting a hike along the John Muir Trail from Curry Village adds 1 mile to the hike,

and a start from LeConte Memorial Lodge adds 1¹/₂ miles.

The Snow Creek Trail ends (or begins) at Mirror Lake, at the far northeast end of The Valley. Private vehicles can only go as far as the stables near North Pines Campground. Either take the shuttle bus or walk the ¹/₄ mile to the start of the bicycle path that leads to Mirror Lake, which is approximately 1 mile uphill from the bus stop.

Tioga Road

The trailhead for the Forsyth Trail is located near the campground on the western shore of Tenaya Lake.

The John Muir Trail follows the roads around Tuolumne Meadows for approximately 3 miles, so this could be considered the biggest trailhead in the High Sierra. To help narrow things down somewhat, the eastern trailhead for the John Muir Trail is located near the hikers' parking area along the road leading to the Tuolumne Meadows Lodge; take the Pacific Crest Trail south from the parking area, across the Lyell Fork to meet the John Muir Trail. The western trailhead is the Cathedral Lakes Trailhead, just west of Budd Creek along the Tioga Road. There is a parking area here, and this is where the John Muir Trail (or Sunrise Trail) leads to Cathedral Lakes and Cathedral Pass.

Trails

Isberg Pass Trail   (23 miles)

This trail, also known as the "Little Jackass Trail," leads from Granite Creek over Isberg Pass into Yosemite National Park to the Vogelsang Pass Trail, along Lewis Creek. The trail goes north from Granite Creek Campground and, after 2¹/₂ miles, it passes through a notch west of Green Mountain to a trail junction. The right fork leads to Cora Creek and the North Fork of the San Joaquin River. The Isberg Pass Trail goes left from the fork, passes Cora Lake (no camping or campfires along its north and east shores) and meets a side trail after 2¹/₄ miles. The side trail goes east to Detachment Meadow; the Isberg Pass Trail continues northwest another 2¹/₂ miles to meet the trail that comes down from Joe Crane Lake. The Isberg Pass Trail continues another 1¹/₂ miles to Sadler Lake, where camping and campfires are prohibited along its eastern and northern shores. The trail climbs another 2 miles to the top of Isberg Pass. The trail descends the west side of the pass for ½ mile to meet the Post Peak Pass Trail. The Isberg Pass Trail goes west from the junction before turning north and gradually descending for another 1¼ miles to meet a side trail that leads to the Red Peak Trail, along Triple Peak Fork of the Merced River. The Isberg Pass Trail goes north from the junction, travels along a bench high above Triple Peak Fork for 4½ miles, and then makes a steep descent down to the Lyell Fork. The trail crosses the stream and travels northwest along another bench above the Merced River for 6 miles to meet the Vogelsang Pass Trail.

Fernandez Pass Trail *(13¼ miles)*

The lower portion of this trail has also been called the "Clover Meadow Trail." The trailhead is at the campground near Clover Meadows; or, you can reach the trail from the Fernandez Pass Trailhead 1½ miles farther east. The trail goes west, and passes forks to the Norris Lake Trailhead after ¼ mile and another 1 mile beyond that. A half-mile beyond the second fork it meets a trail that leads west to Vandeburg Lake. The Fernandez Pass Trail continues another 3 miles, descends to the north, turns northwest and west to meet a side trail to Lillian Lake, and continues north another 1½ miles to meet the Post Peak Pass Trail. The Fernandez Pass Trail turns west from this junction and climbs for 2¼ miles to the top of Fernandez Pass, then descends to the west for 3½ miles to meet the Moraine Meadow Trail. The Fernandez Pass Trail continues west another 1¼ miles to meet the Merced Pass Trail.

Post Peak Pass Trail *(6½ miles)*

This trail starts along the Fernandez Pass Trail at 2¼ miles east of Fernandez Pass. The trail makes a gentle climb to the northeast before turning north, passing Porphyry Lake, and climbing to the top of the Post Peak Pass after 5¼ miles. The trail then makes two big switchbacks for 1 mile to meet the Isberg Pass Trail, ½ mile west of Isberg Pass.

Chiquito Pass Trail *(7 miles)*

To reach the trailhead for this trail, leave the Beasore Road 20.3 miles from Bass Lake and take the side road that goes left (north-

west) from this junction 2.4 miles to the trailhead. The trail ascends the Chiquito Creek drainage for 2¼ miles to Chiquito Lake, then continues another ¾ mile to the top of Chiquito Pass and a fork. One fork goes north for 3 miles to meet the Moraine Meadow Trail below Chain Lakes. The other fork goes left (west) from the junction for 1 mile, crosses the South Fork of the Merced River, and passes the southern shore of Swamp Lake. The trail climbs and descends for another 3 miles to meet the Moraine Meadow Trail.

Moraine Meadow and Chain Lakes Trail *(7¼ miles)*

This trail leaves the Fernandez Pass Trail at Moraine Meadow. The trail goes south for 1¾ miles to a junction. The left fork goes another ¼ mile to meet a branch of the Chiquito Pass Trail, and continues upstream another 1½ miles to the beautiful Chain Lakes. The Moraine Meadow Trail goes west from the junction for 2¾ miles to meet another branch of the Chiquito Pass Trail near Givens Creek, then crosses Givens Creek and makes a gentle climb for 1 mile to meet the Merced Pass Trail.

Buena Vista Trail *(15½ miles)*

The Buena Vista Trail starts from Glacier Point and goes south for 1½ miles to meet the Panorama Trail. It continues descending south and southeast to Illilouette Creek, and follows its west bank another 2¼ miles to the junction with the Mono Meadow Trail and the Merced Pass Trail. The Buena Vista Trail continues to follow the southwest bank of Illilouette Creek and gently climbs before turning southwest into the Buena Vista Creek drainage. The trail eventually crosses Buena Vista Creek and meets the Chilnualna Creek Trail, 8¾ miles from the junction with the Mono Meadow and Merced Pass trails. (The Chilnualna Creek Trail leads west to some beautiful lakes, and eventually to Wawona.) The Buena Vista Trail goes east from the junction and crosses a pass northeast of Buena Vista Peak; excellent views, as the name says. The trail goes downhill to the south to meet the Merced Pass Trail 3 miles from the junction.

Merced Pass Trail *(17 miles)*

This trail starts along the Mono Meadow

Trail, just north of its crossing of Illilouette Creek. The Merced Pass Trail goes east for 1½ miles to the Nevada Fall Trail. The Merced Pass Trail continues east, across the Clark Fork, and turns southeast for 7¾ miles to the junction with the Red Peak Pass Trail. It then crosses Merced Pass and continues south another 2¾ to meet the Fernandez Pass Trail. The Merced Pass Trail makes a gentle climb to the southeast, passes a side trail leading to Givens Lake, and goes downhill for 4½ miles to meet the western end of the Moraine Meadow Trail. The Merced Pass Trail continues southwest from this junction and makes a steep climb to meet the Buena Vista Trail.

Red Peak Pass Trail (21½ miles)

The Red Peak Pass Trail connects the upper reaches of Illilouette Creek with the upper portion of the Merced River. The trail starts by leaving the Merced Pass Trail north of Merced Pass, then climbs to the northeast for 2½ miles to Lower Ottoway Lake. It makes a steep ascent from the lake for another 2½ miles to the top of Red Peak Pass, and descends the north side of the pass before turning east and traveling 7 miles to the Triple Peak Fork of the Merced River. (A side trail leads south from here and climbs the east wall of the canyon for 1¼ miles to meet the Isberg Pass Trail.) The Red Peak Pass Trail goes downstream from this junction for 7 miles to beautiful Washburn Lake. The trail continues downstream for 2½ miles to meet the Vogelsang Pass Trail.

Mono Meadow Trail (6¾ miles)

This trail starts along the Glacier Point Road, approximately 10½ miles from Highway 41. The trail descends to the northeast, passes Mono Meadow, and continues down to Illilouette Creek, where it meets the Buena Vista Trail at 2¾ miles. The Mono Meadow Trail crosses the creek, goes past the Merced Pass Trail, and continues north another 1¼ miles to meet the northwest end of the Nevada Fall Trail. The Mono Meadow Trail continues north another 2¾ miles to the Panorama Trail.

Panorama Trail (3½ miles)

The Panorama Trail starts along the Buena Vista Trail, approximately 1½ miles from

Glacier Point. It goes downstream, crosses Illilouette Creek, and climbs and then follows the edge of Panorama Cliff for 2½ miles to the junction with the Mono Meadow Trail. The Panorama Trail continues east another 1 mile, and descends to meet the John Muir Trail (or Sunrise Trail) near Nevada Fall.

John Muir Trail (22¾ miles)

This trail, also known as the Sunrise Trail, starts at Happy Isles and ascends the east bank of the Merced River before crossing the river on a bridge. After 1 mile it meets the Mist Trail, which passes close to Vernal Fall and Nevada Fall to meet the John Muir Trail above Nevada Fall, 1½ miles from the junction. The John Muir Trail, however, turns south and climbs from this junction, passes a side trail leading to the Mist Trail, and meets the Panorama Trail after 1¼ miles. The John Muir Trail continues east from this junction and passes above Nevada Fall, a truly spectacular sight. The trail continues upstream into Little Yosemite Valley for 1½ miles to the junction with the Merced Lake Trail. The John Muir Trail turns to the north from the junction and meets the side trail leading to the top of Half Dome after 1½ miles, and the Clouds Rest Trail ½ mile farther. The John Muir Trail continues east along Sunrise Creek for 2 miles to a junction with the Forsyth Trail and a side trail that leads to Merced Lake. The John Muir Trail goes east from this junction and then climbs to the northeast, past Sunrise High Sierra Camp (a side trail leads west from here to Sunrise Lakes and the Forsyth Trail), through Long Meadow, over Cathedral Pass, and down past Cathedral Lakes after 9 miles. A side trail leads southwest from here to the westernmost Cathedral Lakes. The John Muir trail goes north before turning northeast and, after 3 miles, it meets the Tioga Road just west of Budd Creek at the Cathedral Lakes Trailhead.

The John Muir Trail then proceeds toward the east on the south side of the Tioga Road. It passes the Tuolumne Meadows Visitor Center and Tuolumne Meadows Campground, and meets the Pacific Crest Trail after 3 miles. The Pacific Crest Trail leads north a short distance to the hikers' parking area along the road leading to the Tuolumne Meadows Lodge.

Half Dome Trail *(2 miles)*

The Half Dome Trail leaves the John Muir Trail approximately 6¼ miles from Happy Isles. It heads northwest before turning southwest and climbing the east face of Half Dome via a system of cables and ladders. (These cables are usually in place from June until the end of October.) So many hikers have followed this route to the summit of Half Dome that the 46-degree rock slope between the cables has become polished, and in places it is disagreeably slippery. But there is an outstanding view from the summit, and every hiker who spends much of his or her free time in the High Sierra should hike up Half Dome at least once.

Clouds Rest Trail *(5½ miles)*

This trail leaves the John Muir Trail ½ mile east of the junction with the Half Dome Trail. The Clouds Rest Trail goes north, and after many switchbacks and 3¾ miles, it leads to the summit of Clouds Rest, an outstanding viewpoint. The trail goes over the summit of Clouds Rest and heads northeast for 1¾ miles to meet the Forsyth Trail.

Merced Lake Trail *(9 miles)*

The Merced Lake Trail leaves the John Muir Trail in Little Yosemite Valley and ascends via the north bank of the Merced River. The upper portion of Little Yosemite Valley has some impressive domes, cliffs, and cascades. The trail crosses to the south bank of the river on a bridge above Lost Valley and eventually crosses the river again on another bridge before meeting a side trail in Echo Valley, 6½ miles from the start. The trail continues upstream along the north bank of the River to Merced Lake, skirts the north shore of the lake, and arrives at the Merced Lake High Sierra Camp after 1¾ miles. The trail continues upstream another ¾ mile to the junction with the Vogelsang Pass Trail and the Red Peak Pass Trail; the Merced Lake Ranger Station is nearby.

Another trail that leads to Merced Lake leaves the John Muir Trail at its junction with the Forsyth Trail. It gradually descends to Echo Valley and meets the Merced Lake Trail after 4 miles.

Tuolumne Pass Trail *(12 miles)*

This trail leaves the John Muir Trail near Tuolumne Meadows and ascends the west bank of Rafferty Creek for 5 miles to Tuolumne Pass. The trail continues another ½ mile to a junction with a side trail, which leads another ¼ mile to meet the Vogelsang Pass Trail. The Tuolumne Pass Trail turns north from this junction, then turns southwest at the southern shore of Booth Lake. The trail goes downstream another 2½ miles to another junction, where a trail leads southwest for ½ mile to Emeric Lake; another trail heads east along Fletcher Creek for 2¼ miles to meet the Vogelsang Pass Trail. The Tuolumne Pass Trail goes south, crosses Fletcher Creek, and continues down its east bank for 3¾ miles to meet the Vogelsang Pass Trail along Lewis Creek.

Elizabeth Lake Trail *(2¼ miles)*

The Elizabeth Lake Trail starts from the Tuolumne Meadows Campground and ascends the east bank of Unicorn Creek to lovely Elizabeth Lake.

Budd Lake Trail *(2½ miles)*

The Budd Lake Trail leaves the John Muir Trail approximately ¼ mile from the Tioga Road near Budd Creek. An excellent use trail ascends the west bank of the creek to Budd Lake.

Vogelsang Pass Trail *(7½ miles)*

This trail starts upstream from Merced Lake, where the Red Peak Pass Trail and the Merced Lake Trail meet. The Vogelsang Pass Trail ascends the canyon of Lewis Creek for 1 mile to the junction of the Tuolumne Pass Trail. It continues upstream another 1 mile to a junction with the Isberg Pass Trail, then goes northeast up beautiful Lewis Creek, past a side trail leading to Bernice Lake, for another 4¼ miles to the summit of Vogelsang Pass and an outstanding view. The trail descends the north side of the pass and crosses the outlet of Vogelsang Lake before meeting the Evelyn Lake Trail and the Vogelsang High Sierra Camp, 1¼ miles from Vogelsang Pass.

Evelyn Lake Trail *(6¼ miles)*

The Evelyn Lake Trail leaves the John Muir Trail approximately 5 miles from Tuolumne Meadows in Lyell Canyon. It ascends the west bank of Ireland Creek for

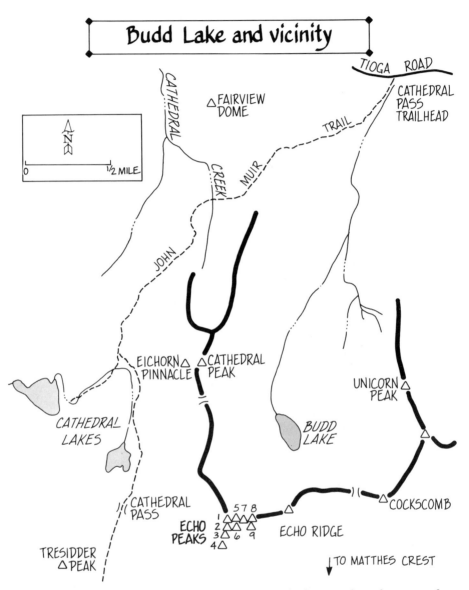

Budd Lake and vicinity

2³/₄ miles to a junction, where a trail leads south to Ireland Lake, in 3 miles. The Evelyn Lake Trail goes west from the junction for 2 miles to where it crosses the outlet of Evelyn Lake. The trail continues southwest, passing the north shore of Fletcher Lake to meet the Vogelsang Pass Trail after 1¹/₂ miles.

Forsyth Trail (7 miles)

This trail leaves the campground on the western shore of Tenaya Lake and goes for 4 miles to the south, where it meets the Clouds

Rest Trail. The Forsyth Trail turns east from this junction and descends for 3 miles to meet the John Muir Trail along Sunrise Creek.

Snow Creek Trail (9 miles)

This trail has also been called the Tenaya Lake Trail and the May Lake Trail. Construction of roads around May Lake and Tenaya Lake over the years has interfered with the aesthetics of hiking some branches of this trail. Because this route is frequently used by skiers during ski tours from Tuolumne Meadows to Yosemite Valley, it is described here from top to bottom.

The trail descends from May Lake and crosses the Tioga Road approximately 2¼ miles west from Tenaya Lake; this crossing can be identified in winter or spring as the crest of the first ridge beyond Olmsted Point; this ridge divides Snow Creek from Tenaya Creek. The trail goes southwest, more or less along the crest of the ridge, and descends for 2¼ miles to a trail junction. A trail leads east from here 6 miles to Tenaya Lake. The Snow Creek Trail continues downhill, crosses Snow Creek, and meets the North Dome Trail after 1½ miles. (This area is typically bare ground by late March to April.) The trail continues to the rim of the canyon and switchbacks down to Tenaya Creek and Mirror Lake after 4 miles. Continue down the bicycle path (a paved road, in reality) to the shuttle-bus route near North Pines Campground in Yosemite Valley.

Cross-Country Routes

Cross-country travel is relatively easy in the Clark and Cathedral Ranges, and there are many more routes than those listed below. The Clark Range can be approached from the west via the Merced Pass Trail along Illilouette Creek by hiking through the vast forests; skill with a compass, an accurate map (see Wrinkles, at the end of this chapter), and perhaps an altimeter are needed to ensure that you are in the correct drainage.

"Blue Lake Pass"
(11,240 ft+; 11,200 ft+; 0.3 mi S of Foerster Peak)

Class 2. This pass leads between the drainages of the North Fork of the San Joaquin River and the Merced River. Steep talus is encountered on the west side of the pass, grassy benches on the east. Further reading: Steve Roper, *Timberline Country,* Sierra Club Books, San Francisco, 1982, pp. 233–36.

"Ingraham Pass"
(11,520 ft+; 11,440 ft+; 1.5 mi SW of Mt. Lyell)

Class 2 from either the northwest or southeast. Robin Ingraham, Jr. specifically asked me to name this pass after him. This pass has been used during ascents of Rodgers

Peak, Electra Peak, Mt. Ansel Adams, and Foerster Peak, from the upper portion of Hutching Creek.

"Lyell–Maclure Col"
(12,400 ft+; 12,400 ft+; 0.3 mi NW of Mt. Lyell)

Class 3–4. This provides a direct route between Lyell Canyon and Hutching Creek. Cross the Lyell Glacier to the low point between Mt. Lyell and Mt. Maclure. A steep, loose chute (class 3, with a 10-foot section of class 4) on the southwest side of the pass leads down to the upper portion of Hutching Creek.

"Russell Pass"
(12,240 ft+; 12,160 ft+; 0.5 mi NW of Mt. Maclure; UTM 984800)

Class 2. This pass, named here in honor of Bill T. Russell, leads between the Lyell Fork of the Tuolumne River and Hutching Creek; it is an easier route than Lyell–Maclure Col. Ascend Maclure Creek from the John Muir Trail. Slabs lead to the highest lake along this creek, which which is followed by talus and the low-angle Maclure Glacier to the top of the pass. Descend talus on the southwest side of the pass to the highest lake in the Hutching Creek drainage.

Tenaya Canyon
Class 3–4. This adventurous cross-country route should only be attempted by experienced mountaineers; many tourists are rescued from this canyon each year. Two days should be allowed to travel from Mirror Lake to Tenaya Lake.

Take the trail that heads upstream from Mirror Lake in Yosemite Valley. Keep to the northwest bank of Tenaya Creek until you are past Quarter Domes. During high water it is necessary to climb about 250 feet above Tenaya Creek; the northwest bank is preferred, as it seems to have less brush. Traverse east until it is possible to traverse diagonally down into Lost Valley, a hanging valley in the middle of Tenaya Canyon.

During low water, a more interesting, more technical, and less brushy route can be taken. Follow Tenaya Creek to the first waterfall, where the creek divides around a chockstone. Bypass this on the left by following a scree-covered ledge that is 50 feet above the creek. Follow this ledge until you are well beyond the chockstone. Descend to the creek and pass through a split rock. Climb 150 feet through brush on the left and continue upstream over a series of narrow, exposed ledges into Lost Valley. One of the ledges, known as "Initial Ledge," was marked by S. L. Foster, who made annual trips through the canyon from 1909 to 1937.

Continue upstream through Lost Valley and cross to the southeast bank of Tenaya Creek. Ascend Pywiack Cascade on its right side via talus, granite slabs, and brush. The rest of the route is easy walking to Tenaya Lake. Further reading: Steve Roper, "Tenaya: John Muir's Canyon of Glistening Rocks," *Summit, The Mountain Journal*, Spring 1990, pp. 40–43.

Other Routes

Grayling Lake is surrounded by cliffs on three sides, and it is best approached directly from Red Creek.

An old cavalry trail was established in the late 1800s from the vicinity of Nevada Fall to Starr King Meadow; some blazes can still be seen along this route.

Another army trail goes up the Gray Peak Fork from the vicinity of Merced Lake. Portions of this trail can still be seen. It leads to Adair Lake; the route of the trail crossed the Clark Range at the first saddle north of Gray Peak.

Peaks

Madera Peak   *(10,509 ft; 10,509 ft)*

First ascent August 1931 by Mrs. Hermina Daulton, Mr. Garthwaite, Mrs. Garthwaite, and their seven-year-old son, Jed. The southwest slope is class 2.

Red Top   *(9,973 ft; 9,977 ft)*

First ascent prior to 1919 by William Frederick Bade. Class 2 via the west slope.

Sing Peak   *(10,520 ft+; 10,552 ft)*

The south slope is class 2.

Gale Peak   *(10,680 ft+; 10,693 ft)*

First ascent 1920 by Lawrence Fley, Freeman Jones, and Thomas Jones. The northwest and northeast ridges are class 2.

Triple Divide Peak

(11,611 ft; 11,607 ft)

First ascent 1920 by Norman Clyde. The northwest ridge is class 2, as is the southeast slope.

Merced Peak   *(11,726 ft; 11,726 ft)*

First ascent prior to 1870 by the California Geological Survey.

Northeast Ridge. Class 2. Leave the Red Peak Pass Trail near Upper Ottoway Lake, and climb to the saddle between Merced Peak and Ottoway Peak. Ascend the east side of the northeast ridge, taking care to avoid some loose talus blocks.

North Face. III, 5.7. First ascent July 1971 by Ken Boche and Mary Bomba. A ramp ascends up and right across the north face. Loose 5.7 climbing leads to the bottom of the ramp. Climb the poorly protected diagonal ramp to where a short, moderate section at the top of the ramp leads to easier climbing and the summit.

West Arete. Class 3. Descended August 1949 by Alfred R. Dole, Stewart Kimball, Elizabeth Kimball, and Richard Leonard. It is necessary to traverse across the southern side of this ridge in many places.

Ottoway Peak   *(11,480 ft+; 11,440 ft+)*

First ascent September 16, 1934, by Ansel Adams. Class 2 from Red Peak Pass, and from the saddle between Ottoway Peak and Merced Peak.

Red Peak   *(11,699 ft; 11,669 ft)*

First ascent 1870 by the California Geological Survey. The south slope is class 2; traverse west from Red Peak Pass across the south slope to a point beyond the gendarmes west of the trail. Follow the loose south slope to the summit. The northwest slope from Red Peak Fork is also class 2.

Gray Peak   *(11,573 ft; 11,574 ft)*

First ascent 1920 by Ansel Adams. The ridge running west from the summit consists of easy class 3 blocks. The ridge can be easily reached from either Red Peak or Mt. Clark.

Mt. Clark   *(11,522 ft; 11,522 ft)*

Southeast Arete. Class 4. First ascent July 12, 1866, by Clarence King and James T. Gardiner. First winter ascent February 21, 1937, by Ken Adam, Ken Davis, Hervey Voge, and David Brower. The base of this arete can be reached from either the Merced Pass Trail along Illilouette Creek (easier), or from the Red Peak Pass Trail along the Merced River (harder). Follow the ridge that connects Mt. Clark with Gray Peak to the base of the cliffs on the arete leading to Mt. Clark. Pass through a small gap on the arete and diagonally ascend high on the east side of the arete to just below the summit block. An exposed move on the south side of the summit block leads to the top.

Northeast Face. Class 4. First ascent July 4, 1916, by Francis Farquhar. The start of this route can be reached from the base of the southeast arete by traversing low across the east face of Mt. Clark. Climb the right side of the northeast face via a series of broad, sandy ledges. Pass through a notch on the north ridge of the peak, and traverse south across the west side of the north ridge until you are just beneath the summit. An exposed pitch up a crack and chimney leads to the summit.

North Face. III, 5.6. First ascent September 1958 by Henry Kendall, Herb Swedlund, Hobey DeStaebler, and Tom Frost. Cross the small glacier on the northern side of the peak, and start climbing the face to the left of a point directly below the summit. Climb to a ledge that runs across the face. Two class 4 pitches go straight up from the far end of the ledge to a pair of chimneys. Climb the right-hand chimney (5.6). This is followed by a 5.4 pitch, which ends on the crest of the northwest ridge. *Variation:* The left-hand chimney has been rated as 5.8.

Northwest Arete. Class 4. First ascent October 1934 by Neil Ruge and Douglas Olds. This arete is a striking sight. Most of the route is class 3.

Southwest Face. IV, 5.8, A2. First ascent August 19, 1970, by Ken Boche and Joe McKeown. Begin by climbing left of the chimney system on this face. Climb about 200 feet to some loose blocks, and traverse to the right into the chimney. Continue up the chimney, where a short aid crack leads up and left. Traverse right, back into the chimney, to a hanging belay. Continue up the chimney to a ledge with a bolt. A 30-foot pendulum to the left leads to a small dihedral. Mixed climbing in this dihedral leads to its top and a ramp. Follow the ramp up and

Mt. Clark from the northeast (photo by R. J. Secor)

right, across the chimney, to a ridge. Free and aid climbing on the right side of this ridge leads to the southeast arete. Follow the arete to the summit.

Peak 10,480
(10,400 ft+; 1.0 mi NE of Mt. Clark)

First ascent June 30, 1990, by Greg Foerstal, Sigrid Hutto, Rick Beatty, and R. J. Secor. The north peak is the high point. Climb slabs and benches up from the east shore of Obelisk Lake to the class 3 south ridge. Follow the ridge to the class 4 summit rocks.

Mt. Starr King   *(9,092 ft; 9,092 ft)*

Southeast Saddle. I, 5.0. First ascent August 23, 1877, by George C. Anderson, James M. Hutchings, and J. B. Lembert. First winter ascent March 9, 1937, by David Brower and Joseph Specht. Climb to the first saddle southeast of this beautiful dome rising above Illilouette Creek. Friction climbing leads up and left from a slab to a small right-facing open book. Traverse to the right under a flake and up to a big ledge. The second pitch is class 4, and goes up and left from the belay ledge past an ancient bolt to some slabs. Scramble up to the summit. Two ropes are recommended to rappel this route.

Northeast Side. I, 5.2. First ascent August 1876 by George Bayley and E. S. Schuyler. Climb to the saddle northwest of the dome and ascend to the high point of the shoulder on the northeast side of the dome. Climb class 3 rock slabs to where the angle steepens appreciably. Traverse diagonally up and right across a 43-degree face for 40 feet to a small ledge. Climb up and right from the ledge, following a two-inch-wide, munge-filled crack to easier ground above.

Further reading: Mark and Shirley Spencer, *Southern Yosemite Rock Climbs,* Condor Designs, Oakhurst, California, 1988, pp. 10–17.

Half Dome   *(8,836 ft; 8,842 ft)*

The cable route (see Trails, earlier in this chapter) was first climbed in October 1875 by George Anderson. He climbed barefoot, and drilled holes for some big iron spikes for protection. The cables were placed in 1919. The face on either side of the cables is class 5, and was first climbed 1931 by Warren Loose, Eldon Dryer, and Judd Boynton.

The base of the cables can also be reached via an interesting cross-country route from Mirror Lake. The cliffs above Mirror Lake go class 3 at either end. Climb the brush-covered slabs above the left end of the cliffs. Ascend talus to the trail and cables on the east face of Half Dome. Further reading: George Myers and Don Reid, *Yosemite Rock Climbs,* Chockstone Press, Denver, 1987, pp. 262–75.

"Sugarloaf Dome"
(7,683 ft; 7,480 ft+; 0.7 mi WNW of Bunnell Pt.)

This dome is located at the head of Little Yosemite Valley.

South Face. III, 5.9. First ascent 1960 by Tom Frost and Yvon Chouinard. Climb to a brushy ledge halfway up the south face. Continue straight up from the ledge for several pitches. The crux is a friction traverse that goes up and right several pitches above the brushy ledge.

South and Southwest Faces. Class 5 and A. First ascent November 6, 1951, by John Salathe and Cliff Hopson. This first ascent of this route involved much direct aid. Go up and left from the brushy ledge on the south face of the dome.

Bunnell Point   *(8,193 ft; 8,193 ft)*

Northwest Face. IV, 5.9. First ascent June 1983 by Alan Bartlett and Robb Dellinger. There are two dikes just to the right of center on the northwest face. These dikes slant up and left and meet about halfway up the face. This route follows the right dike, and slants up and left for fourteen pitches. There are fifteen bolts on this climb, but beware of some off-route bolts that lead to the right at about mid-height. Further reading: Mark and Shirley Spencer, *Southern Yosemite Rock Climbs,* Condor Designs, Oakhurst, California, 1988, p. 18.

The Golden Bear. V, 5.10b. First ascent July 1989 by Bart O'Brien and Mike Jauregui. This route follows the left-hand dike that goes up and left from the center of the northwest face. Follow the dike up and over a roof for two pitches to a belay from the higher of two ledges. The third and fourth pitches are the crux. Follow bolts left into a right-facing open book, then climb the book to a belay at a flake. Climb dikes over the book past two bolts to another belay. This is followed by several more dike pitches up and left to a ledge that is east of an open book with a small pine. Face climbing then leads over a small, prominent white scar to a series of small, right-facing inside corners, which become left-facing higher up. Continue climbing up these corners to the lonely summit pine.

Post Peak *(11,009 ft; 11,009 ft)*

First ascent 1922 by Ansel Adams. Class 1 from Post Peak Pass.

Sadler Peak *(10,567 ft; 10,567 ft)*

Class 1 from the south.

Isberg Peak *(10,996 ft; 10,996 ft)*

First ascent April 20, 1924, by Ansel Adams. Class 1 from the west.

Long Mountain *(11,502 ft; 11,502 ft)*

First ascent August 1922 by Ansel Adams. Class 2 from the south.

Foerster Peak *(12,057 ft; 12,058 ft)*

First ascent 1914 by Norman Clyde. The south slope is class 2. A chute on the southwest side of the peak is also class 2; it was climbed August 20, 1973, by Mary Sue Miller, Neko Colevins, Kes Teter, Bill Schuler, and Andy Smatko. The west side of the north ridge is class 2–3, and was climbed July 1954 by George Whitmore.

Mt. Ansel Adams *(11,760 ft+; 11,760 ft+)*

This the impressive peak at the head of the Lyell Fork of the Merced River. First ascent July 11, 1934, by Glen Dawson, Jack Riegelhuth, and Neil Ruge. Ascend the Lyell Fork of the Merced River to the south face of the peak. Climb a chute that curves to the west-southwest, and ascend the south face to the summit. Class 3.

Another route was climbed by Robin Ingraham, Jr. Climb to the notch between Mt. Ansel Adams and the sharp peak to the northeast. Climb onto the class 3 south face from the notch, and up to the summit.

Electra Peak *(12,442 ft; 12,442 ft)*

First ascent 1914 by Norman Clyde. The north ridge is class 2, as is the southeast face.

Peak 12,573
(12,560 ft+; 0.7 mi S of Rodgers Peak)

First ascent July 10, 1924, by Ansel Adams,

Cedric Wright, and Willard Grinnell. The east and northwest slopes of this peak are class 2.

Rodgers Peak *(12,978 ft; 12,978 ft)*

First ascent August 5, 1897, by Robert M. Price. This peak is class 3 from the west, and class 3 from the north. The east ridge is class 2–3; climb to the middle portion of the east ridge from either the north or south, and follow the ridge to the summit.

Mt. Lyell *(13,114 ft; 13,114 ft)*

This is the highest peak in Yosemite National Park. Its glacier is the second largest in the High Sierra. This peak is frequently climbed, and there is a grand view from the summit.

Lyell Glacier. Class 2–3. First ascent August 29, 1871, by John B. Tileston. First winter ascent March 2, 1936, by David Brower, Lewis Clark, Boynton Kaiser, Einar Nilsson, and Bestor Robinson. Leave the John Muir Trail where it crosses the Lyell Fork of the Tuolumne River, below Donohue Pass. Ascend talus and benches to the western part of the Lyell Glacier. Cross the glacier, aiming for the notch between Mt. Lyell and Mt. Maclure. Climb toward the summit of Mt. Lyell along ledges, above the snow but below a rock face, to a chute that leads up to the summit ridge. This route is open to many variations, due to changing snow levels each year on the glacier.

Lyell–Maclure Col. Class 3–4. Descended July 11, 1934, by Ted Waller, Marjory Bridge, Ray Brothers, John Cahill, Leland Curtis, Louise Hildebrand, Helen LeConte, May Pridham, and Helen Simpson. There are two steep, narrow chutes that lead to the notch between Mt. Lyell and Mt. Maclure from the Hutching Creek drainage. Climb the left-hand chute to the notch; there is a 10-foot class 4 move at the bottom of this otherwise class 3 chute. The top of this chute is about 50 feet above and east of the low point between Mt. Lyell and Mt. Maclure. Keep to the north side of the ridge before climbing a chute that leads to the crest of the summit ridge.

West Face. Class 5. First ascent August 24, 1963, by Les Wilson, Dennis Schmitt, Tim Gerson, and Peter Haan. The wide west face of Mt. Lyell features a vertical prow. Climb two class 4 pitches directly below the prow, in a loose chimney. Go up and then left over better rock to a ledge at the bottom of a broken section on the face. Two class 4 pitches lead straight up over cluttered ledges to where the face steepens against the prow. Climb a shallow open book to the left (class 4), and traverse left around a bulge almost to the prominent diving board that is visible from below. Class 5 climbing then leads up and around an overhang to a ledge above the bulge. Another pitch of class 5 goes straight up the face and leads to some fractured blocks. A short class 4 pitch up and right leads to a ridge that is just northwest of the top of the prow. Follow the ridge to the summit.

Southwest Ridge. Class 4. First ascent July 19, 1955, by George Whitmore. Climb to the saddle between Peak 12,767 (12,720 ft+) and Mt. Lyell. Follow the southwest ridge from the saddle to where the ridge merges with the south face. Several hundred feet of class 3 and class 4 climbing lead to the northwest ridge at a point about 100 feet from the summit.

South Face. Class 4. First ascent July 12, 1934, by Glen Dawson, Tony Chorlton, Milton Hildebrand, Elizabeth Mason, David Parish, Thomas Saunders, and George Shochat. Ascend a talus chute on the south face that leads directly to the summit. The upper part of this chute consists of loose class 4 climbing.

East Arete. Class 3. Cross the Lyell Glacier,

Mt. Lyell and Mt. Maclure from the northeast, September 2, 1965 (photo by Austin Post, #F655-185, USGS Ice and Climate Project, Tacoma, WA)

aiming for the first col to the east of the summit of Mt. Lyell. Follow the east arete to the summit.

East Arete from Marie Lakes. Class 4. First ascent July 3, 1977, by Sonny Lawrence, Diane Rosentreter, and Ian Clarke. Climb onto the crest of the east arete from Marie Lakes, and follow the south side of the arete until progress is stopped by some gendarmes. Pass these on the north side of the ridge and continue to the col that is east of the summit of Mt. Lyell. Follow the east arete to the summit.

Mt. Maclure *(12,880 ft+; 12,960 ft+)*

Southeast Ridge. Class 3. First ascent 1883 by Willard D. Johnson. Climb talus and ledges to the summit from the Lyell–Maclure Col.

South Face. Class 3. First ascent July 11, 1934, by Ted Waller, Marjory Bridge, Ray Brothers, John Cahill, Leland Curtis, Louise Hildebrand, Helen LeConte, May Pridham, and Helen Simpson. Climb the left side of a prominent chute on the south face. Traverse east to the southeast ridge and follow the ridge to the summit.

Northwest Ridge. Class 4. First ascent by Allen Steck and George Steck. Climb to the v-shaped pass northwest of Mt. Maclure and follow the ridge to the summit.

Mt. Florence *(12,561 ft; 12,561 ft)*

First ascent August 1897 by Theodore S. Solomons and F. W. Reed. The south and west slopes are class 2. The east slope consists of loose class 3; it is better to traverse around to the southern side of the mountain from high on Hutching Creek and climb the south slope rather than the east slope.

Simmons Peak *(12,497 ft; 12,503 ft)*

First ascent by a Sierra Club party in 1931. The southwest slope is class 2.

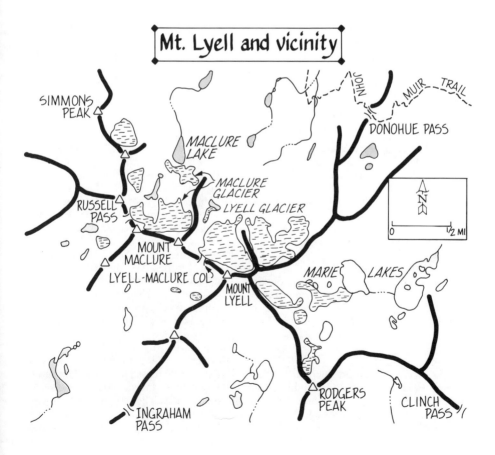

Mt. Lyell and vicinity

Mt. Lyell from the north, August 1904 (photo by W. T. Lee, #109, USGS Photographic Library, Denver, CO)

East Arete. III, 5.8. First ascent August 1982 by Evelyn Lees and Alan Bartlett. Climb the crest of this striking arete for five pitches to a horizontal section of class 3 and class 4. One more pitch along this ridge includes some 5.8 moves on the face to the left of the prow of the arete.

Amelia Earhart Peak
(11,974 ft; 11,982 ft)

The northeast ridge is class 2. The west face has a class 4 couloir. Climb the couloir to where it meets a steep wall, then traverse left to the northeast ridge; this was first climbed July 1973 by Allen Steck and Lee Steck.

Parsons Peak *(12,147 ft; 12,080 ft+)*

First ascent by Marion Randall Parsons prior to 1931. Class 2 from Ireland Lake or the Bernice Lake area. The north ridge is class 3, and was first climbed August 4, 1982, by Chris Keith.

Vogelsang Peak *(11,493 ft; 11,516 ft)*

First ascent 1923 by Francois Matthes. Class 2 via the northeast slope, or via the ridge from Vogelsang Pass.

Nightingale Arete. II, 5.9. First ascent July 1981 by Gary Colliver and Alan Bartlett. This arete leads northwest from the lower, west summit of Vogelsang Peak. Climb slanting cracks (easy class 5) on the left side of the lower buttress. Some 5.7 sections lead to the class 2–3 horizontal ridge that leads to the upper arete. Follow the arete to the summit; a 5.9 pitch in an obvious corner halfway up the upper arete is the crux.

West Face. IV, 5.10, A2. First ascent August 1981 by Evelyn Lees and Alan Bartlett. There are two right-slanting chimneys on the west face. Climb the most obvious crack to the right of these chimneys. Traverses to the right on the fourth and fifth pitches lead to more cracks. The sixth pitch starts with a long traverse left, followed by 30 feet of aid up to an overhanging corner and easier climbing. The first-ascent party used one point of aid on the second pitch, and one point of aid on the fifth pitch. There is much loose rock on this route.

Fletcher Peak *(11,410 ft; 11,408 ft)*

Southwest Slope. Class 2. Climb this slope from the outlet of Vogelsang Lake. Brush, scree, and talus is encountered before reaching the summit.

Northwest Couloir. Class 4. First ascent August 1959 by Ronald Smith and Bob Happle. Ascend the right side of this couloir to avoid the ice. Higher, traverse back and forth to a large crack. Climb the crack and go left to a small clump of trees, and ascend the southwest slope to the summit.

Modesto Surfer. II, 5.9. First ascent September 1989 by Tom Downey, Todd Handy, Tim Kluender, and Johno Alexander. This route is on the northwest face; it follows a prominent, right-facing open book on the right side of the face. Class 3 scrambling across slabs beneath the face leads to the start of the route. Climb the left crack (5.9) to the bottom of the book. Continue up the book, but move left and face climb (5.7) around a slab. This is followed by a 5.9 chimney and crack to a belay ledge. One more pitch in the open book (5.6) leads up and right to easier climbing.

Drop Your Bungy. II, 5.10b. First ascent August 1990 by Todd Handy and Richard Villa. This route ascends the center of the northwest face of Fletcher Peak. There is a small triangular block on the lower part of the face. A long 5.7 crack leads up and left, along the left side of this block, to the right-ascending crack or ledge system in the middle of the face. A 5.10a move is followed by a pair of 5.9 cracks that barely touch. These lead to a right-ascending crack. This crack, a poorly protected 5.10a traverse, is followed by 5.10c face climbing past two bolts to a stance in a crack that is left of Modesto Surfer. Continue up the crack (5.7) to the top. *Variation:* Face climb (5.10a) horizontally left from the top of the second pitch to the Arrowhead route.

Moldy Sole. II, 5.10b. First ascent August 1990 by Richard Villa, Todd Handy, and Tom Downey. This route starts from the top of the first pitch of Drop Your Bungy. Some 5.10b crack climbing is followed by a 5.9 crack. Follow this crack up and right to the right-ascending crack of Drop Your Bungy.

Arrowhead. Class 5. This route follows the left side of the prominent triangular face on the northwest side of Fletcher Peak.

Peak 11,357
(11,282 ft; 1.0 mi SW of Rafferty Peak)

Southeast Slope. Class 2. First ascent 1931 by Julie Mortimer, Alice Carter, and Eleanor Bartlett.

Crowley Buttress. II, 5.8. First ascent July 1968 by Chuck Pratt and Doug Robinson. The far right side of the north face, as seen from Nelson Lake, features many buttresses and ribs. This route ascends the northernmost buttress on this side of the peak. A single crack or chimney descends the buttress from a point just right of the lower, western summit of Peak 11,357 (11,282 ft). Begin climbing this chimney (5.7), which is surprisingly deep. Climb out of the top of the chimney on the third pitch and into the dihedral above. Easier climbing in this dihedral leads to the crux, a bulge on the last pitch. This is an enjoyable, direct route.

Northwest Corner. II, 5.9. First ascent September 22, 1974, by Fred Beckey and Pete Metcalf. This three-pitch climb is right of Crowley Buttress.

Eagle Eyes. IV, 5.9. First ascent July 1973 by Mark Gaylor, Ken Boche, and Chris Vandiver. This route climbs the west face. Climb a chimney on the right side of the face. After 100 feet leave the chimney on its left side and climb a 100-foot 5.9 jam crack. Continue up and left for 600 feet of 5.7 to 5.9 climbing to the lower, western summit of Peak 11,357 (11,282 ft).

Rafferty Peak *(11,110 ft; 11,120 ft+)*

First ascent by Edward W. Harnden. Class 2 from the east.

Johnson Peak *(11,064 ft; 11,070 ft)*

First ascent 1933 by H. B. Blanks. Class 2 from Elizabeth Lake.

"Sunrise Wall"

This east-facing wall rises above the left bank of Echo Creek between the Cockscomb and Peak 10,160+ (10,160 ft+). (The wall is approximately at UTM 900885.) It is most easily approached from Elizabeth Lake. A good use trail leads over the pass southwest of the lake and into the Echo Creek drainage.

Pamplona. II, 5.9. First ascent July 1984 by

Alan Bartlett, Steve Gerberding, and Dimitri Barton. This route starts in a large, left-facing dihedral on the right side of the Sunrise Wall. Two pitches lead to a ledge atop the dihedral. Unprotected face climbing to the right of the ledge leads to a crack. Follow the crack to the top.

Blood Test. II, 5.9. First ascent July 1984 by Alan Bartlett, Steve Gerberding, and Dimitri Barton. This route is a short distance to the left of Pamplona. Climb the right-hand of two parallel cracks. The first pitch ends by traversing left into the left-hand crack to a belay. Climb this crack and then traverse left on a long ledge system to the next crack on the wall.

Dihedral Route. III, 5.8, A3. First ascent October 13, 1974, by Fred Beckey, Reed Cundiff, and Karl Kaiyala. This route climbs the obvious right-facing dihedral of the Sunrise Wall. The first three pitches go free, but the fourth pitch uses aid with some bottoming cracks.

Matthes Crest   *(10,918 ft; 10,880 ft+)*

This is an impressive, knife-edged fin. The high point is the north peak, and it was first climbed July 26, 1931, by Jules Eichorn, Glen Dawson, and Walter Brem. Head for the obvious saddle between Echo Peaks No. 7 and No. 8 from Budd Lake. Cross the saddle, and ascend the north ridge of Matthes Crest to the west side of the north peak. One easy class 5 pitch up steep cracks leads to the summit.

Traverse, South to North. II, 5.6. First ascent June 1947 by Charles Wilts and Ellen Wilts. This is a classic climb, and it deserves more attention. The climb starts from a group of trees at the extreme southern end of Matthes Crest. Four class 4–5 pitches lead to the top of the crest. Many spectacular and enjoyable class 3–4 pitches over slabs, pinnacles, and knife-edges lead to the base of the north peak. Drop down to the west side of the north peak and climb steep cracks to the summit. Two long rappels down the west face of the north peak lead to the bottom.

East Face. Class 5. First ascent July 1954 by Donald Harmon and Robert Dohrmann. Climb the east face of the north peak. Slabs lead up to a short chimney just below the summit block.

South Tooth, West Face. II, 5.9. First ascent

July 1973 by Roger Gocking, Mike Warburton, and Ken Dekleva. This peak is east of Echo Lake, at UTM 887880. Climb the west face to the summit.

South Tooth, East Face. III, 5.8. First ascent July 1973 by Roger Gocking, Mike Warburton, and Ken Dekleva. Climb the east face to the summit.

Columbia Finger
(10,360 ft+; 10,320 ft+)

North Ridge. Class 3. First ascent July 22, 1921, by William H. Staniels, Donald E. Tripp, and B. H. Bochmer. Climb the north ridge to the summit rocks. Ascend the west side of the summit rocks to the top.

Digital Manipulation. II, 5.11b. First ascent September 1988 by Bob Palais and Galen Rowell. Ascend cracks on the northeast face. The crux is a long, rounded, fist-joint layback with tiny footholds, on the second pitch.

Southeast Face. II, 5.4, A1. First ascent September 13, 1970, by Richard Hechtel and Jan Mostowski. Go approximately 150 feet to the right of the south buttress to an open book. Ascend the open book, which leads to the right after 140 feet, for two pitches to a small ledge. Overcome the overhang above the small ledge to a series of small ledges. Follow the highest ledge to its far right side. Climb a small open book and chimney up to the south ridge.

Tresidder Peak   *(10,600 ft+; 10,560 ft+)*

The south summit is the high point, and the south arete is class 4. The north arete, also class 4, was first climbed July 4, 1966, by Bruce Kinnison, Alan Zetterberg, and Pierre Zetterberg.

Echo Peaks
(11,160 ft+; 11,040 ft+)

There are nine summits in this massif, which is located east of Cathedral Pass.

"Echo Peak No. 1"
(11,120 ft+; UTM 886899)

East Face. Class 3. First ascent August 4, 1936, by Owen L. Williams. Ascend the center of the east face to the notch between peaks No. 1 and No. 2. Follow the east side of the ridge north to the summit.

West Face. Class 4. Climb the west face to the notch between peaks No. 1 and No. 2, and follow the ridge north to the summit.

Direct West Face. I, 5.8. First ascent July

1972 by Ron Cagle and Jerry Anderson. Climb the west face directly to the summit of Echo Peak No. 1.

North Arete. Class 5. First ascent June 1967 by Bruce Kinnison and Ken Gobalet.

"Echo Peak No. 2"
(11,080 ft+; UTM 886898)

East Face. Class 3. Climb the east face to the notch between peaks No. 1 and No. 2, and follow the ridge south to the summit.

"Echo Peak No. 3"
(11,160 ft+; 11,040 ft+; UTM 886897)

This is the highest of the Echo Peaks, and was first climbed July 7, 1931, by Norman Clyde and Carl Sharsmith.

East Face. Class 4. Climb the gully on the east face leading to the notch between peaks No. 2 and No. 3. Follow the ridge south to the summit.

West Face. Class 3. Ascend the west face to the notch between peaks No. 2 and No. 3, and follow the ridge south to the summit.

"Echo Peak No. 4"
(11,040 ft+; UTM 885896)

First ascent August 6, 1936, by Owen L. Williams and Ethyl Mae Hill.

Traverse from Echo Peak No. 3. Class 4. Descend the east side of the ridge between peaks No. 3 and No. 4 to a point 30 feet below the notch between the two peaks. Ascend the northeast face from here to the summit of peak No. 4.

Northeast Face. Class 4. There is a prominent row of shrubs at the base of the northeast face. Start climbing from the left of these shrubs directly up the face to the summit.

"Echo Peak No. 5"
(11,120 ft+; UTM 887899)

The north ridge is class 3.

"Echo Peak No. 6"
(11,000 ft+; UTM 887898)

Ascend the vague northeast ridge; class 3.

"Echo Peak No. 7"
(11,040 ft+; UTM 888899)

The northeast ridge is class 3.

"Echo Peak No. 8"
(11,080 ft+; UTM 889899)

The north face is class 3.

"Echo Peak No. 9"
(11,040 ft+; UTM 889898)

This is the most attractive, and most difficult, of the Echo Peaks.

Southwest Side. I, 5.7. First ascent 1945 by Charles Wilts and Spencer Austin. Traverse across the west side of peak No. 9 from the notch between peaks No. 7 and No. 8. Class 3 ramps and ledges lead upward to the wall on the southwest side of peak No. 9. Climb straight up the wall for 120 feet before traversing left on knobs to a belay ledge. One short pitch in a corner leads to an arete. Follow the arete to the summit.

Northeast Corner. I, 5.9. First ascent June 1981 by Gary Colliver, Alan Roberts, and Alan Bartlett. This climb starts from the notch between peaks No. 8 and No. 9. Follow a discontinuous corner system up and right for two pitches. The crux is on the second pitch.

"Echo Ridge"
(11,168 ft; 11,120 ft+; 0.5 mi S of Budd Lake)

West Ridge. Class 2. Climb to the saddle between Echo Peaks and Echo Ridge from Budd Lake, and follow the ridge to the summit.

North Face and East Ridge. Class 4. First ascent 1949 by Joe Firey, Peter Hoessly, Ron Hahn, and Ed Robbins. There is a lot of loose rock on this route. Climb to the base of the left-hand chimney at the bottom of the north face. Climb the chimney to the broad east ridge, and follow the ridge to the summit.

Cockscomb   *(11,065 ft; 11,040 ft+)*

First ascent 1914 by Lipman and Chamberlin.

West Face. Class 4. First ascent 1931 by Glen Dawson and Jules Eichorn. Traverse up and right across the west face from the northwest corner of the peak. Climb to a large, flat ledge and traverse south to a wide notch. The summit is the knife-edge east of this notch. *Variation:* Climb a prominent crack above the large, flat ledge to a fingertip traverse which leads to the notch. Further reading: *Summit,* May–June 1981, pp. 18–19.

Unicorn Peak   *(10,823 ft; 10,880 ft+)*

There are three summits for this peak; the north peak is the high point. First ascent 1911 by Francis Farquhar and James Rennie, via the northeast face. The regular route is

Cockscomb from the northeast (photo by F. E. Matthes, #460a, USGS Photographic Library, Denver, CO)

class 3–4, and ascends slabs and talus to the notch between the north and middle summits. A short class 4 move along an arete leads to the summit. Other routes have been done on the north and northwest faces.

The direct north face has been rated II, 5.8, A3 and was climbed September 1965 by Alex Bertulis and Half Zantop.

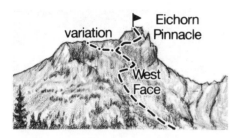

Cathedral Peak from the northwest

Cathedral Peak *(10,911 ft; 10,940 ft+)*

West Face. Class 4. First ascent September 1869 by John Muir. Leave the John Muir Trail along the northwest side of the peak and ascend slabs and talus up the west face to a point between the summit of Cathedral Peak and its west peak, Eichorn Pinnacle. Climb a series of ledges to the southern side of the summit block. A 15-foot class 4 crack leads to the summit. *Variation:* The summit rocks can also be reached from Budd Creek. Leave Budd Creek at the 9,500-foot level and climb a brushy talus slope to a small notch on the ridge north of the summit. Descend the west side of this notch a short way before turning south and climbing to a point between Eichorn Pinnacle and the summit of Cathedral Peak.

North Face. I, 5.5. First ascent July 1961 by Wally Reed and Cathy Warne. This climb begins about 100 feet below the east side of the notch on the north ridge of Cathedral Peak. Traverse south and climb an 8-foot-wide, chimneylike depression with an overhang near its top. Continue up to the notch left of the summit block. A 5.8 variation is left of the depression.

Northeast Face. Class 5. First ascent July 1953 by Frank Tarver and Gordon Petrequin. This climb begins approximately 300 feet to the right of the toe of the southeast buttress. Climb up and left to a shallow ridge. Follow the ridge to the summit.

Southeast Buttress. II, 5.5. First ascent 1945 by Charles Wilts and Spencer Austin. A short approach, combined with excellent climbing on a beautiful peak in one of the most scenic locations in the world, makes this a classic climb. The climb starts about 200 feet to the right of the toe of the southeast buttress at a prominent bush. Climb up and left over right-facing (but downward-sloping) flakes to a ledge. Go directly up the middle of the buttress to a large ledge beneath a chimney. Start the next pitch by climbing the chimney, a knobby face to its right, or a crack farther right. After starting this pitch, continue straight up to a belay stance above a small horn. The next pitch involves some ledges and tricky cracks before it ends on a big ledge 80 feet beneath the summit. Climb a prominent crack to the summit bolt. Further reading: Don Reid and Chris Falkenstein, *Tuolumne Meadows Rock Climbs,* Chockstone Press, Denver, 1986, p. 60; Allan Bard, *Southeast Buttress of Cathedral Peak,* Shooting Star

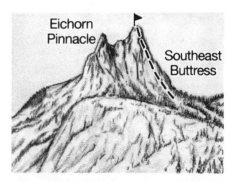

Cathedral Peak from the south

Guides, Bishop, California, 1991 (a route card).

South Face. I, 5.6. First ascent July 1962 by Wally Reed and Don Harmon. This face ends at the broad saddle between Eichorn Pinnacle and the summit of Cathedral Peak. The right side of the face features a crack that leads straight up to another crack, which leads just right of the summit ridge. Climb these cracks, or the faces on their sides, to the top.

"Eichorn Pinnacle"

This is the spectacular west summit of Cathedral Peak.

Eichorn Pinnacle (photo by Pete Yamagata)

North Face. I, 5.4. First ascent July 24, 1931, by Glen Dawson and Jules Eichorn. Climb up and right over cracks and ledges on the north side of the pinnacle to a ledge just below the summit on its west side. A single 165-foot rope suffices for the rappel.

A Celebrity's Holiday. III, 5.10. First ascent June 1984 by Bruce Brossman and Alan Bartlett. This route climbs the long crack system on the left side of the west face of Eichorn Pinnacle. (This crack system does not reach the ground.) Four pitches of poorly protected climbing lead to the upper pitches of the West Pillar route.

West Pillar. III, 5.9. First ascent July 1972 by Gary Colliver and Mike Cohen. Climb a 4-inch-wide jam crack for one pitch and then ascend a rib. Traverse down and right to another crack, and climb this crack to easier climbing.

Southwest Buttress. II, 5.8. First ascent June 1966 by Wally Reed and Gary Colliver. Scramble up some ledges and slabs on the south side of the buttress. Ascend and then traverse into a prominent crack. Continue up the crack for three pitches, and then move left off of the buttress to a wide chimney. Climb the chimney before moving left to a slanting ledge. Climb steep jam cracks to the summit.

Direct South Face. III, 5.7, A2. First ascent July 1972 by Jim Mitchell and Larry Corona. Climb a chimney on the left side of the south face. The chimney is followed by a 5.7 crack and some aid climbing to a ledge. Traverse left from the ledge to the shoulder west of the summit. A chimney then leads to the summit.

Wrinkles

Tuolumne Pass Trail vs. Vogelsang Pass Trail. You can hike either of these two trails between Merced Lake and Vogelsang High Sierra Camp. The Tuolumne Pass Trail is shorter, but it does not have the outstanding views of the Vogelsang Pass Trail.

Errors on the Merced Peak 15-minute map. An approach to Mt. Clark from the west involves cross-country travel through a beautiful, but dense, forest. Rigorous use of the map, compass, and perhaps an altimeter are needed to ensure that you arrive at Mt. Clark, and not one of the cirques surrounding Gray Peak. Unfortunately, some editions of the Merced Peak 15-minute quadrangle are in error regarding the terrain west of Mt. Clark. For example, Red Creek does not flow into the Clark Fork at UTM 807732; it instead flows south of Point 7,232 (on the Merced Peak 15-minute map, at UTM 798730). And there is another fork of the Clark Fork, which does not appear on some editions of the Merced Peak 15-minute map; this fork flows from the west side of Mt. Clark to meet the Clark Fork at UTM 828737. These errors also appear on the Yosemite National Park and Vicinity (1:125,000) map. But it seems that they have been corrected on the new Merced Peak 7.5-minute map.

Northern Yosemite

THE NORTHERN PORTION OF YOSEMITE National Park is the last wilderness of the High Sierra. Much of it is at lower elevations than other portions of the park, and its deep canyons, dense with old-growth forests, still hold historical artifacts from Native Americans, shepherds, and the cavalry. Because it is not as awesome as other regions of the range, it is less visited—so solitude is a part of the wilderness experience of northern Yosemite.

The southern limit of this region is the Tioga Road, and it is marked on the west by a line drawn from Mt. Hoffman, Pate Valley, Wilmer Lake, and Dorothy Lake Pass. The northern boundary is Buckeye Creek.

History

There was no National Park Service when Yosemite National Park was created in 1890. The U.S. Cavalry took charge of administering the park, and their priority was to oust the shepherds and their flocks. The cavalry was at a serious disadvantage, however, because the shepherds had been in the Yosemite backcountry for decades, and had an intimate knowledge of the passes, meadows, and trails. The cavalry established patrols to the boundaries of the new park, and worked out their own system of trails, marked by the "T" (for "trail") blazes in northern Yosemite, and the pointed "Obelisk" blazes in the southern portion of the park. The cavalry named places, began to draw maps, and worked out a system to pursue and capture the herders.

In 1894 First Lieutenant N. F. McClure of the Fifth Cavalry led an expedition to scout for shepherds. His party of twelve mounted soldiers left Wawona and headed for Tuolumne Meadows. He arrested four herders and their pack train near Mt. Conness, and had them escorted back to Wawona. He continued his patrol, and at Virginia Canyon he came across two large flocks of sheep. He wrote, "The herders fled up into the rocks, and we were unable to capture them; so I had one or two shots fired to frighten them. I do not think they have stopped running yet." He sent patrols up and down Return Creek, and found thousands of sheep apparently abandoned by the herders.

But there were no penalties for grazing in the national park; all that the cavalry could do was to confiscate the stock, herd, supplies, and camping equipment, and order the shepherds out of the park. Seizing thousands of sheep was almost impossible, so Lieutenant Benson of the U.S. Cavalry worked out a plan to scatter the flocks beyond the park boundary on one side of the park, and the herders and their dogs on the other side, several days of travel away. In 1898, 189,550 sheep, 350 horses, and 1,000 head of cattle were expelled from the park, and 27 firearms were confiscated.

The ever-resourceful shepherds countered this by hiring spies. A cavalry patrol could not leave Wawona without word being sent far ahead of their approach. Signal fires were lit during the night, and warning notices were nailed to trees along the trails. But the cavalry prevailed in the end, with the help of law and public opinion, and the era of the shepherds in the High Sierra came to an end in the early twentieth century.

Maps

United States Geological Survey: 7.5-minute series: Mt. Dana, Tioga Pass, Falls Ridge, Tenaya Lake, Yosemite Falls, Ten Lakes, Tiltill Mtn., Piute Mtn., Matterhorn Peak, Dunderberg Peak, Twin Lakes, Buckeye Ridge, Tower Peak; 15-minute series: Tuolumne Meadows, Hetch Hetchy Reservoir, Matterhorn Peak, Tower Peak; national park maps: Yosemite National Park and Vicinity (1:125,000).

United States Forest Service: Hoover Wilderness (1:63,360).

Wilderness Permits

For east-side entry to the Hoover Wilderness from Saddlebag Lake to Lundy Lake: Inyo National Forest, Mono Lake Ranger District, Lee Vining, CA 93541.

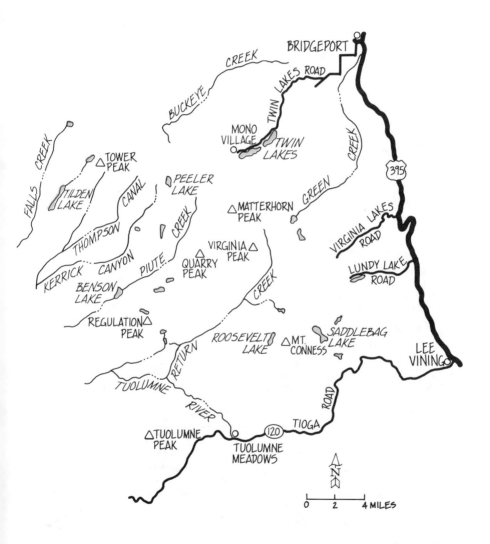

For east-side entry to the Hoover Wilderness from Virginia Lakes to Buckeye Creek: Toiyabe National Forest, Bridgeport Ranger District, Bridgeport, CA 93517.

For entry to the Yosemite backcountry: Backcountry Office, P.O. Box 577, Yosemite National Park, CA 95389.

Roads

Tioga Road

The Tioga Road serves as the southern boundary of this chapter's region. A side road leaves the Tioga Road 9.8 miles from Lee Vining and goes north for 2.5 miles to Saddlebag Lake.

The Gaylor Lakes Trail starts from the Tioga Road 3.4 miles west of Tioga Pass.

A side road leads north off of the Tioga Road 6.9 miles west of Tioga Pass. This road leads to the trailhead serving the Dog Lake Trail and the Pacific Crest Trail near Soda Springs.

The trailhead for the McGee Lake Trail is near the north shore of Tenaya Lake, 15.3 miles west of Tioga Pass along the Tioga Road.

The trailhead for the May Lake Trail is located at Snow Flat. Leave the Tioga Road either 19.4 miles west of Tioga Pass, or 26.6 miles east of Crane Flat, and drive north on the side road 1.9 miles to the trailhead.

Lundy Lake Road

The Lundy Lake Road goes west from the junction of Highways 395 and 167, approximately 7.2 miles north of Lee Vining on Highway 395. The road ascends Lundy Canyon for 6.3 miles to the trailhead of the Lundy Pass Trail.

Virginia Lakes Road

The Virginia Lakes Road goes west from the top of Conway Summit along Highway 395, approximately 13 miles north of Lee Vining, or 13.3 miles south of Bridgeport. The road goes for 6 miles to Virginia Lakes and the trailhead for the Summit Lake Trail.

Green Creek Road

The Green Creek Road leaves Highway 395 approximately 5 miles south of Bridgeport. The road heads south from the highway and goes for 0.9 mile to a fork. Take the left fork for 1.7 miles to another fork. Go left

another 0.8 mile to a junction. Turn right, and continue up the road another 5.8 miles to the end of the road and the trailhead for the Green Lake Trail.

Twin Lakes Road

The Twin Lakes Road heads south from the western edge of Bridgeport. It leads 13.4 miles to Twin Lakes and Mono Village. The trailheads for the Peeler Lake Trail, Rock Island Pass Trail, and the Horse Creek Trail are in the private campground at Mono Village. The hiker parking area is on private land at Mono Village, and a parking fee is charged.

Buckeye Creek Road

The Buckeye Creek Road starts along the Twin Lakes Road at 7.1 miles from Bridgeport. The road goes north for 2.8 miles to a junction. Go left another 1.3 miles to the trailhead for the Buckeye Pass Trail. As of this writing, this trailhead is on private land and is subject to the control of the owner.

Trails

May Lake Trail (4¼ miles)

The May Lake Trail starts from Snow Flat, along the old Tioga Road. The trail goes north 1 mile to May Lake and the May Lake High Sierra Camp. It then continues another 3¼ miles to meet the Ten Lakes Trail.

Ten Lakes Trail (20¼ miles)

The Ten Lakes Trail leaves the Tioga Road at the northern shore of Tenaya Lake. The trail ascends Murphy Creek for 2½ miles before meeting the McGee Lake Trail. The Ten Lakes Trail turns southwest from the junction and continues another ¾ mile to meet the May Lake Trail. The Ten Lakes Trail then climbs to the north, and turns west and then southwest around Tuolumne Peak. The trail descends the South Fork of Cathedral Creek before making a steep climb out of this canyon and continuing on to the westernmost of the Ten Lakes, 10¾ miles from the May Lake Trail. The trail climbs out of the Ten Lakes basin on its western side, and descends to Yosemite Creek to meet the Tioga Road, 6¼ miles from Ten Lakes.

McGee Lake Trail (3¾ miles)

This trail leaves the Pacific Crest Trail at

Glen Aulin and heads southwest for ³/₄ mile to McGee Lake. The trail continues southwest from the lake, crosses Cathedral Creek, and meets the Ten Lakes Trail after 3 miles.

Tuolumne Canyon Trail (13³/₄ miles)

The Tuolumne Canyon Trail starts at Glen Aulin, which is reached via the Pacific Crest Trail from Tuolumne Meadows. The trail follows the north bank of the Tuolumne River down the canyon, and after 3 miles it passes Waterwheel Falls, a sight to behold. The trail continues downstream and crosses Return Creek. It continues to descend the canyon and, after 6 miles, it comes to Muir Gorge, where the river roars through a deep chasm. This is shortly followed by the crossing of Register Creek. The trail continues downstream to Pate Valley, where it meets the Rodgers Canyon Trail.

The lower portion of the Tuolumne Canyon Trail may be flooded during high water, and the stream crossings may be extraordinarily difficult if not impossible. On the other hand, the Tuolumne River is an awesome sight during high water.

Rodgers Canyon Trail (10¹/₂ miles)

The Rodgers Canyon Trail goes north from Pate Valley and makes a steep climb for 4³/₄ miles to meet the Pleasant Valley Trail. It goes southeast from the junction and makes a slight climb before making a gentle descent to Rodgers Canyon. The trail continues upstream and meets the Rodgers Lake Trail 4³/₄ miles from the junction with the Pleasant Valley Trail. The Rodgers Canyon Trail goes north from this junction another 1 mile to meet the Pacific Crest Trail.

Rodgers Lake Trail (3 miles)

This trail leaves the Pacific Crest Trail southwest of Smedberg Lake. After crossing a small saddle, it descends and circles around the west shore of Rodgers Lake. The trail continues descending, crosses the outlet of Neall Lake, and leads to the Rodgers Canyon Trail, approximately 1 mile south of its junction with the Pacific Crest Trail.

Pleasant Valley Trail (5 miles)

The Pleasant Valley Trail leaves the Rodgers Canyon Trail 4³/₄ miles from Pate Valley. The trail goes north from the junction, traversing at first, and then makes a steep descent into Pleasant Valley, meeting a side trail after 2 miles. The side trail leads north to Irwin Bright Lake; the Pleasant Valley Trail wanders through the valley before climbing out of the western side of the valley to meet the Bear Valley Trail after 3 miles.

Bear Valley Trail (5¹/₂ miles)

This trail leaves the Pacific Crest Trail in the lower portion of Kerrick Canyon and makes a steep ascent to the south for 1 mile to the lake at Bear Valley. The trail crosses the outlet of the lake and goes downstream to a small lake, where it turns southeast and makes a short, steep climb to a saddle. It then descends to meet the Pleasant Valley Trail, 4¹/₂ miles from Bear Valley. The Rancheria Trail goes southwest from this junction and leads to Hetch Hetchy Reservoir.

Pacific Crest Trail (54¹/₂ miles)

This section of the Pacific Crest Trail starts from the Tioga Road near Lembert Dome. The trail follows a dirt road for ³/₄ mile to Soda Springs and some stables. It then leaves the road and becomes a real trail and, after ¹/₂ mile, it meets the Young Lakes Trail. The Pacific Crest Trail takes the left fork and descends the upper part of Tuolumne Canyon, passing some impressive waterfalls. After 3¹/₂ miles it meets the McGee Lake Trail. It then descends to the Tuolumne River, crosses it on a bridge, and meets the Tuolumne Canyon Trail at Glen Aulin. The Pacific Crest Trail heads northeast from this junction, and after two river crossings it ascends Cold Canyon for 7 miles to meet the side trail leading to McCabe Lakes, which goes east from the junction before turning south and arriving at the lower McCabe Lake after 1³/₄ miles. The Pacific Crest Trail goes north, crossing McCabe Creek, and descending into Virginia Canyon. It then crosses Return Creek and meets the Summit Lake Trail 1¹/₄ miles from the McCabe Lakes Trail.

The Pacific Crest Trail turns southwest from the junction and descends Virginia Canyon before turning northwest and climbing through a small pass; it then arrives at Miller Lake after 3¹/₂ miles. The trail goes north from the lake and descends into Matterhorn Canyon to meet the Burro Pass Trail after 2¹/₄ miles. The trail turns southwest from this junction, crosses the stream, and descends the canyon before turning northwest and ascending the Wilson Creek drainage to climb to the summit of Benson Pass after 4¹/₂ miles. It then descends the west side of the pass and circles around Volunteer Peak, passing Smedberg Lake and meeting the Rodgers Lake Trail after 3 miles. The Pacific Crest Trail goes west from this junction for ¹/₂ mile to meet the Rodgers Canyon Trail, then goes north and descends for 3 miles to cross Piute Creek. (A half-mile side trail goes west from here to beautiful Benson Lake, the Riviera of northern Yosemite.) The Pacific Crest Trail then makes a steep climb to the north over Seavey Pass for 3¹/₂ miles to meet the Buckeye Pass Trail in Kerrick Canyon. It then descends Kerrick Canyon for 3¹/₄ miles to meet the Bear Valley Trail.

After crossing Rancheria Creek, the Pacific Crest Trail makes a steep climb to the north, crosses a pass, and then makes a steep descent to another major stream crossing after 2 miles. The trail continues west another 2¹/₂ miles, and after crossing Macomb Ridge it meets the Tilden Lake Trail. A trail leads south down Tilden Canyon from this junction; the Pacific Crest Trail continues west and descends to Wilmer Lake (spelled "Wilma" on some maps) after 1³/₄ miles. There is a trail junction just west of Wilmer Lake. The Jack Main Canyon Trail goes south and leads to Hetch Hetchy Reservoir; the Pacific Crest Trail ascends Jack Main Canyon for 1¹/₂ miles to meet the Tilden Lake Trail. The Pacific Crest Trail continues north up Jack Main Canyon another 6³/₄ miles to the Bond Pass Trail junction, turns northeast, passes Dorothy Lake, and reaches the summit of Dorothy Lake Pass after 1¹/₂ miles. The trail descends the east side of the pass and gradually moves north. It descends Cascade Creek and, after 2 miles, it comes to a junction. The Pacific Crest Trail goes west from this junction, continuing on to Cinko Lake and eventually the Canadian border. A side trail leads northeast from this junction for 1¹/₄ miles and descends to the West Walker River, meeting the Kirkwood Pass Trail below Upper Piute Meadows.

Young Lakes Trail (5¹/₄ miles)

The Young Lakes Trail leaves the Pacific Crest Trail ¹/₂ mile from Soda Springs in Tuolumne Meadows. It goes to the right from the junction, crosses Delaney Creek, and makes a gradual ascent to the northeast for 4 miles to meet the Dog Lake Trail. The Young Lakes Trail goes around Ragged Peak for another 1¹/₄ miles to Young Lakes.

Dog Lake Trail (4¹/₂ miles)

This trail starts from the parking area west of Lembert Dome in Tuolumne Meadows. It goes north and climbs around to the north side of Lembert Dome for 1 mile to meet another trail which comes from the eastern side of Lembert Dome. The Dog Lake Trail goes north from the junction, passes Dog Lake after ¹/₂ mile, and continues north another 3 miles to the junction with the Young Lakes Trail.

Gaylor Lakes Trail (2¹/₄ miles)

The Gaylor Lakes Trail goes north from the Tioga Road, about 3¹/₂ miles west of Tioga Pass. It then goes north for 2¹/₄ miles to the lowest of the Gaylor Lakes. Cross-country travel is easy to the other lakes in the basin above.

Another trail leads from Tioga Pass to the Gaylor Lakes. This trail goes west for 1 mile from the Tioga Pass Entrance Station and crosses a saddle before descending to the southeastern lake.

Lundy Pass Trail (6³/₄ miles)

This trail starts from the southern shore of Saddlebag Lake. (A good trail goes around Saddlebag Lake on its western shore, and a road circles the lake on its eastern shore.) The trail goes north over Lundy Pass and makes a steep descent into Lundy Canyon. Campfires are prohibited between Lake Helen and Hummingbird Lake.

Summit Lake Trail (9¹/₂ miles)

The Summit Lake Trail starts from the end of the Virginia Lakes Road. It passes the upper lakes in this basin and crosses a small saddle to meet the Green Lake Trail after 4¹/₄ miles. The trail continues another 1 mile, around Summit Lake to the small pass on its western shore, which is atop the Sierra crest. It then descends into Virginia Canyon. After 4¹/₄ miles it meets the Pacific Crest Trail.

Green Lake Trail (6¹/₄ miles)

The Green Lake Trail starts from the end of the Green Creek Road and climbs southwest for 2 miles to Green Lake. A trail leads northwest from Green Lake to West Lake after 1½ miles, and a good use trail continues from West Lake up into Glimes Canyon. The Green Lake Trail goes south and climbs for 1½ miles to East Lake. The trail continues south another 1 mile to Gilman Lake, passes Hoover Lakes, and meets the Summit Lake Trail after 1¾ miles.

Tamarack Lake Trail (4½ miles)

This trail starts from Twin Lakes Campground, along the Twin Lakes Road from Bridgeport. It switchbacks up the steep slope to the south of the campground and ascends Tamarack Creek to Tamarack Lake.

Horse Creek Trail (5¼ miles)

The Horse Creek Trail switchbacks up the steep slope south of Mono Village for 1½ miles to the hanging valley portion of Horse Creek. A good use trail continues up Horse Creek from here. The Horse Creek Trail goes east, gradually descending to the isthmus of Twin Lakes.

Barney Lake Trail (6¾ miles)

The Barney Lake Trail goes west from Mono Village and ascends Robinson Creek for 4 miles to Barney Lake. (Some maps may show a trail crossing a pass to the west and descending to the South Fork of Buckeye Creek; this trail has been abandoned for a long time.) The trail passes the western shore of Barney Lake and continues upstream another 2¾ miles to meet the Peeler Lake Trail and the Burro Pass Trail.

Peeler Lake Trail (2¼ miles)

The Peeler Lake Trail climbs to the west from the junction of the Barney Lake Trail and the Rock Island Pass Trail. It passes through some enormous boulders before circling around the northern shore of Peeler Lake. Peeler Lake has two outlets during high water: One outlet feeds the Pacific Ocean, and the other drains into the Great Basin. The trail continues west another ¾ mile to the Buckeye Pass Trail.

Rock Island Pass Trail (3¼ miles)

This trail leaves the Buckeye Pass Trail near the southern end of Kerrick Meadow. The trail climbs to the southeast before turning east and finally northeast to cross Rock Island Pass after 2 miles. It then descends the

northeast side of the pass for 1¼ miles to meet the Burro Pass Trail above Crown Lake. The trail continues downhill another ¾ mile to Crown Lake, then continues another 1½ miles to meet the Peeler Lake Trail and the Barney Lake Trail.

Burro Pass Trail (10 miles)

This trail leaves the Rock Island Pass Trail ¾ mile above Crown Lake. The trail makes a steep ascent for 1½ miles to Mule Pass and then continues east another 3 miles to the top of Burro Pass. It then descends Matterhorn Canyon 5½ miles to meet the Pacific Crest Trail.

Kirkwood Pass Trail (15¾ miles)

The Kirkwood Pass Trail ascends Buckeye Creek for 9¼ miles to meet the Buckeye Pass Trail. The trail continues west and makes a steep climb for 2½ miles to the summit of Kirkwood Pass. (This pass is unnamed on most maps.) It descends the west side of the pass for 4 miles, past Upper Piute Meadows, to meet the Tower Lake Trail. The trail continues downstream another 1¼ miles to meet the side trail that leads southwest to the Pacific Crest Trail. A trail continues north from here for 10½ miles to Leavitt Meadows.

Buckeye Pass and
Kerrick Canyon Trail (11 miles)

This trail leaves the Kirkwood Pass Trail and ascends the South Fork of Buckeye Creek for 4 miles to the summit of Buckeye Pass. The trail descends the south side of the pass for ¾ mile to meet the Peeler Lake Trail. The Kerrick Canyon Trail heads south through Kerrick Meadow for 1½ miles to meet the Rock Island Pass Trail. The Kerrick Canyon Trail continues its descent, passing many meadows and forests, for 4¾ miles to meet the Pacific Crest Trail at the head of Kerrick Canyon.

Tower Lake Trail (3¾ miles)

This trail goes south from the northern end of Lower Piute Meadows and ascends Tower Canyon to Tower Lake.

Tilden Lake Trail (4¾ miles)

The Tilden Lake Trail leaves the Pacific Crest Trail in Jack Main Canyon and leads to the lower end of Tilden Lake after 1¼ miles. A side trail follows the western shore of the lake from here, and the main trail continues another ¾ mile along the eastern shore of the lake. The trail then goes south, descending Tilden Canyon Creek for 2¾ miles to meet the Pacific Crest Trail between Wilmer Lake and Macomb Ridge.

Cross-Country Routes

"Conness Pass"

(11,280 ft+; 11,280 ft+; 1.2 mi ENE of Mt. Conness; UTM 981051)

Class 2. This route crosses the east ridge of Mt. Conness. Head northwest from the Carnegie Institute Experimental Station (located ½ mile southwest of Saddlebag Lake), pass a flat area, and climb onto the crest of the east ridge of the peak. Climb the east ridge of the peak to the 11,280-foot level, where a steep spur ridge drops down to the north and leads to the lowest of the Conness Lakes.

"North Peak Pass"

(11,720 ft+; 11,680 ft+; 0.3 mi SW of North Peak)

Class 2. This pass crosses the Sierra crest between Conness Lakes and Roosevelt Lake. Tedious sand slopes lead up the southeast side of the pass. Head northwest for ½ mile from the top of the pass before turning southwest to Roosevelt Lake.

"Don't Be A Smart Pass"

(11,160 ft+; 11,000 ft+; 0.7 mi NW of North Peak)

Class 2. This pass leads between Upper McCabe Lake and Roosevelt Lake. Loose talus, interspersed with patches of snow, leads up the north slope of the pass. The south side is easy.

"McCabe Pass"

(11,160 ft+; 11,200 ft+; 1.3 mi N of North Peak; UTM 971081)

Class 2. This pass crosses the Sierra crest south of Shepherd Crest. An abandoned mining road leads from the north end of Saddlebag Lake to Steelhead Lake. A good use trail leads around the west shore of Steelhead Lake to the summit of the pass. The west side of this pass is class 2 down to Upper McCabe Lake.

"Sky Pilot Col"

(11,640 ft+; 11,600 ft+; 1.4 mi S of Excelsior Mtn.; UTM 972086)

Class 2. This pass leads between Steelhead Lake and Shepherd Lake. A good use trail leads from Steelhead Lake up the eastern side of McCabe Pass. The route to Sky Pilot Col goes north from here over talus to a small bowl. Climb out of this bowl on its left (west) side over talus to a scree slope, which leads to the top of Sky Pilot Col, immediately east of Shepherd Crest. Descend loose talus on the north side of the col down and to the northwest, descending to Shepherd Lake. Further reading: Steve Roper, *Timberline Country*, Sierra Club Books, San Francisco, 1982, pp. 266–68.

Virginia Pass *(10,480 ft+; 10,480 ft+)*

Class 1. This pass leads from Green Creek to the upper portion of Virginia Canyon. A good use trail leads from Green Lake up Glimes Canyon to the summit of Virginia Pass. The easiest descent of the west side of the pass is to contour northwest to the gentler terrain along Return Creek, on the floor of Virginia Canyon.

"Horse Creek Pass"

(10,680 ft+; 10,640 ft+; 0.9 mi NW of Twin Peaks; UTM 921181)

Class 2. This provides a direct cross-country route between Twin Lakes and Spiller Creek. Leave the Horse Creek Trail at the point where it switchbacks away from the canyon, and continue up the canyon over a good use trail. The class 2 portion is just north of the summit. Travel down the Spiller Creek drainage is easy. Further reading: Steve Roper, *Timberline Country*, Sierra Club Books, San Francisco, 1982, pp. 272–73.

"Stanton Pass"

(11,160 ft+; 11,120 ft+; 0.3 mi NE of Stanton Peak)

Class 3. This pass leads between Virginia Canyon and Spiller Creek. It is located between Virginia Peak and Stanton Peak. A ledge system on the east side of the pass is used to approach a notch atop the pass near the northeast ridge of Stanton Peak. Descend the west side of the pass via class 3 ledges and loose gullies for a short distance, then head down and across the west side of Stanton Peak to Spiller Creek. A direct descent of the west side of the pass may result in the hiker becoming stranded on some cliffs. Further reading: Steve Roper, *Timberline Country*, Sierra Club Books, San Francisco, 1982, pp. 268–72.

"Twin Peaks Pass"

(11,480 ft+; 11,520 ft+; 0.8 mi S of Twin Peaks)

Class 2. This pass is between Twin Peaks and Virginia Peak; it leads from Spiller Creek to upper Virginia Canyon. The easiest approach to this pass from the west is to traverse diagonally up and right to the pass from a point in the Spiller Creek drainage, which is west of Twin Peaks; a direct ascent leads to cliffs beneath the pass. The east side of the pass has no hidden obstacles.

"Matterhorn Pass"

(11,320 ft+; 11,360 ft+; 0.5 mi S of Matterhorn Peak)

Class 3. This pass leads between Spiller Creek and upper Matterhorn Canyon. When crossing the pass from Spiller Creek, approach the top of the pass from the right (north) on a ledge system. The west side of the pass is class 2.

Avalanche Lake and Glacier Lake

This cross-country route leads to the Sawtooth Ridge from Twin Lakes. Take the Horse Creek Trail from Mono Village and cross Robinson Creek. Leave the trail here, and make a diagonal climb up and to the right to Blacksmith Creek, aiming for a point above the falls at approximately 7,500 feet. This leads to the first hanging valley, where the creek forks. Those bound for Avalanche Lake take the left (east) fork; those headed for Glacier Lake take the right (west). Wood campfires are prohibited north of the Sawtooth Ridge, and the maximum party size allowed is eight persons.

"Polemonium Pass"

(11,520 ft+; 11,760 ft+; 0.5 mi NW of Matterhorn Peak; UTM 907192)

Class 3; ice axe required. This pass crosses the Sawtooth Ridge between the Dragtooth and the Doodad. The north side of this pass is a wide chute, 500 feet of 45-degree snow/ice, and is a worthwhile climb in its own right. The south side of the pass is class 2 scree.

"Col de Doodad"

(11,400 ft+; 11,440 ft+; 0.7 mi NW of Matterhorn Peak; UTM 905194)

Class 3. This pass crosses the Sawtooth Ridge between the Southeast Tooth and the Doodad. The easiest route on the northeast side of the pass ascends the right (west) gully, which is next to the Southeast Tooth. Ascend this 35-degree snow/ice gully, passing under an overhanging block, and gain the ridge crest. Go to the right for 30 feet to a platform, then go left to a chockstone at the top of a short, steep chimney. Descend this class 3 chimney to the scree slopes that lead down into Slide Canyon. *Variation:* Class 4. The route described above is difficult to locate when crossing the pass from the southwest to the northeast, and some parties have climbed easy scree from Slide Canyon to the most prominent notch between the Southeast Tooth and the Doodad. The 45-degree couloir to the north of this notch is usually filled with snow; otherwise, it is full of loose rock. Rappel down the snow or rock in the couloir for 100 feet to a ledge. Traverse 10 feet horizontally left to the top of a loose chimney. Rappel 90 feet down the chimney to its right (as you look down) wall. This is followed by a third rappel of 60 feet directly to the snowfield below. It is better to develop your route-finding ability and avoid this variation completely.

"Glacier Col"

(11,560 ft+; 11,600 ft+; 0.7 mi S of Avalanche Lake; UTM 900200)

Class 2; ice axe needed. This pass crosses the Sawtooth Ridge between Cleaver Peak and Blacksmith Peak. The north side of the pass consists of steep snow/ice; the south side has scree and benches, which leads down to Slide Canyon.

"Cleaver Notch"

(10,880 ft+; 10,880 ft+; 0.3 mi SE of Avalanche Lake; UTM 905204)

Class 2. This is the obvious notch in The Cleaver. Cross the notch on its southern side, only 30 feet above the benches on its east and west sides.

"Ice Lake Pass"

(10,000 ft+; 10,000 ft+; 0.7 mi SSE of Kettle Peak; UTM 874209)

Class 2. This route ascends Little Slide Canyon from Robinson Creek, crosses the Sierra crest, and descends into Slide Canyon. Leave the Barney Lake Trail at the mouth of the canyon and cross Robinson Creek at a conveniently located beaver dam. Ascend the east side of the canyon, keeping above the willows and aspens that choke the streambed, and cross to the west bank of the stream near the point where the stream makes a sharp turn to the left. Ascend the west bank to a small meadow just below the falls of the outlet stream of Maltby Lake. Traverse east into the east fork of Little Slide Canyon and ascend a ravine next to a rock dome in the middle of the canyon. Circle Ice Lake on its east side and go above the cliffs that drop into the lake. The best approach to Ice Lake Pass is to descend to its low point from the higher, eastern end of the saddle. Benches and meadows on the southwest side of the pass lead to the Burro Pass Trail.

"Tower Pass"

(10,080 ft+; 10,080 ft+; 0.7 mi NW of Tower Peak)

Class 2. This pass leads from Tower Lake over the Sierra crest to Mary Lake and downstream to Tilden Lake. Climb to the broad saddle south of Tower Lake and descend the west bank of Tilden Creek to join the trail along the western shore of Tilden Lake.

Peaks

Mt. Hoffman   *(10,850 ft; 10,850 ft)*

This is a frequently climbed peak, and there is an outstanding view from the summit (if you ignore the radio repeater installed there).

South Slope. Class 2. First ascent June 24, 1863, by Josiah D. Whitney, William H. Brewer, and Charles F. Hoffman. The south slope can be easily reached from either May Lake or the Tioga Road.

Southwest Ridge. Class 3. This ridge can be approached from either Hoffman Creek or from Wegner Lake. Follow the ridge to the summit.

Crimson Corner. III, 5.9. First ascent August 1982 by Terri Counts and Alan Bartlett. This route is on the north face of Mt. Hoffman; it is to the right of the Merle Alley Route. Two pitches lead to the base of a large, left-facing, reddish corner. Three more pitches in the corner lead to the top. Generally, keep to the right wall of the corner. The crux is an off-width section on the fourth pitch.

Merle Alley Route. III, 5.7. First ascent July 1957 by Merle Alley and George Sessions. Ascend the snowfield on the north side of Mt. Hoffman to the base of a chimney that is 200 feet west of the overhanging summit block. Climb the chimney all the way to the ridge.

There are three overhangs in this 500-foot crack-and-chimney system.

North Face. III, 5.7, A2. First ascent August 1969 by George Sessions and Bob Summers. This route directly ascends the north face to the overhanging summit blocks. Begin by climbing cracks on the steep face through overhangs for several pitches to a belay stance about 50 feet below a small, red overhang. Climb to the base of this overhang (5.7), and overcome it with aid. The next pitch traverses left above the overhanging wall and climbs steep cracks (5.7) to a belay ledge. Three more pitches of easy class 5 over flakes and cracks lead to the summit.

East Face. II, 5.7. First ascent September 1970 by Steve Williams and Richard Doleman. This is the face that rises above May Lake. Climb cracks that are to the right of an obvious left-facing open book. These cracks lead to a ramp, which goes left and up to the top.

Approach Face. II, 5.5. First ascent August 1974 by Vern Clevenger and Virginia Wallblom. This is the obvious face that is to the right of the summit when viewed from Snow Flat. The route is reportedly somewhere on this face.

"Hoffman's Thumb"

This is the impressive spire a few hundred feet southwest of the true summit of Mt. Hoffman.

Regular Route. I, 5.6. First ascent October 16, 1932, by Jules Eichorn. Begin by climbing the southwest face of the thumb. Climb to a sloping ledge, which leads out onto the exposed east face. Climb the east face to the summit.

Other class 4 and 5 routes have been done on the northeast and west faces.

"Hoffman Turret"

(10,280 ft+; 10,240 ft+; 0.3 mi NW of Mt. Hoffman)

This pinnacle is at the end of the low northwest ridge of Mt. Hoffman.

Northeast Face. I, 5.9. First ascent August 1958 by Jerry Gray, George Ewing, and Les Overstreet. First free ascent August 1982 by Terri Counts and Alan Bartlett. Begin by climbing the right-hand crack of two cracks on the face, and climb to a large, v-shaped opening. Ascend the left side of the v to a hand crack that traverses left to the highest of three steps. Go right, around a buttress and across a friction slab, to a difficult open chimney. Climb the chimney; this is followed by easy scrambling to the summit.

"The Bowmaiden"
(10,633 ft; 10,480 ft+; 1.0 mi N of May Lake; UTM 808903)

Lucky Sailor's Route. III, 5.10. First ascent July 1981 by Evelyn Lees, Louise Sheperd, and Alan Bartlett. This route rises above the headwaters of the South Fork of Cathedral Creek. It is the most impressive of the north faces between Mt. Hoffman and Tuolumne Peak. Begin by climbing cracks leading to the right-hand of two obvious open books on the prow of the buttress on the north side of the peak. Exit right after climbing the book halfway, and climb to a large, tree-covered ledge that runs across the north side of the Bowmaiden. Walk right along the ledge, and climb toward another large, left-facing open book, but climb a smaller open book to its left. From the top of this smaller book, go left and climb a 5.10 overhang, then climb up and left to a crack that divides the summit overhang.

Tuolumne Peak *(10,845 ft; 10,845 ft)*
The south side of this peak is class 2 from May Lake; the northeast face from the Ten Lakes Trail is also class 2.

East Face, Right Side. II, 5.6. First ascent July 1968 by Bruce Kinnison and Ken Gobalet. Climb a prominent, left-facing open book on the right side of the east face. Climb up and left from the top of the book to the upper left side of a tree-covered terrace. A long class 4 pitch then leads to the summit.

East Face, Left Side. II, 5.7. First ascent September 10, 1974, by Bruce Kinnison, Ken Gobalet, and George Gray. There is an obvious chimney on the left side of the east face. This route starts approximately 50 feet left of this chimney. Fifty feet of easy class 5 climbing leads into the chimney. Climb the right side of the chimney and belay from chockstones in the chimney itself. Climb up the chimney for another long pitch, followed by a traverse left under a roof. Continue upward by climbing cracks to the summit plateau.

Southwest Face. II, 5.7. First ascent July 1972 by Bruce Kinnison and Bob Ashworth. This route climbs the center of the face and ascends a prominent 250-foot chimney. Climb up and left from the top of the chimney to a class 4 buttress. *Variation:* II, 5.9. First ascent August 1987 by Dan Ward and Dave Harden. Climb a steep, right-facing corner directly above the prominent 250-foot chimney.

Giardiasis. II, 5.10. First ascent June 1981 by Kim Walker and Alan Bartlett. The route begins just left of the center portion of the southwest face. Climb up and left through a dirty, black-stained area. Cleaner rock leads up, and then up and right for three more pitches.

Wildcat Point *(9,455 ft; 9,455 ft)*
Class 2 from Mattie Lake.

Wildcat Buttress. IV, 5.9, A4. First ascent August 1972 by Galen Rowell and Dale Bard. This route climbs the buttress above California Falls. The route starts to the right of a prominent dihedral. The first pitch consists of difficult mixed climbing. This is followed by a short 5.9 crack, easier face climbing, and an awesome but easy jam crack behind a huge flake. Two sections of aid pass giant ledges. The second section is in an overhanging dihedral with difficult aid placements. Traverse left from the top of the dihedral for 50 feet along a narrow ledge to a shallow corner, which leads to the top.

Cold Mountain *(10,301 ft; 10,301 ft)*
Class 2. First ascent 1929 by Glen Dawson and party.

Peak 8,886
(8,880 ft+; 0.5 mi NNW of Glen Aulin)

Southwest Buttress. III, 5.8. First ascent September 1972 by Joe Kelsey, Galen Rowell, and TM Herbert. Climb the prominent dihedral on the buttress.

Ragged Peak *(10,912 ft; 10,912 ft)*
Southwest Slope. Class 2. First ascent July 6, 1863, by William H. Brewer and Charles Hoffman. This slope can be approached from the Dog Lake Trail, or from Young Lakes via the saddle east of the summit. The high point is the southernmost of the three summits clustered together.

Northwest Face. Class 5. First ascent August 25, 1939, by Boynton Kaiser and party. Slabs and chimneys lead up this face to the summit.

Northeast Face. I, 5.6. First ascent July 1971 by Jeff Genest and Adrian Rosenthal. This route begins in a v-shaped trough midway up the face.

East Face. Class 5. First ascent August 16, 1953, by Warren Harding, Ray Alcott, and Norah Straley. The route is reportedly somewhere on this face.

Peak 11,255
(11,255 ft; 1.1 mi ESE of Ragged Peak)

First ascent October 15, 1967, by John Simon and Mike Etherton. The summit rocks are class 3 from the southeast.

Gaylor Peak   *(11,004 ft; 11,004 ft)*

This fine viewpoint is class 1 from Tioga Pass. There is a good ski tour on Gaylor Peak's northeast slope. Further reading: Hans Joachim Burhenne, *Sierra Spring Ski-Touring*, Mountain Press, San Francisco, 1971, p. 71.

Tioga Peak   *(11,526 ft; 11,513 ft)*
Class 2 from Gardinsky Lake.

Mono Dome   *(10,622 ft; 10,614 ft)*
The north slope is class 2.

Lee Vining Peak   *(11,690 ft; 11,691 ft)*
The southeast slope is class 2.

Mt. Warren   *(12,327 ft; 12,327 ft)*
First ascent prior to 1868 by a Mr. Wackenreyder. The north and south slopes are both class 2.

Peak 12,002
(12,002 ft; 1.0 mi SE of White Mtn.)

First ascent June 24, 1969, by Daniel Zucker. The southeast slope is class 2.

White Mountain
(12,057 ft; 12,000 ft+)

First ascent 1917 by Walter L. Huber. The south slope is class 2.

Mt. Conness   *(12,590 ft; 12,590 ft)*

From Young Lakes. Class 2. First ascent September 1, 1866, by Clarence King and James T. Gardiner. This is a very popular climb, and a use trail has appeared over the years. Go east from Young Lakes to Lake 10,560+ (10,560 ft+; 1.3 mi S of Mt. Conness). Go north up sand and scree into the valley and onto the plateau southeast of the summit. Climb over blocks to the summit from the plateau.

Southwest Face, Right Corner. IV, 5, A. First ascent July 15, 1959, by John Merriam and Don Harmon. Ascend the huge, deep chimney on the right side of the southwest face. Climb the chimney, and leave it via a more difficult chimney that leads directly up, or via a class 4 gully that goes right. There is an awful lot of loose rock on this route.

Morning Thunder. III, 5.9. First ascent August 1976 by Bob Harrington, Bob Locke, and Rick Wheeler. This route ascends the buttress that is left of the huge, deep chimney on the right side of the southwest face. Face climbing leads onto the crest of the buttress, followed by five more pitches. The climb ends with 200 feet of class 4 below the summit. Further reading: Don Reid and Chris Falkenstein, *Rock Climbs of Tuolumne Meadows*, Chockstone Press, Denver, 1986, p. 57.

Flakes of Fury. IV, 5.10a. First ascent July 11, 1984, by Eric Perlman and Chris Vandiver. This route ascends the right side of the southwest face of Mt. Conness. Begin by climbing a prominent groove with vegetation (5.8). This is followed by a loose 5.10a overhang that leads to rotten flakes and a lichen-infested squeeze chimney. Two 5.9 dihedrals lead to the final crux pitch: a 5.10a layback followed by overhanging flakes. A class 4 ramp then leads to the summit ridge. There is much loose rock on this route.

Rosy Crown Route. IV, 5.9, A2. First ascent June 1974 by Gary Colliver and Chris Vandiver. This route begins approximately 300 feet to the right of the Harding Route. The first pitch goes free, and the second pitch also goes free until the crack becomes shallow. Some aid moves are needed to pass a roof, followed by free climbing to a loose-appearing flake. Eight more pitches straight up the face lead to the summit.

Harding Route. V, 5.11. First ascent September 1959 by Warren Harding, Glen Denny, and Herb Swedlund. First free ascent July 1, 1976, by Galen Rowell and Chris Vandiver. First winter ascent March 6, 1976, by Mike Graber, Dennis Hennek, and Galen Rowell. This is one of the classic big-wall climbs in the High Sierra. The route begins just left of the center portion of the southwest face; a cairn, erected in memory of Don Goodrich (killed during an early attempt), marks the base of the route. The first pitch (5.9) goes straight up. The second pitch is the crux: a long, poorly protected traverse that goes right and up over a small roof to a slot. Climb up and left (5.8) to a ledge. Move slightly left and climb 250 feet straight up along a crack that eventually becomes off-width. This section ends on a ledge. Leave the ledge on its right side and climb a difficult inside corner. The next pitch climbs a chimney at first and then goes right. A few more pitches lead to a ramp, which goes up and right to the summit slabs. Further reading: *American Alpine Journal,* 1977, pp. 73–78; Don Reid and Chris Falkenstein, *Rock Climbs of Tuolumne Meadows,* Chockstone Press, Denver, 1986, p. 56.

West Ridge. Class 5. First ascent 1957 by Dick Long and friends. This highly enjoyable route ascends the far right side of the west face, close to the edge of the southwest face.

West Face. Class 4. First ascent June 1988 by Sam Roberts. The west face of Mt. Conness has many chutes and shallow ribs. The main problem is selecting the easiest chute for the 1,500 feet of class 3–4 climbing over solid

Mt. Conness from the northeast, September 2, 1965 (photo by Austin Post, #F655-174, USGS Ice and Climate Project, Tacoma, WA)

rock. This side of Mt. Conness deserves more attention.

North Ridge. II, 5.6. First ascent July 1969 by Barry Hagen and Galen Rowell. Scramble up the ridge from the saddle between North Peak and Mt. Conness to the top of the huge tower where the ridge changes direction. Down-climb and rappel the south side of this tower into the notch and follow the crest of the ridge for several pitches over beautiful rock to the summit. This is a very nice climb, with outstanding views and moderate climbing.

Northeast Face. Class 5. First ascent July 1958 by George Harr, Lynn Grey, and Ray Van Aken. Cross the glacier north of Mt. Conness to the base of the northeast face, to a point almost directly below the summit. Ascend a gully that goes up and left to a prominent buttress that divides the face. Traverse to the north from the top of the gully and cross the buttress. Many class 4 pitches lead to an overhang, followed by a class 5 traverse to a crack that leads to a recess. More pitches lead up to a notch about 200 feet north of the summit.

Glacier Route. Class 3. Cross the Conness Glacier and ascend rock ribs or gullies to the low point of the east ridge of Mt. Conness. Follow the ridge to the plateau southeast of the summit.

Y Couloir. First ascent August 1986 by Dave Haake and Chris Keith. Ascend the left branch of this prominent chute to the crest of the east ridge. The angle of the snow is approximately 45 degrees.

East Ridge. Class 3. The entire east ridge can be followed from the vicinity of Saddlebag Lake. Keep to the southern side of the ridge until the summit plateau is reached.

From Saddlebag Lake. Class 2. This roundabout route seems to be the most popular approach from the east. Cross to the west side of the dam at Saddlebag Lake and make a gradual descent to the southwest, passing the Carnegie Institute Experimental Station (camping and campfires and prohibited in this area). Ascend to the lowest saddle between Mt. Conness and White Mountain along the Sierra crest. This is Pass 11,400+ (11,360 ft+; 1.1 mi SSE of Mt. Conness; UTM 970029). Head northwest from the pass and climb onto the plateau that is southeast of the summit. Scrambling over blocks leads to the summit.

North Peak   *(12,242 ft; 12,242 ft)*

Southwest Slope. Class 2. First ascent June 26, 1937, by Smoke Blanchard, Hubert North, and Gary Leech. This slope rises above the highest of the Conness Lakes and leads to long, flat southern slope of the peak. The right side of this slope is easier to climb because it has more solid footing. The left side is sandy, and it makes a good descent route.

Way Up North. III, 5.10a. First ascent September 1983 by David Harden and Dick Leversee. This four-pitch route is on the left side of the broad northeast face. Climb cracks in a smooth wall that is to the right of a large, right-facing dihedral.

Northeast Chimney. IV, 5.8. First ascent August 1969 by Bob Summers and John Gibbins. This is the long, steep chimney that is left of the snow/ice couloir on the northeast side of the peak. Remain deep inside this chimney for the first six pitches.

Deliverance. IV, 5.9. First ascent August 1980 by Jack Roberts and Alan Bartlett. This route climbs the narrow face between the chimney and the snow couloir on the northeast face of North Peak. Nine pitches over loose rock lead to several hundred feet of scrambling and the summit.

Northeast Couloir. Class 4. This 50-degree couloir has approximately 600 feet of snow/ice climbing. From some angles there may appear to be three couloirs. The correct couloir is the one farthest left (southeast), which leads to a deep notch.

Northeast Face. III, 5.8. First ascent July 1969 by Galen Rowell and Barry Hagen. This route climbs the face to the right of the northeast couloir. The climb starts from a small glacier and heads directly for the summit. The first three pitches are the steepest and most difficult.

Northeast Chute. Class 4+. First ascent October 3, 1987, by Pete Lowery and Chris Keith. Climb to the highest point of the glacier to the northeast of North Peak. Follow a chute with loose rock and gravel to the ridge that is right of the summit.

Northwest Ridge. II, 5.3. First ascent August 1973 by Kevin Sutter and David Harden. Follow the crest of the ridge to the summit.

Sheep Peak   *(11,842 ft; 11,840 ft+)*

First ascent July 1, 1934, by Kenneth May

and Howard Twining. Class 2 from Roosevelt Lake; the summit block is class 3.

Shepherd Crest *(12,000 ft+; 12,015 ft)*

First ascent July 13, 1933, by Herbert B. Blanks, Kenneth May, and Elliot Sawyer, via the class 3 avalanche chute on the south side of the peak. The northeast ridge is class 2, and was climbed July 5, 1941, by W. Ryland Hill and Charles W. Chesterman. Further reading: *Sierra Club Bulletin*, 1933, pp. 68–80; *Sierra Club Bulletin*, 1949, pp. 82–86.

Northwest Face. II, 5.7. First ascent July 1975 by Steve Porcella, Bob Porcella, and Royal Robbins. This route is on perfect rock, with five superb pitches ranging from class 4 to 5.7.

Excelsior Mountain
(12,446 ft; 12,446 ft)

First ascent June 13, 1931, by Howard Sloan. This peak is class 2 from the pass at the head of Virginia Creek. Leave the trail at the pass, and cross talus to the north ridge of Excelsior Mountain. Follow the ridge to the summit.

Peak 12,126
(12,126 ft; 0.7 mi N of Excelsior Mtn.)

The east slope and south ridge are class 2.

Black Mountain *(11,797 ft; 11,760 ft+)*

First ascent by the U.S. Geological Survey in 1905. The north slope and south slope are class 2. Further reading: Hans Joachim Burhenne, *Sierra Spring Ski-Touring*, Mountain Press, San Francisco, 1971, pp. 74–75.

Dunderberg Peak *(12,374 ft; 12,374 ft)*

First ascent 1878 by Lt. M. M. Macomb and party of the Wheeler Survey. The southeast ridge is class 2, as are the south and southeast slopes rising above Virginia Lakes. There is an outstanding view from the summit.

Epidote Peak *(10,964 ft; 10,880 ft+)*

Southeast Slope. Class 2. First ascent 1917 by a Sierra Club party. Climb the prominent red chute rising above Hoover Lake. This chute ends on the ridge left of the summit.

Southeast Face. Class 3. First ascent June 11, 1989, by Robin Ingrahm, Jr. and Jim

Chapman. This route follows the chute to the right of the prominent chute on the southeast slope. This less prominent chute ascends the face from right to left, and is blocked about 200 feet below the summit. Move left, out of the chute, and climb onto an exposed, knife-edged arete. An impasse is turned to the left via a narrow ledge. The summit is a short scramble above.

Page Peaks *(10,920 ft+; 10,880 ft+)*

Class 2 from East Lake. The traverse from Gabbro Peak is class 3.

Gabbro Peak *(11,033 ft; 10,960 ft+)*

Class 2 from either Green Lake or East Lake.

Camiaca Peak *(11,739 ft; 11,739 ft)*

First ascent 1917 by Walter L. Huber. The south slope is class 2.

Hooper Peak *(9,575 ft; 9,520 ft+)*

An ascent of this peak would involve hours of drudgery for rather dubious rewards.

West Peak *(10,529 ft; 10,480 ft+)*

First ascent July 17, 1931, by Kenneth May and Gus Smith. This peak is class 2 from Regulation Peak.

Regulation Peak
(10,560 ft+; 10,560 ft+)

First ascent 1921 by Ralph Chase. Class 2 from Rodgers Lake, or from Pettit Peak.

Pettit Peak *(10,788 ft; 10,788 ft)*

First ascent August 1, 1934, by Lewis F. Clark and Virginia Geever. Class 2 from Rodgers Lake. It is also class 2 from either Regulation Peak, West Peak, or Volunteer Peak. The best route from Volunteer Peak is to traverse across the west side of Peak 10,640+ (10,640 ft+) at approximately the 10,000-foot level.

Volunteer Peak *(10,481 ft; 10,479 ft)*

First ascent 1895 by Lt. Benson and Lt. McBride of the United States Cavalry. This is a short class 2 climb from the 9,600-foot level of the Rodgers Lake Trail. The traverse from Pettit Peak is class 2. The best route is at the 10,000-foot level, across the west face of Peak 10,640+ (10,640 ft+).

Piute Mountain　*(10,541 ft; 10,541 ft)*

First ascent July 27, 1911, by Francis Farquhar, James Rennie, and Frank Bumstead. This peak is class 2 from Bear Valley. It is also class 2 from Benson Lake; be sure to pass Peak 10,320+ (10,368 ft) over its western shoulder.

The northeast ridge is class 2 from Seavey Pass. Leave the Pacific Crest Trail south of Seavey Pass at the 8,600-foot level. Head northwest up a steep, grassy slope to the crest of the northeast ridge of Piute Mountain. Follow the crest of the ridge to where it ends against the east face of the peak. Drop 100 feet to the right and cross a small, flat bowl at the top of the mountain's north chute. Two chutes leave this bowl and end on the north ridge. The chute on the right is steep and sandy; the chute or ramp on the left is not as steep and has some vegetation in it, along with more secure footing. Follow the ridge to the summit from the top of either chute.

Price Peak　*(10,717 ft; 10,716 ft)*

First ascent July 28, 1945, by A. J. Reyman on a class 2 traverse from Acker Peak. Price Peak is also class 2 from Thomson Canyon.

Slide Mountain　*(10,458 ft; 10,479 ft)*

This is the Slide Mountain that is south of the other Slide Mountain in northern Yosemite. This peak is not named on some editions of the Matterhorn Peak 7.5-minute map. It appears to be easy from any direction.

Bath Mountain　*(10,520 ft+; 10,558 ft)*

First ascent July 30, 1934, by Glen Dawson and John Cahill, via the easy north ridge.

West Face. IV, 5.10, A1. First ascent September 1974 by Bill Dougherty and Vern Clevenger. This route climbs the long, left-facing open book on the left side of the west face.

Doghead Peak　*(11,059 ft; 11,102 ft)*

First ascent 1911 by Harold Bradley. Class 2 from Wilson Creek. There is an outstanding view of Quarry Peak from the summit.

Quarry Peak　*(11,161 ft; 11,161 ft)*

First ascent 1905 by George R. Davis, A. H. Sylvester, and Pearson Chapman of the U.S. Geological Survey. Class 2 from Wilson Creek.

East Face. IV, 5.10. First ascent August

1977 by Vern Clevenger and Alan Bartlett. This route ascends the smooth left side of the east face of Quarry Peak. It follows a right-leaning, left-facing chimney and open book system. The eighth pitch, a shallow, flared slot, is the crux.

Karen's Wall. III, 5.9, A2. First ascent September 11, 1980, by Dwight Kroll. This route ascends the central buttress of the east face. Begin by climbing a right-facing open book (5.8) to the right of the large chimney at the toe of the buttress. Next, traverse to the right to some left-facing books and climb them to their tops. Tension traverse to the right for 20 feet to a right-facing open book. Climb this book about halfway, and follow a large crack (5.9) to some smaller books and a narrow crack that leads to a roof. Move slightly left to a belay stance. A short bit of free climbing leads to two aid bolts, followed by a tension traverse to the right and another left-facing dihedral. Class 3 climbing to the right and slightly down leads to a ramp in a large corner. Climb the corner for two pitches to its end, where a 5.8 crack up and left leads to a short ramp. Traverse to the far left over class 3 rock to another ramp that climbs up and right to some trees, which mark the end of the climb.

East Face, Right Side. III, 5.9. First ascent September 1984 by Fred Beckey and Gary Slate. This route on the northern quarter of the east face can be identified by a dihedral and the reddish tone of the granite to the right of the dihedral. The crux of this eight-pitch route is passing an overhanging block in a dihedral system.

Gray Butte　*(11,365 ft; 11,365 ft)*

First ascent August 1934 by Howard Twining. Class 2 from Virginia Canyon.

Stanton Peak　*(11,695 ft; 11,695 ft)*

First ascent May 31, 1934, by Richard G. Johnson, Kenneth May, and Howard Twining. The north ridge is class 2.

Virginia Peak　*(12,001 ft; 12,001 ft)*

First ascent July 3, 1934, by Howard Twining and Kenneth May. This peak is easy class 3 from Twin Peaks Pass and from Stanton Pass.

Twin Peaks　*(12,323 ft; 12,240 ft+)*

The west peak is the high point. The ridge

rising from Twin Peaks Pass is class 3; a better route is to traverse northeast across class 2 talus and scree to the basin between the two peaks, and climb the main summit from there. There are two chutes on the west face of the mountain. They are both loose class 2–3 and have been used to climb the peaks from upper Horse Creek.

"Horse Creek Peak"
(11,600 ft+; 11,600 ft+; 0.6 mi NW of Twin Peaks)

The southwest side of this peak is class 2.
North Buttress. III, 5.4. First ascent July 1972 by Jim Orey and Gene Drake. This route begins by climbing a narrow snow couloir left of the buttress. Ascend it for 200 feet to a headwall. A ramp leads up and right from the headwall onto the buttress. One class 5 pitch on the prow of the buttress is followed by 800 feet of class 4 climbing to the summit.

Whorl Mountain   *(12,033 ft; 12,029 ft)*
The middle peak is the high point.
Southeast Chute. Class 4. First ascent July 9, 1933, by Herbert Blanks, Kenneth May, and Eliot Sawyer. First winter ascent March 18, 1966, by Lucien Desaulniers and John Simon. Climb the chute that leads to the saddle between the middle and south peaks of Whorl Mountain from Spiller Creek. Leave this chute 150 feet below the saddle and traverse right (north) across a second chute to the third chute. Ascend the third chute, passing a chockstone on its left side. The summit ridge is just above the chockstone, and it is a short, easy climb from there to the top of the middle peak. *Variation:* Class 4. First ascent July 23, 1978, by Harold McFadden, George Toby, Fred Camphausen, and party. Climb a small chute that is about 50 feet south of the chockstone to the south ridge of the middle peak. An exposed ledge on the west side of the ridge leads to a narrow slot back across the ridge to the east side of the peak. The middle peak is an easy scramble from there.
Southeast Chute and West Face. Class 3. First ascent July 19, 1980, by R. J. Secor. Ascend the southeast chute from Spiller Creek until you are 150 feet below the saddle between the middle and south peaks of Whorl Mountain. Traverse right (north) past one chute to the second chute. Ascend this chute

and cross the south ridge of the middle peak. Traverse north across the west face of the middle peak on a system of ledges to a gully that leads up to the notch just north of the middle peak. Climb this gully to the notch, and follow the ridge south to the summit of the middle peak.
North Peak. First ascent July 17, 1921, by Ralph A. Chase and party. This is class 2 from the saddle to the south.
South Peak. First ascent July 23, 1911, by J. W. Combs, R. W. Messer, and William T. Goldsborough. The southeast slope is class 2.

Finger Peaks   *(11,498 ft; 11,440 ft)*
The middle peak is the high point.
West Face. Class 3 with a class 4 summit block. First ascent July 19, 1931, by Jules Eichorn, Glen Dawson, and Walter Brem. Climb to the saddle between the west peak and the middle peak. Ascend the south side of the west arete to a large notch about halfway up. Traverse north about 200 feet from the notch to the northwest gully and climb the gully to the summit block on the middle peak. The summit block is easy class 4.
The west peak is class 2 from the west.
The east peak is class 2 from the south and southwest. The east ridge is class 3; follow the southern side of the ridge. The north face is class 3–4.

"Horse Creek Tower"
(11,320 ft+; 0.5 mi N of Matterhorn Pk.; UTM 912195)

This tower is northeast of the Dragtooth, and can be seen from Twin Lakes.
South Face. II, 5.8, A3. First ascent May 16, 1973, by Fred Beckey, Mike McGoey, and Leland Davis. The climb begins from a big ledge. Go up and right from the ledge on bolts to a vertical aid crack. This crack leads to the southeast corner of the spire, followed by a tension traverse into a dihedral. Free and aid climbing in the dihedral lead to a belay ledge. A short bolt ladder leads to the summit from here.

"Petite Capucin"
(11,240 ft+; 11,280 ft+; 0.4 mi NE of Matterhorn Pk.; UTM 916192)

This is the northernmost tower on the ridge that is northeast of Matterhorn Peak.

North Face. II, 5.8. First ascent July 1972 by Gene Drake, Rich Stevenson, and Jim Orey. This route consists of four pitches.

Pillar Route. II, 5.10. First ascent August 1979 by Rick Erker and Harry Marinakis. This route is also on the north side of this spire. Start from a belay ledge that is just above the glacier. Climb an easy, right-sloping ramp to a belay stance beneath a small overhang. The second pitch at first climbs a wide crack to the left of the chimney, and then moves right into the chimney itself; belay in the notch between the pillar and the main spire. Climb to the top of the pillar and jump(!) to a small ledge on the main spire. A short scramble then leads to a nice belay ledge. The fourth pitch follows a left-facing arch and open book (5.10) to a good belay ledge just beneath the summit. The last pitch is a short layback along a flake to the summit.

Descent Route. Rappel 60 feet into the notch between Petite Capucin and the spire to its northwest. Walk off to another notch to the southeast.

Matterhorn Peak   *(12,279 ft; 12,264 ft)*

This peak, which has an outstanding view from the summit, appears to be poorly named, especially during an ascent of the snow-free southeast slope in August. But in the spring, however, a ski tour from the summit can be one of the finest mountaineering experiences on the continent.

Southwest Side. Class 2. First ascent 1899 by M. R. Dempster, James S. Hutchinson, Lincoln Hutchinson, and Charles A. Noble. Ascend the broad scree gully in the center of the southwest slope. This side of the peak is easily reached from Burro Pass.

Southeast Slope. Class 2. This is an easy climb from Horse Creek Pass.

East Couloir. Class 3. Climb the obvious couloir on the east side of the northeast ridge. This leads to the top of the east ridge, which is followed to the upper part of the southeast slope. Further reading: Hans Joachim Burhenne, *Sierra Spring Ski-Touring,* Mountain Press, San Francisco, 1971, pp. 72–73.

North Arete. II, 5.5. First ascent September 1954 by Jerry Gallwas, Wally Kodis, and Don Wilson. This is the prominent arete that divides the north faces of Matterhorn Peak. The arete begins from a platform partway up the north side of the peak. (This platform is reached by climbing three class 4 pitches on the left side of the face.) Ascend the arete for one pitch and then traverse 75 feet out onto the west face of the arete. Climb a steep crack for two pitches of 5.5 to a large ledge that is to the right of the arete. Traverse left from the large ledge, past the arete, and ascend a chimney with a chockstone. Climb another arete that is left of the main north arete. This is followed by one more pitch to the summit. *Variation:* First ascent July 1956 by James Derby, Peter Lipman, and Thomas Vaughn. The above-mentioned platform can also be reached by climbing the class 4 face on the right side of the face. *Variation:* First ascent July 1974 by Rupert Kammerlander and Bruce McCubbrey. The platform can also be reached by climbing the 5.8 face directly above the glacier. *Variation:* First ascent July 1970 by Mike Hane and Frank Uher. The arete can be ascended directly from the large ledge (5.7). *Variation:* Follow the arete for one pitch above the large ledge and then go right to a small notch (5.7). *Variation:* It is also possible to climb the prominent dihedral above the large ledge, and continue to the summit over the Double Dihedral Route (5.8). Further reading: Allan Bard, *North Buttress of Matterhorn Peak,* Shooting Star Guides, Bishop, California, 1991 (a route card).

Double Dihedral Route. II, 5.8. First ascent July 4, 1965, by Rich Gnagy, Burt Turney, Gen Turney, and Rick Brosch. This route is on the face to the right of the north arete; it ascends the two prominent dihedrals that go up and right. Climb the glacier north of Matterhorn Peak to the base of the right-hand dihedral; the bottom of this dihedral may be filled with snow. A 5.7 pitch up the dihedral leads to a large flake on the left. Descend 20 feet behind the flake to the bottom of the second dihedral. Climb a 5.7 crack in the lower portion of this dihedral for 150 feet to a large ledge that is to the right of the north arete. Climb the upper dihedral to its top; this is followed by a 5.8 move to the left, which leads out onto the exposed face. One long pitch up and left leads to a good belay ledge. A thin, flaring crack that gradually widens then leads up to the summit ridge. *Variation:* It is possible to traverse left from the large ledge and continue to the summit via the North Arete route or its variations.

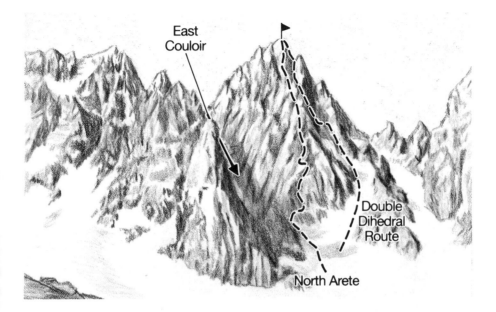

East Couloir

Double Dihedral Route

North Arete

Matterhorn Peak, North Face

Northwest Face. Class 3. First ascent July 20, 1931, by Walter Brem, Glen Dawson, and Jules Eichorn. Climb a gully, or the face on either side of the gully, from the notch between Dragtooth or Matterhorn Peak. This notch can be reached from either the Burro Pass area or the glacier north of Matterhorn Peak.

"The Dragtooth"
(12,080 ft+; 12,160 ft+; 0.4 mi NW of Matterhorn Pk.; UTM 910192)

Southwest Slope. Class 2. First ascent July 20, 1931, by Walter Brem, Glen Dawson, and Jules Eichorn. This is a straightforward climb from the basin north of Burro Pass.

Northeast Buttress. Class 4. First ascent 1952 by Joe Firey, Norm Goldstein, Chuck Wharton, and John Ohrenschall. This buttress divides the glaciers between Matterhorn Peak and the Dragtooth. Climb onto the base of the buttress from the glacier that is north of the Dragtooth. Ascend the east side of the buttress before moving onto the very crest of the upper buttress. The climb ends in a short chimney just below the summit.

North Face. Class 4. First ascent July 16, 1941, by J. C. Southard and Hervey Voge. This route ascends the broad face above the glacier north of the Dragtooth. Ascend steep snow on the lower portion of the face to a point about 100 feet to the left of the main chute that descends the north face. Climb ledges leading up and left to a less prominent chute that is 200 feet east of the main chute. Ascend this chute for 200 feet and cross over to the right into the main chute. Ascend the left side of this chute until you are 100 feet beneath the summit ridge. Climb a 75-foot chimney leading up to the ridge to a point about 50 feet northwest of the summit.

North Buttress. III, 5.10. First ascent June 16, 1971, by Reed Cundiff and Jack Miller. First free ascent 1983 by Jay Smith and Paul Crawford. One of the classic climbs in the High Sierra, this route deserves more traffic. The route ascends the prominent buttress that extends farther out onto the glacier than any other part of the Dragtooth. There is a triangular pedestal at the bottom of this buttress. Rope up at a sloping, sandy ledge beneath a wide chimney along the left edge of the pedestal. Climb the chimney (5.7) for 120 feet to a belay with two bolts. Continue straight up for another 100 feet (5.7) and traverse to the right to the base of the prominent dihedral that marks the route. Two pitches (5.9 and 5.10) in the dihedral, with hand, fist, and off-width cracks, lead to a belay alcove. A finger crack (5.9) above the alcove leads to scrambling along the summit ridge. Chocks to 5 inches are needed for protection on this route. *Variation:* Traverse up and right from the belay alcove, across blocks to a trough, to exit right to easier climbing.

West Chimney. III, 5.8. First ascent July 1970 by Mary Bomba and Ken Boche. Climb toward Polemonium Pass from the glacier north of the Dragtooth. From a point approximately 100 feet below the northeast side of the pass, climb cracks and chimneys up and left to a large broken area. Continue climbing up and left to a large chimney and climb it to its top. Exit the chimney on its right side (5.8) and climb onto the top of the west ridge. Easy climbing along the southern side of the west ridge leads to the summit.

"The Doodad"

(11,680 ft+; 11,600 ft+; 0.5 NW of Matterhorn Pk.; UTM 906192)

The Doodad is a 25-foot-high cube, overhanging on all sides, perched on a ridge 500 feet above the glacier.

South Side. Class 4. First ascent July 7, 1934, by Kenneth May and Howard Twining. Class 3 climbing starts this climb along an arete on the left (west) side of the south face. Climb diagonally right, over a short but difficult pitch, to the east ridge. Follow the east ridge around a pinnacle to the main summit. The Doodad itself is 5.2, and is climbed via a crack on its south side.

Northeast Face. Class 5. First ascent July 1956 by James Derby, Peter Lipman, and Thomas Vaughn. Climb the long, left-leaning gully on the northeast face. It is necessary to deviate from one side of the gully to the other to pass chockstones. A hand traverse from the top of the gully leads left to a ledge system beneath the summit block.

"The Three Teeth"

(11,680 ft+; 11,600 ft+; 0.8 mi NW of Matterhorn Pk.)

These three pinnacles are atop the Sawtooth Ridge, between the Sawblade and the Col de Doodad. Further reading: *Sierra Club Bulletin*, 1934, pp. 31–33.

The Northwest Tooth is seen to the right when viewed from the north. The deep notch to the left of the Northwest Tooth is the West Notch. Left of the West Notch is the Middle Tooth, and the small notch to its left is the East Notch. The Southeast Tooth is left of the East Notch and right of the Col de Doodad.

Traverse, Northwest to Southeast. III, 5.5 with rappels. First ascent July 2, 1933, by Henry Beers, Bestor Robinson, and Richard M. Leonard. Two 150-foot ropes are needed for the rappels on this route. Climb a series of ledges in a broad depression on the center of the northeast face of the Northwest Tooth. At a point about one-third of the way up the face, traverse diagonally up to the right toward ledges that lead up to the northwest arete. Follow the arete upward to the tunnel underneath the summit block. The tunnel comes out on the southeast side of the summit block. Climb the summit block of the Northwest Tooth on its northwest side.

A long rappel (140 feet) leads down to the West Notch. Climb a loose chimney for 40 feet, then go left and climb another loose chimney to a flat ledge on the right. A 5.5 layback and face climbing lead to the summit of the Middle Tooth.

Descend a short chimney near the northeast side of the summit of the Middle Tooth. After 75 feet, a 100-foot rappel leads down to the gully below; this gully is on the Slide Canyon side of the East Notch. Ascend the gully to the highest ledge on the Southeast Tooth. Traverse right 75 feet along ledges to a narrow, steep chimney. Climb this squeeze chimney to a chockstone, then traverse right a few feet on small holds to a crack. Ascend this crack to the summit of the Southeast Tooth.

And now the fun really begins (I am being sarcastic; I hate to rappel). There is a pinnacle located immediately northwest of the summit of the Southeast Tooth. Rappel 145 feet down the southeast side of this pinnacle to the lowest of two ledges. Go southeast on this ledge for 50 feet and climb down to a block below a small pinnacle. Another 145-foot rappel to an area of broken rock is followed by another short rappel to more broken rock. Head toward the base of the Middle Tooth and rappel 80 feet down to the scree below. This leaves you on the Slide Canyon side of the Sawtooth Ridge, and it is necessary to cross the Col de Doodad to return to the northeast side of the Sawtooth Ridge.

Traverse, Southeast to Northwest. III, 5.6

with rappels. First ascent July 25, 1934, by Glen Dawson and Jack Riegelhuth. Two 150-foot ropes are needed for the rappels. This traverse starts from the Slide Canyon side of the Col de Doodad. Climb the short chimney with an overhanging chockstone that leads to an arete. Ascend the arete to the base of a

tall pinnacle. Pass this pinnacle on the left by crawling through a tunnel. More difficult climbing leads back to the southeast arete. Ascend the arete to the top of the Southeast Tooth. *Variation:* You may prefer climbing to the Southeast Tooth from the Slide Canyon base of the Middle Tooth. This would be the

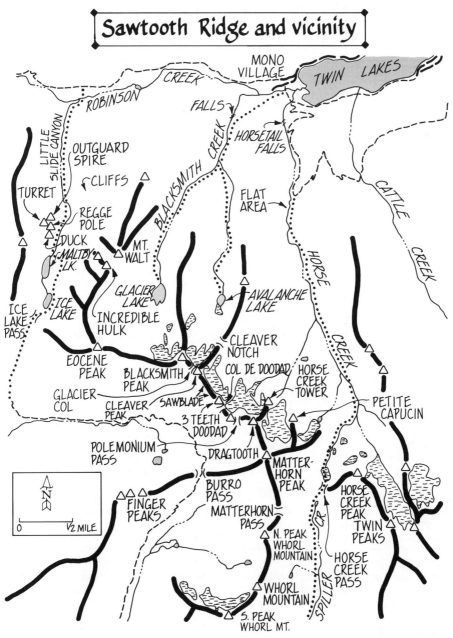

Sawtooth Ridge and vicinity

Sawtooth Ridge from the north (photo by W. D. Johnson, #430, USGS Photographic Library, Denver, CO)

reverse of the descent of the Southeast Tooth as described in the Traverse, Northwest to Southeast write-up, above.

A long rappel leads from the summit of the Southeast Tooth to the East Notch. Descend the Slide Canyon side of the East Notch and climb a large chimney on the southeast side of the Middle Tooth. Ascend cracks and a short chimney to the summit of the Middle Tooth.

Another long rappel leads to the West Notch from the summit of the Middle Tooth. Descend the gully leading down into Slide Canyon from the West Notch. Climb up and right on the southeast face of the Northwest Tooth over steep ledges and cracks for about 100 feet to a 3-foot-wide ledge. Climb thin cracks and narrow ledges (5.6) up a steep face for 75 feet (loose rock) to the southeast side of the summit block of the Northwest Tooth.

Descend the tunnel underneath the summit block of the Northwest Tooth to the northwest arete. Descend the arete to where it is possible to descend to the glacier via ledges leading down the northeast face of the Northwest Tooth.

Northwest Tooth, Southwest Face. II, 5.6. First ascent July 23, 1941, by David Brower, Bruce Meyer, and Art Argiewicz. Climb the buttress that is left of the scree slope coming down from the West Notch. Go diagonally left toward a ledge at the top of the lowest chimney. A fingertip traverse across the top of the chimney leads to a scree chute above the chimney. Ascend the scree chute to a point about 30 feet below its top and traverse left on an easy ledge. Swing around a flake that is left of and above this ledge and climb a classic chimney to its top. Leave the top of this chimney on its left side, and continue up and right across the southwest face to the 3-foot-wide ledge on the southeast side of the Northwest Tooth. A 75-foot 5.6 pitch over loose rock leads up to the summit block.

Northwest Tooth, West Notch. Class 4–5. First ascent 1949 by Oscar Cook, Joe Firey, Larry Taylor, and Jack Hansen. Ascend the couloir leading to the West Notch from the glacier. From the notch, traverse right on a hand ledge that ends in a chimney. Ascend the chimney to the tunnel underneath the summit block.

Middle Tooth, Northeast Face. II, 5.5. First ascent July 2, 1933, by Lewis F. Clark, Richard G. Johnson, Oliver Kehrlein, and Randolph May. Climb the steep snow couloir leading to the West Notch from the glacier. Leave the couloir about 100 feet above a chockstone in this couloir and traverse diagonally left on a ledge. Leave the ledge at a prominent chimney and climb it and more ledges up and right to a loose chimney. This chimney leads to a flat ledge

Sawtooth Ridge from the south (photo by H. W. Turner, #47, USGS Photographic Library, Denver, CO)

on the right, where a 5.5 layback and face climbing lead to the summit of the Middle Tooth.

Middle Tooth, Southwest Face. III, 5.9, A1. First ascent August 1972 by Mike Heath and Bill Sumner. Climb steep jam cracks to the left of the center portion of the face for 300 feet. Pendulum right across a smooth section to another crack system near the right edge of the face. Three more strenuous and moderately difficult pitches lead to the summit.

Middle Tooth, Southwest Face Direct. III, 5.10. First ascent October 1976 by Jack Roberts and Fred Beckey. This route starts from the gully on the left side of the southwest face. Climb diagonally right to the crack system at the left edge of the prominent orange pillar on the face. Continue up the crack system to the summit. The rock on the lower section of this face is quite friable, but it improves higher up.

Southeast Tooth, Northeast Face. III, 5.7. First ascent June 1969 by Jim Jones, Fred Beckey, and Galen Rowell. There are four prominent cracks splitting the center of this face. Two are parallel and about 15 feet apart. Start climbing from the base of these two cracks, and climb steep rock for 40 feet to an easy traverse up and right to a belay. Step left into the crack and jam (5.7) up to a small, exposed belay ledge on the right. A long pitch straight up (5.7) leads to a prominent

ledge that traverses across most of the northeast face. Go left along this ledge to two cracks, which lead up to the summit. Ascend these cracks over an overhang (5.7) to a ledge just beneath the summit. A strenuous move then leads to the flat summit.

Southeast Tooth, Left Side of Northeast Face. III, 5.10. First ascent September 1987 by Bruce Runnals and Al Swanson. This route ascends the left side of the face. Five 5.10 pitches lead to the summit.

Descent Routes. The Northwest Tooth has been descended by going down the northwest arete to near the junction with the Sawblade. Four rappels down the south side of the ridge lead to Slide Canyon.

The southeast side of the Northwest Tooth also involves four rappels down the southeast buttress. The last rappel starts from a ledge and is free for over 100 feet.

It is possible to rappel from the West Notch down to the glacier; the last rappel is over 120 feet long.

The south chimney of the East Notch has also been rappelled. This leads down to Slide Canyon.

The Northeast Face route of the Middle Tooth has been rappelled. The last rappel is free. Ugh!

Finally, the north side of the East Notch has been rappelled. One of the intermediate stances involves standing in slings. Ugh!

"The Sawblade"

(11,760 ft+; 11,600 ft+; 1.0 mi NW of Matterhorn Pk.; UTM 901199)

Traverse, Southeast to Northwest. Class 4. First ascent July 25, 1934, by David Brower and Hervey Voge. Climb from Slide Canyon to the notch that is northwest of the pinnacle on the northwest arete of the West tooth. Traverse the ridge leading northwest. Two 150-foot ropes are needed for the rappels.

The Cleaver

This is the long ridge that runs down and northeast from the summit of Cleaver Peak.

Goldfinger. I, 5.6, A3. First ascent October 27, 1968, by Fred Beckey and Joe Brown. This is the 125-foot spire atop the Cleaver. It is climbed on its west side. Further reading: *Summit,* December 1968, pp. 6–7.

"Cleaver Peak"

(11,760 ft+; 11,760 ft+; 1.1 mi NW of Matterhorn Pk.; UTM 901200)

Northwest Face. Class 3. First ascent July 3, 1933, by Henry Beers and Oliver Kehrlein. Traverse up and left from Glacier Col to a broad depression on the northwest face. Follow the depression to the summit.

Northeast Face. Class 3. First ascent July 27, 1934, by Glen Dawson and Jack Riegelhuth. Ascend a series of ledges and blocks on the northeast face of Cleaver Peak to the crest of the arete of The Cleaver. Follow the arete to the summit of Cleaver Peak.

South Face. Class 5. First ascent August 6, 1950, by M. L. Wade and F. Chisholm. Climb an easy class 4 chute that leads to the notch between Cleaver Peak and the Sawblade. Approximately 150 feet below this notch, a block leans against Cleaver Peak. (A passage underneath this block leads to the notch.) Go left at the lower side of this block, and climb several interesting class 5 pitches on the south face to the summit of Cleaver Peak.

"Blacksmith Peak"

(11,760 ft+; 11,680 ft+; 1.3 mi NW of Matterhorn Pk.; UTM 898202)

Southwest Face. Class 3. First ascent July 3, 1933, by Bestor Robinson and Richard Leonard. Climb the prominent gully on the southwest face to its top, among the four summit pinnacles. The northwest pinnacle is the high point, and is rated 5.6. The register is 30 feet below the top of the northwest pinnacle.

Northwest Face, Right Side. II, 5.8, A2. First ascent July 1973 by Lito Tejada-Flores and Chris Jones. Climb slabs on the right side of the face to steep rock that leads to an overhang. Use aid over the overhang, and climb slightly left to a steep crack system, which also requires aid. Continue up to the summit ridge.

Northwest Face, Left Side. II, 5.8. First ascent July 1973 by Doug Robinson and friend. This route starts left of the central, steep portion of the northwest face. Go up and right over broken rock to the summit.

Northeast Gully. II, 5.6. First ascent September 8, 1936, by Bestor Robinson and Carl Jensen. Climb a steep, sloping ledge from the base of the north arete. This ledge leads left and rises above the glacier north of Cleaver Peak. After 200 feet this ledge dead-ends against a face. Climb up and right for about 20 feet (5.5) on small holds to the northeast gully. Ascend the gully to the summit.

South Face. II, 5.8. First ascent August 1976 by Willie Sare and Paul Willis. Climb a large, left-facing dihedral for three pitches to its head. Then angle up and left for one pitch to the summit area.

"Eocene Peak"

(11,569 ft; 11,851 ft; 1.3 mi SE of Kettle Pk.)

First ascent July 16, 1932, by Herbert B. Blanks and Richard M. Leonard. The southwest slope is class 2.

"The Incredible Hulk"

(11,480 ft+; 11,520 ft+; 0.9 mi ESE of Kettle Peak; UTM 886216)

This peak was thought to be unclimbed for many years, while a register on the summit named it "Middle Peak of Outpost Peak" and recorded an ascent on September 6, 1936, by Bestor Robinson, Florence Robinson, Carl Jensen, and Don Woods. The current name, which has been in use for many years, refers to the large, west-facing mass on the ridge north of Eocene Peak. All of the routes on the west face end atop the ridge northwest of the true summit, Point 11,280+ (11,120 ft+; UTM 885218).

Mountaineer's Route. Class 4–5. First ascent May 23, 1971, by Bob Grow and Joe Kiskis. Ascend Little Slide Canyon to where the stream forks. Follow the east branch to the base of the Hulk. Climb the right couloir (snow-filled in early season; loose rock later in the summer) for several hundred feet. A steep chute on the left wall of this couloir leads to a high notch. Three pitches of roped climbing lead from the notch to the summit.

Positive Vibrations. V, 5.10, A2. First ascent August 1981 by Bob Harrington and Alan Bartlett. To the left of the Mountaineer's Route is a huge rock wall with a triangle at its base. Three class 4 pitches on the right side of this triangle lead to a large ledge. Go to the left end of this ledge and climb six pitches up crack systems that are just to the right of a huge outside corner. These lead to Point 11,280+, a long way from the true summit.

West Face. V, 5.8, A3. First ascent 1970 by Greg Donaldson, Joe Kiskis, and Bob Grow. Climb the left side of the triangle at the base of the west face for two pitches to a ledge. Climb straight up for 70 feet to some overhangs, then traverse right to a hanging belay beneath a chimney. Climb the chimney, which features some good ledges, and leave it to the right. Some nailing leads to a hanging flake in an open book beneath some ceilings. Climb the flake and the book, then traverse to the right to a ledge in the middle of the face. A very thin crack leads up and right for one pitch. Continue traversing up and right to the buttress on the far right side of the wall. Climb to a notch on the buttress, and continue up the buttress, with progressively easier climbing, to the top of the face. Ten rappels down the west face lead back to the base of the climb.

Macedonian Route. V, 5.9, A4. First ascent July 1976 by Rick Wheeler and Dave Bircheff. Climb to the top of the triangle at the base of the west face and continue up the chimney above. Climb straight up the face from the chimney to the top of the face. This route includes one pitch of excellent free climbing, followed by five pitches of difficult aid climbing. Seven rappels down the east side of the west face lead to the bottom.

Polish Route. V, 5.10. First ascent August 1976 by Rick Wheeler and Bob Harrington. This route starts about 100 feet to the left of the triangle at the base of the west face. Climb a difficult crack in a left-facing corner. Higher up, this crack widens considerably, with three pitches of fist jams and off-width climb-

ing with hanging belays. The climb ends on a large, flat ledge. Traverse along this ledge to the east. This leads to rappels and to the chute on the north side of the Incredible Hulk.

Northwest Couloir. Class 4. First ascent October 1978 by Dick Benoit, Bill Peppin, John McCartney, and Alvin R. McLane. This 2,000-foot snow/ice climb ascends the chute that is north of the west face of the Incredible Hulk.

A route (III, 5.7, A1) has been done on the east side of Little Slide Canyon, near its entrance. Climb the obvious gully on the three-toothed cliff. First ascent 1973 by Darien Hopkins, Roger Gocking, Dave Warburton, and Mike Warburton.

"Mt. Walt"
(11,480 ft+; 11,581 ft; 0.6 mi NW of Glacier Lake; UTM 888218)

First ascent September 6, 1936, by Bestor Robinson, Florence Robinson, Carl Jensen, and Don Woods. The northeast slope is class 2 from the middle portion of Blacksmith Creek; this has been done as a ski tour.

This peak has been unofficially named in memory of Walter W. Herbert. Further reading: Hans Joachim Burhenne, *Sierra Spring Ski-Touring,* Mountain Press, San Francisco, 1971, pp. 68–69.

"Outguard Spire"
(10,280 ft+; UTM 876224)

This is the northernmost spire on the west side of Little Slide Canyon.

Southeast Corner. II, 5.8. First ascent September 5, 1968, by John York, Joe Kiskis, and Robert Grow. Ascend a narrow talus gully on the west side of the spire to the southeast corner. Climb a rotten chimney for about 80 feet to a short jam crack (5.8) protected by some large chocks. Easier climbing goes up and right to a good ledge, followed by more easy climbing to a notch behind a small pinnacle. Traverse left and get behind a flake, where steep face climbing leads for 70 feet directly up the southeast corner to a ledge. A short pitch up the exposed summit ridge leads to the top, a tiny summit.

East Face. III, 5.10, A2. First ascent July 1973 by Mike Warburton and Roger Gocking. Climb a corner on the right side of the east face to a small overhang. Go up and right along a ramp to a belay ledge on the corner between the east and north faces. Traverse right across the north face to a scary chimney behind a flake, and climb to a ledge above. Go to the far right side of the ledge and layback to a sloping ledge on the west corner of the spire. A short stretch of aid climbing leads to a hanging belay to the left of a prominent crack. A jam crack then leads to the summit.

"The Turret"
(10,320 ft+; UTM 876224)

This is the highest of the four pinnacles on the west side of Little Slide Canyon. It is climbed from the notch on its west side. Class 3–4 climbing leads to a short 5.8 section. First ascent 1970 by Joe Kiskis. First free ascent July 1972 by Margaret Quick and Bob Grow.

"Regge Pole"
(10,280 ft+; UTM 876223)

South Face. III, 5.7, A2. First ascent July 1970 by Greg Donaldson and Joe Kiskis. Ascend the chute on the south side of this spire and climb a large dihedral for four pitches; it is sometimes necessary to move out onto the left wall of this dihedral with some aid points. Follow a large ledge out across the west side of the spire from the top of the dihedral, and climb a chimney on the west face.

South Face, Right Side. IV, 5.7, A3. First ascent August 1973 by Mike Warburton and Roger Gocking. Traverse to the right from the bottom of the dihedral on the south face. This leads to a crack system, which is followed to a small ledge. Overcome a roof via nailing, and belay in slings. Go left and use more aid to another hanging belay. Bypass a large, rotten flake to its right to yet another hanging belay. More nailing leads up to a ledge, at last. Climb straight up for a short distance, where a hand traverse goes left to a chimney system, which leads to the summit.

"The Duck"

First ascent July 1970 by Greg Donaldson and Joe Kiskis. This formation is just south of Regge Pole. This is easily climbed via a class 4 route.

Kettle Peak *(11,000 ft+; 11,010 ft)*

First ascent August 1948 by Bill Dunmire and Bob Swift. Class 2 from Ice Lake Pass.

Suicide Ridge *(11,047 ft; 11,089 ft)*

First ascent May 31, 1934, by Glen Dawson and John Cahill. Class 2 from Rock Island Lake.

Slide Mountain *(11,084 ft; 11,040 ft+)*

This peak is north of the other Slide Mountain in this region of the High Sierra. Class 2 from the Burro Pass Trail.

"The Juggernaut"
(11,040 ft+; 11,040 ft+; 0.7 mi E of Rock Island Pass)

There is a steep cliff on the north side of this modest peak.

Arches Route. III, 5.9, A2. First ascent September 15, 1973, by Jack Roberts, Fred Beckey, and Dave Black. This route follows the obvious crack system near the center of the prow on the north side of the peak, just right of two huge, overhanging arches. The climb consists of five long hard pitches, with some aid climbing on the second pitch.

Dihedral Route. III, 5.10. First ascent 1974 by Bill Dougherty, Vern Clevenger, Mike Farrell, and Galen Rowell. This route ascends the long, left-facing dihedral that is to the left of the Arches Route. The first pitch goes up a chimney that narrows down to a slot and, finally, a 5.10 layback. Higher in the dihedral, you have a choice between an intimidating 5.8 traverse on the outside of the dihedral, or a frightening 5.10 overhang in the dihedral. The last pitch consists of moderate climbing up a broken, open headwall immediately to the right of the overhangs at the top of the dihedral.

Crown Point *(11,346 ft; 11,346 ft)*

First ascent 1905 by George R. Davis, A. H. Sylvester, and Pearson Chapman of the U.S. Geological Survey. This peak is class 2 from Snow Lake.

Peeler Pillar. II, 5.6. First ascent September 1971 by Larry Johnson, Geert Dijkhuis, and Greg Donaldson. The route starts about 100 feet to the right of the north buttress, between an overhanging chimney and a sandy gully. About 200 feet of easy class 5 leads to a large ledge, followed by a short class 3 section. Climb a white face above this easy section. This face is left of a large open book, and is lined with cracks. Four pitches of 5.5

to 5.6 lead to the summit. *Variation:* II, 5.8. First ascent August 1989 by Dan Ward and David Harden. Climb cracks to the left of the overhanging chimney for two pitches to the white ledge.

Cirque Mountain
(10,713 ft; 10,714 ft)

First ascent August 16, 1948, by A. J. Reyman. The northwest slope is class 1.

Eagle Peak *(11,847 ft; 11,845 ft)*

First ascent September 1905 by George Davis, A. H. Sylvester, and Pearson Chapman of the U.S. Geological Survey. This peak is class 2 from either Buckeye Creek or Robinson Creek.

Victoria Peak *(11,706 ft; 11,732 ft)*

First ascent September 8, 1946, by A. J. Reyman. Class 2 from either the north or south.

Hunewill Peak *(11,713 ft; 11,680 ft+)*

First ascent August 1946 by Ken Crowley, R. Dickey, Jr., Ken Hargreaves, and H. Watty. Class 2 from Barney Lake.

Center Mountain *(11,271 ft; 11,273 ft)*

First ascent 1905 by the U.S. Geological Survey. The south slope is class 1.

Grouse Mountain *(10,734 ft; 10,775 ft)*

First ascent August 3, 1949, by A. J. Reyman, via the class 1 northwest couloir and west ridge. The east face is class 3, and was first climbed August 1953 by LeRoy Johnson, Fred Schaub, and Ken Hondsinger.

Ehrnbeck Peak *(11,240 ft; 11,240 ft)*

First ascent July 27, 1945, by A. J. Reyman, via the class 2 south ridge. The northeast ridge is class 3.

Hawksbeak Peak
(11,341 ft; 11,120 ft+)

West Face. III, 5.9. First ascent September 1988 by Al Swanson and John Nye. This route consists of nine pitches.

Wells Peak *(11,109 ft; 11,118 ft)*

First ascent July 27, 1945, by A. J. Reyman. The north ridge is class 2.

Acker Peak *(10,988 ft; 11,015 ft)*

First ascent July 27, 1945, by A. J. Reyman. The east slope is class 2.

Snow Peak *(10,945 ft; 10,950 ft)*

First ascent 1938 by John Dyer. The south slope is class 2.

Craig Peak *(11,087 ft; 11,090 ft)*

First ascent 1938 by John Dyer. Class 2 from either the north or south. A traverse from Tower Peak is class 3.

Tower Peak *(11,755 ft; 11,755 ft)*

This is the prominent peak that rises above the headwaters of the West Walker River. The first ascent may have been made by Native Americans; arrowhead fragments were found just beneath the summit in 1941.

Northwest Chute. Class 3. First ascent 1870 by Charles F. Hoffman, William A. Goodyear, and Alfred Craven. Climb a ridge on the northwest side of the peak to a staircase chute, which leads to the summit.

West Face. Class 4. First ascent July 15, 1941, by Raffi Bedayan and Barbara Norris. Some belaying is required on the face that rises above Mary Lake.

Southeast Chute. Class 3. Descended July 1941 by David Brower, Dorothy Markwad, Pat Goldsworthy, Ted Grubb, and Bruce Meyer. This chute rises above the head of Stubblefield Canyon.

Northeast Face. III, 5.9. First ascent September 1988 by John Nye and Alan Swanson. This five-pitch route ascends a long, shallow dihedral next to the pillar on the northeast face.

Saurian Crest *(11,040 ft+; 11,095 ft)*

First ascent September 7, 1938, by John Dyer. Long talus slopes from all sides lead to the class 3 summit rocks.

Keyes Peak *(10,618 ft; 10,670 ft)*

First ascent September 1, 1942, by A. J. Reyman. The south ridge is class 2.

Forsyth Peak *(11,177 ft; 11,180 ft)*

First ascent July 10, 1937, by Rene Kast, Don Hersey, Paul Hersey, Al Teakle, Harry Tenney, Jr., Arthur Evans, and Leon Casou. The south and west slopes are class 2. The north ridge is class 3, and was first climbed

Tower Peak from the north (photo by H. W. Turner, #34, USGS Photographic Library, Denver, CO)

August 23, 1953, by LeRoy Johnson, Fred Schaub, and Ken Hondsinger.

Wrinkles

Horse Creek vs. Green Lake. The most obvious approach to the upper part of Spiller Creek is from Twin Lakes via Horse Creek. An often overlooked alternative is an approach from Green Lake and over Virginia Pass. This alternate route has less elevation gain and features a good use trail over Virginia Pass. Spiller Creek can be reached by crossing Twin Peaks Pass or Stanton Pass.

Sawtooth Ridge in a day. Sawtooth Ridge is an exception to the generalization that solitude can be found in northern Yosemite. There is a strict quota in effect in this area, and the best option for many climbers is to climb the peaks in a day from Twin Lakes. But this is realistic only for competent climbers who are in excellent physical condition.

Appendix A
Glossary

What follows are some rough definitions for some of the esoteric words found in this book.

Aid: direct aid climbing, i.e., climbing a pitch by hanging from equipment that has been placed in or on the rock.

Alcove: a belay ledge that is surrounded on all sides by vertical rock.

Arete: a steep, narrow ridge.

Bergschrund or **'schrund:** a crevasse in a glacier or snowfield, formed when the movement of snow or ice diverges away from the fixed mountainside.

Black ice: very old ice that has been mixed with scree and gravel. This is usually found deep in couloirs in late autumn during drought years.

Bolts: small metal spikes that are hammered into holes that have been drilled into rock.

Bongs: extra-wide pitons, now virtually non-existent; they have been replaced by large chocks.

Buttress: a very steep arete on the face of a mountain. **Nose** and **pillar** are synonymous with buttress.

Ceiling: see **Roof.**

Chickenheads: see **Horns.**

Chimney: either a steep, narrow chute with parallel walls, or a wide crack that the climber can fit into.

Chocks: rock protection that is wedged into cracks by hand. **Nuts** is a synonym.

Chockstones: rocks that are wedged into cracks, either by nature or by a desperate leader who doesn't have any other protection left.

Chute: this is usually steeper than a gully, and may be subject to rockfall.

Cirque: a deep recess in a mountain; it resembles an amphitheater with steep walls.

Col: a steep, high pass.

Corn snow: unconsolidated granular snow that has gone through a short freeze-and-thaw process. This type of snow is prevalent throughout the High Sierra in April and May.

Couloir: a steep chute, which may have snow or ice.

Crack: the separation of two rock faces, ranging in size from the width of a chimney to microscopically narrow.

Crest: the very top of a ridge or arete.

Dihedral: see **Open book.**

Face: the sides of a mountain, a slope being more gentle (less steep) than a face.

Firn: consolidated granular snow left over from the previous year. Closer to ice than snow in density, it may require the use of crampons.

Flakes: long, narrow horns, or a huge rock slab leaning against a cliff. The sides of such a slab may form dihedrals.

Flared: a crack or chimney whose sides are not parallel, but instead form two converging planes of rock.

Free: free climbing, i.e., doing a climb or pitch without resorting to aid.

Gully: this usually refers to a wide, shallow ravine on a mountainside.

Headwall: where the face of a mountain steepens dramatically.

Horns: spikes of rock that are used for protection or holds. **Chickenheads** is a synonym.

Lead: see **Pitch.**

Mixed climbing: either a combination of free and aid climbing, or a combination of rock, snow, and ice climbing.

Moat: the gap between snow or ice and a rock wall.

Move: see **Pitch.**

Munge: dirt and vegetation that fills a crack.

Nailing: an ancient term used to describe direct-aid climbing with pitons.

Nevé: consolidated granular snow. This is common on glaciers and snowfields during the height of the summer.

Nose: see **Buttress.**

Notch: a small col.

Nuts: see **Chocks.**

Off-width: a crack or chimney too wide to climb but too narrow to climb into.

Open book: the junction of two planes of

rock; in other words, an inside corner. The corner can be either acute or obtuse, and can face right or left. **Dihedral** is a synonym.

Outside corner: see **Rib.**

Overhang: a section of rock that exceeds the vertical.

Pass: the lowest or easiest crossing of a ridge.

Pitch or lead: a section of a climb between belays. A very short pitch is a **move.**

Pillar: see **Buttress.**

Pitons: metal spikes that are hammered into cracks.

Ramp: an ascending ledge.

Rib: a short, small buttress. An **outside corner** is even smaller.

Ridge: a high divide extending out from a peak.

Roof: an overhang that forms a horizontal plane. **Ceiling** is a synonym.

Runners: loops of nylon webbing that are threaded or looped around chockstones, flakes, horns, or chickenheads for protection.

Saddle: a high pass that is not as steep as a col.

Scree: small rocks that slide under the climber's feet.

Sierra crest: the divide that runs along the very top of the High Sierra, separating the Great Basin and the Pacific Ocean watersheds.

Sierra wave: a lenticular cloud.

Slope: see **Face.**

Summit: the high point of a peak or the top of a pass.

Talus: large blocks of rock.

Tarn: a small lake.

Toe: the bottom of a buttress.

Verglas: thin water ice on rock.

Water ice: solid ice that contains few air bubbles. This is typically found in the couloirs of the High Sierra in autumn.

Appendix B
The Yosemite Decimal System: The Fine Print

The Yosemite Decimal System has its roots in the Sierra Club classification system first created in 1936. This divided climbs into six classes, class 1 being easy and class 6 severe. A 1936 class 1 would be class 1 or 2 today. A 1936 class 2 would be class 3 today. A 1936 class 3 would be class 4 today. A 1936 class 4 covers everything from class 4 to 5.6 today. A 1936 class 5 would be in the 5.6 to 5.7 range today. No class 6 climbs were identified in 1936.

To confuse matters further, the Sierra Club classification system was changed in 1938. A 1938 class 1 would be class 1 today. A 1938 class 2 would be class 2 to 3 today. A 1938 class 3 would be class 3 to 4 today. A 1938 class 4 would be class 4 to 5.4 today. A 1938 class 5 would be from 5.4 to 5.6 today. In 1938, aid climbing was identified as class 6.

It must be remembered that there weren't very many climbers in the 1930s, and communication was not as good as it is today, so no one could be sure that the numbers being used actually matched in reality. Also, many routes were climbed before this rating system first came into existence. And some routes that were first climbed fifty years ago are awaiting their second ascent. Combine all of this with the change in the rating system, and the confusion is rampant.

After having written all of this, I am sure that someone will attempt a class 4 route, only to find it to be 5.6 at his or her favorite bouldering area, and use this incident to vilify me in the alpine media. It is rewarding to know that my work has brought so much happiness to the world, and joy to those who disagree with me.

Index

About the Author

R. J. Secor has been hiking and skiing since he learned to walk. An enthusiastic peak-bagger, he has attained List Completion status in the Sierra Peaks Section of the Sierra Club and has made more than 350 mountain ascents in the High Sierra, climbing as many as sixty peaks in a single year. Other mountain adventures have taken him as far afield as the Himalaya in Tibet, the Andes in Argentina, and the volcanoes of Mexico.

The High Sierra: Peaks, Passes, and Trails is a compilation of over twenty years of Secor's copious notes and exchanges with other Sierra hikers, climbers, and skiers. His other book is *Mexico's Volcanoes: A Climbing Guide*, also from The Mountaineers. (Photo by Rene MeVay)

About the Mountaineers

THE MOUNTAINEERS, founded in 1906, is a non-profit outdoor activity and conservation club, whose mission is "to explore, study, preserve and enjoy the natural beauty of the outdoors . . ." Based in Seattle, Washington, the club is now the third largest such organization in the United States, with 12,000 members and four branches throughout Washington State.

The Mountaineers sponsors both classes and year-round outdoor activities in the Pacific Northwest, which include hiking, mountain climbing, ski-touring, snow-shoeing, bicycling, camping, kayaking and canoeing, nature study, sailing, and adventure travel. The club's conservation division supports environmental causes through educational activities, sponsoring legislation, and presenting informational programs. All club activities are led by skilled, experienced volunteers, who are dedicated to promoting safe and responsible enjoyment and preservation of the outdoors.

The Mountaineers Books, an active, non-profit publishing program of the club, produces guidebooks, instructional texts, historical works, natural history guides, and works on environmental conservation. All books produced by The Mountaineers are aimed at fulfilling the club's mission.

If you would like to participate in these organized outdoor activities or the club's programs, consider a membership in The Mountaineers. For information and an application, write or call The Mountaineers, Club Headquarters, 300 Third Avenue West, Seattle, Washington 98119; (206) 284-6310.

Other books you may enjoy from The Mountaineers

Mountaineering: The Freedom of the Hills, 5th edition, Graydon, editor.
225,000 copies sold! New edition of the classic text on mountaineering and climbing, from expeditions to ice climbing. Entirely revamped to include recent advances in technique and technology. $32.00 cloth, $22.95 paper.

Bugaboo Rock: A Climber's Guide, Green and Bensen.
Peak-by-peak, pitch-by-pitch descriptions of more than 200 routes in Canada's Bugaboos. Contains topo sketches, photographs with route overlays. $16.95

Cascade Alpine Guide: Climbing and High Routes Series, Beckey.
Comprehensive climbing, approach, route guides to Washington's Cascades. Sketches, photos with route overlays. **Volume 1, 2nd Ed.: Columbia River to Stevens Pass. Volume 2, 2nd Ed.: Stevens Pass to Rainy Pass. Volume 3: Rainy Pass to Fraser River.** $25.00 each.

Exploring Idaho's Mountains: A Guide for Climbers, Scramblers, and Hikers, Lopez.
Route directions and descriptions for more than 700 summits in Idaho. Maps and photos. $16.95.

Mexico's Volcanoes: A Climbing Guide, Secor.
Approach and climbing routes for Popo, Ixta, Orizaba, others; plus information on food, medicine, transportation, supplies. Maps, photos, bilingual mountaineering glossary. $10.95.

Medicine for Mountaineering, 3rd Ed., Wilkerson, M.D., editor.
The "bible" for travelers more than 24 hours away from medical aid, and for climbing expeditions. $12.95.

Glacier Travel and Crevasse Rescue, Selters.
Comprehensive how-to covers knowledge of glaciers, how to cross them: reading glaciers, rescue techniques, team travel, routefinding, expedition skills, and more. $12.95.

Available from your local book or outdoor store, or from The Mountaineers Books, 1011 SW Klickitat Way, Seattle, WA 98134. 1-800-553-4453.